Integrated Mathematics 1

Volume 1

TIMOTHY D. KANOLD

EDWARD B. BURGER

JULI K. DIXON

MATTHEW R. LARSON

STEVEN J. LEINWAND

Authors

Timothy D. Kanold, Ph.D., is an award-winning international educator, author, and consultant. He is a former superintendent and director of mathematics and science at Adlai E. Stevenson High School District 125 in Lincolnshire, Illinois. He is a past president of the National Council of Supervisors of Mathematics (NCSM) and the Council for the Presidential Awardees of Mathematics (CPAM). He  has served on several writing and leadership commissions for NCTM during the past decade. He presents motivational professional development seminars with a focus on developing professional learning communities (PLC's) to improve the teaching, assessing, and learning of students. He has recently authored nationally recognized articles, books, and textbooks for mathematics education and school leadership, including *What Every Principal Needs to Know about the Teaching and Learning of Mathematics*.

Edward B. Burger, Ph.D., is the President of Southwestern University, a former Francis Christopher Oakley Third Century Professor of Mathematics at Williams College, and a former vice provost at Baylor University. He has authored or coauthored more than sixty-  five articles, books, and video series; delivered over five hundred addresses and workshops throughout the world; and made more than fifty radio and television appearances. He is a Fellow of the American Mathematical Society as well as having earned many national honors, including the Robert Foster Cherry Award for Great Teaching in 2010. In 2012, Microsoft Education named him a "Global Hero in Education."

Juli K. Dixon, Ph.D., is a Professor of Mathematics Education at the University of Central Florida. She has taught mathematics in urban schools at the elementary, middle, secondary, and post-secondary levels. She is an active researcher and speaker with numerous publications and conference presentations. Key areas of focus are deepening teachers' content knowledge and communicating and justifying  mathematical ideas. She is a past chair of the NCTM Student Explorations in Mathematics Editorial Panel and member of the Board of Directors for the Association of Mathematics Teacher Educators.

Matthew R. Larson, Ph.D., is the K-12 mathematics curriculum specialist for the Lincoln Public Schools and served on the Board of Directors for the National Council of Teachers of Mathematics from 2010 to 2013. He is a past chair of NCTM's Research Committee and was a member of NCTM's Task Force on Linking Research and Practice.  He is the author of several books on implementing the Common Core Standards for Mathematics. He has taught mathematics at the secondary and college levels and held an appointment as an honorary visiting associate professor at Teachers College, Columbia University.

Steven J. Leinwand is a Principal Research Analyst at the American Institutes for Research (AIR) in Washington, D.C., and has over 30 years in leadership positions in mathematics education. He is past president of the National Council of Supervisors of Mathematics and served on the NCTM Board of Directors. He is the author of  numerous articles, books, and textbooks and has made countless presentations with topics including student achievement, reasoning, effective assessment, and successful implementation of standards.

Performance Task Consultant

Robert Kaplinsky
Teacher Specialist, Mathematics
Downey Unified School District
Downey, California

STEM Consultants
Science, Technology, Engineering, and Mathematics

Michael A. DiSpezio
Global Educator
North Falmouth, Massachusetts

Michael R. Heithaus
Executive Director, School of Environment, Arts,
and Society
Professor, Department of Biological Sciences
Florida International University
North Miami, Florida

Reviewers

Mindy Eden
Richwoods High School
Peoria School District
Peoria, IL

Dustin Johnson
Badger High School Math Teacher
Department Chair
Lake Geneva-Genoa City Union
High School District
Lake Geneva, WI

Ashley D. McSwain
Murray High School
Murray City School District
Salt Lake City, UT

Rebecca Quinn
Doherty Memorial High School
Worcester Public Schools District
Worcester, MA

Ted Ryan
Madison LaFollette High School
Madison Metropolitan School District
Madison, WI

Tony Scoles
Fort Zumwalt School District
O'Fallon, MO

Cynthia L. Smith
Higley Unified School District
Gilbert, AZ

Phillip E. Spellane
Doherty Memorial High School
Worcester Public Schools District
Worcester, MA

Mona Toncheff
Math Content Specialist
Phoenix Union High School District
Phoenix, AZ

Quantities and Modeling

MODULE 1

Quantitative Reasoning

MODULE 2

Algebraic Models

UNIT 2
Volume 1

Understanding Functions

MODULE 3

Functions and Models

MODULE 4

Patterns and Sequences

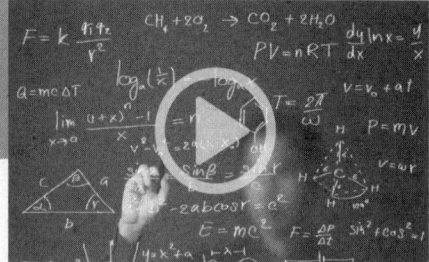

Linear Functions, Equations, and Inequalities

MODULE 5

Linear Functions

MODULE 6

Forms of Linear Equations

MODULE 7

Linear Equations and Inequalities

Statistical Models

© Houghton Mifflin Harcourt Publishing Company • Image Credits: (t) ©Daniel Padavona/Shutterstock; (b) ©Duane Osborn/Somos Images/Corbis

Multi-Variable Categorical Data

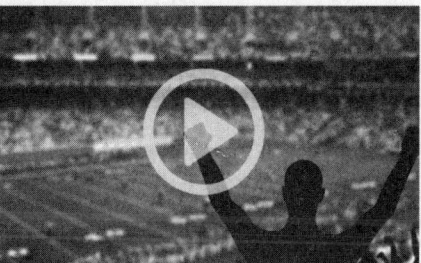

One-Variable Data Distributions

MODULE 10

Linear Modeling and Regression

© Houghton Mifflin Harcourt Publishing Company • Image Credits: ©John Elk III/Alamy

Linear Systems and Piecewise-Defined Functions

UNIT 5

Volume 1

MODULE 11

Solving Systems of Linear Equations

© Houghton Mifflin Harcourt Publishing Company • Image Credits: (t) ©Richard Green/Alamy (b) ©Fuse/Getty Images

Exponential Relationships

MODULE 14

Geometric Sequences and Exponential Functions

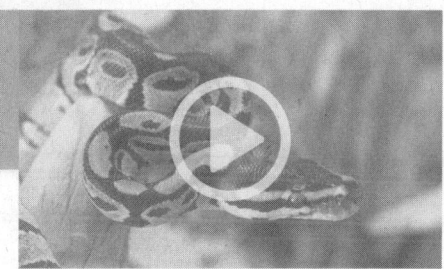

Real-World Video 635
Are You Ready? 636

MODULE 15

Exponential Equations and Models

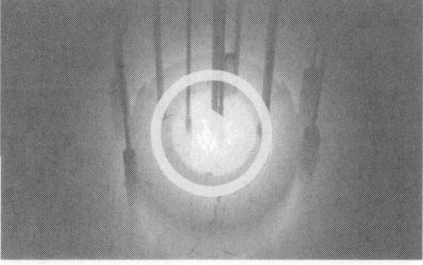

Real-World Video 707
Are You Ready? 708

UNIT 7

Volume 2

Transformations and Congruence

MODULE 16

Tools of Geometry

MODULE 17

Transformations and Symmetry

MODULE 18

Congruent Figures

UNIT 8

Volume 2

Lines, Angles, and Triangles

MODULE 19

Lines and Angles

MODULE 20

Triangle Congruence Criteria

Applications of Triangle Congruence

Properties of Triangles

MODULE 23

Special Segments in Triangles

Real-World Video 1127
Are You Ready? 1128

© Houghton Mifflin Harcourt Publishing Company • Image Credit: ©AugustSnow/Alamy

Quadrilaterals and Coordinate Proof

UNIT 9

Volume 2

MODULE 24

Properties of Quadrilaterals

MODULE 25

Coordinate Proof Using Slope and Distance

Real-World Video 1263
Are You Ready? 1264

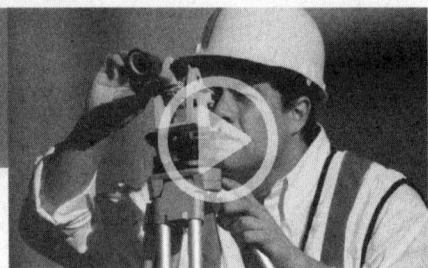

© Houghton Mifflin Harcourt Publishing Company • Image Credit: ©©Sportstock/iStockPhoto.com

HMH Integrated Math 1
Online State Resources

Scan the QR code or visit:
my.hrw.com/nsmedia/osp/2015/ma/hs/tempint
for correlations and other state-specific resources.

Succeeding with HMH Integrated Math 1

HMH Integrated Math 1 is built on the 5E instructional model--Engage, Explore, Explain, Elaborate, Evaluate--to develop strong conceptual understanding and mastery of key mathematics standards.

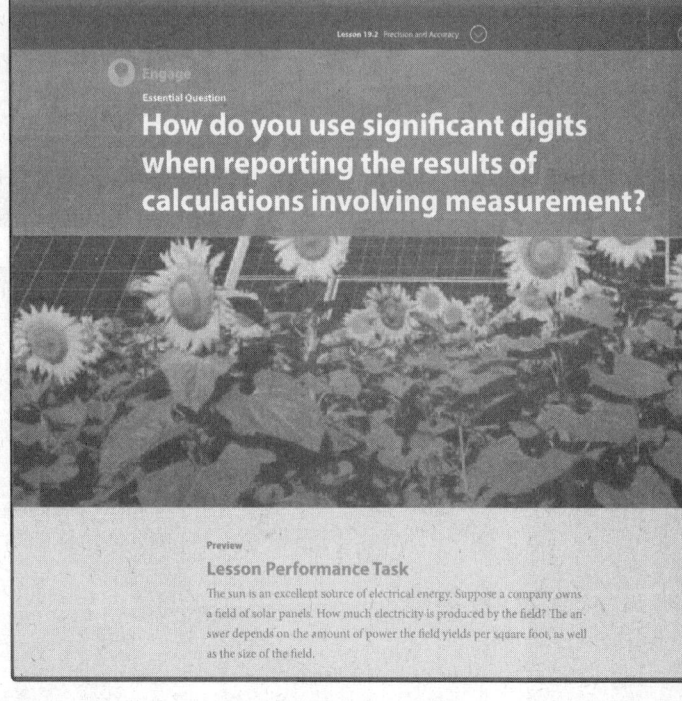

Lesson 19.2 Precision and Accuracy

Engage

Essential Question

How do you use significant digits when reporting the results of calculations involving measurement?

Preview

Lesson Performance Task

The sun is an excellent source of electrical energy. Suppose a company owns a field of solar panels. How much electricity is produced by the field? The answer depends on the amount of power the field yields per square foot, as well as the size of the field.

ENGAGE

Preview the Lesson Performance Task in the Interactive Student Edition.

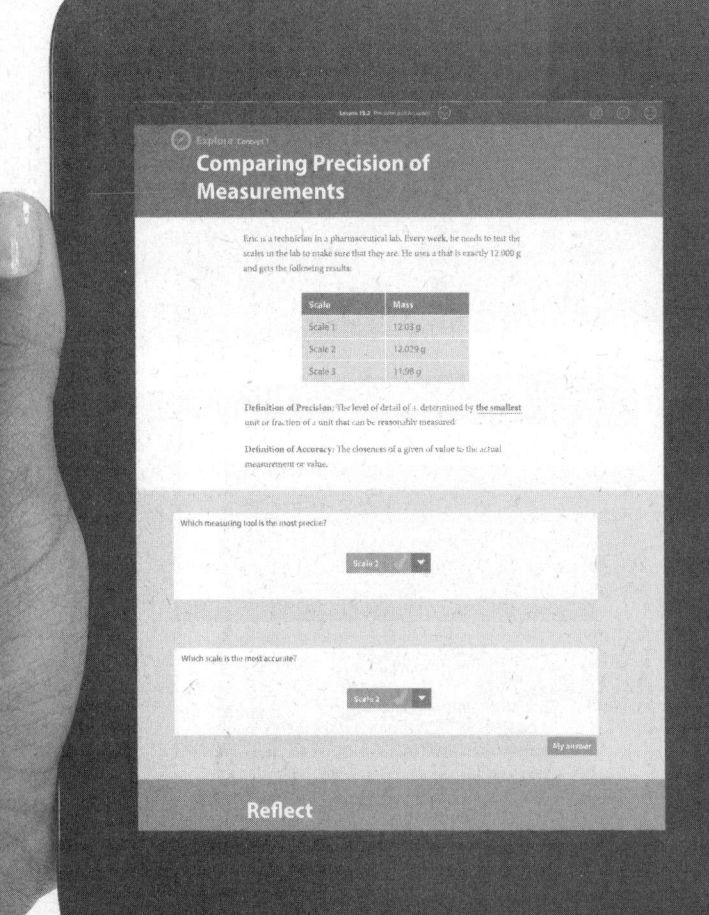

Explore Concept 1

Comparing Precision of Measurements

Eric is a technician in a pharmaceutical lab. Every week, he needs to test the scales in the lab to make sure that they are. He uses a that is exactly 12.000 g and gets the following results:

Scale	Mass
Scale 1	12.03 g
Scale 2	12.029 g
Scale 3	11.98 g

Definition of Precision: The level of detail of a determined by the smallest unit or fraction of a unit that can be reasonably measured.

Definition of Accuracy: The closeness of a given of value to the actual measurement or value.

Which measuring tool is the most precise?

Which scale is the most accurate?

My answer

Reflect

EXPLORE

Explore and interact with new concepts to develop a deeper understanding of mathematics in your book and the Interactive Student Edition.

Scan the QR code to access engaging videos, activities, and more in the Resource Locker for each lesson.

Name _____ Class _____ Date _____

1.3 Reporting with Precision and Accuracy

Essential Question: How do you use significant digits when reporting the results of calculations involving measurement?

Explore **Comparing Precision of Measurements.**

Numbers are values without units. They can be used to compute or to describe measurements. Quantities are real-word values that represent specific amounts. For instance, 15 is a number, but 15 grams is a quantity.

Precision is the level of detail of a measurement, determined by the smallest unit or fraction of a unit that can be reasonably measured.

Accuracy is the closeness of a given measurement or value to the actual measurement or value. Suppose you know the actual measure of a quantity, and someone else measures it. You can find the accuracy of the measurement by finding the absolute value of the difference of the two.

Ⓐ Complete the table to choose the more precise measurement.

Measurement 1	Measurement 2	Smaller Unit	More Precise Measurement
4 g	4.3 g		
5.71 oz	5.7 oz		
4.2 m	422 cm		
7 ft 2 in.	7.2 in.		

Ⓑ Eric is a lab technician. Every week, he needs to test the scales in the lab to make sure that they are accurate. He uses a standard mass that is exactly 8.000 grams and gets the following results.

Scale	Mass
Scale 1	8.02 g
Scale 2	7.9 g
Scale 3	8.038 m

EXPLAIN

Learn concepts with step-by-step interactive examples. Every example is also supported by a Math On the Spot video tutorial.

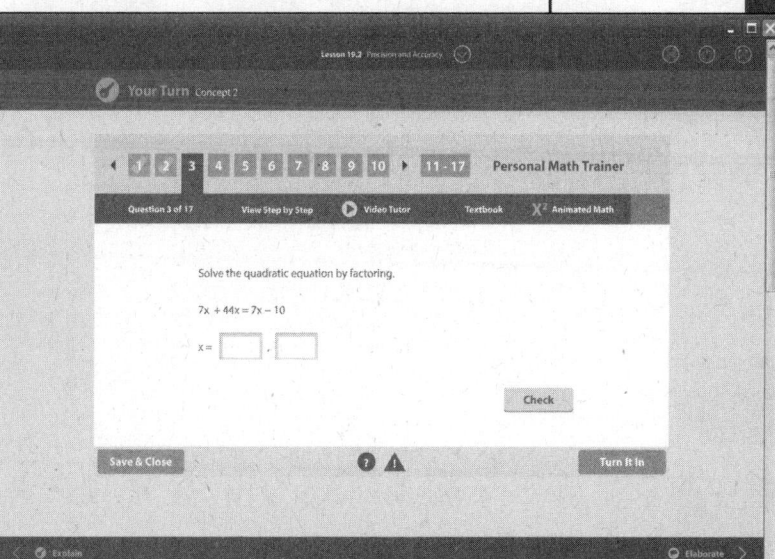

Explain Concept 2

Determining Precision

As you have seen, measurements are given to a certain precision. Therefore, the value reported does not necessarily represent the actual value of the measurement. For example, a measurement of 5 centimeters, which is given to the nearest whole unit, can actually range from 0.5 units below the reported value, 4.5 centimeters, up to, but not including, 0.5 units above it, 5.5 centimeters. The actual length, l, is within a range of possible values: centimeters. Similarly, a length given to the nearest tenth can actually range from 0.05 units below the reported value up to, but not including, 0.05 units above it. So a length reported as 4.5 cm could actually be as low as 4.45 cm or as high as nearly 4.55 cm.

Converting Areas
The area of a yard is 170 ft2. How large is the yard in square meters? Write your answer with the correct number of significant digits. Use 1 m ≈ 3.28 ft.

Conversion factor: $\frac{1\ m}{3.28\ ft}$

Your Turn Concept 2

◀ ✓ 2 3 4 5 6 7 8 9 10 ▶ 11 - 17   **Personal Math Trainer**

Question 3 of 17 | View Step by Step | ▶ Video Tutor | Textbook | X² Animated Math

Solve the quadratic equation by factoring.

$7x + 44x = 7x - 10$

$x = \boxed{} , \boxed{}$

Check

Save & Close   ? ⚠   Turn It In

◀ Explain   Elaborate ▶

Check your understanding of new concepts and skills with Your Turn exercises in your book or online with Personal Math Trainer.

Personal **Math** Trainer

ⓒ Find the accuracy of each of the measurements in Step B.

Scale 1: Accuracy = |8.000 − _____| = _____

Scale 2: Accuracy = |8.000 − _____| = _____

Scale 3: Accuracy = |8.000 − _____| = _____

Complete each statement: the measurement for Scale _____, which is _____ grams,

is the most accurate because _____.

Reflect

1. Discussion Given two measurements of the same quantity, is it possible that the more precise measurement is not the more accurate? Why do you think that is so?

_____

Explain 1 Determining Precision of Calculated Measurements

As you have seen, measurements are reported to a certain precision. The reported value does not necessarily represent the actual value of the measurement. When you measure to the nearest unit, the actual length can be 0.5 unit less than the measured length or less than 0.5 unit greater than the measured length. So, a length reported as 4.5 centimeters could actually be anywhere between 4.45 centimeters and 4.55 centimeters, but not including 4.55 centimeters. It cannot include 4.55 centimeters because 4.55 centimeters reported to the nearest tenth would round up to 4.6 centimeters.

Example 1 Calculate the minimum and maximum possible areas. Round your answers to the nearest square centimeter.

Ⓐ The length and width of a book cover are 28.3 centimeters and 21 centimeters, respectively.

Find the range of values for the actual length and width of the book cover.

Minimum length = (28.3 − 0.05) cm and maximum length = (28.3 + 0.05) cm, so 28.25 cm ≤ length < 28.35 cm.

Minimum width = (21 − 0.5) cm and maximum width = (21 + 0.5) cm, so 20.5 cm ≤ width < 21.5 cm.

Find the minimum and maximum areas.

Minimum area = minimum length · minimum width

$= 28.25\ cm \cdot 20.5\ cm \approx 579\ cm^2$

Maximum area = maximum length · maximum width

$= 28.35\ cm \cdot 21.5\ cm \approx 610\ cm^2$

So $579\ cm^2 \leq$ area $< 610\ cm^2$.

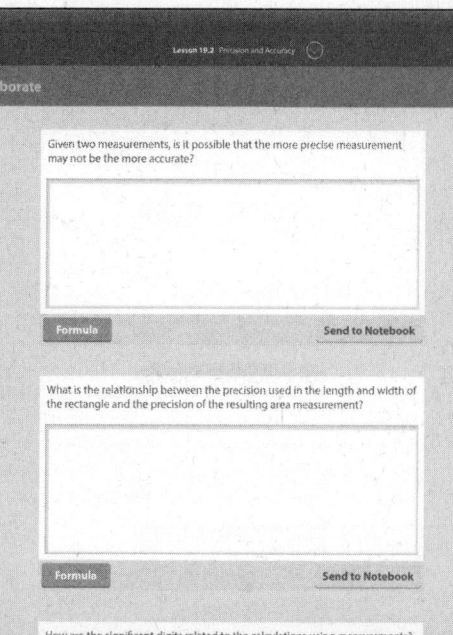

Elaborate

Given two measurements, is it possible that the more precise measurement may not be the more accurate?

[ ]

Formula   Send to Notebook

What is the relationship between the precision used in the length and width of the rectangle and the precision of the resulting area measurement?

[ ]

Formula   Send to Notebook

How are the significant digits related to the calculations using measurements?

ELABORATE

Show your understanding and reasoning with Reflect and Elaborate questions.

Elaborate

17. Given two measurements, is it possible that the more accurate measurement is not the more precise? Justify your answer.

_____

18. What is the relationship between the range of possible error in the measurements used in a calculation and the range of possible error in the calculated measurement?

_____

19. Essential Question Check-In How do you use significant digits to determine how to report a sum or product of two measurements?

_____

EVALUATE

Practice and apply skills and concepts with Evaluate exercises and a Lesson Performance Task in your book with plenty of workspace, or complete these exercises online with Personal Math Trainer.

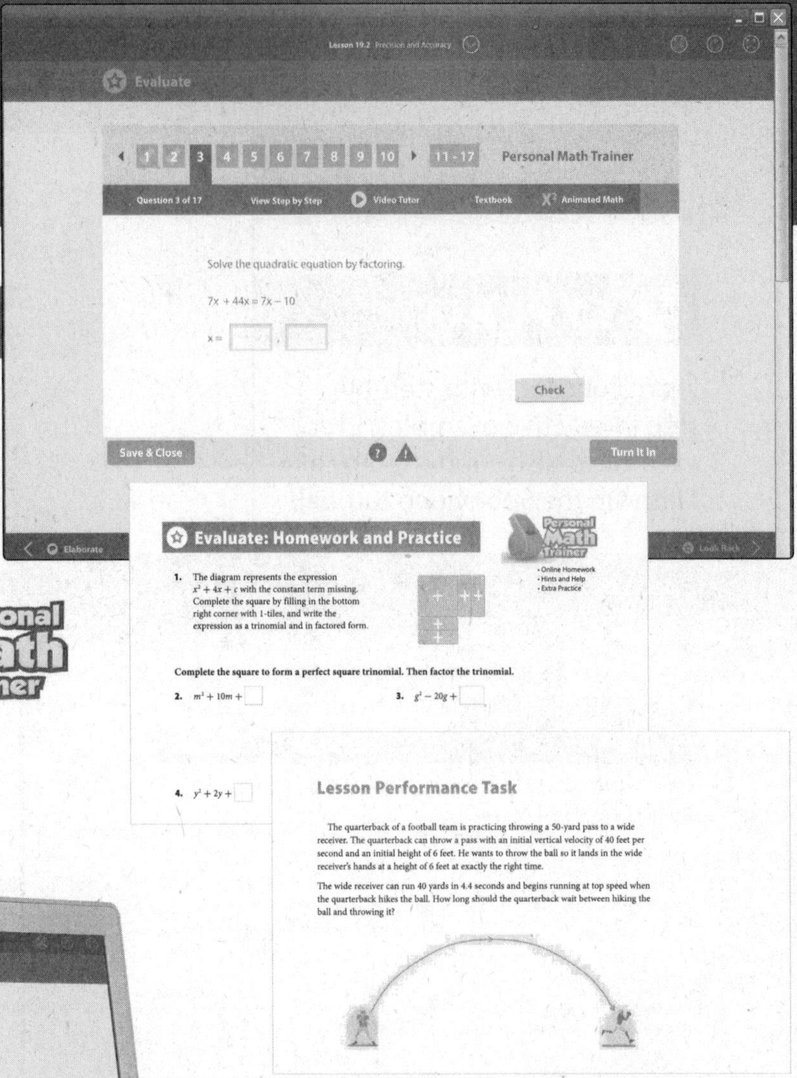

Personal Math Trainer

Lesson 19.2 Precision and Accuracy

Evaluate

| 1 | 2 | 3 | 4 | 5 | 6 | 7 | 8 | 9 | 10 | ► | 11 – 17 | **Personal Math Trainer** |

Question 3 of 17 | View Step by Step | ▶ Video Tutor | Textbook | X³ Animated Math

Solve the quadratic equation by factoring.

$7x + 44x = 7x - 10$

$x = \boxed{} , \boxed{}$

Check

Save & Close | ? ⚠ | Turn It In

Evaluate: Homework and Practice

Personal Math Trainer
· Online Homework
· Hints and Help
· Extra Practice

1. The diagram represents the expression $x^2 + 4x + c$ with the constant term missing. Complete the square by filling in the bottom right corner with 1-tiles, and write the expression as a trinomial and in factored form.

Complete the square to form a perfect square trinomial. Then factor the trinomial.

2. $m^2 + 10m + \boxed{}$

3. $g^2 - 20g + \boxed{}$

4. $y^2 + 2y + \boxed{}$

Lesson Performance Task

The quarterback of a football team is practicing throwing a 50-yard pass to a wide receiver. The quarterback can throw a pass with an initial vertical velocity of 40 feet per second and an initial height of 6 feet. He wants to throw the ball so it lands in the wide receiver's hands at a height of 6 feet at exactly the right time.

The wide receiver can run 40 yards in 4.4 seconds and begins running at top speed when the quarterback hikes the ball. How long should the quarterback wait between hiking the ball and throwing it?

LOOK BACK

Review what you have learned and prepare for high-stakes tests with a variety of resources, including Study Guide Reviews, Performance Tasks, and Assessment Readiness test preparation.

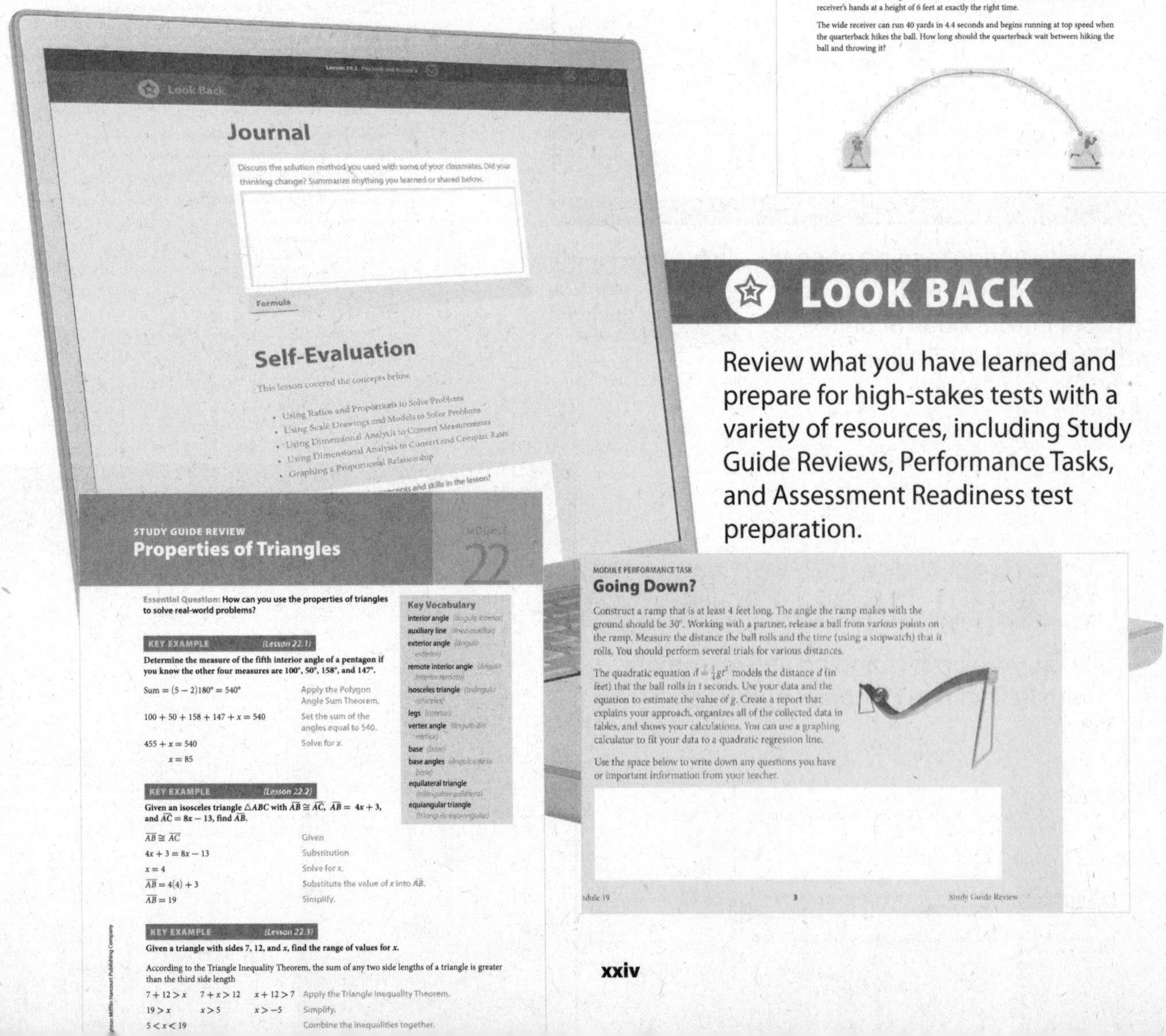

Journal

Discuss the solution method you used with some of your classmates. Did your thinking change? Summarize anything you learned or shared below.

Formula

Self-Evaluation

This lesson covered the concepts below.

· Using Ratios and Proportions to Solve Problems
· Using Scale Drawings and Models to Solve Problems
· Using Dimensional Analysis to Convert Measurements
· Using Dimensional Analysis to Convert and Compare Rates
· Graphing a Proportional Relationship

STUDY GUIDE REVIEW
Properties of Triangles

MODULE **22**

Essential Question: How can you use the properties of triangles to solve real-world problems?

Key Vocabulary
interior angle *(ángulo interior)*
auxiliary line *(línea auxiliar)*
exterior angle *(ángulo exterior)*
remote interior angle *(ángulo interior remoto)*
isosceles triangle *(triángulo isósceles)*
legs *(catetos)*
vertex angle *(ángulo del vértice)*
base *(base)*
base angles *(ángulos de la base)*
equilateral triangle *(triángulo equilátero)*
equiangular triangle *(triángulo equiángulo)*

KEY EXAMPLE *(Lesson 22.1)*
Determine the measure of the fifth interior angle of a pentagon if you know the other four measures are 100°, 50°, 158°, and 147°.

Sum $= (5 - 2)180° = 540°$	Apply the Polygon Angle Sum Theorem.
$100 + 50 + 158 + 147 + x = 540$	Set the sum of the angles equal to 540.
$455 + x = 540$	Solve for x.
$x = 85$	

KEY EXAMPLE *(Lesson 22.2)*
Given an isosceles triangle $\triangle ABC$ with $\overline{AB} \cong \overline{AC}$, $\overline{AB} = 4x + 3$, and $\overline{AC} = 8x - 13$, find $\overline{AB}$.

$\overline{AB} \cong \overline{AC}$	Given
$4x + 3 = 8x - 13$	Substitution
$x = 4$	Solve for x.
$\overline{AB} = 4(4) + 3$	Substitute the value of x into $\overline{AB}$.
$\overline{AB} = 19$	Simplify.

KEY EXAMPLE *(Lesson 22.3)*
Given a triangle with sides 7, 12, and x, find the range of values for x.

According to the Triangle Inequality Theorem, the sum of any two side lengths of a triangle is greater than the third side length.

$7 + 12 > x$	$7 + x > 12$	$x + 12 > 7$	Apply the Triangle Inequality Theorem.
$19 > x$	$x > 5$	$x > -5$	Simplify.
$5 < x < 19$			Combine the inequalities together.

MODULE PERFORMANCE TASK
Going Down?

Construct a ramp that is at least 4 feet long. The angle the ramp makes with the ground should be 30°. Working with a partner, release a ball from various points on the ramp. Measure the distance the ball rolls and the time (using a stopwatch) that it rolls. You should perform several trials for various distances.

The quadratic equation $d = \frac{1}{2}gt^2$ models the distance d (in feet) that the ball rolls in t seconds. Use your data and the equation to estimate the value of g. Create a report that explains your approach, organizes all of the collected data in tables, and shows your calculations. You can use a graphing calculator to fit your data to a quadratic regression line.

Use the space below to write down any questions you have or important information from your teacher.

Module 19 — 3 — Study Guide Review

UNIT 1

Quantities and Modeling

MODULE 1
Quantitative Reasoning

MODULE 2
Algebraic Models

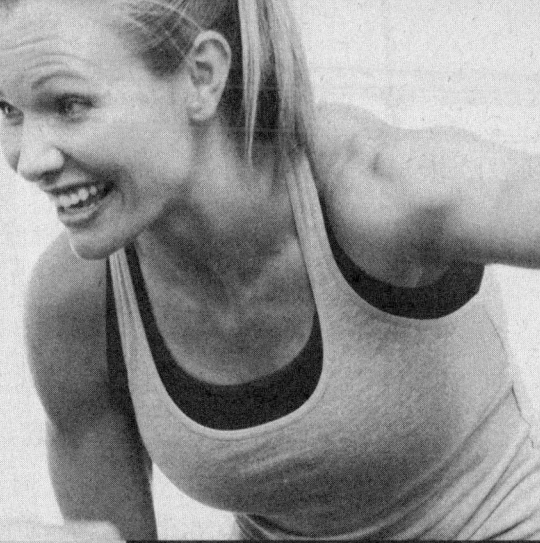

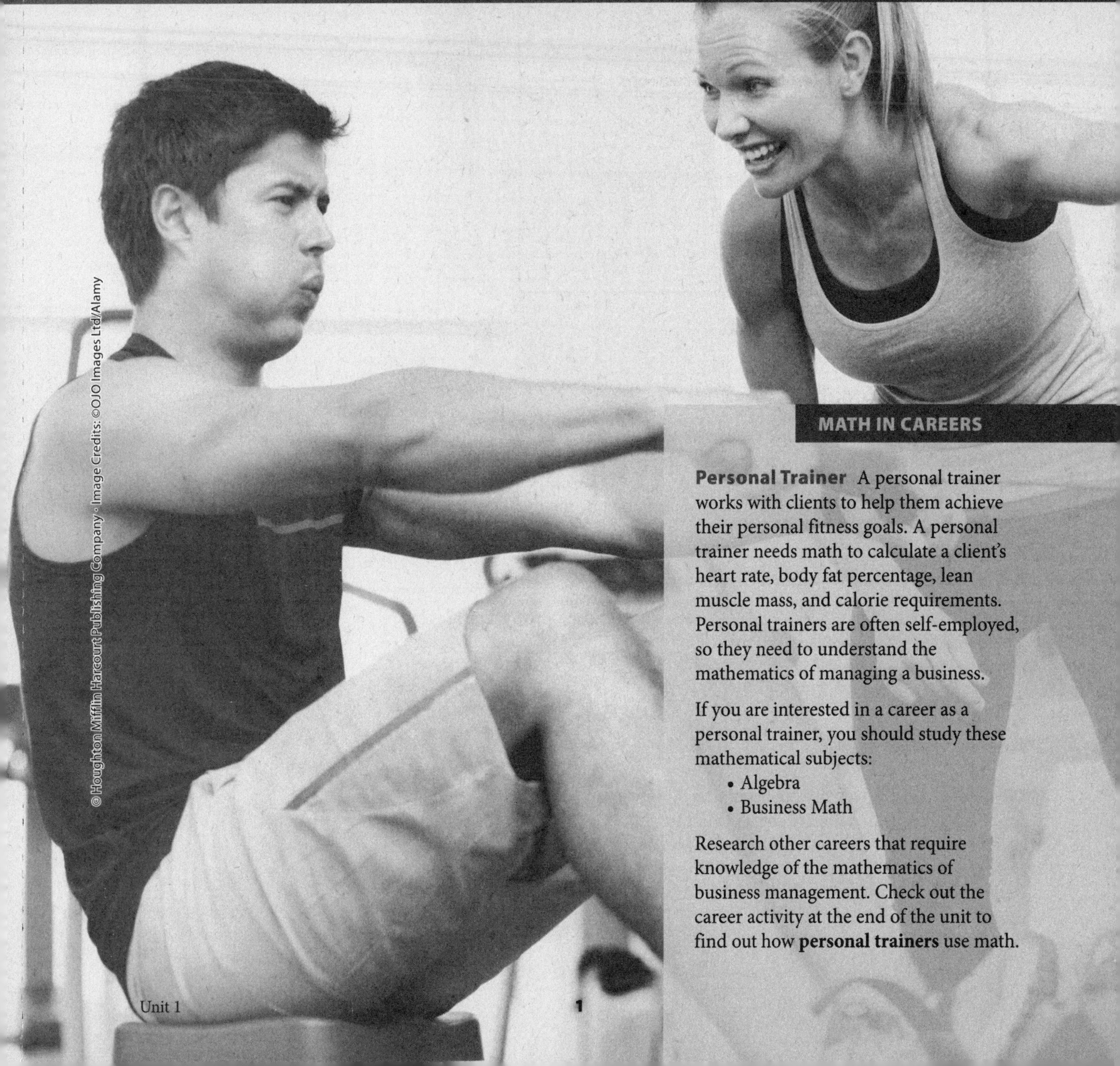

MATH IN CAREERS

Personal Trainer A personal trainer works with clients to help them achieve their personal fitness goals. A personal trainer needs math to calculate a client's heart rate, body fat percentage, lean muscle mass, and calorie requirements. Personal trainers are often self-employed, so they need to understand the mathematics of managing a business.

If you are interested in a career as a personal trainer, you should study these mathematical subjects:

- Algebra
- Business Math

Research other careers that require knowledge of the mathematics of business management. Check out the career activity at the end of the unit to find out how **personal trainers** use math.

Reading Start-Up

Vocabulary

Review Words

✔ absolute value
   (*función de valor absoluto*)

✔ algebraic expression
   (*expresión algebraica*)

✔ coefficient (*coeficiente*)

✔ constant (*constante*)

✔ numerical expression
   (*expresión numérica*)

✔ simplify (*simplificar*)

✔ solution (*solución*)

✔ term (*término*)

✔ variable (*variable*)

Preview Words

accuracy (*exactitud*)

literal equation
   (*ecuación literal*)

precision (*precisión*)

proportion (*proporción*)

ratio (*razón*)

scale model (*modelo a escala*)

Visualize Vocabulary

Use the ✔ words to complete the graphic. Put one term in each section of the square.

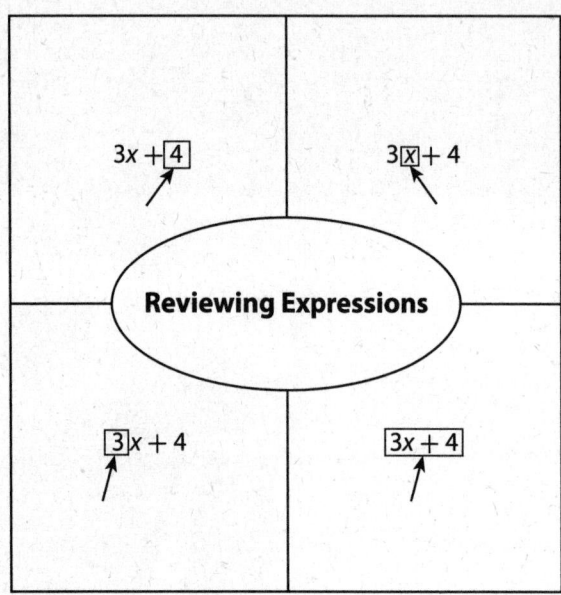

Understand Vocabulary

To become familiar with some of the vocabulary terms in this unit, consider the following. You may refer to the module, the glossary, or a dictionary.

1. The level of detail of a measurement, determined by the unit of measure,

   is _____ .

2. A statement that two ratios are equal is called a _____ .

3. A _____ is a comparison of two quantities by division.

Active Reading

Two-Panel Flip Book Before beginning the lessons, create a two-panel flip chart to help you compare concepts in this unit. Label the flaps "Creating and Solving Equations" and "Creating and Solving Inequalities." As you study each lesson, write important ideas under the appropriate flap. Include any examples that will help you remember the concepts later when you look back at your notes.

Quantitative Reasoning

Essential Question: How do you use quantitative reasoning to solve real-world problems?

REAL WORLD VIDEO
In order to function properly and safely, electronics must be manufactured to a high degree of precision. Material tolerances and component alignment must be precisely matched in order to not interfere with each other.

MODULE PERFORMANCE TASK PREVIEW

What an Impossible Score!

Darts is a game of skill in which small pointed darts are thrown at a circular target mounted on a wall. The target is divided into regions with different point values, and scoring depends on which segment the dart hits. Is there some score that is impossible to achieve no matter how many darts are thrown in a simple game of darts? Keep your eye on the target and let's figure it out!

Are YOU Ready?

Complete these exercises to review skills you will need for this module.

• Online Homework
• Hints and Help
• Extra Practice

One-Step Equations

Example 1   Solve.

$$y - 11 = 7$$
$$y - 11 + 11 = 7 + 11 \quad \text{Isolate the variable by adding 11}$$
$$y = 18 \qquad\qquad \text{to both sides of the equation.}$$

Solve each equation.

1. $4x = 32$

2. $9 + a = 23$

3. $\dfrac{n}{3} = 16$

Scale Factor and Scale Drawings

Example 2   Length of car: 132 in. Length of model of car: 11 in.

$$\frac{\text{model length}}{\text{actual length}} = \frac{11}{132} \qquad \text{Write a ratio using the given dimensions}$$
$$\text{comparing the model length to the actual length.}$$
$$= \frac{1}{12} \qquad \text{Simplify.}$$

The scale factor is $\dfrac{1}{12}$.

Identify the scale factor.

4.   Length of room: 144 in.
Length of room on scale drawing: 18 in.

5.   Wingspan of airplane: 90 ft
Wingspan of model of airplane: 6 ft

Significant Digits

Example 3   Determine the number of significant digits in 37.05.

The significant digits in 37.05 are 3, 7, 0, and 5.

37.05 has 4 significant digits.

Significant digits are nonzero digits, zeros at the end of a number and to the right of a decimal point, and zeros between significant digits.

Determine the number of significant digits.

6.   0.0028

7.   970.0

8.   50,000

9.   4000.01

1.1 Solving Equations

Essential Question: How do you solve an equation in one variable?

Resource
Locker

◈ Explore   Solving Equations by Guess-and-Check or by Working Backward

An **equation** is a mathematical sentence that uses the equal sign $=$ to show two expressions are equivalent. The expressions can be numbers, variables, constants, or combinations thereof.

There are many ways to solve an equation. One way is by using a method called *guess-and-check*. A guess-and-check method involves guessing a value for the variable in an equation and checking to see if it is the solution by substituting the value in the equation. If the resulting equation is a true statement, then the value you guessed is the solution of the equation. If the equation is not a true statement, then you adjust the value of your guess and try again, continuing until you find the solution.

Another way to solve an equation is by *working backward*. In this method, you begin at the end and work backward toward the beginning.

Solve the equation $x - 6 = 4$ using both methods.

Use the *guess-and-check* method to find the solution of the equation $x - 6 = 4$.

(A) Guess 11 for *x*.

$$x - 6 = 4$$

$$\boxed{} - 6 \overset{?}{=} 4$$

$$\boxed{} \overset{?}{=} 4$$

Is 11 the solution

of $x - 6 = 4$? _____

(B) The value 11 is too high.

Guess 10 for *x*.

$$x - 6 = 4$$

$$\boxed{} - 6 \overset{?}{=} 4$$

$$\boxed{} \overset{?}{=} 4$$

Is 10 the solution

of $x - 6 = 4$? _____

(C) Use the *working backward* method to find the solution of the equation $x - 6 = 4$.

$4 + 6 = \boxed{}$ Is this the value of *x* before taking away 6?

$\boxed{} - 6 \overset{?}{=} 4$ _____

Reflect

1. **Discussion** Which method of solving do you think is more efficient? Explain your answer.

_____

_____

© Houghton Mifflin Harcourt Publishing Company

⊘ Explain 1 Solving One-Variable Two-Step Equations

A **solution of an equation** is a value for the variable that makes the equation true. To determine the solution of an equation, you will use the Properties of Equality.

Properties of Equality		
Words	**Numbers**	**Algebra**
Addition Property of Equality You can add the same number to both sides of an equation, and the statement will still be true.	$3 = 3$ $3 + 2 = 3 + 2$ $5 = 5$	$a = b$ $a + c = b + c$
Subtraction Property of Equality You can subtract the same number from both sides of an equation, and the statement will still be true.	$7 = 7$ $7 - 5 = 7 - 5$ $2 = 2$	$a = b$ $a - c = b - c$
Multiplication Property of Equality You can multiply both sides of an equation by the same number, and the statement will still be true.	$3 = 3$ $3 \cdot 4 = 3 \cdot 4$ $12 = 12$	$a = b$ $a \cdot c = b \cdot c$
Division Property of Equality You can divide both sides of an equation by the same nonzero number, and the statement will still be true.	$15 = 15$ $\dfrac{15}{3} = \dfrac{15}{3}$ $5 = 5$	$a = b$ $\dfrac{a}{c} = \dfrac{b}{c}$, where $c \neq 0$

Example 1 Solve the equation by using Properties of Equality.

 $3x - 2 = 6$

Use the Addition Property of Equality. $3x - 2 + 2 = 6 + 2$

Combine like terms. $3x = 8$

Now use the Division Property of Equality. $\dfrac{3x}{3} = \dfrac{8}{3}$

Simplify. $x = \dfrac{8}{3}$

 $\dfrac{1}{2}z + 4 = 10$

Use the Subtraction Property of Equality. $\dfrac{1}{2}z + 4 - \boxed{} = 10 - \boxed{}$

Combine like terms. $\dfrac{1}{2}z = \boxed{}$

Now use the Multiplication Property of Equality to multiply each side by 2. $2 \cdot \dfrac{1}{2}z = 2 \cdot \boxed{}$

Simplify. $z = \boxed{}$

© Houghton Mifflin Harcourt Publishing Company

2. Discussion What is the goal when solving a one-variable equation?

Solve the equation by using Properties of Equality.

3. $5x - 10 = 20$

4. $\frac{1}{3}x + 9 = 21$

🔑 Explain 2 Solving Equations to Define a Unit

One useful application of algebra is to use an equation to determine what a unit of measure represents. For instance, if a person uses the unit of time "score" in a speech and there is enough information given, you can solve an equation to find the quantity that a "score" represents.

Example 2 Solve an equation to determine the unknown quantity.

(A) In 1963, Dr. Martin Luther King, Jr., began his famous "I have a dream" speech with the words "Five score years ago, a great American, in whose symbolic shadow we stand, signed the Emancipation Proclamation." The proclamation was signed by President Abraham Lincoln in 1863. But how long is a score? We can use algebra to find the answer.

Let *s* represent the quantity (in years) represented by a score.

s = number of years in a score

Calculate the quantity in years after President Lincoln signed the Emancipation Proclamation.

$$1963 - 1863 = 100$$

Dr. Martin Luther King, Jr. used "five score" to describe this length of time. Write the equation that shows this relationship.

$$5s = 100$$

Use the Division Property of Equality to solve the equation.

$$\frac{5s}{5} = \frac{100}{5}$$

$$s = 20$$

A score equals 20 years.

Ⓑ An airplane descends in altitude from 20,000 feet to 10,000 feet. A gauge at Radar Traffic Control reads that the airplane's altitude drops 1.8939 miles. How many feet are in a mile?

Let m represent the quantity (in feet) represented by a mile.

$m =$ number of feet in a mile

Calculate the quantity in feet of the descent. $\qquad$ $20{,}000 - \boxed{} = \boxed{}$

A gauge described this quantity as 1.8939 miles. Write the equation that shows this relationship.

$$1.8939m = \boxed{}$$

Use the Division Property of Equality to solve the equation. $\qquad \dfrac{1.8939m}{\boxed{}} = \dfrac{\boxed{}}{\boxed{}}$

Round to the nearest foot. $\qquad\qquad m \approx \boxed{}$

There are 5280 feet in a mile.

Your Turn

Solve an equation to determine the unknown quantity.

5. An ostrich that is 108 inches tall is 20 inches taller than 4 times the height of a kiwi. What is the height of a kiwi in inches?

6. An emu that measures 60 inches in height is 70 inches less than 5 times the height of a kakapo. What is the height of a kakapo in inches?

💬 Elaborate

7. How do you know which operation to perform first when solving an equation?

_____

8. How can you create an equivalent equation by using the Properties of Equality?

_____

9. When a problem involves more than one unit for a characteristic (such as length), how can you tell which unit is more appropriate to report the answer in?

_____

_____

10. Essential Question Check-In Describe each step in a solution process for solving an equation in one variable.

_____

_____

Use the *guess-and-check* method to find the solution of the equation. Show your work.

1. $2x + 5 = 19$

Use the *working backward* method to find the solution of the equation. Show your work.

2. $4y - 1 = 7$

Solve each equation using the Properties of Equality. Check your solutions.

3. $4a + 3 = 11$

4. $8 = 3r - 1$

5. $42 = -2d + 6$

6. $3x + 0.3 = 3.3$

7. $15y + 31 = 61$

8. $9 - c = -13$

9. $\dfrac{x}{6} + 4 = 15$

10. $\dfrac{1}{3}y + \dfrac{1}{4} = \dfrac{5}{12}$

11. $\dfrac{2}{7}m - \dfrac{1}{7} = \dfrac{3}{14}$

12. $15 = \dfrac{a}{3} - 2$

13. $4 - \dfrac{m}{2} = 10$

14. $\dfrac{x}{8} - \dfrac{1}{2} = 6$

Justify each step.

15. $2x - 5 = -20$

$\quad\quad 2x = -15$ _____

$\quad\quad\quad x = -\dfrac{15}{2}$ _____

16. $\dfrac{x}{3} - 7 = 11$

$\quad\quad\quad \dfrac{x}{3} = 18$ _____

$\quad\quad\quad x = 6$ _____

17. $\dfrac{9x}{4} = -9$

$\quad\quad 9x = -36$ _____

$\quad\quad\quad x = -4$ _____

18. In 2003, the population of Zimbabwe was about 12.6 million people, which is 1 million more than 4 times the population in 1950. Write and solve an equation to find the approximate population p of Zimbabwe in 1950.

19. Julio is paid 1.4 times his normal hourly rate for each hour he works over 30 hours in a week. Last week he worked 35 hours and earned $436.60. Write and solve an equation to find Julio's normal hourly rate, r. Explain how you know that your answer is reasonable.

20. The average weight of the top 5 fish caught at a fishing tournament was 12.3 pounds. Some of the weights of the fish are shown in the table.

Top 5 Fish	
Caught by	**Weight (lb)**
Wayne S.	
Carla P.	12.8
Deb N.	12.6
Vincente R.	11.8
Armin G.	9.7

What was the weight of the heaviest fish?

11

21. Paul bought a student discount card for the bus. The card allows him to buy daily bus passes for $1.50. After one month, Paul bought 15 passes and spent a total of $29.50. How much did he spend on the student discount card?

22. Jennifer is saving money to buy a bike. The bike costs $245. She has $125 saved, and each week she adds $15 to her savings. How long will it take her to save enough money to buy the bike?

23. Astronomy The radius of Earth is 6378.1 km, which is 2981.1 km greater than the radius of Mars. Find the radius of Mars.

24. Maggie's brother is 3 years younger than twice her age. The sum of their ages is 24. How old is Maggie?

25. **Analyze Relationships** One angle of a triangle measures 120°. The other two angles are congruent. Write and solve an equation to find the measure of the congruent angles.

26. **Explain the Error** Find the error in the solution, and then solve correctly.

$$9x + 18 + 3x = 1$$
$$9x + 18 = -2$$
$$9x = -20$$
$$x = -\frac{20}{9}$$

27. **Check for Reasonableness** Marietta was given a raise of $0.75 per hour, which gave her a new wage of $12.25 per hour. Write and solve an equation to determine Marietta's hourly wage before her raise. Show that your answer is reasonable.

Lesson Performance Task

The formula $p = 8n - 30$ gives the profit p when a number of items n are each sold at $8 and expenses totaling $30 are subtracted.

a. If the profit is $170.00, how many items were bought?

b. If the same number of items were bought but the expenses changed to $40, would the profit increase or decrease, and by how much? Explain.

1.2 Modeling Quantities

Essential Question: How can you use rates, ratios, and proportions to solve real-world problems?

Resource Locker

⊘ Explore Using Ratios and Proportions to Solve Problems

Ratios and *proportions* are very useful when solving real-world problems. A **ratio** is a comparison of two numbers by division. An equation that states that two ratios are equal is called a **proportion**.

A totem pole that is 90 feet tall casts a shadow that is 45 feet long. At the same time, a 6-foot-tall man casts a shadow that is x feet long.

The man and the totem pole are both perpendicular to the ground, so they form right angles with the ground. The sun shines at the same angle on both, so similar triangles are formed.

90 ft

6 ft

45 ft x ft

Ⓐ Write a ratio of the man's height to the totem pole's height. ⬚/⬚

Ⓑ Write a ratio of the man's shadow to the totem pole's shadow. ⬚/⬚

Ⓒ Write a proportion.

$$\frac{\text{man's height}}{\text{pole's height}} = \frac{\text{man's shadow}}{\text{pole's shadow}} \qquad \frac{\square}{\square} = \frac{\square}{\square}$$

Ⓓ Solve the proportion by _____ both sides by 45.

Ⓔ Solve the proportion to find the length of the man's shadow in feet. $x = \boxed{}$

Reflect

1. **Discussion** What is another ratio that could be written for this problem? Use it to write and solve a different proportion to find the length of the man's shadow in feet.

    _____

    _____

2. **Discussion** Explain why your new proportion and solution are valid.

    _____

    _____

⚙ Explain 1 Using Scale Drawings and Models to Solve Problems

A **scale** is the ratio of any length in a *scale drawing* or *scale model* to the corresponding actual length. A drawing that uses a scale to represent an object as smaller or larger than the original object is a **scale drawing**. A three-dimensional model that uses a scale to represent an object as smaller or larger than the actual object is called a **scale model**.

Example 1 Use the map to answer the following questions.

Waukegan

North Chicago

Highland Park

Evanston

1 inch: 18 miles

Chicago

(A) The actual distance from Chicago to Evanston is 11.25 mi. What is the distance on the map?

Write the scale as a fraction.

$$\frac{\text{map}}{\text{actual}} \rightarrow \frac{1 \text{ in.}}{18 \text{ mi}}$$

Let d be the distance on the map.

$$\frac{1}{18} = \frac{d}{11.25}$$

Multiply both sides by 11.25.

$$\frac{11.25}{18} = d$$

$$0.625 = d$$

The distance on the map is about 0.625 in.

(B) The actual distance between North Chicago and Waukegan is 4 mi. What is this distance on the map? Round to the nearest tenth.

Write the scale as a fraction.

$$\frac{\text{map}}{\text{actual}} \rightarrow \frac{\boxed{}}{\boxed{}}$$

Let d be the distance on the map.

$$\frac{\boxed{}}{\boxed{}} = \frac{\boxed{}}{\boxed{}}$$

Multiply both sides by 4.

$$\frac{\boxed{}}{\boxed{}} = d$$

$$\boxed{} \approx d$$

The distance on the map is about _____ in.

Your Turn

3. A scale model of a human heart is 196 inches long. The scale is 32 to 1. How many inches long is the actual heart? Round your answer to the nearest whole number.

Dimensional analysis is a method of manipulating unit measures algebraically to determine the proper units for a quantity computed algebraically. The comparison of two quantities with different units is called a **rate**. The ratio of two equal quantities, each measured in different units, is called a **conversion factor**.

Example 2 Use dimensional analysis to convert the measurements.

(A) A large adult male human has about 12 pints of blood. Use dimensional analysis to convert this quantity to gallons.

Step 1 Convert pints to quarts.

Multiply by a conversion factor whose first quantity is quarts and whose second quantity is pints.

$$12 \text{ pt} \cdot \frac{1 \text{ qt}}{2 \text{ pt}} = 6 \text{ qt}$$

12 pints is 6 quarts.

Step 2 Convert quarts to gallons.

Multiply by a conversion factor whose first quantity is gallons and whose second quantity is quarts.

$$6 \text{ qt} \cdot \frac{1 \text{ gal}}{4 \text{ qt}} = \frac{6}{4} \text{ gal} = 1\frac{1}{2} \text{ gal}$$

A large adult male human has about $1\frac{1}{2}$ gallons of blood.

(B) The length of a building is 720 in. Use dimensional analysis to convert this quantity to yards.

Step 1 Convert inches to feet.

Multiply by a conversion factor whose first quantity is feet and whose second quantity is inches.

$$720 \text{ in.} \cdot \frac{\boxed{} \text{ ft}}{\boxed{} \text{ in.}} = \boxed{} \text{ ft}$$

720 inches is $\boxed{}$ feet.

Step 2 Convert feet to yards.

Multiply by a conversion factor whose first quantity is yards and whose second quantity is feet.

$$\boxed{} \text{ ft} \cdot \frac{\boxed{} \text{ yd}}{\boxed{} \text{ ft}} = \boxed{} \text{ yd}$$

$\boxed{}$ feet is $\boxed{}$ yards.

Therefore, 720 inches is _____ yards.

Your Turn

Use dimensional analysis to convert the measurements. Round answers to the nearest tenth.

4. 7500 seconds ≈ _____ hours

5. 3 feet ≈ _____ meters

6. 4 inches ≈ _____ yards

Using Dimensional Analysis to Convert and Compare Rates

Use dimensional analysis to determine which rate is greater.

Example 3   During a cycling event for charity, Amanda traveled 105 kilometers in 4.2 hours and Brenda traveled at a rate of 0.2 mile per minute. Which girl traveled at a greater rate? Use 1 mi = 1.61 km.

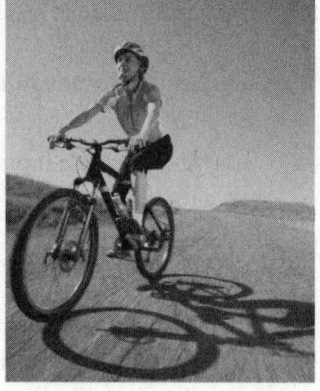

Ⓐ Convert Amanda's rate to the same units as Brenda's rate.
Set up conversion factors so that both kilometers and hours cancel.

$$\frac{x \text{ miles}}{\text{minute}} \approx \frac{105 \text{ km}}{4.2 \text{ h}} \cdot \frac{1 \text{ mi}}{1.61 \text{ km}} \cdot \frac{1 \text{ h}}{60 \text{ min}}$$

$$\approx \frac{105 \text{ mi}}{4.2 \cdot 1.61 \cdot 60 \text{ min}}$$

$$\approx 0.2588 \text{ mi/min}$$

Amanda traveled approximately 0.26 mi/min.

Amanda traveled faster than Brenda.

Ⓑ A box of books has a mass of 4.10 kilograms for every meter of its height. A box of magazines has a mass of 3 pounds for every foot of its height. Which box has a greater mass per unit of height? Use 1 lb = 0.45 kg and 1 m = 3.28 ft. Round your answer to the nearest tenth.

Convert the mass of the box of books to the same units as the mass of the box of magazines. Set up conversion factors so that both kilograms and meters cancel.

$$\frac{x \text{ lb}}{\text{ft}} \approx \frac{4.10 \text{ kg}}{1 \text{ m}} \cdot \frac{\boxed{} \text{ lb}}{\boxed{} \text{ kg}} \cdot \frac{\boxed{} \text{ m}}{\boxed{} \text{ ft}} \approx \frac{\boxed{} \text{ lb}}{\boxed{} \text{ ft}} \approx \boxed{} \text{ lb/ft}$$

The box of _____ has a greater mass per unit of height.

Reflect

7.   Why is it important to convert rates to the same units before comparing them?

_____

_____

_____

Your Turn

Use dimensional analysis to determine which rate is greater.

8.   Alan's go-kart travels 1750 feet per minute, and Barry's go-kart travels 21 miles per hour. Whose go-kart travels faster? Round your answer to the nearest tenth.

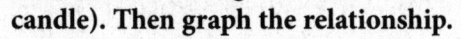 **Explain 4** **Graphing a Proportional Relationship**

To graph a proportional relationship, first find the unit rate, then create scales on the *x*- and *y*-axes and graph points.

Example 4 Simon sold candles to raise money for the school dance. He raised a total of $25.00 for selling 10 candles. Find the unit rate (amount earned per candle). Then graph the relationship.

Ⓐ Find the unit rate. $\dfrac{\text{Amount earned}}{\text{Candles sold}} : \dfrac{25}{10} = \dfrac{x}{1}$

$$2.5 = x$$

Simon's Earnings

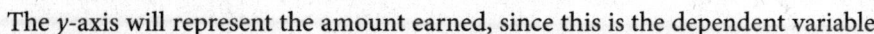

The unit rate is $2.50 per candle.

Using this information, create scales on the *x*- and *y*-axes.

The *x*-axis will represent the candles sold, since this is the independent variable.

The *y*-axis will represent the amount earned, since this is the dependent variable.

The origin represents what happens when Simon sells 0 candles. The school gets $0.

Simon sold a total of 10 candles, so the *x*-axis will need to go from 0 to 10.

Since the school gets a total of $25 from Simon, the *y*-axis will need to go from 0 to 25.

Plot points on the graph to represent the amount of money the school earns for the different numbers of candles sold.

A local store sells 8 corn muffins for a total of $6.00. Find the unit rate. Then graph the points.

Ⓑ Find the unit rate. $\dfrac{\text{Amount earned}}{\text{Muffins sold}} : \dfrac{\boxed{}}{\boxed{}} = \dfrac{x}{1}$

$$\boxed{} = x$$

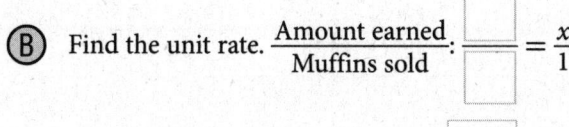

The unit rate is _____ per muffin.

Using this information, create scales on the *x*- and *y*-axes.

The *x*-axis will represent the _____ , since this is the independent variable.

The *y*-axis will represent the _____ , since this is the dependent variable.

The origin in this graph represents what happens when _____ .

The *x*-axis will need to go from _____ to _____ .

The *y*-axis will need to go from _____ to _____ .

Plot points on the graph to represent the earnings from the different numbers of muffins sold.

Reflect

9. In Example 4A, Simon raised a total of $25.00 for selling 10 candles. If Simon raised $30.00 for selling 10 candles, would the unit rate be higher or lower? Explain.

Find the unit rate, create scales on the *x*- and *y*-axes, and then graph the function.

10. Alex drove 135 miles in 3 hours at a constant speed.

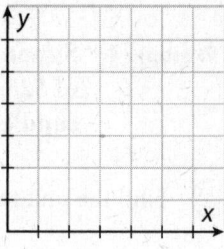

11. Max wrote 10 pages of his lab report in 4 hours.

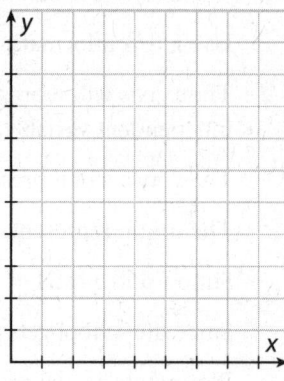

💬 Elaborate

12. Give three examples of proportions. How do you know they are proportions? Then give three nonexamples of proportions. How do you know they are not proportions?

_____

_____

_____

_____

13. If a scale is represented by a ratio less than 1, what do we know about the actual object? If a scale is represented by a ratio greater than 1, what do we know about the actual object?

_____

_____

_____

14. How is dimensional analysis useful in calculations that involve measurements?

_____

_____

15. **Essential Question Check In** How is finding the unit rate helpful before graphing a proportional relationship?

_____

_____

☆ Evaluate: Homework and Practice

1. **Represent Real-World Problems** A building casts a shadow 48 feet long. At the same time, a 40-foot-tall flagpole casts a shadow 9.6 feet long. What is the height of the building?

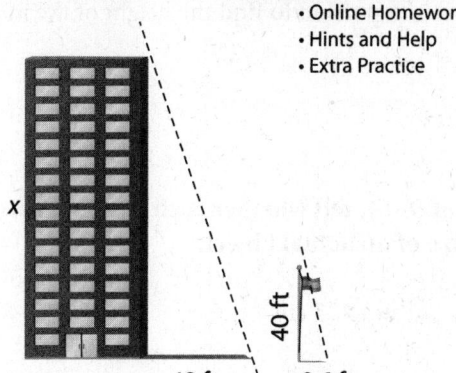

Use the table to answer questions 2–4. Select the best answer. Assume the shadow lengths were measured at the same time of day.

2. The flagpole casts an 8-foot shadow, as shown in the table. At the same time, the oak tree casts a 12-foot shadow. How tall is the oak tree?

Object	Length of Shadow (ft)	Height (ft)
Flagpole	8	20
Oak tree	12	
Goal post	18	
Fence		6.5

3. How tall is the goal post?

4. What is the length of the fence's shadow?

5. **Decorating** A particular shade of paint is made by mixing 5 parts red paint with 7 parts blue paint. To make this shade, Shannon mixed 12 quarts of blue paint with 8 quarts of red paint. Did Shannon mix the correct shade? Explain.

6. **Geography** The scale on a map of Virginia shows that 1 inch represents 30 miles. The actual distance from Richmond, VA, to Washington, D.C., is 110 miles. On the map, how many inches are between the two cities?

7. Sam is building a model of an antique car. The scale of his model to the actual car is 1:10. His model is $18\frac{1}{2}$ inches long. How long is the actual car?

8. Archaeology Stonehenge II in Hunt, Texas, is a scale model of the ancient construction in Wiltshire, England. The scale of the model to the original is 3 to 5. The Altar Stone of the original construction is 4.9 meters tall. Write and solve a proportion to find the height of the model of the Altar Stone.

For 9–11, tell whether each scale *reduces*, *enlarges*, or *preserves* the size of an actual object.

9. 1 m to 25 cm

10. 8 in. to 1 ft

11. 12 in. to 1 ft

12. Analyze Relationships When a measurement in inches is converted to centimeters, will the number of centimeters be greater or less than the number of inches? Explain.

Use dimensional analysis to convert the measurements.

13. Convert 8 milliliters to fluid ounces. Use 1 mL ≈ 0.034 fl oz.

14. Convert 12 kilograms to pounds. Use 1 kg ≈ 2.2 lb.

15. Convert 950 US dollars to British pound sterling. Use 1 US dollar = 0.62 British pound sterling.

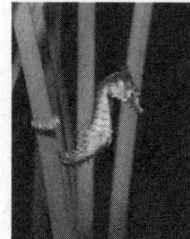

16. The dwarf sea horse *Hippocampus zosterae* swims at a rate of 52.68 feet per hour. Convert this speed to inches per minute.

Use dimensional analysis to determine which rate is greater.

17. Tortoise A walks 52.0 feet per hour and tortoise B walks 12 inches per minute. Which tortoise travels faster? Explain.

18. The pitcher for the Robins throws a baseball at 90.0 miles per hour. The pitcher on the Bluebirds throws a baseball 121 feet per second. Which pitcher throws a baseball faster? Explain.

19. For a science experiment Marcia dissolved 1.0 kilogram of salt in 3.0 liters of water. For a different experiment, Bobby dissolved 2.0 pounds of salt in 7.0 pints of water. Which person made a more concentrated salt solution? Explain. Use 1 L = 2.11 pints. Round your answer to the nearest hundredth.

20. Will a stand that can hold up to 40 pounds support a 21-kilogram television? Explain. Use 2.2 lb = 1 kg.

Find the unit rate, create scales on the *x*- and *y*-axes, and then graph the function.

21. Brianna bought a total of 8 notebooks and got 16 free pens.

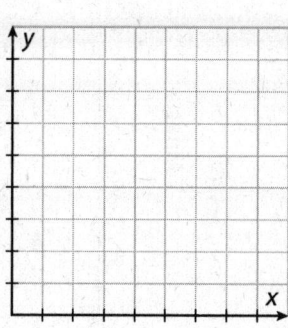

22. Mason sold 10 wristbands and made a total of 5 dollars.

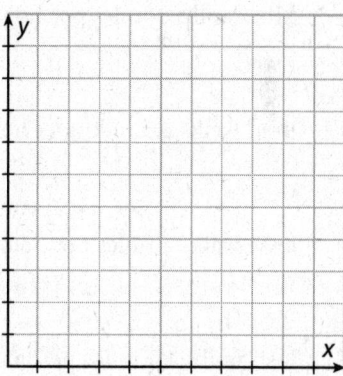

23. Match each graph to the data it goes with. Explain your reasoning.

A.

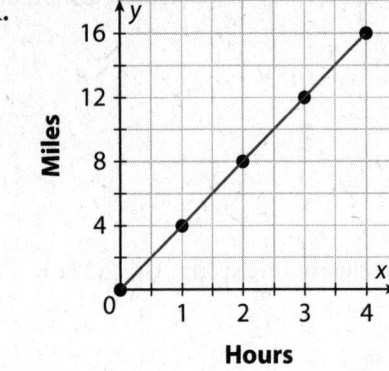

B.

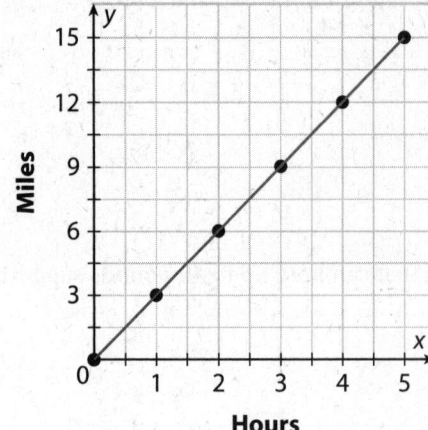

C.

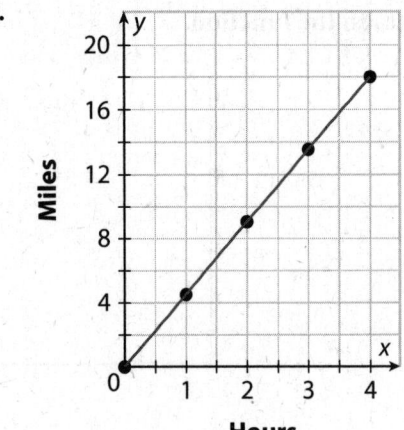

D.

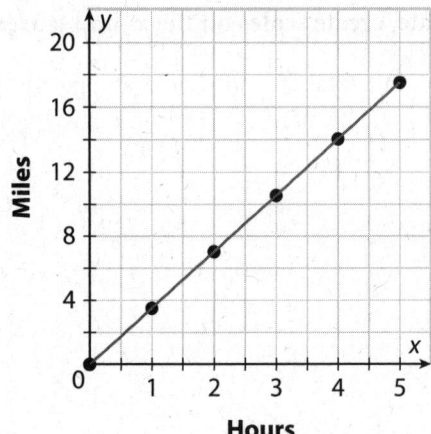

Mike walks 3 miles per hour for 5 hours.

Brad walks 3.5 miles per hour for 5 hours.

Jesse walks 4 miles per hour for 4 hours.

Josh walks 4.5 miles per hour for 4 hours.

24. Multi-Step A can of tuna has a shape similar to the shape of a large water tank. The can of tuna has a diameter of 3 inches and a height of 2 inches. The water tank has a diameter of 6 yards. What is the height of the water tank in both inches and yards?

25. Represent Real-World Problems Write a real-world scenario in which 12 fluid ounces would need to be converted into liters. Then make the conversion. Use 1 fl oz = 0.0296 L. Round your answer to the nearest tenth.

26. Find the Error The graph shown was given to represent this problem. Find the error(s) in the graph and then create a correct graph to represent the problem.

Jamie took an 8-week keyboarding class. At the end of each week, she took a test to find the number of words she could type per minute and found out she improved the same amount each week. Before Jamie started the class, she could type 25 words per minute, and by the end of week 8, she could type 65 words per minute.

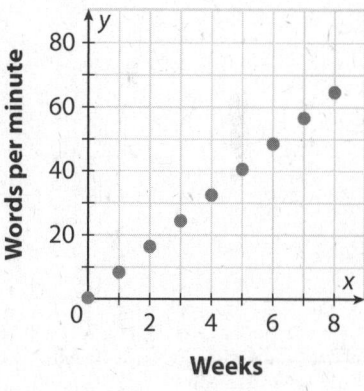

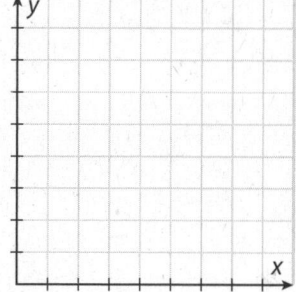

Lesson Performance Task

The Wright Flyer was the first successful powered aircraft. A model was made to display in a museum with the length of 35 cm and a wingspan of about 66.9 cm. The length of the actual plane was 21 ft 1 in., and the height was 2.74 m. Compare the length, height, and wingspan of the model to the actual plane and explain why any errors may occur. (Round any calculations to the nearest whole number.)

1.3 Reporting with Precision and Accuracy

Essential Question: How do you use significant digits when reporting the results of calculations involving measurement?

Resource Locker

⊙ Explore   Comparing Precision of Measurements

Numbers are values without units. They can be used to compute or to describe measurements. Quantities are real-word values that represent specific amounts. For instance, 15 is a number, but 15 grams is a quantity.

Precision is the level of detail of a measurement, determined by the smallest unit or fraction of a unit that can be reasonably measured.

Accuracy is the closeness of a given measurement or value to the actual measurement or value. Suppose you know the actual measure of a quantity, and someone else measures it. You can find the accuracy of the measurement by finding the absolute value of the difference of the two.

(A) Complete the table to choose the more precise measurement.

Measurement 1	Measurement 2	Smaller Unit	More Precise Measurement
4 g	4.3 g		
5.71 oz	5.7 oz		
4.2 m	422 cm		
7 ft 2 in.	7.2 in.		

(B) Eric is a lab technician. Every week, he needs to test the scales in the lab to make sure that they are accurate. He uses a standard mass that is exactly 8.000 grams and gets the following results.

Scale	Mass
Scale 1	8.02 g
Scale 2	7.9 g
Scale 3	8.029 g

Scale 1   Scale 2   Scale 3

Complete each statement:

The measurement for Scale _____ is the most precise

because it measures to the nearest _____, which is smaller than the smallest unit measured on the other two scales.

Ⓒ Find the accuracy of each of the measurements in Step B.

Scale 1: Accuracy = $\left| 8.000 - \underline{\hspace{2cm}} \right| = \underline{\hspace{2cm}}$

Scale 2: Accuracy = $\left| 8.000 - \underline{\hspace{2cm}} \right| = \underline{\hspace{2cm}}$

Scale 3: Accuracy = $\left| 8.000 - \underline{\hspace{2cm}} \right| = \underline{\hspace{2cm}}$

Complete each statement: the measurement for Scale _____, which is _____ grams,

is the most accurate because _____.

Reflect

1. **Discussion** Given two measurements of the same quantity, is it possible that the more precise measurement is not the more accurate? Why do you think that is so?

_____

_____

_____

⚙ Explain 1   Determining Precision of Calculated Measurements

As you have seen, measurements are reported to a certain precision. The reported value does not necessarily represent the actual value of the measurement. When you measure to the nearest unit, the actual length can be 0.5 unit less than the measured length or less than 0.5 unit greater than the measured length. So, a length reported as 4.5 centimeters could actually be anywhere between 4.45 centimeters and 4.55 centimeters, but not including 4.55 centimeters. It cannot include 4.55 centimeters because 4.55 centimeters reported to the nearest tenth would round *up* to 4.6 centimeters.

Example 1   **Calculate the minimum and maximum possible areas. Round your answers to the nearest square centimeter.**

Ⓐ The length and width of a book cover are 28.3 centimeters and 21 centimeters, respectively.

Find the range of values for the actual length and width of the book cover.

Minimum length = $(28.3 - 0.05)$ cm and maximum length = $(28.3 + 0.05)$ cm, so 28.25 cm $\leq$ length < 28.35 cm.

Minimum width = $(21 - 0.5)$ cm and maximum width = $(21 + 0.5)$ cm, so 20.5 cm $\leq$ width < 21.5 cm.

Find the minimum and maximum areas.

Minimum area = minimum length · minimum width

$= 28.25 \text{ cm} \cdot 20.5 \text{ cm} \approx 579 \text{ cm}^2$

Maximum area = maximum length · maximum width

$= 28.35 \text{ cm} \cdot 21.5 \text{ cm} \approx 610 \text{ cm}^2$

So 579 cm^2 $\leq$ area < 610 cm^2.

Ⓑ The length and width of a rectangle are 15.5 centimeters and 10 centimeters, respectively.

Find the range of values for the actual length and width of the rectangle.

Minimum length = (15.5 − _____) cm and maximum length = (15.5 + _____) cm,

so _____ ≤ length < _____ .

Minimum width = (10 − _____) cm and maximum width = (10 + _____) cm,

so _____ ≤ width < _____ .

Find the minimum and maximum areas.

Minimum area = minimum length · minimum width

= _____ cm · _____ cm ≈ _____ cm²

Maximum area = maximum length · maximum width

= _____ cm · _____ cm ≈ _____ cm²

So _____ cm² ≤ area < _____ cm².

Reflect

2. How do the ranges of the lengths and widths of the books compare to the range of the areas? What does that mean in terms of the uncertainty of the dimensions?

_____

_____

_____

Your Turn

Calculate the minimum and maximum possible areas. Round your answers to the nearest whole square unit.

3. Sara wants to paint a wall. The length and width of the wall are 2 meters and 1.4 meters, respectively.

4. A rectangular garden plot measures 15 feet by 22.7 feet.

⊘ Explain 2 Identifying Significant Digits

Significant digits are the digits in measurements that carry meaning about the precision of the measurement.

Identifying Significant Digits	
Rule	**Examples**
All nonzero digits are significant.	55.98 has 4 significant digits. 115 has 3 significant digits.
Zeros between two other significant digits are significant.	102 has 3 significant digits. 0.4000008 has 7 significant digits.
Zeros at the end of a number to the right of a decimal point are significant.	3.900 has 4 significant digits. 0.1230 has 4 significant digits.
Zeros to the left of the first nonzero digit in a decimal are *not* significant.	0.00035 has 2 significant digits. 0.0806 has 3 significant digits.
Zeros at the end of a number without a decimal point are assumed to be *not* significant.	60,600 has 3 significant digits. 77,000,000 has 2 significant digits.

Example 2 Determine the number of significant digits in a given measurement.

(A) 6040.0050 m

Significant Digits Rule	Digits	Count
Nonzero digits:	⑥ 0 ④ 0 . 0 0 ⑤ 0	3
Zeros between two significant digits:	6 ⓪ 4 ⓪ . ⓪ ⓪ 5 0	4
End zeros to the right of a decimal:	6 0 4 0 . 0 0 5 ⓪	1
	Total	8

So, 6040.0050 m has 8 significant digits.

(B) 710.080 cm

Significant Digits Rule	Digits	Count
Nonzero digits:	7 1 0 . 0 8 0	
Zeros between two significant digits:	7 1 0 . 0 8 0	
End zeros to the right of a decimal:	7 1 0 . 0 8 0	
	Total	

710.080 cm has _____ significant digit(s).

5. **Critique Reasoning** A student claimed that 0.045 and 0.0045 m have the same number of significant digits. Do you agree or disagree?

_____

_____

Your Turn

Determine the number of significant digits in each measurement.

6. 0.052 kg

7. 10,000 ft

8. 10.000 ft

Explain 3   Using Significant Digits in Calculated Measurements

When performing calculations with measurements of different precision, the number of significant digits in the solution may differ from the number of significant digits in the original measurements. Use the rules from the following table to determine how many significant digits to include in the result of a calculation.

Rules for Significant Digits in Calculated Measurements	
Operation	**Rule**
Addition or Subtraction	The sum or difference must be rounded to the same place value as last significant digit of the least precise measurement.
Multiplication or Division	The product or quotient must have no more significant digits than the least precise measurement.

Example 3   **Find the perimeter and area of the given object. Make sure your answers have the correct number of significant digits.**

(A) A rectangular swimming pool measures 22.3 feet by 75 feet.

Find the perimeter of the swimming pool using the correct number of significant digits.

$$\text{Perimeter} = \text{sum of side lengths}$$
$$= 22.3 \text{ ft} + 75 \text{ ft} + 22.3 \text{ ft} + 75 \text{ ft}$$
$$= 194.6 \text{ ft}$$

The least precise measurement is 75 feet. Its last significant digit is in the ones place. So round the sum to the ones place. The perimeter is 195 ft.

Find the area of the swimming pool using the correct number of significant digits.

$$\text{Area} = \text{length} \cdot \text{width}$$
$$= 22.3 \text{ ft} \cdot 75 \text{ ft} = 1672.5 \text{ ft}^2$$

The least precise measurement, 75 feet, has two significant digits, so round the product to a number with two significant digits. The area is 1700 ft^2.

(B) A rectangular garden plot measures 21 feet by 25.2 feet.

Find the perimeter of the garden using the correct number of significant digits.

Perimeter = sum of side lengths

= [   ] + [   ] + [   ] + [   ] = [   ]

The least precise measurement is _____. Its last significant digit is in the ones place. So round the sum

to the _____ place. The perimeter is _____.

Find the area of the garden using the correct number of significant digits.

Area = length · width

= [   ] · [   ] = [   ]

The least precise measurement, _____ has _____ significant digit(s), so round to a number with

_____ significant digit(s). The area is _____.

Reflect

9. In the example, why did the area of the garden and the swimming pool each have two significant digits?

_____

10. Is it possible for the perimeter of a rectangular garden to have more significant digits than its length or width does?

_____

_____

Your Turn

Find the perimeter and area of the given object. Make sure your answers have the correct number of significant digits.

11. A children's sandbox measures 7.6 feet by 8.25 feet.

_____

_____

12. A rectangular door measures 91 centimeters by 203.2 centimeters.

_____

_____

Explain 4 **Using Significant Digits in Estimation**

Real-world situations often involve estimation. Significant digits play an important role in making reasonable estimates.

> A city is planning a classic car show. A section of road 820 feet long will be closed to provide a space to display the cars in a row. In past shows, the longest car was 18.36 feet long and the shortest car was 15.1 feet long. Based on that information, about how many cars can be displayed in this year's show?

Analyze Information

- Available space: _____

- Length of the longest car: _____

- Length of the shortest car: _____

Formulate a Plan

The word *about* indicates that your answer will be a(n) _____.

Available Space = Number of Cars · _____

Find the number of longest cars and the number of shortest cars, and then use the average.

Solve

Longest:

$$820 = L \cdot \boxed{}$$

$$L = \frac{820}{\boxed{}} \approx \boxed{}$$

Shortest:

$$820 = S \cdot \boxed{}$$

$$S = \frac{820}{\boxed{}} \approx \boxed{}$$

To find a numerical estimate for the number of cars, average the two estimates.

$$\text{Number of cars} = \frac{L + S}{2} = \frac{\boxed{} + \boxed{}}{2} \approx \boxed{}$$

So, the on average, _____ cars can be displayed.

Justify and Evaluate

Because the cars will probably have many different lengths, a reasonable estimate is a

whole number between _____.

13. In the example, why wouldn't it be wise to use the length of a shorter car?

14. Critical Thinking How else might the number of cars be estimated? Would you expect the estimate to be the same? Explain.

Estimate the quantity needed in the following situations. Use the correct number of significant digits.

15. Claire and Juan are decorating a rectangular wall of 433 square feet with two types of rectangular pieces of fabric. One type has an area of 9.4 square feet and the other has an area of 17.2 square feet. About how many decorative pieces can Claire and Juan fit in the given area?

16. An artist is making a mosaic and has pieces of smooth glass ranging in area from 0.25 square inch to 3.75 square inches. Suppose the mosaic is 34.1 inches wide and 50.0 inches long. About how many pieces of glass will the artist need?

💬 Elaborate

17. Given two measurements, is it possible that the more accurate measurement is not the more precise? Justify your answer.

18. What is the relationship between the range of possible error in the measurements used in a calculation and the range of possible error in the calculated measurement?

19. Essential Question Check-In How do you use significant digits to determine how to report a sum or product of two measurements?

1. Choose the more precise measurement from the pair 54.1 cm and 54.16 cm. Justify your answer.

Choose the more precise measurement in each pair.

2. 1 ft; 12 in.   **3.** 5 kg; 5212 g   **4.** 7 m; 7.7 m   **5.** 123 cm; 1291 mm

6. True or False? A scale that measures the mass of an object in grams to two decimal places is more precise than a scale that measures the mass of an object in milligrams to two decimal places. Justify your answer.

7. Every week, a technician in a lab needs to test the scales in the lab to make sure that they are accurate. She uses a standard mass that is exactly 4 g and gets the following results.

   a. Which scale gives the most precise measurement?

Scale 1   Scale 2   Scale 3

   b. Which scale gives the most accurate measurement?

8. A manufacturing company uses three measuring tools to measure lengths. The tools are tested using a standard unit exactly 7 cm long. The results are as follows.

   a. Which tool gives the most precise measurement?

Measuring Tool	Length
Tool 1	7.033 cm
Tool 2	6.91 cm
Tool 3	7.1 cm

   b. Which tool gives the most accurate measurement?

Given the following measurements, calculate the minimum and maximum possible areas of each object. Round your answer to the nearest whole square unit.

9. The length and width of a book cover are 22.2 centimeters and 12 centimeters, respectively.

10. The length and width of a rectangle are 19.5 centimeters and 14 centimeters, respectively.

11. Chris is painting a wall with a length of 3 meters and a width of 1.6 meters.

12. A rectangular garden measures 15 feet by 24.1 feet.

Show the steps to determine the number of significant digits in the measurement.

13. 123.040 m

14. 0.00609 cm

Determine the number of significant digits in each measurement.

15. 0.0070 ft   **16.** 3333.33 g   **17.** 20,300.011 lb

Find the perimeter and area of each garden. Report your answers with the correct number of significant digits.

18. A rectangular garden plot measures 13 feet by 26.6 feet.

19. A rectangular garden plot measures 24 feet by 25.3 feet.

20. Samantha is putting a layer of topsoil on a garden plot. She measures the plot and finds that the dimensions of the plot are 5 meters by 21 meters. Samantha has a bag of topsoil that covers an area of 106 square meters. Should she buy another bag of topsoil to ensure that she can cover her entire plot? Explain.

21. Tom wants to tile the floor in his kitchen, which has an area of 320 square feet. In the store, the smallest tile he likes has an area of 1.1 square feet and the largest tile he likes has an area of 1.815 square feet. About how many tiles can be fitted in the given area?

22. Communicate Mathematical Ideas Consider the calculation 5.6 mi ÷ 9s = 0.62222 mi/s. Why is it important to use significant digits to round the answer?

23. Find the Error A student found that the dimensions of a rectangle were 1.20 centimeters and 1.40 centimeters. He was asked to report the area using the correct number of significant digits. He reported the area as 1.7 cm². Explain the error the student made.

24. Make a Conjecture Given two values with the same number of decimal places and significant digits, is it possible for the sum or product of the two values to have a different number of decimal places or significant digits than the original values?

Lesson Performance Task

The sun is an excellent source of electrical energy. A field of solar panels yields 16.22 Watts per square feet. Determine the amount of electricity produced by a field of solar panels that is 305 feet by 620 feet.

Quantitative Reasoning

Essential Question: How do you use quantitative reasoning to solve real-world problems?

KEY EXAMPLE   (Lesson 1.1)

Two fortnights have passed from January 3rd to January 31st. How many days long is a fortnight?

$31 - 3 = 28$	*Calculate the number of days that have passed.*
$2f = 28$	*Write an equation.*
$\dfrac{2f}{2} = \dfrac{28}{2}$	*Use the division property of equality.*
$f = 14$	

A fortnight equals 14 days.

KEY EXAMPLE   (Lesson 1.2)

The scale on a map is 1 in: 8 mi. The distance from Cedar Park, TX to Austin, TX on the map is 2.5 in. How long is the actual distance?

$\dfrac{actual}{map} \rightarrow \dfrac{8 \text{ mi}}{1 \text{ in.}}$	*Write the scale as a fraction.*
$\dfrac{8}{1} = \dfrac{d}{2.5}$	*Let d be the actual distance.*
$2.5 \times 8 = 2.5 \times \dfrac{d}{2.5}$	*Multiply both sides by 2.5.*
$20 = d$	

The actual distance is 20 mi.

KEY EXAMPLE   (Lesson 1.3)

Find the sum and product of the following measurements using the correct number of significant digits: 15 ft and 9.25 ft.

$15 \text{ ft} + 9.25 \text{ ft} = 24.25 \text{ ft}$	*Round to the place value of the last significant digit of the least precise measurement.*
24 ft	*The last significant digit of 15 is in the ones place.*
$15 \text{ ft} \times 9.25 \text{ ft} = 138.75 \text{ ft}^2$	*Round so it has the number of significant digits of the least precise measurement.*
140 ft^2	*15 has 2 significant digits.*

Key Vocabulary

accuracy *(exactitud)*

conversion factor
   (factor de conversión)

dimensional analysis
   (análisis dimensional)

equation *(ecuación)*

precision *(precisión)*

proportion *(proporción)*

rate *(tasa)*

ratio *(razón)*

scale *(escala)*

significant digits
   (dígitos significativos)

solution of an equation
   (solución de una ecuación)

Solve. Check your solutions. *(Lesson 1.1)*

1. $z - 12 = 30$

2. $-\dfrac{y}{7} = 8$

3. $5x + 13 = 48$

4. $25 - 3p = -11$

5. The height of a scale model building is 15 in. The scale is 5 in. to 32 in. Find the height of the actual building in inches and in feet. *(Lesson 1.2)*

6. Which of the following measurements is least precise, and how many significant digits does it have? *(Lesson 1.3)*

$$50.25 \text{ cm}, 12.5 \text{ cm}, 101 \text{ cm}$$

7. A square countertop has a side length of 28 inches. Find the perimeter and area of the countertop using the correct number of significant digits. *(Lesson 1.3)*

MODULE PERFORMANCE TASK

What an Impossible Score!

The simple dartboard shown has two sections, a 5-point outer ring and a 7-point inner circle. What is the largest integer score that is impossible to achieve for this simple dartboard, even if you are allowed to throw as many darts as you want?

Start by listing in the space below how you plan to tackle the problem. Then use your own paper to complete the task. Be sure to write down all your data and assumptions. Then use graphs, numbers, words, or algebra to explain how you reached your conclusion.

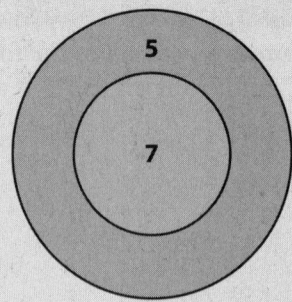

(Ready) to Go On?

1.1–1.3 Quantitative Reasoning

• Online Homework
• Hints and Help
• Extra Practice

Solve. *(Lesson 1.1)*

1. $7 = 4s + 19$

2. $\frac{x}{4} + 8 = 16$

3. A student's pay of $23 an hour at a new job is $6 more than twice the amount the student earned per hour at an internship. Write and solve an equation to find the hourly pay of the internship. *(Lesson 1.1)*

4. Susan enlarged to scale a rectangle with a height of 4 cm and length of 11 cm on her computer. The length of the new rectangle is 16.5 cm. Find the height of the new rectangle. *(Lesson 1.2)*

5. An instructional video is 5.4 minutes long. How long is the video in seconds? How long is it in hours? *(Lesson 1.2)*

Solve using the correct number of significant digits. *(Lesson 1.3)*

6. $70.8 \text{ m} \times 11 \text{ m}$

7. $16.5 \text{ ft} + 2.25 \text{ ft} + 12.5 \text{ ft}$

ESSENTIAL QUESTION

8. How do you calculate correctly with real-world measurements?

Assessment Readiness

1. Look at each equation and possible solution. Is the solution correct? Select Yes or No for each equation.

    A. $-3x = -30; x = -10$ ○ Yes   ○ No

    B. $25 - 2y = 13; y = 6$ ○ Yes   ○ No

    C. $\frac{z}{3} + 2 = 6; z = 16$ ○ Yes   ○ No

2. During a 5-kilometer run to raise money for the school band, Tabitha ran 0.08 kilometer per minute. Use 1 mi ≈ 1.61 km. Choose True or False for each statement.

    A. Tabitha ran 4.8 miles per hour.   ○ True   ○ False

    B. Tabitha ran about 0.05 mile per minute.   ○ True   ○ False

    C. Tabitha ran faster than 4 kilometers per hour.   ○ True   ○ False

3. A carpenter took the following measurements: 3.4 m, 10.25 m, 20.2 m, and 19 m. Choose True or False for each statement.

    A. The most precise measurement has 4 significant digits.   ○ True   ○ False

    B. The least precise measurement has 2 significant digits.   ○ True   ○ False

    C. Written using the correct number of significant digits, the sum of the measurements should be rounded to the tenths place.   ○ True   ○ False

4. Stanley is putting wallpaper strips on his bathroom walls that have a total area of 450 square feet. Each strip of wall paper covers between 20 and 24 square feet. Estimate how many strips of wallpaper Stanley will need. Explain how you solved this problem.

Algebraic Models

 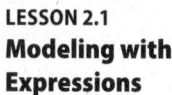

Essential Question: How can you use algebraic models to solve real-world problems?

REAL WORLD VIDEO
In a grocery store receipt, some items are taxed and some items are not taxed. You can write an expression that shows a simplified method for calculating the total grocery bill.

MODULE PERFORMANCE TASK PREVIEW
Menu Math

What if you opened a menu in a restaurant and saw this: "Special Today!!! All G's just $2.95 a piece! M's reduced 20%!" You might decide to try another restaurant. On the other hand, you might decide that you wanted to decipher the code. Deciphering codes is one way of describing what you do when you solve equations. In this module, you'll decipher a lot of codes and then use what you've learned to discover the mathematics of menus!

Are (YOU) Ready?

Complete these exercises to review skills you will need for this module.

One-Step Inequalities

Example 1   Solve.

$$x + 8 < 15$$

$$x + 8 - 8 < 15 - 8 \qquad \text{Isolate the variable by subtracting 8}$$

$$x < 7 \qquad\qquad\quad\ \text{from both sides of the inequality.}$$

Solve each inequality.

1. $n - 23 \geq 17$ _____

2. $p + 14 \leq 9$ _____

3. $\frac{n}{5} > -13$ _____

Two-Step Equations

Example 2   Solve.

$$6k - 12 = 18$$

$$6k - 12 + 12 = 18 + 12 \quad \text{Add 12 to both sides of the equation.}$$

$$6k = 30$$

$$\frac{6k}{6} = \frac{30}{6} \qquad\qquad \text{Divide both sides of the equation by 6.}$$

$$k = 5$$

Solve each equation.

4. $3n + 19 = 28$ _____

5. $34 - 4b = 18$ _____

6. $\frac{2}{3}y + 7 = 15$ _____

Two-Step Inequalities

Example 3   Solve.

$$15 - 3f > 75$$

$$15 - 15 - 3f > 75 - 15 \quad \text{Subtract 15 from both sides of the inequality.}$$

$$-3f > 60$$

$$\frac{-3f}{-3} < \frac{60}{-3} \qquad\qquad \text{Divide both sides of the inequality by } -3.$$

$$\qquad\qquad\qquad\qquad\quad \text{Reverse the inequality symbol.}$$

$$f < -20$$

Solve each inequality.

7. $8c - 21 < 35$ _____

8. $-6h + 17 > 41$ _____

9. $\frac{r}{5} - 2 \leq 9$ _____

2.1 Modeling with Expressions

Essential Question: How do you interpret algebraic expressions in terms of their context?

Resource Locker

⊘ Explore — Interpreting Parts of an Expression

An **expression** is a mathematical phrase that contains operations, numbers, and/or variables. The **terms** of an expression are the parts that are being added. A **coefficient** is the numerical factor of a variable term. There are both *numerical expressions* and *algebraic expressions*. A **numerical expression** contains only numbers while an **algebraic expression** contains at least one variable.

Ⓐ Identify the terms and the coefficients of the expression $8p + 2q + 7r$.

terms: _____ ; coefficients: _____

Ⓑ Identify the terms and coefficients of the expression $18 - 2x - 4y$. Since the expression involves _____ rather than addition, rewrite the expression as the _____ of the terms:

$18 - 2x - 4y =$ _____. So, the terms of the expression are _____

and the coefficients are _____.

Ⓒ Identify the terms and coefficients in the expression $2x + 3y - 4z + 10$. Since the expression involves both _____ and addition, rewrite the expression as the _____

of the terms: $2x + 3y - 4z + 10 =$ _____. So, the terms of the

expression are _____ and the coefficients are _____.

Tickets to an amusement park are $60 for adults and $30 for children. If a is the number of adults and c is the number of children, then the cost for a adults and c children is $60a + 30c$.

Ⓓ What are the terms of the expression? _____

Ⓔ What are the factors of $60a$? _____

Ⓕ What are the factors of $30c$? _____

Ⓖ What are the coefficients of the expression? _____

Ⓗ Interpret the meaning of the two terms of the expression. _____

_____

The price of a case of juice is $15.00. Fred has a coupon for 20 cents off each bottle in the case. The expression to find the final cost of the case of juice is $15 - 0.2b$, wherein b is the number of bottles.

Ⓘ What are the terms of the expression? _____

(J) What are the factors of each term? _____ is the only factor of the _____ term and _____ and _____ are the factors of the _____ term.

(K) Do both terms have coefficients? Explain. _____ _____ What are the coefficients? _____

(L) What does the expression $15 - 0.2b$ mean in the given situation?

_____

_____

Reflect

1. Sally identified the terms of the expression $9a + 4b - 18$ as $9a$, $4b$, and 18. Explain her error.

_____

2. What is the coefficient of b in the expression $b + 10$? Explain. _____

Explain 1 Interpreting Algebraic Expressions in Context

In many cases, real-world situations and algebraic expressions can be related. The coefficients, variables, and operations represent the given real-world context.

Interpret the algebraic expression corresponding to the given context.

Example 1

(A) Curtis is buying supplies for his school. He buys p packages of crayons at \$1.49 per package and q packages of markers at \$3.49 per package. What does the expression $1.49p + 3.49q$ represent?

Interpret the meaning of the term $1.49p$. What does the coefficient 1.49 represent?

The term $1.49p$ represents the cost of p packages of crayons. The coefficient represents the cost of one package of crayons, \$1.49.

Interpret the meaning of the term $3.49q$. What does the coefficient 3.49 represent?

The term $3.49q$ represents the cost of q packages of markers. The coefficient represents the cost of one package of markers, \$3.49.

Interpret the meaning of the entire expression.

The expression $1.49p + 3.49q$ represents the total cost of p packages of crayons and q packages of markers.

(B) Jill is buying ink jet paper and laser jet paper for her business. She buys 8 more packages of ink jet paper than p packages of laser jet paper. Ink jet paper costs \$6.95 per package and laser jet paper costs \$8 per package. What does the expression $8p + 6.95(p + 8)$ represent?

Interpret the meaning of the first term, $8p$. What does the coefficient 8 represent?

The term $8p$ represents the cost of _____. The coefficient represents _____, \$8.

Interpret the meaning of the second expression, $6.95(p + 8)$. What do the factors 6.95 and $(p + 8)$ represent?

The term $6.95(p + 8)$ represents _____. 6.95 represents the cost

of _____. $(p + 8)$ represents _____ that

Jill bought.

Interpret the expression $8p + 6.95(p + 8)$.

The expression represents _____ that Jill bought.

Your Turn

Interpret the algebraic expression corresponding to the given context.

3. George is buying watermelons and pineapples to make fruit salad. He buys w watermelons at $4.49 each and p pineapples at $5 each. What does the expression $4.49w + 5p$ represent?

4. Sandi buys 5 fewer packages of pencils than p packages of pens. Pencils costs $2.25 per package and pens costs $3 per package. What does the expression $3p + 2.25(p - 5)$ represent?

🔑 Explain 2 Comparing Algebraic Expressions

Given two algebraic expressions involving two variables, we can compare whether one is greater or less than the other. We can denote the inequality between the expressions by using $<$ or $>$ symbols. If the expressions are the same, or **equivalent expressions**, we denote this equality by using $=$.

Suppose x and y give the populations of two different cities where $x > y$. Compare the expressions and tell which of the given pair is greater.

Example 1

(A) $x + y$ and $2x$

The expression $2x$ is greater.

- Putting the lesser population, y, together with the greater population, x, gives a population that is less than double the greater population.

(B) $\frac{x}{y}$ and $\frac{y}{x}$

Since $x > y$, $\frac{x}{y}$ will be _____ than 1 and $\frac{y}{x}$ will be _____ than 1.

So $\frac{x}{y}$ _____ $\frac{y}{x}$.

Your Turn

Suppose x and y give the populations of two different cities where $x > y$ and $y > 0$. Compare the expressions and tell which of the given pair is greater.

5. $\frac{x}{x + y}$ and $\frac{x + y}{x}$

6. $2(x + y)$ and $(x + y)^2$

⏺ Explain 3 Modeling Expressions in Context

The table shows some words and phrases associated with the four basic arithmetic operations. These words and phrases can help you translate a real-world situation into an algebraic expression.

Operation	Words	Examples
Addition	the sum of, added to, plus, more than, increased by, total, altogether, and	1. A number increased by 2 2. The sum of n and 2 3. $n + 2$
Subtraction	less than, minus, subtracted from, the difference of, take away, taken from, reduced by	1. The difference of a number and 2 2. 2 less than a number 3. $n - 2$
Multiplication	times, multiplied by, the product of, percent of	1. The product of 0.6 and a number 2. 60% of a number 3. $0.6n$
Division	divided by, division of, quotient of, divided into, ratio of,	1. The quotient of a number and 5 2. A number divided by 5 3. $n \div 5$ or $\frac{n}{5}$

Example 3   Write an algebraic expression to model the given context. Give your answer in simplest form.

Ⓐ the price of an item plus 6% sales tax

Price of an item   +   6% sales tax

   p + $0.06p$

The algebraic expression is $p + 0.06p$, or $1.06p$.

Ⓑ the price of a car plus 8.5% sales tax

The price of a car   +   _____

_____   +   _____

The algebraic expression is _____,

or _____.

Reflect

7. Use the Distributive Property to show why $p + 0.06p = 1.06p$.

_____

8. What could the expression $3(p + 0.06p)$ represent? Explain.

_____

_____

Your Turn

Write an algebraic expression to model the given context. Give your answer in simplest form.

9. the number of gallons of water in a tank, that already has 300 gallons in it, after being filled at 35 gallons per minute for m minutes

_____

10. the original price p of an item less a discount of 15%

_____

11. When given an algebraic expression involving subtraction, why is it best to rewrite the expression using addition before identifying the terms?

_____

_____

12. How do you interpret algebraic expressions in terms of their context?

_____

_____

13. How do you simplify algebraic expressions?

_____

_____

14. **Essential Question Check In** How do you write algebraic expressions to model quantities?

_____

_____

_____

 ☆ **Evaluate: Homework and Practice**

- Online Homework
- Hints and Help
- Extra Practice

Identify the terms and the coefficients of the expression.

1. $-20 + 5p - 7z$

2. $8x - 20y - 10$

Identify the factors of the terms of the expression.

3. $5 + 6a + 11b$

4. $13m - 2n$

5. Erin is buying produce at a store. She buys c cucumbers at \$0.99 each and a apples at \$0.79 each. What does the expression $0.99c + 0.79a$ represent?

6. The number of bees that visit a plant is 500 times the number of years the plant is alive, where t represents the number of years the plant is alive. What does the expression $500t$ represent?

7. Lorenzo buys 3 shirts at s dollars apiece and 2 pairs of pants at p dollars a pair. What does the expression $3s + 2p$ represent?

8. If a car travels at a speed of 25 mi/h for t hours, then travels 45 mi/h for m hours, what does the expression $25t + 45m$ represent?

9. The price of a sandwich is $1.50 more than the price of a smoothie, which is d dollars. What does the expression $d + 1.5$ represent?

10. A bicyclist travels 1 mile in 5 minutes. If m represents minutes, what does the expression $\frac{m}{5}$ represent?

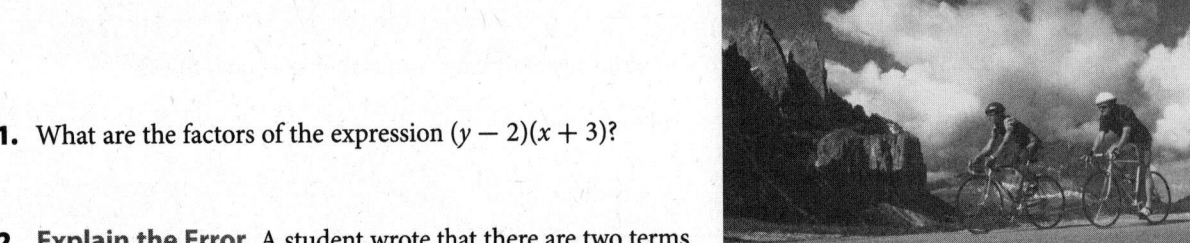

11. What are the factors of the expression $(y - 2)(x + 3)$?

12. **Explain the Error** A student wrote that there are two terms in the expression $3p - (7 - 4q)$. Explain the student's error.

13. Yolanda is buying supplies for school. She buys n packages of pencils at $1.40 per package and m pads of paper at $1.20 each. What does each term in the expression $1.4n + 1.2m$ represent? What does the entire expression represent?

14. Chris buys p pairs of pants and 4 more shirts than pairs of pants. Shirts cost $18 each and pair of pants cost $25 each. What does each term in the expression $25p + 18(p + 4)$ represent? What does the entire expression represent?

Suppose a and b give the populations of two states where $a > b$. Compare the expressions and tell which of the given pair is greater or if the expressions are equal.

15. $\dfrac{b}{a+b}$ and 0.5

16. $a + 13c$ and $b + 13c$, where c is the population of a third state

17. $\dfrac{a-b}{2}$ and $a - \dfrac{b}{2}$

18. $a + b$ and $2b$

19. $5(a+b)$ and $(a+b)5$

Write an algebraic expression to model the given context. Give your answer in simplest form.

20. the price s of a pair of shoes plus 5% sales tax.

21. the original price p of an item less a discount of 20%

22. the price h of a recently bought house plus 10% property tax

23. the principal amount P originally deposited in a bank account plus 0.3% interest

24. Match each statement with the algebraic expression that models it.

A. the price of a winter coat and a 20% discount

_____ $x + 0.02x = 1.02x$

B. the base salary of an employee and a 2% salary increase

_____ $x - 0.20x = 0.80x$

C. the cost of groceries and a 2% discount with coupons

_____ $x + 0.20x = 1.20x$

D. the number of students attending school last year and a 20% increase from last year

_____ $x - 0.02x = 0.98x$

25. Critique Reasoning A student is given the rectangle and the square shown. The student states that the two figures have the same perimeter. Is the student correct? Explain your reasoning.

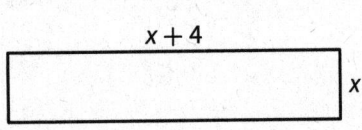

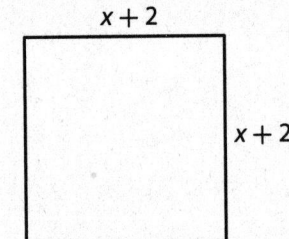

26. Multi-Step Yon buys tickets to a concert for himself and a friend. There is a tax of 6% on the price of the tickets and an additional booking fee of $20 for the transaction. Write an algebraic expression to represent the price per person. Simplify the expression if possible.

27. Persevere in Problem Solving Jerry is planting white daisies and red tulips in his garden and he wants to choose a pattern in which the tulips surround the daisies. He uses tiles to generate patterns starting with two rows of three daisies. He surrounds these daisies with a border of tulips. The design continues as shown.

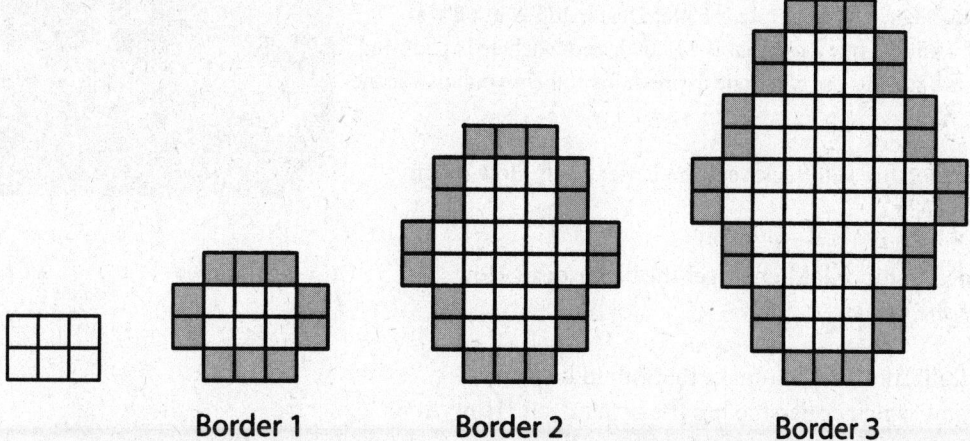

Border 1   Border 2   Border 3

a. Jerry writes the expression $8(b - 1) + 10$ for the number of tulips in each border, wherein b is the border number and $b \geq 1$. Explain why Jerry's expression is correct.

b. Elaine wants to start with two rows of four daisies. Her reasoning is that Jerry started with two rows of three daisies and his expression was $8(b - 1) + 10$, so if she starts with two rows of four daisies, her expression will be $10(b - 1) + 10$. Is Elaine's statement correct? Explain.

Lesson Performance Task

Becky and Michele are both shopping for a new car at two different dealerships. Dealership A is offering $500 cash back on any purchase, while Dealership B is offering $1000 cash back. The tax rate is 5% at Dealership A but 8% at Dealership B. Becky wants to buy a car that is $15,000, and Michele is planning to buy a car that costs $20,000. Use algebraic expressions to help you answer the following questions.

a. At which dealership will Becky get the better deal? How much does she save?

b. At which dealership will Michele get the better deal? How much does she save?

c. What generalization can you make that would help any shopper know which dealership has the better deal? [Hint: At what price point would the two deals be equal?]

2.2 Creating and Solving Equations

Essential Question: How do you use an equation to model and solve a real-world problem?

Resource
Locker

⊘ Explore   Creating Equations from Verbal Descriptions

You can use what you know about writing algebraic expressions to write an equation that represents a real-world situation.

Suppose Cory and his friend Walter go to a movie. Each of their tickets costs the same amount, and they share a frozen yogurt that costs $5.50. The total amount they spend is $19.90. How can you write an equation that describes the situation?

(A) Identify the important information.

The word _____ tells you that the relationship describes an equation.

The word *total* tells you that the operation involved in the relationship is _____.

What numerical information do you have? _____

_____

What is the unknown quantity? _____

(B) Write a verbal description.

Choose a name for the variable. In this case, use *c* for _____.

The verbal description is: Twice the cost of _____ plus the cost

of _____ equals _____.

(C) To write an equation, write a numerical or _____ expression for each quantity

and insert an equal sign in the appropriate place. An equation is: _____.

Reflect

1. How can you use a verbal model to write an equation for the situation described?

2. Could you write a different equation to describe the situation? Explain your reasoning.

_____

_____

⏺ Explain 1 Creating and Solving Equations Involving the Distributive Property

When you create an equation to model a real-world problem, your equation may involve the Distributive Property. When you solve a real-world problem, you should always check that your answer makes sense.

Example 1 Write and solve an equation to solve each problem.

Ⓐ Aaron and Alice are bowling. Alice's score is twice the difference of Aaron's score and 5. The sum of their scores is 320. Find each student's bowling score.

Write a verbal description of the basic situation.

The sum of Aaron's score and Alice's score is 320.

Choose a variable for the unknown quantity and write an equation to model the detailed situation.

Let a represent Aaron's score. Then $2(a - 5)$ represents Alice's score.

$$a + 2(a - 5) = 320$$

Solve the equation for a.

$$a + 2(a - 5) = 320$$

$\quad a + 2a - 10 = 320 \qquad$ Distributive Property

$\qquad\quad 3a - 10 = 320$

$3a - 10 + 10 = 320 + 10 \qquad$ Addition Property of Equality

$\qquad\qquad\quad 3a = 330$

$\qquad\qquad \dfrac{3a}{3} = \dfrac{330}{3} \qquad$ Division Property of Equality

$\qquad\qquad\quad\; a = 110$

So, Aaron's score is 110 and Alice's score is $2(a - 5) = 2(110 - 5) = 2(105) = 210$.

Check that the answer makes sense.

$110 + 210 = 320$, so the answer makes sense.

Ⓑ Mari, Carlos, and Amanda collect stamps. Carlos has five more stamps than Mari, and Amanda has three times as many stamps as Carlos. Altogether, they have 100 stamps. Find the number of stamps each person has.

Write a verbal description of the basic situation.

Choose a variable for the unknown quantity and write an equation to model the detailed situation.

Let s represent the number of stamps Mari has. Then Carlos has _____ stamps, and Amanda has _____ stamps.

$$s + \boxed{} + 3\left(\boxed{}\right) = \boxed{}$$

Solve the equation for s.

$$s + \boxed{} + 3\left(\boxed{}\right) = \boxed{}$$

$s + s + 5 + 3s + \boxed{} = \boxed{}$ Distributive Property

$\boxed{} + \boxed{} = \boxed{}$ Combine like terms

$\boxed{}\ s = \boxed{}$ Subtraction Property of Equality

$s = \boxed{}$ Division Property of Equality

So, Mari has _____ stamps, Carlos has _____ stamps, and Amanda has _____ stamps.

Check that the answer makes sense.

$\boxed{} + \boxed{} + \boxed{} = \boxed{}$; the answer makes sense.

$\boxed{} = \boxed{}$

Reflect

3. Would a fractional answer make sense in this situation?

_____

_____

_____

4. Discussion What might it mean if a check revealed that the answer to a real-world problem did not make sense?

_____

_____

_____

Write and solve an equation to solve the problem.

5. A rectangular garden is fenced on all sides with 256 feet of fencing. The garden is 8 feet longer than it is wide. Find the length and width of the garden.

$(w + 8)$ feet

w feet

⚙ Explain 2 Creating and Solving Equations with Variables on Both Sides

In some equations, variables appear on both sides. You can use the properties of equality to collect the variable terms so that they all appear on one side of the equation.

Example 2 Write and solve an equation to solve each problem.

(A) Janine has job offers at two companies. One company offers a starting salary of $28,000 with a raise of $3000 each year. The other company offers a starting salary of $36,000 with a raise of $2000 each year. In how many years would Janine's salary be the same with both companies? What will the salary be?

Write a verbal description of the basic situation.

Let n represent the number of years it takes for the salaries to be equal.

Base Salary A plus $3000 per year raise = Base Salary B + $2000 per year raise

$$28,000 + 3000n = 36,000 + 2,000n$$

$$28,000 + 3000n - 2000n = 36,000 + 2,000n - 2000n \qquad \text{Subtraction Property of Equality}$$

$$28,000 + 1000n = 36,000 \qquad \text{Combine like terms.}$$

$$28,000 + 1000n - 28,000 = 36,000 - 28,000 \qquad \text{Subtraction Property of Equality}$$

$$1000n = 8000$$

$$\frac{1000n}{1000} = \frac{8000}{1000} \qquad \text{Division Property of Equality}$$

$$n = 8$$

$$28,000 + 3,000(8) = 36,000 + 2,000(8)$$

$$52,000 = 52,000$$

In 8 years, the salaries offered by both companies will be $52,000.

(B) One moving company charges \$800 plus \$16 per hour. Another moving company charges \$720 plus \$21 per hour. At what number of hours will the charge by both companies be the same? What is the charge?

Write a verbal description of the basic situation. Let t represent the number of hours that the move takes.

Moving Charge A plus \$16 per hour = Moving Charge B plus \$21 per hour

$$800 + \boxed{}\, t = 720 + \boxed{}\, t$$

$$800 + \boxed{}\, t - \boxed{}\, t = 720 + \boxed{}\, t - \boxed{}\, t \qquad \text{Subtraction Property of Equality}$$

$$800 = 720 + \boxed{}\, t$$

$$800 - 720 = 720 + \boxed{}\, t - 720 \qquad \text{Subtraction Property of Equality}$$

$$\boxed{} = \boxed{}\, t$$

$$\frac{\boxed{}}{\boxed{}} = \frac{\boxed{}}{\boxed{}}\, t \qquad \text{Division Property of Equality}$$

$$t = \boxed{}$$

The charges are the same for a job that takes _____ hours.

Substitute the value 16 in the original equation.

$$800 + 16t = 720 + 21t$$

$$800 + 16\left(\boxed{}\right) = 720 + 21\left(\boxed{}\right)$$

$$800 + \boxed{} = 720 + \boxed{}$$

$$\boxed{} = \boxed{}$$

After _____ hours, the moving charge for both companies will be _____.

Reflect

6. Suppose you collected the variable terms on the other side of the equal sign to solve the equation. Would that affect the solution?

_____

_____

Write and solve an equation to solve each problem.

7. Claire bought just enough fencing to enclose either a rectangular garden or a triangular garden, as shown. The two gardens have the same perimeter. How many feet of fencing did she buy?

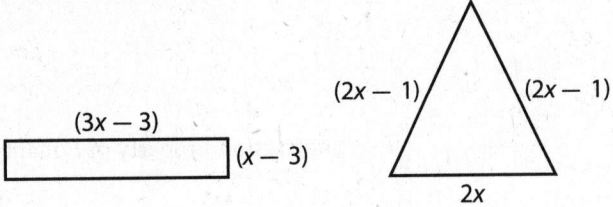

8. A veterinarian is changing the diets of two animals, Simba and Cuddles. Simba currently consumes 1200 Calories per day. That number will increase by 100 Calories each day. Cuddles currently consumes 3230 Calories a day. That number will decrease by 190 Calories each day. The patterns will continue until both animals are consuming the same number of Calories each day. In how many days will that be? How many Calories will each animal be consuming each day then?

🔑 **Explain 3** **Constructing Equations from an Organized Table**

You can use a table to organize information and see relationships.

Example 3 **Construct and solve an equation to solve the problem.**

Kim works 4 hours more each day than Jill does, and Jack works 2 hours less each day than Jill does. Over 2 days, the number of hours Kim works is equal to the difference of 4 times the number of hours Jack works and the number of hours Jill works. How many hours does each person work each day?

🧩 **Analyze Information**

Identify the important information.

- Kim works ☐ hours more per day than Jill does.

- Jack works ☐ hours less per day than Jill does.

🧩 **Formulate a Plan**

Make a table using the information given. Let x be the number of hours Jill works in one day.

	Hours Worked Per Day	Hours Worked Over 2 Days
Kim		
Jill		
Jack		

Over 2 days, the number of hours Kim works is equal to the difference of 4 times the number of hours Jack works and the number of hours Jill works.

Solve

$$2(x + 4) = 4 \cdot 2(x - 2) - 2x$$

$$2(x + 4) = \boxed{}(x - 2) - 2x \qquad \text{Simplify.}$$

$$2x + \boxed{} = 8x - \boxed{} - 2x \qquad \text{Distributive Property}$$

$$2x + 8 = \boxed{}x - 16 \qquad$$

$$2x + 8 + \boxed{} = 6x - 16 + \boxed{} \qquad \text{Addition Property of Equality}$$

$$2x + \boxed{} = 6x \qquad$$

$$2x + 24 - \boxed{}x = 6x - \boxed{}x \qquad \text{Subtraction Property of Equality}$$

$$24 = \boxed{}x \qquad$$

$$\frac{24}{\boxed{}} = \frac{\boxed{}x}{\boxed{}} \qquad \text{Division Property of Equality}$$

$$\boxed{} = x$$

Jill works $\boxed{}$ hours per day, Kim works $\boxed{}$ hours per day, and Jack works $\boxed{}$ hours per day.

Justify and Evaluate

Substitute $x = 6$ into the original equation.

$$2(6 + 4) = 4 \cdot 2(6 - 2) - 2x$$

$$2\left(\boxed{}\right) = 8\left(\boxed{}\right) - 2\left(\boxed{}\right)$$

$$\boxed{} = \boxed{}$$

Your Turn

Write and solve an equation to solve the problem.

9. Lisa is 10 centimeters taller than her friend Ian. Ian is 14 centimeters taller than Jim. Every month, their heights increase by 2 centimeters. In 7 months, the sum of Ian's and Jim's heights will be 170 centimeters more than Lisa's height. How tall is Ian now?

10. How can you use properties to solve equations with variables on both sides?

_____

_____

11. How is a table helpful when constructing equations?

_____

_____

12. When solving a real-world problem to find a person's age, would a negative solution make sense? Explain.

_____

_____

13. Essential Question Check-In How do you write an equation to represent a real-world situation?

_____

_____

_____

☆ Evaluate: Homework and Practice

- Online Homework
- Hints and Help
- Extra Practice

Write an equation for each description.

1. The sum of 14 and a number is equal to 17.

2. A number increased by 10 is 114.

3. The difference between a number and 12 is 20.

4. Ten times the sum of half a number and 6 is 8.

5. Two-thirds a number plus 4 is 7.

6. Tanmayi wants to raise $175 for a school fundraiser. She has raised $120 so far. How much more does she need to reach her goal?

7. Hector is visiting a cousin who lives 350 miles away. He has driven 90 miles. How many more miles does he need to drive to reach his cousin's home?

8. The length of a rectangle is twice its width. The perimeter of the rectangle is 126 feet.

Write and solve an equation for each situation.

9. In one baseball season, Peter hit twice the difference of the number of home runs Alice hit and 6. Altogether, they hit 18 home runs. How many home runs did each player hit that season?

10. The perimeter of a parallelogram is 72 meters. The width of the parallelogram is 4 meters less than its length. Find the length and the width of the parallelogram.

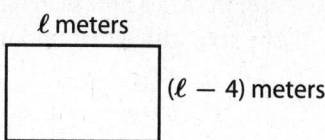

ℓ meters

$(\ell - 4)$ meters

11. One month, Ruby worked 6 hours more than Isaac, and Svetlana worked 4 times as many hours as Ruby. Together they worked 126 hours. Find the number of hours each person worked.

12. In one day, Annie traveled 5 times the sum of the number of hours Brian traveled and 2. Together they traveled 20 hours. Find the number of hours each person traveled.

13. Xian and his cousin Kai both collect stamps. Xian has 56 stamps, and Kai has 80 stamps. The boys recently joined different stamp-collecting clubs. Xian's club will send him 12 new stamps per month. Kai's club will send him 8 new stamps per month. After how many months will Xian and Kai have the same number of stamps? How many stamps will each have?

14. Kenya plans to make a down payment plus monthly payments in order to buy a motorcycle. At one dealer she would pay $2,500 down and $150 each month. At another dealer, she would pay $3,000 down and $125 each month. After how many months would the total amount paid be the same for both dealers? What would that amount be?

15. Community Gym charges a $50 membership fee and a $55 monthly fee. Workout Gym charges a $200 membership fee and a $45 monthly fee. After how many months will the total amount of money paid to both gyms be the same? What will the amount be?

16. Tina is saving to buy a notebook computer. She has two options. The first option is to put $200 away initially and save $10 every month. The second option is to put $100 away initially and save $30 every month. After how many months would Tina save the same amount using either option? How much would she save with either option?

Use the table to answer each question.

	Starting Salary	Yearly Salary Increase
Company A	$24,000	$3000
Company B	$30,000	$2400
Company C	$36,000	$2000

17. After how many years are the salaries offered by Company A and Company B the same?

18. After how many years are the salaries offered by Company B and Company C the same?

19. Paul started work at Company B ten years ago at the salary shown in the table. At the same time, Sharla started at Company C at the salary shown in the table. Who earned more during the last year? How much more?

20. George's page contains twice as many typed words as Bill's page and Bill's page contains 50 fewer words than Charlie's page. If each person can type 60 words per minute, after one minute, the difference between twice the number of words on Bill's page and the number of words on Charlie's page is 210. How many words did Bill's page contain initially? Use a table to organize the information.

21. Geometry Sammie bought just enough fencing to border either a rectangular plot or a square plot, as shown. The perimeters of the plots are the same. How many meters of fencing did she buy?

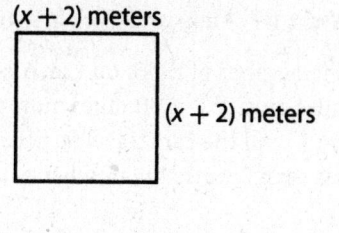

$(x + 2)$ meters

$(x + 2)$ meters

$(3x + 2)$ meters $(x - 1)$ meters

22. Justify Reasoning Suppose you want to solve the equation $2a + b = 2a$, where a and b are nonzero real numbers. Describe the solution to this equation. Justify your description.

23. Multi-step A patio in the shape of a rectangle, is fenced on all sides with 134 feet of fencing. The patio is 5 feet less wide than it is long.

ℓ feet

$(\ell - 5)$ feet

a. What information can be used to solve the problem? How can you find the information?

b. Describe how to find the area of the patio. What is the area of the patio?

24. Explain the Error Kevin and Brittany write an equation to represent the following relationship, and both students solve their equation. Who found the correct equation and solution? Why is the other person incorrect?

5 times the difference of a number and 20 is the same as half the sum of 4 more than 4 times a number.

Kevin: Brittany:

$5(x - 20) = \frac{1}{2}(4x + 4)$ $5(20 + x) = \frac{1}{2}(4x + 4)$

$5x - 100 = 2x + 2$ $100 - 5x = 2x + 2$

$3x - 100 = 2$ $100 - 7x = 2$

$3x = 102$ $-7x = -98$

$x = 34$ $x = 14$

25. What If? Alexa and Zack are solving the following problem.

The number of miles on Car A is 50 miles more than the number of miles on Car B, and the number of miles on Car B is 30 miles more than the number of miles on Car C. All the cars travel 50 miles in 1 hour. After 1 hour, twice the number of miles on Car A is 70 miles less than 3 times the number of miles on Car C. How many miles were there on Car B initially?

Alexa assumes there are m miles on Car B. Zack assumes there are m miles on Car C. Will Zack's answer be the same as Alexa's answer? Explain.

Lesson Performance Task

Stacy, Oliver, and Jivesh each plan to put a certain amount of money into their savings accounts that earn simple interest of 6% per year. Stacy puts $550 more than Jivesh, and Oliver puts in 2 times as much as Jivesh. After a year, the amount in Stacy's account is 2 times the sum of $212 and the amount in Oliver's account. How much does each person initially put into his or her account? Who had the most money in his or her account after a year? Who had the least? Explain.

© Houghton Mifflin Harcourt Publishing Company

Name_____ Class_____ Date_____

2.3 Solving for a Variable

Essential Question: How do you rewrite formulas and literal equations?

Resource Locker

⊙ Explore   Rearranging Mathematical Formulas

Literal Equations are equations that contain two or more variables. There are many literal equations in the form of math, science, and engineering formulas. These formulas may seem like they can only be solved for the variable that is isolated on one side of the formula. By using inverse operations and the properties of equality, a formula can be rearranged so any variable in the formula can be isolated. It is no different than how equations are solved by using inverse operations and the properties of equality.

How can you solve the equation $42 = 6x$?

Ⓐ $\dfrac{42}{\square} = \dfrac{6x}{\square}$ What is the reason for dividing?_____

_____

Why divide by $\square$?_____

$\square = x$ By rearranging the equation x was isolated and the solution was found.

The mathematical formula for the volume of a rectangular prism, $B = Vh$ or $V = \ell wh$, is a literal equation. V represents volume, ℓ represents length, w represents width, and h represents height. Using inverse operations, the formula can be rearranged to solve for any one of the variables that might be unknown. Like solving for x, a formula can be rearranged to isolate a variable.

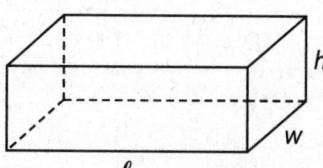

Ⓑ In the formula $V = \ell wh$, the variable h needs to be isolated.

The operation of _____ is used in the formula. The inverse

operation, _____, should be used

to isolate $\square$.

Ⓒ $\dfrac{V}{\square} = \dfrac{\ell wh}{\square}$

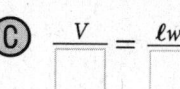

$\dfrac{V}{\square} = \square$

The formula rearranged in this way can easily produce the height of the rectangular prism, when the volume, length, and width are known.

Reflect

1. Using the formula for a rectangular prism, rewrite the formula to solve for ℓ.

© Houghton Mifflin Harcourt Publishing Company

⚙ Explain 1 Rearranging Scientific Formulas

Use inverse operations to isolate the unknown variable in a scientific formula.

The formula for density is $D = \frac{m}{V}$. Lead has a very high density of 11,340 kg/m³. Plastic foam has a very low density of 75 kg/m³. The formula for density can be rearranged to solve for V, volume or m, mass.

Example 1

(A) A sinker on a fishing line is made of lead and has a volume of 0.000015 m³. What is the mass of the sinker?

The density formula can be rearranged to isolate m, the mass. The values for volume and density can then be substituted into the formula to find the mass.

$$D = \frac{m}{V}$$
$$DV = \left(\frac{m}{V}\right)V$$
$$DV = m$$
$$\left(11{,}340 \text{ kg/m}^3\right)\left(0.000015 \text{ m}^3\right) = m$$
$$0.17 \text{ kg} \approx m$$

(B) The design for a life preserver requires 0.3 kilogram of plastic foam to provide proper buoyancy. What is the volume of the plastic foam required?

Rearrange the density formula to isolate V.

$$D = \frac{m}{V}$$
$$(D)V = \frac{m}{V}\,\Box$$
$$DV = \Box$$
$$\frac{DV}{\Box} = \frac{m}{\Box}$$
$$V = \Box$$

Now substitute the given values.

$$V = \frac{\Box}{\Box}$$
$$V = \Box \quad \text{m}^3$$

Your Turn

2. For altitudes up to 36,000 feet, the relationship between ground temperature and atmospheric temperature can be described by the formula $t = -0.0035a + g$, in which t is the atmospheric temperature in degrees Fahrenheit, a is the altitude, in feet, at which the atmospheric temperature is measured, and g is the ground temperature in degrees Fahrenheit. Determine the altitude in feet when t is $-27.5\,°F$ and g is $60\,°F$.

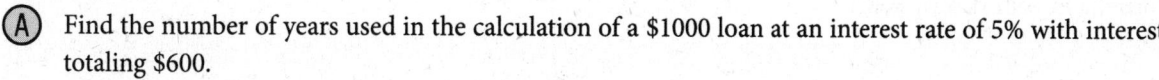 **Explain 2** **Rearranging Literal Equations**

Using inverse operations to rearrange literal equations can be applied to any formula. The interest formula, $I = prt$, is another example of a literal equation. In the formula, I represents interest, p the principal or the initial amount to which interest will be applied, r the rate at which interest will be paid, and t is the time in years.

Example 2

(A) Find the number of years used in the calculation of a $1000 loan at an interest rate of 5% with interest totaling $600.

Solve the formula for t.

$$I = prt$$

$$\frac{I}{pr} = \frac{prt}{pr}$$

$$\frac{I}{pr} = t$$

Substitute the given values. Since the interest rate is 5%, $r = 0.05$.

$$\frac{\$600}{\$1000 \cdot 0.05} = t$$

$$12 = t$$

So the length of time for the loan is 12 years.

(B) Determine the interest rate for a $2000 loan that will be paid off in 4 years with interest totaling $640. In order to find the interest rate, solve the formula for r.

$$I = prt$$

$$\frac{I}{\boxed{}} = \frac{prt}{\boxed{}}$$

$$\frac{\boxed{}}{\boxed{}} = r$$

Now substitute the values and simplify.

$$\frac{\boxed{}}{\left(\boxed{}\right)\left(\boxed{}\right)} = r$$

$$0.08 = r$$

So the interest rate is _____% per year.

Your Turn

3. The formula $y = mx + b$ is the slope-intercept form of the equation of a line. Solve the equation for m.

4. **Discussion** What could be a reason for isolating a variable in a literal equation?

_____

_____

5. Describe a situation in which a formula could be used more easily if it were rearranged. Include the formula in your description.

_____

_____

6. **Essential Question Check-In** How do you isolate a variable?

_____

_____

⊛ Evaluate: Homework and Practice

- Online Homework
- Hints and Help
- Extra Practice

Solve for the indicated variable in each mathematical formula.

1. $C = 2\pi r$ for r

2. $A = \frac{1}{2}bh$ for b

3. $y = mx + b$ for x

4. $A = \frac{1}{2}(a + b)h$ for h

5. $V = \pi r^2 h$ for h

6. $SA = 2\pi r^2 + 2\pi rh$ for h

Solve for the indicated variable in each scientific formula.

7. $d = rt$ for t

8. $PV = nRT$ for T

9. $A = \frac{FV - OV}{T}$ for OV

10. $C = \frac{Wtc}{1000}$ for W

Solve for the indicated variable in each literal equation.

11. $2p + 5r = q$ for p

12. $-10 = xy + z$ for x

13. $\frac{a}{b} = c$ for b

14. $\frac{h - 4}{j} = k$ for j

15. $\frac{x}{5} - g = a$ for x

16. $5p + 9c = p$ for c

17. $\frac{2}{5}(z + 1) = y$ for z

18. $g\left(h + \frac{2}{3}\right) = 1$ for h

19. $a(n - 3) + 8 = bn$ for n

20. Which is a possible way to rewrite the equation $y = 3x + 3b$ to solve for b?

A. $b = \dfrac{y - 3x}{3}$

C. $b = \dfrac{y - 3}{3x}$

B. $b = 3(y - 3x)$

D. $b = x(y - 3)$

21. Sports To find a baseball pitcher's earned run average (ERA), you can use the formula $Ei = 9r$, in which E represents ERA, i represents the number of innings pitched, and r represents the number of earned runs allowed. Solve the equation for E. What is a pitcher's ERA if he allows 5 earned runs in 18 innings pitched?

22. Meteorology For altitudes up to 36,000 feet, the relationship between ground temperature and atmospheric temperature can be described by the formula $t = -0.0035a + g$, in which t is the atmospheric temperature in degrees Fahrenheit, a is the altitude, in feet, at which the atmospheric temperature is measured, and g is the ground temperature in degrees Fahrenheit. Solve the equation for a. If the atmospheric temperature is $-65.5\,°F$ and the ground temperature is $57\,°F$, what is the altitude?

23. Explain the Error A student was asked to use the formula for the perimeter of a rectangle, $P = 2\ell + 2w$, to solve for ℓ. The student came up with an answer, $P - 2w = 2\ell$. What error did the student make? Explain. Then solve for ℓ.

24. Multi-Step The formula $c = 5p + 215$ relates c, the total cost in dollars of hosting a birthday party at a skating rink, to p, the number of people attending. If Allie's parents are willing to spend $300 for a party, how many people can attend?

25. Multi-Step The formula for the area of a triangle is $A = \frac{1}{2}bh$, in which b represents the length of the base and h represents the height. If a triangle has an area of 192 mm² and the height is 12 mm, what is the measure of the base?

Lesson Performance Task

The following table sh⌐ ⌐ the average low temperatures in Fahrenheit for the city of Boston for several months during the ye⌐ ⌐ ⌐e formula $F = \frac{9}{5}C + 32$ allows you to determine the temperature in Fahrenheit when given the temper⌐ ⌐e in Celsius.

Month	Temperature in Fahrenheit	Temperature in Celsius
January	22°	
April	41°	
July	65°	
October	47°	
December	28°	

a. Use the information given to determine the average low temperatures in Celsius.

b. Would it ever be possible for the temperature in Celsius to have a greater value than the temperature in Fahrenheit? Explain why or why not.

2.4 Creating and Solving Inequalities

Essential Question: How do you write and solve an inequality that represents a real-world situation?

⊘ Explore   Creating Inequalities from Verbal Descriptions

An **inequality** is a statement that compares two expressions that are not strictly equal by using one of the following inequality signs.

Symbol	Meaning
$<$	is less than
$\leq$	is less than or equal to
$>$	is greater than
$\geq$	is greater than or equal to
$\neq$	is not equal to

You have probably seen a sign at an amusement park saying something like, "You must be at least 48 inches tall to ride this ride." This statement could be written as $h \geq 48$ in., where h represents the height of a person allowed to ride.

Nora is planning a birthday party for her little sister, Colleen. Nora's budget will allow her to spend no more than $50 for party supplies. Eight children, including Colleen, will attend the party, and Nora wants to determine how much she could spend on party favors for each child. She will also purchase a cake for $10. Write an inequality that represents the situation, and find possible solutions.

Ⓐ First, let c represent the cost of a party favor for each child. Write an expression for the total cost of the party as a function of c.

$$\boxed{}\, c + \boxed{}$$

Ⓑ Which inequality symbol should be used to represent the phrase "no more than"? _____

Ⓒ Write the inequality that represents Nora's budget goal.

$$8c + 10 \leq \boxed{}$$

Ⓓ Suppose Nora finds party favors that cost $4 each. Use a value of 4 for c and check to see if this inequality is true.

$$8 \cdot 4 + 10 \overset{?}{\leq} 50$$

$$\boxed{} \overset{?}{\leq} 50$$

(E) Is the inequality true? _____

(F) Could Nora buy $6 party favors for all of her guests without going over budget?

_____

_____

Reflect

1. Why does an inequality represent Nora's budget calculation better than an equation?

_____

_____

2. The solution set of an inequality consists of all values that make the statement true. Describe the whole dollar amounts that are in the solution set for this situation.

_____

_____

🔧 Explain 1 Creating and Solving Inequalities Involving the Distributive Property

You may need to use the Distributive Property before you can solve an inequality.

Distributive Property	If a, b, and c are real numbers, then $a(b + c) = ab + ac$.

The inequality sign must be reversed when multiplying or dividing both sides of an inequality by a negative number.

Example 1

(A) Trina is buying 12 shirts for the drama club. She will choose a style for the blank shirts and then pay an additional charge of $2.75 for each shirt to have the club logo. If Trina cannot spend more than $99, how much can she spend on each blank shirt? Write and solve an inequality to find the possible cost of each blank shirt.

Let s represent the cost of each blank shirt.

Write an inequality to represent the situation. $12(s + 2.75) \leq 99$

Use the Distributive Property. $12s + 33 \leq 99$

Subtraction Property of Inequality $12s + 33 - 33 \leq 99 - 33$

Simplify. $12s \leq 66$

Division Property of Inequality $\frac{12s}{12} \leq \frac{66}{12}$

Simplify. $s \leq 5.5$

Check your answer.

Since $s \leq 5.5$, check a smaller number. $12(5 + 2.75) \overset{?}{\leq} 99$

Trina can order blank shirts that cost $5.50 or less. $93 \leq 99$ true

(B) Sergio needs to buy gifts for 8 friends. He wants to give the same gift to all his friends and he plans to have the gifts wrapped for an additional charge of $1.50 each. If Sergio spends at least $70, he will receive free shipping on his order. Write and solve an inequality to determine how much Sergio needs to spend on each gift in order to receive free shipping.

Let g be the cost of one gift.

Write an inequality to represent the situation. $\boxed{}\left(g + \boxed{}\right) \geq 70$

Use the Distributive Property. $\boxed{}g + \boxed{} \geq 70$

Subtraction Property of Inequality $\boxed{}g + 12 - \boxed{} \geq 70 - \boxed{}$

Simplify. $8g \geq \boxed{}$

Division Property of Inequality $\dfrac{8g}{\boxed{}} \geq \dfrac{58}{\boxed{}}$

Simplify. $g \geq \boxed{}$

Check your answer.

Since $g \geq 7.25$, check a larger number. $8(8 + 1.50) \overset{?}{\geq} 70$

Sergio must spend at least $\boxed{}$ on each gift. $\boxed{} \overset{?}{\geq} 70$

Reflect

3. **Discussion** Why is the first step in solving the inequality to use the Distributive Property instead of working inside the parentheses?

_____

_____

Your Turn

4. Zachary is planning to send a video game to each of his two brothers. If he buys the same game for both brothers and pays $4.75 to ship each game, how much can he spend on each game without spending more than $100? Write and solve an inequality for this situation.

Solve each inequality.

5. $\frac{4}{3}(6x + 9) < 4$ 6. $-2\left(\frac{1}{4}x + 2\right) \geq 5$

Some inequalities have variable terms on both sides of the inequality symbol. You can solve these inequalities the same way you solved equations with variables on both sides. Use the properties of inequality to collect all the variable terms on one side and all the constant terms on the other side.

Example 2

(A) The *Daily Info* charges a fee of $650 plus $80 per week to run an ad. The *People's Paper* charges $145 per week. For how many weeks must an ad run for the total cost at the *Daily Info* to be less expensive than the cost at the *People's Paper*? Let w be the number of weeks the ad runs in the paper.

Write an inequality to represent the situation.	$650 + 80w < 145w$
Subtraction Property of Inequality	$650 + 80w - 80w < 145w - 80w$
Simplify.	$650 < 65w$
Division Property of Inequality	$\dfrac{650}{65} < \dfrac{65w}{65}$
Simplify.	$10 < w$

The total cost at the *Daily Info* is less than the cost at the *People's Paper* if the ad runs for more than 10 weeks.

(B) The Home Cleaning Company charges $312 to power-wash the siding of a house plus $12 for each window. Power Clean charges $36 per window, and the price includes power-washing the siding. How many windows must a house have to make the total cost from The Home Cleaning Company less expensive than Power Clean? Let w be the number of windows.

Write an inequality to represent the situation.	$\boxed{} + 12w < 36w$
Subtraction Property of Inequality	$312 + 12w - \boxed{} < 36w - \boxed{}$
Simplify.	$312 < \boxed{}$
Division Property of Inequality	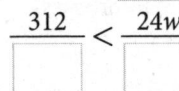
Simplify.	$\boxed{} < w$

A house must have more than 13 windows for The Home Cleaning Company to be less expensive than Power Clean.

Reflect

7. How would the final inequality change if you divided by −24 in the next to last step?

_____

Your Turn

8. The school band will sell pizzas to raise money for new uniforms. The supplier charges $100 plus $4 per pizza. The band members sell the pizzas for $7 each. Write and solve an inequality to find how many pizzas the band members will have to sell to make a profit?

9. Which inequality symbol would you use to represent the following words or phrases? Can you come up with more examples?

    a. at most   **b.** farther than   **c.** younger than   **d.** up to

10. **Discussion** How are the steps to solving an inequality similar to those for solving an equation? How are they different?

11. **Essential Question Check-In** How can you write an inequality that represents a real-world situation?

☆ Evaluate: Homework and Practice

- Online Homework
- Hints and Help
- Extra Practice

Write an inequality that represents the description, and then solve.

1. Max has more than 5 carrots (number of carrots Max has $= c$).

2. Brigitte is shorter than 5 feet (Brigitte's height $= h$).

3. Twice a number (x) is less than 10.

4. Six more than five times a number (x) is at least twenty-one.

5. Dave has $15 to spend on an $8 book and two birthday cards (c) for his friends. How much can he spend on each card if he buys the same card for each friend?

6. Toni can carry up to 18 lb in her backpack. Her lunch weighs 1 lb, her gym clothes weigh 2 lb, and her books (b) weigh 3 lb each. How many books can she carry in her backpack?

Solve each inequality.

7. $3(x - 2) > -3$

8. $5 + 5(x + 4) \leq 20$

9. $3 + \frac{1}{2}(3 - x) < -7$

10. $3(x + 6) - 2(x + 2) \geq 10$

11. $5(3 - x) - 4(2 - 3x) > 2$

12. $\frac{1}{2}(4x - 2) - \frac{2}{3}(6x + 9) \leq 4$

13. $x + 1 > -5(7 - 2x)$

14. $\frac{5}{3}(6x + 3) \leq 2x - 7$

15. $2x \leq -\frac{2}{3}(4x + 4)$

16. $\frac{1}{2}(-2x - 10) > 3(4 - 6x)$

17. $-5 - 3x \geq 2(10 + 2x) + 3$

18. $-3(9x + 20) \geq 15x - 20$

19. $8\left(\frac{1}{4}x - 3\right) + 24 < 4(x + 5)$

20. $6x - 2(x + 2) > 2 - 3(x + 3)$

21. Physics A crane cable can support a maximum load of 15,000 kg. If a bucket has a mass of 2,000 kg and gravel has a mass of 1,500 kg for every cubic meter, how many cubic meters of gravel (g) can be safely lifted by the crane?

22. Find the solution set of each inequality below, and then determine which inequalities have the same solution set as $\frac{1}{3}(-5x - 3) < 14$.

a. $\frac{1}{3}(5x + 3) > -14$

b. $\frac{2}{5}(10x + 20) > 44$

c. $-\frac{2}{5}(10x + 20) < -44$

d. $-\frac{1}{3}(5x + 3) < 14$

e. $\frac{2}{5}(10x - 20) > -44$

f. $\frac{1}{3}(5x + 3) < -14$

H.O.T. Focus on Higher Order Thinking

23. Explain the Error Sven is trying to find the maximum amount of time he can spend practicing the five scales of piano music he is supposed to be working on. He has 60 minutes to practice piano and would like to spend at least 35 minutes playing songs instead of practicing scales. So, Sven sets up the following inequality, where t is the number of minutes he spends on each scale, and solves it.

$$60 - 5t \leq 35$$
$$-5t \leq -25$$
$$t \geq 5$$

Sven has concluded that he should spend 5 minutes or more on each scale. Is this correct? If not, what mistake did he make? Then solve for the correct answer.

24. Critical Thinking Anika wants to determine the maximum number of tulip bulbs (*t*) she can purchase if each bulb costs $1.50. She will also need to purchase separate pots for each bulb at $1.25 each and a bag of potting soil for $10.00. Set up an inequality to determine how many tulip bulbs Anika can purchase without spending more than $20.00, and solve it. Can Anika buy exactly enough bulbs and pots to spend the full $20.00? Explain. Can you think of a better inequality to describe the answer?

25. Geometry The area of the triangle shown is no more than 10 square inches.

a. Write an inequality that can be used to find *x*.

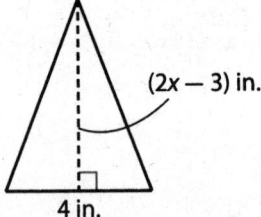

$(2x - 3)$ in.

4 in.

b. Solve the inequality from part **a**.

c. What is the maximum height of the triangle?

Lesson Performance Task

When planning an airplane route, the trip planner must be careful to consider the range the aircraft can travel and the availability of airports to stop and refuel.

A large commercial jet airplane burns approximately 5 gallons of fuel per mile flown, plus about 8500 gallons of fuel per trip to reach cruising altitude. With a useable fuel capacity of 50,000 gallons (there is additional fuel reserved for emergencies), describe the acceptable distance for which an airline could establish a non-stop flight.

For flights originating from Chicago, determine which cities could be safely reached by a non-stop flight.

City	Distance from Chicago (miles)
Bangalore, India	8530
Jakarta, Indonesia	9810
Johannesburg, South Africa	8680
Moscow, Russia	4970
Paris, France	4130
Perth, Australia	10,970
Tokyo, Japan	6300

2.5 Creating and Solving Compound Inequalities

Essential Question: How can you solve a compound inequality and graph the solution set?

Resource Locker

🧭 Explore   Truth Tables and Compound Statements

A **compound statement** is formed by combining two or more simple statements. A compound statement can be true or false. A compound statement involving **AND** is true when *both* simple statements are true. A compound statement involving **OR** is true when *either* one simple statement *or both* are true.

Ⓐ Complete the truth table.

P	Q	P True or False?	Q True or False?	P AND Q True or False?
A dog is a mammal.	Red is a color.			
A dog is a mammal.	Red is not a color.			
A dog is a fish.	Red is a color.			
A dog is a fish.	Red is not a color.			

Ⓑ *P* **AND** *Q* is true when _____.

Ⓒ Complete the truth table.

P	Q	P True or False?	Q True or False?	P OR Q True or False?
1 is an odd number.	2 is an even number.			
1 is an odd number.	2 is an odd number.			
1 is an even number.	2 is an even number			
1 is an even number.	2 is an odd number.			

Ⓓ *P* **OR** *Q* is true when _____.

Reflect

1. Give two simple statements *P* and *Q* for which *P* **AND** *Q* is false and *P* **OR** *Q* is true.

_____

_____

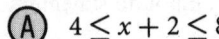 **Explain 1** **Solving Compound Inequalities Involving AND**

Combining two or more simple inequalities forms a **compound inequality**. The graph of a compound inequality involving **AND** is the **intersection**, or the overlapping region, of the simple inequality graphs.

Compound Inequalities: AND		
Words	**Algebra**	**Graph**
All real numbers greater than 2 **AND** less than 6	$x > 2$ **AND** $x < 6$ $2 < x < 6$	← $\longmapsto$ 0 1 2 3 4 5 6 7 8 9 10
All real numbers greater than or equal to 2 **AND** less than or equal to 6	$x \geq 2$ **AND** $x \leq 6$ $2 \leq x \leq 6$	← $\longmapsto$ 0 1 2 3 4 5 6 7 8 9 10

Example 1 Solve each compound inequality and graph the solutions.

(A) $4 \leq x + 2 \leq 8$

$4 \leq x + 2$ **AND** $x + 2 \leq 8$ Write the compound inequality using AND.

$4 - 2 \leq x + 2 - 2$ $x + 2 - 2 \leq 8 - 2$ Subtract 2 from both sides of each simple inequality.

$2 \leq x$ $x \leq 6$ Simplify.

Graph $2 \leq x$.

Graph $x \leq 6$.

Graph the intersection by finding where the two graphs overlap.

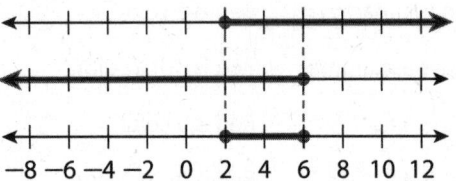

(B) $-5 \leq 2x + 3 < 9$

$-5 - \boxed{} \leq 2x + 3 - \boxed{} < 9 - \boxed{}$ Subtract $\boxed{}$ from each part of the inequality.

$\boxed{} \leq 2x < \boxed{}$ Simplify.

$\dfrac{-8}{\boxed{}} \leq \dfrac{2x}{\boxed{}} < \dfrac{6}{\boxed{}}$ Divide each part of the inequality by $\boxed{}$.

$\boxed{} \leq x < \boxed{}$ Simplify.

Graph $-4 \leq x$.

Graph $x < 3$.

Graph the intersection by finding where the two graphs overlap.

2. **Discussion** Explain why $2 \leq x \leq 6$ can be considered the *short method* for writing the **AND** compound inequality $x \geq 2$ **AND** $x \leq 6$.

_____

Solve each compound inequality and graph the solutions.

3. $-2 < x - 3 < 5$

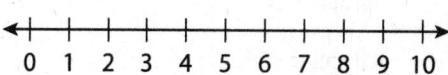

4. $-10 < 3x + 2 \leq 8$

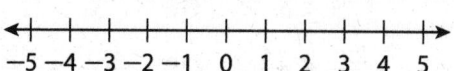

🔑 Explain 2 Solving Compound Inequalities Involving OR

The graph of a compound inequality involving **OR** is the **union**, or the combined region, of the simple inequality graphs.

Compound Inequalities: OR		
Words	**Algebra**	**Graph**
All real numbers less than 2 **OR** greater than 6	$x < 2$ **OR** $x > 6$	← 0 1 2 3 4 5 6 7 8 9 10 →
All real numbers less than or equal to 2 **OR** greater than or equal to 6	$x \leq 2$ **OR** $x \geq 6$	← 0 1 2 3 4 5 6 7 8 9 10 →

Example 2 Solve each compound inequality and graph the solutions.

(A) $-4 + x > 1$ OR $-4 + x < -3$

$\quad\quad -4 + x > 1 \quad$ OR $\quad\quad -4 + x < -3 \quad$ Write the compound inequality using OR.

$\quad -4 + 4 + x > 1 + 4 \quad -4 + 4 + x < -3 + 4 \quad$ Add 4 to both sides of each simple inequality.

$\quad\quad\quad x > 5 \quad\quad\quad\quad\quad\quad x < 1 \quad$ Simplify.

Graph $x > 5$.

Graph $x < 1$.

Graph the union by combining the graphs.

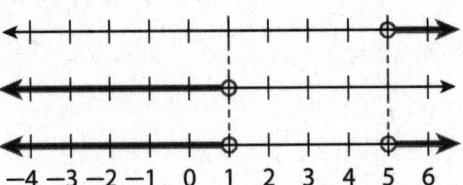

(B) $2x \leq 6$ OR $3x > 12$

$\quad\quad 2x \leq 6 \quad\quad$ OR $\quad\quad 3x > 12 \quad$ Write the compound inequality using OR.

$\quad \dfrac{2x}{\boxed{}} \leq \dfrac{6}{\boxed{}} \quad$ OR $\quad \dfrac{3x}{\boxed{}} > \dfrac{12}{\boxed{}} \quad$ Divide the first simple inequality by $\boxed{}$.

Divide the second simple inequality by $\boxed{}$.

$\quad\quad x \leq \boxed{} \quad$ OR $\quad x > \boxed{}$. Simplify.

Graph $x \leq 3$.

Graph $x > 4$.

Graph the union by combining the graphs.

Reflect

5. **Critical Thinking** What kind of compound inequality has no solution?

_____

_____

_____

Your Turn

Solve each compound inequality and graph the solutions.

6. $x - 5 \geq -2$ OR $x - 5 \leq -6$

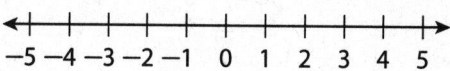

7. $4x - 1 < 15$ OR $8x \geq 48$

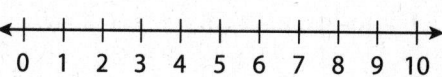

🔑 Explain 3   Creating Compound Inequalities From Graphs

Given a number line graph with a solution set graphed, you can create a compound inequality to fit the graph.

Example 3   Write the compound inequality shown by each graph.

Ⓐ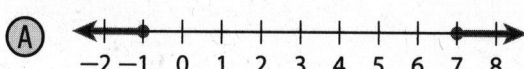

The shaded portion of the graph is not between two values, so the compound inequality involves OR.

On the left, the graph shows an arrow pointing left from -1 and a solid circle, so use $\leq$.

The inequality is $x \leq -1$.

On the right, the graph shows an arrow pointing right from 7 and a solid circle, so use $\geq$.

The inequality is $x \geq 7$.

The compound inequality is $x \leq -1$ OR $x \geq 7$.

Ⓑ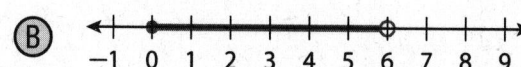

The graph is shaded between the values ☐ and ☐ , so the compound inequality involves **AND**.

The graph is shaded to the right/left of ☐ and the circle is open/solid, so use the inequality

symbol _____ .

The inequality is _____ .

The graph is shaded to the right/left of ☐ and the circle is open/solid, so use the inequality

symbol _____ .

The inequality is _____ .

The compound inequality is _____ .

© Houghton Mifflin Harcourt Publishing Company

8. What is a *short method* to write the compound inequality $x \geq 0$ AND $x < 6$?

_____

Your Turn

Write the compound inequality shown by each graph.

9.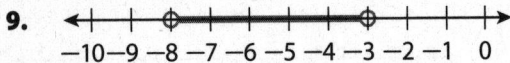

10.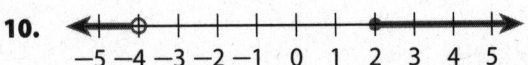

⚙ Explain 4 ## Expressing Acceptable Levels with Compound Inequalities

You can express quality-controls levels in real-world problems using compound inequalities.

Example 4 **Write a compound inequality to represent the indicated quality-control level, and graph the solutions.**

Ⓐ The recommended pH level for swimming pool water is between 7.2 and 7.6, inclusive.

Let p be the pH level of swimming pool water.

7.2	is less than or equal to	pH level	is less than or equal to	7.6
7.2	$\leq$	p	$\leq$	7.6

The compound inequality is $7.2 \leq p \leq 7.6$.

Graph the solutions.

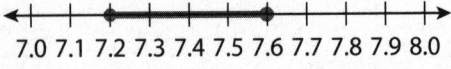

(B) The recommended free chlorine level for swimming pool water is between 1.0 and 3.0 parts per million, inclusive.

Let c be the free chlorine level in the pool.

	is less than or equal to	free chlorine level	is less than or equal to	

$$c$$

The compound inequality is $\boxed{} \leq c \leq \boxed{}$.

Graph the solutions.

```
←+—+—+—+—+—+—+—+—+—+—+→
  0  1  2  3  4  5  6  7  8  9  10
```

Reflect

11. Discussion What does the phrase "between 7.2 and 7.6, inclusive" mean?

_____

_____

Your Turn

Write a compound inequality to represent the indicated quality-control level, and graph the solutions.

12. The recommended alkalinity level for swimming pool water is between 80 and 120 parts per million, inclusive.

```
←+—+—+—+—+—+—+—+—+—+—+→
  0    40    80   120   160   200
```

⊙ Elaborate

13. Explain the difference between graphing a compound inequality involving **AND** and graphing a compound inequality involving **OR**.

_____

_____

_____

14. How can you tell whether a compound inequality involves **AND** or **OR** from looking at its graph?

_____

_____

_____

15. Essential Question Check-In Explain how to find the solutions of a compound inequality.

_____

_____

_____

Complete the truth tables.

1.

P	Q	P True or False?	Q True or False?	P AND Q True or False?
An apple is a fruit.	A carrot is a vegetable.			
An apple is a fruit.	A carrot is a fruit.			
An apple is a vegetable.	A carrot is a vegetable.			
An apple is a vegetable.	A carrot is a fruit.			

2.

P	Q	P True or False?	Q True or False?	P OR Q True or False?
Blue is a color.	Five is a number.			
Blue is a color.	Five is a color.			
Blue is a number.	Five is a number.			
Blue is a number.	Five is a color.			

Solve each compound inequality and graph the solutions.

3. $-3 < 3x \le 9$

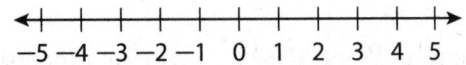

4. $0 \le 2x - 10 \le 20$

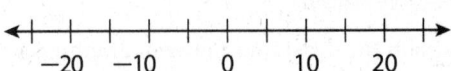

5. $x - 5 < 3$ OR $x - 5 \ge 8$

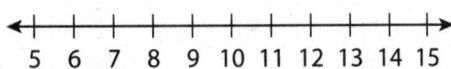

6. $1 \le x + 7 < 7$

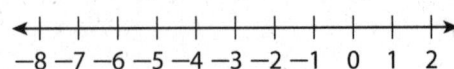

7. $4x + 3 < -5$ OR $4x + 3 > 23$

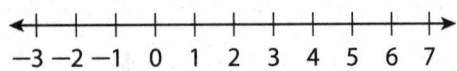

8. $\frac{x}{5} - 2 \le -6$ OR $8x + 1 \ge 41$

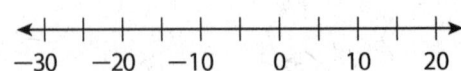

9. $-6 < \frac{x - 12}{4} < -2$

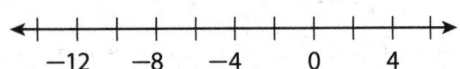

10. $x + 7 \le 7$ OR $5 + 2x > 7$

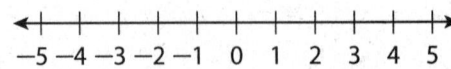

24. **Multi-Step** Jenna's band is going to record a CD at a recording studio. They will pay $225 to use the studio for one day and $80 per hour for sound technicians. Jenna has $200 and can reasonably expect to raise up to an additional $350 by taking pre-orders for the CDs.

   a. Explain how the inequality $200 \leq 225 + 80n \leq 550$ can be used to find the number of hours Jenna and her band can afford to use the studio and sound technicians.

   b. Solve the inequality. Are there any numbers in the solution set that are not reasonable in this situation?

   c. Suppose Jenna raises $350 in pre-orders. How much more money would she need to raise if she wanted to use the studio and sound technicians for 6 hours?

25. **Explain the Error** A student solves the compound inequality $15 \leq 2x + 5 \leq 17$ and finds the solutions of the compound inequality to be all real numbers. Explain and correct the student's mistake. Graph the actual solutions to back up your answer.

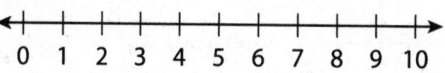

26. **Communicate Mathematical Thinking** Describe the solutions of the compound inequalities.

   $x > 9$ AND $x < 9$

   $x < 9$ OR $x > 9$

   $x \geq 9$ AND $x \leq 9$

   $x \leq 9$ OR $x \geq 9$

Lesson Performance Task

The table gives the melting point and boiling point of various elements. Write a compound inequality for each element to show the temperature range of the element in its liquid state. Graph the solutions of each. Suppose you were to set the temperature of each element to its melting point and increase the temperature of each element at the same rate. Which element will remain liquid for the longest amount of time? Which element will reach its boiling point first? Explain.

Element	Melting Point (°C)	Boiling Point (°C)
Gold	1064	2856
Copper	1085	2562
Iron	1538	2861
Lead	327	1749
Aluminum	660	2519

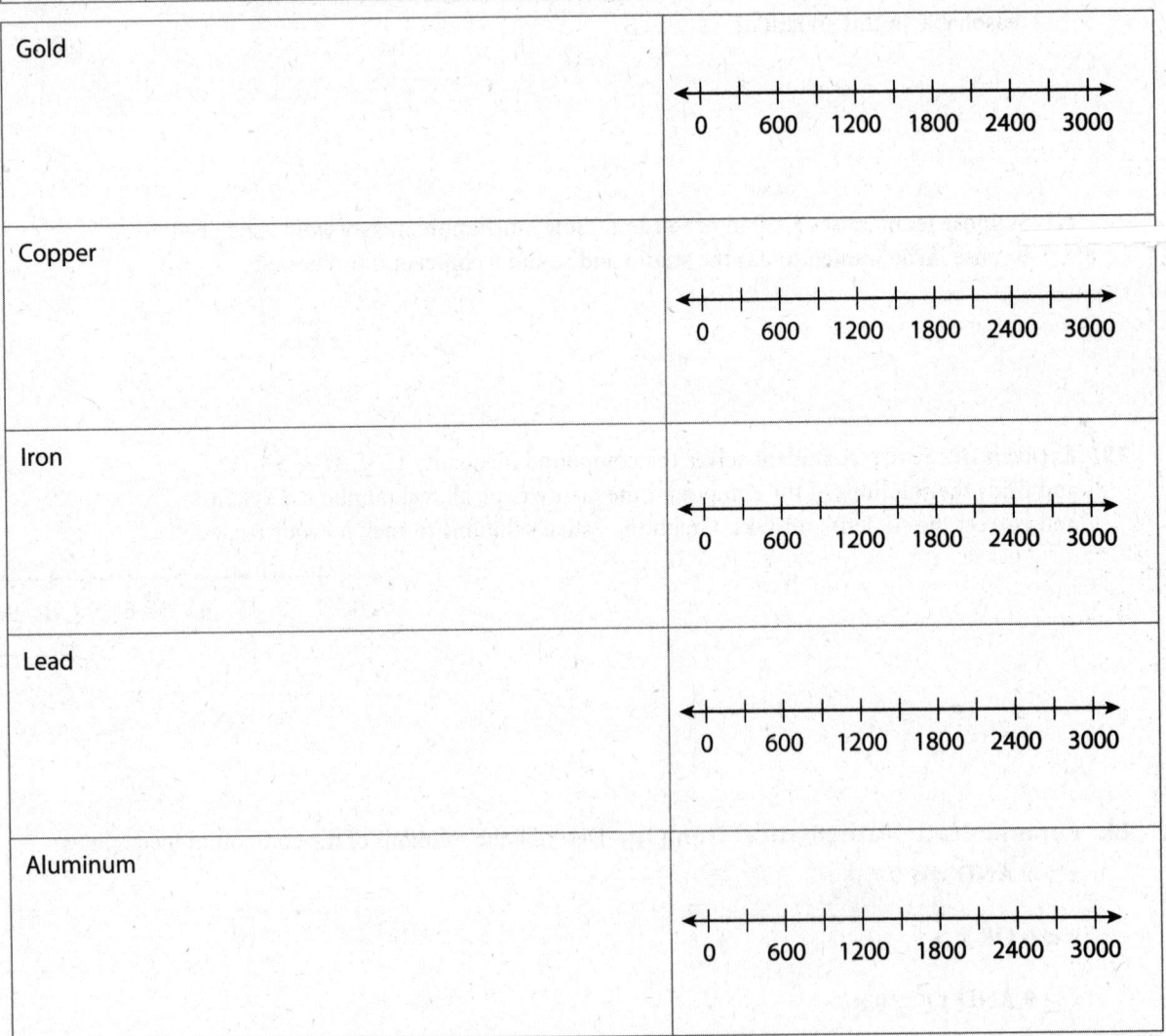

(Ready) to Go On?

2.1–2.5 Algebraic Models

• Online Homework
• Hints and Help
• Extra Practice

Write an expression in simplest form for each verbal description. *(Lesson 2.1)*

1. The sum of the cost of dinner d and a \$12 tip divided equally between 3 people

2. The total pay for 12 hours of work at a base rate of p per hour plus a temporary raise of \$2.50 per hour

3. Given $x < y$, compare the following expressions and determine which is greater: $2x - y$; $2y - x$. Explain your answer. *(Lesson 2.1)*

4. The formula $y - y_1 = m(x - x_1)$ is the point-slope form of the equation of a line where m is the slope of the line and (x, y) and (x_1, y_1) are points of the line. Solve the equation for m, and find the slope of a line that includes the points $(4, -2)$ and $(5, 0)$. *(Lesson 2.3)*

Solve. *(Lessons 2.2, 2.4, 2.5)*

5. $-17 - 5(x + 3) = 3x$

6. $100x - 200 > 50x - 75$

7. $12 < 2x + 2 \leq 22$

8. $-13 < -x + 5 < 8$

ESSENTIAL QUESTION

9. What is the general process for solving an equation with one variable?

Assessment Readiness

1. Consider the new expression that is obtained by simplifying $8(x - 1) + 15$. Select True or False for each statement.

   A. The new expression has 3 terms. ○ True ○ False

   B. The coefficient of x in the new expression is 8. ○ True ○ False

   C. The constant in the new expression is 14. ○ True ○ False

2. Look at each equation and possible solution. Is the solution correct? Select Yes or No for each equation.

   A. $3 - m = -2(m + 6); m = -15$ ○ Yes ○ No

   B. $5(p + 3) = -35; p = -4$ ○ Yes ○ No

   C. $8q = 3(10 + q); q = 6$ ○ Yes ○ No

3. The formula for finding the volume of a triangular prism $V = \frac{1}{2}(bh)\ell$ where b represents the base length, h represents the base height, and ℓ represents the length of the prism. Select True or False for each statement.

   A. The formula solved for h is $h = \frac{2V\ell}{b}$. ○ True ○ False

   B. The formula solved for ℓ is $\ell = \frac{2V}{bh}$. ○ True ○ False

   C. The formula solved for b is $b = \frac{2V}{bh}$. ○ True ○ False

4. Sherman hopes to get at least a 90 average on his science tests. He has one more test before the end of the school year. His past test scores are 79, 94, 91, and 92. Write and solve an inequality that represents this situation. What is the lowest score Sherman can get on his final test and reach his goal? Show your work.

1. Consider each equation and solution. Is each solution correct?
   Select Yes or No.

   A. $6 = -\dfrac{r}{3}$; $r = -2$ ◯ Yes   ◯ No

   B. $1 - 2s = 3$; $s = 5$ ◯ Yes   ◯ No

   C. $4 + 6t = -20$; $t = -4$ ◯ Yes   ◯ No

2. The distance from Town A to Town B on a map is 6 inches. The actual distance from Town B to Town C is 12 miles. The scale on the map is 1 in: 4 mi. Determine if each statement is True or False.

   A. The actual distance from A to B is 24 mi.   ◯ True   ◯ False

   B. The distance from B to C on the map is 36 in.   ◯ True   ◯ False

   C. The actual distance from A to C is 4.5 mi.   ◯ True   ◯ False

3. The dimensions of a storage container in the shape of a rectangular prism are 54 in. × 32.25 in. × 24.5 in. Choose True or False for each statement.

   A. The most precise dimension has 4 significant digits.   ◯ True   ◯ False

   B. Written using the correct number of significant digits, the volume of the container has 3 significant digits.   ◯ True   ◯ False

   C. Written using the correct number of significant digits, the surface area of the container is rounded to the ones place.   ◯ True   ◯ False

4. Hank bought 3 more boxes of cereal than gallons of milk. He bought x boxes of cereal at $2.79 each. Each gallon of milk costs $4.49. Consider the expression $2.79x + 4.49(x - 3)$. Determine if each statement is True or False.

   A. The term $x - 3$ represents the number of gallons of milk.   ◯ True   ◯ False

   B. The coefficient 2.79 represents the cost of one box of cereal.   ◯ True   ◯ False

   C. The expression represents the total number of boxes of cereal and gallons of milk.   ◯ True   ◯ False

5. The formula $y = mx + b$ is the slope-intercept form of the equation of a line where m is the slope of the line, b is the y-intercept, and (x, y) is a solution of the equation.

   A. The equation solved for b is $b = y - mx$.   ○ True   ○ False

   B. The equation solved for x is $x = \dfrac{y - b}{m}$.   ○ True   ○ False

   C. The equation solved for m is $m = x(y - b)$.   ○ True   ○ False

6. Carla and Ross competed in the long-jump at a track meet. Carla jumped 3.5 meters. Ross jumped 99 inches. Who jumped farther and by approximately how many feet? Use 1 m ≈ 3.27 ft. Explain how you solved this problem.

7. Solve the following equation for x: $\dfrac{1}{2}(5x + 12) = 2x - 3$. Show your work.

8. A factory produces 5-packs of pencils. To be within the weight specifications, a pack of 5 pencils should weigh between 60 grams and 95 grams. The cardboard for each package has a mass of 15 grams. Write a compound inequality to represent the mass of a single pencil in a pack. Can each pencil have a mass of 10.5 grams? Explain.

Performance Tasks

★ **9.** Fernando is starting a new sales job and needs to decide which of two salary plans to choose from. For plan A, he will earn $100/week plus 15% commission on all sales. For plan B, he will earn $150/week plus 10% commission on all sales.

   A. Write an expression for each salary plan if Fernando's total weekly sales are s.

   B. For what amount of weekly sales is plan B better than plan A?

★★**10.** An electronics company has developed a new hand-held device. The company predicts that the start-up cost to manufacture the new product will be $125,000, and the cost to make one device will be $6.50.

A. If the company plans on selling the device at a wholesale price of $9, write and solve an inequality to determine how many must be sold for the company to make a profit. Show your work.

B. The cost of making one device is 10% more than the company predicted. What is the new cost of making one device? How many devices must it now sell at the same wholesale price to make a profit?

C. Suppose the company wants to start making a profit after selling the same number of devices you found in part **A**. What should the new wholesale price be? Explain how you found this price.

★★★**11.** A company that sells computers and other electronic equipment wants to hire some new sales staff. The company offers salary packages that combine a base salary and commissions from sales. It is willing to pay a base salary of between $20,000 and $30,000 per year and a commission rate between 2.5% and 6.5% of total sales per year. The company has a rule that if someone makes the maximum base salary, he or she cannot earn the highest commission rate, and vice versa.

A. Javier is very confident in his ability to generate large sales. What salary package would appeal to him? Explain your reasoning, and write an algebraic expression for Javier's salary package.

B. Catherine prefers to have a more stable income that is less affected by sales. What salary package would appeal to her? Explain your reasoning, and write an algebraic expression for her salary package.

C. For what amounts of sales will Catherine make more than Javier? Use your expressions from parts **A** and **B** to write and solve an inequality to find the answer.

Personal Trainer Kayla is a personal trainer and is working with Jed to devise a plan to help him lose weight. Kayla explained to Jed that each pound of body fat is equal to 3500 Calories. So, if Jed eliminates 500 Calories per day through diet and exercise, he will lose one pound per week. The table shows how many Calories are burned per hour of exercise for people of different weights who are walking or running at various speeds.

Calories Burned per Hour of Exercise by Body Weight				
	Body Weight			
Exercise (1 Hour)	**130 lb**	**155 lb**	**180 lb**	**205 lb**
Walking 2.0 mph	148	176	204	233
Walking 3.0 mph	195	232	270	307
Walking 4.0 mph	295	352	409	465
Running 5.0 mph	472	563	654	745
Running 6.0 mph	590	704	817	931
Running 7.0 mph	649	774	899	1024

Jed currently weighs 205 pounds. He walks on a treadmill at a speed of 3 miles per hour and runs at a speed of 5 miles per hour, and he exercises for 30 minutes each day.

a. Use the information in the table to find an expression for the number of Calories Jed burns while walking for t minutes.

b. If Jed exercises for 30 minutes, then $30 - t$ is the number of minutes Jed runs at 5.0 miles per hour. Write an expression for the number of Calories Jed burns while running for t minutes.

c. Write an equation relating the total number of Calories Jed burns to the number of minutes he walks each day.

d. What is the domain of the equation you found in part c?

e. Is it possible for Jed to burn 500 Calories per day from exercising for 30 minutes? Explain how you determined your answer.

Understanding Functions

© Houghton Mifflin Harcourt Publishing Company • Image Credits: ©Design Pics Inc./Alamy

MATH IN CAREERS

Interior Designer Interior designers create and improve interior spaces in homes and buildings, making them safe, functional, and visually pleasing. Interior designers must understand the geometry of spaces and how to interpret measurements on blueprints. They also need to be able to calculate the amount and cost of materials needed for a project.

If you are interested in a career as an interior designer, you should study these mathematical subjects:
- Algebra
- Geometry
- Trigonometry
- Business Math

Research other careers that require determining costs and amounts of materials for a project. Check out the career activity at the end of the unit to find out how **interior designers** use math.

Reading Start-Up

Vocabulary

Review Words

✔ coordinate plane
   (*plano cartesiano*)

✔ input (*entrada*)

✔ ordered pair
   (*par ordenado*)

✔ origin (*origen*)

✔ output (*salida*)

✔ x-axis (*eje x*)

✔ y-axis (*eje y*)

Preview Words

continuous graph
   (*gráfica continua*)

discrete graph
   (*gráfica discreta*)

domain (*dominio*)

function (*función*)

function rule (*regla de función*)

range (*rango*)

relation (*relación*)

sequence (*sucesión*)

Visualize Vocabulary

Use the ✔ words to identify a–e in the graphic. Put one term on each line and one term in the circle.

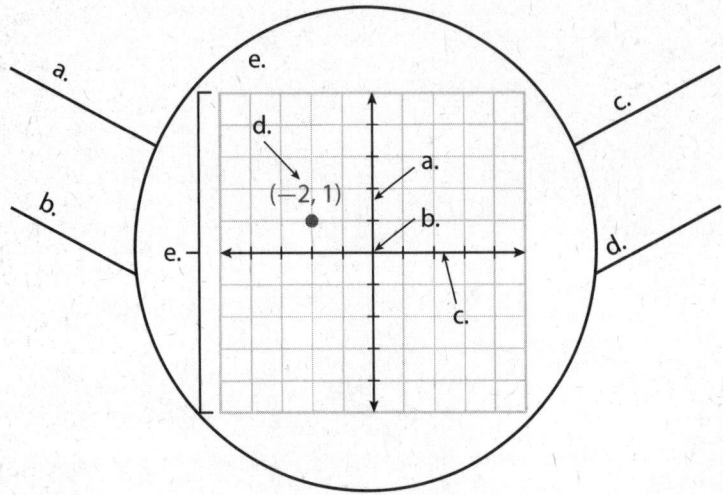

Understand Vocabulary

Match the term on the left to the correct expression on the right.

1. __ discrete graph

2. __ function rule

3. __ continuous graph

4. __ relation

A. a graph made up of connected lines or curves

B. a graph made up of unconnected points

C. a set of ordered pairs

D. an algebraic expression that describes how the output comes from the input

Active Reading

Booklet Before beginning the unit, create a booklet for taking notes as you learn the concepts in this unit. Write the main idea of each module on the appropriate pages to create an outline of the unit. As you study each lesson, write the important details that support the main idea, such as vocabulary and formulas. Refer to your finished booklet as you work on assignments and study for tests.

Functions and Models

Essential Question: How can you use functions to solve real-world problems?

REAL WORLD VIDEO
A function can be thought of as an industrial machine, only accepting certain predefined inputs, performing a series of operations on what it's been fed, and delivering an output dependent on the initial input.

MODULE PERFORMANCE TASK PREVIEW
Season Passes

Decisions, decisions! Wild Planet Theme Park has just opened, and you've decided to buy a season pass but aren't sure which payment option is the least expensive. How can you decide? Looks like the theme of this theme park is mathematics!

Are (YOU) Ready?

Complete these exercises to review skills you will need for this module.

Graphing Linear Relationships

Example 1   Tell whether the graph represents a linear nonproportional or proportional relationship.

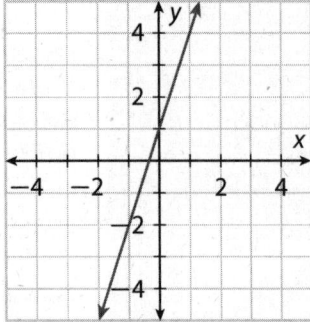

The graph of a linear nonproportional relationship is a straight line that does not pass through the origin.

The graph of a linear proportional relationship is a straight line that passes through the origin.

The graph represents a linear nonproportional relationship because it is a straight line that does not pass through the origin.

Tell whether the graph represents a linear nonproportional or proportional relationship.

1.

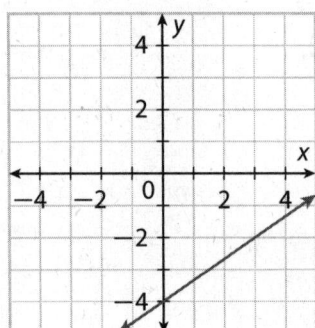

2.

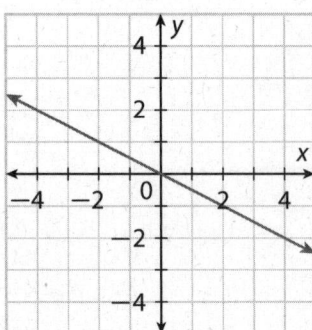

Linear Functions

Example 2   Tell whether $y = x^2 + 5$ represents a linear function.

$y = x^2 + 5$ does not represent a linear function because x has an exponent of 2.

When a linear equation is written in standard form, the following are true.

• x and y both have exponents of 1.

• x and y are not multiplied together.

• x and y do not appear in denominators, exponents, or radicands.

Tell whether the equation represents a linear function.

3. $0.3x + y = 7$

4. $xy - 2 = 9$

5. $y = 2^x + 5$

3.1   Graphing Relationships

Essential Question: How can you describe a relationship given a graph and sketch a graph given a description?

Resource
Locker

⊘ Explore   Interpreting Graphs

The distance a delivery van is from the warehouse varies throughout the day. The graph shows the distance from the warehouse for a day from 8:00 am to 5:00 pm.

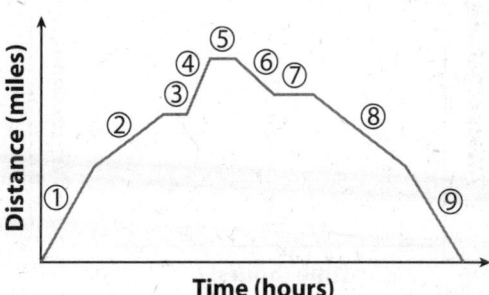

Ⓐ Segment 1 shows that the delivery van moved away from the warehouse. What does segment 2 show?

_____

_____

Ⓑ Based on the time frame, what change in the distance from the warehouse is represented by segment 6?

_____

_____

Ⓒ Which line segments show intervals where the distance did not change?

_____

Ⓓ What is a possible explanation for these segments?

_____

Reflect

1.   **Discussion** Explain how the slope of each segment of the graph is related to whether the delivery truck is not moving, is moving away from, or is moving toward the warehouse.

_____

_____

_____

⊘ Explain 1 Relating Graphs to Situations

Graphs can often be drawn to represent real life situations. These graphs are not always easily derived from equations, but rather represent certain situations. For example, these graphs may include the amount of rain over a certain period of time, or the height of a bouncing ball over a certain period of time.

Example 1 Three hoses fill three different water barrels. A green hose fills a water barrel at a constant rate. A black hose is slowly opened when filling the barrel. A blue hose is completely open at the beginning and then slowly closed. The three graphs of the situations are shown.

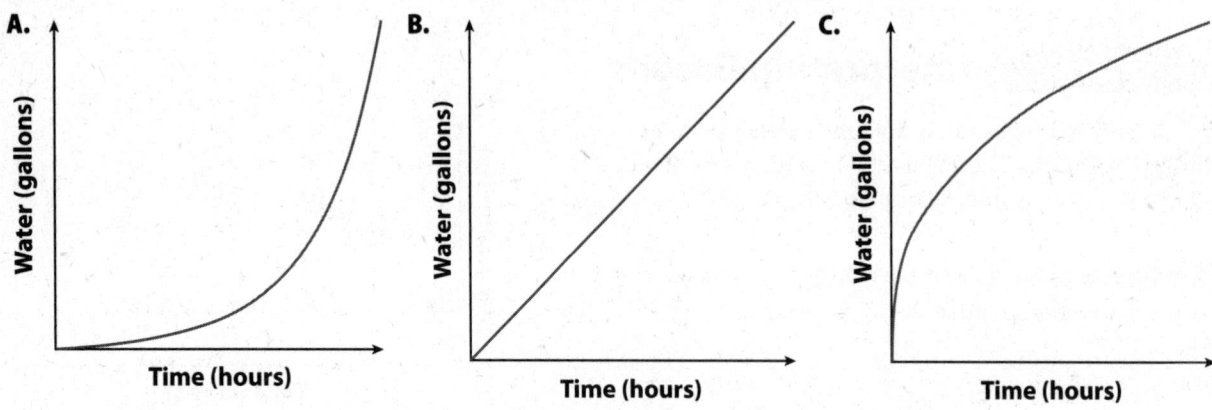

(A) Which graph best represents the amount of water in the barrel filled by the green hose?

Since the flow of the water is constant, the amount of water in the barrel should be a steady increase. Thus, graph B best represents the situation.

(B) Describe the water level represented by each graph. Then determine which graph represents each situation.

Describe the water level for graph A.

_____

Describe the water level for graph C.

_____

Graph A represents the _____ hose and graph C represents the _____ hose.

© Houghton Mifflin Harcourt Publishing Company

Reflect

2. Could a graph of the amount of water in a water barrel slant downward from left to right? Explain.

_____

You and a friend are playing catch. You throw three different balls to your friend. You throw the first ball in an arc and your friend catches it. You throw the second ball in an arc, but this time the ball gets stuck in a tree. You throw the third ball directly at your friend, but it lands in front of your friend, and rolls the rest of the way on the ground. The three graphs of these situations are shown.

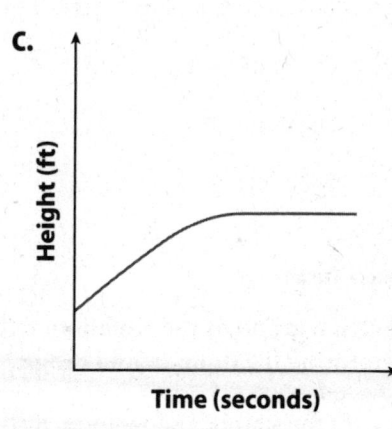

A.   **B.**   **C.**

Height (ft) — Time (seconds)

3. Which graph represents the situation where the ball gets stuck in the tree?

_____

4. Describe the height of the ball represented by the other two graphs.

_____

_____

_____

⏃ Explain 2 **Sketching Graphs for Situations**

Some graphs that represent real-world situations are drawn without any interruptions. In other words, they are *continuous graphs*. A **continuous graph** is a graph that is made up of connected lines or curves. Other types of graphs are not continuous. They are made up of distinct, unconnected points. These graphs are called **discrete graphs**.

Example 2   **Sketch a graph of the situation, tell whether the graph is continuous or discrete, and determine the domain and range.**

Ⓐ A student is taking a test. There are 10 problems on the test. For each problem the student answers correctly, the student received 10 points.

The graph is made up of multiple unconnected points, so the graph is discrete.

The student can get anywhere from 0 to 10 questions right, so the domain is the whole numbers from 0 to 10.

If the student gets 0 problems correct, the student gets 0 points. If the student gets 10 problems correct, the student gets 100 points. So the range is whole number multiples of 10 from 0 to 100.

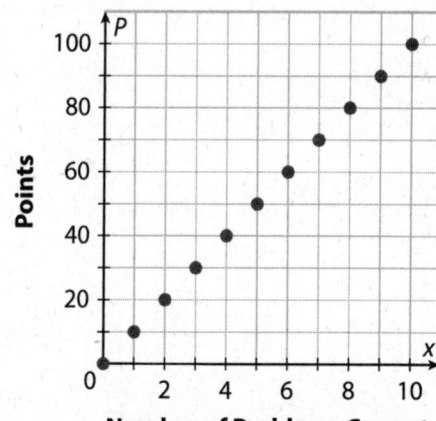

Number of Problems Correct

B A bathtub is being filled with water. After 10 minutes, there are 75 quarts of water in the tub. Then someone accidentally pulls the drain plug while the water is still running, and the tub begins to empty. The tub loses 15 quarts in 5 minutes, and then someone plugs the drain and the tub fills for 6 more minutes, gaining another 45 quarts of water. After a 15-minute bath, the person gets out and pulls the drain plug. It takes 11 minutes for the tub to drain.

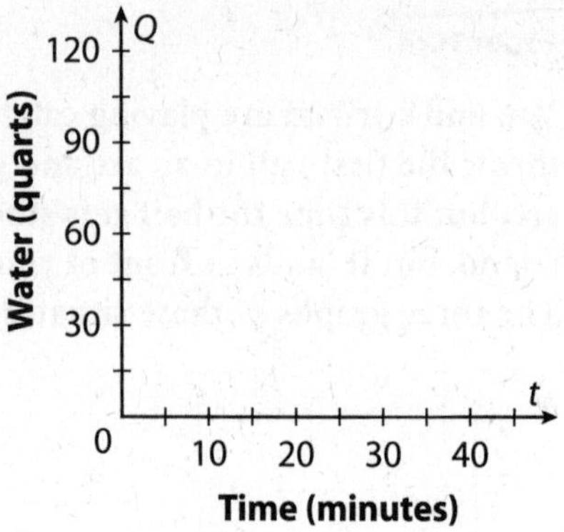

The graph is a _____ graph.

The domain is _____ .

The range is _____ .

Your Turn

Sketch a graph of the situation, tell whether the graph is continuous or discrete, and determine the domain and range.

5. At the start of a snowstorm, it snowed two inches an hour for two hours, then slowed to one inch an hour for an additional hour before stopping. Three hours after the snow stopped, it began to melt at one-half an inch an hour for two hours.

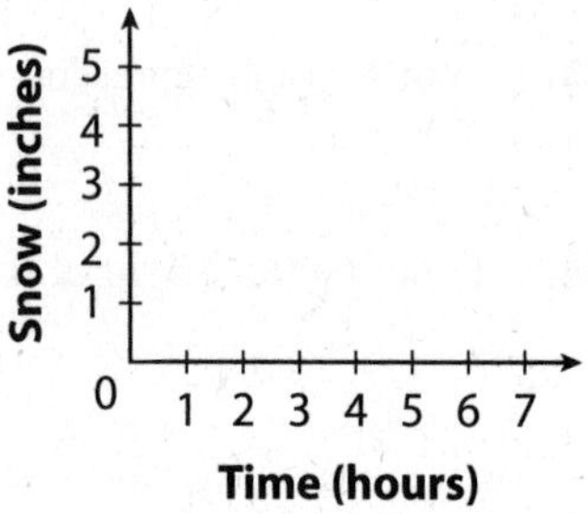

_____

_____

_____

6. A local salesman is going door to door trying to sell vacuums. For every vacuum he sells, he makes $20. He can sell a maximum of 10 vacuums a day.

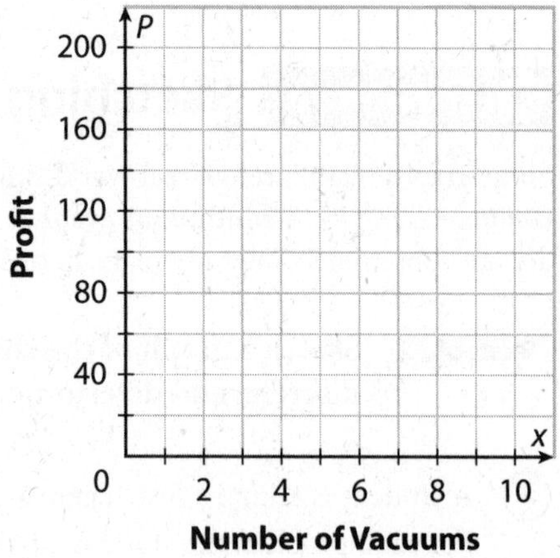

_____

_____

_____

7. When interpreting graphs of real world situations, what can the slope of each part tell you about the situation?

_____

_____

8. **Discussion** What is the best way to sketch the graph of a situation?

_____

_____

9. **Essential Question Check-In** How can you tell when to use a discrete graph as opposed to using a continuous graph? Give an example of each.

_____

_____

_____

_____

☆ Evaluate: Homework and Practice

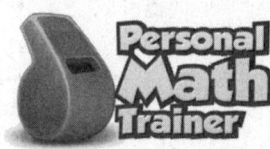

- Online Homework
- Hints and Help
- Extra Practice

The graph shows the attendance at a hockey game, and the rate at which the fans enter and exit the arena.

1. Compare segments 1 and 2. What do they represent?

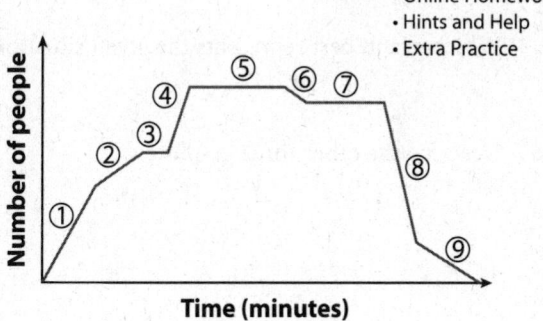

2. What does segment 8 represent in terms of the game?

3. What is the significance of segments 5 and 7?

4. What does segment 6 mean?

Use Graphs A–D for Exercises 5–8. Janelle alternates between running and walking. She begins by walking for a short period, and then runs for the same amount of time. She takes a break before beginning to walk again. Consider the graphs shown.

A.

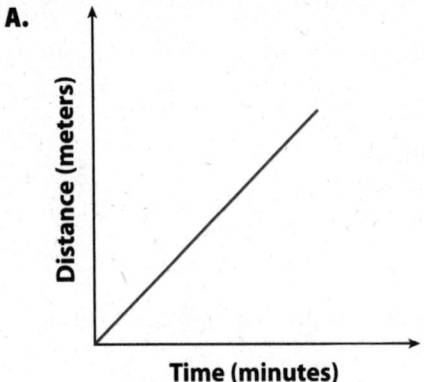

B.

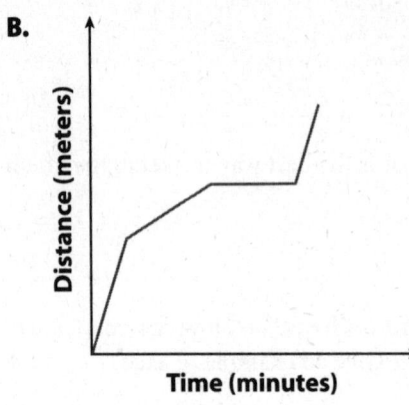

C.

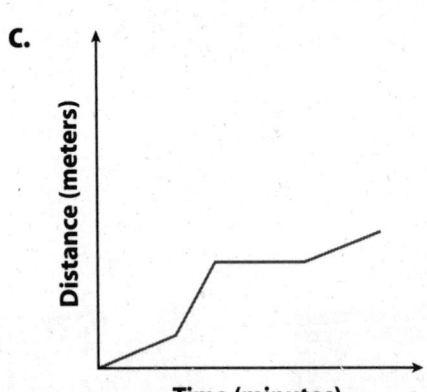

D.

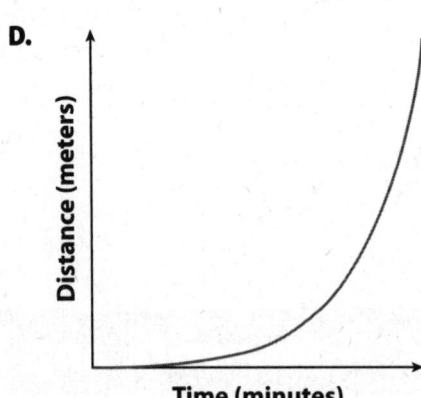

5. Which graph best represents the given situation?

6. Describe the other three graphs.

7. What if Janelle began by running, then slowed to a walk, stopped, and then began running again. Which graph would represent this situation?

8. What are possible situations for graphs A and D?

Use Graphs A–D for Exercises 9–11. **During the winter, the amount of water that flows down a river remains at a low constant. In the spring, when the snow melts, the flow of water increases drastically, until it decreases to a steady rate in the summer. The flow then slowly decreases through the fall into the winter. Consider the graphs shown.**

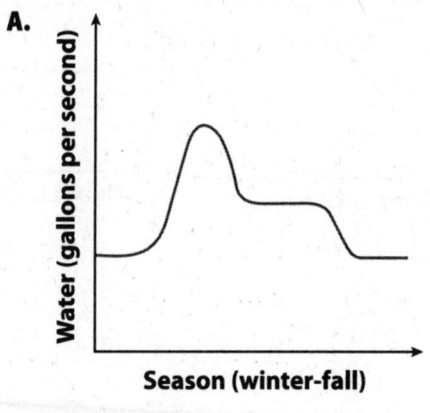

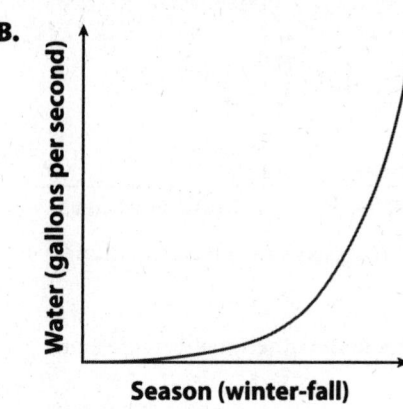

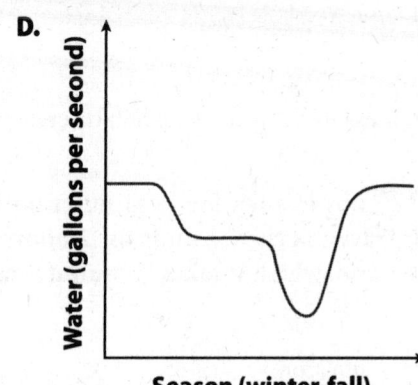

9. Which graph best represents the given situation?

10. Describe the other three graphs.

11. What are possible situations for graphs B, C, and D?

Two children are selling lemonade. They are charging $1 for a cup. They only sell 10 cups. Consider the graphs shown.

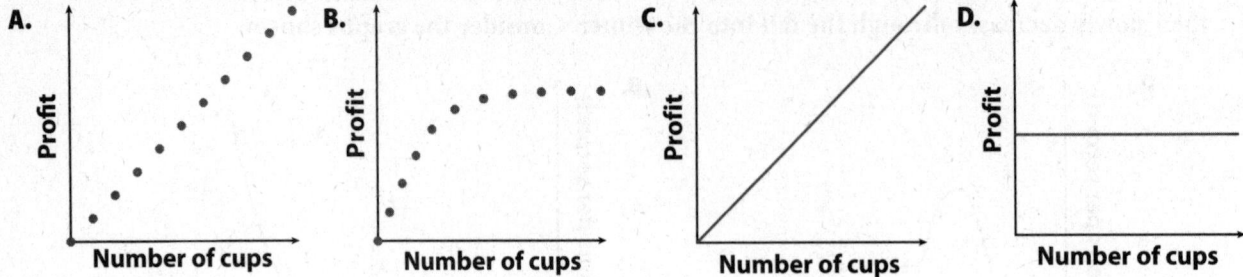

A. Profit / Number of cups

B. Profit / Number of cups

C. Profit / Number of cups

D. Profit / Number of cups

12. Which graph best represents the given situation?

13. What situations could the other graphs represent?

14. Is the graph that represents the given situation discrete or continuous?

A plane takes off and climbs steadily for 15 minutes until it reaches 30,000 feet. It travels at that altitude for 2 hours until it begins to descend to land, which it takes 15 minutes at a constant rate.

15. Sketch a graph of the situation.

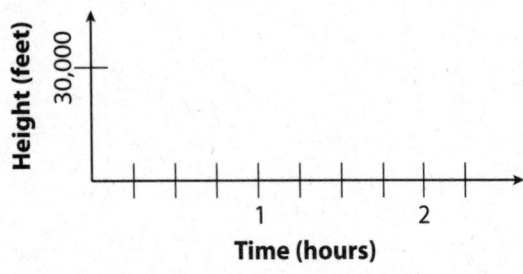

16. Is the graph discrete or continuous?

17. Determine the domain and range.

A contestant on a game show is given $100 and is asked five questions. The contestant loses $20 for every wrong answer.

18. Sketch a graph of the situation.

19. Is the graph discrete or continuous?

20. Determine the domain and range.

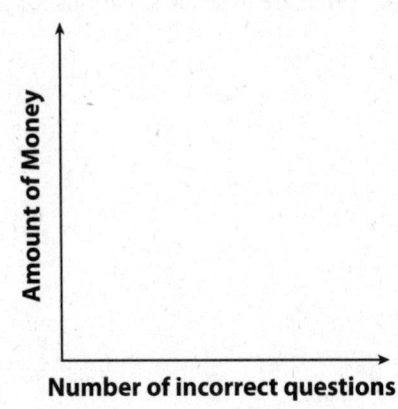

You decide to hike up a mountain. You climb steadily for 2 hours, then take a 30 minute break for lunch. Then you continue to climb, faster than before. When you make it to the summit, you enjoy the view for an hour. Finally, you decide to climb down the mountain, but stop halfway down for a short break. Then you continue down at a slower pace than before.

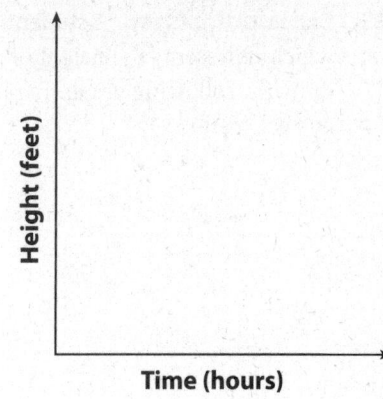

21. Sketch a graph of the situation.

22. Is the graph discrete or continuous?

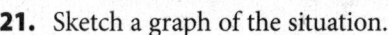

23. Analyze Relationships Write a possible situation for the graph shown.

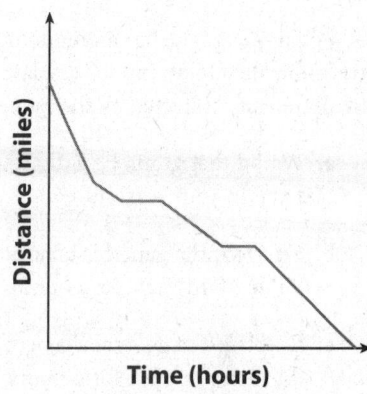

24. Represent Real-World Problems Scientists are conducting an experiment on a bacteria colony that causes its population to fluctuate. The population of a bacteria colony is shown in the graph.

a. What happened to the bacteria colony before time t?

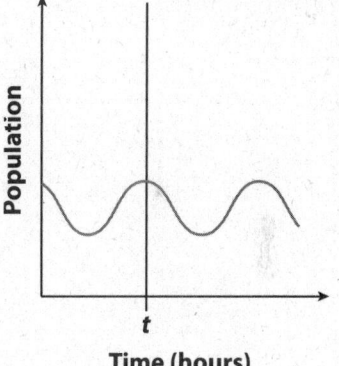

b. Suppose at time t, a second colony of bacteria is added to the first. Draw a new graph to show how this action might affect the population after time t.

c. Suppose at some point after time t, scientists add a substance to the colony that destroys some of the bacteria. Describe how your graph from part b might change.

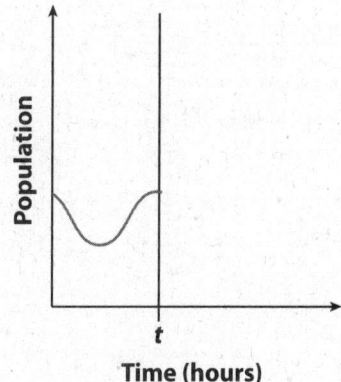

25. Explain the Error A student is told to draw a graph of the situation which represents the height of a skydiver with respect to time. He drew the following graph. Explain the student's error and draw the correct graph.

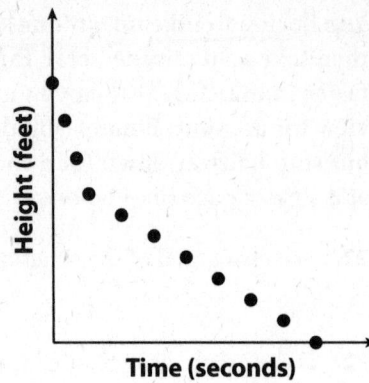

Lesson Performance Task

A digital rain gauge has an outdoor sensor that collects rainfall and transmits data to an indoor display. Assume you produced a graph of all the data collected by the rain gauge over a 24-hour period.

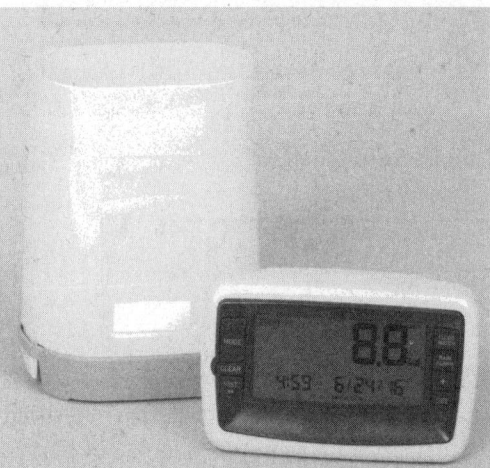

   a. Would that graph be a discrete graph or a continuous graph? Explain your reasoning.

   b. Describe the general shape of the graph assuming it rained at a rate of 0.1 inch per hour for the entire 24-hour period.

   c. Describe the general shape of the graph assuming it rained 0.1 inch per hour for 6 hours, stopped raining for 6 hours, and then rained 0.2 inch for 12 hours.

3.2 Understanding Relations and Functions

Essential Question: How do you represent relations and functions?

Explore   Understanding Relations

A **relation** is a set of ordered pairs (x, y) where x is the input value and y is the output value. The **domain** is all possible inputs of a relation, and the **range** is all possible outputs of a relation. For example, the given relation represents the number of whole-wheat cracker boxes sold and the money earned.

$\{(1, 4), (2, 8), (3, 12), (4, 16)\}$.

Domain: $\{1, 2, 3, 4\}$ Range: $\{2, 8, 12, 16\}$

Ⓐ For the following relation, the input, x, is the ages of boys and the output, y, is their corresponding height, in inches.

$\{(7, 41), (8, 45), (9, 49), (10, 52), (10, 53), (11, 55), (12, 59)\}$

Ⓑ Fill the values in the table.

x	y

Ⓒ Plot the points on the graph.

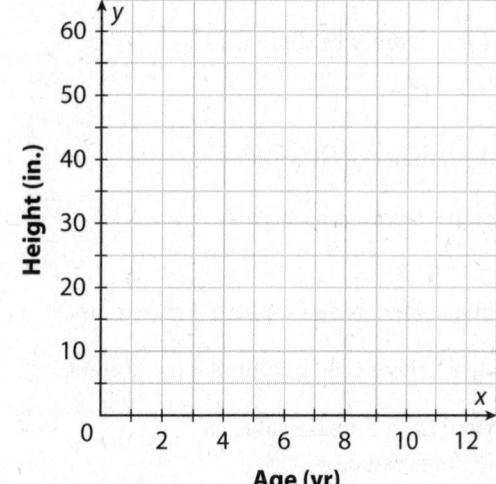

Complete the mapping diagram.

Age (yr)	Height (in.)
7	41
8	45
9	49
10	52
11	53
12	55
	59

E State the domain of the relation.

_____

F State the range of the relation.

_____

Reflect

1. **Discussion** The number 10 appears twice in the *x* column of the table. How many times is it written in the domain? Explain.

_____

_____

⏱ Explain 1   Recognizing Functions

A **function** is a type of relation in which there is only one output value for each input value.

For every input value, there is a unique output value.

Example: $y = x^2$. When $x = 3$, y will always be equal to 9.

Example 1   **Give the domain and range of each relation. State the corresponding outputs for the given inputs in context and explain whether the relation is a function.**

A The given relation represents the number of students and the number of classrooms the school has to have for the corresponding number of students.

Students x	Classrooms y
40	2
45	3
50	4

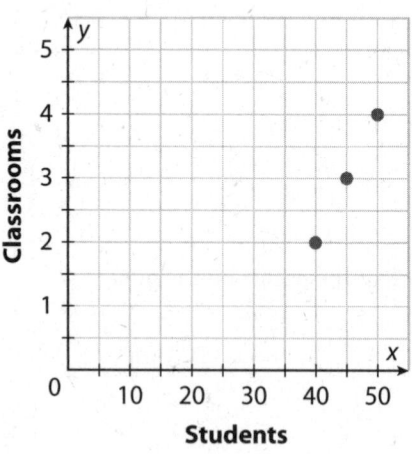

Domain: {40, 45 50}

The domain represents the number of students.

Range: {2, 3, 4}

The range represents the number of classrooms.

For an input of 40 students, there is an output of 2 classrooms.

For an input of 45 students, there is an output of 3 classrooms.

For an input of 50 students, there is an output of 4 classrooms.

This relation is a function. Each domain value is paired with exactly one range value.

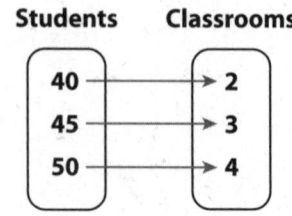

© Houghton Mifflin Harcourt Publishing Company

Ⓑ The given relation represents the amount of gas in gallons and the distance traveled in miles from that amount of gas.

Gas (gal)	Distance (mi)
10	150
16	240
17	240
20	300

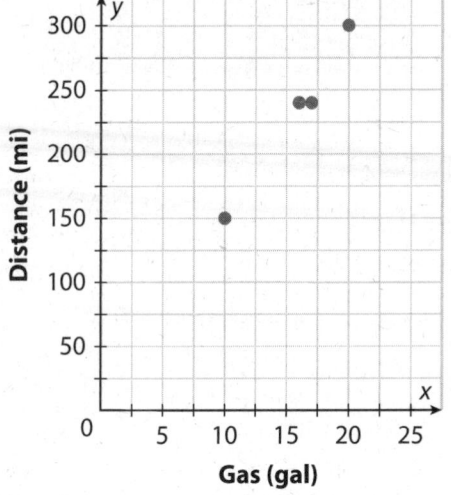

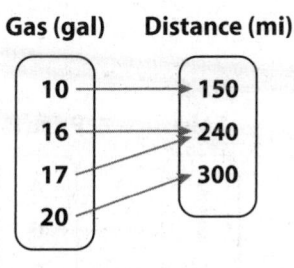

Domain: _____

The domain represents _____

Range: _____

The range represents _____.

For an input of _____, there is an output of _____.

For an input of _____, there is an output of _____.

For an input of _____, there is an output of _____.

For an input of _____, there is an output of _____.

This relation _____ a function. Each domain value is paired with _____ range value.

Reflect

2. If each month in a year was paired with all the possible numbers of days in the month, will the result be a function? Explain.

_____

Give the domain and range of each relation and interpret them in context. State the corresponding outputs for the given inputs in context and explain whether the relation is a function.

3. The relation represents the number of books sold and the price for the corresponding number of books.

Number of books sold	Price ($)
2	4
3	6
4	7
5	9

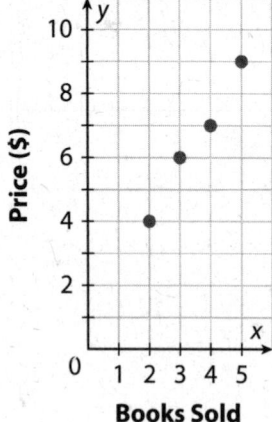

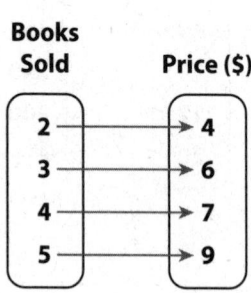

_____

_____

_____

_____

_____

_____

_____

4. The relation represents the time spent exercising and the number of calories burned during that time.

Time (min)	Calories burned
20	50
30	85
35	85
60	100

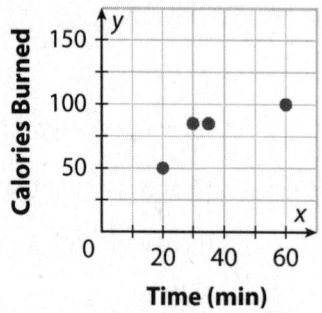

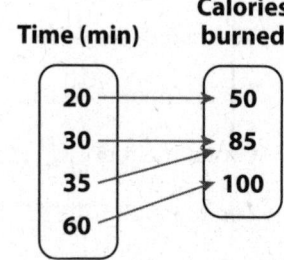

_____

_____

_____

_____

_____

_____

🔧 Explain 2 Understanding the Vertical Line Test

A test, called the *vertical line test*, can be used to determine if a relation is a function. The **vertical line test** states that a relation is a function if and only if a vertical line does not pass through more than one point on the graph of the relation.

Example 2   Use the vertical line test to determine if each relation is a function. Explain.

Ⓐ Draw a vertical line through each point of the graph.

Does any vertical line touch more than one point? Yes

Since a vertical line does pass through more than one point, the graph fails the vertical line test. So, the relation is not a function.

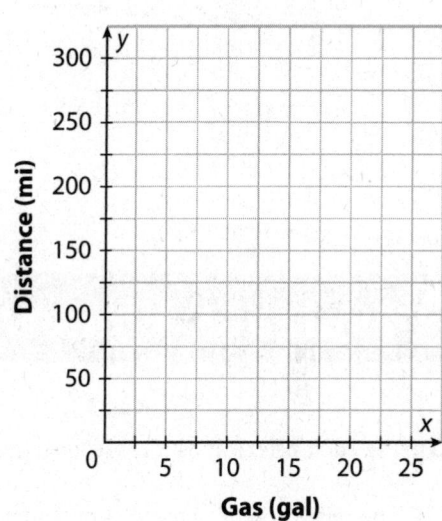

Ⓑ Draw a vertical line through each point of the graph.

Does any vertical line touch more than one point? _____

Since a vertical line _____ pass through more than

one point, the graph _____ the vertical line test. So,

the relation _____ a function.

Reflect

5.   Why does the vertical line test work?

_____

Your Turn

Use the vertical line test to determine if each relation is a function.

6.
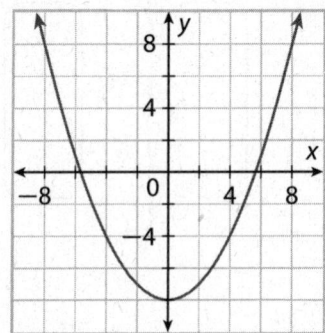

7.
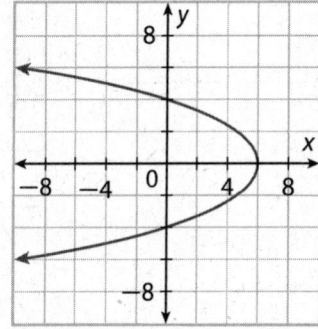

8. How can you use a mapping diagram to determine the domain and the range of a relation?

_____

_____

9. **Discussion** For a discrete function, can the number of elements in the range be greater than the number of elements in the domain? Explain.

_____

_____

10. Is a relation a function if its graph intersects the y-axis twice?

_____

_____

11. **Essential Question Check-In** You are asked to determine if the relation $y = x^2 - 8x + 4$ is a function. What would be the best way to represent this relation in order to determine if it is a function or not? Explain.

_____

_____

_____

_____

✪ Evaluate: Homework and Practice

- Online Homework
- Hints and Help
- Extra Practice

Express each relation as a table, as a graph, and as a mapping diagram.

1. The relation represents ages of students and the number of words they can write per minute.

$$\{(5, 10), (6, 20), (6, 23), (7, 35)\}$$

x	y

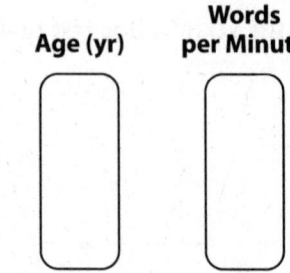

Age (yr)   Words per Minute

Express each relation as a table, as a graph, and as a mapping diagram.

2. The relation represents the place won in a track meet and the number of points that place finish is worth.

$$\{(1, 5), (2, 3), (3, 2), (4, 1), (5, 0)\}$$

x	y

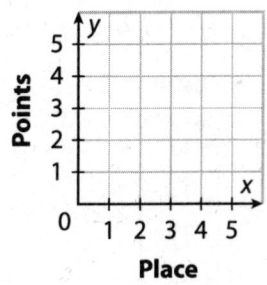

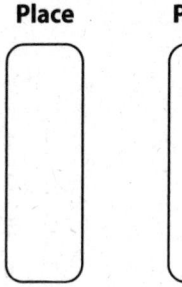

State the domain and range of each relation.

3.

x	y
2	5
7	8
8	15
11	12
15	19

4.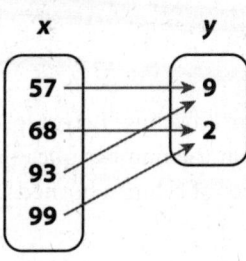

5.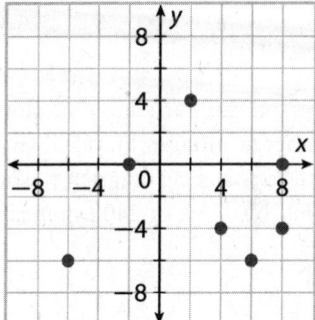

State the domain and range of each relation, interpret in context, and explain if it is a function or not.

6. The relation represents the age of each student and the number of pets the student has.

Age	Number of Pets
6	3
8	2
9	0
11	1
11	2

7. The relation represents time driven in hours and the number of miles traveled at the end of each hour.

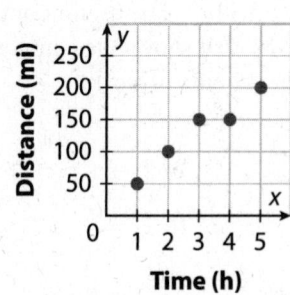

State the domain and range of each relation, interpret in context, and explain if it is a function or not.

8. The relation represents the number of hours a person is able to rent a canoe and the cost of renting the canoe for that many hours.

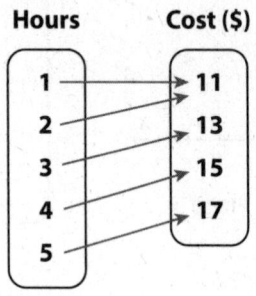

9. A person can burn about 6 calories per minute bicycling. Let *x* represent the number of minutes bicycled, and let *y* represent the number of calories burned. Create a mapping diagram to show the number of calories burned by bicycling for 60, 120, 180, or 240 minutes.

Minutes	Calories

10. The table represents a sample of ages of people and their shoe size.

Age	Shoe Size
x	y
11	7
12	8
13	10
15	10
15	10.5
16	11

11. An electrician charges a base fee of $75 plus $50 for each hour of work. The minimum the electrician charges is $175. Create a table that shows the amount the electrician charges for 1, 2, 3, and 4 hours of work.

x	y

12. The graph represents the average soccer goals scored for players of different ages. Determine the domain and range of the relation in context and explain whether or not this represents a function.

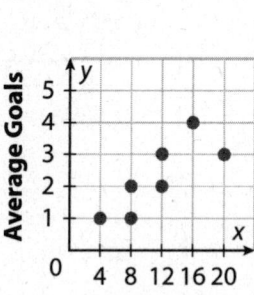

Express each relation as a mapping diagram and explain whether or not the relation represents a function.

13. $\{(13, 33), (17, 25), (22, 22), (25, 17), (33, 17)\}$

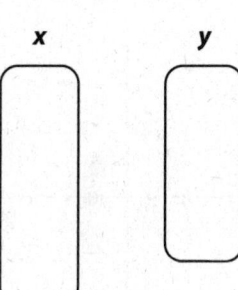

14. $\{(1, 2), (5, 2), (5, 4), (7, 6), (11, 6)\ (11, 8)\}$

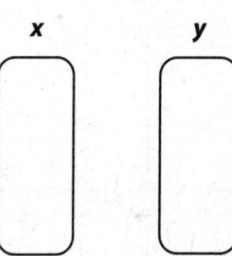

Use the vertical line test to determine if each relation is a function.

15.

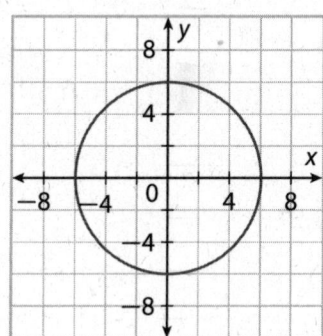

16.

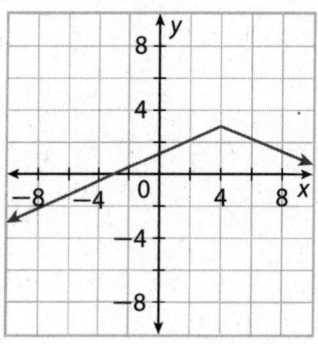

Use the vertical line test to determine if each relation is a function.

17.

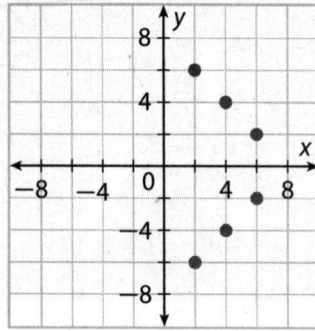

18.

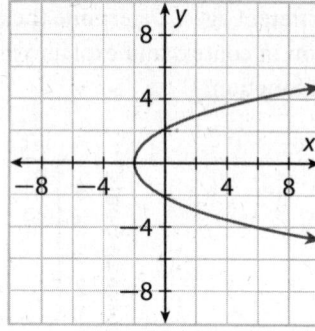

19.

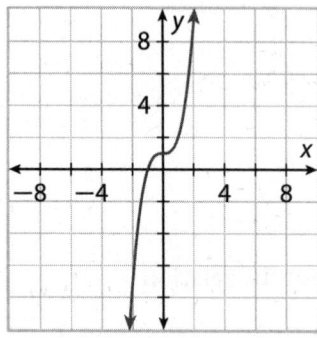

20.

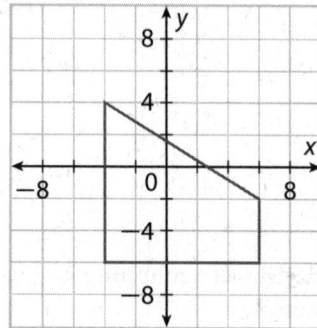

21.

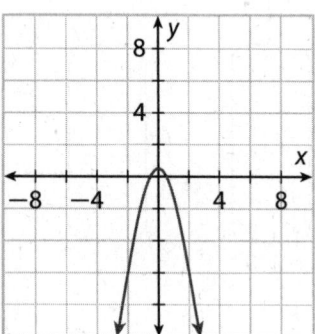

22.

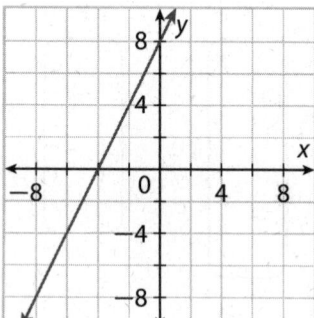

23. Draw Conclusions Examine the mapping diagram. The first set is the months of the year, and the second set is the possible number of days per month. Is the relation a function? Explain.

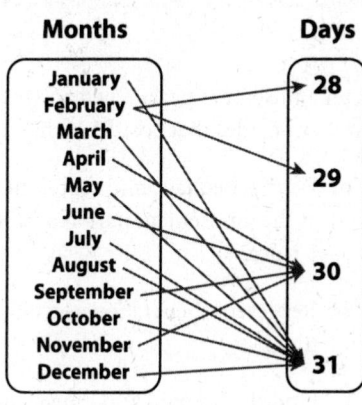

24. Justify Reasoning Tell whether each situation represents a function. Explain your reasoning. If the situation represents a function, give the domain and range.

a. Each U.S. coin is mapped to its monetary value.

b. A $1, $5, $10, $20, $50, or $100 bill is mapped to all the sets of coins that are the same as the total value of the bill.

25. Explain the Error A student was given a graph and asked to use the vertical line test to determine if the relation was a function or not. The student said that the relation failed the vertical line test and the graph was not a function. What error did the student make? Explain the error and give the correct answer.

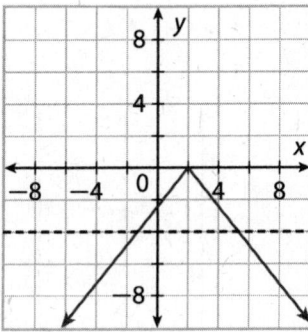

Lesson Performance Task

At an amusement park, a person spends $30 on admission and food, and then goes on *r* number of rides that cost $2 each.

a. Write an equation to represent the total amount *A* spent at the amusement park if a person goes on anywhere from 0 to 5 rides.

b. Represent the relation as a table, as a graph, and as a mapping diagram.

c. Find the domain and range, and then determine whether the relation is a function or not.

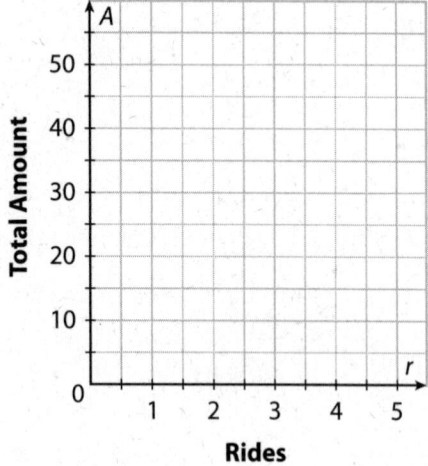

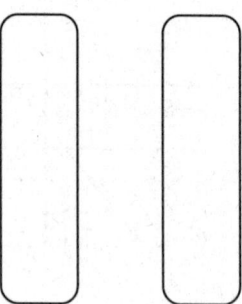

3.3 Modeling with Functions

Essential Question: What is function notation and how can you use functions to model real-world situations?

🧭 Explore 1 Identifying Independent and Dependent Variables

The input of a function is the **independent variable**. The output of the function is the **dependent variable**. The value of the dependent variable depends on, or is a function of, the value of the independent variable.

Identify dependent and independent variables in each situation.

In the winter, more electricity is used when the outside temperature goes down, and less is used when the outside temperature rises.

Ⓐ The _____ depends on the _____.

Ⓑ Dependent: _____

Independent: _____

Ⓒ The cost of shipping a package is based on its weight.

The _____ depends on the _____.

Ⓓ Dependent: _____ Independent: _____

Ⓔ The faster Tom walks, the quicker he gets home.

The _____ depends on the _____.

Ⓕ Dependent: _____ Independent: _____

Reflect

1. **Discussion** Give a situation where "time" is the dependent variable and "distance" is the independent variable.

_____

_____

2. In Explore 1, explain how you know that the amount of electricity used is not the independent variable.

_____

⊘ Explore 2 Applying Function Notation

If x is the independent variable and y is the dependent variable, then you can use **function notation** to write $y = f(x)$, which is read "y equals f of x," where f names the function. When an equation in two variables describes a function, you always can use function notation to write it.

The dependent variable	is	a function of	the independent variable.
y	is	a function of	x.
y	=	f	(x)

Write an equation in function notation.

Amanda babysits and charges $5 per hour.

Time Worked in Hours (x)	1	2	3	4
Amount Earned in Dollars (y)	5	10	15	20

(A) The _____ is $5 times the _____.

(B) An algebraic expression that defines a function is a **function rule**. Write an equation using two variables to show this relationship.

Amount earned	is	$5	times	the number of hours worked.
↓	↓	↓	↓	↓
_____	=	5	•	_____

(C) The dependent variable is a function of the independent variable. Write the equation in function notation.

Amount earned	is	$5	times	the number of hours worked.
↓	↓	↓	↓	↓
y	=	5	•	x
_____	=	5	•	x

Reflect

3. **Discussion** Can y be used instead of $f(x)$ in function notation? If so, tell why. If not, give an example of a function not written in function notation and the same function written in function notation.

_____

_____

Explain 1 Modeling Using Function Notation

The value of the dependent variable depends on, or is a function of, the value of the independent variable. If x is the independent variable and y is the dependent variable, then the function notation for y will read "f of x," where f names the function. When an equation in two variables describes a function, you can use function notation to write it.

Example 1 For each example identify the independent and dependent variables. Write an equation in function notation for each situation, and then use the equation to solve the problem.

(A) A lawyer's fee is \$180 per hour for his services. How much does the lawyer charge for 5 hours?

The fee for the lawyer depends on how many hours he works.

Dependent: fee; Independent: hours

Let h represent the number of hours the lawyer works.

The function for the lawyer's fee is $f(h) = 180h$.

$$f(h) = 180h$$
$$f(5) = 180(5) \quad \text{Substitute 5 for } h.$$
$$\quad\;\; = 900 \quad\quad\; \text{Simplify.}$$

The lawyer charges \$900 for 5 hours of work.

(B) The admission fee at a carnival is \$9. Each ride costs \$1.75. How much does it cost to go to the carnival and then go on 12 rides?

The _____ depends on the _____, plus \$9.

Dependent: _____ Independent: _____

Let r represent the _____. The function for the total cost of the carnival is

$f(r)=$ _____.

Substitute 12 for r into the function for the total cost of the carnival, and find the total cost.

$$f\left(\boxed{}\right) = \boxed{}$$
$$f\left(\boxed{}\right) = \boxed{}$$

It costs _____ to go to the carnival and go on _____ rides.

For each example identify the independent and dependent variables. Write an equation in function notation for each situation. Then use the equation to solve the problem.

4. Kate earns \$7.50 per hour. How much money will she earn after working 8 hours?

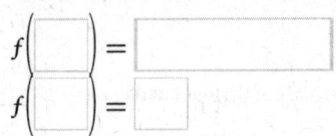

© Houghton Mifflin Harcourt Publishing Company • Image Credits: ©Photodisc/Getty Images

⚙ Explain 2 Choosing a Reasonable Domain and Range

When a function describes a real-world situation, every real number is not always a reasonable choice for the domain and range. For example, a number representing the length of an object cannot be negative, and only whole numbers can represent a number of people.

Example 2 Write a function in function notation for each situation. Find a reasonable domain and range for each function.

(A) Manuel has already sold $20 worth of tickets to the school play. He has 4 tickets left to sell at $2.50 per ticket. Write a function for the total amount collected from ticket sales.

Let t represent the number of tickets to sell.

Total amount collected from ticket sales	is	$2.50	per	ticket	plus	tickets already sold
$f(t)$	=	$2.50	•	t	+	20

Manuel has only 4 tickets left to sell, so a reasonable domain is {0, 1, 2, 3, 4}.

Substitute these values into the function rule $2.50t + 20$ to find the range values.

The range is {$20, $22.50, $25, $27.50, $30}.

(B) A telephone company charges $0.25 per minute for the first 5 minutes of a call plus a $0.45 connection fee per call. Write a function for the total cost in dollars of making a call.

Let m represent the number of minutes used.

Total cost for one call	is	$0.25	per	minute	plus	$0.45 fee.
$f(m)$	=	_____	•	_____	+	_____

The charges only occur if a call is made, so a reasonable domain is {_____}.

Substitute these values into the function rule $0.25m + 0.45$ to find the range values.

The range is _____.

Your Turn

Write a function in function notation for each situation. Find a reasonable domain and range for each function.

5. The temperature early in the morning is 17 °C. The temperature increases by 2 °C for every hour for the next 5 hours. Write a function for the temperature in degrees Celsius.

6. Takumi earns $8.50 per hour proofreading advertisements at a local newspaper. He works no more than 5 hours a day. Write a function for his earnings.

7. How can you identify the independent variable and the dependent variable given a situation?

_____

_____

8. Describe how to write $3x + 2y = 12$ in function notation. Assume that y represents the dependent variable.

_____

_____

_____

_____

9. Discussion What is the advantage of using function notation instead of using y?

_____

_____

10. Essential Question Check-In Explain how to find reasonable domain values for a function.

_____

_____

⭐ Evaluate: Homework and Practice

- Online Homework
- Hints and Help
- Extra Practice

Identify the dependent and independent variables in each situation.

1. Identify the dependent and independent variables in each situation.

   A. The total cost of running a business is based on its expenses.

   B. The price of a house depends on its area.

   C. The time it takes you to run a certain distance depends on the distance.

   D. The number of items in a carton depends on the size of the carton.

2. Charles will babysit for up to 4 hours and charges $7 per hour.

Write a function in function notation for this situation.

For each situation, identify the independent and dependent variables. Write a function in function notation. Then use the function to solve the problem.

3. Almira earns $50 an hour. How much does she earn in 6 hours?

4. Stan, a local delivery driver, is paid $3.50 per mile driven plus a daily amount of $75. On Monday, he is assigned a route that is 30 miles long. How much is he being paid for that day?

5. Bruce owns a small grocery store and charges $4.75 per pound of produce. If a customer orders 5 pounds of produce, how much does Bruce charge the customer?

6. Georgia, a florist, charges $10.95 per flower bundle plus a $15 delivery charge per order. If Charlie orders 8 bundles of flowers and has them delivered, how much does Georgia charge Charlie?

7. Allison owns a music store and sells DVDs at $17.75 per DVD. If Craig orders 5 DVDs, how much does it cost?

8. Anne buys used cars at auction for $2000 per car. There is a $150 fee to take part in the auction. If Anne buys 13 used cars, how much does she pay in total?

9. Harold, a real estate developer, sells houses at $250,000 per house. If he sells 9 houses, how much does he earn?

10. Gordon buys 3 HD TVs for $1200 each. There is a shipping charge of $90 to have the TVs delivered to his house. How much does Gordon pay in total?

11. Cindy is buying jackets for her local community charity's auction. Each jacket costs $50. If Cindy bought 23 jackets, what is the total cost?

12. Autumn sells laptop computers for $600 each. If she sells 68 computers, how much money does she earn?

Write a function using function notation to describe each situation. Find a reasonable domain and range for each function.

13. Elijah has already sold $40 worth of tickets for a local raffle.
He has 5 tickets left to sell at $5 per ticket.

14. Mary has already sold $55 worth of tickets to the benefit concert. She has 3 tickets left to sell at $7 per ticket.

15. A law firm charges $100 per hour for the first 3 hours plus a $300 origination fee for its services.

16. A pay-for-service Internet company charges $5 per hour for the first 3 hours of service plus a $10 connection fee.

17. A high definition radio station charges $200 per year in addition to $50 per month for the first 3 months to receive its broadcast.

18. A newspaper charges $3 per line for the first 4 lines plus a $20 fee to advertise.

19. Matt has already sold $72 worth of tickets to the benefit concert. He has 6 tickets left to sell at $9 per ticket.

20. Sarah has sold $33 worth of tickets to the comedy show. She has 4 tickets left to sell at $11 per ticket.

21. Justify Reasoning The function $f(x) = -6x + 11$ has a range given by $\{-37, -25, -13, -1\}$. Select the domain values of the function from the list 1, 2, 3, 4, 5, 6, 7, 8. Explain how you arrived at your answer.

22 a. Represent Real-World Problems Victor needs to find the volume of 6 cube-shaped boxes with sides lengths of between 2 feet and 7 feet. The side lengths of the boxes can only be whole numbers. The volume of a cube-shaped box with a side length of s is given by the function $V(s) = s^3$.

What is a reasonable domain for this situation? Explain.

b. What is a reasonable range for this situation? Explain.

22 a. Represent Real-World Problems Tanya is printing a report. There are 100 sheets of paper in the printer, and the number of sheets of paper p left after t minutes of printing is given by the function $p(t) = -8t + 100$.

How many minutes would it take the printer to use all 100 sheets of paper? Show your work.

b. What is a reasonable domain for this situation? Explain.

c. What is a reasonable range for this situation? Explain.

Lesson Performance Task

Jenna's parents have given her an interest-free loan of $100 to buy a new pair of running shoes. She plans to pay back the loan with monthly payments of $20 each.

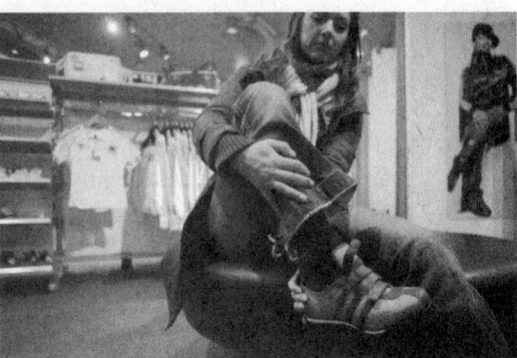

a. Write a function rule for the balance function $B(p)$, where p represents the number of payments that Jenna has made.

b. After how many payments will Jenna have paid back more than half the loan? Explain your reasoning.

c. Suppose the loan amount were $120 and the monthly payments were $15. Write a rule for the new balance function and use it to determine how long it would take Jenna to pay off the loan.

3.4 Graphing Functions

Essential Question: How do you graph functions?

⊘ Explore   Graphing Functions Using a Given Domain

Recall that the domain of a function is the set of input values, or x-values, of the function and that the range is the set of corresponding output values, or y-values, of the function. One way to understand a function and its features is to graph it. You can graph a function by finding ordered pairs that satisfy the function.

Graph the function for the given domain.

$x + 3y = 15$ D: {0, 3, 6, 9}

(A) You have been given the input values, x, of the domain. You need to solve the function for y.

$x + 3y = 15$

$\underline{-x \qquad -x}$ Subtract x from both sides.

$3y = \boxed{}$

$\dfrac{3y}{3} = \dfrac{\boxed{}}{3}$ Since y is multiplied by 3, divide both sides by 3.

$y = \boxed{} + \boxed{}$ Rewrite the right side as two separate fractions.

$y = \boxed{} + \boxed{}$ Simplify.

(B) Substitute the given values of the domain for x to find the values of y.

(C) Graph the ordered pairs.

x	$y = -\frac{1}{3}x + 5$	(x, y)
0	$y = -\frac{1}{3}(0) + 5 = \boxed{}$	$\left(0, \boxed{}\right)$
3	$y = -\frac{1}{3}\left(\boxed{}\right) + 5 = 4$	$\left(\boxed{}, 4\right)$
6	$y = -\frac{1}{3}(6) + 5 = \boxed{}$	$\left(6, \boxed{}\right)$
9	$y = -\frac{1}{3}\left(\boxed{}\right) + 5 = 2$	$\left(\boxed{}, \boxed{}\right)$

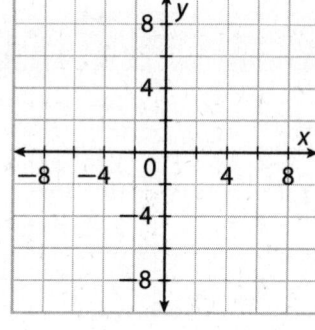

1. **Discussion** Why do you not connect the points of the graph?

_____

_____

_____

2. **Discussion** How would the graph be different if the domain was $0 \leq x \leq 9$?

_____

_____

_____

🔑 Explain 1 — Graphing Functions Using a Domain of All Real Numbers

If the domain of a function is all real numbers, any number can be used as an input value producing an infinite number of ordered pairs that satisfy the function. Arrowheads are drawn at both ends of a smooth line or curve to represent the infinite number of ordered pairs. If a domain is not provided, it should be assumed that the domain is all real numbers.

Graphing Functions Using a Domain of All Real Numbers	
Step 1	Use the function to generate ordered pairs by choosing several values of x.
Step 2	Plot enough points to see a pattern for the graph.
Step 3	Connect the points with a line or smooth curve.

Example 1 Graph each function.

Ⓐ $y = x^2$

Use several values of x to generate ordered pairs. Plot the points from the table, and draw a smooth curve through the points. Include an arrowhead at each end.

x	$y = x^2$	(x, y)
-3	$y = (-3)^2 = 9$	$(-3, 9)$
-2	$y = (-2)^2 = 4$	$(-2, 4)$
-1	$y = (-1)^2 = 1$	$(-1, 1)$
0	$y = (0)^2 = 0$	$(0, 0)$
1	$y = (1)^2 = 1$	$(1, 1)$
2	$y = (2)^2 = 4$	$(2, 4)$
3	$y = (3)^2 = 9$	$(3, 9)$

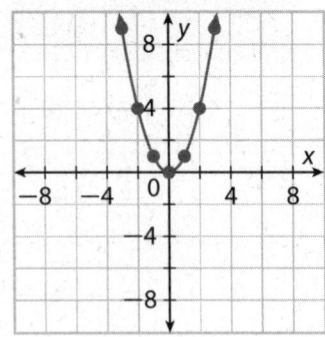

Ⓑ $f(x) = 3x - 5$

Use several values of x to generate ordered pairs.

x	$f(x) = 3x - 5$	$(x, f(x))$
−1	$f(-1) = 3(-1) - 5 = \boxed{}$	$\left(-1, \boxed{}\right)$
0	$f\boxed{} = 3\left(\boxed{}\right) - 5 = -5$	$\left(\boxed{}, -5\right)$
1	$f(1) = 3(1) - 5 = \left(\boxed{}\right)$	$\left(1, \boxed{}\right)$
2	$f\boxed{} = 3\left(\boxed{}\right) - 5 = 1$	$\left(\boxed{}, 1\right)$
3	$f(3) = 3(3) - 5 = \left(\boxed{}\right)$	$\left(3, \boxed{}\right)$
4	$f\boxed{} = 3\left(\boxed{}\right) - 5 = 7$	$\left(\boxed{}, \boxed{}\right)$

Plot the points from the table to see a pattern.

The points appear to form a _____. Draw a _____
through all the points to show the ordered pairs that satisfy the function.
Draw _____ on both ends of the graph.

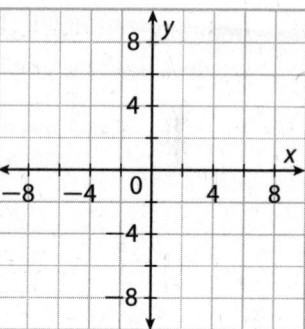

Reflect

3. When graphing a function, does it matter if the function is written in function notation? Explain.

_____

_____

Your Turn

Graph each function.

4. $y = -x^2$

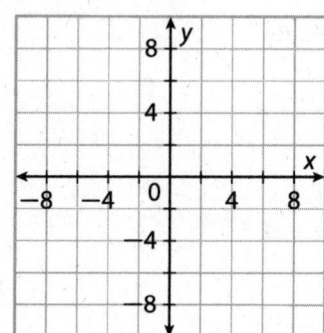

5. $y = -4x + 2$

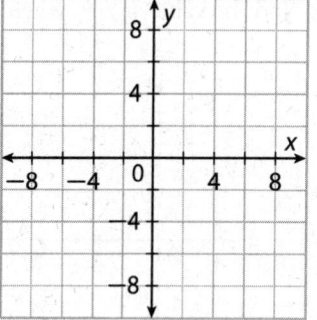

© Houghton Mifflin Harcourt Publishing Company

⚙ Explain 2 Using a Graph to Find Values

To find the value of a function for a given value of x using a graph, locate the value of x on the x-axis, move up or down to the graph of the function, and then move left or right to the y-axis to find the corresponding value of y.

Example 2 Use a graph to find the value of $f(x)$ when $x = -2$ for each function.

Ⓐ $f(x) = -\frac{1}{2}x + 3$

Use a graphing calculator to graph $y = -\frac{1}{2}x + 3$, and use TRACE to find the function value when $x = -2$.

Therefore, the value of y is 4 when x is -2.

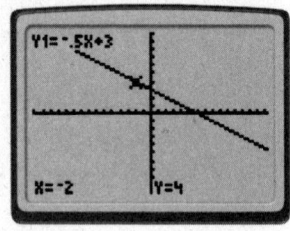

Ⓑ $f(x) = \frac{3}{2}x - 4$

First graph the line. Locate _____ on the x-axis. Draw a vertical line segment

from _____ on the x-axis to the graph of the function and a horizontal line segment from the graph of the function to the y-axis.

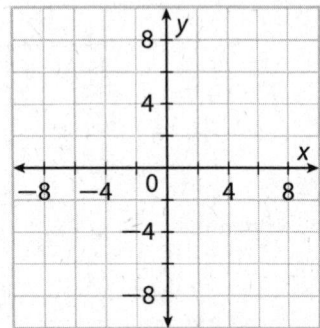

The value of y on the y-axis is the value of the function. Therefore,

the value of $f(x)$ is _____ when x is -2.

Your Turn

6. Use a graph to find the value of $f(x)$ when $x = 3$ for the function $f(x) = -x + 7$.

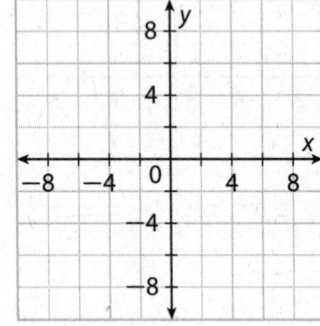

© Houghton Mifflin Harcourt Publishing Company

Explain 3 **Modeling Using a Function Graph**

The domain of a real-world situation may have to be limited in order to have reasonable answers. Only nonnegative numbers can be used to represent quantities such as time, distance, and the number of people. When both the domain and the range of a function are limited to nonnegative values, the function is graphed only in Quadrant I.

Example 3 The Mid-Atlantic Ridge separates the North and South American Plates from the Eurasian and African Plates. The function $y = 2.5x$ relates the number of centimeters y the Mid-Atlantic Ridge spreads after x years. Graph the function and use the graph to estimate how many centimeters the Mid-Atlantic Ridge spreads in 4.5 years.

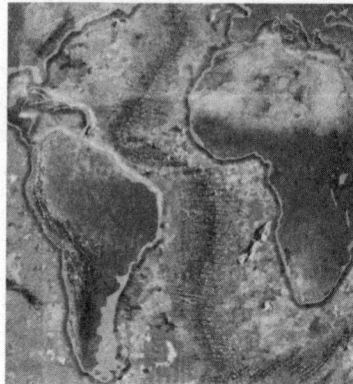

 Analyze Information

Identify the important information:

- The function _____ describes how many centimeters the Mid-Atlantic Ridge spreads after _____ years.

Formulate a Plan

Only use _____ values of x and y. Use a graph to find the value of _____ when x is _____.

Solve

Choose several values of x that are in the domain of the function to find values of y.

x	$y = 2.5x$	(x, y)
0	$y = 2.5\left(\boxed{}\right) = 10$	$\left(\boxed{}, 0\right)$
2	$y = 2.5\,(2) = \boxed{}$	$\left(2, \boxed{}\right)$
4	$y = 2.5\left(\boxed{}\right) = 10$	$\left(\boxed{}, 10\right)$
5	$y = 2.5\,(5) = \boxed{}$	$\left(5, \boxed{}\right)$

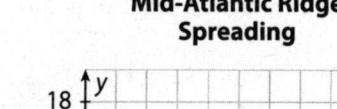

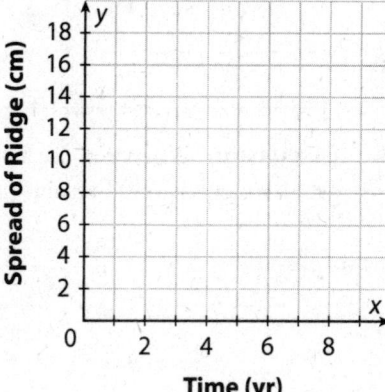

Plot the points that represent the ordered pairs on the graph.

Draw a _____ through all of the points because the points appear to form a _____.

Use the graph to estimate the y-value when x is 4.5.

The Mid-Atlantic Ridge spreads about _____ centimeters after 4.5 years.

Justify and Evaluate

The distance of the Mid-Atlantic Ridge spread _____ as the number of years increases, so the graph is reasonable. When x is between 4 and 5, y is

between _____ and _____ . Since 4.5 is between 4 and 5, it is

reasonable to estimate y to be _____ when x is 4.5.

7. A cruise ship is currently 5 kilometers away from its port and is traveling away from the port at 15 kilometers per hour. The function $y = 15x + 5$ relates the number of kilometers y the ship will be from its port x hours from now. How far will the cruise ship be from its port 2.5 hours from now?

x	$y = 15x + 5$	(x, y)

Distance from Port

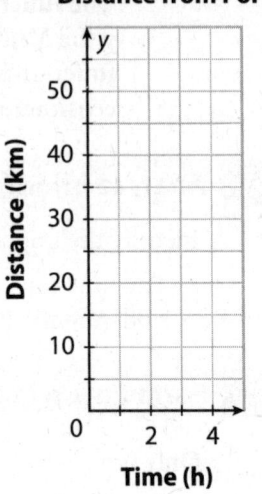

⊙ Elaborate

8. Is it enough to plot two points to see a pattern for a graph? Explain.

_____

_____

_____

9. **Discussion** When you use a graph to find the value of a function for a specific value of x, do you always get an exact answer? Explain.

_____

_____

_____

_____

10. **Essential Question Check-In** How do you graph a function that has a domain of all real numbers?

_____

_____

_____

• Online Homework
• Hints and Help
• Extra Practice

Graph each function for the given domain.

1. $y = 2x$ D:$\{-2, 0, 2, 4\}$

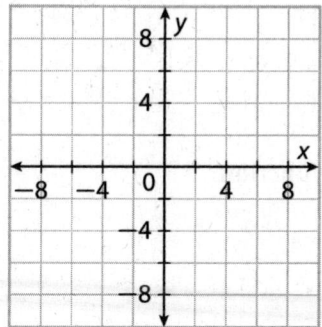

2. $y = \frac{1}{4}x + 5$ D:$\{-8, -4, 0, 4\}$

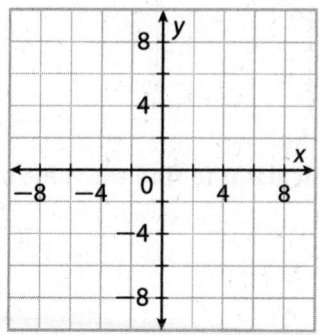

3. $-3x - 5y = 20$ D:$\{-10, -5, 0, 5\}$

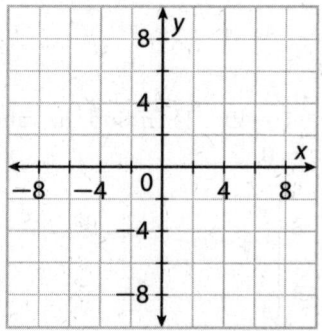

4. $y = x^2 - 3$ D:$\{-2, -1, 0, 1, 2\}$

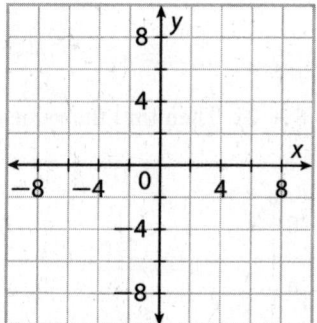

Graph each function.

5. $y = -x^2 + 5$

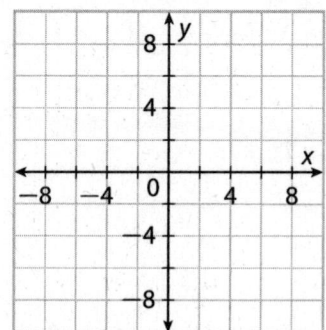

6. $y = \frac{2}{3}x - 1$

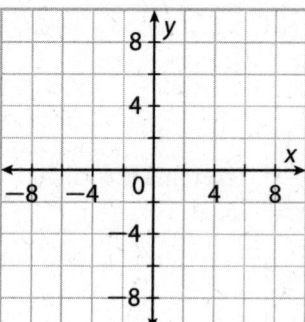

7. $x + y = 0$

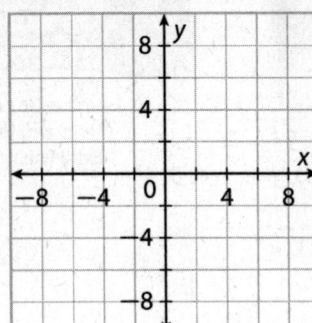

8. $y = \frac{1}{4}x^2 - 8$

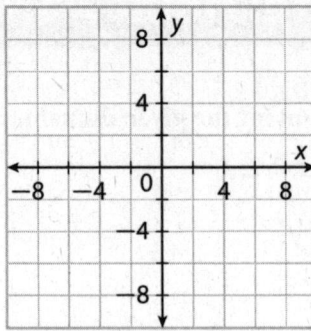

Use a graphing calculator to find the value of $f(x)$ when $x = 3$ for each function.

9. $f(x) = \frac{1}{3}x - 2$

10. $f(x) = -x^2 - 4$

Use a graphing calculator to find the value of $f(x)$ when $x = -4$ for each function.

11. $fx = x^2 - 3$

12. $f(x) = -4x - \frac{3}{2}$

13. $f(x) = -\frac{9}{2}x^2 - 5$

14. Graph $f(x) = 8 + 2x$. Then find the value of $f(x)$ when $x = \frac{1}{2}$.

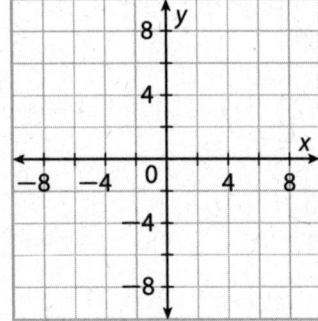

15. Graph $f(x) = 0.5 - 2x^2$. Then find the value of $f(x)$ when $x = 0$.

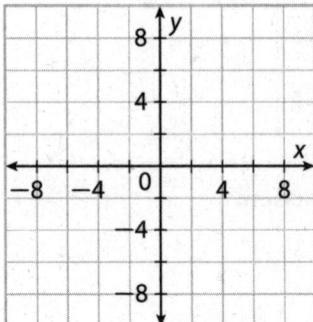

16. Graph $f(x) = \frac{1}{4}x^2$. Then find the value of $f(x)$ when $x = -6$.

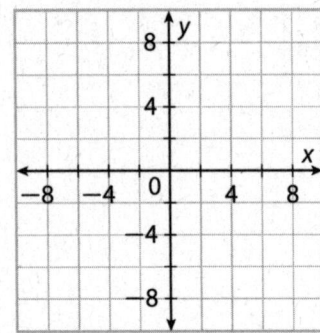

17. The fastest recorded Hawaiian lava flow moved at an average speed of 6 miles per hour. The function $y = 6x$ describes the distance y the lava moved on average in x hours. Graph the function. Use the graph to estimate how many miles the lava moved after 4.5 hours.

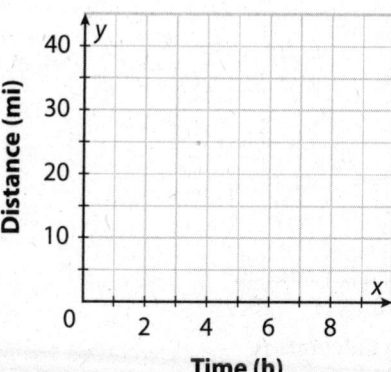

18. The total cost of a cab ride can be represented by the function $f(x) = 3x + 2.5$, where x is the number of miles driven. Graph the function. Use the graph to estimate how much the cab will cost if the cab ride is 8 miles.

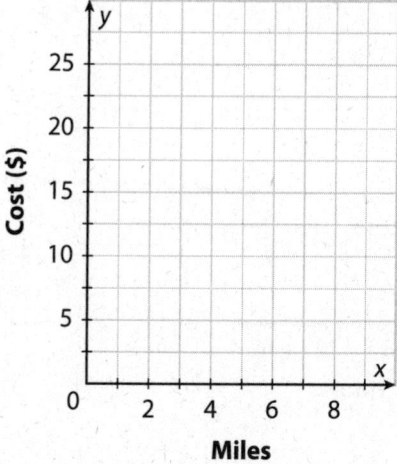

19. Joshua is driving to the store. The average distance d in miles he travels over t minutes is given by the function $d(t) = 0.5t$. Graph the function. Use the graph to estimate how many miles he drove after 5 minutes.

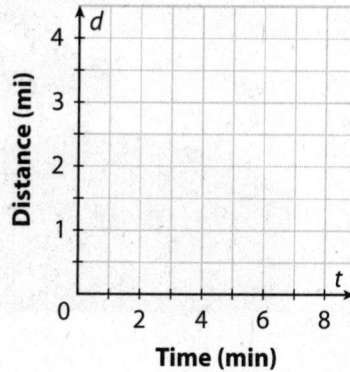

20. The production cost for g graphing calculators is $C(g) = 15g$. Graph the function and then evaluate it when $g = 15$. What does the value of the function at $g = 15$ represent?

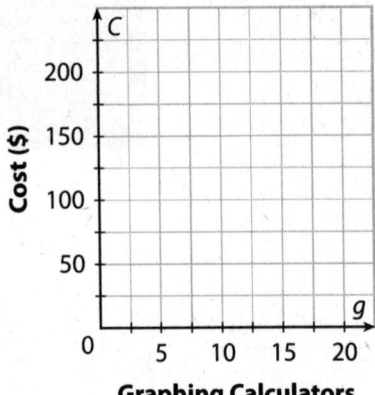

Graphing Calculators

21. The temperature, in degrees Fahrenheit, of a liquid that is increasing can be represented by the equation $f(t) = 64 + 4t$, where t is the time in hours. Graph the function to show the temperatures over the first 10 hours. Use the graph to find the temperature after 7 hours.

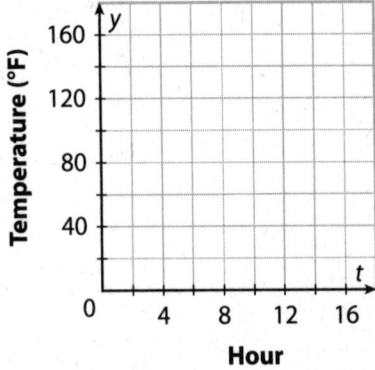

Hour

22. A snowboarder's elevation, in feet, can be represented by the function $E(t) = 3000 - 70t$, where t is in seconds. Graph the function and find the elevation of the snowboarder after 30 seconds.

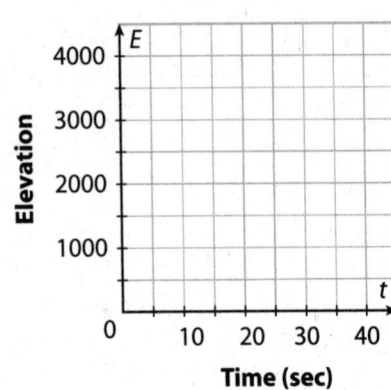

Time (sec)

23. **Explain the Error** Student A and student B were given the following graph and asked to find the value of $f(x)$ when $x = 1$. Student A gave an answer of 0 while student B gave an answer of -2. Who is incorrect? Explain the error.

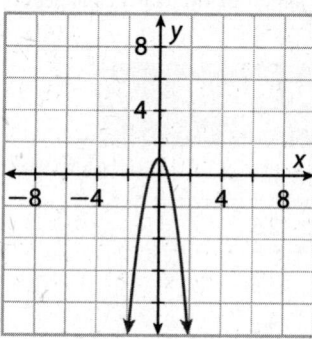

24. **Justify Reasoning** Without graphing, tell which statement(s) are true for the graph of the function $y = x^2 + 1$. Explain your choices.

   I. All points on the graph are above the origin.

   II. All points on the graph have positive x-values.

   III. All points on the graph have positive y-values.

Lesson Performance Task

The Japanese Shinkansen, or bullet train, can accelerate rapidly to reach its maximum traveling speed of about 170 miles per hour. The table gives the speed of the train in feet per second at several different times.

Time (seconds)	Speed (feet per second)
0	0
1	2.5
4	10
6	15
10	25

a. Convert the data from the table to a set of ordered pairs and graph them on a coordinate grid. Connect the points with a line. What does the line represent?

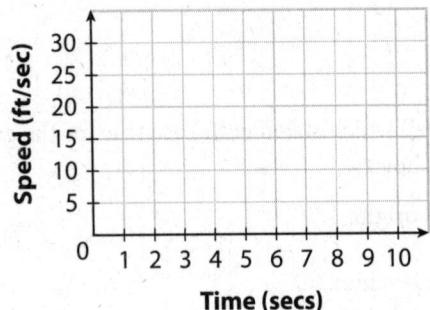

b. What is the slope of the line? What does the slope represent?

c. If the acceleration remains constant, how long will it take the train to reach its maximum speed of 170 miles per hour (mph)? [1 mph equals about 1.5 feet per second]

Functions and Models

Essential Question: How can you use functions to solve real-world problems?

KEY EXAMPLE   *(Lesson 3.1)*

The graph below represents Robert's total distance traveled during his walk to school. Write a possible situation for the graph.

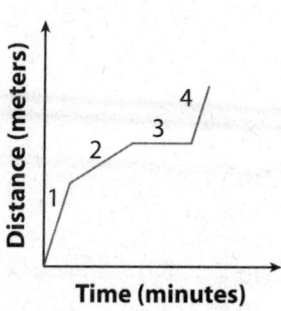

Sections 1 and 4 are steeper than section 2, so Robert was walking faster during these times.

Section 3 is horizontal, so Robert was not moving during this time.

Possible Situation: Robert walked quickly at the beginning of his walk, then he walked at a slower pace. He stopped for a while to talk to some friends. Then, he walked quickly the rest of the way to school.

KEY EXAMPLE   *(Lesson 3.2)*

Give the domain and range of the relation. Explain whether the relation is a function.

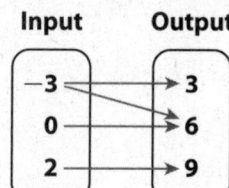

The domain is all inputs, or $\{-3, 0, 2\}$.

The range is all outputs, or $\{3, 6, 9\}$.

A function has at most one output value for each input. The relation is not a function, because the input value -3 has more than one output.

KEY EXAMPLE   *(Lessons 3.3, 3.4)*

Write an equation in function notation for the following example, and graph the function.

A study skills tutor charges $8 an hour for sessions lasting 1, 2, 3, or 4 hours.

The independent variable x is the number of hours.

The dependent variable $f(x)$ is the total cost.

The function for the total cost is $f(x) = 8x$.

The ordered pairs for the function $f(x) = 8x$ for the domain $\{1, 2, 3, 4\}$ are $(1, 8)$, $(2, 16)$, $(3, 24)$, and $(4, 32)$.

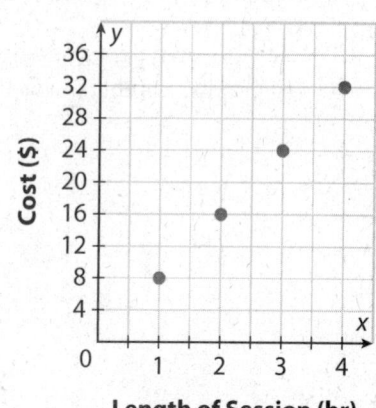

Length of Session (hr)

Key Vocabulary

continuous graph
  (gráfica continua)
dependent variable
  (variable dependiente)
discrete graph
  (gráfica discreta)
domain *(dominio)*
function *(función)*
function notation
  (notación de función)
independent variable
  (variable independiente)
range *(rango)*
relation *(relación)*

EXERCISES

1. Sketch a graph that represents the following situation. A person gets on a ride at an amusement park. The ride rises slowly and then quickly to its highest point. Then, to build anticipation, the ride stops for a period of time before quickly falling. Then, the ride descends more slowly before coming to a stop. *(Lesson 3.1)*

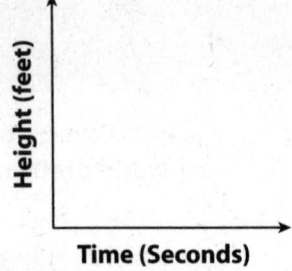

2. Identify the independent and dependent variables of the following relation. Give the domain and range, and explain whether the relation is a function.

A farmer has up to 3 pigs at a time on his farm. The given relation represents the average number of pounds of feed needed for x pigs daily. *(Lesson 3.2)*

Number of Pigs, x	Pounds of Feed, y
1	55
2	110
3	165

3. A store sells roasted peanuts in 1, 2, 2.5, and 4 pound bags. The peanuts cost $4 per pound. Write an equation in function notation that represents the cost of the peanuts in terms of the number of pounds, and graph the function. *(Lessons 3.3, 3.4)*

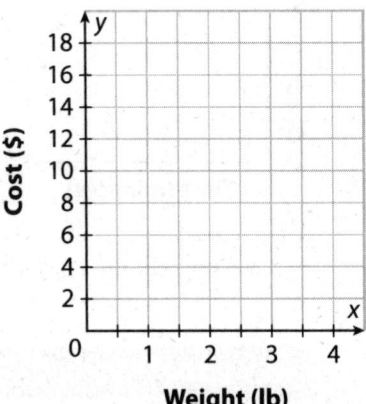

MODULE PERFORMANCE TASK
Season Passes

Wild Planet Theme Park offers three season-pass purchase options.

Plan A	Plan B	Plan C
One payment of $500	$80 down payment 6 payments of $75 every other month	$60 down payment 11 monthly payments of $45

Which payment option is the least expensive?

Use your own paper to complete the task. Be sure to write down all your data. Then use graphs, numbers, words, or algebra to explain how you reached your conclusion.

(Ready) to Go On?

3.1–3.4 Functions and Models

1. The graph shown represents the altitude of a hiker during a period of time. Write a possible situation represented by the graph. *(Lesson 3.1)*

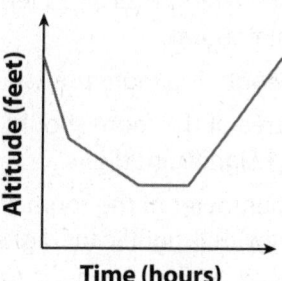

2. Use the vertical line test to determine if the relation represented on the graph from **Exercise 1** is a function. Explain. *(Lesson 3.2)*

3. A math test is made up of 7 problems, each worth 10 points. There is no partial credit. Every test taker receives 30 points for taking the test. Write a function to describe the test score determined by the number of correct answers. Graph the function using a reasonable domain and range. *(Lessons 3.3, 3.4)*

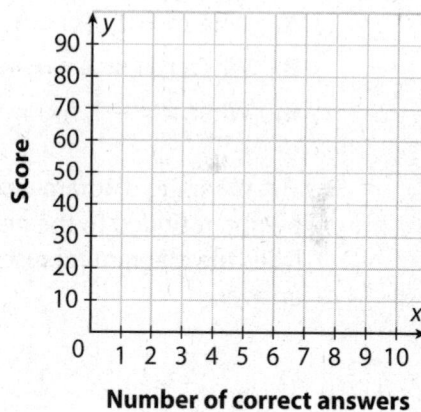

ESSENTIAL QUESTION

4. What is a function?

Assessment Readiness

1. Kyle is installing new baseboards and carpet in his rectangular living room. He measured the length as 24.25 feet and the width as 16.4 feet. Select Yes or No for each statement.

   A. The length is a more precise measurement. ◯ Yes ◯ No

   B. The area of the room should be given with 3 significant digits. ◯ Yes ◯ No

   C. The perimeter of the room should be given with 4 significant digits. ◯ Yes ◯ No

2. The graph represents the function $f(x) = -x^2 + 2$. Select True or False for each statement.

   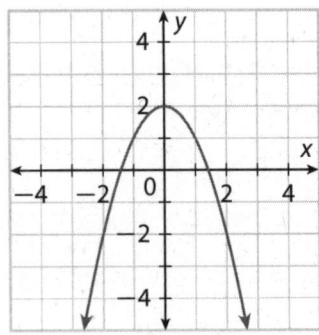

   A. When $x = 1$, $f(x) = 1$. ◯ True ◯ False

   B. When $f(x) = 2$, $x = -2$. ◯ True ◯ False

   C. When $x = -1$, $f(x) = 1$. ◯ True ◯ False

3. The mapping diagram represents the age, in years, and height, rounded to the nearest inch, of a group of friends. Does the diagram represent a function? Explain your answer.

   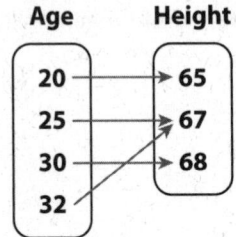

4. An amusement park charges an entrance fee of $25 plus $3.50 per ride. Write a function to represent this situation. How much would it cost to go to the park and ride 8 rides?

Patterns and Sequences

Essential Question: How are patterns and sequences used to solve real-world problems?

REAL WORLD VIDEO
Today's calculators, apps, and computer software can perform even the most complex calculations almost instantly. Programming based on patterns and sequences makes these modern marvels possible.

MODULE PERFORMANCE TASK PREVIEW

There Has to Be an Easier Way

Carl Friedrich Gauss, one of the greatest mathematicians of all time, showed his genius at a very early age. When he was just ten, his teacher presented a math problem that the teacher thought would keep the class occupied for a long time. Surprise! Gauss solved the problem almost before the teacher had finished stating it. In this module, you'll get a chance to tackle the same problem Gauss solved. Use a creative method to find the answer and you'll be famous too!

Are YOU Ready?

Complete these exercises to review skills you will need for this module.

• Online Homework
• Hints and Help
• Extra Practice

Number Patterns

Example 1   Find the next three numbers in the pattern 2, 5, 8, 11, …

2   5   8   11

+3   +3   +3

$11 + 3 = 14$

$14 + 3 = 17$

$17 + 3 = 20$

Study the pattern in the sequence.

Each number is 3 more than the number before it.

The next 3 numbers will be 14, 17, and 20.

Find the next three numbers in each pattern.

1. 2, 4, 8, 16, …

2. 5, 11, 17, 23, …

3. 50, 43, 36, 29, …

4. 1, 4, 9, 16, …

Algebraic Expressions

Example 2   Evaluate $2x + 3y$ for $x = 4$ and $y = -5$.

$2x + 3y$

$2(4) + 3(-5)$ Substitute 4 for *x* and −5 for *y*.

$8 + (-15)$ Multiply.

-7 Add.

Evaluate each expression for the given values of the variables.

5. $4p - 7p$ for $p = 8$ and $q = 5$

6. $(n - 1)^2$ for $n = -4$

7. $8d + 5e - 11$ for $d = 6$ and $e = -9$

8. $a^2 - b$ for $a = 7$ and $b = 12$

4.1 Identifying and Graphing Sequences

Essential Question: What is a sequence and how are sequences and functions related?

Explore Understanding Sequences

A go-kart racing track charges $5 for a go-kart license and $2 for each lap. If you list the charges for 1 lap, 2 laps, 3 laps, and so on, in order, the list forms a sequence of numbers:

$$7, 9, 11, 13, \ldots$$

A **sequence** is a list of numbers in a specific order. Each element in a sequence is called a **term**. In a sequence, each term has a position number. In the sequence $7, 9, 11, 13, \ldots$, the second term is 9, so its position number is 2.

(A) The total cost (term) of riding a go-kart for different numbers of laps (position) is shown below. Complete the table.

Position number, n	1	2	3		5		Domain
Term of the sequence, $f(n)$	7	9		13		17	Range

(B) You can use the term and position number of a sequence to write a function. Using function notation, $f(2) = 9$ indicates that the second term is 9. Use the table to complete the following statements.

$f(1) = \boxed{}$ $f(3) = \boxed{}$ $f(6) = \boxed{}$ $f\left(\boxed{}\right) = 13$ $f\left(\boxed{}\right) = 15$

(C) Identify the domain of the function $f(n)$. _____

(D) Identify the range of the function $f(n)$. _____

Reflect

1. **Discussion** What does $f(4) = 13$ mean in the context of the go-kart problem?

_____

2. **Discussion** Explain how to find the missing values in the table.

_____

3. **Communicate Mathematical Ideas** Explain why the relationship between the position numbers and the corresponding terms of a sequence can be considered a function.

_____

✏ Explain 1   Generating Sequences Using an Explicit Rule

An **explicit rule** for a sequence defines the nth term as a function of n for any whole number n greater than 0. Explicit rules can be used to find any specific term in a sequence without finding any of the previous terms.

Example 1   Write the first 4 terms of the sequence defined by the explicit rule.

(A) $f(n) = n^2 + 2$

Make a table and substitute values for $n = 1, 2, 3, 4$ to find the first 4 terms.

The first 4 terms of the sequence defined by the explicit rule $f(n) = n^2 + 2$ are 3, 6, 11, and 18.

n	$f(n) = n^2 + 2$	$f(n)$
1	$f(1) = 1^2 + 2 = 3$	3
2	$f(2) = 2^2 + 2 = 6$	6
3	$f(3) = 3^2 + 2 = 11$	11
4	$f(4) = 4^2 + 2 = 18$	18

(B) $f(n) = 3n^2 + 1$

Make a table and substitute values for $n = $ _____.

The first 4 terms are _____.

n	$f(n) = 3n^2 + 1$	$f(n)$
1	$f\left(\boxed{}\right) = 3\left(\boxed{}\right)^2 + 1 = \boxed{}$	$\boxed{}$
2	$f\left(\boxed{}\right) = 3\left(\boxed{}\right)^2 + 1 = \boxed{}$	$\boxed{}$
3	$f\left(\boxed{}\right) = 3\left(\boxed{}\right)^2 + 1 = \boxed{}$	$\boxed{}$
4	$f\left(\boxed{}\right) = 3\left(\boxed{}\right)^2 + 1 = \boxed{}$	$\boxed{}$

Reflect

4. Communicate Mathematical Ideas Explain how to find the 20th term of the sequence defined by the explicit rule $f(n) = n^2 + 2$.

5. Justify Reasoning The number 125 is a term of the sequence defined by the explicit rule $f(n) = 3n + 2$. Which term in the sequence is 125? Justify your answer.

6. Write the first 4 terms of the sequence defined by the explicit rule. $f(n) = n^2 - 5$

7. Find the 15th term of the sequence defined by the explicit rule. $f(n) = 4n - 3$.

🔑 **Explain 2** **Generating Sequences Using a Recursive Rule**

A **recursive rule** for a sequence defines the nth term by relating it to one or more previous terms.

The following is an example of a recursive rule:

$f(1) = 4, f(n) = f(n - 1) + 10$ for each whole number n greater than 1

This rule means that after the first term of the sequence, every term $f(n)$ is the sum of the pervious term $f(n - 1)$ and 10.

Example 2 **Write the first 4 terms of the sequence defined by the recursive rule.**

(A) $f(1) = 2, f(n) = f(n - 1) + 3$ for each whole number n greater than 1

For the first 4 terms, the domain of the function is 1, 2, 3, and 4.

The first term of the sequence is 2.

n	$f(n) = f(n - 1) + 3$	$f(n)$
1	$f(1) = 2$	2
2	$f(2) = f(1) + 3 = 2 + 3 = 5$	5
3	$f(3) = f(2) + 3 = 5 + 3 = 8$	8
4	$f(4) = f(3) + 3 = 8 + 3 = 11$	11

The first 4 terms are 2, 5, 8, and 11.

(B) $f(1) = 4, f(n) = f(n - 1) + 5$ for each whole number n greater than 1

For the first 4 terms, the domain of the function is _____

The first term of the sequence is ☐ .

n	$f(n) = f(n - 1) + 5$	$f(n)$
1	$f(1) = $ ☐	☐
2	$f(2) = f\left(\Box\right) + 5 = \Box + 5 = \Box$	☐
3	$f(3) = f\left(\Box\right) + 5 = \Box + 5 = \Box$	☐
4	$f(4) = f\left(\Box\right) + 5 = \Box + 5 = \Box$	☐

The first 4 terms are _____ .

© Houghton Mifflin Harcourt Publishing Company

8. Describe how to find the 12th term of the sequence in Example 2A.

_____

_____

9. Suppose you want to find the 40th term of a sequence. Would you rather use a recursive rule or an explicit rule? Explain your reasoning.

_____

_____

Your Turn

Write the first 5 terms of the sequence.

10. $f(1) = 35$ and $f(n) = f(n-1) - 2$ for each whole number n greater than 1.

11. $f(1) = 45$ and $f(n) = f(n-1) - 4$ for each whole number n greater than 1.

⚷ Explain 3   Constructing and Graphing Sequences

You can graph a sequence on a coordinate plane by plotting the points $(n, f(n))$ indicated in a table that you use to generate the terms.

Example 3   Construct and graph the sequence described.

(A) The go-kart racing charges are $5 for a go-kart license and $2 for each lap. Use the explicit rule $f(n) = 2n + 5$.

Complete the table to represent the cost for the first 4 laps.

n	$f(n) = 2n + 5$	f(n)
1	$f(1) = 2(1) + 5 = 2 + 5 = 7$	7
2	$f(2) = 2(2) + 5 = 4 + 5 = 9$	9
3	$f(3) = 2(3) + 5 = 6 + 5 = 11$	11
4	$f(4) = 2(4) + 5 = 8 + 5 = 13$	13

The ordered pairs are (1, 7), (2, 9), (3, 11), (4, 13).

Graph the sequence using the ordered pairs.

Notice that the graph is a set of points that are not connected.

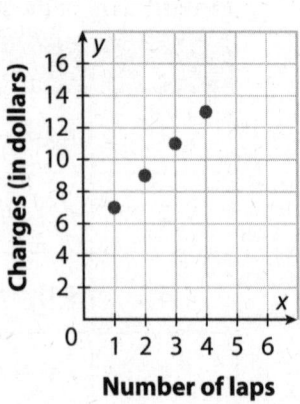

(B) A movie rental club charges $20 a month plus a $5 membership fee. Use the explicit rule $f(n) = 20n + 5$.

Complete the table to represent the charges paid for 6 months.

n	$f(n) = \boxed{}n + \boxed{}$			$f(n)$
1	$f\left(\boxed{}\right) = \boxed{}\left(\boxed{}\right) + \boxed{} = \boxed{}$			$\boxed{}$
2	$f\left(\boxed{}\right) = \boxed{}\left(\boxed{}\right) + \boxed{} = \boxed{}$			$\boxed{}$
3	$f\left(\boxed{}\right) = \boxed{}\left(\boxed{}\right) + \boxed{} = \boxed{}$			$\boxed{}$
4	$f\left(\boxed{}\right) = \boxed{}\left(\boxed{}\right) + \boxed{} = \boxed{}$			$\boxed{}$
5	$f\left(\boxed{}\right) = \boxed{}\left(\boxed{}\right) + \boxed{} = \boxed{}$			$\boxed{}$
6	$f\left(\boxed{}\right) = \boxed{}\left(\boxed{}\right) + \boxed{} = \boxed{}$			$\boxed{}$

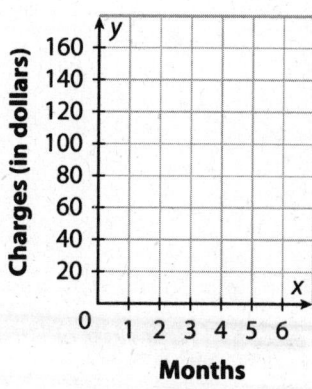

The ordered pairs are _____ .

Graph the sequence using the ordered pairs.

Notice that the graph is a set of points that are not connected.

Reflect

12. Explain why the points in the graphs in Example 3 are not connected.

_____

_____

Your Turn

Construct and graph the sequence described.

13. A pizza place is having a special. If you order a large pizza for a regular price $17, you can order any number of additional pizzas for $8.50 each. Use the recursive rule $f(1) = 17$ and $f(n) = f(n - 1) + 8.5$ for each whole number n greater than 1.

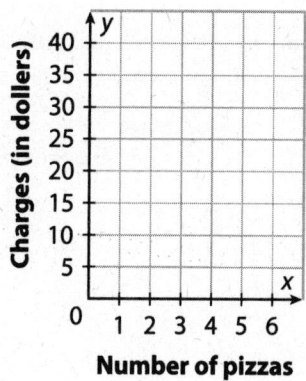

14. A gym charges $100 as the membership fee and $20 monthly fee. Use the explicit rule $f(n) = 20n + 100$ to construct and graph the sequence.

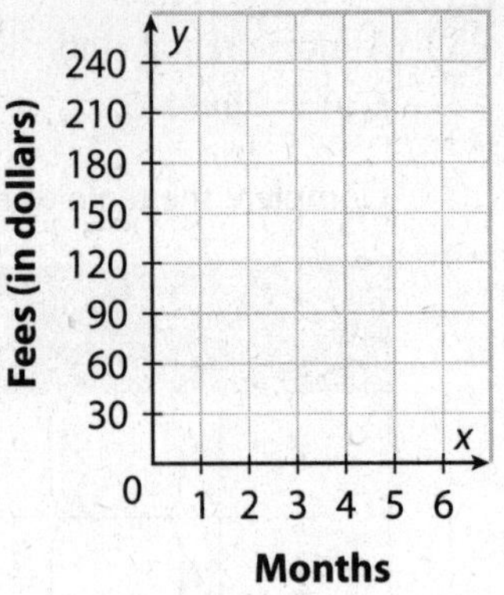

💬 Elaborate

15. What is the difference between an explicit rule and a recursive rule?

_____

_____

_____

16. Describe how to use an explicit rule to find the position number of a given term in a sequence.

_____

_____

_____

17. Explain why the graph of a sequence is a set of points that are not connected.

_____

_____

_____

18. Essential Question Check-In Why can the rule for a sequence be considered a function?

_____

_____

_____

Complete the table, and state the domain and range for the sequence it represents. Assume that the sequence continues without end.

1.

n	1	2	3		5	
f(n)	15	30		60		90

2.

n	1		3	4		6
f(n)	6	8	10		14	

Write the first 4 terms of the sequence defined by the given rule.

3. $f(1) = 65{,}536, f(n) = \sqrt{f(n-1)}$

4. $f(n) = n^3 - 1$

5. $f(1) = 7, f(n) = -4 \cdot f(n-1) + 15$

6. $f(n) = 2n^2 + 4$

7. $f(1) = 3, f(n) = [f(n-1)]^2$

8. $f(n) = (2n-1)^2$

Find the 10th term of the sequence defined by the given rule.

9. $f(1) = 2, f(n) = f(n-1) + 7$

10. $f(n) = \sqrt{n+2}$

11. $f(1) = 30, f(n) = 2 \cdot f(n-1) - 50$

12. $f(n) = \frac{1}{2}(n-1) + 3$

The explicit rule for a sequence and one of the specific terms is given. Find the position of the given term.

13. $f(n) = 1.25n + 6.25;\ 25$

14. $f(n) = -3(n-1);\ -51$

15. $f(n) = (2n-2) + 2;\ 52$

The recursive rule for a sequence and one of the specific terms is given. Find the position of the given term.

16. $f(1) = 8\frac{1}{2};\ f(n) = f(n-1) - \frac{1}{2};\ 5\frac{1}{2}$

17. $f(1) = 99, f(n) = f(n-1) + 4;\ 119$

18. $f(1) = 33.3, f(n) = f(n-1) + 0.2;\ 34.9$

Graph the sequence that represents the situation on a coordinate plane.

19. Jessica had $150 in her savings account after her first week of work. She then started adding $35 each week to her account for the next 5 weeks. The savings account balance can be represented by a sequence.

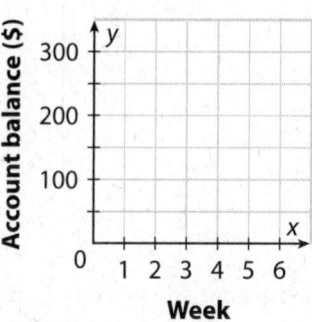

20. Carrie borrowed $840 from a friend to pay for a car repair. Carrie promises to repay her friend in 8 equal monthly payments. The remaining amount Carrie has to repay can be represented by a sequence.

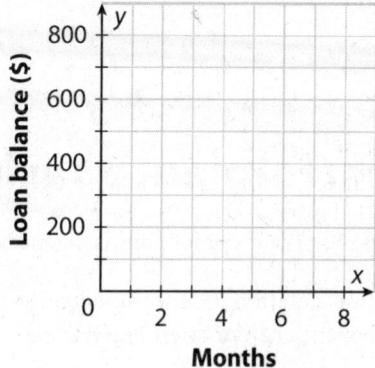

H.O.T. **Focus on Higher Order Thinking**

21. A park charges $12 for one round of miniature golf and a reduced fee for each additional round played. If Tom paid $47 for 6 rounds of miniature golf, what is the reduced fee for each additional round played?

22. **Analyze Relationships** Construct a recursive rule to describe the sequence: 2, 4, 6, 8,…

23. Explain the Error To find the 5th term of a sequence where $f(1) = 4$ and $f(n) = 2 \cdot f(n-1) + 1$ for each whole number greater than 1, Shane calculates $(4 \cdot 2 \cdot 2 \cdot 2 \cdot 2) + 1 = 65$. Is this correct? Justify your answer.

24. Critical Thinking Write a recursive rule for a sequence where every term is the same.

Lesson Performance Task

A museum charges $10 per person for admission and $2 for each of 8 special exhibits.

   a. Use function notation to write an equation to represent the cost for attending n events.

   b. Make a table to represent the total cost of admission plus 1, 2, and 3 special exhibits.

   c. What would $f(0) = 10$ represent?

   d. What would the total cost be for going to all 8 special exhibits?

   e. Determine an explicit rule for the total cost if the first special exhibit were free.

4.2 Constructing Arithmetic Sequences

Essential Question: What is an arithmetic sequence?

Resource Locker

⊘ Explore   Exploring Arithmetic Sequences

You can order tickets for the local theater online. There is a fee of $2 per order. Matinee tickets cost $10 each. The total cost, in dollars, of ordering n matinee tickets online can be found by using $C(n) = 10n + 2$. The table shows the cost of 1, 2, 3, and 4 tickets.

(A) Complete the table of values for $C(n) = 10n + 2$.

Tickets	1	2	3	4
Total Cost ($)				

What is the domain of the sequence? _____

(B) What is the range of the sequence? _____

(C) What is the first term of the sequence? _____

(D) Find the difference between each two consecutive terms in the sequence:

22 − 12 = _____   32 − 22 = _____   42 − 32 = _____

Reflect

1. **Discussion** Suppose you extended the table for up to 15 tickets. Would you expect the difference between consecutive terms to be the same? Explain your reasoning.

_____

_____

_____

2. **Communicate Mathematical Ideas** Explain how the domain is limited in this situation.

_____

_____

_____

🔑 Explain 1   Constructing Rules for Arithmetic Sequences

In an **arithmetic sequence**, the difference between consecutive terms is always equal. This difference, written as d, is called the **common difference**.

An arithmetic sequence can be described in two ways, explicitly and recursively. As you saw earlier, in an **explicit** rule for a sequence, the nth term of the arithmetic sequence is defined as a function of n. In a **recursive** rule for a sequence, the first term of the sequence is given and the nth term is defined by relating it to the previous term. An arithmetic sequence can be defined using either a recursive rule or an explicit rule.

Example 1   Write a recursive rule and an explicit rule for the sequence described by each table.

(A)   The table shows the monthly balance in a savings account with regular monthly deposits. The savings account begins with $2000, and $500 is deposited each month.

Time (months)	n	1	2	3	4	5
Balance	$f(n)$	2000	2500	3000	3500	4000

Write a recursive rule.

$f(1) = 2000$, and the common difference d is 500.

The recursive rule is $f(1) = 2000$, $f(n) = f(n - 1) + 500$ for $n \geq 2$.

Write an explicit rule.

n	$f(n)$	$f(1) + d \cdot x = f(n)$
1	2000	$2000 + 500(0) = 2000$
2	2500	$2000 + 500(1) = 2500$
3	3000	$2000 + 500(2) = 3000$

Since d is always multiplied by a number equal to $(n - 1)$, you can generalize the result from the table. The explicit rule is $f(n) = 2000 + 500(n - 1)$.

(B)   The table shows the monthly balance in a savings account with regular monthly deposits.

Time (months)	n	1	2	3	4	5
Balance	$f(n)$	5000	6000	7000	8000	9000

Write a recursive rule.

$f(1) = $ _____ and the common difference d is _____.

The recursive rule is $f(1) = $ _____, $f(n) = f(n - 1) + $ _____ for $n \geq 2$.

Write an explicit rule.

n	$f(n)$	$f(1) + d \cdot x = f(n)$
1	5000	$5000 + 1000(0) = 5000$
2		
3		

Since d is always multiplied by a number equal to _____, you can generalize the result from

the table. $f(n) = $ _____ $+$ _____.

© Houghton Mifflin Harcourt Publishing Company

3. **Critique Reasoning** Jerome says that the sequence 1, 8, 27, 64, 125,... is not an arithmetic sequence. Is that correct? Explain.

_____

_____

4. An arithmetic sequence has a common difference of 3. If you know that the third term of the sequence is 15, how can you find the fourth term? _____

YourTurn

5. The table shows the number of plates left at a buffet after n hours. Write a recursive rule and an explicit rule for the arithmetic sequence represented by the table.

Time (hours)	n	1	2	3	4	5
Number of plates	$f(n)$	155	141	127	113	99

_____

_____

_____

⊘ Explain 2 Using a General Form to Construct Rules for Arithmetic Sequences

Arithmetic sequences can be described by a set of general rules. Values can be substituted into these rules to find a recursive and explicit rule for a given sequence.

General Recursive Rule	General Explicit Rule
Given $f(1)$, $f(n) = f(n-1) + d$ for $n \geq 2$	$f(n) = f(1) + d(n-1)$

Example 2 Write a general recursive and general explicit rule for each arithmetic sequence.

Ⓐ 100, 88, 76, 64, ...

$f(1) = 100$, common difference $= 88 - 100 = -12$

The recursive rule is $f(1) = 100$, $f(n) = f(n-1) - 12$ for $n \geq 2$.

The explicit rule is $f(n) = 100 - 12(n-1)$.

Ⓑ 0, 8, 16, 24, 32,...

$f(1) =$ _____, common difference $=$ _____ $-$ _____ $=$ _____.

The recursive rule is $f(1) =$ _____, $f(n) = f(n-1) +$ _____ for $n \geq 2$.

The explicit rule is $f(n) =$ _____ $+$ _____ $(n-1)$.

6. What is the recursive rule for the sequence $f(n) = 2 + (-3)(n - 1)$? How do you know?

_____

_____

7. Write a recursive rule and an explicit rule for the arithmetic sequence 6, 16, 26, 36,...

_____

_____

Explain 3   Relating Arithmetic Sequences and Functions

The explicit rule for an arithmetic sequence can be expressed as a function. You can use the graph of the function to write an explicit rule.

Example 3   Write an explicit rule in function notation for each arithmetic sequence.

Ⓐ   The cost of a whitewater rafting trip depends on the number of passengers. The base fee is $50, and the cost per passenger is $25. The graph shows the sequence.

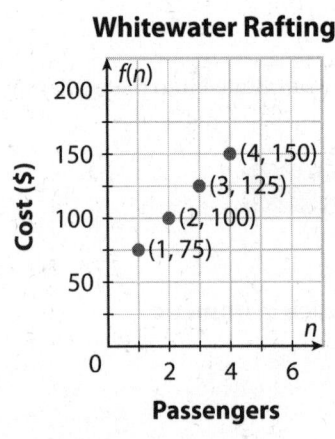

Whitewater Rafting

Step 1 Represent the sequence in a table.

Number of passengers n	1	2	3	4
Cost ($) $f(n)$	75	100	125	150

Step 2 Find the common difference.

$f(2) - f(1) = 100 - 75 = 25$

$f(3) - f(2) = 125 - 100 = 25$

$f(4) - f(3) = 150 - 125 = 25$

The common difference d is 25.

Step 3 Write an explicit rule for the sequence.

Substitute 75 for $f(1)$ and 25 for d.

$f(n) = f(1) + d(n - 1)$

$f(n) = 75 + 25(n - 1)$

Ⓑ The number of seats per row in an auditorium depends on which row it is. The first row has 6 seats, the second row has 9 seats, the third row has 12 seats, and so on. The graph shows the sequence.

Auditorium Seats

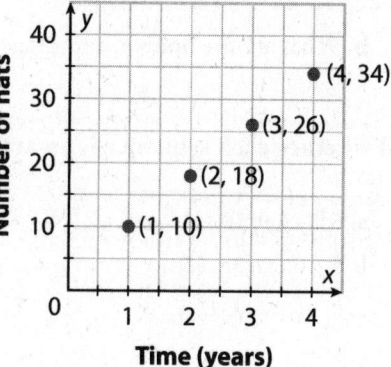

Step 1 Represent the sequence in a table.

Row number n	1	2	3	4
Number of seats $f(n)$				

Step 2 Find the common difference.

$f(2) - f(1) =$ ☐ $-$ ☐ $=$ ☐

$f(3) - f(2) =$ ☐ $-$ ☐ $=$ ☐

$f(4) - f(3) =$ ☐ $-$ ☐ $=$ ☐   The common difference is $d =$ _____.

Step 3 Write an explicit rule for the sequence. $f(n) = f(1) + d(n - 1)$

Substitute _____ for $f(1)$ and _____ for d. $f(n) =$ ☐ $+$ ☐ $(n - 1)$

Reflect

8. **Analyze Relationships** Compare the graph of the function $f(x) = 3 + 5(x - 1)$ and the graph of the sequence $f(n) = 3 + 5(n - 1)$.

_____

_____

_____

YourTurn

9. Jerry collects hats. The total number of hats in Jerry's collection depends on how many years he has been collecting hats. After the first year, Jerry had 10 hats. Each year he has added the same number of hats to his collection. The graph shows the sequence. Write an explicit rule in function notation for the arithmetic sequence.

Number of Hats over Time

Elaborate

10. What information do you need to write a recursive rule for an arithmetic sequence that you do not need to write an explicit rule?

_____

_____

11. Suppose you want to be able to determine the ninetieth term in an arithmetic sequence and you have both an explicit and a recursive rule. Which rule would you use? Explain.

_____

_____

_____

12. Essential Question Check-In The explicit equation for an arithmetic sequence and a linear equation have a similar form. How is the value of m in the linear equation $y = mx + b$ similar to the value of d in the explicit equation $f(n) = f(1) + d(n - 1)$?

_____

_____

⭐ Evaluate: Homework and Practice

- Online Homework
- Hints and Help
- Extra Practice

1. Farah pays a $25 signup fee to join a car sharing service and a $7 monthly charge. The total cost of using the car sharing service for n months can be found using $C(n) = 25 + 7n$. The table shows the cost of the service for 1, 2, 3, and 4 months.

a. Complete the table for $C(n) = 25 + 7n$

Months	n	1	2	3	4
Cost ($)	$f(n)$				

b. What are the domain and range of the sequence?

c. What is the common difference d?

Tell whether each sequence is an arithmetic sequence.

2.
a. 6, 7, 8, 9, 10,…

b. 5, 10, 20, 35, 55,…

c. 0, −1, 1, −2, 2,…

d. 1, 16, 81, 625, 1296

e. −2, −4, −6, −8, −10, …

3. Chemistry A chemist heats up several unknown substances to determine their boiling point. Use the table to determine whether the sequence is arithmetic. If it is arithmetic, write an explicit rule and a recursive rule for the sequence. If not, explain why it is not arithmetic.

Substance	1	2	3	4	5
Boiling Point (°F)	100	135	149	165	188

Write a recursive rule and an explicit rule for the arithmetic sequence described by each table.

4.

Month	n	1	2	3	4	5
Account balance ($)	$f(n)$	35	32	29	26	23

5.

Tickets	n	1	2	3	4	5
Total cost (S)	$f(n)$	58	65	72	79	86

6.

Month	n	1	2	3	4	5
Total deposits ($)	$f(n)$	84	100	116	132	148

7.

Delivery number	n	1	2	3	4	5
Weight of truck (lb)	$f(n)$	4567	3456	2345	1234	123

8.

Week	n	1	2	3	4	5
Account owed ($)	$f(n)$	125	100	75	50	25

9.

Skaters	n	1	2	3	4	5
Charge for lesson ($)	$f(n)$	60	80	100	120	140

Write a recursive rule and an explicit rule for each arithmetic sequence.

10. 95, 90, 85, 80, 75, . . .

11. 63, 70, 77, 84, 91, . . .

12. 86, 101, 116, 131, 146, . . .

13. 112, 110, 108, 106, 104, . . .

14. 5, 9, 13, 17, 21, . . .

15. 67, 37, 7, −23, −53, . . .

Write an explicit rule in function notation for each arithmetic sequence.

16. A student loan needs to be paid off beginning the first year after graduation. Beginning at Year 1, there is $52,000 remaining to be paid. The graduate makes regular payments of $8,000 each year. The graph shows the sequence.

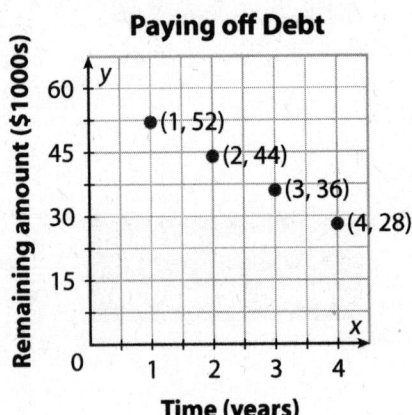

Paying off Debt

17. A grocery cart is 38 inches long. When the grocery carts are put away in a nested row, the length of the row depends on how many carts are nested together. Each cart added to the row adds 12 inches to the row length. The graph shows the sequence.

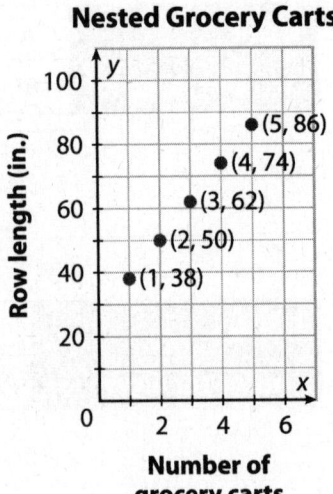

Nested Grocery Carts

18. A dog food for overweight dogs claims that a dog weighing 85 pounds will lose about 2 pounds per week for the first 4 weeks when following the recommended feeding guidelines. The graph shows the sequence.

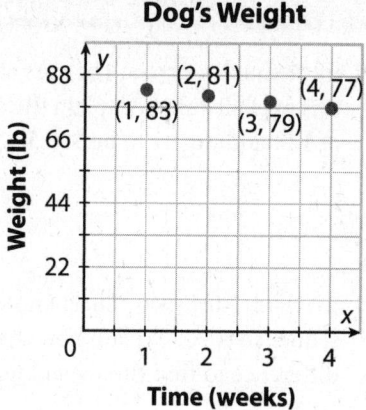

Dog's Weight

19. A savings account is opened with $6300. Monthly deposits of $1100 are made. The graph shows the sequence.

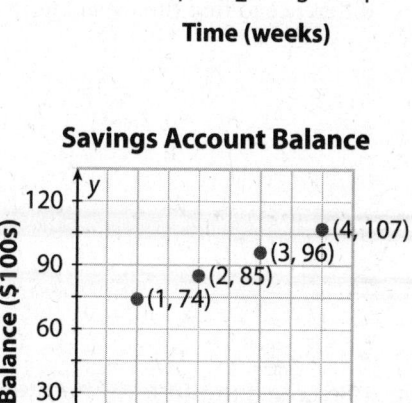

Savings Account Balance

20. Biology The wolf population in a local wildlife area is currently 12. Due to a new conservation effort, conservationists hope the wolf population will increase by 2 animals each year for the next 50 years. Assume that the plan will be successful. Write an explicit rule for the population sequence. Use the rule to predict the number of animals in the wildlife area in the fiftieth year.

21. How are the terms in the sequence in the table related? Is the sequence an arithmetic sequence? Explain.

n	1	2	3	4	5
f(n)	3	9	27	81	243

22. **Explain the Error** The cost of a hamburger is $2.50. Each additional hamburger costs $2.00. Sully wrote this explicit rule to explain the sequence of costs: $f(n) = 2 + 2.5(n - 1)$. Using this rule, he found the cost of 12 hamburgers to be $29.50. Is this number correct? If not, identify Sully's error.

23. **Critical Thinking** Lucia knows the fourth term in a sequence is 55 and the ninth term in the same sequence is 90. Explain how she can find the common difference for the sequence. Then use the common difference to find the second term of the sequence.

24. **Represent Real-World Problems** Write and solve a real-world problem involving a situation that can be represented by the sequence $f(n) = 15 + 2(n - 1)$.

Lesson Performance Task

For Carl's birthday, his grandparents gave him a $50 gift card to a local movie theater. The theater charges $6 admission for each movie. How can Carl use an arithmetic sequence to determine the value left on his card after each movie he sees?

a. Write an explicit rule for the arithmetic sequence and use it to determine how much value is left on the card after Carl has seen 4 movies.

b. How much is left on the card after Carl has seen the maximum number of movies?

4.3 Modeling with Arithmetic Sequences

Essential Question: How can you solve real-world problems using arithmetic sequences?

⊘ Explore Interpreting Models of Arithmetic Sequences

You can model real-world situations and solve problems using models of arithmetic sequences. For example, suppose watermelons cost $6.50 each at the local market. The total cost, in dollars, of n watermelons can be found using $c(n) = 6.5n$.

(A) Complete the table of values for 1, 2, 3, and 4 watermelons.

Watermelons n	1	2	3	4
Total cost ($) $c(n)$				

(B) What is the common difference?

_____

_____

(C) What does n represent in this context?

_____

_____

(D) What are the dependent and independent variables in this context?

_____

_____

(E) Find $c(7)$. What does this value represent?

_____

_____

Reflect

1. **Discussion** What domain values make sense for $c(n) = 6.5n$ in this situation?

_____

_____

⚙ Explain 1 Modeling Arithmetic Sequences From a Table

Given a table of data values from a real-world situation involving an arithmetic sequence, you can construct a function model and use it to solve problems.

Example 1 Construct an explicit rule in function notation for the arithmetic sequence represented in the table. Then interpret the meaning of a specific term of the sequence in the given context.

Ⓐ Suppose the table shows the cost, in dollars, of postage per ounce of a letter.

Number of ounces	n	1	2	3	4
Cost ($) of postage	$f(n)$	0.35	0.55	0.75	0.95

Determine the value of $f(9)$, and tell what it represents in this situation.

Find the common difference, d. $d = 0.55 - 0.35 = 0.20$

Substitute 0.35 for $f(1)$ and 0.20 for d.

$f(n) = f(1) + d(n - 1)$

$f(n) = 0.35 + 0.20(n - 1)$

$f(9) = 0.35 + 0.20(8) = 1.95$

So, the cost of postage for a 9-ounce letter is $1.95.

Ⓑ The table shows the cumulative total interest paid, in dollars, on a loan after each month.

Number of months	n	1	2	3	4
Cumulative total ($)	$f(n)$	160	230	300	370

Determine the value of $f(20)$ and tell what it represents in this situation.

Find the common difference, d. $d = \boxed{} - 160 = \boxed{}$

Substitute $\boxed{}$ for $f(1)$ and $\boxed{}$ for d.

$f(n) = f(1) + d(n - 1)$

$f(n) = \boxed{} + \boxed{}(n - 1)$

Find $f(20)$ and interpret the value in context.

$$f(n) = f(1) + d(n - 1)$$

$f\left(\boxed{}\right) = \boxed{} + \boxed{}\left(\boxed{}\right) = \boxed{}$

So, the cumulative total _____ paid after _____ months is _____.

Construct an explicit rule in function notation for the arithmetic sequence represented in the table. Then interpret the meaning of a specific term of the sequence in the given context.

2. The table shows $f(n)$, the distance, in miles, from the store after Mila has traveled for n hours.

Time (h)	n	1	2	3	4
Distance (mi)	$f(n)$	20	32	44	56

Determine the value of $f(10)$ and tell what it represents in this situation.

3. The table below shows the total cost, in dollars, of purchasing n battery packs.

Number of battery packs	n	1	2	3	4
Total cost ($)	$f(n)$	4.90	8.90	12.90	16.90

Determine the value of $f(18)$ and tell what it represents in this situation.

⊙ Explain 2 Modeling Arithmetic Sequences From a Graph

Given a graph of a real-world situation involving an arithmetic sequence, you can construct a function model and use it to solve problems.

Example 2 Construct an explicit rule in function notation for the arithmetic sequence represented in the graph, and use it to solve the problem.

(A) D'Andre collects feather pens. The graph shows the number of feather pens D'Andre has collected over time, in weeks. According to this pattern, how many feather pens will D'Andre have collected in 12 weeks?

Represent the sequence in a table.

n	1	2	3	4
$f(n)$	18	37	56	75

Find the common difference.

$d = 37 - 8 = 19$

Use the general explicit rule for an arithmetic sequence to write the rule in function notation. Substitute 18 for $f(1)$ and 19 for d.

$f(n) = f(1) + d(n - 1)$

$f(n) = 18 + 19(n - 1)$

To determine the number of feather pens D'Andre will have collected after 12 weeks,

find $f(12)$.

$f(n) = 18 + 19(n - 1)$

$f(12) = 18 + 19(11)$

$f(12) = 18 + 209$

$f(12) = 227$

So, if this pattern continues, D'Andre will have collected 227 feather pens in 12 weeks.

Ⓑ Eric collects stamps. The graph shows the number of stamps that Eric has collected over time, in months. According to this pattern, how many stamps will Eric have collected in 10 months?

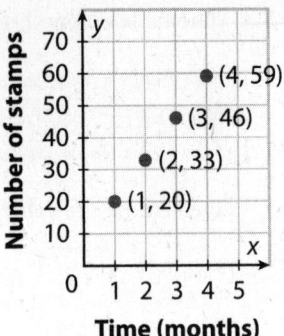

Represent the sequence in a table.

n	1	2	3	4
$f(n)$				

Find the common difference.

$d = \boxed{} - 20 = \boxed{}$

Use the general explicit rule for an arithmetic sequence to write the rule in function notation.

Substitute $\boxed{}$ for $f(1)$ and $\boxed{}$ for d.

$f(n) = f(1) + d(n - 1)$

$f(n) = \boxed{} + \boxed{}(n - 1)$

To determine the number of stamps Eric will have collected in 10 months, find $f\left(\boxed{}\right)$.

$f(n) = f(1) + d(n - 1)$

$f\left(\boxed{}\right) = \boxed{} + \boxed{}\left(\boxed{}\right) = \boxed{}$

So, if this pattern continues, Eric will have collected _____ in _____ months.

Reflect

4. How do you know which variable is the independent variable and which variable is the dependent variable in a real-world situation involving an arithmetic sequence?

_____

_____

Your Turn

Construct an explicit rule in function notation for the arithmetic sequence represented in the graph, and use it to solve the problem.

5. The graph shows the height, in inches, of a stack of boxes on a table as the number of boxes in the stack increases. Find the height of the stack with 7 boxes.

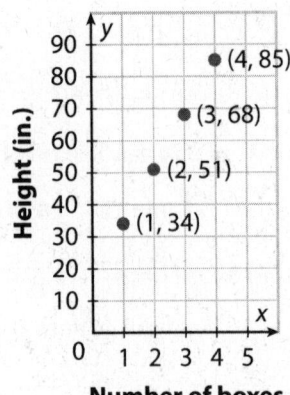

6. Quynh begins to save the same amount each month to save for a future shopping trip. The graph shows total amount she has saved after each month, *n*. What will be the total amount Quynh has saved after 12 months?

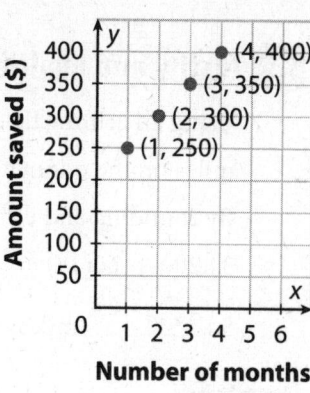

🔧 Explain 3 Modeling Arithmetic Sequences From a Description

Given a description of a real-world situation involving an arithmetic sequence, you can construct a function model and use it to solve problems.

Example 3 Construct an explicit rule in function notation for the arithmetic sequence represented, and use it to solve the problem. Justify and evaluate your answer.

The odometer on a car reads 34,240 on Day 1. Every day the car is driven 57 miles. If this pattern continues, what will the odometer read on Day 15?

🧩 Analyze Information

- The odometer on the car reads _____ miles on Day 1.

- Every day the car is driven _____ miles.

$f(1) =$ _____ and
$d =$ _____

🧩 Formulate a Plan

Write an explicit rule in function notation for the arithmetic sequence, and use it to

find _____, the odometer reading on Day 15.

🧩 Solve

$$f(n) = f(1) + d(n - 1)$$

$$f(n) = \boxed{} + \boxed{} (n - 1)$$

$$f\left(\boxed{}\right) = \boxed{} + \boxed{} \left(\boxed{}\right)$$

$$f\left(\boxed{}\right) = \boxed{}$$

On the Day 15, the odometer will show _____ miles.

Justify and Evaluate

Using an arithmetic sequence model _____ reasonable because the number of miles on the odometer increases by the same amount each day.

By rounding and estimation:

$34{,}200 + 60(14) =$ ⬚ $+$ ⬚ $=$ ⬚ miles

So _____ miles is a reasonable answer.

Your Turn

Construct an explicit rule in function notation for the arithmetic sequence represented, and use it to solve the problem. Justify and evaluate your answer.

7. Ruby signed up for a frequent-flier program. She receives 3400 frequent-flier miles for the first round-trip she takes and 1200 frequent-flier miles for all additional round-trips. How many frequent-flier miles will Ruby have after 5 round-trips?

8. A gym charges each member $100 for the first month, which includes a membership fee, and $50 per month for each month after that. How much money will a person spend on their gym membership for 6 months?

Elaborate

9. What domain values usually make sense for an arithmetic sequence model that represents a real-world situation?

10. When given a graph of an arithmetic sequence that represents a real-world situation, how can you determine the first term and the common difference in order to write a model for the sequence?

11. What are some ways to justify your answer when creating an arithmetic sequence model for a real-world situation and using it to solve a problem?

12. **Essential Question Check-In** How can you construct a model for a real-world situation that involves an arithmetic sequence?

1. A T-shirt at a department store costs $7.50. The total cost, in dollars, of a T-shirts is given by the function $C(a) = 7.5a$.

   a. Complete the table of values for 4 T-shirts.

T-shirts	1	2	3	4
Cost ($)				

   b. Determine the common difference.

   c. What does the variable a represent? What are the reasonable domain values for a?

2. A car dealership sells 5 cars per day. The total number of cars C sold over time in days is given by the function $C(t) = 5t$.

   a. Complete the table of values for the first 4 days of sales.

Time (days)	1	2	3	4
Number of Cars				

   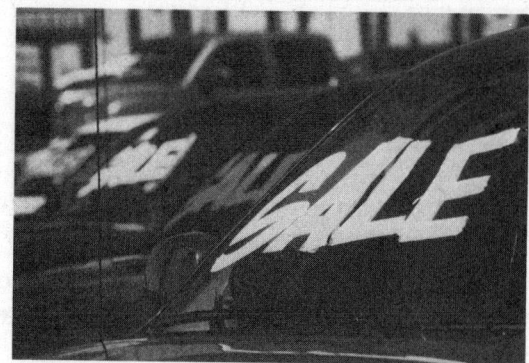

   b. Determine the common difference.

   c. What do the variables represent? What are the reasonable domain and range values for this situation?

3. A telemarketer makes 82 calls per day. The total number of calls made over time, in days, is given by the function $C(t) = 82t$.

   a. Complete the table of values for 4 days of calls.

Time (days)	1	2	3	4
Number of Calls				

   b. Determine the common difference.

   c. What do the variables represent? What are the reasonable domain and range values for this situation?

Construct an explicit rule in function notation for the arithmetic sequence represented in the table. Then determine the value of the given term, and explain what it means.

4. Darnell starts saving the same amount from each week's paycheck. The table shows the total balance $f(n)$ of his savings account over time in weeks.

Time (weeks) n	1	2	3	4
Savings Account Balance($) $f(n)$	$250	$380	$510	$640

Determine the value of $f(9)$, and explain what it represents in this situation.

5. Juan is traveling to visit universities. He notices mile markers along the road. He records the mile markers every 10 minutes. His father is driving at a constant speed. Complete the table.

a.

Time Interval	Mile Marker
1	520
2	509
3	498
4	
5	
6	

b. Find $f(10)$, and tell what it represents in this situation.

Construct an explicit rule in function notation for the arithmetic sequence represented in the graph. Then determine the value of the given term, and explain what it means.

6. The graph shows total cost of a whitewater rafting trip and the corresponding number of passengers on the trip. Find $f(8)$, and explain what it represents.

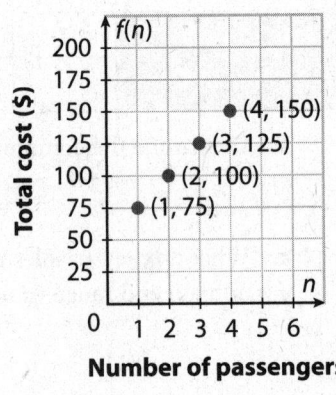

7. Ed collects autographs. The graph shows the total number of autographs that Ed has collected over time, in weeks. Find $f(12)$, and explain what it represents.

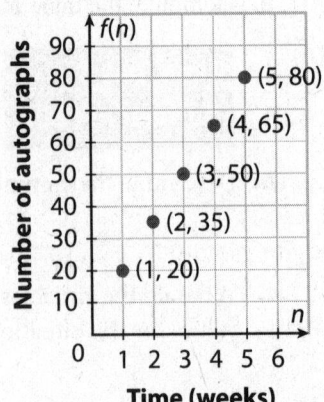

8. Finance Bob purchased a bus pass card with 320 points. Each week costs 20 points for unlimited bus rides. The graph shows the points remaining on the card over time in weeks. Determine the value of $f(10)$, and explain what it represents.

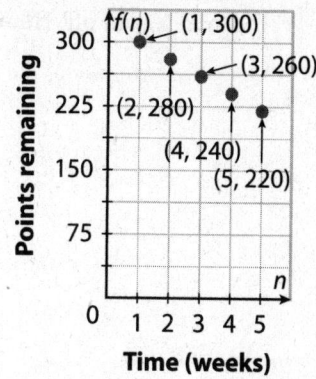

9. Biology The local wolf population is declining. The graph shows the local wolf population over time, in weeks.

Find $f(9)$, and explain what it represents.

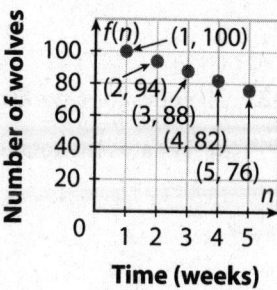

Construct an explicit rule in function notation for the arithmetic sequence. Then determine the value of the given term, and explain what it means.

10. Economics To package and ship an item, it costs $5.75 for the first pound and $0.75 for each additional pound. Find the 12th term, and explain what it represents.

11. A new bag of cat food weighs 18 pounds. At the end of each day, 0.5 pound of food is removed to feed the cats. Find the 30th term, and explain what it represents.

12. Carrie borrows $960 interest-free to pay for a car repair. She will repay $120 monthly until the loan is paid off. How many months will it take Carrie to pay off the loan? Explain.

13. The rates for a go-kart course are shown.

   a. What is the total cost for 15 laps?

Number of Laps n	1	2	3	4
Total cost ($) $f(n)$	7	9	11	13

   b. Suppose that after paying for 9 laps, the 10th lap is free. Will the sequence still be arithmetic? Explain.

14. **Multi-Part** Seats in a concert hall are arranged in the pattern shown.

   a. The numbers of seats in the rows form an arithmetic sequence. Write a rule for the arithmetic sequence.

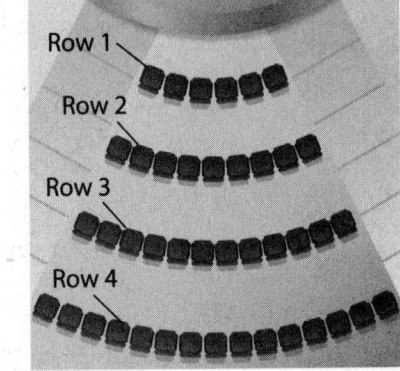

Row 1
Row 2
Row 3
Row 4

   b. How many seats are in Row 15?

   c. Each ticket costs $40. If every seat in the first 10 rows is filled, what is the total revenue from those seats?

   d. An extra chair is added to each row. Write the new rule for the arithmetic sequence and find the new total revenue from the first 10 rows.

15. Explain the Error The table shows the number of people who attend an amusement park over time, in days.

Time (days) n	1	2	3	4
Number of people $f(n)$	75	100	125	150

Sam writes an explicit rule for this arithmetic sequence: $f(n) = 25 + 75(n - 1)$

He then claims that according to this pattern, 325 people will attend the amusement park on Day 5. Explain the error that Sam made.

16. Communicate Mathematical Ideas Explain why it may be harder to find the nth value of an arithmetic sequence from a graph if the points are not labeled.

17. Make a prediction Verona is training for a marathon. The first part of her training schedule is given in the table.

Session n	1	2	3	4	5	6
Distance (mi) $f(n)$	3.5	5	6.5	8	9.5	11

a. Is this training schedule an arithmetic sequence? Explain. If it is, write an explicit rule for the sequence.

b. If Verona continues this pattern, during which training session will she run 26 miles?

18. If Verona's training schedule starts on a Monday and she runs every third day, on which day will she run 26 miles?

19. Multiple Representations Determine whether the following graph, table, and verbal description all represent the same arithmetic sequence.

Time (months) n	1	2	3	4
Amount of money ($) $f(n)$	250	300	350	400

A person deposits $250 dollars into a bank account. Each month, he adds $25 dollars to the account, and no other transactions occur in the account.

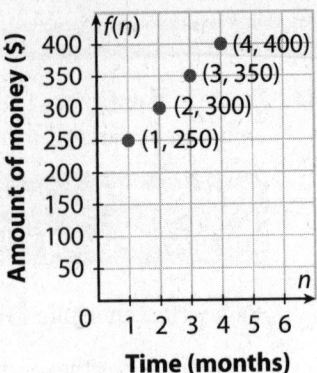

Lesson Performance Task

The graph shows the population of Ivor's ant colony over the first four weeks. Assume the ant population will continue to grow at the same rate.

   a. Write an explicit rule in function notation.

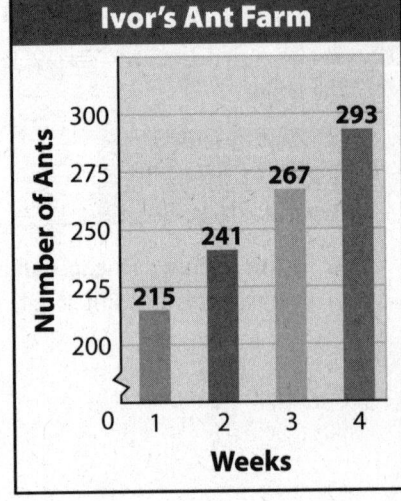

   b. If Ivor's ants have a mass of 1.5 grams each, what will be the total mass of all of his ants in 13 weeks?

   c. When the colony reaches 1385 ants, Ivor's ant farm will not be big enough for all of them. In how many weeks will the ant population be too large?

Essential Question: How are patterns and sequences used to solve real-world problems?

Key Vocabulary

arithmetic sequence
(sucesión aritmética)

common difference
(diferencia común)

explicit rule (fórmula explícita)

recursive rule
(fórmula recurrente)

sequence (sucesión)

term (término)

KEY EXAMPLE (Lesson 4.1)

A software subscription is $4 a month plus a start-up fee of $8. Use the explicit rule $f(n) = 4n + 8$. Construct and graph the first 4 terms of the sequence described.

n	1	2	3	4
$f(n)$	12	16	20	24

Represent the sequence in a table.

$(1, 12), (2, 16), (3, 20), (4, 24)$ *Generate ordered pairs.*

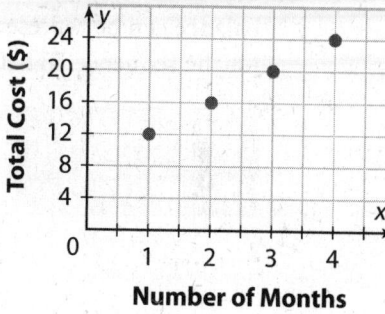

KEY EXAMPLE (Lesson 4.2)

Write a recursive rule and an explicit rule for the sequence 20, 14, 8, 2 ....

$f(1) = 20, d = 14 - 20 = -6$ *Find the first term and common difference.*

Given $f(1)$, $f(n) = f(n-1) + d$ for $n \geq 2$.   *Use the general form of the recursive rule.*

Recursive Rule: $f(1) = 20, f(n) = f(n-1) - 6$

$f(n) = f(1) + d(n-1)$ *Use the general form of the explicit rule.*

Explicit Rule: $f(n) = 20 - 6(n-1)$

KEY EXAMPLE (Lesson 4.3)

Construct an explicit rule in function notation for the arithmetic sequence represented in the graph, and use it to solve the problem.

The graph shows the total predicted sales $f(n)$ for the next n days at a clothing store. What are the total predicted sales on day 10?

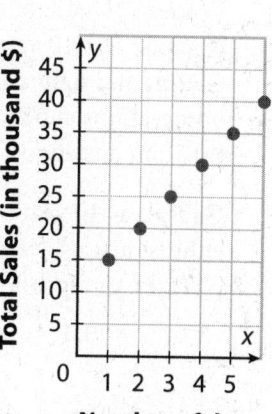

15, 20, 25, 30...   *Write a sequence to represent the information.*

$d = 20 - 15 = 5$ *Find the common difference.*

$f(n) = f(1) + d(n-1)$ *Use the general explicit rule.*

$f(n) = 15 + 5(n-1)$

$f(10) = 15 + 5(10-1)$ *Find $f(10)$.*

$f(10) = 60$

The total predicted sales on day 10 are $60,000.

EXERCISES

Write the first 4 terms of each sequence following the given rule. *(Lesson 4.1)*

1. $f(n) = n^2 - 4$

2. $f(1) = -12, f(n) = 2f(n-1)$

Determine if each of the following sequences is arithmetic. If so, write a recursive rule and an explicit rule for the sequence. If not, explain why. *(Lesson 4.2)*

3. $-8, -1, 6, 13...$

4. $1, 8, 27, 81...$

5. The table below shows the balance of a savings account each month after being opened. The balance can be represented with an arithmetic sequence. Write an explicit rule and a recursive rule for the sequence. What will the account balance be after 10 months? *(Lesson 4.3)*

Time (months)	1	2	3	4
Balance ($)	750	715	680	645

MODULE PERFORMANCE TASK

There Has to Be an Easier Way

Quick, now, what's the sum: $1 + 2$?

Okay, you got that one. How about this: $1 + 2 + 3$?

You're really sailing along! Okay, how about this one: $1 + 2 + 3 + ... + 98 + 99 + 100$?

Whoops. That's the problem that mathematician Carl Friedrich Gauss solved quickly when he was 10 years old. And that's the problem you're being asked to solve now. Getting the right answer isn't as important as coming up with some interesting observations about the problem or some ideas that might lead you in the direction of the right answer.

Gauss was 10 years old in 1787, so he didn't have a calculator! No calculator for you either—just use your own paper to work on the task. Then use numbers, words, pictures, or algebra to explain how you reached your conclusion.

(Ready) to Go On?

4.1–4.3 Patterns and Sequences

Write the first 4 terms of each sequence defined by the rule given. *(Lesson 4.1)*

1. $f(1) = 8, f(n) = f(n-1) - 4$

2. $f(n) = \dfrac{n^2}{2}$

• Online Homework
• Hints and Help
• Extra Practice

Write a recursive rule and an explicit rule for each arithmetic sequence. Then, find the 20th term of each sequence. *(Lessons 4.2, 4.3)*

3. $2, 0, -2, -4\ldots$

4. $45, 55, 65, 75\ldots$

5. Each Saturday, Tina mows lawns to earn extra money which she puts into a savings account. The graph shows the balance of Tina's savings account over the first six weeks of mowing lawns. Write an explicit function to describe this sequence. According to this pattern, how much will Tina have in her account after 15 weeks of mowing lawns? *(Lesson 4.3)*

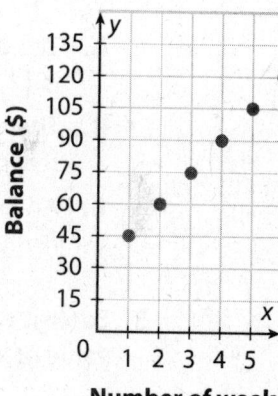

ESSENTIAL QUESTION

6. What are two ways of representing an arithmetic sequence?

Assessment Readiness

1. Consider a sequence defined by the recursive rule $f(1) = 15$; $f(n) = f(n-1) - 6$ for $n \geq 2$. Choose True or False for each statement.

   A. The second term of the sequence is 8. ○ True ○ False

   B. The third term of the sequence is 3. ○ True ○ False

   C. The fourth term of the sequence is −3. ○ True ○ False

2. The cost of renting a moped for 1, 2, 3, or 4 hours and can be represented by an arithmetic sequence. The base fee is $30, and the cost per hour is $15. The graph shows the sequence. Choose True or False for each statement.

   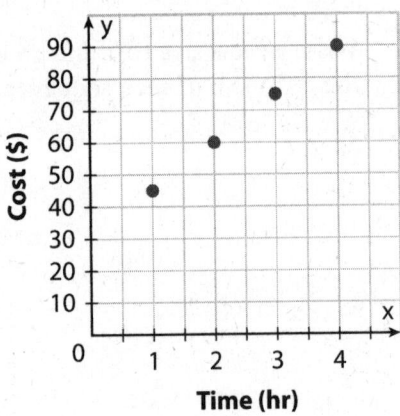

   A. The domain of the sequence is $\{1, 2, 3, 4\}$. ○ True ○ False

   B. The range of the sequence is the set of all real numbers. ○ True ○ False

   C. An explicit rule for the sequence is $f(n) = 15 + 30n$. ○ True ○ False

3. Look at each possible solution of the inequality $-12 < 2x + 8 < -6$ below. Is the value of x actually a solution of the inequality? Select Yes or No for each value of x.

   A. $x = -10$ ○ True ○ False

   B. $x = -8$ ○ True ○ False

   C. $x = -14$ ○ True ○ False

4. On Monday, Mr. Sanchez started reading a 225-page biography. He plans to read 15 pages each day until he finishes the book. Write an explicit function to represent the number of pages he has left to read depending on the day number; Monday is day number 1, Tuesday is day number 2, and so on. Find $f(5)$ and interpret its meaning in this situation.

1. Write $18z - 7(-3 + 2z)$ in simplest form. Select True or False for each statement.

   A. The expression has 2 terms.   ◯ True   ◯ False

   B. The coefficient of z is 13.   ◯ True   ◯ False

   C. The constant is 21.   ◯ True   ◯ False

2. The relation shown in the table represents the number of various books sold and their total cost.

Number of books sold, x	Cost ($), y
1	5
2	6
2	8
4	12

   Is each statement True?

   A. The domain is all real numbers.   ◯ Yes   ◯ No

   B. The range is {5, 6, 8, 12}.   ◯ Yes   ◯ No

   C. The relation is a function.   ◯ Yes   ◯ No

3. A dog walker charges a flat rate of $6 per walk plus an hourly rate of $30. How much does the dog walker charge for a 45 minute walk? Write an equation in function notation for the situation, and then use it to solve the problem. Determine if the given statement is True or False.

   A. The dependent variable is the number of hours.   ◯ True   ◯ False

   B. The function for the walker's fee is $f(h) = 30h + 6$.   ◯ True   ◯ False

   C. The dog walker charges $22.50 for a 45 minute walk.   ◯ True   ◯ False

4. Consider a sequence defined by the explicit rule $f(n) = -8 + 3(n - 1)$. Choose True or False for each statement.

   A. $f(1) = -8$ ◯ True   ◯ False

   B. The common difference is 3.   ◯ True   ◯ False

   C. The fifth term of the sequence is 7.   ◯ True   ◯ False

5. Graph $f(x) = -2x + 4$. What is x when $f(x) = -8$? Explain how you found x.

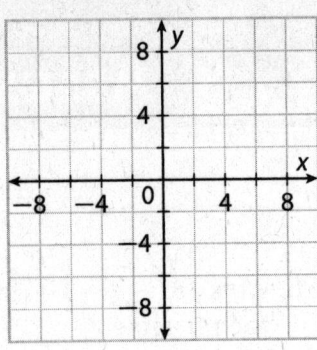

6. Find the first 4 terms of the sequence defined by the explicit rule $f(n) = 7(n - 1) - 10$. Is it an arithmetic sequence? Explain your answer.

Performance Tasks

★ **7.** A construction company's cost to build a new home is $35,000 plus $95 for each square foot of floor space.

A. Find a function for the cost c to build a house with f square feet of floor space.

B. Use your function to determine how much it will cost to build a house that contains 1600 square feet.

★★ **8.** The weight in pounds that can be supported by a diving board is given by the function $w(x) = \frac{5000}{x}$, where x is the distance in feet from the base to a point along the length of the diving board.

A. What is the domain of the function? Can the domain include zero? Explain.

B. Make a table of values and generate five ordered pairs to represent the function.

C. Plot the ordered pairs (x, w), and draw a smooth curve connecting the points.

★★★ **9.** The results of a test of an alloy are shown in the table. Stress is the tension force per unit area, and strain is deformation of the alloy.

Strain (m/m)	0.01	0.02	0.03	0.04	0.05	0.06	0.07	0.08	0.09
Stress (MPa)	100	200	300	400	500	540	560	550	525

A. Make a graph of the data using strain on the horizontal axis.

B. Hooke's law states that stress is directly proportional to strain. For what domain does the material obey Hooke's law? How did you determine your answer?

C. Write a function to represent Hooke's law for this material.

D. The ultimate tensile strength is the maximum stress value on the stress-strain curve. What are the stress and strain values for this material's ultimate tensile strength?

Interior Designer Ben is an interior designer and plans to have part of a floor tiled with 36 square tiles. The tiles come in whole-number side lengths from 2 to 6 inches.

a. Write a function for the area, $A(s)$, where s is the side length of the tile.

b. Identify the domain of this function.

c. Make a table of values for this domain. Write the results as ordered pairs in the form (independent variable, dependent variable).

d. Graph the function by plotting the ordered pairs.

e. What does the function evaluated at $s = 3$ mean in this context?

Linear Functions, Equations, and Inequalities

MATH IN CAREERS

Wildlife Field Researcher Wildlife field researchers observe wildlife and their habitats. Wildlife field researchers utilize geometry and trigonometry when surveying habitats. They use statistics, exponential functions, and differential equations to study population changes.

If you are interested in a career as a wildlife field researcher, you should study these mathematical subjects:

- Algebra
- Geometry
- Trigonometry
- Calculus
- Differential Equations

Research other careers that require using exponential equations to understand populations. Check out the career activity at the end of the unit to find out how **wildlife field researchers** use math.

© Houghton Mifflin Harcourt Publishing Company · Image Credits: ©DLILLC/ Corbis

Reading Start-Up

Vocabulary

Review Words

✔ function (*función*)

✔ reflection (*reflexión*)

✔ rotation (*rotación*)

✔ transformation (*transformación*)

Preview Words

boundary line (*línea de límite*)

constant of variation (*constante de variación*)

parent function (*función madre*)

rate of change (*tasa de cambio*)

slope (*pendiente*)

x-intercept (*intersección con el eje x*)

y-intercept (*intersección con el eje x*)

Visualize Vocabulary

Use the ✔ words to complete the graphic. You will put one word in each oval.

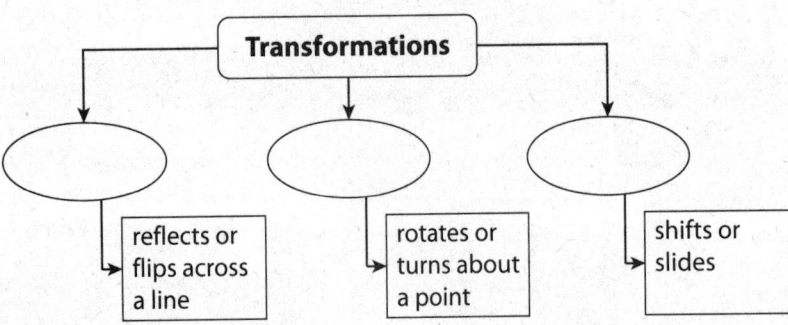

Transformations

reflects or flips across a line	rotates or turns about a point	shifts or slides

Understand Vocabulary

Complete the sentences using the preview words.

1. The _____ of a graph is the *y*-coordinate of the point where the graph intersects the *y*-axis.

2. The _____ of a graph is the *x*-coordinate of the point where the graph intersects the *x*-axis.

3. A _____ is a line that divides a coordinate plane into two halves.

Active Reading

Layered Book Before beginning the unit, create a layered book to help you learn the concepts in this unit. Label the flaps "Linear Functions," "Forms of Linear Equations," and "Linear Equations and Inequalities." As you study the lessons in each module, write important ideas, such as vocabulary, and sample problems under the appropriate flap.

Linear Functions

Essential Question: How can you use a linear function to solve real-world problems?

REAL WORLD VIDEO
Cyclists adjust their gears to climb up a steep grade or through rocky terrain. Check out how gear ratios, rates of speed, and slope ratios can be used to solve problems involving speed, distance, and time when mountain biking.

MODULE PERFORMANCE TASK PREVIEW

How Many Cups Do You Need?

Paper or foam cups are convenient for drinking out of, but they can also be used to explore mathematical concepts. They can be used to build a structure by stacking individual cups. Just how many cups would you need to build a structure the same height as your math teacher? Get ready to discover the mathematics of cup-stacking!

Are (YOU) Ready?

Complete these exercises to review skills you will need for this module.

Slope

Example 1   Describe the slope of the line that joins the points.

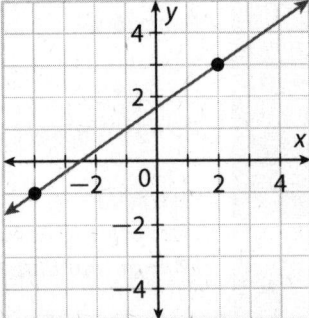

The slope is positive if the line slants up.

The slope is negative if the line slants down.

The slope is 0 if the line is horizontal.

The slope is undefined if the line is vertical.

The line slants up, so the slope is positive.

Describe the slope of the line that joins the points.

1.

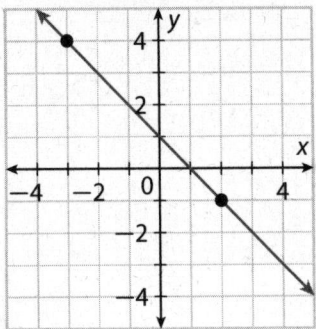

2.

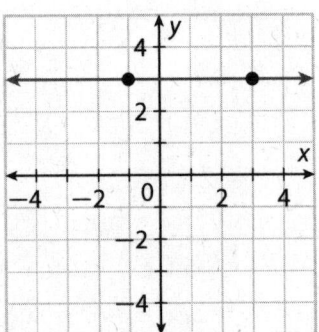

_____   _____

Multi-Step Equations

Example 2   Solve.

$$3x + 5 + 4x - 9 = 24$$

$$7x - 4 = 24$$ Combine like terms.

$$7x - 4 + 4 = 24 + 4$$ Add 4 to both sides of the equation.

$$7x = 28$$

$$\frac{7x}{7} = \frac{28}{7}$$ Divide both sides of the equation by 7.

$$x = 4$$

Solve each equation.

3. $3(2n - 7) + 12 = 39$ _____

4. $4a + 23 - 9a - 17 = 21$ _____

5.1 Understanding Linear Functions

Essential Question: What is a linear function?

Resource
Locker

⊘ Explore 1 Recognizing Linear Functions

A race car can travel up to 210 mph. If the car could travel continuously at this speed, $y = 210x$ gives the number of miles y that the car would travel in x hours. Solutions are shown in the graph below.

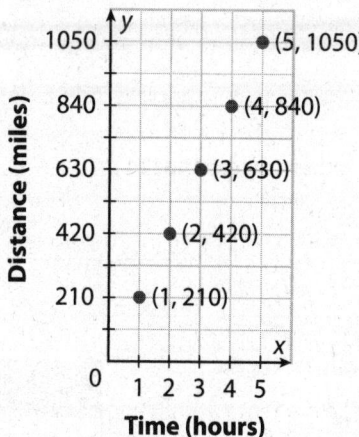

The graph of the car's speed is a function because every x-value is paired with exactly one y-value. Because the graph is a non-vertical straight line, it is also a **linear function.**

(A) Fill in the table using the data points from the graph above.

(B) Using the table, check that x has a constant change between consecutive terms.

x	y

C Now check that *y* has a constant change between consecutive terms.

D Using the answers from before, what change in *x* corresponds to a change in *y*?

E All linear functions behave similarly to the one in this example. Based on this information,

a generalization can be made that a _____ change in *x* will correspond to a _____

change in *y*.

Reflect

1. **Discussion** Will a non-linear function have a constant change in *x* that corresponds to a constant change in *y*?

   _____

   _____

2. $y = x^2$ represents a typical non-linear function. Using the table of values, check whether a constant change in *x* corresponds to a constant change in *y*.

   _____

   _____

   _____

x	$y = x^2$
1	1
2	4
3	9
4	16
5	25

Linear functions change by a constant amount (change by equal differences) over equal intervals. Now you will explore the proofs of these statements. $x_2 - x_1$ and $x_4 - x_3$ represent two intervals in the x-values of a linear function.

It is also important to know that any linear function can be written in the form $f(x) = mx + b$, where m and b are constants.

Complete the proof that linear functions grow by equal differences over equal intervals.

Given: $x_2 - x_1 = x_4 - x_3$

f is a linear function of the form $f(x) = mx + b$.

Prove: $f(x_2) - f(x_1) = f(x_4) - f(x_3)$

Proof: 1. $x_2 - x_1 = x_4 - x_3$ Given.

2. $m(x_2 - x_1) = \boxed{}(x_4 - x_3)$ Mult. Property of Equality

3. $mx_2 - \boxed{} = mx_4 - \boxed{}$ _____

4. $mx_2 + b - mx_1 - b = mx_4 + \boxed{} - mx_3 - \boxed{}$ _____

5. $mx_2 + b - (mx_1 + b) = mx_4 + b - \boxed{}$ _____

6. $f(x_2) - f(x_1) = \boxed{}$ Definition of $f(x)$

Reflect

3. **Discussion** Consider the function $y = x^3$. Use two equal intervals to determine if the function is linear. The table for $y = x^3$ is shown.

x	$y = x^3$
1	1
2	8
3	27
4	64
5	125

_____

_____

_____

_____

_____

_____

_____

4. In the given of the proof it states that: f is a linear function of the form $f(x) = mx + b$. What is the name of the form for this linear function?

_____

_____

_____

Explain 1 Graphing Linear Functions Given in Standard Form

Any linear function can be represented by a linear equation. A **linear equation** is any equation that can be written in the **standard form** expressed below.

Standard Form of a Linear Equation

$Ax + By = C$ where A, B, and C are real numbers and A and B are not both 0.

Any ordered pair that makes the linear equation true is a **solution of a linear equation in two variables**. The graph of a linear equation represents all the solutions of the equation.

Example 1 Determine whether the equation is linear. If so, graph the function.

(A) $5x + y = 10$

The equation is linear because it is in the standard form of a linear equation:

$A = 5$, $B = 1$, and $C = 10$.

To graph the function, first solve the equation for y.

Make a table and plot the points. Then connect the points.

x	−1	0	1	2	3
y	15	10	5	0	−5

Note that because the domain and range of functions of a non-horizontal line are all real numbers, the graph is continuous.

$$5x + y = 10$$
$$y = 10 - 5x$$

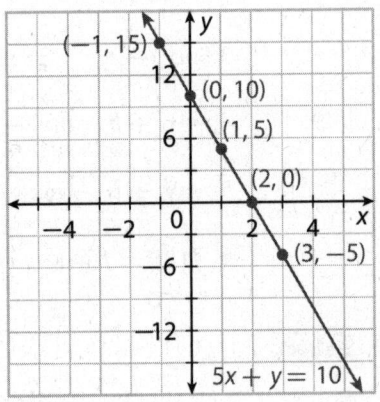

(B) $-4x + y = 11$

The equation is linear because it is in the _____ form of a linear equation:

$A = $ _____, $B = $ _____, and $C = $ _____.

To graph the function, first solve the equation for _____.

$$-4x + y = 11$$
$$y = 11 + \underline{\quad} x$$

Make a table and plot the points. Then connect the points.

x	−4	−2	0	2	4
y					

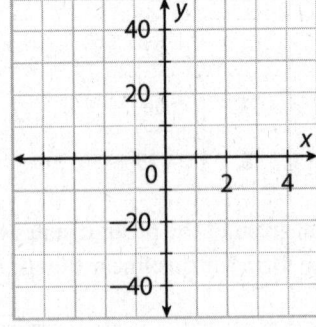

© Houghton Mifflin Harcourt Publishing Company

Reflect

5. Write an equation that is linear but is not in standard form.

_____

6. If $A = 0$ in an equation written in standard form, how does the graph look?

_____

Your Turn

7. Determine whether $6x + y = 12$ is linear. If so, graph the function.

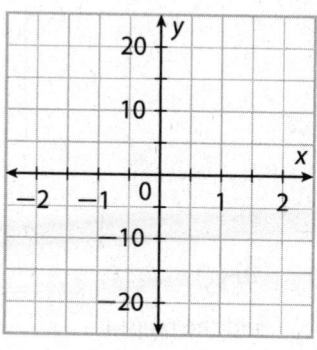

Explain 2 Modeling with Linear Functions

A **discrete function** is a function whose graph has unconnected points, while a **continuous function** is a function whose graph is an unbroken line or curve with no gaps or breaks. For example, a function representing the sale of individual apples is a discrete function because no fractional part of an apple will be represented in a table or a graph. A function representing the sale of apples by the pound is a continuous function because any fractional part of a pound of apples will be represented in a table or graph.

Example 2 Graph each function and give its domain and range.

(A) Sal opens a new video store and pays the film studios $2.00 for each DVD he buys from them. The amount Sal pays is given by $f(x) = 2x$, where x is the number of DVDs purchased.

x	$f(x) = 2x$
0	$f(0) = 2(0) = 0$
1	$f(1) = 2(1) = 2$
2	$f(2) = 2(2) = 4$
3	$f(3) = 2(3) = 6$
4	$f(4) = 2(4) = 8$

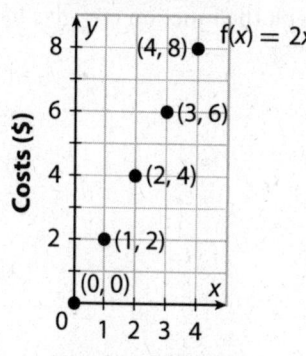

DVD Purchases

This is a discrete function. Since the number of DVDs must be a whole number, the domain is $\{0, 1, 2, 3, \ldots\}$ and the range is $\{0, 2, 4, 6, 8 \ldots\}$.

B Elsa rents a booth in her grandfather's mall to open an ice cream stand. She pays $1 to her grandfather for each hour of operation. The amount Elsa pays each hour is given by $f(x) = x$, where x is the number of hours her booth is open.

x	$f(x) = x$
0	$f(0) = $
1	$f(1) = $
2	$f(2) = $
3	$f(3) = $
4	$f(4) = $

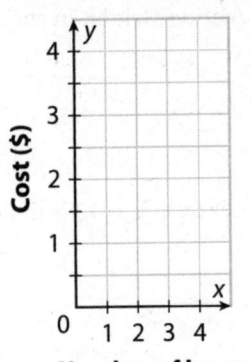

Ice Cream Booth Rental

Cost ($) / Number of hours

This is a _____ function. The domain is _____

and the range is _____.

Reflect

8. Why are the points on the graph in Example 2B connected?

_____

_____

9. **Discussion** How is the graph of the function in Example 2A related to the graph of an arithmetic sequence?

_____

_____

Your Turn

10. Kristoff rents a kiosk in the mall to open an umbrella stand. He pays $6 to the mall owner for each umbrella he sells. The amount Kristoff pays is given by $f(x) = 6x$, where x is the number of umbrellas sold. Graph the function and give its domain and range.

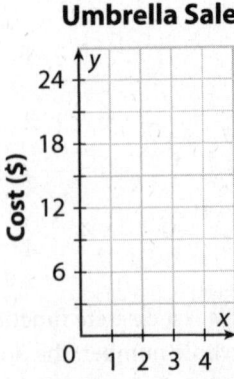

Umbrella Sales

Cost ($) / Number of umbrellas

11. What is a solution of a linear equation in two variables?

_____

_____

12. What type of function has a graph with a series of unconnected points?

_____

_____

13. **Essential Question Check-In** What is the standard form for a linear equation?

_____

_____

⭐ Evaluate: Homework and Practice

• Online Homework
• Hints and Help
• Extra Practice

Determine if the equation is linear. If so, graph the function.

1. $2x + y = 4$

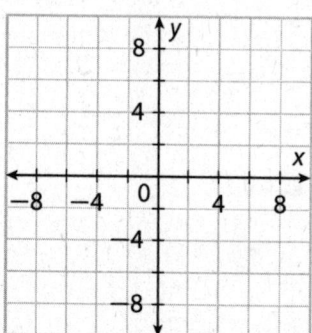

2. $2x^2 + y = 6$

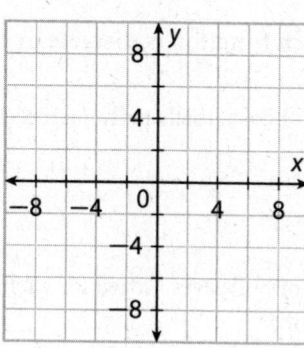

3. $\frac{2}{x} + \frac{y}{4} = \frac{3}{2}$

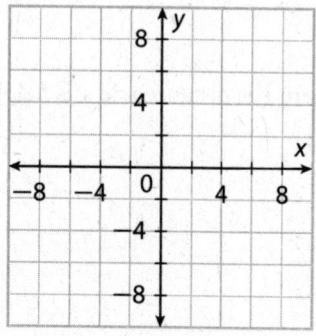

4. $3x + 4y = 8$

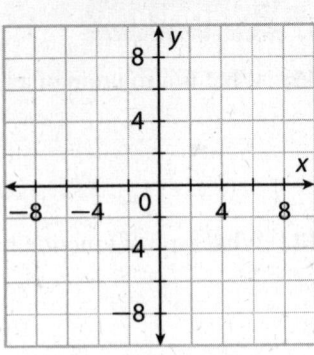

5. $x + y^2 = 1$

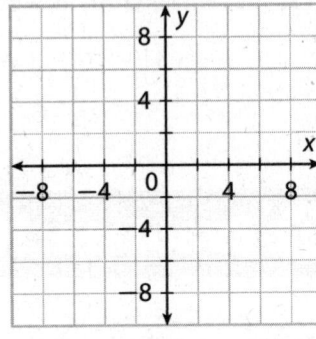

6. $x + y = 1$

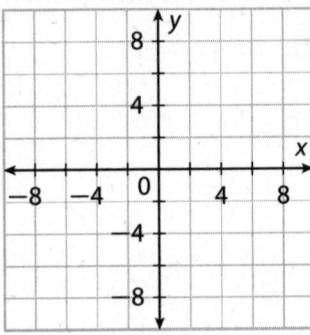

State whether each function is discrete or continuous.

7. The number of basketballs manufactured per day

8. $x = \dfrac{y}{4}$, where x is the number of hours and y is the miles walked

9. The number of bulls eyes scored for each hour of practice

10. $y = 4^4 x$, where x is the time and y is gallons of water

11. $y = 35x^1$, where x is distance and y is height

12. The amount of boxes shipped per shift

Graph each function and give its domain and range.

13. Hans opens a new video game store and pays the gaming companies $5.00 for each video game he buys from them. The amount Hans pays is given by $f(x) = 5x$, where x is the number of video games purchased.

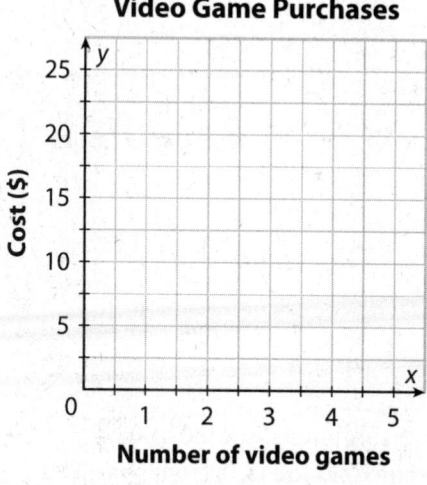

Video Game Purchases

y-axis: Cost ($), values 5, 10, 15, 20, 25
x-axis: Number of video games, values 1, 2, 3, 4, 5

14. Peter opens a new bookstore and pays the book publisher $3.00 for each book he buys from them. The amount Peter pays is given by $f(x) = 3x$, where x is the number of books purchased.

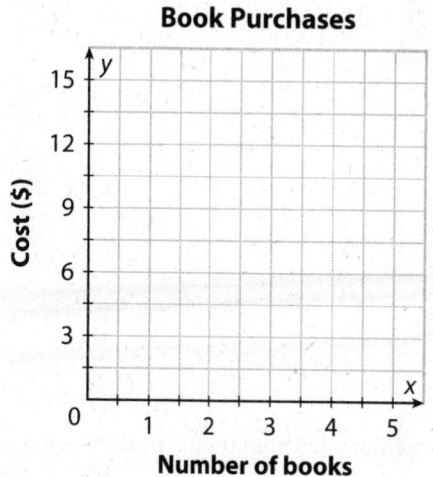

Book Purchases

y-axis: Cost ($), values 3, 6, 9, 12, 15
x-axis: Number of books, values 1, 2, 3, 4, 5

15. Steve opens a jewelry shop and makes $15.00 profit for each piece of jewelry sold. The amount Steve makes is given by $f(x) = 15x$, where x is the number of pieces of jewelry sold.

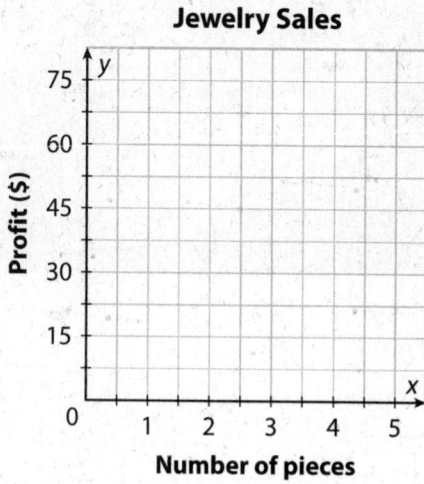

Jewelry Sales

y-axis: Profit ($), values 15, 30, 45, 60, 75
x-axis: Number of pieces, values 1, 2, 3, 4, 5

16. Anna owns an airline and pays the airport $35.00 for each ticket sold. The amount Anna pays is given by $f(x) = 35x$, where x is the number of tickets sold.

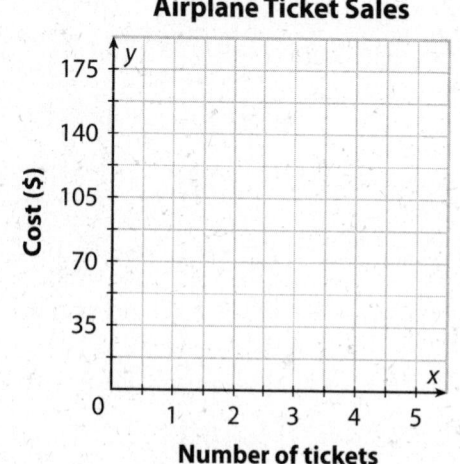

Airplane Ticket Sales

y-axis: Cost ($), values 35, 70, 105, 140, 175
x-axis: Number of tickets, values 1, 2, 3, 4, 5

17. A hot air balloon can travel up to 85 mph. If the balloon travels continuously at this speed, $y = 85x$ gives the number of miles y that the hot air balloon would travel in x hours.

Fill in the table using the data points from the graph. Determine whether x and y have constant change between consecutive terms and whether they are in a linear function.

x					
y					

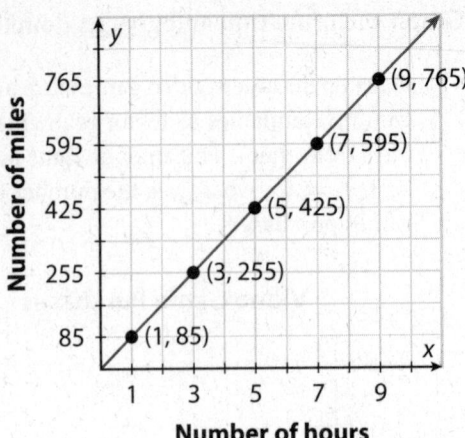

18. State whether each equation is in standard form.

   a. $3x + y = 8$

   b. $x - y = 15z$

   c. $x^2 + y = 11$

   d. $3xy + y^2 = 4$

   e. $x + 4y = 12$

   f. $5x + 24y = 544$

19. **Physics** A physicist working in a large laboratory has found that light particles traveling in a particle accelerator increase velocity in a manner that can be described by the linear function $-4x + 3y = 15$, where x is time and y is velocity in kilometers per hour. Use this function to determine when a certain particle will reach 30 km/hr.

20. Travel The graph shows the costs of a hotel for one night for a group traveling. The total cost depends on the number of hotel rooms the group needs. Does the plot follow a linear function? Is the graph discrete or continuous?

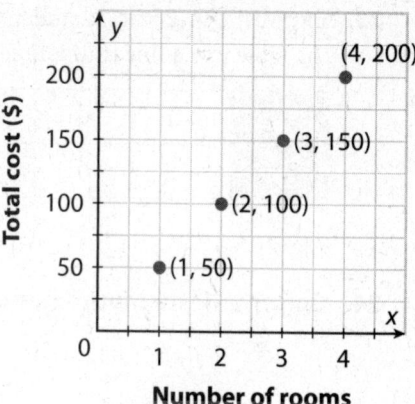

21. Biology The migration pattern of a species of tree frog to different swamp areas over the course of a year can be described using the graph below. Fill in the table and express whether this pattern follows a linear function. If the migration pattern is a linear function, express what constant change in *y* corresponds to a constant change in *x*.

x	y
1	
2	
3	
4	
5	

22. Representing Real-World Problems Write a real-world problem that is a discrete non-linear function.

23. **Explain the Error** A student used the following table of values and stated that the function described by the table was a linear function. Explain the student's error.

x	−1	0	2	3	4
y	−5	0	5	10	15

24. **Communicate Mathematical Ideas** Explain how graphs of the same function can look different.

Lesson Performance Task

Jordan has started a new dog-walking service. His total profits over the first 4 weeks are expressed in this table.

a. Show that his profits can be described by a linear function.

Time (weeks)	Profits($)
1	150
2	300
3	450
4	600

b. Graph this function and use the graph to predict his business profit 9 weeks after he opens.

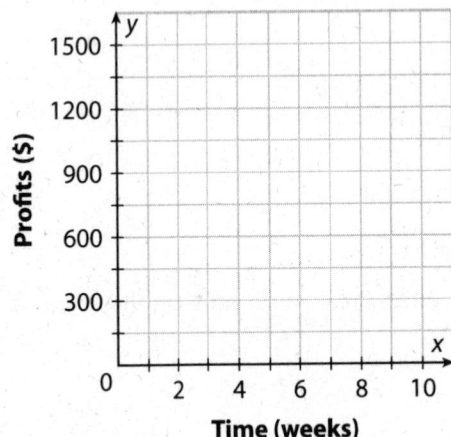

c. Explain why it is or is not a good idea to project his profits so far into the future. Give examples to support your answer.

5.2 Using Intercepts

Essential Question: How can you identify and use intercepts in linear relationships?

⊘ Explore   Identifying Intercepts

Miners are exploring 90 feet underground. The miners ascend in an elevator at a constant rate over a period of 3 minutes until they reach the surface. In the coordinate grid, the horizontal axis represents the time in minutes from when the miners start ascending, and the vertical axis represents the miners' elevation relative to the surface in feet.

(A) What point represents the miners' elevation at the beginning of the ascent?

_____ Plot this point.

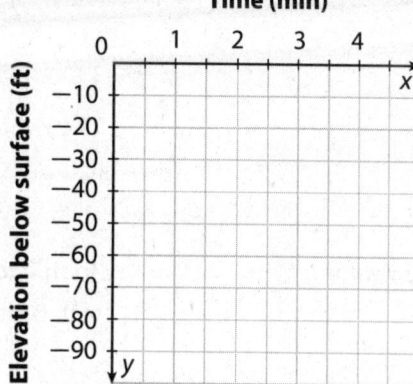

(B) What point represents the miners' elevation at the end of the ascent?

_____ Plot this point.

(C) Connect the points with a line segment.

(D) What is the point where the graph crosses the y-axis? _____ the x-axis? _____

Reflect

1. **Discussion** The point where the graph intersects the y-axis represents the beginning of the miners' ascent. Will the point where a graph intersects the y-axis always be the lowest point on a linear graph? Explain.

_____

_____

_____

⊘ Explain 1   Determining Intercepts of Linear Equations

The graph in the Explore intersected the axes at $(0, -90)$ and $(3, 0)$.

The **y-intercept** of a graph is the y-coordinate of the point where the graph intersects the y-axis. The x-coordinate of this point is always 0. The y-intercept of the graph in the Explore is -90.

The **x-intercept** of a graph is the x-coordinate of the point where the graph intersects the x-axis. The y-coordinate of this point is always 0. The x-intercept of the graph in the Explore is 3.

Example 1   **Find the x- and y-intercepts.**

Ⓐ $3x - 2y = 6$

To find the x-intercept, replace y with 0 and solve for x.

$$3x - 2(0) = 6$$

$$3x = 6$$

$$x = 2$$

The x-intercept is 2.

To find the y-intercept, replace x with 0 and solve for y.

$$3(0) - 2y = 6$$

$$-2y = 6$$

$$y = -3$$

The y-intercept is -3.

Ⓑ $-5x + 6y = 60$

To find the x-intercept, replace y with _____ and solve for x.

$$-5x + 6\left(\boxed{}\right) = 60$$

$$-5x = 60$$

$$x = \boxed{}$$

The x-intercept is _____.

To find the y-intercept, replace _____ with 0 and solve for _____.

$$-5\left(\boxed{}\right) + 6y = 60$$

$$6y = 60$$

$$y = \boxed{}$$

The y-intercept is _____.

Reflect

2.   If the point $(5, 0)$ is on a graph, is $(5, 0)$ the y-intercept of the graph? Explain.

_____

Your Turn

Find the x- and y-intercepts.

3. $8x + 7y = 28$

4. $-6x - 8y = 24$

Interpreting Intercepts of Linear Equations

You can use intercepts to interpret a situation that is modeled by a linear function.

Example 2 Find and interpret the *x*- and *y*-intercepts for each situation.

Ⓐ The Sandia Peak Tramway in Albuquerque, New Mexico, travels a distance of about 4500 meters to the top of Sandia Peak. Its speed is 300 meters per minute. The function $f(x) = 4500 - 300x$ gives the tram's distance in meters from the top of the peak after *x* minutes.

To find the *x*-intercept, replace $f(x)$ with 0 and solve for *x*.

$f(x) = 4500 - 300x$

$0 = 4500 - 300x$

$x = 15$

It takes 15 minutes to reach the peak.

To find the *y*-intercept, replace *x* with 0 and find $f(0)$.

$f(x) = 4500 - 300x$

$f(0) = 4500 - 300(0) = 4500$

The distance from the peak when it starts is 4500 m.

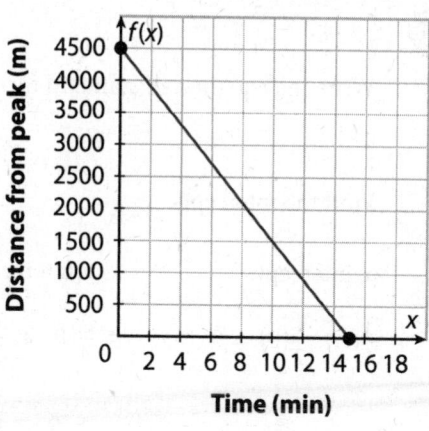

Sandia Peak Tramway

Ⓑ A hot air balloon is 750 meters above the ground and begins to descend at a constant rate of 25 meters per minute. The function $f(x) = 750 - 25x$ represents the height of the hot air balloon after *x* minutes.

To find the *x*-intercept, replace $f(x)$ with 0 and solve *x*.

$f(x) = 750 - 25x$

$\boxed{} = 750 - 25x$

$x = \boxed{}$

It takes _____ to reach the ground.

To find the *y*-intercept, replace *x* with 0 and find $f(0)$.

$f(x) = 750 - 25x$

$f(0) = 750 - 25\left(\boxed{}\right) = 750$

The height above ground when it starts is _____.

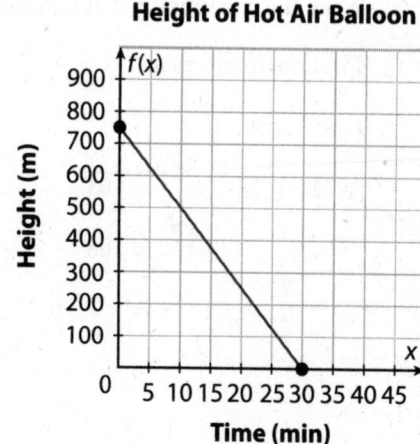

Height of Hot Air Balloon

Reflect

5. Critique Reasoning A classmate says that the graph shows the path of the tram. Do you agree?

_____

Your Turn

6. The temperature in an experiment is increased at a constant rate over a period of time until the temperature reaches 0 °C. The equation $y = \frac{5}{2}x - 70$ gives the temperature *y* in degrees Celsius *x* hours after the experiment begins. Find and interpret the *x*- and *y*-intercepts.

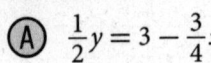 **Explain 3** **Graphing Linear Equations Using Intercepts**

You can use the x- and y-intercepts to graph a linear equation.

Example 3 Use intercepts to graph the line described by each equation.

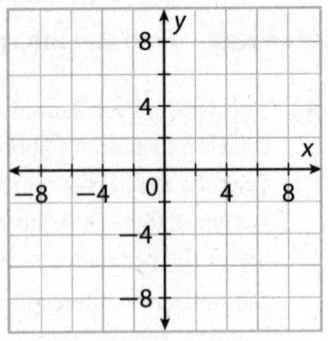

(A) $\frac{1}{2}y = 3 - \frac{3}{4}x$

Write the equation in standard form. $\frac{3}{4}x + \frac{1}{2}y = 3$

Find the intercepts.

x-intercept: y-intercept:

$\frac{3}{4}x + \frac{1}{2}(0) = 3$ $\frac{3}{4}(0) + \frac{1}{2}y = 3$

$\frac{3}{4}x = 3$ $\frac{1}{2}y = 3$

$x = 4$ $y = 6$

Graph the line by plotting the points $(4, 0)$ and $(0, 6)$ and drawing a line through them.

(B) $18y = 12x + 108$

Write the equation in standard form. $\boxed{} = 108$

Find the intercepts.

x-intercept: y-intercept:

$-12x + 18\left(\boxed{}\right) = 108$ $-12\boxed{} + 18y = 108$

$-12x = 108$ $18y = 108$

$x = \boxed{}$ $y = \boxed{}$

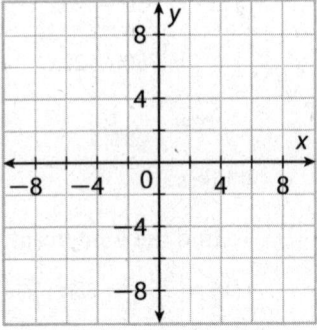

Graph the line by plotting the points _____ and _____

and draw _____ through them.

Your Turn

7. Use intercepts to graph $3y = -5x - 30$.

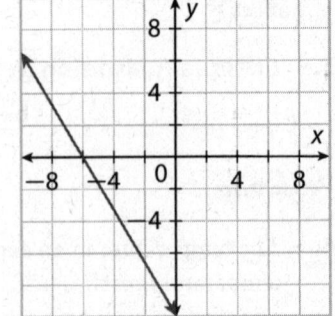

8. A line intersects the *y*-axis at the point (a, b). Is $a = 0$? Is $b = 0$? Explain.

_____

_____

_____

9. What does a negative *y*-intercept mean for a real-world application?

_____

_____

_____

10. **Essential Question Check-in** How can you find the *x*-intercept of the graph of a linear equation using the equation? How is using the graph of a linear equation to find the intercepts like using the equation?

_____

_____

⭐ Evaluate: Homework and Practice

• Online Homework
• Hints and Help
• Extra Practice

Identify and interpret the intercepts for each situation, plot the points on the graph, and connect the points with a line segment.

1. An electronics manufacturer has 140 capacitors, and the same number of capacitors is needed for each circuit board made. The manufacturer uses the capacitors to make 35 circuit boards.

2. A dolphin is 42 feet underwater and ascends at a constant rate for 14 seconds until it reaches the surface.

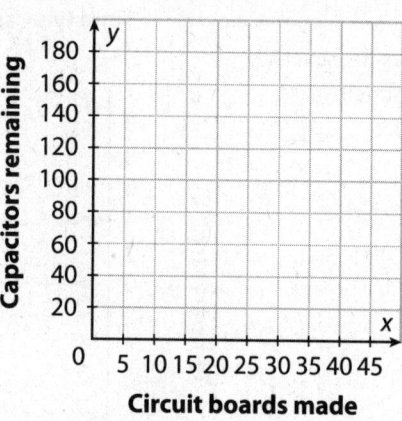

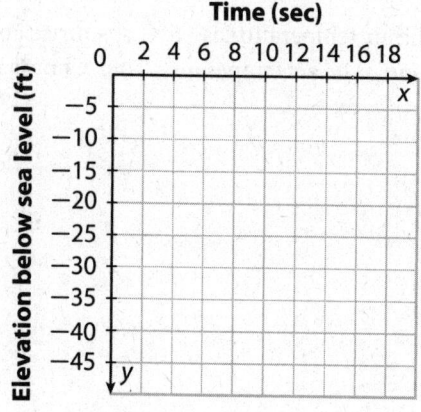

Find the *x*- and *y*-intercepts.

3. $2x - 3y = -6$

4. $-4x - 5y = 40$

5. $8x + 4y = -56$

6. $-9x + 6y = 72$

7. $\frac{3}{5}x + \frac{1}{2}y = 30$

8. $-\frac{3}{4}x + \frac{5}{6}y = 15$

Interpret the intercepts for each situation. Use the intercepts to graph the function.

9. Biology A lake was stocked with 350 trout. Each year, the population decreases by 14. The population of trout in the lake after *x* years is represented by the function $f(x) = 350 - 14x$.

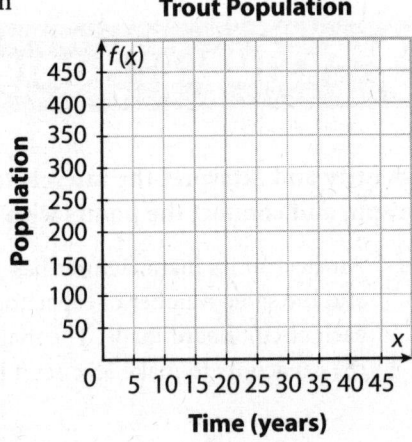

Trout Population

10. The air temperature is −6 °C at sunrise and rises 3 °C every hour for several hours. The air temperature after *x* hours is represented by the function $f(x) = 3x - 6$.

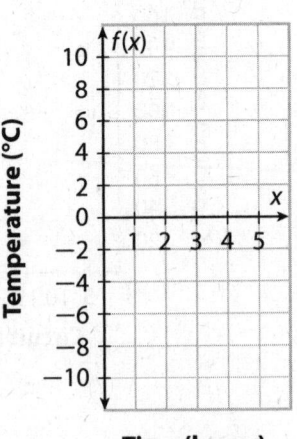

11. The number of brake pads needed for a car is 4, and a manufacturing plant has 480 brake pads. The number of brake pads remaining after brake pads have been installed on x cars is $f(x) = 480 - 4x$.

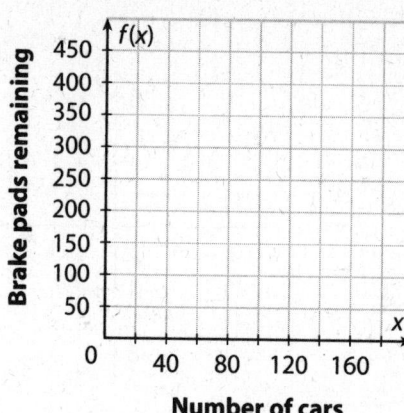

12. Connor is running a 10-kilometer cross country race. He runs 1 kilometer every 4 minutes. Connor's distance from the finish line after x minutes is represented by the function $f(x) = 10 - \frac{1}{4}x$.

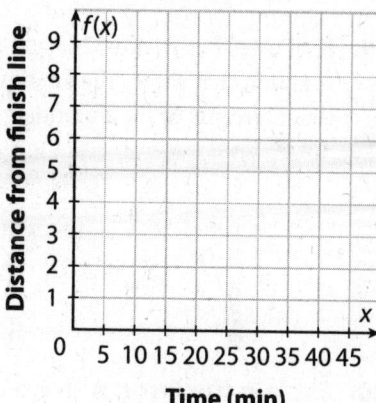

Use intercepts to graph the line described by each equation.

13. $-6y = -4x + 24$

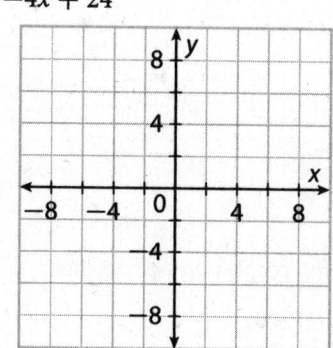

14. $9y = 3x + 18$

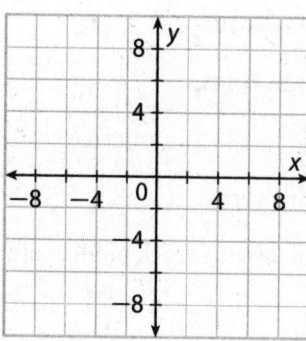

15. $y = \frac{1}{5}x + 2$

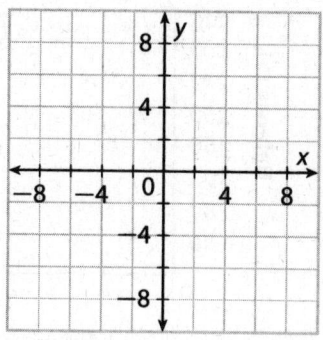

16. $-3y = 7x - 21$

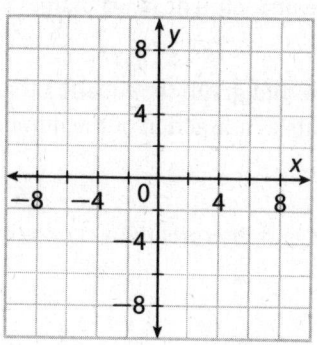

17. $\frac{3}{2}x = -4y - 12$

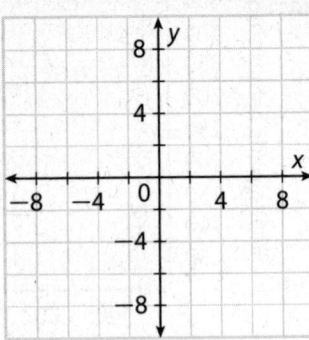

18. $\frac{2}{3}y = 2 - \frac{1}{2}x$

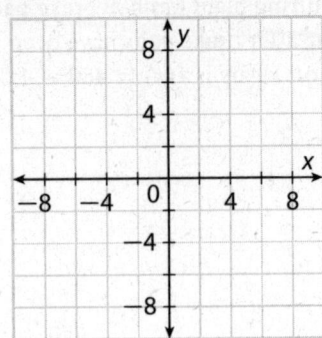

19. Kim owes her friend $245 and plans to pay $35 per week. Write an equation of the function that shows the amount Kim owes after x weeks. Then find and interpret the intercepts of the function.

20. Explain the Error Arlo incorrectly found the x-intercept of $9x + 12y = 144$. His work is shown.

$$9x + 12y = 144$$

$$9(0) + 12y = 144$$

$$12y = 144$$

$$y = 12 \text{ The } x\text{-intercept is 12.}$$

Explain Arlo's error.

21. Determine whether each point could represent an x-intercept, y-intercept, both, or neither.

A. $(0, 5)$ **B.** $(0, 0)$ **C.** $(-7, 0)$

D. $(3, -4)$ **E.** $(19, 0)$

22. A bank employee notices an abandoned checking account with a balance of $360. The bank charges an $8 monthly fee for the account.

a. Write and graph the equation that gives the balance $f(x)$ in dollars as a function of the number of months, x.

b. Find and interpret the x- and y-intercepts.

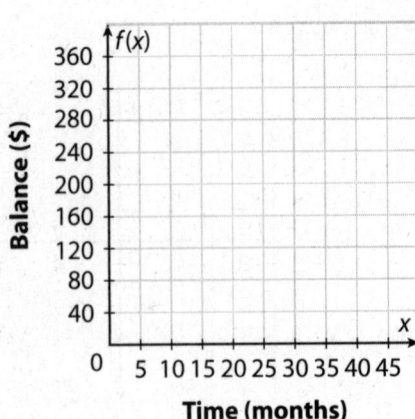

23. Kathryn is walking on a treadmill at a constant pace for 30 minutes. She has programmed the treadmill for a 2-mile walk. The display counts backward to show the distance remaining.

   a. Write and graph the equation that gives the distance $f(x)$ left in miles as a function of the number x of minutes she has been walking.

   b. Find and interpret the x- and y-intercepts.

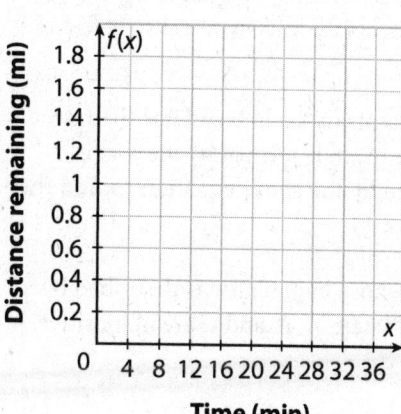

---

24. Represent Real-World Problems Write a real-world problem that could be modeled by a linear function whose x-intercept is 6 and whose y-intercept is 60.

25. Draw Conclusions For any linear equation $Ax + By = C$, what are the intercepts in terms of A, B, and C?

26. Multiple Representations Find the intercepts of $3x + 40y = 1200$. Explain how to use the intercepts to determine appropriate scales for the graph and then create a graph.

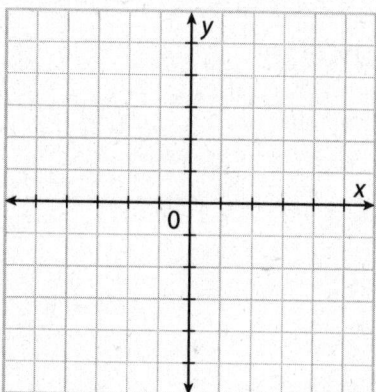

Lesson Performance Task

A sail on a boat is in the shape of a right triangle. If the sail is superimposed on a coordinate plane, the point where the horizontal and vertical sides meet is (0, 0) and the sail is above and to the right of (0, 0). The equation of the line that represents the sail's hypotenuse in feet is $10x + 4y = 240$.

a. Find and interpret the intercepts of the line and use them to graph the line. Then use the triangle formed by the x-axis, y-axis, and the line described by the above equation to find the area of the sail.

b. Now find the area of a sail whose hypotenuse is described by the equation $Ax + By = C$, where A, B, and C are all positive.

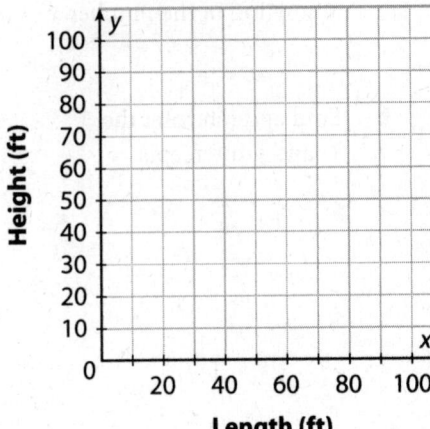

5.3 Interpreting Rate of Change and Slope

Essential question: How can you relate rate of change and slope in linear relationships?

⊘ Explore Determining Rates of Change

For a function defined in terms of x and y, the **rate of change** over a part of the domain of the function is a ratio that compares the change in y to the change in x in that part of the domain.

$$\text{rate of change} = \frac{\text{change in } y}{\text{change in } x}$$

The table shows the year and the cost of sending 1-ounce letter in cents.

Years after 2000 (x)	3	4	6	8	13
Cost (cents)	37	37	39	42	46

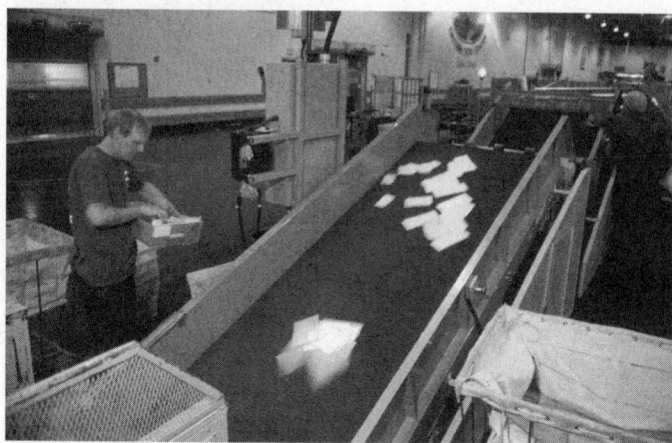

Find the rate of change, $\dfrac{\text{change in postage}}{\text{change in year}}$, for each time period using the table.

(A) From 2003 to 2004: $\dfrac{\boxed{} - \boxed{}}{4-3} = \boxed{}$ cent(s) per year

(B) From 2004 to 2006: $\dfrac{\boxed{} - \boxed{}}{6-4} = \boxed{} = \boxed{}$ cent(s) per year

(C) From 2006 to 2008: $\dfrac{\boxed{} - \boxed{}}{8-6} = \boxed{} = \boxed{}$ cent(s) per year

(D) From 2008 to 2013: $\dfrac{\boxed{} - \boxed{}}{13-8} = \boxed{} = \boxed{}$ cent(s) per year

(E) Plot the points represented in the table. Connect the points with line segments to make a statistical line graph.

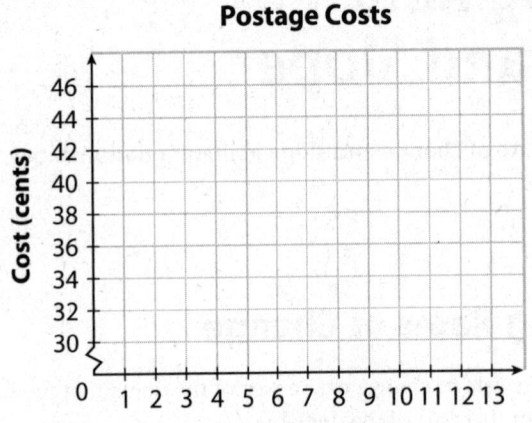

Postage Costs

Find the rate of change for each time period using the graph.

(F) Label the vertical increase (*rise*) and the horizontal increase (*run*) between points (4, 37) and (6, 39). Then find the rate of change, $\frac{\text{rise}}{\text{run}}$.

$$\frac{\text{rise}}{\text{run}} = \frac{\boxed{}}{\boxed{}} = \boxed{} \text{ cent(s) per year}$$

(G) Label the vertical increase (*rise*) and the horizontal increase (*run*) between points (6, 39) and (8, 42). Then find the rate of change, $\frac{\text{rise}}{\text{run}}$.

$$\frac{\text{rise}}{\text{run}} = \frac{\boxed{}}{\boxed{}} = \boxed{} \text{ cent(s) per year}$$

(H) Label the vertical increase (*rise*) and the horizontal increase (*run*) between points (8, 42) and (13, 46). Then find the rate of change, $\frac{\text{rise}}{\text{run}}$.

$$\frac{\text{rise}}{\text{run}} = \frac{\boxed{}}{\boxed{}} = \boxed{} \text{ cent(s) per year}$$

Reflect

1. **Discussion** Between which two years is the rate of change $\frac{\text{change in postage}}{\text{change in years}}$ the greatest?

_____

2. **Discussion** Compare the line segment between 2006 and 2008 with the line segment between 2008 and 2013. Which is steeper? Which represents a greater rate of change?

_____

_____

3. **Discuss** How do you think the steepness of the line segment between two points is related to the rate of change it represents?

_____

_____

⊘ Explain 1 Determining the Slope of a Line

The rate of change for a linear function can be calculated using the rise and run of the graph of the function. The **rise** is the difference in the y-values of two points on a line. The **run** is the difference in the x-values of two points on a line.

The **slope** of a line is the ratio of rise to run for any two points on the line.

$$\text{Slope} = \frac{\text{rise}}{\text{run}} = \frac{\text{difference in } y\text{-values}}{\text{difference in } x\text{-values}}$$

Example 1 Determine the slope of each line.

(A) Use $(3, 4)$ as the first point. Subtract y-values to find the change in y, or rise. Then subtract x-values to find the change in x, or run.

$$\text{slope} = \frac{4 - 1}{3 - 2} = \frac{3}{1} = 3.$$

Slope of the line is 3.

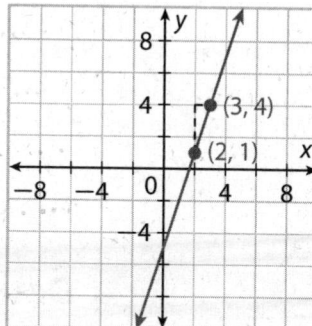

(B) Use $\left(-2, \boxed{}\right)$ as the first point. Subtract y-values to find the change in y, or rise. Then subtract x-values to find the change in x, or run.

$$\text{slope} = \frac{\boxed{} - \boxed{}}{\boxed{} - \boxed{}} = \frac{\boxed{}}{\boxed{}} = \boxed{}.$$

The slope of the line is $\boxed{}$.

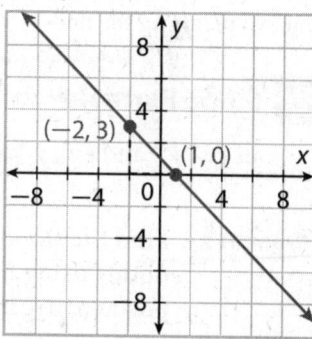

Reflect

4. Find the rise of a horizontal line. What is the slope of a horizontal line?

_____

_____

5. Find the run of a vertical line. What is the slope of a vertical line?

_____

_____

6. **Discussion** If you have a graph of a line, how can you determine whether the slope is positive, negative, zero, or undefined without using points on the line?

_____

_____

Find the slope of each line.

7.
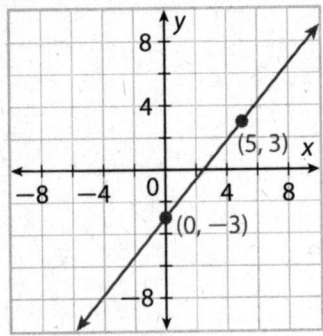

8.
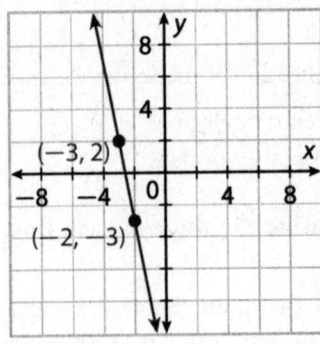

⚙ Explain 2 Determining Slope Using the Slope Formula

The **slope formula** for the slope of a line is the ratio of the difference in y-values to the difference in x-values between any two points on the line.

🧩 Slope Formula

If (x_1, y_1) and (x_2, y_2) are any two points on a line, the slope of the line is $m = \dfrac{y_2 - y_1}{x_2 - x_1}$.

Example 2 Find the slope of each line passing through the given points using the slope formula. Describe the slope as positive, negative, zero, or undefined.

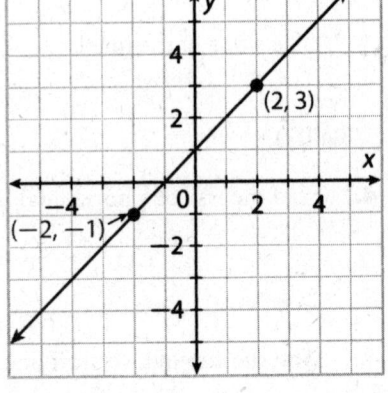

(A) The graph shows the linear relationship.

$y_2 - y_1 = 3 - (-1) = 3 + 1 = 4$

$x_2 - x_1 = 2 - (-2) = 2 + 2 = 4$

$m = \dfrac{y_2 - y_1}{x_2 - x_1} = \dfrac{4}{4} = 1$

The slope is positive. The line rises from left to right.

(B)

x	3	3	3	3
y	2	4	6	8

Let $\left(\boxed{}, 4\right)$ be (x_1, y_1) and $\left(\boxed{}, 8\right)$ be (x_2, y_2).

$y_2 - y_1 = 8 - \boxed{} = \boxed{}$

$x_2 - x_1 = \boxed{} - \boxed{} = \boxed{}$

$m = \dfrac{y_2 - y_1}{x_2 - x_1} = \dfrac{\boxed{}}{\boxed{}}$

The slope is _____ and the line is _____.

Find the slope of each line passing through the given points using the slope formula. Describe the slope as positive, negative, zero, or undefined.

9. The graph shows the linear relationship.

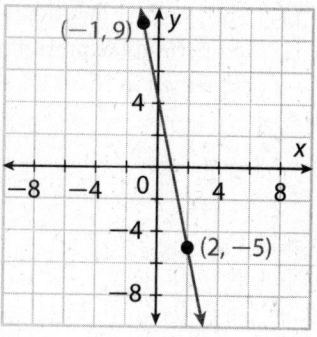

10.

x	1	2	3	4
y	5	5	5	5

🔑 Explain 3   Interpreting Slope

Given a real-world situation, you can find the slope and then interpret the slope in terms of the context of the situation.

Example 3   Find and interpret the slope for each real-world situation.

(A) The graph shows the relationship between a person's age and his or her estimated maximum heart rate.

Use the two points that are labeled on the graph.

$$\text{slope} = \frac{\text{rise}}{\text{run}} = \frac{180 - 150}{50} = \frac{30}{-30} = -1$$

Interpret the slope.

The slope being -1 means that for every year a person's age increases, his or her maximum heart rate decreases by 1 beat per minute.

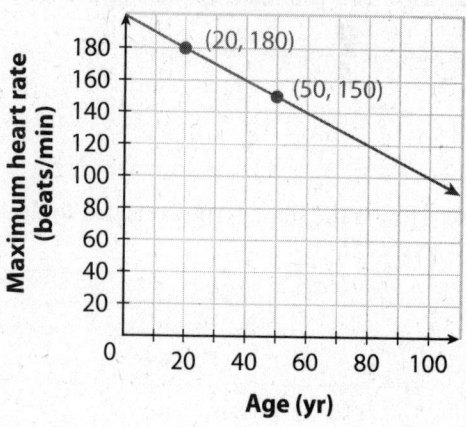

Estimated Maximum Heart Rate

(B) The height of a plant y in centimeters after x days is a linear relationship. The points (30, 15) and (40, 25) are on the line.

Use the two points that are given.

$$\text{slope} = \frac{\text{rise}}{\text{run}} = \frac{\boxed{} - 15}{\boxed{} - \boxed{}} = \frac{\boxed{}}{\boxed{}} = \boxed{}$$

Interpret the slope.

The slope being _____ means _____.

Find and interpret the slope.

11. The graph shows the relationship between the temperature expressed in °F and the temperature expressed in °C.

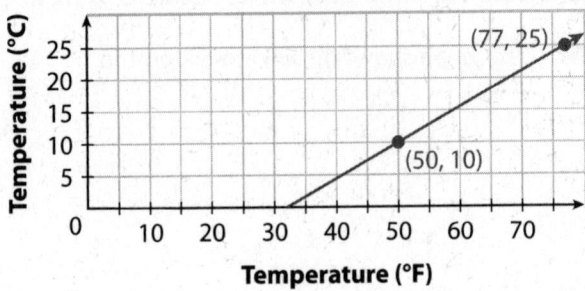

12. The number of cubic feet of water y in a reservoir x hours after the water starts flowing into the reservoir is a linear function. The points (40, 3000) and (60, 4000) are on the line of the function.

💬 Elaborate

13. How can you relate the rate of change and slope in the linear relationships?

_____

_____

_____

14. How is the slope formula related to the definition of slope?

_____

_____

_____

15. How can you interpret slope in a real-world situation?

_____

_____

_____

Determine the slope of each line.

1.

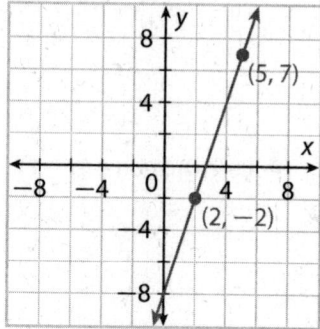

(5, 7)

(2, −2)

2.

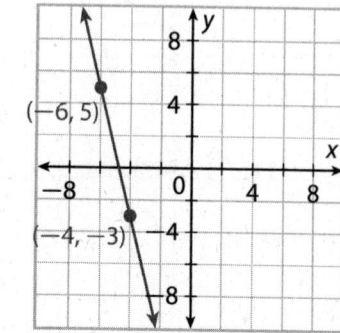

(−6, 5)

(−4, −3)

3.

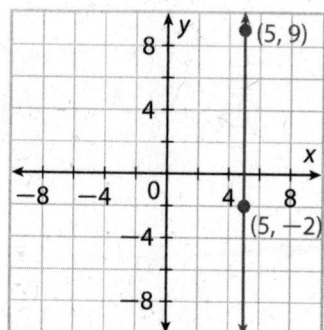

(5, 9)

(5, −2)

4.

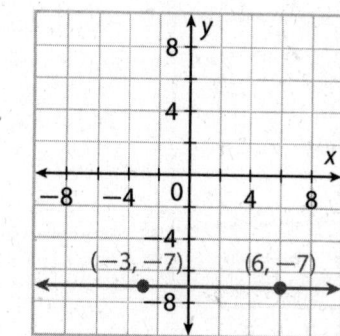

(−3, −7)   (6, −7)

5.

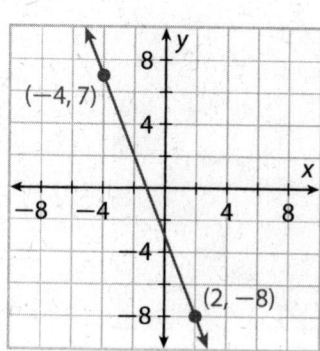

(−4, 7)

(2, −8)

6.

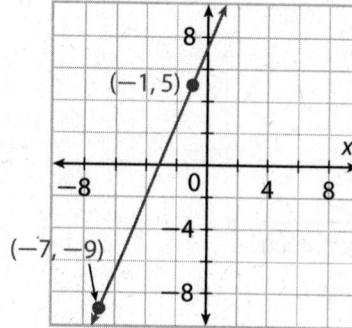

(−1, 5)

(−7, −9)

Find the slope of each line passing through the given points using the slope formula. Describe the slope as positive, negative, zero, or undefined.

7. $(5, 3)$ and $(10, 8)$

8. $(-5, 14)$ and $(-1, 2)$

9. $(-5, 6)$ and $(8, 6)$

10. $(-4, -17)$ and $(-4, -3)$

11. $(12, -7)$ and $(2, -2)$

12. $(-3, -10)$ and $(-1, -1)$

Find and interpret the slope for each real-world situation.

13.

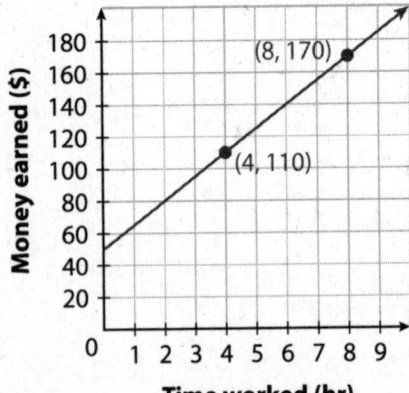

14.

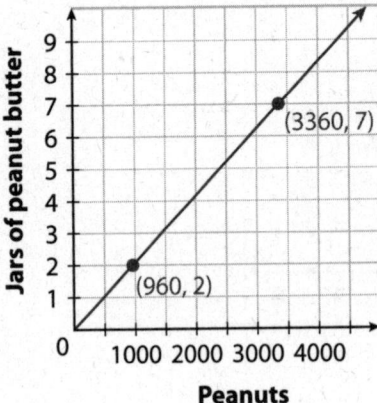

15.

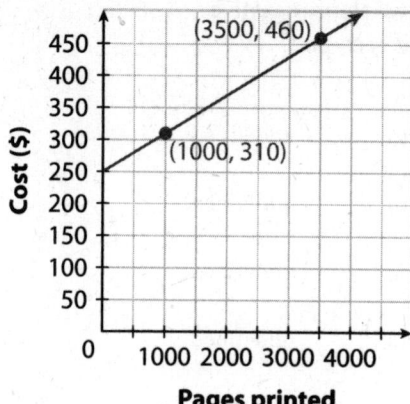

16.

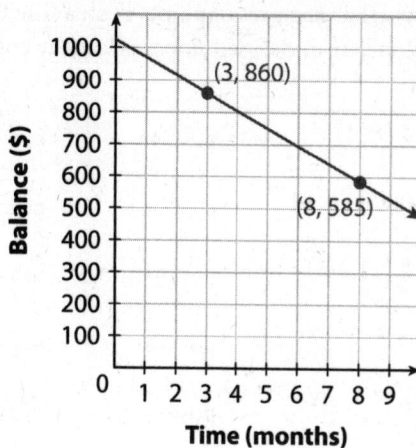

17. a. The table shows the distance that a group of hikers has traveled from the start of the trail.

Time (hr)	0.5	1	2	3
Distance (km)	3	5	7	13

Use the table to plot the 4 points on the graph and join the points using line segments.

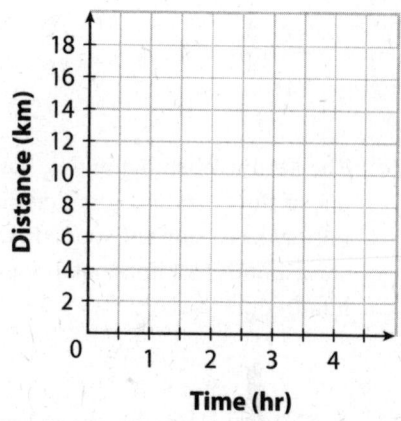

b. Find the slope for each of the three line segments.

c. Which line segment has the greatest slope? Does this line segment appear to be the steepest on the graph?

18. Determine whether each set of points is on a line that has a positive slope, negative slope, zero slope, or undefined slope. Select the correct answer for each part.

a. $(5, 0)$ and $(8, 4)$ ☐ positive ☐ negative ☐ zero ☐ undefined

b. $(-6, 1)$ and $(-6, 9)$ ☐ positive ☐ negative ☐ zero ☐ undefined

c. $(2, 6)$ and $(11, -3)$ ☐ positive ☐ negative ☐ zero ☐ undefined

d. $(3, 4)$ and $(-2, 12)$ ☐ positive ☐ negative ☐ zero ☐ undefined

e. $(-3, 5)$ and $(7, 5)$ ☐ positive ☐ negative ☐ zero ☐ undefined

19. What is the slope of the segment shown for a staircase with 10-inch treads and 7.75-inch risers? As you walk up (or down) the stairs, your vertical distance from the floor is a linear function of your horizontal distance from the point on the floor where you started. Is the function discrete or continuous? Explain.

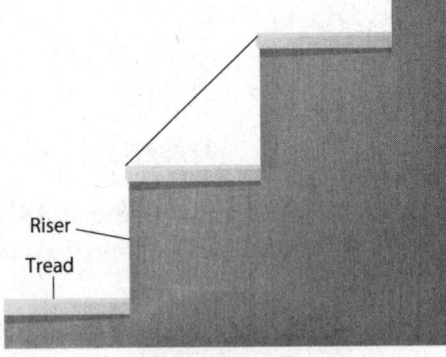

Riser —

Tread

20. The Mount Washington Cog Railway in New Hampshire is one of the steepest cog railways in the world. A section of the railway has a slope of approximately 0.37. In this section, a vertical change of 1 unit corresponds to a horizontal change of what length? Round your answer to the nearest hundredth.

21. a. Biology The table shows how the number of cricket chirps per minute changes with the air temperature.

Temperature (°F)	40	50	60	70	80	90
Chirps per minute	0	40	80	120	160	200

Find the rates of change.

b. Is the graph of the data a line? If so, what is the slope? If not, explain why not.

22. **Explain the Error** A student is asked to find the slope of a line containing the points (4, 3) and (−2, 15) and finds the slope as shown. Explain the error.

$$\text{slope} = \frac{\text{rise}}{\text{run}} = \frac{4 - (-2)}{3 - 15} = \frac{6}{-12} = -\frac{1}{2}$$

23. **Critical Thinking** In this lesson, you learned that the slope of a line is constant. Does this mean that all lines with the same slope are the same line? Explain.

24. **a. Represent Real-World Problems** A ladder is leaned against a building. The bottom of the ladder is 11 feet from the building. The top of the ladder is 19 feet above the ground. What is the slope of the ladder?

   b. What does the slope of the ladder mean in the real world?

   c. If the ladder were set closer to the building, would it be harder or easier to climb? Explain in terms of the slope of the ladder.

25. **a.** The table shows the cost, in dollars, charged by an electric company for various amounts of energy in kilowatt-hours. Graph the data and show the rates of change.

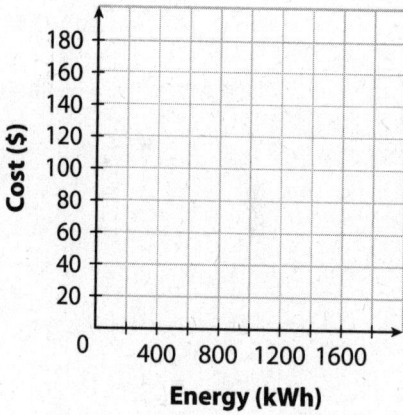

Energy (kWh)	0	200	400	600	1000	2000
Cost ($)	8	8	34	60	112	157

   b. Compares the rates of change for each interval. Are they all the same? Explain.

   c. What do the rates of change represent?

   d. Describe in words the electric company's billing plan.

Lesson Performance Task

A city has three Internet service providers (ISP), each of which charges a usage fee when a subscriber goes over 100 megabytes (MB) per billing cycle. The table below relates the amount of data a subscriber uses with the cost for each ISP.

ISP	100 MB	200 MB	400 MB
A	$54	$74	$94
B	$42	$57	$87
C	$60	$72	$96

Use the table to find the rate of change for each interval of each ISP, and use the rates of change to determine whether the usage fee is constant for each ISP. Interpret the meaning of the rates of change for each ISP. Then determine and explain which ISP would be the least expensive and which ISP would be the most expensive for a subscriber that uses a high amount of data.

Linear Functions

Essential Question: How can you use a linear function to solve real-world problems?

KEY EXAMPLE   *(Lesson 5.1)*

Determine whether $4x + y = 7$ is linear. If so, graph the function.

The equation is linear because it is in the standard form of a linear equation: $A = 4$, $B = 1$, and $C = 7$.

To graph the function, first solve the equation for y.

$$4x + y = 7$$
$$\underline{-4x \qquad\qquad -4x}$$
$$y = 7 - 4x$$

Make a table and plot the points. Then connect the points.

x	-1	0	1	2
y	11	7	3	-1

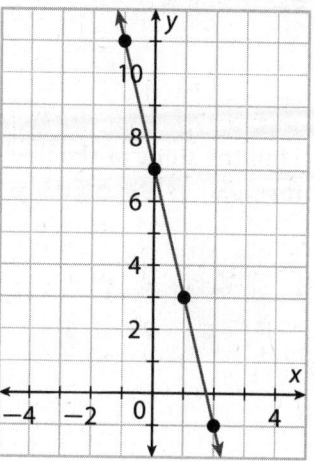

KEY EXAMPLE   *(Lesson 5.3)*

Find the slope of the line passing through the given points using the slope formula. Describe the slope as positive, negative, zero, or undefined.

x	1	2	3	4
y	7	7	7	7

Let $(1, 7)$ be (x_1, y_1) and $(3, 7)$ be (x_2, y_2).

$$y_2 - y_1 = 7 - 7 = 0$$

$$x_2 - x_1 = 3 - 1 = 2$$

$$m = \frac{y_2 - y_1}{x_2 - x_1} = \frac{0}{2} = 0$$

The slope is zero.

EXERCISES

Determine whether each equation is linear. *(Lesson 5.1)*

1. $4x^2 + y = 8$

2. $7x + y = 3$

Find the x- and y-intercepts. *(Lesson 5.2)*

3. $2x - 3y = 12$

4. $-6x + 8y = 24$

5. $3x + y = 5$

6. $5x - 2y = 0$

Find the slope of the line passing through the given points using the slope formula. *(Lesson 5.3)*

7.

x	0	1	2	3
y	2	5	8	11

8.

x	0	2	4	6
y	6	5	4	3

MODULE PERFORMANCE TASK

How Many Stacked Cups Do You Need?

You want to stack paper, plastic, or foam cups one inside the next so that the height of the stack is equal to your math teacher's height. How can you determine the number of cups you would need?

Start by listing in the space the questions you will need to answer in order to tackle the problem. Then use your own paper to complete the task. Be sure to write down all your data and assumptions. Then use graphs, numbers, words, or algebra to explain how you reached your conclusion.

(Ready) to Go On?

5.1–5.3 Linear Functions

- Online Homework
- Hints and Help
- Extra Practice

Determine whether each equation is linear. If it is linear, graph the equation, determine the slope, and find the *x*- and *y*-intercepts. *(Lessons 5.1, 5.2, 5.3)*

1. $x^3 + y = 8$

2. $4x + 2y = 6$

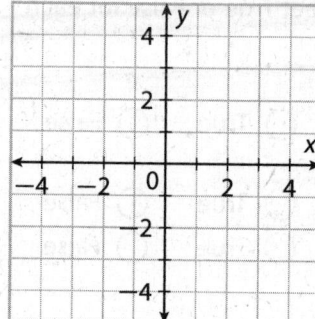

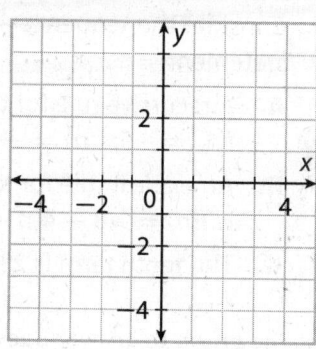

3. $-5x + 4y = 0$

4. $5xy + y = 9$

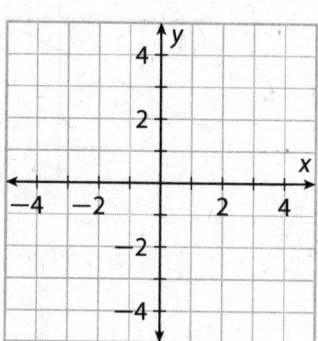

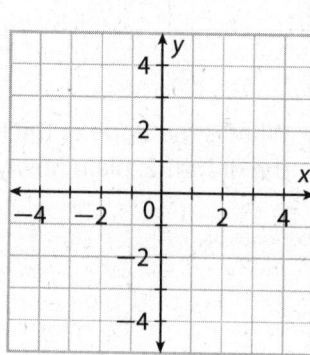

ESSENTIAL QUESTION

5. What do the slope and *y*-intercept of a real-world linear function represent?

Assessment Readiness

1. Look at each equation. Is the equation linear? Select Yes or No.

   A. $\frac{1}{3}x - 2y = 7$ ◯ Yes   ◯ No

   B. $y = x^2 - 8$ ◯ Yes   ◯ No

   C. $3x + \frac{7}{y} = -5$ ◯ Yes   ◯ No

2. Consider the equation $8x - 2y = 24$. Select True or False for each statement.

   A. The x-intercept is 3.   ◯ True   ◯ False

   B. The y-intercept is 12.   ◯ True   ◯ False

   C. It is equivalent to $y = 4x - 12$.   ◯ True   ◯ False

3. Consider the sequence –8, –4, 0, 4, 8, 12, …. Select True or False for each statement.

   A. A recursive rule for the sequence is
      $f(1) = -8; f(n) = -4(n - 1)$ for all $n \geq 2$.   ◯ True   ◯ False

   B. An explicit rule for the sequence
      is $f(n) = -8 + 4(n - 1)$.   ◯ True   ◯ False

   C. The tenth term is 28.   ◯ True   ◯ False

Use the graph to answer questions 4 and 5.

4. Is the relation represented on the graph a function? Explain.

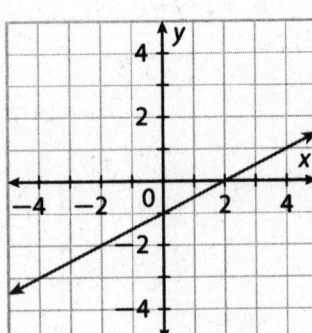

5. What is the slope of the line shown on the graph? Explain how you got your answer.

Forms of Linear Equations

Essential Question: How can you use different forms of linear equations to solve real-world problems?

REAL WORLD VIDEO
Periodic comets have orbital periods of less than 200 years. Halley's comet is the only short-period comet that is visible to the naked eye. It returns every 76 years. You can build functions to represent and model predictable occurrences, such as the return of Halley's comet.

MODULE PERFORMANCE TASK PREVIEW
Who Wins the Race

A marathon is a long-distance run that is 26.2 miles long. Marathon events are hosted all over the world, and participants are a mix of athletes with different skill levels. Most runners train for many months to prepare for a marathon. How can linear equations be used to compare the running speeds of two different runners? Stay on track and find out!

Are (YOU) Ready?

Complete these exercises to review skills you will need for this module.

Constant Rate of Change

Example 1 Tell if the rate of change is constant.

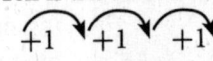

x	1	2	3	4
y	16	22	28	34

The rate of change, $\frac{6}{1}$, is constant.

For a function defined in terms of x and y, the rate of change of the function is a ratio that compares the change in y to the change in x.

$$\text{rate of change} = \frac{\text{change in } y}{\text{change in } x} = \frac{6}{1}$$

Tell if the rate of change is constant.

1.

x	2	5	8	11
y	6	15	24	33

_____

2.

x	3	6	9	12
y	2	6	11	17

_____

Two-Step Equations

Example 2 Solve.

$$10 = 3x - 11$$
$$10 + 11 = 3x - 11 + 11 \qquad \text{Add 11 to both sides of the equation.}$$
$$21 = 3x$$
$$\frac{21}{3} = \frac{3x}{3} \qquad \text{Divide both sides of the equation by 3.}$$
$$7 = x$$

Solve each equation.

3. $7n + 17 = 59$ _____

4. $24 - 4y = 20$ _____

5. $34 = 49 - 3b$ _____

Linear Functions

Example 3 Tell whether $y = \frac{4}{x} - 8$ represents a linear function.

$y = \frac{4}{x} - 8$ does not represent a linear function because x appears in the denominator.

When a linear equation is written in standard form, the following are true.

• x and y both have exponents of 1.

• x and y are not multiplied together.

• x and y do not appear in denominators, exponents, or radicands.

Tell whether the equation represents a linear function.

6. $8x^2 + y = 16$ _____

7. $6x + y = 12$ _____

8. $3y = 2x + 5$ _____

6.1 Slope-Intercept Form

Essential Question: How can you represent a linear function in a way that reveals its slope and *y*-intercept?

Resource Locker

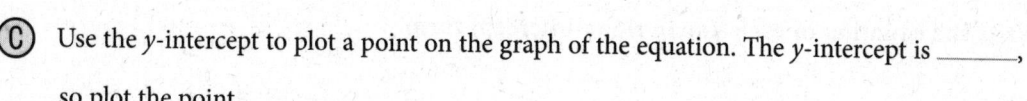 **Explore** **Graphing Lines Given Slope and *y*-intercept**

Graphs of linear equations can be used to model many real-life situations. Given the slope and *y*-intercept, you can graph the line, and use the graph to answer questions.

Andrew wants to buy a smart phone that costs $500. His parents will pay for the phone, and Andrew will pay them $50 each month until the entire amount is repaid. The loan repayment represents a linear situation in which the amount *y* that Andrew owes his parents is dependent on the number *x* of payments he has made.

(A) When $x = 0$, $y =$ _____.

The *y*-intercept of the graph of the equation that represents

the situation is _____

(B) The rate of change in the amount Andrew owes over

time is _____ per month.

The slope is _____.

(C) Use the *y*-intercept to plot a point on the graph of the equation. The *y*-intercept is _____,

so plot the point _____.

(D) Using the definition of slope, plot a second point.

$$\text{Slope} = \frac{\text{Change in } y}{\text{Change in } x} = \frac{\boxed{}}{1} = \boxed{}.$$

Start at the point you plotted. Count _____ units down

and _____ unit right and plot another point.

(E) Draw a line through the points you plotted.

Amount Andrew Owes

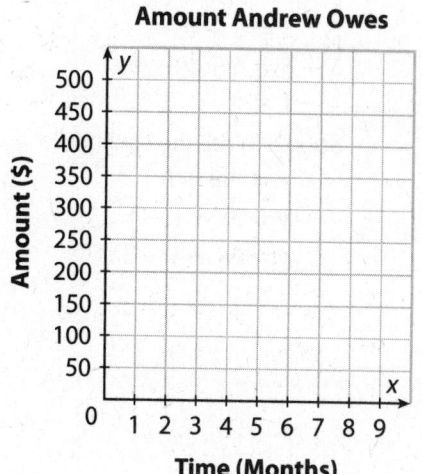

Time (Months)

1. **Discussion** How can you use the same method to find two more points on that same line?

_____

_____

2. How many months will it take Andrew to pay off his loan? Explain your answer.

_____

_____

🔑 Explain 1 Creating Linear Equations in Slope-Intercept Form

You can use the slope formula to derive the slope-intercept form of a linear equation.

Consider a line with slope m and y-intercept b.

The slope formula is $m = \dfrac{y_2 - y_1}{x_2 - x_1}$.

Substitute $(0, b)$ for (x_1, y_1) and (x, y) for (x_2, y_2).

$$m = \frac{y - b}{x - 0}$$

$$m = \frac{y - b}{x}$$

$$mx = y - b \qquad \text{Multiply both sides by } x \left(x \neq 0\right).$$

$$mx + b = y \qquad \text{Add } b \text{ to both sides.}$$

$$y = mx + b$$

Slope-Intercept Form of an Equation
If a line has slope m and y-intercept $(0, b)$, then the line is described by the equation $y = mx + b$.

Example 1 Write the equation of each line in slope-intercept form.

Ⓐ Slope is 3, and $(2, 5)$ is on the line.

Step 1: Find the y-intercept.

$y = mx + b$	Write the slope–intercept form.
$5 = 3(2) + b$	Substitute 3 for m, 2 for x, and 5 for y.
$5 = 6 + b$	Multiply.
$5 - 6 = 6 + b - 6$	Subtract 6 from both sides.
$-1 = b$	Simplify.

Step 2: Write the equation.

$y = mx + b$	Write the slope–intercept form.
$y = 3x + (-1)$	Substitute 3 for m and -1 for b.
$y = 3x - 1$	

B The line passes through $(0, 5)$ and $(2, 13)$.

Step 1: Use the points to find the slope.

$m = \dfrac{\boxed{}}{\boxed{}}$

Substitute $(0, 5)$ for (x_1, y_1) and $\left(\boxed{}, \boxed{}\right)$ for (x_2, y_2).

$m = \dfrac{\boxed{}}{\boxed{}} = \dfrac{\boxed{}}{\boxed{}} = \boxed{}$

Step 2: Substitute the slope and x- and y-coordinates of either of the points in the equation $y = mx + b$.

Step 3: Substitute _____ for m and _____ for b in the equation $y = mx + b$.

The equation of the line is $\boxed{}$.

$y = mx + b$

$\boxed{} = \boxed{} \left(\boxed{}\right) + b$

$\boxed{} = \boxed{} + b$

$\boxed{} - \boxed{} = \boxed{} + b - \boxed{}$

$\boxed{} = b$

Your Turn

Write the equation of each line in slope-intercept form.

3. Slope is -1, and $(3, 2)$ is on the line.

4. The line passes through $(1, 4)$ and $(3, 18)$.

 Explain 2 **Graphing from Slope-Intercept Form**

Writing an equation in slope-intercept form can make it easier to graph the equation.

Example 2 **Write each equation in slope-intercept form. Then graph the line.**

A $y = 5x - 4$

The equation $y = 5x - 4$ is already in slope-intercept form.

Slope: $m = 5 = \dfrac{5}{1}$

y-intercept: $b = -4$

Step 1: Plot $(0, -4)$

Step 2: Count 5 units up and 1 unit to the right and plot another point.

Step 3: Draw a line through the points.

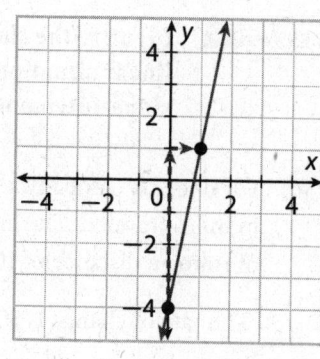

(B) $2x + 6y = 6$

Step 1: Write the equation in slope-intercept form by solving for y.

$2x + 6y - 2x = 6 - \boxed{}$ Slope: $\boxed{}$

$6y = \boxed{} + 6$ y-intercept: $\boxed{}$

$y = \boxed{} x + \boxed{}$

Step 2: Graph the line.

Plot $\left(\boxed{}, \boxed{} \right)$. Move _____ unit down and _____ units to the right to plot a second point. Draw a line through the points.

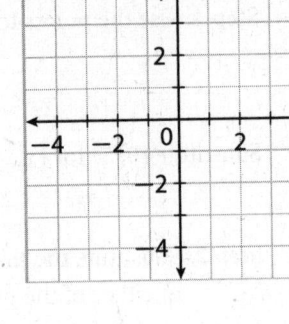

Your Turn

Write each equation in slope-intercept form. Then graph the line.

5. $2x + y = 4$

6. $2x + 3y = 6$

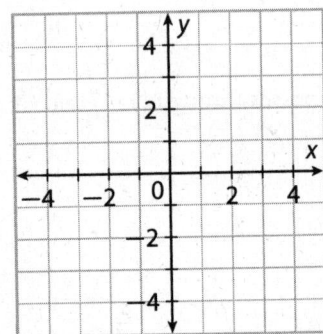

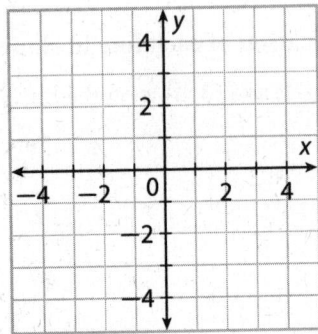

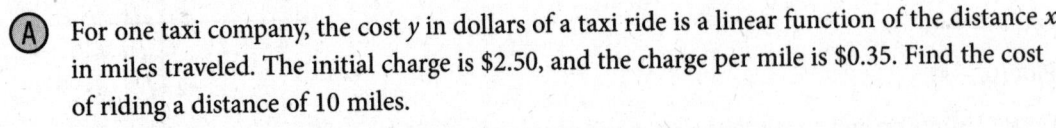

Explain 3   **Determining Solutions of Equations in Two Variables**

Given a real-world linear situation described by a table, a graph, or a verbal description, you can write an equation in slope-intercept form. You can use that equation to solve problems.

Example 3   Identify the slope and y-intercept of the graph that represents each linear situation and interpret what they mean. Then write an equation in slope-intercept form and use it to solve the problem.

(A)   For one taxi company, the cost y in dollars of a taxi ride is a linear function of the distance x in miles traveled. The initial charge is $2.50, and the charge per mile is $0.35. Find the cost of riding a distance of 10 miles.

The rate of change is $0.35 per mile, so the slope, m, is 0.35.

The initial cost is the cost to travel 0 miles, $2.50, so the y-intercept, b, is 2.50.

Then an equation is $y = 0.35x + 2.50$.

$y = 0.35x + 2.50$

To find the cost of riding 10 miles, substitute 10 for x.

$= 0.35(10) + 2.50$

$= 6$

$(6, 10)$ is a solution of the equation, and the cost of riding a distance of 10 miles is $6.

(B) A chairlift descends from a mountain top to pick up skiers at the bottom. The height in feet of the chairlift is a linear function of the time in minutes since it begins descending as shown in the graph. Find the height of the chairlift 2 minutes after it begins descending.

Height of a Chairlift

The graph contains the points (0, _____) and (____, 2400).

The slope is $\dfrac{\boxed{} - 5400}{\boxed{} - 0} = \boxed{}$.

It represents the rate at which the chairlift _____.

The graph passes through the point (0, _____), so the y-intercept is _____. It represents the height of the chairlift _____ minutes after it begins descending.

Let x be the time in minutes after the chairlift begins to descend.

Let y be the height of the chairlift in feet.

The equation is _____.

To find the height after 2 minutes, substitute 2 for x and simplify.

$$\boxed{} = \boxed{} \left(\boxed{} \right) + 5400$$

$$= \boxed{} + 5400$$

$$= \boxed{}$$

_____ is a solution of the equation, and the height of the chairlift 2 minutes after it begins descending is _____ feet.

Reflect

7. In the example involving the taxi, how would the equation change if the cost per mile increased or decreased? How would this affect the graph?

_____

_____

Identify the slope and *y*-intercept of the graph that represents the linear situation and interpret what they mean. Then write an equation in slope-intercept form and use it to solve the problem.

8. A local club charges an initial membership fee as well as a monthly cost. The cost *C* in dollars is a linear function of the number of months of membership. Find the cost of the membership after 4 months.

Membership Cost	
Time (months)	**Cost ($)**
0	100
3	277
6	454

⊙ Elaborate

9. What are some advantages to using slope-intercept form?

_____

_____

10. What are some disadvantages of slope-intercept form?

_____

_____

11. **Essential Question Check-In** When given a real-world situation that can be described by a linear equation, how can you identify the slope and *y*-intercept of the graph of the equation?

_____

_____

_____

⊛ Evaluate: Homework and Practice

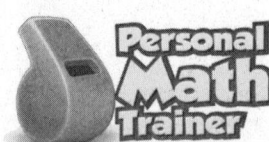

• Online Homework
• Hints and Help
• Extra Practice

For each situation, determine the slope and *y*-intercept of the graph of the equation that describes the situation.

1. John gets a new job and receives a $500 signing bonus. After that, he makes $200 a day.

2. Jennifer is 20 miles north of her house, and she is driving north on the highway at a rate of 55 miles per hour.

Sketch a graph that represents the situation.

3. Morwenna rents a truck. She pays $20 plus $0.25 per mile.

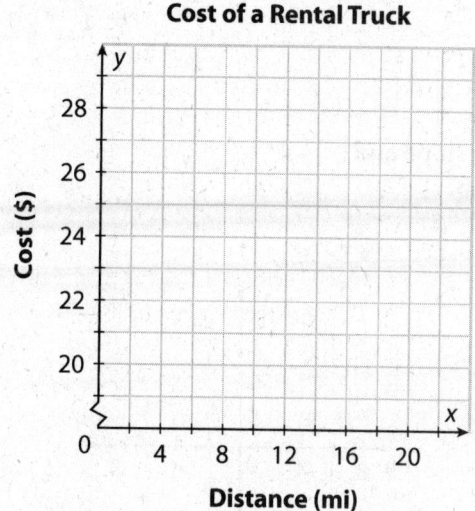

Cost of a Rental Truck

4. An investor invests $500 in a certain stock. After the first six months, the value of the stock has increased at a rate of $20 per month.

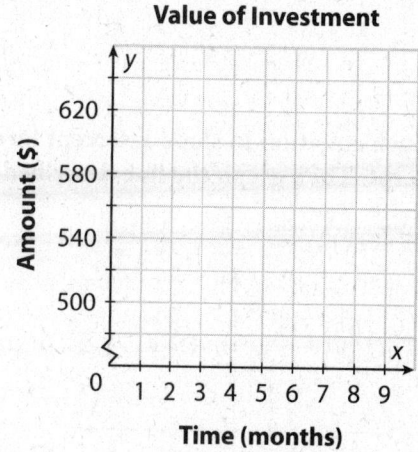

Value of Investment

Write the equation of each line in slope-intercept form.

5. Slope is 3, and $(1, 5)$ is on the line.

6. Slope is -2, and $(5, 3)$ is on the line.

7. Slope is $\frac{1}{4}$, and $(4, 2)$ is on the line.

8. Slope is 5, and $(2, 6)$ is on the line.

9. Slope is $-\frac{2}{3}$, and $(-6, -5)$ is on the line.

10. Slope is $-\frac{1}{2}$, and $(-3, 2)$ is on the line.

11. Passes through $(5, 7)$ and $(3, 1)$

12. Passes through $(-6, 10)$ and $(-3, -2)$

13. Passes through $(6, 6)$ and $(-2, 2)$

14. Passes through $(-1, -5)$ and $(2, 6)$

Write each equation in slope-intercept form. Identify the slope and y-intercept. Then graph the line described by the equation.

15. $y = 2x + 3$

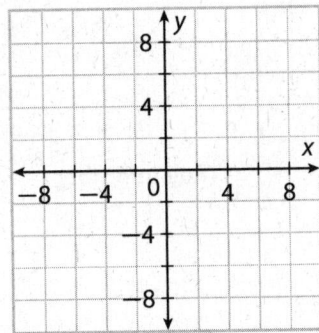

16. $y = -x + 2$

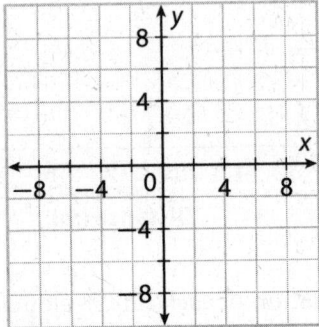

17. $y = \frac{2}{3}x - 4$

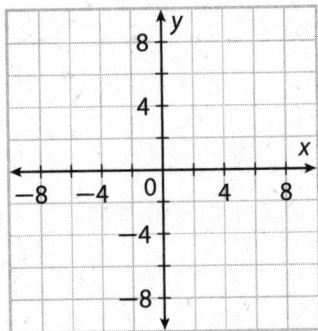

18. $y = -\frac{1}{2}x - 1$

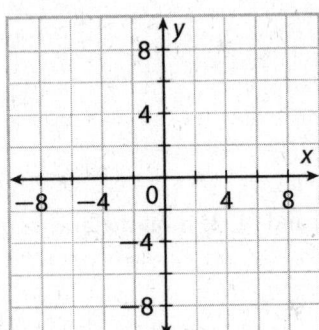

19. $-4x + 2y = 10$

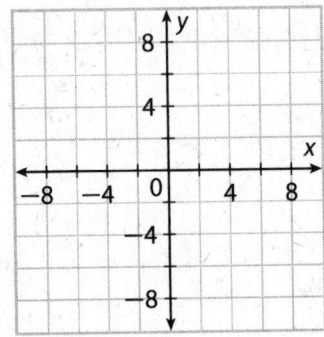

20. $3x - 6y = -12$

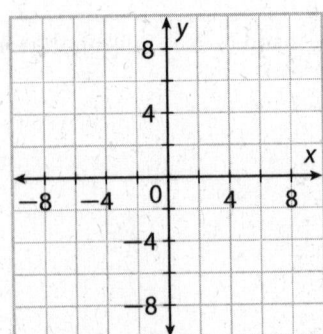

21. $-5x - 2y = 8$

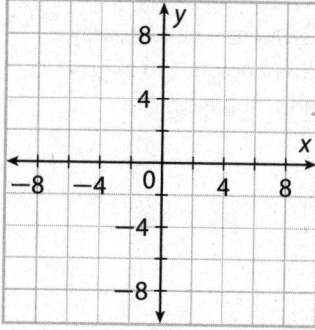

22. $3x + 4y = -12$

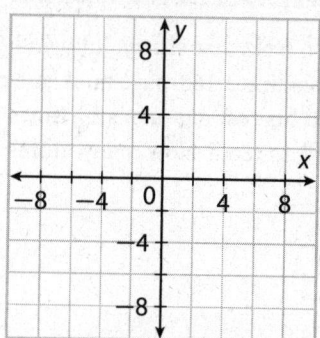

23. Sports A figure skating school offers introductory lessons at $25 per session. There is also a registration fee of $30. Write a linear equation in slope-intercept form that represents the situation. You want to take at least 6 lessons. Can you pay for those lessons using a $200 gift certificate? If so, how much money, if any, will be left on the gift certificate? If not, explain why not.

24. Represent Real World Problems Lorena and Benita are saving money. They began on the same day. Lorena started with $40. Each week she adds $8. The graph describes Benita's savings plan. Which girl will have more money in 6 weeks? How much more will she have? Explain your reasoning.

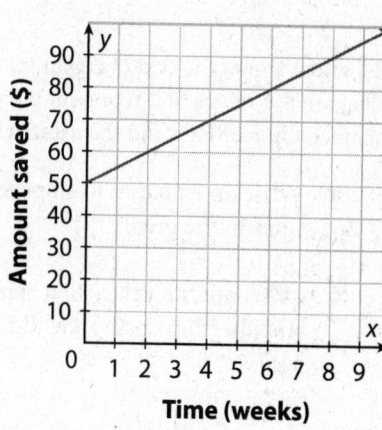

25. Analyze Relationships Julio and Jake start their reading assignments the same day. Jake is reading a 168-page book at a rate of 24 pages per day. Julio's book is 180 pages long and his reading rate is $1\frac{1}{4}$ times Jake's rate. After 5 days, who will have more pages left to read? How many more? Explain your reasoning.

26. Explain the Error John has $2 in his bank account when he gets a job. He begins making $107 dollars a day. A student found that the equation that represents this situation is $y = 2x + 107$. What is wrong with the student's equation? Describe and correct the student's error.

27. Justify Reasoning Is it possible to write the equation of every line in slope-intercept form? Explain your reasoning.

Lesson Performance Task

The graph shows the cost of a gym membership in each of two years. What are the values that represent the sign-up fee and the monthly membership fee? How did the values change between the years?

   a. Write an equation in slope-intercept form for each of the two lines in the graph.

   b. What are the values that represent the sign-up fee and the membership cost? How did the values change between the years?

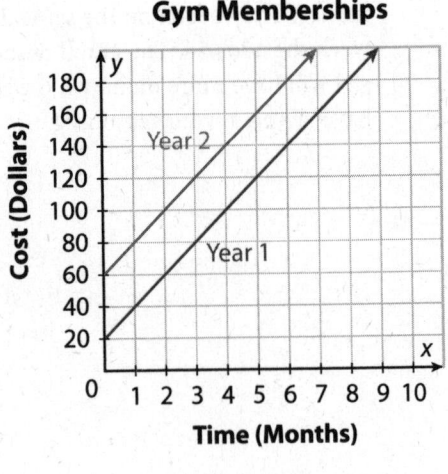

Gym Memberships

6.2   Point-Slope Form

Essential Question: How can you represent a linear function in a way that reveals its slope and a point on its graph?

Resource
Locker

⊘ Explore   Deriving Point-Slope Form

Suppose you know the slope of a line and the coordinates of one point on the line. How can you write an equation of the line?

(A)   A line has a slope m of 4, and the point $(2, 1)$ is on the line. Let (x, y) be any other point on the line. Substitute the information you have in the slope formula.

$$m = \frac{y_2 - y_1}{x_2 - x_1}$$

$$\boxed{} = \frac{y - \boxed{}}{x - \boxed{}}$$

(B)   Use the Multiplication Property of Equality to get rid of the fraction.

$$\boxed{}\left(x - \boxed{}\right) = \left(\frac{y - \boxed{}}{x - \boxed{}}\right)\left(x - \boxed{}\right)$$

(C)   Simplify.

$$\boxed{}\left(x - \boxed{}\right) = \left(y - \boxed{}\right)$$

Reflect

1.   **Discussion** The equation that you derived is written in a form called *point-slope form*. The equation $y = 2x + 1$ is in slope-intercept form. How can you rewrite it in point-slope form?

_____

_____

_____

⊘ Explain 1   Creating Linear Equations Given Slope and a Point

Point-Slope Form

The line with slope m that contains the point (x_1, y_1) can be described by the equation $y - y_1 = m(x - x_1)$.

Example 1   Write an equation in point-slope form for each line.

(A)   Slope is 3.5, and $(-3, 2)$ is on the line.

$y - y_1 = m(x - x_1)$	Point-slope form
$y - 2 = 3.5\big(x - (-3)\big)$	Substitute.
$y - 2 = 3.5(x + 3)$	Simplify.

(B)   Slope is 0, and $(-2, -1)$ is on the line.

$y - y_1 = m(x - x_1)$	Point-slope form
$y - \boxed{} = \boxed{}\left(x - \boxed{}\right)$	Substitute.
$y + \boxed{} = \boxed{}$	Simplify.

2. **Communicate Mathematical Ideas** Suppose that you are given that the slope of a line is 0. What is the only additional information you need to write an equation of the line? Explain.

_____

_____

Your Turn

Write an equation in point-slope form for each line.

3. Slope is 6, and (1, 2) is on the line.

4. Slope is $\frac{1}{3}$, and $(-3, 1)$ is on the line.

🔑 **Explain 2** **Creating Linear Models Given Slope and a Point**

You can write an equation in point-slope form to describe a real-world linear situation. Then you can use that equation to solve a problem.

Example 2 **Solve the problem using an equation in point-slope form.**

Ⓐ Paul wants to place an ad in a newspaper. The newspaper charges $10 for the first 2 lines of text and $3 for each additional line of text. Paul's ad is 8 lines long. How much will the ad cost?

Let x represent the number of lines of text. Let y represent the cost in dollars of the ad. Because 2 lines of text cost $10, the point $(2, 10)$ is on the line. The rate of change in the cost is $3 per line, so the slope is 3.

Write an equation in point-slope form.

$y - y_1 = m(x - x_1)$ Point-slope form

$y - 10 = 3(x - 2)$ Substitute 3 for m, 2 for x_1, and 10 for y_1.

To find the cost of 8 lines, substitute 8 for x and solve for y.

$y - 10 = 3(8 - 2)$ Substitute

$y - 10 = 18$ Simplify.

$y = 28$

The cost of 8 lines is $28.

(B) Paul would like to shop for the best price to place the ad. A different newspaper has a base cost of $15 for 3 lines and $2 for every extra line. How much will an 8-line ad cost in this paper?

$$y - y_1 = m(x - x_1)$$ Point-slope form

$$y - \boxed{} = 2\left(x - \boxed{}\right)$$ Substitute.

$$y - \boxed{} = 2\left(\boxed{} - \boxed{}\right)$$ Substitute for x.

$$y - \boxed{} = \boxed{}$$ Simplify the right side.

$$y = \boxed{}$$ Solve for y.

The cost of 8 lines is $ \boxed{} .

Reflect

5. **Analyze Relationships** Suppose that you find that the cost of an ad with 8 lines in another publication is $18. How is the ordered pair (8, 18) related to the equation that represents the situation? How is it related to the graph of the equation?

_____

_____

Your Turn

6. Daisy purchases a gym membership. She pays a signup fee and a monthly fee of $11. After 4 months, she has paid a total of $59. Use a linear equation in point-slope form to find the signup fee.

🖋 Explain 3 Creating Linear Equations Given Two Points

You can use two points on a line to create an equation of the line in point-slope form. There is more than one such equation.

Example 3 Write an equation in point-slope form for each line.

(A) (2, 1) and (3, 4) are on the line.

Let $(2, 1) = (x_1, y_1)$ and let $(3, 4) = (x_2, y_2)$.

Find the slope of the line by substituting the given values in the slope formula.

$$m = \frac{y_2 - y_1}{x_2 - x_1}$$
$$= \frac{4 - 1}{3 - 2}$$
$$= 3$$

You can choose either point and substitute the coordinates in the point-slope form.

$$y - y_1 = m(x - x_1)$$ Point-slope form

$$y - 1 = 3(x - 2)$$ Substitute 3 for m, 2 for x_1, and 1 for y_1.

Or:

$$y - y_1 = m(x - x_1)$$ Point-slope form

$$y - 4 = 3(x - 3)$$ Substitute 3 for m, 3 for x_1, and 4 for y_1.

(B) (1, 3) and (2, 3) are on the line.

Let $(1, 3) = (x_1, y_1)$ and let $(2, 3) = (x_2, y_2)$.

Find the slope of the line by substituting the given values in the slope formula.

$$m = \frac{y_2 - y_1}{x_2 - x_1}$$

$$= \frac{\boxed{} - \boxed{}}{\boxed{} - \boxed{}}$$

$$= \boxed{}$$

Choose either point and substitute the coordinates in the point-slope form.

$y - y_1 = m(x - x_1)$ Point-slope form

$y - \boxed{} = \boxed{}\left(x - \boxed{}\right)$ Substitute 0 for m, 1 for x_1, and 3 for y_1.

Or:

$y - y_2 = m(x - x_2)$ Point-slope form

$y - \boxed{} = \boxed{}\left(x - \boxed{}\right)$ Substitute 0 for m, 2 for x_2, and 3 for y_2.

Reflect

7. Given two points on a line, Martin and Minh each found the slope of the line. Then Martin used (x_1, y_1) and Minh used (x_2, y_2) to write the equation in point-slope form. Each student's equation was correct. Explain how they can show both equations are correct.

_____

_____

Your Turn

Write an equation in point-slope form for each line.

8. $(2, 4)$ and $(3, 1)$ are on the line.

9. $(0, 1)$ and $(1, 1)$ are on the line.

🔑 Explain 4   Creating a Linear Model Given Two Points

In a real-world linear situation, you may have information that represents two points on the line. You can write an equation in point-slope form that represents the situation and use that equation to solve a problem.

Example 4   **Solve the problem using an equation in point-slope form.**

An animal shelter asks all volunteers to take a training session and then to volunteer for one shift each week. Each shift is the same number of hours. The table shows the numbers of hours Joan and her friend Miguel worked over several weeks. Another friend, Lili, plans to volunteer for 24 weeks over the next year. How many hours will Lili volunteer?

Volunteer	Weeks worked	Hours worked
Joan	6	15
Miguel	10	23

Analyze Information

Identify the important information.

- Joan worked for _____ weeks for a total of _____ hours.
- Miguel worked for _____ weeks for a total of _____ hours.
- Lili will work for _____ weeks.

 Formulate a Plan

To create the equation, identify the two ordered pairs represented by the situation. Find the _____ of the line that contains the two points. Write the equation in point-slope form. Substitute the _____ that Lili works for x to find y, the _____.

Let x represent the number of weeks worked and y represent the number of hours worked.

The points _____ and _____ are on the line. Substitute the coordinates in the slope formula to find the slope.

$$m = \frac{y_2 - y_1}{x_2 - x_1}$$

$$m = \frac{\boxed{} - \boxed{}}{\boxed{} - \boxed{}}$$

$$m = \boxed{}$$

Next choose one of the points and find an equation of the line in point-slope form.

$y - y_1 = m(x - x_1)$ Point-slope form

$y - \boxed{} = \boxed{}\left(x - \boxed{}\right)$ Substitute $\boxed{}$ for m, $\boxed{}$ for x_1, and $\boxed{}$ for y_1.

Or:

$y - y_2 = m(x - y_2)$ Point-slope form

$y - \boxed{} = \boxed{}\left(x - \boxed{}\right)$ Substitute $\boxed{}$ for m, $\boxed{}$ for x_2, and $\boxed{}$ for y_2.

Finally, substitute _____ in the equation to find y.

$y - \boxed{} = \boxed{}\left(x - \boxed{}\right)$ Substitute $\boxed{}$ for m, $\boxed{}$ for x_1, and $\boxed{}$ for y_1.

$y - \boxed{} = \boxed{}\left(\boxed{} - \boxed{}\right)$ Substitute $\boxed{}$ for x.

$y - \boxed{} = \boxed{}\left(\boxed{}\right)$ Simplify.

$y = \boxed{}$ Simplify.

Or:

$y - \boxed{} = \boxed{}\left(x - \boxed{}\right)$ Substitute $\boxed{}$ for m, $\boxed{}$ for x_2, and $\boxed{}$ for y_2.

$y - \boxed{} = \boxed{}\left(\boxed{} - \boxed{}\right)$ Substitute $\boxed{}$ for x.

$y - \boxed{} = \boxed{}\left(\boxed{}\right)$ Simplify.

$y = \boxed{}$ Simplify.

Lili will work a total of _____ hours.

The ordered pair $\left(\boxed{}, \boxed{} \right)$ is a solution of both equations obtained using the given information.

$y - \boxed{} = \boxed{}\left(x - \boxed{} \right)$ Substitute 2 for m, 6 for x_1, and 15 for y_1.

$\boxed{} - \boxed{} = \boxed{}\left(\boxed{} - \boxed{} \right)$ Substitute $\boxed{}$ for x and $\boxed{}$ for y.

$\boxed{} = \boxed{}$ Simplify.

Or:

$y - \boxed{} = \boxed{}\left(x - \boxed{} \right)$ Substitute 2 for m, 10 for x_2, and 23 for y_2.

$\boxed{} - \boxed{} = \boxed{}\left(\boxed{} - \boxed{} \right)$ Substitute $\boxed{}$ for x and $\boxed{}$ for y.

$\boxed{} = \boxed{}$ Simplify.

The answer makes sense because the rate of change in the number of hours is the

slope, _____. Because Lili will work _____ more weeks than Miguel, she will work

$23 + 2$ _____ hours, or _____ hours.

Your Turn

Solve the problem using an equation in point-slope form.

10. A gas station has a customer loyalty program. The graph shows the amount y dollars that two members paid for x gallons of gas. Use an equation in point-slope to find the amount a member would pay for 22 gallons of gas.

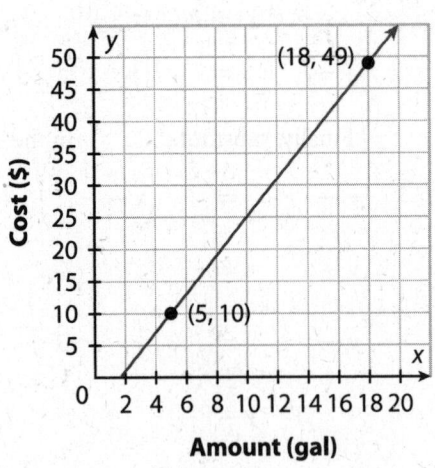

11. A roller skating rink offers a special rate for birthday parties. On the same day, a party for 10 skaters cost $107 and a party for 15 skaters cost $137. How much would a party for 12 skaters cost?

12. Can you write an equation in point-slope form that passes through any two given points in a coordinate plane?

_____

_____

13. Compare and contrast the slope-intercept form of a linear equation and the point-slope form.

_____

_____

_____

_____

_____

14. **Essential Question Check-In** Given a linear graph, how can you write an equation in point-slope form of the line?

_____

_____

_____

 **Evaluate: Homework and Practice**

• Online Homework
• Hints and Help
• Extra Practice

1. Is the equation $y + 1 = 7(x + 2)$ in point-slope form? Justify your answer.

Write an equation in point-slope form for each line.

2. Slope is 1 and $(-2, -1)$ is on the line.

3. Slope is -2, and $(1, 1)$ is on the line.

4. Slope is 0, and $(1, 2)$ is on the line.

5. Slope is $\frac{1}{4}$, and $(1, 2)$ is on the line.

6. $(1, 6)$ and $(2, 3)$ are on the line.

7. $(-1, 1)$ and $(1, -1)$ are on the line.

8. $(7, 7)$ and $(-3, 7)$ are on the line.

9. $(0, 3)$ and $(2, 4)$ are on the line.

Solve the problem using an equation in point-slope form.

10. An oil tank is being filled at a constant rate. The depth of the oil is a function of the number of minutes the tank has been filling, as shown in the table. Find the depth of the oil one-half hour after filling begins.

Time (min)	Depth (ft)
0	3
10	5
15	6

11. James is participating in a 5-mile walk to raise money for a charity. He has received $200 in fixed pledges and raises $20 extra for every mile he walks. Use a point-slope equation to find the amount he will raise if he completes the walk.

12. Keisha is reading a 325-page book at a rate of 25 pages per day. Use a point-slope equation to determine whether she will finish reading the book in 10 days.

13. Lizzy is tiling a kitchen floor for the first time. She had a tough time at first and placed only 5 tiles the first day. She started to go faster, and by the end of day 4, she had placed 35 tiles. She worked at a steady rate after the first day. Use an equation in point-slope form to determine how many days Lizzy took to place all of the 100 tiles needed to finish the floor.

14. The amount of fresh water left in the tanks of a nineteenth-century clipper ship is a linear function of the time since the ship left port, as shown in the table. Write an equation in point-slope form that represents the function. Then find the amount of water that will be left in the ship's tanks 50 days after leaving port.

Time (days)	Amount (gal)
1	3555
8	3240
15	2925

15. At higher altitudes, water boils at lower temperatures. This relationship between altitude and boiling point is linear. At an altitude of 1000 feet, water boils at 210 °F. At an altitude of 3000 feet, water boils at 206 °F. Use an equation in point-slope form to find the boiling point of water at an altitude of 6000 feet.

16. In art class, Tico is copying a detail from a painting. He paints slowly for the first few days, but manages to increase his rate after that. The graph shows his progress after he increased his rate. How many square centimeters of his painting will he finish in 5 days after the increase in rate?

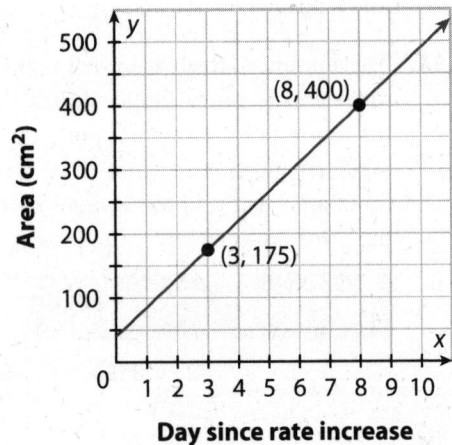

Day since rate increase

17. A hot air balloon in flight begins to ascend at a steady rate of 120 feet per minute. After 1.5 minutes, the balloon is at an altitude of 2150 feet. After 3 minutes, it is at an altitude of 2330 feet. Use an equation in point-slope form to determine whether the balloon will reach an altitude of 2500 feet in 4 minutes.

18. A candle burned at a steady rate. After 32 minutes, the candle was 11.2 inches tall. Eighteen minutes later, it was 10.75 inches tall. Use an equation in point-slope form to determine the height of the candle after 2 hours.

19. Volume A rectangular swimming pool has a volume capacity of 2160 cubic feet. Water is being added to the pool at a rate of about 20 cubic feet per minute. Determine about how long it will take to fill the pool completely if there were already about 1200 gallons of water in the pool. Use the fact that 1 cubic foot of space holds about 7.5 gallons of water.

20. Multi-Step Marisa is walking from her home to her friend Sanjay's home. When she is 12 blocks away from Sanjay's home, she looks at her watch. She looks again when she is 8 blocks away from Sanjay's home and finds that 6 minutes have passed.

    a. What do you need to assume in order to treat this as a linear situation?

    b. Identify the variables for the linear situation and identify two points on the line. Explain the meaning of the points in the context of the problem.

    c. Find the slope of the line and describe what it means in the context of the problem.

    d. Write an equation in point-slope form for the situation and use it to find the number of minutes Marisa takes to reach Sanjay's home. Show your work.

21. Match each equation with the pair of points used to create the equation.

    a. $y - 10 = 1(x + 2)$ _____ $(0, 0), (-1, 1)$

    b. $y - 0 = 1(x - 0)$ _____ $(1, 1), (-1, -1)$

    c. $y - 3 = -1(x + 3)$ _____ $(-2, 10), (0, 12)$

    d. $y - 3 = 0(x - 2)$ _____ $(1, 3), (-3.5, 3)$

22. Explain the Error Carlota wrote the equation $y + 1 = 2(x - 3)$ for the line passing through the points $(-1, 3)$ and $(2, 9)$. Explain and correct her error.

23. Communicate Mathematical Ideas Explain why it is possible for a line to have no equation in point-slope form or to have infinitely many, but it is not possible that there is only one.

24. Persevere in Problem Solving If you know that $A \neq 0$ and $B \neq 0$, how can you write an equation in point-slope form of the equation $Ax + By = C$?

Lesson Performance Task

Alberto is snow boarding down a mountain with a constant slope. The slope he is on has an overall length of 1560 feet. The top of the slope has a height of 4600 feet, and the slope has a vertical drop of 600 feet. It takes him 24 seconds to reach the bottom of the slope.

   a. If we assume that Alberto's speed down the slope is constant, what is his height above the bottom of the slope at 10 seconds into the run?

   b. Alberto says that he must have been going 50 miles per hour down the slope. Do you agree? Why or why not?

6.3 Standard Form

Essential Question: How can you write a linear equation in standard form given properties of the line including its slope and points on the line?

Resource
Locker

⊕ Explore   Comparing Forms of Linear Equations

You have seen that the standard form of a linear equation is $Ax + By = C$ where A and B are not both zero. For instance, the equation $2x + 3y = -12$ is in standard form. You can write equivalent equations in slope-intercept form and point-slope form. For instance, the equation in slope-intercept form and an equation in point-slope are shown.

$$\text{Standard form: } 2x + 3y = -12$$

$$\text{Slope-intercept form: } y = -\tfrac{2}{3}x - 4$$

$$\text{Point-slope from: } y + 8 = -\tfrac{2}{3}(x - 6)$$

Use the three forms of the equation shown to complete each step.

(A) Circle true or false.   **(B)** The slope is _____.

You can read the slope from the equation.

Standard form	True	False
Slope-intercept form	True	False
Point-slope form	True	False

(C) Circle true or false.   **(D)** Identify the y-intercept _____

You can read the y-intercept from the equation.

Standard form	True	False
Slope-intercept form	True	False
Point-slope form	True	False

Reflect

1. Explain how you can find both intercepts using the standard form.

_____

_____

2. How can you find a point on the line using the slope-intercept form?

_____

_____

⊘ Explain 1   Creating Linear Equations in Standard Form Given Slope and a Point

Given the slope of a line and a point on the line, you can write an equation of the line in standard form.

Example 1   Write an equation in standard form for each line.

(A) Slope is 2 and $(-2, 2)$ is on the line.

Method 1: Use the point-slope form. Substitute the given slope and the coordinates of the given point.

$$y - 2 = 2(x - (-2))$$ Point-slope form   Rewrite in standard form.

$$y - 2 = 2x + 4$$ Simplify. $$y - 2 = 2x + 4$$

$$-2x + y = 6$$

Method 2: Use the slope-intercept form. Substitute the given slope and the coordinates of the given point. Solve for b.

$$y = mx + b$$ Slope-intercept form   The slope-intercept form is $y = 2x + 6$.

$$2 = 2(-2) + b$$ Substitute for x.   Rewrite in standard form as in Method 1: $-2x + y = 6$

$$6 = b$$ Simplify.

(B) Slope is 5, and $(-2, 4)$ is on the line.

Method 1: Use the point-slope form. Substitute the given slope and the coordinates of the given point.

$$y - \boxed{} = \boxed{} \left(x - \left(\boxed{} \right) \right)$$ Point-slope form

$$y - \boxed{} = \boxed{} x + \boxed{}$$ Simplify.

Rewrite in standard form.

$$y - \boxed{} = \boxed{} x + \boxed{}$$

$$\boxed{} x + y = \boxed{}$$

Method 2: Use the slope-intercept form and substitute the slope and point into the equation to solve for b.

$$\boxed{} = \boxed{} \cdot \boxed{} + b$$ This gives the equation $y = \boxed{} x + \boxed{}$.

$$\boxed{} = \boxed{} + b$$ Rewrite in standard form as in Method 1:

$$\boxed{} = b$$ $$\boxed{} x + y = \boxed{}$$

Reflect

3. Discussion Which method do you prefer? Why?

_____

_____

_____

_____

Your Turn

Write an equation in standard form for each line.

4. Slope is -2, and $(-7, -10)$ is on the line.

5. Slope is 4, and $(-3, 0)$ is on the line.

⟐ Explain 2 Creating Linear Equations in Standard Form Given Two Points

You can use two points on a line to create an equation of the line in standard form.

Example 2 Write an equation in standard form for each line.

Ⓐ $(-2, -1)$ and $(0, 4)$ are on the line.

Find the slope using the given points.

$$m = \frac{y_2 - y_1}{x_2 - x_1} = \frac{4 - (-1)}{0 - (-2)} = \frac{5}{2}$$

Substitute the slope and the coordinates of either of the given points in the point-slope form.

$$y - y_1 = m(x - x_1)$$

$$y - 4 = \frac{5}{2}(x - 0)$$

$$y - 4 = \frac{5}{2}x$$

Rewrite in standard form.

$$2y - 8 = 5x$$

$$5x - 2y = -8$$

Ⓑ $(5, 2)$ and $(3, -6)$ are on the line.

Find the slope.

$$m = \frac{y_2 - y_1}{x_2 - x_1} = \frac{\boxed{} - \boxed{}}{\boxed{} - \boxed{}} = \frac{\boxed{}}{\boxed{}} = \boxed{}$$

Substitute the slope and the coordinates of either of the given points in the point-slope form.

$$y - y_1 = m(x - x_1)$$

$$y - \boxed{} = \boxed{}\left(x - \boxed{}\right)$$

$$y - \boxed{} = \boxed{}\ x - \boxed{}$$

Or:

$$y - \boxed{} = \boxed{}\left(x - \boxed{}\right)$$

$$y + \boxed{} = \boxed{}\ x - \boxed{}$$

Rewrite in standard form.

_____

Reflect

6. Why does it not matter which of the two given points you use in the point-slope form?

_____

Write an equation in standard form for each line.

7. $(4, -7)$ and $(2, -3)$ are on the line.

8. $(1, 5)$ and $(-10, -6)$ are on the line.

🔑 Explain 3 Creating Linear Models in Standard Form

Equations in standard form can be used to model real-world linear situations.

Example 3 **Write an equation in standard form to model the linear situation.**

Ⓐ A tank is filling up with water at a rate of 3 gallons per minute. The tank already had 3 gallons in it before it started being filled.

Let x represent the time in minutes since the filling began and y represent the amount of water in gallons. Since 3 gallons were in the tank before filling started, the point $(0, 3)$ is on the line.

The rate is 3 gallons per minute, so $m = 3$.

Substitute the slope and the coordinates of the point in the point-slope form and rewrite in standard form.

$y - 3 = 3(x - 0)$

$y - 3 = 3x$

$3x - y = -3$

Ⓑ A hot tub filled with 440 gallons of water is being drained. After 1.5 hours, the amount of water had decreased to 320 gallons.

The initial amount of water in the hot tub was 440 gallons, so $(0, 440)$ is on the line.

After 1.5 hours, the amount of water had decreased to 320 gallons, so $(1.5, 320)$ is on the line.

Use the given information to find the slope.

$m = \dfrac{\boxed{} - \boxed{}}{\boxed{} - \boxed{}} = \dfrac{\boxed{}}{\boxed{}} = \boxed{}$

Substitute the slope and the coordinates of one of the points in the point-slope form, and rewrite in standard form.

$y - \boxed{} = \boxed{}\left(x - \boxed{}\right)$

$y - \boxed{} = \boxed{}\,x$

$\boxed{}$

264

9. Your school sells adult and student tickets to a school play. Adult tickets cost $15 and student tickets cost $4. The total value of all the tickets sold is $7000. How could you write an equation in standard form to describe the linear situation?

_____

_____

Your Turn

Write an equation in standard form to model the linear situation.

10. A tank is being filled with gasoline at a rate of 4.5 gallons per minute. The gas tank contained 1.5 gallons of gasoline before filling started.

11. A pool that is being drained contained 18,000 gallons of water. After 2 hours, 12,500 gallons of water remain.

💬 Elaborate

12. Describe a method other than the one given in the example for writing an equation in standard form given two points on a line.

_____

_____

_____

13. Why might you choose the standard form of an equation over another form?

_____

14. **Essential Question Check-In** When writing a linear equation in standard form, what other forms might you need to use?

_____

☆ Evaluate: Homework and Practice

• Online Homework
• Hints and Help
• Extra Practice

Identify the form of each equation.

1. **a.** $5x + 4y = 8$

   b. $y - 3 = 8(x - 2)$

   c. $y = 3x + 6$

   d. $2x - 3y = -7$

Rewrite each equation in standard form.

2. $y = 6x - 4$

3. $y - 2 = -(x + 7)$

© Houghton Mifflin Harcourt Publishing Company

4. $y = \frac{4}{3}x - \frac{2}{3}$

5. $y - 4 = \frac{7}{3}(x - 3)$

Use the information given to write an equation in standard form.

6. Slope is 3, and (1, 4) is on the line.

7. Slope is −2, and (4, 3) is on the line.

8. Slope is −3, and (0, −4) is on the line.

9. Slope is 0, and (0, 5) is on the line.

10. Slope is $\frac{4}{7}$, and (1, 3) is on the line.

11. Slope $= -\frac{3}{2}$, and (2, 3) is on the line.

12. (−1, 1) and (0, 4) are on the line.

13. (6, 11) and (5, 9) are on the line.

14. (2, −5) and (−1, 1) are on the line.

15. (25, 34) and (35, 50) are on the line.

16. Use the information on the graph to write an equation in standard form.

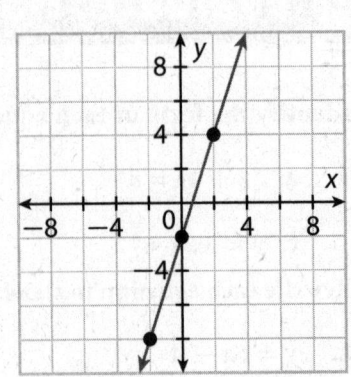

Write an equation in standard form to model the linear situation.

17. A bathtub that holds 32 gallons of water contains 12 gallons of water. You begin filling it, and after 5 minutes, the tub is full.

18. A barrel of oil was filled at a constant rate of 7.5 gal/min. The barrel had 10 gallons before filling began.

19. **Represent Real-World Situations**
A restaurant needs to plan seating for a party of 150 people. Large tables seat 10 people and small tables seat 6. Let x represent the number of large tables and y represent the number of small tables. An expression like the total number of people you can seat using A large tables and B small tables is called a *linear combination*. For instance, 150 people could be seated using 12 large tables and 5 small tables. Use that expression to write an equation in standard form that models all the different combinations of tables the restaurant could use. Then identify at least one possible combination of tables other than $(12, 5)$.

20. Match each equation with an equivalent equation in standard form.

a. $y = \frac{2}{3}x + 3$ _____ $7x + 6y = 6$

b. $6 - y = -5x + 8$ _____ $5x - y = 2$

c. $y - 3 = 4(x - 3)$ _____ $2x - 3y = -9$

d. $-\frac{7}{6}x + 1 = y$ _____ $4x - y = 9$

21. **Explain the Error** Cody was given two points $\left(\frac{1}{2}, 4\right)$ and $\left(\frac{2}{3}, 1\right)$, on a line and asked to create a linear equation in standard form. Cody's work is shown. Identify any errors and correct them.

$$m = \frac{1 - 4}{\frac{2}{3} - \frac{1}{2}} = -\frac{3}{\frac{1}{6}} = -\frac{1}{2}$$

$$y - 1 = -\frac{1}{2}\left(x - \frac{2}{3}\right)$$

$$y - 1 = -\frac{1}{2}x + \frac{1}{3}$$

$$2y - 2 = -x + \frac{2}{3}$$

$$x + 2y = \frac{8}{3}$$

22. **Communicate Mathematical Ideas** In the equation $Ax + By = C$, A and B cannot both be zero. What if only A is zero? What if only B is zero? Explain.

Lesson Performance Task

An airplane takes off with a full tank of 40,000 gallons of fuel and flies at an average speed of 550 miles per hour. After 8 hours in flight, there are 14,000 gallons of fuel left. It will take another 3.5 hours for the plane to reach its destination. How much fuel will be left in the tank when the plane lands? What is the total distance of the flight?

6.4 Transforming Linear Functions

Essential Question: What are the ways in which you can transform the graph of a linear function?

Explore 1 Building New Linear Functions by Translating

Investigate what happens to the graph of $f(x) = x + b$ when you change the value of b.

(A) Use a graphing calculator. Start with the standard viewing window, which you can obtain by pressing Zoom and selecting ZStandard. Because the distances between consecutive tick marks on the x-axis and on the y-axis are not equal, you can make them equal by pressing Zoom again and selecting ZSquare.

What interval on each axis does the viewing window now show? (Press Window to find out.)

_____

(B) Graph the function $f(x) = x$ by pressing Y= and entering the function's rule next to $Y_1 =$. As shown, the graph of the function is a line that makes a 45° angle with each axis.

What are the slope and y-intercept of the graph of $f(x) = x$?

_____

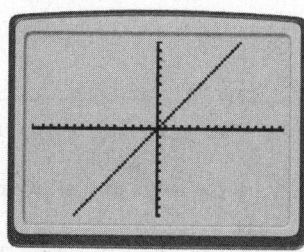

(C) Graph other functions of the form $f(x) = x + b$ by entering their rules next to $Y_2 =$, $Y_3 =$, and so on. Be sure to choose both positive and negative values of b. For instance, graph $f(x) = x + 2$ and $f(x) = x - 3$.

What do the graphs have in common? How are they different?

_____

_____

Reflect

1. **Discussion** A *vertical translation* moves all points on a figure the same distance either up or down. Use the idea of a vertical translation to describe what happens to the graph of $f(x) = x + b$ when you increase the value of b and decrease the value of b.

_____

_____

2. In this Explore, we replaced the linear function $f(x)$ by $f(x) + k$. Show how replacing $f(x)$ by $f(x + k)$ has exactly the same effect.

_____

_____

Building New Linear Functions by Stretching, Shrinking, or Reflecting

Investigate what happens to the graph of $f(x) = mx$ when you change the value of m.

(A) Use a graphing calculator. Press Y= and clear out all but the function $f(x) = x$ from the previous Explore Activity. Then graph other functions of the form $f(x) = mx$ by entering their rules next to $Y_2 =$, $Y_3 =$, and so on. Use only values of m that are greater than 1. For example, graph $f(x) = 2x$ and $f(x) = 6x$.

What do the graphs have in common? How are they different?

As the value of m increases from 1, does the graph become steeper or less steep?

_____

_____

(B) Again, press Y= and clear out all but the function $f(x) = x$. Then graph other functions of the form $f(x) = mx$ by entering their rules next to $Y_2 =$, $Y_3 =$, and so on. This time use only values of m that are less than 1 but greater than 0. For instance, graph $f(x) = 0.5x$ and $f(x) = 0.2x$.

As the value of m decreases from 1 to 0, does the graph become steeper or less steep?

_____

(C) Again, press Y= and clear out all but the function $f(x) = x$. Then graph the function $f(x) = -x$ by entering its rule next to $Y_2 =$.

What are the slope and y-intercept of the graph of $f(x) = -x$?

How are the graphs of $f(x) = x$ and $f(x) = -x$ geometrically related?

_____

_____

_____

(D) Again, press Y= and clear out all the functions. Graph $f(x) = -x$ by entering its rule next to $Y_1 =$. Then graph other functions of the form $f(x) = mx$ where $m < 0$ by entering their rules next to $Y_2 =$, $Y_3 =$, and so on. Be sure to choose values of m that are less than -1 as well as values of m between -1 and 0.

Describe what happens to the graph of $f(x) = mx$ as the value of m decreases from -1, and as it increases from -1 to 0.

_____

_____

3. **Discussion** When $m > 1$, will the graph of $f(x) = mx$ be a *vertical stretch* or a *vertical shrink* of the graph of $f(x) = x$? When $0 < m < 1$, will the graph of $f(x) = mx$ be a *vertical stretch* or a *vertical shrink* of the graph of $f(x) = x$? Explain your answers.

_____

_____

_____

_____

_____

⊘ Explore 3 Understanding Function Families

Investigate what happens to the graph of $f(x) = mx$ when you change the value of m.

Ⓐ A **family of functions** is a set of functions whose graphs have basic characteristics in common. What do all these variations on the original function $f(x) = x$ have in common?

_____

Ⓑ The most basic function of a family of functions is called the **parent function**. What is the parent function of the family of functions explored in the first two Explore Activities?

_____

Ⓒ A **parameter** is one of the constants in a function or equation that determines which variation of the parent function one is considering. For functions of the form $f(x) = mx + b$, what are the two parameters?

_____

4. Discussion For the family of all linear functions, the parent function is $f(x) = x$, where the parameters are $m = 1$ and $b = 0$. Other examples of families of linear functions are shown below. The example on the left shows a family with the same parameter m and differing parameters b. The example on the right shows a family with the same parameter b and differing parameters m.

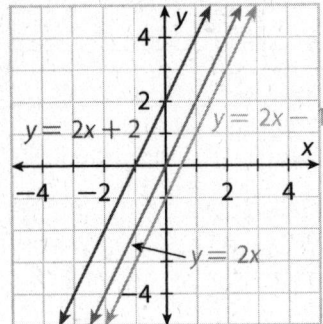
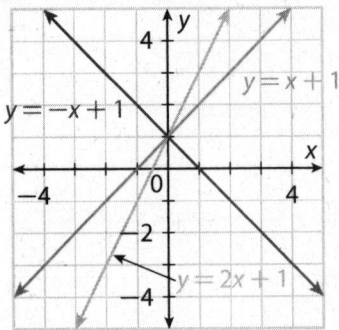

Describe the parameter that is left unchanged in the equations of the lines in the first graph.

⚙ Explain 1 **Interpreting Parameter Changes in Linear Models**

Many real-world scenarios can be modeled by linear functions. Changes in a particular scenario can be analyzed by making changes in the corresponding parameter of the linear function.

Example 1 A gym charges a one-time new member fee of $50 and then a monthly membership fee of $25. The total cost C of being a member of the gym is given by the function $C(t) = 25t + 50$, where t is the time (in months) since joining the gym. For each situation described below, sketch a graph using the given graph of $C(t) = 25t + 50$ as a reference.

Ⓐ The gym decreases its one-time fee for new members.

What change did you make to the graph of $C(t) = 25t + 50$ to represent a lower one-time fee?

I decreased the y-intercept but the slope remained the same.

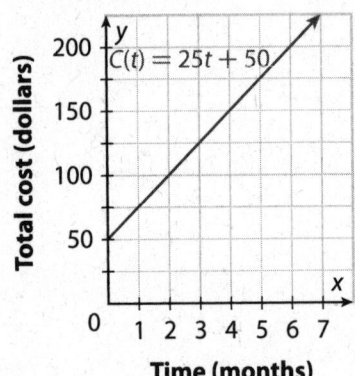

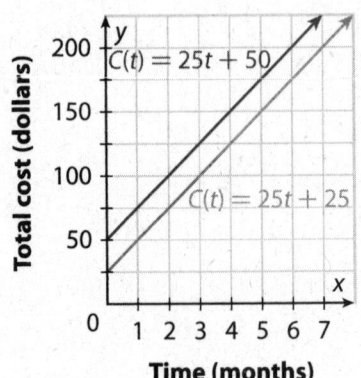

(B) The gym increases its monthly membership fee.

What change did you make to the graph of $C(t) = 25t + 50$ to represent an increased monthly fee?

I increased the slope but the y-intercept remained the same.

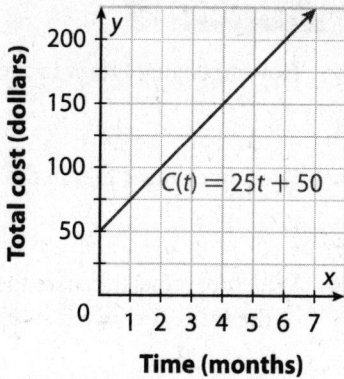

Reflect

5. Suppose the gym increases its one-time new member fee *and* decreases its monthly membership fee. Describe how you would alter the graph of $C(t) = 25t + 50$ to illustrate the new cost function.

_____

_____

Your Turn

Determine what will happen to the graph of the original function when the described changes occur.

6. Once a year the gym offers a special in which the one-time fee for joining is waived for new members. What impact does this special offer have on the graph of the original function $C(t) = 25t + 50$?

7. Suppose the gym increases its one-time joining fee *and* decreases its monthly membership fee. Does this have any impact on the domain of the function? Does this have any impact on the range of the function? Explain your reasoning.

8. How do changes to m in the equation $f(x) = mx$ affect the graph of the equation?

_____

9. How do changes to b in the equation $f(x) = x + b$ affect the graph of the equation?

_____

10. Which parameter causes the steepness of the graph of the line to change for the family of linear functions of the form $f(x) = mx + b$?

_____

11. Essential Question Check-In What are the different types of transformations?

_____

_____

☆ Evaluate: Homework and Practice

- Online Homework
- Hints and Help
- Extra Practice

In Exercises 1–4, the graph of $f(x) = x + 2$ is graphed.

1. Graph two more functions in the same family for which the parameter being changed is the y-intercept, b.

2. Graph two more functions in the same family for which the parameter being changed is the slope, m, and is greater than 1.

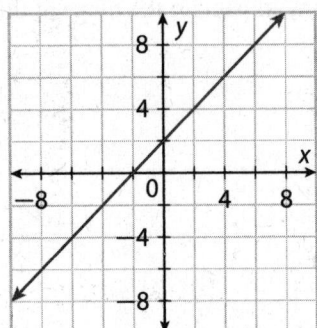

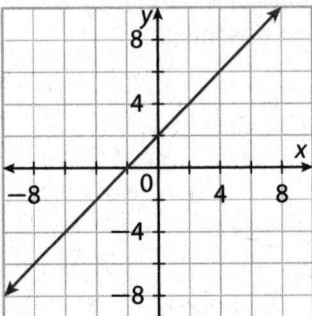

3. Graph two more functions in the same family for which the parameter being changed is the slope, m, and is between 0 and 1.

4. Graph two more functions in the same family for which the parameter being changed is the slope, m, and is less than 0.

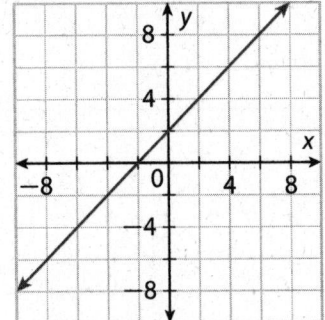

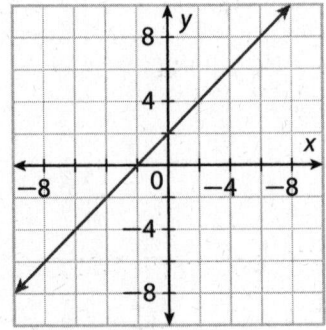

5. The graph of the parent linear function $f(x) = x$ is shown in black on the coordinate grid. Write the function that represents this function with the indicated parameter changes.

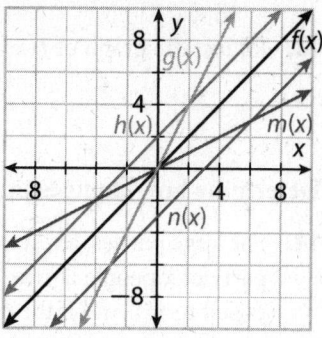

a. m increased, b unchanged _____

b. m decreased, b unchanged _____

c. m unchanged, b increased _____

d. m unchanged, b decreased, _____

6. For each linear function graphed on the coordinate grid, state the value of m and the value of b.

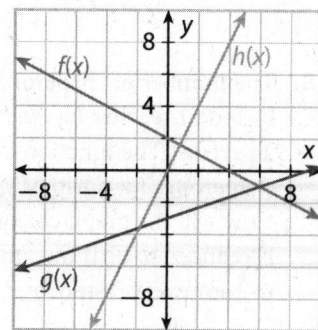

a. $f(x)$: $m =$ _____, $b =$ _____

b. $g(x)$: $m =$ _____, $b =$ _____

c. $h(x)$: $m =$ _____, $b =$ _____

Describe the transformation(s) on the graph of the parent function $f(x) = x$ that results in the graph of $g(x)$.

7. $g(x) = -x + 9$

8. $g(x) = 3x$

9. $g(x) = \frac{1}{4}x$

10. $g(x) = 7x - 8$

11. $g(x) = -\frac{3}{4}x + 5$

Use the parent function and the description of the transformation to write the new function.

12. Transform the graph of $f(x) = -x + 2$ in such a way that it has the same steepness in the opposite direction.

13. Reflect the graph of $f(x) = x - 1$ across the y-axis, and then translate it 4 units down.

Determine how changes in parameters will affect a graph. Write the new function.

14. For large parties, a restaurant charges a reservation fee of $25, plus $15 per person. The total charge for a party of x people is $f(x) = 15x + 25$. How will the graph of this function change if the reservation fee is raised to $50 and if the per-person charge is lowered to $12?

15. The number of chaperones on a field trip must include 1 teacher for every 4 students, plus a total of 2 parents. The function describing the number of chaperones for a trip of x students is $f(x) = \frac{1}{4}x + 2$. How will the graph change if the number of parents is reduced to 0? If the number of teachers is raised to 1 for every 3 students?

16. A satellite dish company charges a one-time installation fee of $75 and then a monthly usage charge of $40. The total cost C of using that satellite service is given by the function $C(t) = 40t + 75$, where t is the time (in months) since starting the service. For the situation given below, describe the new function using the graph of $C(t) = 40t + 75$ as a reference.

a. The satellite dish company reduces its one-time installation fee to $60. What change would you make to the graph of $C(t) = 40t + 75$ to obtain the new graph?

b. The satellite dish company decreases its monthly fee to $30. What change would you make to the graph of $C(t) = 40t + 75$ to obtain the new graph?

c. What is the new function with both changes?

17. A salesperson earns a base monthly salary of $2000 plus a 10% commission on sales. The salesperson's monthly income I (in dollars) is given by the function $I(s) = 0.1s + 2000$, where s is the sales (in dollars) that the salesperson makes. Sketch a graph to illustrate each situation using the graph of $I(s) = 0.1s + 2000$ as a reference.

A. The salesperson's base salary is increased.

B. The salesperson's commission rate is decreased.

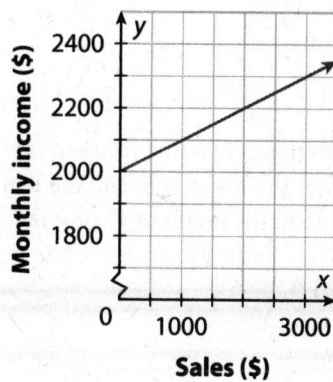 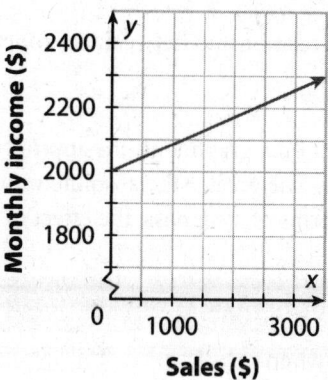

18. Mr. Resnick is driving at a speed of 40 miles per hour to visit relatives who live 100 miles away from his home. His distance d (in miles) from his destination is given by the function $d(t) = 100 - 40t$, where t is the time (in hours) since his trip began. Sketch a graph to illustrate each situation. The graphs shown already represent the function $d(t)$.

a. He increases his speed to get to the destination sooner. (Hint: His distance from the destination decreases faster.)

b. His starting distance from the destination is increased because a detour forces him to take a longer route.

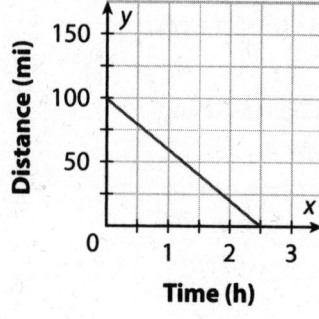 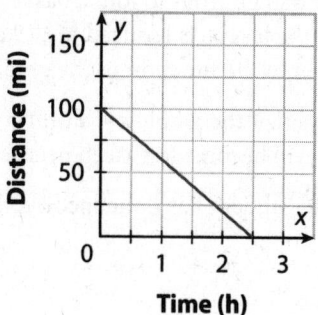

c. Give an example of another linear function within the same family of functions as $d(t) = 100 - 40t$. Explain the meaning of each parameter in your example.

19. A book club charges a membership fee of $20 and then $12 for each book purchased.

    a. Write a function to represent the cost y of membership in the club based on the number of books purchased x.

    b. Write a second function to represent the cost of membership if the club raises its membership fee to $30.

    c. Describe the relationship between the functions from parts A and B.

20. Match each effect on a graph with the appropriate change in m. The *steepness* of a line refers to the absolute value of its slope. The greater the absolute value of the slope, the steeper the line. Complete the table to summarize, in terms of steepness, the effect of changing the value of m on the graph of $f(x) = mx$.

How the Value of m Changes	Effect on the Graph of $f(x) = mx$
A. Increase m when $m > 1$.	_____ Graph becomes steeper.
B. Decrease m when $0 < m < 1$.	_____ Graph becomes less steep.
C. Decrease m when $m < -1$.	_____ Graph becomes steeper.
D. Increase m when $0 > m > -1$.	_____ Graph becomes less steep.

H.O.T. **Focus on Higher Order Thinking**

21. **Explain the Error** A student is asked to explain what happens with each of the parameters for the following situation.

It costs a player $20 up front to join a basketball league and then $5 a week to play. If the cost to join the league is reduced to $19 and the weekly fee increases to $6 a week, what will happen to the function of the graph?

The student says that the graph will shift up because the value of b has increased and then the graph will become less steep because the value of m has decreased.

Explain what the student has done incorrectly.

22. Critique Reasoning Geoff says that changing the value of m while leaving b unchanged in $f(x) = mx + b$ has no impact on the intercepts of the graph. Marcus disagrees with this statement. Who is correct? Explain your reasoning.

23. Multiple Representations The graph of $y = x + 3$ is a vertical translation of the graph of $y = x + 1$, 2 units upward. Examine the intercepts of both lines and state another way that the geometric relationship between the two graphs can be described.

24. Critique Reasoning Stephanie says that the graphs of $y = 3x + 2$ and $y = 3x - 2$ are parallel. Isabella says that the graphs are perpendicular. Who is correct? Explain your reasoning.

25. Critical Thinking It has been shown that the graph of $g(x) = x + 3$ is the result of translating the graph of $f(x) = x$ three units up. However, this can also be thought of as a horizontal translation—that is, a translation left or right. Describe the horizontal translation of $f(x) = x$ to get the graph of $g(x) = x + 3$.

Lesson Performance Task

High-demand cars that are also in low supply tend to retain their value better than other cars. The data in the table is for a car that won a resale value award.

Year	1	3	5
Value (%)	84	64	44

a. Write a function to represent the change in the percentage of the car's value over time. Assume that the function is linear for the first 5 years.

b. According to the model, by what percent did the car's value drop the day it was purchased and driven off the lot?

c. Would the linear model be useful after 10 years? Explain why or why not.

d. Suppose months were used instead of years to write the function. How would the model change? What is the relationship of the new function to the original function?

6.5 Comparing Properties of Linear Functions

Essential Question: How can you compare linear functions that are represented in different ways?

Resource
Locker

🧭 Explore Comparing Properties of Linear Functions Given Algebra and a Description

Comparing linear relationships can involve comparing relationships that are expressed in different ways.

Dan's Plumbing and Kim's Plumbing have different ways of charging their customers. The function $D(t) = 35t$ represents the total amount in dollars that Dan's Plumbing charges for t hours of work. Kim's Plumbing charges \$35 per hour plus a \$40 flat-rate fee.

(A) Define a function $K(t)$ that represents the total amount Kim's Plumbing charges for t hours of work and then complete the tables.

_____

_____

Cost for Dan's Plumbing		
t	$D(t) = 35t$	$(t, D(t))$
0		
1		
2		
3		

Cost for Kim's Plumbing		
t	$K(t) =$	$(t, K(t))$
0		
1		
2		
3		

(B) What domain and range values for the functions $D(t)$ and for $K(t)$ are reasonable in this context? Explain.

_____

_____

_____

_____

_____

(C) Graph the two cost functions for the appropriate domain values.

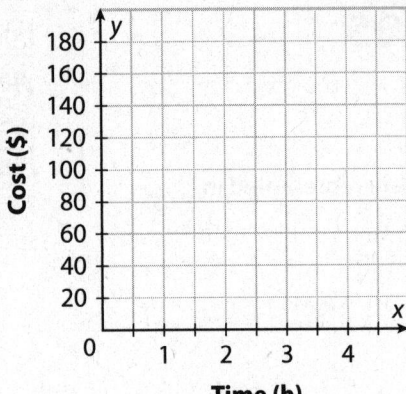

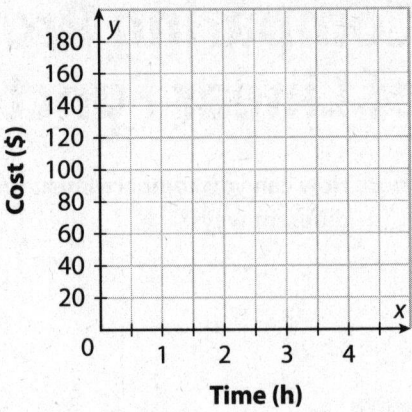

(D) Compare the graphs. How are they alike? How are they different?

_____

Reflect

1. **Discussion** What information could be found about the two functions without changing their representation?

_____

✎ Explain 1 Comparing Properties of Linear Functions Given Algebra and a Table

A table and a rule are two ways that a linear relationship may be expressed. Sometimes it may be helpful to convert one representation to the other when comparing two relationships. There are other times when comparisons are possible without converting either representation.

Example 1 Compare the initial value and the range for each of the linear functions $f(x)$ and $g(x)$.

(A) The domain of each function is the set of all real numbers x such that $5 \leq x \leq 8$. The table shows some ordered pairs for $f(x)$. The function $g(x)$ is defined by the rule $g(x) = 3x + 7$.

x	f(x)
5	20
6	24
7	28
8	32

The initial value is the output that is paired with the least input. The least input for $f(x)$ and $g(x)$ is 5.

The initial value of $f(x)$ is $f(5) = 20$.

The initial value of $g(x)$ is $g(5) = 3(5) + 7 = 22$.

Since $f(x)$ is a linear function and its domain is the set of all real numbers from 5 to 8, its range will be the set of all real numbers from $f(5)$ to $f(8)$. Since $f(5) = 20$ and $f(8) = 32$, the range of $f(x)$ is the set of all real numbers such that $20 \leq f(x) \leq 32$.

Since $g(x)$ is a linear function and its domain is the set of all real numbers from 5 to 8, its range will be the set of all real numbers from $g(5)$ to $g(8)$. Since $g(5) = 22$ and $g(8) = 3(8) + 7 = 31$, the range of $g(x)$ is the set of all real numbers such that $22 \leq g(x) \leq 31$.

(B) The domain of each function is the set of all real numbers x such that $6 \leq x \leq 10$. The table shows some ordered pairs for $f(x)$. The function $g(x)$ is defined by the rule $g(x) = 5x + 11$.

x	f(x)
6	36
7	42
8	48
9	54
10	60

The initial value is the output that is paired with the least input. The least input for $f(x)$ and $g(x)$ is _____.

The initial value of $f(x)$ is _____.

The initial value of $g(x)$ is _____.

Since $f(x)$ is a linear function, and its domain is the set of all real numbers from _____ to 10, its range will be the set of all real numbers from $f\left(\boxed{}\right)$ to $f(10)$. Since $f\left(\boxed{}\right) = \boxed{}$ and $f(10) = \boxed{}$, the range of $f(x)$ is the set of all real numbers such that $\boxed{} \leq f(x) \leq \boxed{}$.

Since $g(x)$ is a linear function and its domain is the set of all real numbers from _____ to 10, its range will be the set of all real numbers from $g\left(\boxed{}\right)$ to $g(10)$. Since $g\left(\boxed{}\right) = \boxed{}$ and

$g(10) = 5\left(\boxed{}\right) + 11 = \boxed{}$, the range of $g(x)$ is the set of all real numbers such that $\boxed{} \leq g(x) \leq \boxed{}$.

Reflect

2. **Discussion** How can you use a table of values to find the rate of change for a linear function?

_____

_____

Your Turn

3. Find the rate of change for the linear function $f(x)$ that is shown in the table.

x	f(x)
3	22
4	29
5	36
6	43
7	50

4. The rule for $f(x)$ in Example 1B is $f(x) = 6x$. If the domains were extended to all real numbers, how would the slopes and y-intercepts of $f(x)$ and $g(x) = 5x + 11$ in Example 1B compare?

© Houghton Mifflin Harcourt Publishing Company

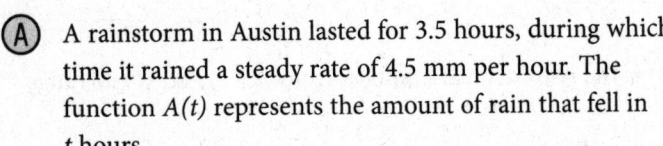

Explain 2   Comparing Properties of Linear Functions Given a Graph and a Description

Information about a linear relationship may have to be inferred from the context given in the problem.

Example 2   Write a rule for each function, and then compare their domain, range, slope, and *y*-intercept.

(A) A rainstorm in Austin lasted for 3.5 hours, during which time it rained a steady rate of 4.5 mm per hour. The function $A(t)$ represents the amount of rain that fell in t hours.

The graph shows the amount of rain that fell during the same rainstorm in Dallas, $D(t)$ (in millimeters), as a function of time t (in hours).

Write a rule for each function. $A(t) = 4.5t$ for $0 \leq t \leq 3.5$

The line representing $D(t)$ has endpoints at $(0, 0)$ and $(4, 20)$. The slope of $D(t)$ is $\frac{20 - 0}{4 - 0} = 5$. The *y*-intercept is 0, so substituting 5 for m and 0 for b in $y = mx + b$ produces the equation $y = 5x$. This can be represented by the function $D(t) = 5t$, for $0 \leq t \leq 4$.

The domains of each function both begin at 0 but end for different values of t, because the lengths of time that it rained in Austin and Dallas were not the same.

The range for $A(t)$ is $0 \leq A(t) \leq 15.75$. The range for $D(t)$ is $0 \leq A(t) \leq 20$.

The slope for $D(t)$ is 5, which is greater than the slope for $A(t)$, which is 4.5.

The *y*-intercepts of both functions are 0.

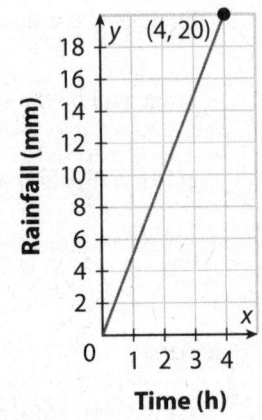

Time (h)

© Houghton Mifflin Harcourt Publishing Company • Image Credits: ©Getty Images

B One group of hikers hiked at a steady rate of 6.5 kilometers per hour for 4 hours. The function $f(t)$ represents the distance this group of hikers hiked in t hours.

The graph shows the distance a second group of hikers hiked, $g(t)$ (in kilometers), as a function of t (in hours).

Write a rule for each function.

$f(t) = \boxed{}$ for $\boxed{} \leq t \leq \boxed{}$

The line representing $g(t)$ has endpoints at $(0, 0)$

and $\left(\boxed{}, \boxed{}\right)$. The slope of $g(t)$ is $\dfrac{\boxed{} - 0}{\boxed{} - 0} = \boxed{}$.

The y-intercept is _____, so substituting _____ for m and _____ for b in $y = mx + b$ produces the equation

$y = \boxed{}$. This can be represented by the function $g(t) = \boxed{}$ for $\boxed{} \leq t \leq \boxed{}$.

The domains of each function both begin at _____ and end at _____ values of t.

The range for $f(t)$ is $\boxed{} \leq f(t) \leq \boxed{}$ and the range for $g(t)$ is $\boxed{} \leq g(t) \leq \boxed{}$.

The slope for _____ is greater than the slope for _____.

The y-intercepts are _____.

Distance (km) — Time (h), with point (4.5, 36)

5. What is the meaning of the y-intercepts for the functions $A(t)$ and $D(t)$ in Example 2A?

_____

_____

_____

Your Turn

6. An experiment compares the heights of two plants over time. A plant was 5 cm tall at the beginning of the experiment and grew 0.3 centimeters each day. The function $f(t)$ represents the height of the plant (in centimeters) after t days. The graph shows the height of the second plant, $g(t)$ (in centimeters), as a function of time t (in days).

Find the rate of change $g(t)$ and compare it to the rate of change for $f(t)$.

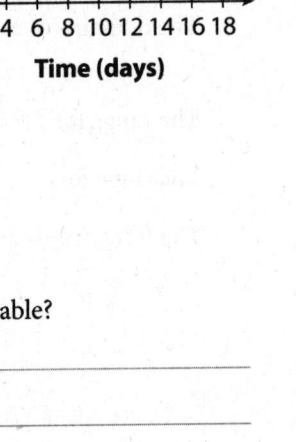

Elaborate

7. When would representing a linear function by a graph be more helpful than by a table?

_____

_____

_____

8. When would representing a linear function by a table be more helpful than by a graph?

_____

_____

_____

9. **Essential Question-Check-In** How can you compare a linear function represented in a table to one represented as a graph?

_____

_____

_____

• Online Homework
• Hints and Help
• Extra Practice

Compare the initial value and the range for each of the linear functions $f(x)$ and $g(x)$.

1. The domain of each function is the set of all real numbers x such that $2 \leq x \leq 5$. The table shows some ordered pairs for $f(x)$. The function $g(x)$ is defined by the rule $g(x) = x + 6$.

x	f(x)
2	5
3	7
4	9
5	11

2. The domain of each function is the set of all real numbers x such that $8 \leq x \leq 12$. The table shows some ordered pairs for $f(x)$. The function $g(x)$ is defined by the rule $g(x) = 7x - 3$.

x	f(x)
8	34
9	38
10	42
11	46
12	50

3. The domain of each function is the set of all real numbers x such that $-4 \leq x \leq -1$. The function $f(x)$ is defined by the rule $f(x) = 2x + 9$. The table shows some ordered pairs for $g(x)$.

x	g(x)
−4	10
−3	9
−2	8
−1	7

4. The domain of each function is the set of all real numbers x such that $0 \leq x \leq 4$. The function $f(x)$ is defined by the rule $f(x) = -3x + 15$. The table shows some ordered pairs for $g(x)$.

x	g(x)
0	23
1	19
2	15
3	11
4	7

5. The domain of each function is the set of all real numbers x such that $10 \leq x \leq 13$. The table shows some ordered pairs for $f(x)$. The function $g(x)$ is defined by the rule $g(x) = \frac{1}{2}x + 12$.

x	f(x)
10	22
11	$\frac{47}{2}$
12	25
13	$\frac{53}{2}$

6. The domain of each function is the set of all real numbers x such that $2 \leq x \leq 6$. The function $f(x)$ is defined by the rule $f(x) = -\frac{3}{4}x + 10$. The table shows some ordered pairs for $g(x)$.

x	g(x)
2	14
3	$\frac{51}{4}$
4	$\frac{23}{2}$
5	$\frac{41}{4}$
6	9

Write a rule for each function f and g, and then compare their domains, ranges, slopes, and y-intercepts.

7. The function $f(x)$ has a slope of 6 and has a y-intercept of 20. The graph shows the function $g(x)$.

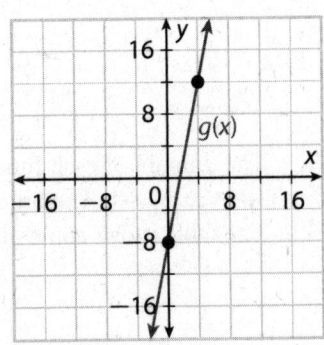

8. The function $f(x)$ has a slope of -3 and has a y-intercept of 5. The graph shows the function $g(x)$.

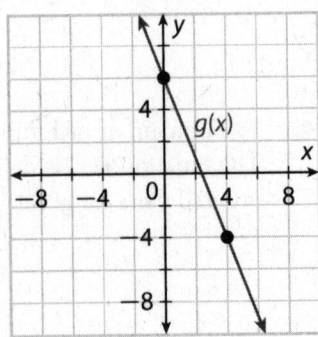

Write a rule for each function, and then compare their domains, ranges, slopes, and y-intercepts.

9. Jeff, an electrician, had a job that lasted 5.5 hours, during which time he earned $32 per hour and charged a $25 service fee. The function $J(t)$ represents the amount Jeff earns in t hours.

Brendan also works as an electrician. The graph of $B(t)$ shows the amount in dollars that Brendan earns as a function of time t in hours.

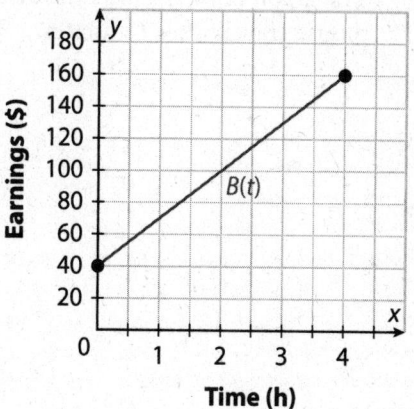

10. Apples can be bought at a farmer's market up to 10 pounds at a time, where each pound costs $1.10. The function $a(w)$ represents the cost of buying w pounds of apples.

The graph of $p(w)$ shows the cost in dollars of buying w pounds of pears.

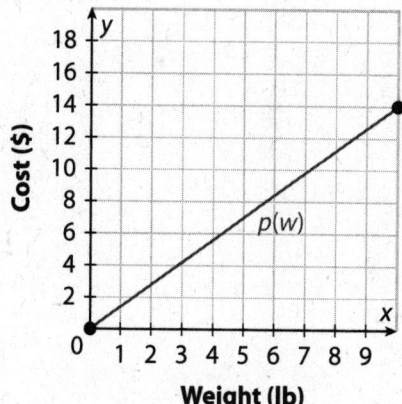

11. **Biology** A gecko travels for 6 minutes at a constant rate of 19 meters per minute. The function $g(t)$ represents the distance the gecko travels after t minutes.

The graph of $m(t)$ shows the distance in meters that a mouse travels after t minutes.

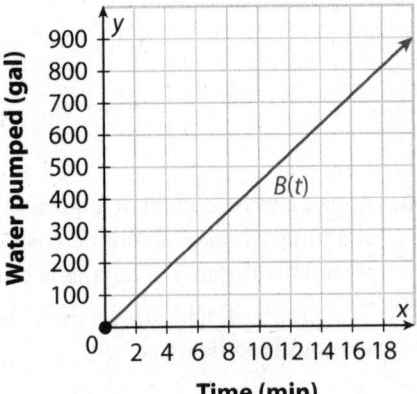

12. Cindy is buying a water pump. The box for Pump A claims that it can move 48 gallons per minute. The function $A(t)$ represents the amount of water (in gallons) Pump A can move after t minutes.

The graph of $B(t)$ shows the amount of water in gallons that Pump B can move after t minutes.

13. Erin is comparing two rental car companies for an upcoming trip. The function $A(d) = 0.20d$ represents the total amount in dollars of driving a car d miles from company A. Company B charges $0.10 per mile and a $10 fee.

a. Define a function $B(d)$ that represents the total amount company B charges for driving d miles and then complete the tables.

Cost for Company A		
d	$A(d) = 0.20d$	$(d, A(d))$
0		
20		
40		

Cost for Company B		
d	$B(d) =$	$(d, B(d))$
0		
20		
40		

b. Graph and label the two cost functions for all appropriate domain values.

c. Compare the graphs. How are they alike? How are they different?

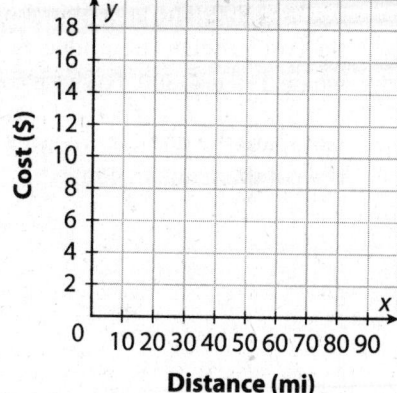

14. Snow is falling in two cities. The function $C(t) = 2t + 8$ represents the amount of snow on the ground, in centimeters, in Carlisle t hours after the snowstorm begins. There was 8 cm of snow on the ground in York when the storm began and the snow accumulates at 1.5 cm per hour.

a. Define a function $Y(t)$ that represents the amount of snow on the ground after t hours in York and then complete the tables.

Carlisle		
t	$C(t) = 2t + 8$	$(t, C(t))$
0		
1		
2		

York		
t	$Y(t) =$	$(t, Y(t))$
0		
1		
2		

b. Graph and label the two cost functions for all appropriate domain values.

c. Compare the graphs. How are they alike? How are they different?

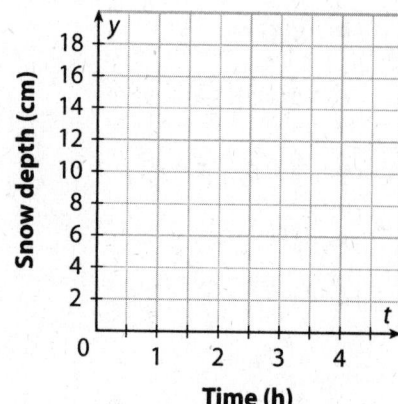

15. Gillian works from 20 to 30 hours per week during the summer. She earns $12.50 per hour. Her friend Emily also has a job. Her pay for t hours each week is given by the function $e(t) = 13t$, where $15 \leq t \leq 25$.

a. Find the domain and range of each function.

b. Compare their hourly wages and the amount they earn per week.

16. The function $A(p)$ defined by the rule $A(p) = 0.13p + 15$ represents the cost in dollars of producing a custom textbook that has p pages for college A, where $0 < p \leq 500$. The table shows some ordered pairs for $B(p)$, where $B(p)$ represents the cost in dollars of producing a custom textbook that has p pages for college B, where $0 < p \leq 500$. For both colleges, only full pages may be printed.

Compare the domain, range, slope, and y-intercept of the functions. Interpret the comparisons in context.

p	B(p)
0	24
50	30
100	36
150	42

17. Complete the table so that $f(x)$ is a linear function with a slope of 4 and a y-intercept of 7. Assume the domain includes all real numbers between the least and greatest values shown in the table. Compare $f(x)$ to $g(x) = 4x + 7$ if the range of $g(x)$ is $-1 \leq g(x) \leq 11$.

x	f(x)
−2	
−1	
0	
1	

18. Which functions have a rate of change that is greater than the one shown in the graph? Select all that apply.

a. $f(x) = \frac{1}{2}x - 5$

b. $g(x) = x + 6$

c. $h(x) = \frac{3}{4}x - 9$

d. $j(x) = \frac{1}{4}x + 8$

e. $k(x) = x$

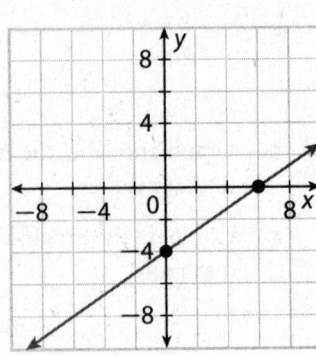

19. Does the function $f(x) = 5x + 5$ with the domain $6 \leq x \leq 8$ have the same domain as function $g(x)$, whose only function values are shown in the table? Explain.

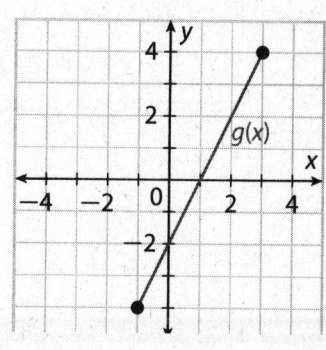

x	g(x)
6	35
7	40
8	45

20. The linear function $f(x)$ is defined by the table, and the linear function $g(x)$ is shown in the graph. Assume that the domain of $f(x)$ includes all real numbers between the least and greatest values shown in the table.

a. Find the domain and range of each function, and compare them.

x	f(x)
−1	−7
0	−4
1	−1
2	2
3	5

b. What is the slope of the line represented by each function? What is the y-intercept of each function?

21. The linear function $f(x)$ is defined by $f(x) = -\frac{1}{4}x + 6$ for all real numbers, and the linear function $g(x)$ is shown in the graph.

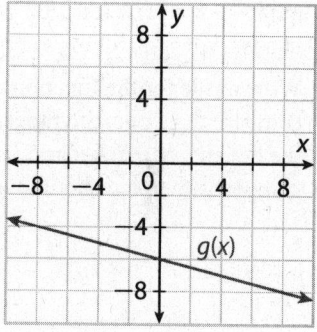

a. Find the domain and range of each function, and compare them.

b. What is the slope of the line represented by each function? What is the y-intercept of each function?

H.O.T. Focus on Higher Order Thinking

22. Communicate Mathematical Ideas Describe a linear function for which the least value in the range does not occur at the least value of the domain (a function for which the least value in the range is not the initial value.)

23. Draw Conclusions Two linear functions have the same slope, same x-intercept, and same y-intercept. Must these functions be identical? Explain your reasoning.

24. Draw Conclusions Let $f(x)$ be a line with slope -3 and y-intercept 0 with domain $\{0, 1, 2, 3\}$, and let $g(x) = \{(0, 0), (1, -1), (2, -4), (3, -9)\}$. Compare the two functions.

25. Draw Conclusions Let $f(x)$ be a line with slope 7 and y-intercept -17 with domain $0 \leq x \leq 5$, and let $g(x) = \Big\{(0, -17), (1, -10), (2, -3), (3, 4), (4, 11), (5, 18)\Big\}$. Compare the two functions.

Lesson Performance Task

Lindsay found a new job as an insurance salesperson. She has her choice of two different compensation plans. Plan F was described to her as a \$450 base weekly salary plus a 10% commission on the amount of sales she made that week. The function $f(x)$ represents the amount Lindsay earns in a week when making sales of x dollars with compensation plan F. Plan G was described to her with the graph shown. The function $g(x)$ represents the amount Lindsay earns in a week when making sales of x dollars with compensation plan G.

Write a rule for the functions $f(x)$ and $g(x)$; then identify and compare their domain, range, slope, and y-intercept. Compare the benefits and drawbacks of each compensation plan. Which compensation plan should Lindsay take? Justify your answer.

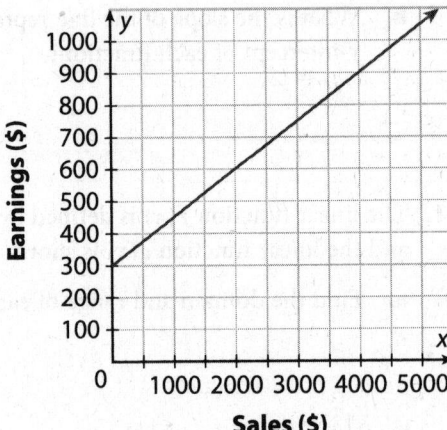

Forms of Linear Equations

Essential Question: How can you use different forms of linear equations to solve real-world problems?

KEY EXAMPLE *(Lesson 6.1)*

For one taxi company, the cost y in dollars of a ride is a linear function of the miles traveled x. The initial charge is $2.00, and the charge per mile is $0.40. Identify the slope and y-intercept of the graph that represents this situation and interpret what they mean. Then write an equation in slope-intercept form and use it to find the cost of riding 15 miles.

The rate of change is $0.40 per mile, so the slope m is 0.4.

The initial cost is the cost to travel 0 miles, $2.00, so the y-intercept b is 2.

So, the equation in slope-intercept form is $y = 0.4x + 2$.

To find the cost of riding 15 miles, substitute 15 for x and simplify.

$$y = 0.4x + 2$$
$$= 0.4(15) + 2$$
$$= 6 + 2$$
$$= 8$$

(15, 8) is a solution of the equation, and the cost of riding 15 miles is $8.

KEY EXAMPLE *(Lesson 6.3)*

Write an equation in standard form for the line that contains $(-3, 4)$ and $(5, 0)$.

Find the slope using the given points.

$$m = \frac{y_2 - y_1}{x_2 - x_1} = \frac{0 - 4}{5 - (-3)} = \frac{-4}{8} = -\frac{1}{2}$$

Substitute the slope and the coordinates of either of the points in point-slope form.

$$y - y_1 = m(x - x_1)$$
$$y - 0 = -\frac{1}{2}(x - 5)$$
$$y = -\frac{1}{2}x + \frac{5}{2}$$

Rewrite in standard form. $x + 2y = 5$

EXERCISES

Write the equation of each line in slope-intercept form. *(Lesson 6.1)*

1. slope is 4 and contains (3, 6)

2. contains (5, 0) and (9, 4)

Write the equation of each line in point-slope form. *(Lesson 6.2)*

3. slope is −1 and contains (2, 7)

4. contains (−2, 8) and (4, −4)

Write the equation of each line in standard form. *(Lesson 6.3)*

5. slope is 3 and contains (1, 6)

6. contains (0, −2) and (10, 2)

7. Describe a series of transformations of the graph of $f(x) = x$ that results in the graph of $g(x) = -x + 6$. *(Lesson 6.4)*

8. Compare the domain and range of $f(x) = -3x + 5$ and $g(x) = 4x - 6$. *(Lesson 6.5)*

MODULE PERFORMANCE TASK

Who Wins the Race?

Jamal and Kendra are running in a 26.2-mile marathon. Jamal's friend is recording his times in the table as shown, while Kendra's friend uses a scatter plot to show her progress. If both runners continue at the same average pace, who will arrive at the finish line first? How much longer will it take for the other person to finish?

Jamal's Race	
Distance (mi)	**Time (min)**
4	26
8	56
12	90
16	128
20	170

Kendra's Distance vs. Time

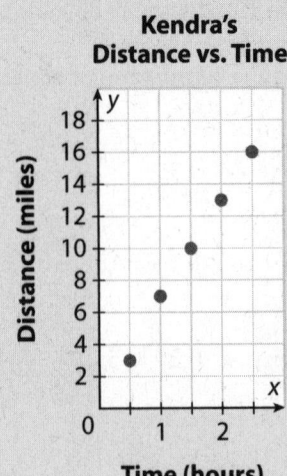

Use your own paper to complete the task. Be sure to write down all your data and assumptions. Then use graphs, numbers, words, or algebra to explain how you reached your conclusion.

(Ready) to Go On?

6.1–6.5 Forms of Linear Equations

• Online Homework
• Hints and Help
• Extra Practice

Write an equation for each line in the given form. *(Lessons 6.1, 6.2, 6.3)*

1. slope is −2 and (1, 7) is on the line; standard form

2. contains the points (3, 4) and (6, 10); slope-intercept form

3. slope is 4 and (−3, 8) is on the line; point-slope form

4. Describe a transformation of the graph of $f(x) = x$ that results in the graph of $g(x) = 4x$.
(Lesson 6.4)

5. Jan works from 30 to 40 hours per week during the summer. She earns $12.00 per hour. Her friend Rachel also has a job. Rachel's pay for t hours is given by the function $r(t) = 11t$, where $20 \leq t \leq 30$. Find the domain and range of each function. Compare their hourly wages and the amount they earn per week. *(Lesson 6.5)*

ESSENTIAL QUESTION

6. What type or types of transformations can affect the slope of a linear function? What type or types cannot?

Assessment Readiness

1. Look at each equation. Does the equation represent a line with slope $m = 5$, containing the point (3, 8)? Select Yes or No for each equation.

   A. $5x - y = 7$ ○ Yes   ○ No

   B. $3x + 8y = 5$ ○ Yes   ○ No

   C. $10x - 2y = 14$ ○ Yes   ○ No

2. Consider the function $f(x) = 3x - 2$. Select True or False for each statement.

   A. The y-intercept is 2.   ○ True   ○ False

   B. The x-intercept is $\frac{2}{3}$.   ○ True   ○ False

   C. The slope is 3.   ○ True   ○ False

3. Look at each statement. Does the statement describe a transformation of the graph of $f(x) = x$ that would result in the graph of $g(x) = x + 2$? Select Yes or No for each statement.

   A. The graph of the parent function is reflected across the y-axis.   ○ Yes   ○ No

   B. The graph of the parent function is translated 2 units up.   ○ Yes   ○ No

   C. The graph of the parent function is translated 2 units down.   ○ Yes   ○ No

4. What is the x-intercept of $y + 12 = 3(x - 9)$? Explain how you solved this problem.

5. Write $5x - 3y = -12$ in slope-intercept form. What is the slope? Show your work.

Linear Equations and Inequalities

Essential Question: How can you use linear equations and inequalities to solve real-world problems?

REAL WORLD VIDEO
In some sports, such as boxing and wrestling, the athletes and their competitions are categorized by weight. The weight divisions are defined by specific upper and lower weight limits, which can be efficiently described using inequalities.

© Houghton Mifflin Harcourt Publishing Company • Image Credit: ©Image Source/Getty Images

MODULE PERFORMANCE TASK PREVIEW

Making Weight

Wrestling is a physically demanding contact sport in which two athletes grapple on a mat with the goal of out-maneuvering and gaining control over the opponent. Opponents are matched up based on weight, and there are several weight classes. How can athletes use models to help them meet their weight class goals? Let's hit the mat and find out!

Are YOU Ready?

Complete these exercises to review skills you will need for this module.

Algebraic Expressions

Example 1 Evaluate $5x + 6y$ for $x = -9$ and $y = 7$.

$5x + 6y$

$5(-9) + 6(7)$ Substitute -9 for x and 7 for y.

$-45 + 42$ Multiply.

-3 Add.

Evaluate each expression for the given values of the variables.

1. $7p + 3q$ for $p = 2$ and $q = -6$

2. $(n + 1)^2$ for $n = -9$

3. $4d - 2e - 13$ for $d = 5$ and $e = -7$

4. $a^2 - b$ for $a = 4$ and $b = 5$

Graphing Linear Proportional Relationships

Example 2 Tell whether the graph represents a linear proportional relationship.

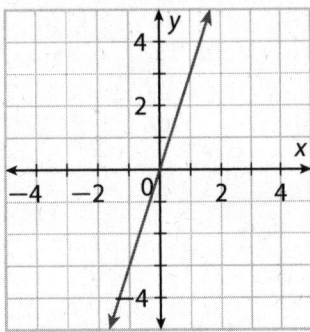

The graph of a proportional relationship is a straight line that passes through the origin.

The graph is a straight line that passes through $(0, 0)$, so it represents a linear proportional relationship.

Tell whether the graph represents a linear proportional relationship.

5.

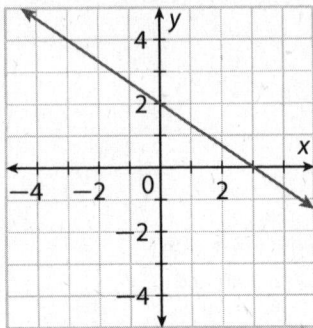

6.

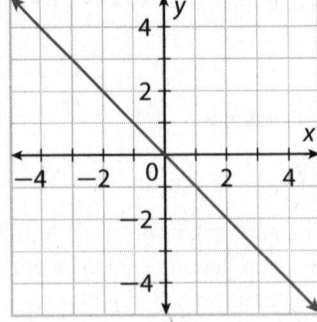

7.1 Modeling Linear Relationships

Essential Question: How can you model linear relationships given limited information?

Resource Locker

⊘ Explore Modeling Linear Relationships with Slope-Intercept Form

A department store offers a frequent-buyers card to earn rewards for purchases customers make at the store. Each transaction is worth 12 points, and customers automatically earn 25 points when they sign up.

Write an equation for the function that gives the card value based on the number of transactions that have occurred.

(A) What units would be associated with the variables in this function?

_____

(B) Complete the verbal model for the frequent-buyers card function. Include units.

Card Value (points) = Initial Value (points) + ⬚ · ⬚

(C) Write the function rule for the card-value function C.

$C(t) = $ ⬚ $+$ ⬚ t, where t is the number of transactions.

(D) For each 100 points, the customer receives a gift certificate. How many transactions will it take for the customer to earn the first gift certificate?

_____

_____

_____

_____

_____

(E) What is the y-intercept for this linear function, and what does it represent?

_____

_____

(F) What is the slope for this linear function, and what does it represent?

_____

_____

1. **Discussion** Use the function rule to show that the units for $C(t)$ are points.

    _____

2. **Critical Thinking** What types of number are appropriate for the domain of $C(t)$?

    _____

    _____

3. Using inequalities, express the restrictions on the range of $C(t)$.

    _____

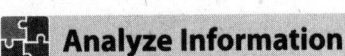 **Explain** **Creating and Interpreting Linear Models**

You can create linear equations and inequalities to model some real-world situations.

Example   **Given the real-world situation, solve the problem.**

Fundraising The Band Booster Club is selling T-shirts and blanket wraps to raise money for a trip. The band director has asked the club to raise at least $1000.

The booster club president wants to know how many T-shirts and how many blanket wraps the club needs to sell to meet their goal of $1000. The T-shirts cost $10 each, and the blanket wraps cost $25 each. Write a linear equation that describes the problem, and then graph the linear equation. How can the booster club president use the sales price of each item to meet the goal?

Analyze Information

Identify the important information.

- T-shirts cost $_____ each.

- Blanket wraps cost $_____ each.

- The booster club needs to raise a total of $_____ .

Formulate a Plan

The total amount of revenue earned by selling T-shirts is $_____ t. The total amount

of revenue earned from selling blanket wraps is $_____ b. These two results can be

added and set equal to the sales goal to find the number of T-shirts and blanket

wraps that need to be sold to reach $_____ . Graph this function to find all of the

possible combinations of T-shirts and blanket wraps sold to reach $_____ .

Solve

Write a linear equation for the sales goal.

$$\boxed{}\, b + \boxed{}\, t = \boxed{}$$

© Houghton Mifflin Harcourt Publishing Company • Image Credits: ©B Christopher/Alamy

Calculate three pairs of values for t and b, and graph a line through those points to find possible solutions. Be sure to label the graph.

t	b
0	
50	
	0

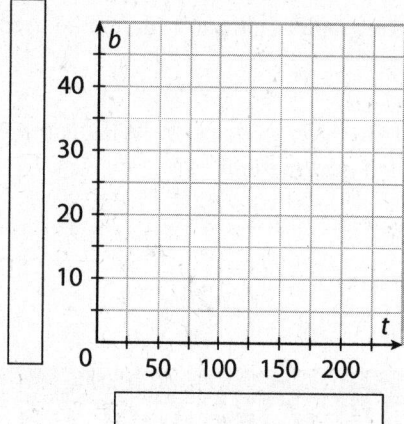

Justify and Evaluate

The x-intercept represents the number of _____ that need to be sold if no _____

are sold. The y-intercept represents the number of _____ to be sold if no _____

are sold. The booster club president can use the _____ to find the possible combinations

of T-shirts and blankets to reach $_____.

Reflect

4. **Critical Thinking** Technically, the graph of possible combinations of T-shirts and blanket wraps that reach the goal of $1000 should be discrete, but for convenience the graph is shown as a connected line. Explain why the solutions to this problem would be only the points on the line that have whole-number coordinates.

_____

_____

Your Turn

5. **Business** A sandwich shop sell sandwiches for $5 each and bottles of water for $1 each. The owner of this shop needs to earn a total of $100 by the end of the day. Write a linear equation that describes the problem; then graph the linear equation. Make sure to label both axes with appropriate titles. Then use the graph to determine how many sandwiches the shop must sell if no waters are sold.

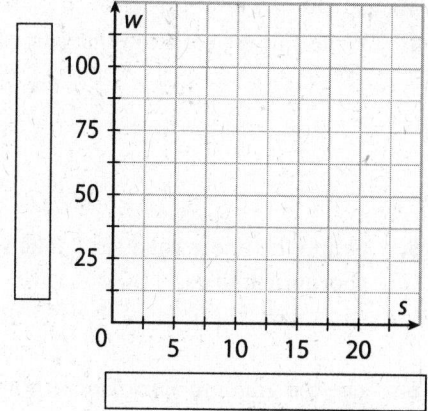

6. How can the graph of a linear function be used to find answers to a real-world problem?

_____

7. **Essential Question Check-In** What is the first step when modeling linear relationships given limited information?

_____

⭐ Evaluate: Homework and Practice

- Online Homework
- Hints and Help
- Extra Practice

Food A baker sells bread for $3 a loaf and rolls for $1 each. The baker needs to sell $24 worth of baked goods by the end of the day.

1. Write a linear equation that describes the problem.

2. Graph the linear equation. Make sure to label both axes with appropriate titles.

3. Use the graph to approximate how many loaves of bread the baker must sell if 12 rolls are sold.

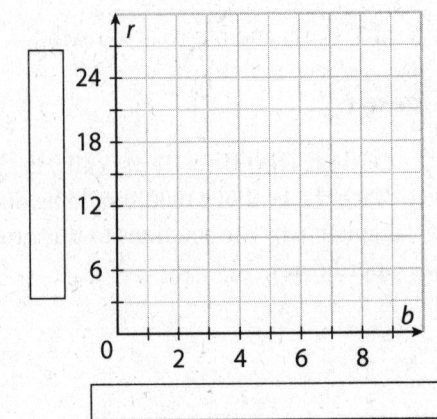

Charity A local charity is selling seats to a baseball game. Seats cost $20 each, and snacks cost an additional $5 each. The charity needs to raise $400 to consider this event a success.

4. Write a linear equation that describes the problem.

5. Graph the linear equation. Make sure to label both axes with appropriate titles.

6. Use the graph to approximate how many snacks the charity must sell if 10 seats are sold.

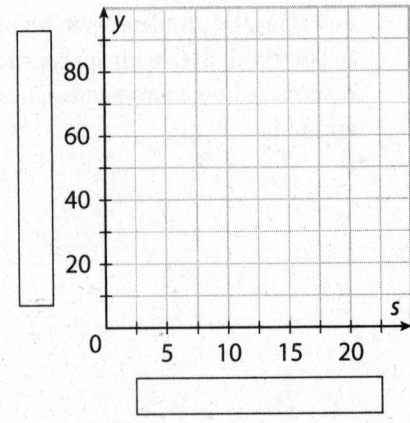

Movies A movie theater sells tickets to a new show for $10 each. The theater also sells small containers of popcorn for $6 each. The theater needs to make $3000 in order to break even on the show.

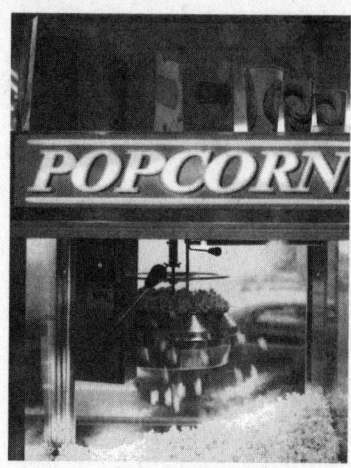

7. Write a linear equation that describes the problem.

8. Graph the linear equation. Make sure to label both axes with appropriate titles.

9. Use the graph to approximate how many buckets of popcorn must the movie theater must sell if it sells 210 movie tickets.

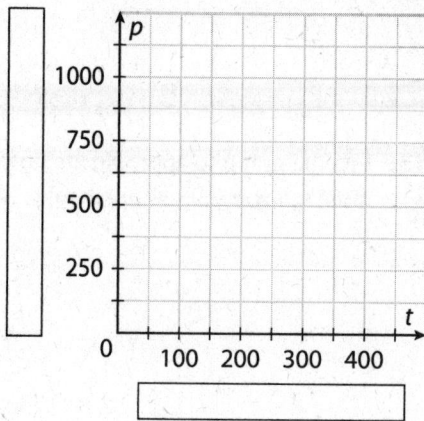

Sports A golf course charges $18 for a package including the full 18-hole course. The course also sells buckets of golf balls for $20 each. The golf course would like to earn $400 by the end of the day.

10. Write a linear equation that describes the problem.

11. Graph the linear equation. Make sure to label both axes with appropriate titles.

12. Use the graph to approximate how many buckets of balls the golf course must sell if it sells 10 course packages.

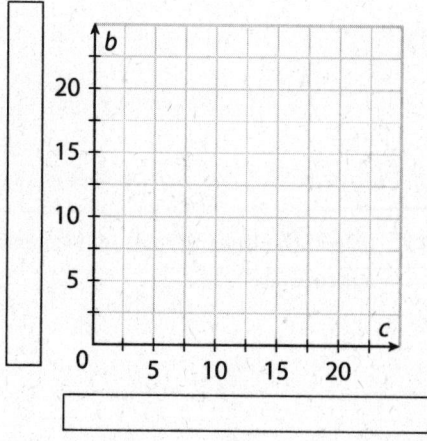

Reading A bookstore sells textbooks for $80 each and notebooks for $4 each. The bookstore would like to sell $800 in merchandise by the end of the week.

13. Write a linear equation that describes the problem.

14. Graph the linear equation. Make sure to label both axes with appropriate titles.

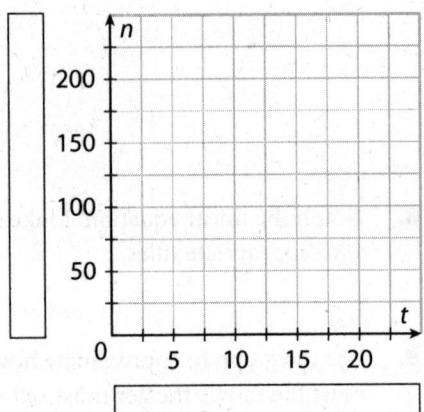

15. Use the graph to approximate how many textbooks the bookstore must sell if it sells 40 notebooks.

Fitness A gym is selling monthly memberships for $30 each and reusable water bottles for $7 each. The gym needs to make $1050 by the end of the month.

16. Write a linear equation that describes the problem.

17. Graph the linear equation. Make sure to label both axes with appropriate titles.

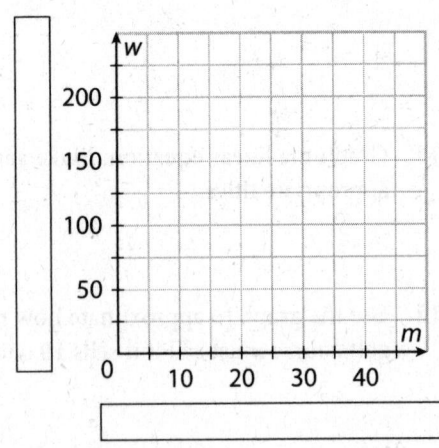

18. Use the graph to approximate the number of water bottles that the gym must sell if it sells 28 gym memberships.

A shoe store offers a frequent-buyers card. Each transaction is worth 8 points, and customers automatically earn 20 points when they sign up.

19. The value of the card is a function of the number of transactions. What are the units for a card?

20. Complete the verbal model for the transaction function. Include units.

Card Value   =   Initial Value   +   [   ]   ·   [   ]
(points)   (points)

21. Write the function rule for the transaction function.

$N(p) = $ [   ] $+$ [   ] p

In graphing the function, _____ would be the slope and _____ would be the y-intercept.

22. In each equation of the form $ax + by = c$, state a, b, and c.

$y = 2$

$3x = 0$

$3x + 2y = 6$

$5x - y = 1$

$4y + 2x = 3$

23. **Critical Thinking** Suppose that you were given the graph of a monthly revenue function that is a linear relationship and are asked to interpret a point. What would it mean if the point were located on the graph, two units to the right of the origin and slightly above the y-intercept?

24. **Represent Real-World Problems** Describe a situation not used in the lesson that is best described by a linear relationship.

25. **Explain the Error** Consider the following situation. Lacie pays a babysitter an initial fee of $35 in addition to $6 per hour.
When trying to model this situation, Juan created the function $y = 35x + 6$.
Explain his error.

Lesson Performance Task

A computer store sells both tablets and laptops. One brand of tablet costs $200. That same brand of laptop costs $400. The store manager wants to sell enough of this brand of tablets and laptops to reach the sales goal of $20,000.

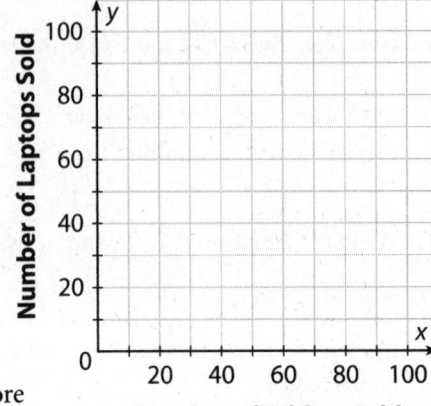

a. Write an equation that models the situation. Then graph the equation.

b. Interpret the *x*- and *y*-intercepts.

c. Will the store manager meet her goal if the sales team sells 45 tablets and 25 laptops? If so, explain. If not, find how many more tablets need to be sold to meet the goal.

d. Will the store manager meet her goal if the sales team sells 80 tablets and 10 laptops? If so, explain. If not, find how many more tablets need to be sold to meet the goal.

7.2 Using Functions to Solve One-Variable Equations

Essential Question: How can you use functions to solve one-variable equations?

Resource
Locker

⊘ Explore **Creating Functions to Solve One-Variable Equations**

Finance Susan wants to hire a babysitter for this weekend for her 3 children. She has two choices. Babysitter A charges $10 per child and $5 per hour. Babysitter B charges $15 per child and $2 per hour. When will they charge the same amount of money?

Ⓐ Write and solve a one-variable equation to find the number of hours for which the two babysitters will charge the same amount of money. Let x represent the number of hours.

Ⓑ Write a function for each babysitting service. Enter the two functions in a graphing calculator. Use the graphing calculator to compare their tables and find the intersection point of their graphs.

x	$f(x) = y_1$	$g(x) = y_2$
0		
1		
2		
3		
4		
5		
6		

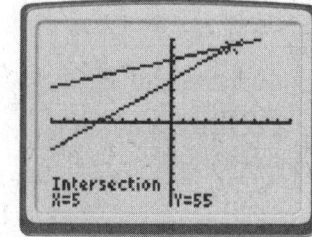

1. **Discussion** Why are the x-coordinates of the points where the graphs of the equations $f(x) = y_1$ and $g(x) = y_2$ intersect the solutions of the equation $f(x) = g(x)$.

_____

_____

_____

_____

2. **Discussion** How should the graph provided by the graphing calculator be changed to make the graph an accurate representation of this situation?

_____

_____

_____

🔑 Explain 1 Using Intersections to Determine Approximate Solutions of One-Variable Equations

You can use tables and graphs of the functions $y_1 = f(x)$ and $y_2 = g(x)$ to solve an equation of the form $f(x) = g(x)$.

Use a table and a graphing calculator to estimate the solution.

Example 1

(A) John needs to hire a painter. Painter A is offering his services for an initial $175 in addition to $14.25 per hour. Painter B is offering her services for an initial $200 in addition to $11 per hour. For what number of hours will the two painters charge the same amount of money?

$f(x) = 175 + 14.25x$
$g(x) = 200 + 11x$

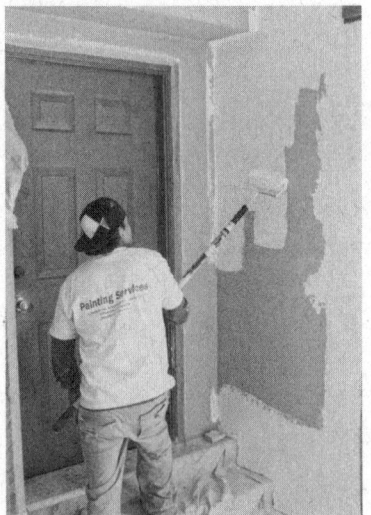

x	f(x)	g(x)
0	175	200
1	189.25	211
2	203.5	222
3	217.75	233
4	232	244
5	246.25	255
6	260.5	266
7	274.75	277
8	289	288

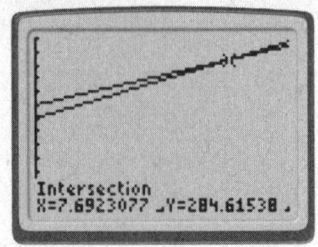

Intersection
X=7.6923077 Y=284.61538

From the table, the solution must be between 7 and 8 hours.

Based on the intersection point in the graph, the solution is approximately 7.7 hours.

Ⓑ Georgia is in need of an electrician. Electrician A is offering his services for an initial fee of $125 in addition to $45 per hour. Electrician B is offering her services for an initial fee of $150 in addition to $38 per hour. For what number of hours will the two electricians charge the same amount of money?

$f(x) = $ _____ $g(x) = $ _____

x	f(x)	g(x)
0		
1		
2		
3		
4		
5		
6		

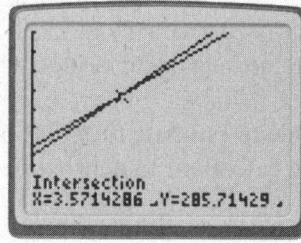

Intersection
X=3.5714286 Y=285.71429

From the table, the solution must be between _____ and _____ hours. From the graph, the solution is about 3.6 hours.

Reflect

3. What limitations, if any, exist on the range of the functions?

_____

_____

4. Why is using a graph better than using a table when finding the solution to a one-variable equation?

_____

_____

_____

Your Turn

5. Sarah would like to hire a clown for her daughter's birthday party. Clown A is offering his services for an initial fee of $100 in addition to $11 per hour. Clown B is offering her services for an initial $150 fee in addition to $8 per hour. When will the two clowns charge the same amount of money? Use a table and a graphing calculator to estimate the solution.

 **Explain 2** **Using Intercepts to Determine Approximate Solutions for One-Variable Equations**

When the amount in a bank account is less than the amount of the payment due, an automatic payment would overdraw the account. That is, the value of the account would be less than zero. In discrete situations like the ones described in the examples, there is no actual point at which the value of the account would be zero, unless the amount in the account is a multiple of the monthly payment. However, you can use the related continuous functions to make an estimation of when the account would theoretically reach zero.

Example 2 Use a table to estimate the solution to the given situation. Then use a graphing calculator to approximate the x-intercept.

(A) Tara has $800 in a bank account that she uses to make automatic payments of her $101.51 monthly cable bill. If Tara stops making deposits to that account, when would automatic payments make the value of the account zero?

The function that describes the amount in the account after x automatic payments is $f(x) = 800 - 101.51x$.

The other function that describes the situation is $g(x) = 0$.

x	f(x)	g(x)
0	800	0
1	698.49	0
2	596.98	0
3	495.47	0
4	393.96	0
5	292.45	0
6	190.94	0
7	89.43	0
8	−12.08	0

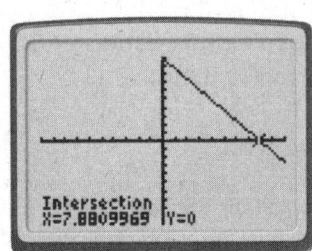

Intersection
X=7.8809969 Y=0

From the table, the value of the account would be 0 between 7 and 8 months. From the graph, the x-intercept is about 7.9.

(B) Craig has $1850 dollars in a bank account that he uses to make automatic payments of $400.73 on his car loan. If Craig stops making deposits to that account, when would automatic payments make the value of the account zero?

The function that describes the amount in the account after x automatic payments is

$f(x) =$ _____ − _____ x.

The other function that describes the situation is $g(x) =$ _____ .

x	f(x)	g(x)
0		
1		
2		
3		
4		
5		

From the table, the value of the account would be 0 between _____

and _____ months. From the graph, the x-intercept is about _____ .

6. How are the examples in this section similar to the examples in the previous section?

_____

_____

7. **Discussion** Name one way to better approximate the solution without the use of technology.

_____

_____

8. Cassandra has $2000 dollars in a bank account that she uses to make automatic $900.01 mortgage payments each month. If Cassandra stops making deposits to that account, when would automatic payments make the value of the account zero? Use a table to estimate the solution. Then use a graphing calculator to approximate the x-intercept.

💬 Elaborate

9. Throe would like to hire a guitarist for his charity concert. Guitarists A and B are offering their services to Throe but each guitarist charges different initial fees and hourly rates. How can Throe check to see when they will charge the same amount of money? Name three ways to perform this task.

_____

_____

_____

10. Essential Question Check-In What is the first step in using functions to solve one-variable equations?

_____

_____

_____

★ Evaluate: Homework and Practice

Use a table to find the solution to each situation.

1. Bridget needs an actor. Actor A is offering her services for an initial $250 in addition to $50 per day. Actor B is offering her services for an initial $200 in addition to $60 per day. When will the two actors charge the same amount of money?

2. Yuma needs a singer. Singer A is offering her services for an initial $50 in addition to $20 per hour. Singer B is offering his services for an initial $100 in addition to $10 per hour. When will the two singers charge the same amount of money?

3. Sam needs a web designer. Designer A is offering her services for an initial $500 in addition to $100 per hour. Designer B is offering her services for an initial $600 in addition to $50 per hour. When will the two designers charge the same amount of money?

4. Lindsey needs a jeweler to repair her earrings. Jeweler A is offering her services for an initial $125 in addition to $15 per hour. Jeweler B is offering his services for an initial $140 in addition to $12 per hour. When will the two jewelers charge the same amount of money?

5. Stan needs a mime. Mime A is offering his services for an initial $75 in addition to $25 per hour. Mime B is offering her services for an initial $30 in addition to $40 per hour. When will the two mimes charge the same amount of money?

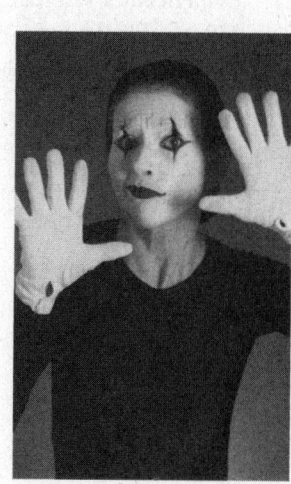

6. Lottie needs a driver. Driver A is offering his services for an initial $200 in addition to $80 per hour. Driver B is offering his services for an initial $230 in addition to $70 per hour. When will the two drivers charge the same amount of money?

7. Garrett needs a baseball coach. Coach A is offering her services for an initial $5000 in addition to $450 per hour. Coach B is offering her services for an initial $4000 in addition to $700 per hour. When will the two coaches charge the same amount of money?

8. Zena needs a salesperson. Salesperson A is offering his services for an initial $50 in addition to $5 per hour. Salesperson B is offering her services for $15 per hour. When will the two salespeople charge the same amount of money?

In Exercises 9–14, each person uses the given bank account to make automatic monthly payments and stops making deposits to the account. Use a table to find when automatic payments would make the value of the account zero.

9. Charles has $1600 dollars in his account and makes automatic $400 monthly payments on a utility bill.

10. Lena has $2800 dollars in her account and makes automatic $700 monthly payments on a cell phone bill.

11. Malcolm has $3600 dollars in his account and makes automatic $600 monthly mortgage payments.

12. Isabelle has $4900 dollars in her account and makes automatic $700 monthly payments on a home loan.

13. Larry's small business has $60,000 dollars in its account and makes automatic monthly payments that total $12,000.

14. Sharon has $12,000 dollars in her account and makes automatic monthly payments that total $6000.

Use a graphing calculator to find the solution to each situation.

15. Aaron needs to hire a waiter. Waiter A is offering his services for an initial $25 in addition to $5.25 per hour. Waitress B is offering her services for an initial $30 in addition to $4.25 per hour. When will the two waiters charge the same amount of money?

16. **Finance** Lucy needs to hire a host. Host A is offering his services for an initial $60 in addition to $13.25 per hour. Hostess B is offering her services for an initial $75 in addition to $11.50 per hour. When will the two hosts charge the same amount of money?

17. Ida needs to hire a singer for her wedding. Singer A is offering his services for an initial $90 in addition to $13.15 per hour. Singer B is offering her services for an initial $100 in addition to $11.85 per hour. When will the two singers charge the same amount of money?

18. Emily needs to hire a pilot. Pilot A is offering his services for an initial $32 in addition to $22.18 per hour. Pilot B is offering her services for an initial $46.75 in addition to $18.24 per hour. When will the two pilots charge the same amount of money?

In Exercises 19–22, each person uses the given bank account to make automatic monthly payments and stops making deposits to the account. Use a graphing calculator to approximate the *x*-intercept of the point where the value of the account would be zero.

19. Rafael has $1875 in his account. and makes automatic monthly payments of $225.18 for a smartphone service plan.

20. Zach has $43,408 dollars in his account. and makes automatic monthly rent payments of $4500.

21. Rebecca has $326.74 dollars in her account. and makes automatic monthly payments of $113.51 for bike rental.

22. Greg has $1464.54 in his account and makes automatic monthly payments of $321.46 for a car loan.

23. Given that $f(x)$ and $g(x)$ are equal, write a one-variable equation. No solutions need to be found for this problem.

    a. $f(x) = 45x + 12, g(x) = 244x + 234$

    b. $f(x) = 13x + 48, g(x) = 24x + 47$

    c. $f(x) = 71x + 145, g(x) = 43x + 17$

    d. $f(x) = 8x + 11, g(x) = 55x + 123$

H.O.T. Focus on Higher Order Thinking

24. Critical Thinking Given a table of values for a one-variable linear equation, how can $f(x)$ be found?

25. Communicate Mathematical Ideas In a real-world problem one variable is solved with a graphing calculator. What quadrants of the graph are never used for the problem?

26. Explain the Error A student was trying to solve a problem and came up with this table as a result:

Time (Weeks)	Profit($)
1	200
2	500
3	800
4	1100
5	1400
6	1700
7	2000
8	2300
9	2600

The student stated that the range of this function is all real numbers. What is wrong with the student's answer?

Lesson Performance Task

Laura wants to hire a lawyer to file deeds for some properties she owns. The graph illustrates costs for her two choices of lawyers. Using the points on the graph, construct a table of results and two equations. Which lawyer is a better choice for her if she has 8 deeds? Which lawyer is a better choice if she has 2 deeds? Why? Over the long run, which lawyer is more cost-effective?

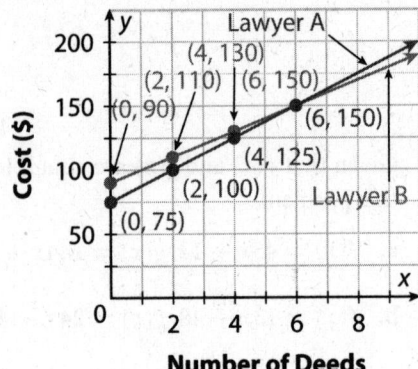

7.3 Linear Inequalities in Two Variables

Essential Question: How do you write and graph linear inequalities in two variables?

⊘ Explore   Graphing Linear Inequalities Involving ≤ or ≥

A **linear inequality in two variables** can be written in one of the following forms: $Ax + By < C$, $Ax + By \leq C$, $Ax + By \geq C$, or $Ax + By > C$, where A, B, and C are constants and A and B are not both 0. The **solution of an inequality in two variables** is one or more ordered pairs that make the inequality true.

Some students at a music recital perform 3-minute pieces and some perform 5-minute pieces. The total time of this part of the recital needs to be at least 30 minutes long. An inequality that represents this is $3x + 5y \geq 30$.

Ⓐ Solve the inequality for y.

Ⓒ Graph the boundary line. The inequality $y \geq -\frac{3}{5}x + 6$ uses the symbol $\geq$, so the line will be solid, to show that the points on the boundary line are part of the solution set.

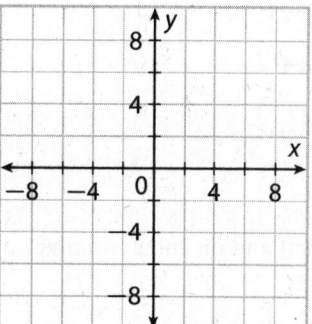

Ⓑ Replace the inequality symbol in the inequality with an equal sign. The inequality is now an equation that will be used to graph a line. The line is called the **boundary line** of the solution set of the inequality. Write the equation of the line.

Ⓓ The part of the coordinate plane containing the solution set to the inequality, which may include the line, is called a **half-plane**. Since the inequality symbol is $\geq$, two conditions must be met. (1) The boundary line is solid, and (2) the half-plane above the boundary line is shaded. Shade the appropriate part of the graph.

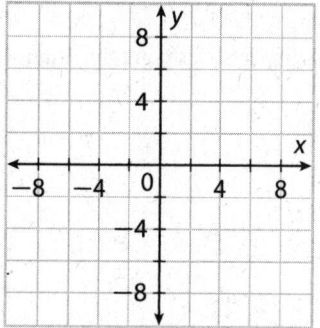

Point	Above or Below Line	Inequality	True or False?
$(0, 0)$		$3\left(\right) + 5\left(\right) \geq 30$	
$(8, 8)$		$3\left(\right) + 5\left(\right) \geq 30$	

Reflect

1. **Discussion** How would the graph change if the inequality were $>$ instead of $\geq$?

🔧 Explain 1   Graphing Linear Inequalities Involving < or >

Example 1   Graph the solution set for the given inequality using the method given.

(A) Graph $21 - 3y < 9x$ using a graphing calculator.

Solve the inequality for y.

$21 - 3y < 9x$

$-3y < 9x - 21$

$y > -3x + 7$

Enter the equation into Y_1 in the graphing calculator.

Go to the far left and hit enter two times until it looks like this.

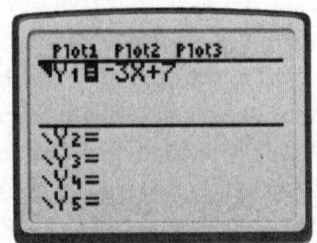

Now view the graph. Note that the calculator will draw a solid line. Determine whether the line should be solid or not.

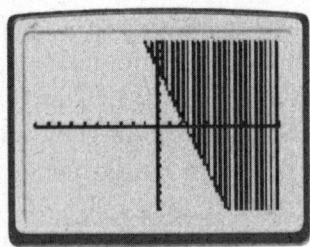

Since the inequality is strictly greater than, the line should be dashed.

(B) Graph $-14 + 2y < -x$ by hand.

Solve the inequality for y.

$$-14 + 2y < -x$$

$$+ 2y < -x + \boxed{}$$

$$y < \frac{-x + \boxed{}}{\boxed{}}$$

$$y < -\boxed{}\,x + \boxed{}$$

Graph the boundary line. The inequality uses the symbol _____, so use a _____ line to show that points on the line _____ part of the solution.

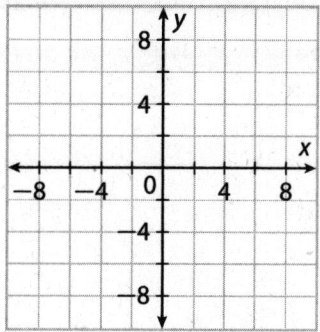

Shade the appropriate part of the graph. The inequality uses the symbol _____, so shade _____ the boundary line.

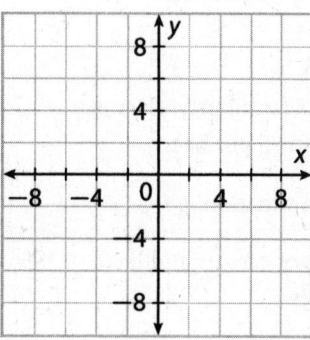

Check the solution by filling in the table.

Point	Above or Below Line	Inequality	True or False?
$(0, 0)$		$-14 + 2\left(\boxed{}\right) < -\left(\boxed{}\right)$	
$(8, 8)$		$-14 + 2\left(\boxed{}\right) < -\left(\boxed{}\right)$	

2. Is $(6, 4)$ part of the solution?

Graph the inequality.

3. $3 - y < -5x$

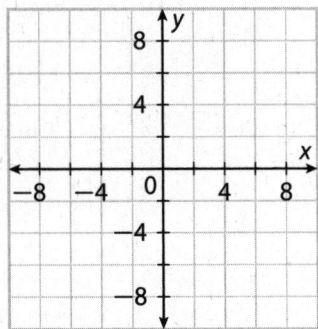

4. $10x + 8y < 64$

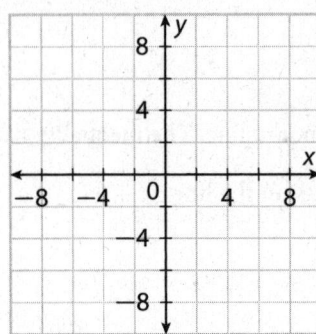

⚙ Explain 2 Creating Models with Linear Inequalities

Example 2 Write a linear inequality to represent the information or graph given.

Ⓐ Elijah can spend at most $8.25 on snacks for a party. Carrots cost $2.00 per package and grapes cost $0.75 per bag.

Write a linear inequality to describe the situation.

Let x represent the number of packages of carrots and let y represent the number of bags of grapes.

Use $\leq$ for "at most".

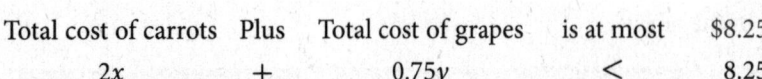

Total cost of carrots	Plus	Total cost of grapes	is at most	$8.25
$2x$	$+$	$0.75y$	$\leq$	8.25

Solve the inequality for y.

$$2x + 0.75y \leq 8.25$$

$$0.75y \leq -2x + 8.25$$

$$y \leq -\frac{8}{3}x + 11$$

Ⓑ

The slope of the line is _____.

The y-intercept of the line is _____.

The boundary line is y = ☐.

The boundary line on the graph is _____ and the shaded

region is _____ the graph so the symbol

will be _____.

So the inequality is ☐.

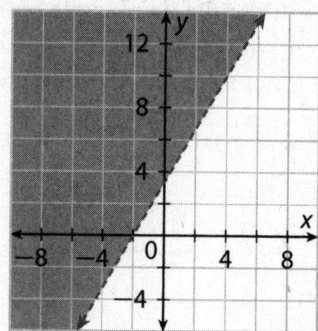

Your Turn

5. Complete the linear inequality that represents the relationship shown in the table: y ☐ 2x

x	y
−3	−8
−2	−10
−1	−2.5
0	0
1	1
2	4
3	0

6. Ramona has $18 that she can spend on food for her dog. Dry dog food costs $5.50 per small bag and wet dog food costs $2.00 per can. Write a linear inequality that describes how many bags and cans of dog food Ramona can buy.

Elaborate

7. Describe a real-world problem situation that can be represented by a linear inequality in two variables. Write an inequality and explain what each part means. Are there any solutions of the solution set that are not solutions to the problem?

8. How can you tell which side of the boundary line should be shaded?

9. **Essential Question Check-In** How do you graph a linear inequality in two variables?

In order to graph the inequality using a graphing calculator, tell what function to enter for the boundary line, whether the graph should be shaded above or below the line, and if the boundary line is included in the solution.

1. $30 + 5y \geq 4x$

2. $-\frac{1}{2} + y \leq 6x$

3. $-\frac{1}{2}y \leq -\frac{3}{4}x + \frac{5}{4}$

4. $-\frac{8}{3}x \geq y + 9$

Graph the inequality.

5. $4x - 4y \geq 28$

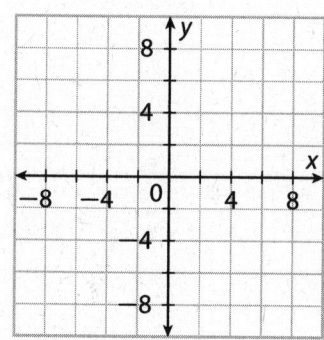

6. $3x + 2y \leq 12$

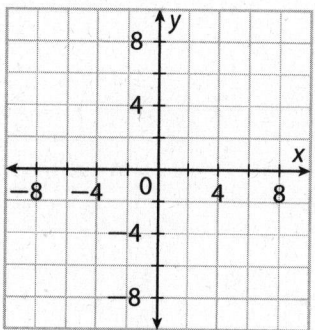

7. $y \leq 3$

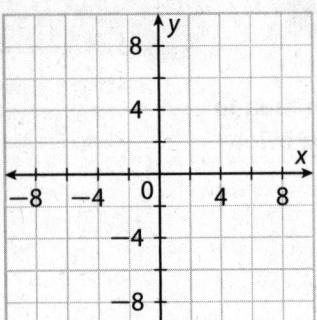

8. $5x - y \geq 4$

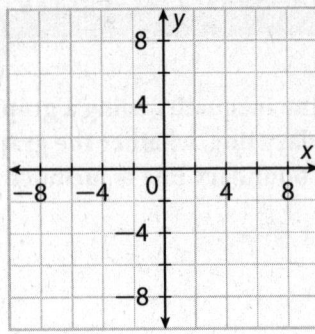

In order to graph the inequality using a graphing calculator, tell what function to enter for the boundary line, whether the graph should be shaded above or below the line, and if the boundary line is included in the solution.

9. $x + 5y > 25$

10. $-x - 7y \geq 0$

11. $-\frac{9}{2}x - y \geq -10y + 3$

12. $15x + 20y < 140$

Graph the inequality.

13. $4y + 3x - y > -6x + 12$

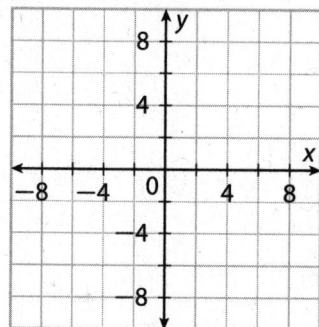

14. $-15y > 30x - 45$

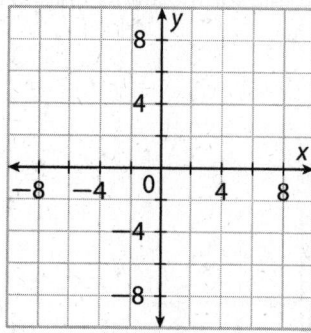

15. $10x - 6y > -36$

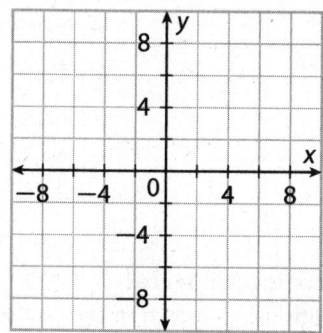

16. $7x + 2y < 2$

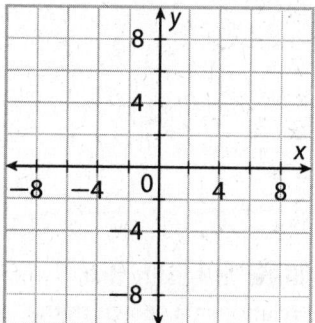

Write a linear inequality to represent the information or graph given.

17. Shanley would like to give $5 gift cards and $4 teddy bears as party favors. Shanley has $120 to spend on party favors. Write an inequality to find the number of gift cards x and teddy bears y Shanley could purchase. Give one solution to the inequality.

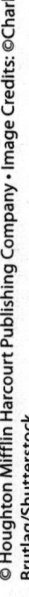

18. The total fees for the high school play are $250. Tickets to the play cost $5 for students and $8 for nonstudents. Write a linear inequality that describes the number of student and nonstudent tickets that need to be sold for the drama class to be able to pay the fees.

19.

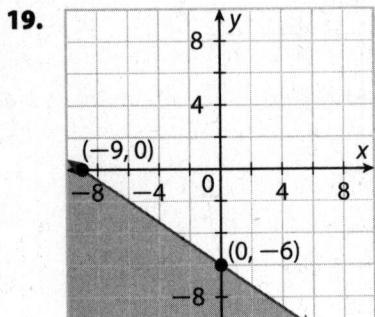

20.

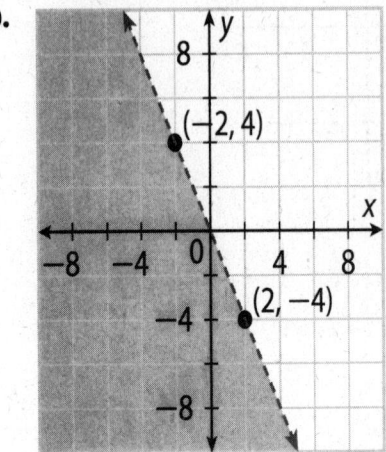

21. Complete the linear inequality that represents the relationship shown in the table:

$$y \boxed{} x + 1$$

x	y
−3	0
−2	−1
−1	5
0	1
1	3
2	4
3	4

22. Complete the linear inequality that represents the relationship shown in the table:

$$y \boxed{} 3x - \frac{1}{2}$$

x	y
−3	−10.5
−2	−7
−1	−4
0	−1
1	1
2	5
3	7.5

23. Critique Reasoning Austin thinks that the inequality $6x - 4y \geq 10$ should be shaded above the boundary line because it uses the $\geq$ inequality symbol. Is he correct? Explain.

24. Analyze Relationships For the graph of $x > 10$, the boundary line is the vertical line $x = 10$. Would you shade to the left or right of the boundary? Explain.

25. Multi-step The fare for a taxi cab is $2.50 per passenger and $0.75 for each mile. A group of friends has $22.00 for cab fare.

a. Write a linear inequality to represent how many miles, y, the group can travel if there are x people in the group.

b. If there are 3 people in the group, how far can they travel by taxi? Show all work.

c. If the group wants to travel 10 miles, what is the greatest number of passengers that can travel by taxi? Explain.

26. Communicate Mathematical Ideas How is graphing a linear inequality on a coordinate plane similar to graphing an inequality on a number line?

Lesson Performance Task

Students are raising money for a field trip by selling candles and soap. The candles cost $0.75 each and will be sold for $2.75, and the soap costs $1.50 per bar and will be sold for $4. The students need to raise at least $300 to cover their trip costs.

a. Write an inequality that relates the number of candles c and the number of bars of soap s to the needed income.

b. The wholesaler can supply no more than 100 bars of soap and no more than 130 candles. Graph the inequality from part a and the inequalities that represent the constraints. Graph the number of candles on the vertical axis.

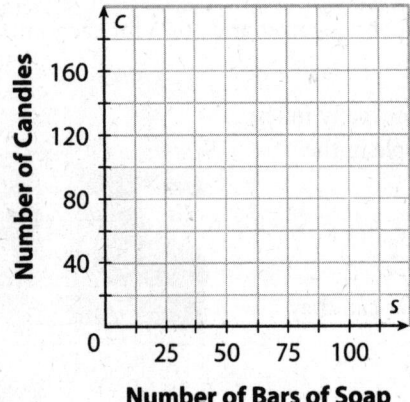

c. What does the shaded area of your graph represent?

Linear Equations and Inequalities

Essential Question: How can you use linear equations and inequalities to solve real-world problems?

Key Vocabulary

linear inequality in two variables *(desigualdad lineal en dos variables)*

solution of an inequality in two variables *(solución de una desigualdad en dos variables)*

KEY EXAMPLE   (Lesson 7.1)

A clothing store offers a rewards program in which customers earn points by making purchases at the store. Every item bought is worth 8 points, and customers earn 20 points when they sign up. Write an equation for the function that gives the number of points based on the number of items bought. How many points will a customer have after making 16 purchases?

Write a verbal model for the situation.

   Total points = Initial points + Points Per Item · Number of Items.

Define the variables that you will use for the function.

   n = number of items; $P(n)$ = total points

Using the verbal model, variables, and information from the problem, write a function rule.

   $P(n) = 20 + 8n$

Substitute $n = 16$ into the function, and solve to find the total points.

   $P(16) = 20 + 8(16)$
   $P(16) = 148$

The customer will have 148 points after making 16 purchases.

KEY EXAMPLE   (Lesson 7.2)

Sandi is in need of an electrician. Electrician A is offering his services for an initial fee of $50 and $12 per hour. Electrician B is offering her services for an initial fee of $32 and $15 per hour. When will the two electricians charge the same amount of money? Use a table to find the solution.

$f(x) = 12x + 50$

$g(x) = 15x + 32$

x	f(x)	g(x)
0	50	32
1	62	47
2	74	62
3	86	77
4	98	92
5	110	107
6	122	122

The solution is 6 hours.

EXERCISES

Write a linear equation that models the situation. *(Lesson 7.1)*

1. A kiosk sells magazines for $4 each and paperback books for $6 each. The owner would like to make $180 by the end of the day.

2. A theater is selling children's tickets at $8 and adult tickets at $18. The theater would like to sell tickets worth a total of $720 for a performance.

3. Maxine needs a stunt driver. Driver A is offering his services for an initial $150 and $90 per hour. Driver B is offering his services for an initial $210 and $70 per hour. When will the two drivers charge the same amount of money? Fill out the table to find the solution. *(Lesson 7.2)*

x	f(x) = _____	g(x) = _____
0		
1		
2		
3		
4		

4. Solve $-9x + 3y \leq 6$ for y and show your work. Graph the solution. *(Lesson 7.3)*

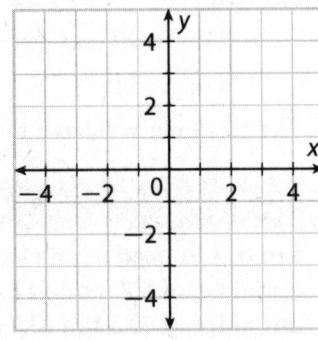

MODULE PERFORMANCE TASK

Making Weight

The National Federation of State High School Associations designates 14 weight classes for wrestlers. Coach Silva has two wrestlers who would like to compete in the 182-pound weight class, Jake and Tawa. Jake weighs 194.6 pounds, Tawa weighs 176 pounds. Coach Silva wants to put each on a diet regimen so that they can meet their weight goal in 6 weeks. For health reasons, neither athlete should lose or gain more than 1.5% of his body weight per week.

If Coach Silva would like for each boy to gain or lose weight at a steady rate over the 6-week time frame, how much does each boy's weight need to change per week? Is this a reasonable goal for each athlete, given the 1.5% per week body weight restriction? Work out your answer on a separate piece of paper.

(Ready) to Go On?

7.1–7.3 Linear Equations and Inequalities

• Online Homework
• Hints and Help
• Extra Practice

Write a linear equation that models the situation. *(Lesson 7.1)*

1. A drugstore sells pens for $1.50 each and notebooks for $4 each. The owner would like to sell $35 of these items each day.

2. A movie theater sells tickets to a film for $12 each. The theater also sells beverages for $3. The theater needs to make $1700 in all in order to break even on the film.

3. Sylvia has $14,000 dollars in a bank account that she uses to make automatic payments that total $7000 each month. If Sylvia stops making deposits to that account, when would automatic payments make the value of the account zero? *(Lesson 7.2)*

x	f(x) = _____
0	
1	
2	

4. Solve $10x + 5y \geq 20$ for y and show your work. Graph the solution. *(Lesson 7.3)*

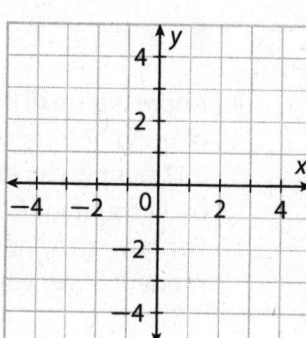

ESSENTIAL QUESTION

5. How can you use the graph of a linear equation to graph an inequality in two variables?

Assessment Readiness

1. Look at each equation. Does the graph of the equation include the point $(-6, 3)$? Select Yes or No for each equation.

   A. $y = -2x - 6$ ◯ Yes   ◯ No

   B. $y + 3 = 2(x + 9)$ ◯ Yes   ◯ No

   C. $y - 4 = \frac{1}{2}(x + 4)$ ◯ Yes   ◯ No

2. Consider the inequality represented by the graph. Choose True or False for each statement.

   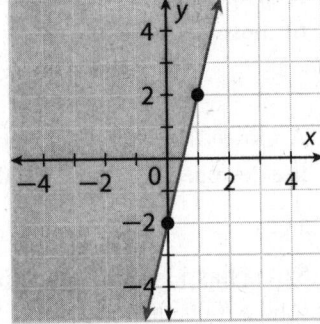

   A. $(1, 4)$ is a solution of the inequality.   ◯ True   ◯ False

   B. $(-3, -2)$ is a solution of the inequality.   ◯ True   ◯ False

   C. The inequality represented is $y < 6x - 2$.   ◯ True   ◯ False

3. Look at each equation. Is the equation linear? Select Yes or No for each equation.

   A. $-3x + y = 8$ ◯ Yes   ◯ No

   B. $3 = xy + 9$ ◯ Yes   ◯ No

   C. $y = x^3 - 3$ ◯ Yes   ◯ No

4. Andre is a small business owner who wants to hire an accountant. Accountant A is offering his services for $50 an hour. Accountant B is offering her services for $35 an hour plus an initial fee of $375. Write a function to represent the cost charged by Accountant A. Write a function to represent the cost charged by Accountant B. For how many hours of work do the two accountants charge the same amount of money? Show your work.

1. Is the given equation linear? Select Yes or No.

A. $-\dfrac{3}{4}x - \dfrac{1}{2}y = 2$ ⭕ Yes ⭕ No

B. $y = x^2 - 5$ ⭕ Yes ⭕ No

C. $-\dfrac{2}{x} = y + 12$ ⭕ Yes ⭕ No

2. Consider the equation $2x - \dfrac{3}{5}y = -6$.

Determine if the given statement is True or False.

A. The y-intercept is 10. ⭕ True ⭕ False

B. It is equivalent to $x = \dfrac{3}{10}y - 3$. ⭕ True ⭕ False

C. It is equivalent to $y = \dfrac{10}{3}x + 10$. ⭕ True ⭕ False

3. A line is represented by the equation $y - 5 = 6\left(x + \dfrac{1}{2}\right)$.

Does the given statement describe the line?

A. The slope of the line is -6. ⭕ Yes ⭕ No

B. $\left(-\dfrac{1}{2}, 5\right)$ is a point on the line. ⭕ Yes ⭕ No

C. The y-intercept of the line is 3. ⭕ Yes ⭕ No

4. Does the given statement describe a step in the transformation of the graph of $f(x) = x$ that would result in the graph of $g(x) = -\dfrac{1}{3}x - 4$?

A. The is reflected across the y-axis. ⭕ Yes ⭕ No

B. The is translated 4 units down. ⭕ Yes ⭕ No

C. The parent function becomes steeper. ⭕ Yes ⭕ No

5. Consider the graph of the inequality $2y - 10 \le -\dfrac{2}{4}x$. Is the given statement true?

A. The boundary line is dashed. ⭕ Yes ⭕ No

B. The boundary line is $y = -\dfrac{1}{2}x + 5$. ⭕ Yes ⭕ No

C. The half-plane below the boundary line is shaded. ⭕ Yes ⭕ No

6. Leia and Thaddeus are reading the same 225 page book. Leia starts reading the book and plans to read 25 pages a day. Thaddeus has already read 45 pages and is reading 20 pages a day. Determine if each statement is True or False.

A. Leia will finish the book in 9 days. ⭕ True ⭕ False

B. $f(x) = 20x$ represents the number of pages Thaddeus has read after x days. ⭕ True ⭕ False

C. They will both finish the book in 9 days. ⭕ True ⭕ False

7. Write $5x = -2y + 6$ in slope-intercept form, and graph the line. Explain how you graphed the line.

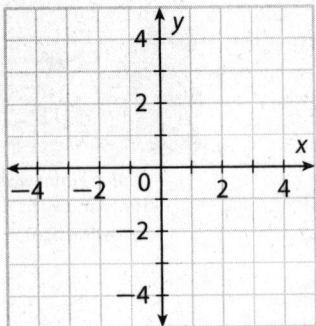

8. Donnie and Tania are math tutors. The amount Donnie charges for a session h hours long is represented by the function $D(h) = 40h + 10$. Tania charges a flat fee of \$30 plus \$15 an hour. Write a function, $T(h)$, that represents the amount in dollars that Tania charges for h hours of tutoring. Graph both functions on the same coordinate grid, and label each line. Compare the slopes and y-intercepts of the graphs.

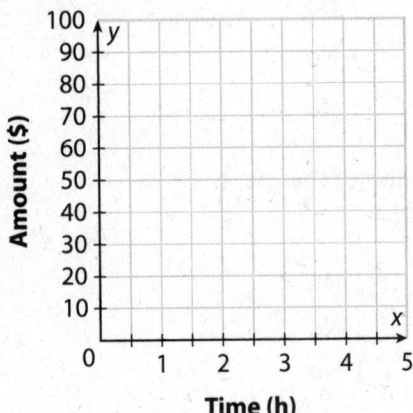

Performance Tasks

★ **9.** A bicycle computer or cyclometer uses a magnetic counter that records each wheel rotation to calculate the bike's total distance traveled. To set up the computer, you select a calibration constant for the bike's wheel size. The computer multiplies this constant times the number of tire rotations to find the total distance in miles. Write a function for the distance d in miles if the calibration number is 0.00125. If the function is incorrect and your tire is actually slightly smaller, how should the function change?

© Houghton Mifflin Harcourt Publishing Company

★★**10.** A marina rents party boats for large social gatherings. They charge the following amounts for a 2-hour rental.

Number of People	10	20	35	50
Cost	$165	$192.50	$233.75	$275

A. Write an equation that represents the data. Include a definition of your variables.

B. What are the intercepts of the graph of your equation? What is the slope? What do they mean in this context?

C. Use your equation to predict the cost of providing a party boat for 75 people.

D. The marina actually charges $460 for 75 people. What might be a reason for the difference?

★★★**11.** High demand cars that are also in low supply tend to retain their value better than other cars. The data in the table are for a car that won a resale value award.

Year	1	3	5
Value (%)	84	64	44

A. Write a function to represent the car's value over time, assuming that the car's value is linear for the first 5 years.

B. According to your model, how much did the car's value drop the day it was purchased and driven off the lot?

C. Do you think the linear model would still be useful after 10 years? Explain.

D. Suppose you used months instead of years to write a function. How would your model change?

Wildlife Field Researcher Alexa is a wildlife field researcher who is studying the American black bear. American black bears are the most common bears in the United States. They can be found in 11 of the 21 counties in New Jersey. Most wild male black bears weigh between 125 and 600 pounds, while females generally weigh between 90 and 300 pounds. Their weight depends upon their age, the season of the year and how much food is available.

a. Write inequalities to show the range of weights for male and female black bears.

b. Black bears hibernate for about 5 months in the winter. They must store 50 to 60 pounds of fat to survive hibernation. During the month before hibernation, a black bear may consume up to 20,000 Calories per day. If a bear consumes an average of 18,500 Calories per day in the month of August, about how many total calories will he consume that month?

c. Use the graph to estimate how much a male bear, weighing $\frac{2}{3}$ pound at birth and 400 pounds at the age of his death, 20 years, weighed when he was 7 years old.

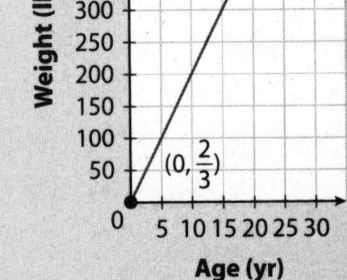

d. A white-tailed deer is running from a black bear at 20 miles per hour. It is $\frac{1}{3}$ mile in front of the bear. The bear is running at 30 miles per hour. How many minutes will it take the bear to catch the deer? Assume both continue running at a constant pace.

e. During the hibernation months, the bear's heart rate slows to about 10 beats per minute. If the bear hibernates for 155 days, how many times will its heart beat?

UNIT 4

Statistical Models

MATH IN CAREERS

Geologist A geologist is a scientist who studies Earth—its processes, materials, and history. Geologists investigate earthquakes, floods, landslides, and volcanic eruptions to gain a deeper understanding of these phenomena. They explore ways to extract materials from the Earth, such as metals, oil, and groundwater. Geologists devise and use mathematical models and use statistical methods to help them understand Earth's geological processes and history.

If you are interested in a career as a geologist, you should study these mathematical subjects:

- Algebra
- Geometry
- Trigonometry
- Statistics
- Calculus

Research other careers that require using statistical methods to understand natural phenomena. Check out the career activity at the end of the unit to find out how **geologists** use math.

© Houghton Mifflin Harcourt Publishing Company · ©Ulrich Doering/Alamy

Reading Start-Up

Vocabulary

Review Words

✔ data *(datos)*

✔ mean *(media)*

✔ median *(mediana)*

✔ range *(rango)*

Preview Words

box plot *(gráfica de caja)*

categorical data *(datos categoricos)*

dot plot *(diagrama de puntos)*

frequency table *(table de frecuencia)*

histogram *(histograma)*

normal distribution *(distribución normal)*

outlier *(valor extremo)*

quartile *(cuartil)*

scatter plot *(diagram de dispersión)*

trend line *(línea de tendencia)*

Visualize Vocabulary

Use the ✔ words to complete the graphic.

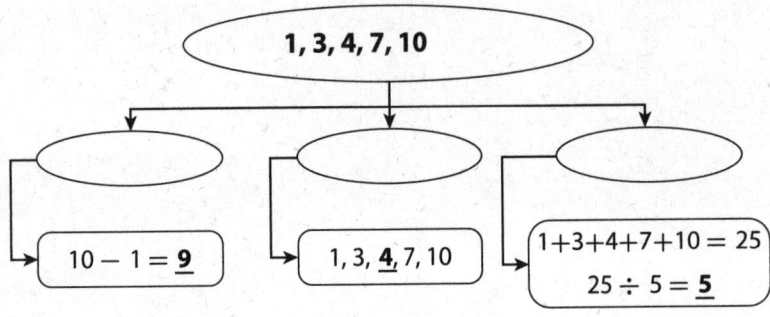

10 − 1 = **9**

1, 3, **4**, 7, 10

1+3+4+7+10 = 25

25 ÷ 5 = **5**

Understand Vocabulary

To become familiar with some of the vocabulary terms in the module, consider the following. You may refer to the module, the glossary, or a dictionary.

1. A _____ is the median of the upper or lower half of a data set.

2. A graph with points plotted to show a possible relationship between two sets of data is a _____.

3. A _____ is a bar graph used to display data grouped in intervals.

4. A data value that is far removed from the rest of the data is an _____.

Active Reading

Booklet Before beginning each module in this unit, create a booklet to help you learn the vocabulary and concepts in the module. Each page of the booklet should contain a main topic from each lesson. As you study each lesson, write details of the main topic, with definitions, diagrams, graphs, and examples, to create an outline that summarizes the main content of the lesson.

Multi-Variable Categorical Data

Essential Question: How can you use multi-variable categorical data to solve real-world problems?

REAL WORLD VIDEO
With emotions riding high, it can be difficult to evaluate popular opinion concerning personal preferences, such as favorite sports teams. Polls and surveys use a methodical, mathematical approach to reduce or eliminate bias.

MODULE PERFORMANCE TASK PREVIEW

Survey Says?

You won't be surprised to learn that the activities people enjoy change with age. Most six-year-olds like climbing on jungle gyms. Most twenty-year-olds don't, but they do like to attend pop music concerts. In this module, you'll learn ways to analyze surveys of public opinions and preferences. Then you'll look at data relating to the vacation preferences of two different age groups and decide what you can learn from the data.

Are (YOU) Ready?

Complete these exercises to review skills you will need for this module.

Percents

Example 1

What percent of 14 is 21?

$$\frac{x}{100} \cdot 14 = 21$$ Write an equation.

$$\frac{x}{100} \cdot 14 \cdot \frac{100}{14} = 21 \cdot \frac{100}{14}$$ Multiply both sides by $\frac{100}{14}$.

$$x = 150$$ Simplify.

21 is 150% of 14.

Solve each equation.

1. What percent of 24 is 18?

2. What percent of 400 is 2?

3. What percent of 880 is 924?

Two-Way Frequency Tables

Example 2

The table shows the number of adults, teens, and children under 13 who visited the local petting zoo one week. How many people visited it on Friday?

	Su	M	Tu	W	Th	F	Sa
Adult	112	40	33	52	29	8	90
Teen	29	0	6	22	4	2	10
Child	61	32	56	65	38	16	48

Friday is the second to last column. It shows that 8 adults, 2 teens, and 16 children visited that day.
The sum is $8 + 2 + 16 = 26$.

The number of people who visited the petting zoo on Friday is 26.

Use the table shown to answer the questions.

4. How many children under 13 visited the petting zoo that week?

5. How many adults visited the petting zoo on the weekend?

6. To the nearest whole percent, what percent of the visitors were teens?

8.1   Two-Way Frequency Tables

Essential Question: How can categorical data for two categories be summarized?

Resource Locker

🧭 **Explore**   **Categorical Data and Frequencies**

Data that can be expressed with numerical measurements are **quantitative data**. In this lesson you will examine qualitative data, or **categorical data**, which cannot be expressed using numbers. Data describing animal type, model of car, or favorite song are examples of categorical data.

(A)   Circle the categorical data variable. Justify your choice.

temperature   weight   height   color

_____

_____

(B)   Identify whether the given data is categorical or quantitative.

large, medium, small _____

120 ft^2, 130 ft^2, 140 ft^2 _____

(C)   A **frequency** table shows how often each item occurs in a set of categorical data. Use the categorical data listed on the left to complete the frequency table.

Ways Students Get to School
bus car walk car car car bus
walk walk walk bus bus car
bus bus walk bus car bus car

Way	Frequency
bus	8
car	☐
_____	☐

Reflect

1.   How did you determine the numbers for each category in the frequency column?

_____

_____

2.   What must be true about the sum of the frequencies in a frequency table?

_____

_____

🔑 Explain 1   Constructing Two-Way Frequency Tables

If a data set has two categorical variables, you can list the frequencies of the paired values in a **two-way frequency table**.

Example 1   **Complete the two-way frequency table.**

Ⓐ A high school's administration asked 100 randomly selected students in the 9th and 10th grades about what fruit they like best. Complete the table.

Grade	Preferred Fruit			
	Apple	Orange	Banana	Total
9th	19	12	23	
10th	22	9	15	
Total				

Row totals:

9th: $19 + 12 + 23 = 54$

10th: $22 + 9 + 15 = 46$

Column totals:

Apple: $19 + 22 = 41$

Orange: $12 + 9 = 21$

Banana: $23 + 15 = 38$

Grand total:

Sum of row totals: $54 + 46 = 100$

Sum of column totals: $41 + 21 + 38 = 100$

Both sums should equal the grand total.

Grade	Preferred Fruit			
	Apple	Orange	Banana	Total
9th	19	12	23	54
10th	22	9	15	46
Total	41	21	38	100

Ⓑ Jenna asked some randomly selected students whether they preferred dogs, cats, or other pets. She also recorded the gender of each student. The results are shown in the two-way frequency table below. Each entry is the frequency of students who prefer a certain pet and are a certain gender. For instance, 8 girls prefer dogs as pets. Complete the table.

Gender	Preferred Pet			
	Dog	Cat	Other	Total
Girl	8	7	1	☐
Boy	10	5	9	☐
Total	☐	☐	☐	☐

Row totals:

Girl: $8 + 7 + 1 =$ ☐

Boy: $10 + 5 + 9 =$ ☐

Column totals:

Dog: $8 + 10 =$ ☐

Cat: $7 + 5 =$ ☐

Other: $1 + 9 =$ ☐

Grand total:

Sum of row totals: $16 +$ ☐ $=$ ☐

Sum of column totals: $18 +$ ☐ $+$ ☐ $=$ ☐

Both sums should equal the grand total.

3. Look at the totals for each row. Was Jenna's survey evenly distributed among boys and girls? Explain.

_____

4. Look at the totals for each column. Which pet is preferred by the most students? Justify your answer.

_____

Your Turn

Complete the two-way frequency table.

5. Antonio surveyed 60 of his classmates about their participation in school activities and whether they have a part-time job. The results are shown in the two-way frequency table below. Complete the table.

Job	Activities				
	Clubs Only	**Sports Only**	**Both**	**Neither**	**Total**
Yes	12	13	16	4	
No	3	5	5	2	
Total					

6. Jen surveyed 100 students about whether they like baseball or basketball. Complete the table.

Like Baseball	Like Basketball		
	Yes	**No**	**Total**
Yes	61	13	
No	16	10	
Total			

🔎 Explain 2   Reading Two-Way Frequency Tables

You can extract information about paired categorical variables by reading a two-way frequency table.

Example 2   **Read and complete the two-way frequency table.**

(A) Suppose you are given the circled information in the table and instructed to complete the table.

Gender	Eat Cereal for Breakfast		
	Yes	**No**	**Total**
Girl	(42)	(12)	(54)
Boy	36	(10)	46
Total	78	22	(100)

Find the total number of boys by subtracting: $100 - 54 = 46$

Find the number of boys who do eat cereal by subtracting: $46 - 10 = 36$

Add to find the total number of students who eat cereal and the total number of students who do not eat cereal.

B One hundred students were surveyed about which beverage they chose at lunch. Some of the results are shown in the two-way frequency table below. Complete the table.

Gender	Lunch Beverage			
	Juice	Milk	Water	Total
Girl	10	☐	17	☐
Boy	15	24	21	60
Total	☐	☐	☐	☐

Find the total number of girls by subtracting: $100 - 60 =$ ☐

So, the total number of girls is ☐ . The number of girls who do not choose milk is ☐ + ☐ = ☐ .

Find the number of girls who chose milk by subtracting: ☐ − ☐ = ☐

Reflect

7. Which lunch beverage is the least preferred? How do you know?

_____

Your Turn

Read and complete the two-way frequency table.

8. 100 students were asked what fruit they chose at lunch. The two-way frequency table shows some of the results of the survey. Complete the table.

Gender	Lunch Fruit			
	Apple	Pear	Banana	Total
Girl		17	11	49
Boy		10	16	
Total				

9. 200 high school teachers were asked whether they prefer to use the chalkboard or projector in class. The two-way frequency table shows some of the results of the survey. Complete the table.

Gender	Preferred Teaching Aid		
	Chalkboard	Projector	Total
Female		56	99
Male	44		
Total	87	113	200

10. You are making a two-way frequency table of 5 fruit preferences among a survey sample of girls and boys. What are the dimensions of the table you would make? How many entries would you need to fill the table with frequencies and totals?

_____

_____

11. A 3 categories-by-3 categories two-way frequency table has a row with 2 numbers, and no row or column totals. Can you fill the row?

_____

_____

_____

12. **Essential Question Check-In** How can you summarize categorical data for 2 categories?

_____

_____

⭐ Evaluate: Homework and Practice

1. Identify whether the given data is categorical or quantitative.

gold medal, silver medal, bronze medal _____

100 m, 200 m, 400 m _____

2. A theater company asked its members to bring in canned food for a food drive. Use the categorical data to complete the frequency table.

Cans Donated to Food Drive
peas corn peas soup corn
corn soup soup corn peas
peas corn soup peas corn
peas corn peas corn soup
corn peas soup corn corn

Cans	Frequency
soup	☐
peas	☐
	☐

Complete the two-way frequency table.

3. James surveyed some of his classmates about what vegetable they like best. Complete the table.

Grade	Preferred Vegetable			
	Carrots	Green Beans	Celery	Total
9th	30	15	24	
10th	32	9	20	
Total				

4. A high school's extracurricular committee surveyed a randomly selected group of students about whether they like tennis and soccer. Complete the table.

	Like Tennis		
Like Soccer	**Yes**	**No**	**Total**
Yes	37	20	
No	16	15	
Total			

5. After a school field trip, Ben surveyed some students about which animals they liked from the zoo. Complete the table.

	Preferred Animal at a Zoo			
Grade	**Lion**	**Zebra**	**Monkey**	**Total**
11th	9	15	14	
12th	4	17	15	
Total				

6. Jill asked some randomly selected students whether they preferred blue, green, or other colors. She also recorded the gender of each student. The results are shown in the two-way frequency table below. Complete the table.

	Preferred Color			
Gender	**Green**	**Blue**	**Other**	**Total**
Girl	15	3	10	
Boy	3	16	6	
Total				

7. Kevin surveyed some students about whether they preferred soccer, baseball, or another sport. He also recorded their gender. Complete the table.

	Preferred Sport			
Gender	**Soccer**	**Baseball**	**Other**	**Total**
Girl	33	7	10	
Boy	15	27	7	
Total				

8. A school surveyed a group of students about whether they like backgammon and chess. They will use this data to determine whether there is enough interest for the school to compete in these games. Complete the table.

Like Chess	Like Backgammon		
	Yes	No	Total
Yes	10	61	
No	5	3	
Total			

9. Hugo surveyed some 9th and 10th graders in regard to whether they preferred math, English, or another subject. The results of the survey are in the following table. Complete the table.

Grade	Preferred Subject			
	Math	English	Other	Total
9th	40	35	20	
10th	41	32	17	
Total				

10. Luis surveyed some middle school and high school students about the type of music they prefer. Complete the table.

School Level	Preferred Music			
	Country	Pop	Other	Total
Middle School	18	13	23	
High School	7	32	15	
Total				

11. Natalie surveyed some teenagers and adults on whether they prefer standard cars, vans, or convertibles. Her results are in the following table. Complete the table.

Age	Preferred Car Type			
	Standard	Van	Convertible	Total
Adults	10	25	9	
Teenagers	11	7	24	
Total				

12. Eli surveyed some teenagers and adults on whether they prefer apples, oranges, or bananas. His results are in the following table. Complete the table.

Age	Preferred Fruit			
	Apple	Orange	Banana	Total
Adults	22	12	10	
Teenagers	24	9	9	
Total				

200 students were asked to name their favorite science class. The results are shown in the two-way frequency table. Use the table for the following questions.

Gender	Favorite Science Class			
	Biology	Chemistry	Physics	Total
Girl	42	39	23	104
Boy		45	32	
Total				

13. How many boys were surveyed? Explain how you found your answer.

14. Complete the table. How many more girls than boys chose biology as their favorite science class? Explain how you found your answer.

The results of a survey of 150 students about whether they own an electronic tablet or a laptop are shown in the two-way frequency table.

Gender	Device				
	Electronic tablet	Laptop	Both	Neither	Total
Girl	15	54		9	88
Boy		35	8	5	
Total					

15. Complete the table. Do the surveyed students own more laptops or more electronic tablets?

16. Which group had more people answer the survey, boys or students who own an electronic tablet only? Explain.

17. The table shows the results of a survey about students' preferred frozen yogurt flavor. Complete the table, and state the flavors that students preferred the most and the least.

Gender	Preferred Flavor			
	Vanilla	Mint	Strawberry	Total
Girl		15	18	45
Boy	17	25		
Total				100

18. Teresa surveyed 100 students about whether they like pop music or country music. Out of the 100 students surveyed, 42 like only pop, 34 like only country, 15 like both pop and country, and 9 do not like either pop or country. Complete the two-way frequency table.

Like Country	Like Pop		
	Yes	No	Total
Yes			
No			
Total			

19. Forty students in a class at an international high school were surveyed about which non-English language they can speak. Complete the table.

Gender	Foreign Language			
	Chinese	Spanish	French	Total
Girl	7	8		
Boy		6	7	18
Total				

Luis surveyed 100 students about whether they like soccer. The number of girls and the number of boys completing the survey are equal.

20. Complete the table.

Gender	Likes Soccer		
	Yes	No	Total
Girl		20	
Boy		35	
Total			100

21. Twice as many girls like soccer as the number that like tennis. The same number of students like soccer as like tennis. Construct a table containing the tennis data.

22. A group of 200 high school students were asked about their use of email and text messages. The results are shown in the two-way frequency table. Complete the table.

	Text Messages		
Email	**Yes**	**No**	**Total**
Yes	72		90
No		45	
Total			

23. Circle the letter of each data set that is categorical. Select all that apply.

A. 75°, 79°, 77°, 85°

B. apples, oranges, pears

C. male, female

D. blue, green, red

E. 2 feet, 5 feet, 12 feet

F. classical music, country music

G. 1 centimeter, 3 centimeters, 9 centimeters

24. Explain the Error Find the mistake in completing the two-way frequency table for a survey involving 50 students. Then complete the table correctly.

	Favorite Foreign Language Class			
Gender	**Russian**	**German**	**Italian**	**Total**
Girl	8	8	8	24
Boy	42	9	7	58
Total	50			

Correct table:

	Favorite Foreign Language Class			
Gender	**Russian**	**German**	**Italian**	**Total**
Girl	8	8	8	24
Boy		9	7	
Total				

25. Justify Reasoning Charles surveyed 100 boys about their favorite color. Of the 100 boys surveyed, 44 preferred blue, 25 preferred green, and 31 preferred red.

a. Explain why it is not possible to make a two-way frequency table from the given data.

b. Suppose Charles also surveyed some girls. Of the girls surveyed, 30 preferred blue and 43 preferred green. Can Charles make a two-way frequency table now? Can he complete it?

26. Persevere in Problem Solving Shown are two different tables about a survey involving students. Each survey had a few questions about musical preferences. All students answered all questions. Complete the tables. What type of music do the students prefer?

Gender	Likes Classical Music		
	Yes	No	Total
Girl	21		
Boy		22	
Total			100

Gender	Likes Blues Music		
	Yes	No	Total
Girl		15	49
Boy		15	
Total			

Lesson Performance Task

Two hundred students were asked about their favorite sport. Of the 200 students surveyed, 98 were female. Some of the results are shown in the following two-way frequency table.

Gender	Favorite Sport				
	Football	Baseball	Basketball	Soccer	Total
Female			36	12	
Male	38	19			
Total	64			36	

a. Complete the table.

b. Which sport is the most popular among the students? Which is the least popular? Explain.

c. Which sport is most popular among the females? Which sport is most popular among the males? Explain.

8.2 Relative Frequency

Essential Question: How can you recognize possible associations and trends between two categories of categorical data?

⊙ Explore   Relative Frequencies

To show what portion of a data set each category in a frequency table makes up, you can convert the data to *relative frequencies*. The **relative frequency** of a category is the frequency of the category divided by the total of all frequencies.

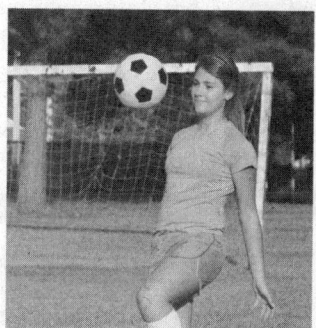

The frequency table below shows the results of a survey Kenesha conducted at school. She asked 80 randomly selected students whether they preferred basketball, football, or soccer.

Favorite Sport	Basketball	Football	Soccer	Total
Frequency	20	32	28	80

Ⓐ Use the frequencies to make a relative frequency table expressed with decimals.

Favorite Sport	Basketball	Football	Soccer	Total
Relative Frequency	$\frac{20}{80} = 0.25$			$\frac{80}{80} =$ ☐

Ⓑ Rewrite the relative frequency table using percents instead of decimals.

Favorite Sport	Basketball	Football	Soccer	Total
Relative Frequency	25%			

Reflect

1. Explain what the numerator and denominator of the ratio $\frac{20}{80}$ refer to in part A.

_____

_____

2. What types of numbers can you use to write relative frequencies?

_____

_____

⊙ Explain 1   Two-Way Relative Frequency Tables

Two types of relative frequencies are found in a relative frequency table:

1. A **joint relative frequency** is found by dividing a frequency that is not in the Total row or the Total column by the grand total. It tells what portion of the total has both of the two specified characteristics.

2. A **marginal relative frequency** is found by dividing a row total or a column total by the grand total. It tells what portion of the total has a specified characteristic.

Example 1   Complete a two-way relative frequency table from the data in a two-way frequency table. Identify the joint relative frequencies and the marginal relative frequencies.

Ⓐ   For her survey about sports preferences, Kenesha also recorded the gender of each student. The results are shown in the two-way frequency table for Kenesha's data.

	Preferred Sport			
Gender	**Basketball**	**Football**	**Soccer**	**Total**
Girl	6	12	18	36
Boy	14	20	10	44
Total	20	32	28	80

To find the relative frequencies, divide each frequency by the grand total.

	Preferred Sport			
Gender	**Basketball**	**Football**	**Soccer**	**Total**
Girl	$\frac{6}{80} = 0.075$	$\frac{12}{80} = 0.15$	$\frac{18}{80} = 0.225$	$\frac{36}{80} = 0.45$
Boy	$\frac{14}{80} = 0.175$	$\frac{20}{80} = 0.25$	$\frac{10}{80} = 0.125$	$\frac{44}{80} = 0.55$
Total	$\frac{20}{80} = 0.25$	$\frac{32}{80} = 0.4$	$\frac{28}{80} = 0.35$	$\frac{80}{80} = 1$

The joint relative frequencies tell what percent of all those surveyed are in each category:

- 7.5% are girls who prefer basketball.
- 15% are girls who prefer football.
- 22.5% are girls who prefer soccer.

- 17.5% are boys who prefer basketball.
- 25% are boys who prefer football.
- 12.5% are boys who prefer soccer.

The marginal relative frequencies tell what percent of totals has a given single characteristic:

- 25% prefer basketball.
- 40% prefer football.
- 35% prefer soccer.

- 45% are girls.
- 55% are boys.

(B) Millie performed a survey of students in the lunch line and recorded which type of fruit each student selected along with the gender of each student. The two-variable frequency data she collected is shown in the table.

	Fruit			
	Apple	**Banana**	**Orange**	**Total**
Girl	16	10	14	40
Boy	25	13	14	52
Total	41	23	28	92

	Fruit			
	Apple	**Banana**	**Orange**	**Total**
Girl	17.4%			
Boy	27.2%			
Total	44.6%			

The joint relative frequencies:

- [ ] are girls who selected an apple.
- [ ] are girls who selected a banana.
- [ ] are girls who selected an orange.

- [ ] are boys who selected an apple.
- [ ] are boys who selected a banana.
- [ ] are boys who selected an orange.

The marginal relative frequencies:

- [ ] selected an apple.
- [ ] selected a banana.
- [ ] selected an orange.

- [ ] are girls.
- [ ] are boys.

Reflect

3. **Discussion** Explain how you can use joint and marginal relative frequencies to check your relative frequency table.

_____

_____

Use the two-way table of data from another student survey to answer the following questions.

Like Weight Lifting	Like Aerobic Exercise		
	Yes	No	Total
Yes	7	14	21
No	12	7	19
Total	19	21	40

4. Find the joint relative frequency of students surveyed who like aerobics exercise but dislike weight lifting.

5. What is the marginal relative frequency of students surveyed who like weight lifting?

🔑 Explain 2   Conditional Relative Frequencies

A **conditional relative frequency** describes what portion of a group with a given characteristic also has another characteristic. A conditional relative frequency is found by dividing a frequency that is not in the Total row or the Total column by the total for that row or column.

Example 2   Use the joint relative frequencies to calculate the associated conditional relative frequencies and describe what each one means.

Ⓐ Use the data from Example 1A. Find the conditional relative frequency that a a person in Kenesha's survey prefers soccer, given that the person is a girl.

Divide the number of girls who prefer soccer by the total number of girls.

$$\frac{\text{Number of girls who prefer soccer}}{\text{Total number of girls}} = \frac{18}{36} = 0.5 = 50\%$$

Half of the girls in the sample prefer soccer.

Ⓑ Use the data from Example 1B. Find the conditional relative frequency that a student in Millie's survey chose an orange, given that the student is a boy.

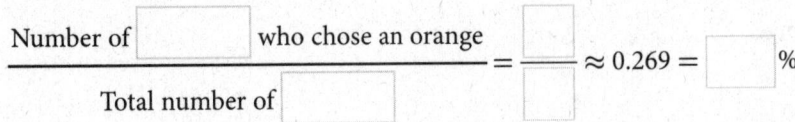

$$\frac{\text{Number of } \boxed{} \text{ who chose an orange}}{\text{Total number of } \boxed{}} = \frac{\boxed{}}{\boxed{}} \approx 0.269 = \boxed{}\%$$

Use the data from Your Turn Exercises 4 and 5 after Example 1.

6. What is the conditional relative frequency that a student likes to lift weights, given that the student does not like aerobics?

7. Find the conditional relative frequency that a student likes to lift weights, given that the student likes aerobics.

🔑 Explain 3 Finding Possible Associations

You can analyze two-way frequency tables to locate possible associations or patterns in the data.

Example 3 **Analyze the results of the surveys to determine preferences by gender.**

Kenesha is interested in the question, "Does gender influence what type of sport students prefer?" If there is no influence, then the distribution of gender within each sport preference will roughly equal the distribution of gender within the whole group. Analyze the results of Kenesha's survey from Example 1. Determine which sport each gender is more likely to prefer.

Ⓐ Analyze the data about girls that were surveyed.

Step 1: Identify the percent of all students surveyed who are girls.

$$\frac{36}{80} = 0.45 = 45\%$$

Step 2: Determine each conditional relative frequency.

Basketball	Football	Soccer
Of the 20 students who prefer basketball, 6 are girls. $\frac{6}{20} = 0.3 = 30\%$	Of the 32 students who prefer football, 12 are girls. $\frac{12}{32} = 0.375 = 37.5\%$	Of the 28 students who prefer soccer, 18 are girls. $\frac{18}{28} \approx 0.643 = 64.3\%$

Step 3: Interpret the results by comparing each conditional relative frequency to the percent of all students surveyed who are girls, 45%.

Basketball	Football	Soccer
30% < 45%	37.5% < 45%	64.3% > 45%
Girls are less likely to prefer basketball.	Girls are less likely to prefer football.	Girls are more likely to prefer soccer.

Ⓑ Analyze the data about boys that were surveyed.

Step 1: Identify the percent of all students surveyed who are boys.

$$\frac{\boxed{}}{80} = 0.\boxed{} = \boxed{}\%$$

Step 2: Determine each conditional relative frequency.

Basketball	Football	Soccer
Of the 20 students who prefer basketball, $\boxed{}$ are boys. $\frac{\boxed{}}{20} = 0.\boxed{} = \boxed{}\%$	Of the $\boxed{}$ students who prefer football, $\boxed{}$ are boys. $\frac{\boxed{}}{\boxed{}} = 0.\boxed{} = \boxed{}\%$	Of the $\boxed{}$ students who prefer soccer, $\boxed{}$ are boys. $\frac{\boxed{}}{\boxed{}} = 0.\boxed{} = \boxed{}\%$

Step 3: Interpret the results by comparing each conditional relative frequency to the percent of all students surveyed who are boys, ☐ %.

Basketball	Football	Soccer
70% > 55%	62.5% > 55%	35.7% < 55%
Boys are more likely to prefer basketball.	Boys are more likely to prefer football.	Boys are less likely to prefer soccer.

Reflect

8. **Making Connections** How can the statement "6 out of the 20 students who prefer basketball are girls" be stated as a conditional relative frequency?

_____

Your Turn

9. Analyze the data given in the Your Turn after Example 1 to determine if liking aerobic exercise influences whether a person also likes weight lifting. Explain.

💬 Elaborate

10. What does it mean to say there is an association between characteristics in a two-way frequency table?

_____

_____

11. **Essential Question Check-In** How can you use two-way frequency data to recognize possible associations between the two categories of categorical data?

_____

_____

_____

_____

⭐ Evaluate: Homework and Practice

- Online Homework
- Hints and Help
- Extra Practice

Use the table of frequency data for Exercises 1–4.

Class Survey of Favorite Colors

Favorite Color	Red	Orange	Yellow	Green	Blue	Purple	Total
Frequency	2	5	1	6	8	2	24

1. Complete the relative frequency table for this data using decimals rounded to the nearest thousandth.

Class Survey of Favorite Colors

Favorite Color	Red	Orange	Yellow	Green	Blue	Purple	Total
Relative Frequency							

2. Complete the relative frequency table for this data using percents rounded to the nearest tenth.

Class Survey of Favorite Colors

Favorite Color	Red	Orange	Yellow	Green	Blue	Purple	Total
Relative Frequency							

3. What is the relative frequency of having blue as a favorite color, expressed as a decimal?

4. Which color is a favorite color with a relative frequency of 25%?

The following frequency data shows the number of states, including the District of Columbia, that favored each party in the presidential popular vote in 1976 and in 2012.

| 1976 Election | 2012 Election | | |
	Democrat	Republican	Total
Democrat	12 =	12 =	24 =
Republican	15 =	12 =	27 =
Total	27 =	24 =	51 =

5. Complete the table above with relative frequencies using percents.

6. What percent switched from Democrat in 1976 to Republican in 2012? What type of frequency is this?

7. What percent voted Republican in 1976? What type of frequency is this?

© Houghton Mifflin Harcourt Publishing Company

The results of a survey of 45 students and the foreign language they are studying are shown in the two-way frequency table.

Gender	Language			
	Chinese	French	Spanish	Total
Girl	2	8	15	25
Boy	4	4	12	20
Total	6	12	27	45

8. Fill in the table of two-way relative frequencies using decimals, rounded to the nearest thousandth.

Gender	Language			
	Chinese	French	Spanish	Total
Girl				
Boy				
Total				

9. What fraction of the surveyed students are boys taking Spanish?

10. What fraction of the surveyed students are taking Chinese?

In some states, a driver of a vehicle may not use a handheld cell phone while driving. In one state with this law, 250 randomly selected drivers were surveyed to determine the association between drivers who know the law and drivers who obey the law. The results are shown in the table below.

11. Complete the table of two-way relative frequencies using percents.

Obeys the Law	Knows the Law		
	Yes	No	Total
Yes	160 =	45 =	
No	25 =	20 =	
Total			

12. What is the relative frequency of drivers who know and obey the law?

13. What is the relative frequency of drivers who know the law?

Refer to the election data from Exercises 5–7. Answer using percents rounded to the nearest tenth.

14. What is the conditional relative frequency of a state's popular vote being won by the Democrat in 2012, given that it was won by the Democrat in 1976?

15. What is the conditional relative frequency of a state's popular vote being won by the Democrat in 1976, given that it was won by the Democrat in 2012?

Refer to the language data from Exercises 8–10. Answer using decimals rounded to the nearest thousandth.

16. What fraction of girls are studying French?

17. What fraction of Spanish students are boys?

Refer to the cell phone law data from Exercises 11–13. Answer using percents rounded to the nearest tenth.

18. What percent of drivers obey the law despite not knowing the law?

19. What is the conditional relative frequency of drivers who obey the law, given that they know the law?

Use the previously described data to determine whether there are associations between the categories surveyed.

20. Refer to the election data from Exercises 5–7. Is there an association between the party that won the popular vote in a state in 1976 and in 2012?

21. Refer to the language data from Exercises 8–10. Can you use gender to predict a preference for taking Spanish?

22. Refer to the language data from Exercises 8–10. Is there an association between gender and a preference for French?

23. Refer to the cell phone law data from Exercises 11–13. Most drivers who don't know that it is illegal to operate a cell phone while driving obey the law anyway, presumably out of a general concern for safe driving. Does this mean there is no association between knowledge of the cell phone law and obeying the cell phone law?

24. Multipart Classification Classify each statement as describing a *joint*, *marginal*, or *conditional* relative frequency.

    a. In a study on age and driving safety, 33% of drivers were considered younger and a high accident risk.

    b. In a study on age and driving safety, 45% of older drivers were considered a high accident risk.

    c. In a study on age and driving safety, 67% of drivers were classified as younger.

    d. In a pre-election poll, 67% of the respondents who preferred the incumbent were men.

    e. In a pre-election poll, 33% of women preferred the challenger.

    f. In a pre-election poll, 16% of respondents were men who preferred the challenger.

25. Explain the Error In the survey on gender and fruit selection (Example 1B), Millicent notices that given a preference for oranges, the conditional relative frequencies of a student being a boy or a girl are the same. She concludes that there is no association between gender and orange preference. Explain her error.

26. Communicate Mathematical Ideas Can a joint relative frequency be greater than either of the conditional relative frequencies associated with it? Explain your reasoning.

27. Explain the Error Refer to the cell phone data from Exercises 11–13. Cole found the conditional relative frequency that a driver surveyed does not know the law, given that the driver obeys the law, by dividing 45 by 250. Explain Cole's error.

Lesson Performance Task

Eighty students were surveyed about playing an instrument. The results are shown in the two-way frequency table.

Gender	Play an Instrument		
	Yes	No	Total
Female	28	17	45
Male	20	15	35
Total	48	32	80

a. Complete the two-way relative frequency table for the data.

Gender	Play an Instrument		
	Yes	No	Total
Female			
Male			
Total			

b. What percent of the students surveyed play an instrument? What percent of the males surveyed do not play an instrument? Identify what type of frequency each percent is.

c. Is there an association between the sex of a student and whether the student plays an instrument? Explain.

Multi-Variable Categorical Data

Essential Question: How can you use multi-variable categorical data to solve real-world problems?

KEY EXAMPLE   *(Lesson 8.1)*

The principal of a high school surveyed 9th and 10th graders as to whether they want to go on a field trip to the museum, zoo, or botanical garden. The results of the survey are in the following table. Complete the table.

Grade	Preferred Field Trip			
	Museum	**Zoo**	**Botanical Garden**	**Total**
9th	42	28	31	
10th		52	62	142
Total	70	80	93	

$42 + 28 + 31 = 101$ Find the 9th grade row total.

$70 - 42 = 28$ Total who prefer the museum — 9th graders who prefer the museum

$70 + 80 + 93 = 243$ and $101 + 142 = 243$ Find the grand total.

Grade	Preferred Field Trip			
	Museum	**Zoo**	**Botanical Garden**	**Total**
9th	42	28	31	101
10th	28	52	62	142
Total	70	80	93	243

KEY EXAMPLE   *(Lesson 8.2)*

The principal wants to know if the percent of 10th graders who prefer the zoo is greater than the percent of total students who prefer the zoo. Find the conditional relative frequency of 10th graders who prefer the zoo and the marginal relative frequency of students who prefer the zoo. Compare the results.

The percent of 10th graders who prefer the zoo is given by the conditional relative frequency:
$$\frac{\text{Number of } 10^{th} \text{ graders who prefer the zoo}}{\text{Total number of 10th graders}} = \frac{52}{142} \approx 0.37$$

The percent of total students who prefer the zoo is given by the marginal relative frequency:
$$\frac{\text{Number of students who prefer the zoo}}{\text{Total number of students}} = \frac{80}{243} \approx 0.33.$$

Since 37% > 33%, the percent of 10th graders who prefer the zoo is greater than the percent of total students who prefer the zoo.

EXERCISES

1. Complete the two-way frequency table. Interpret the meaning of the number in the starred cell of the table. *(Lesson 8.1)*

Age	Preferred Mode of Transportation			
	Bike	Car	Bus	Total
Adults	25	3	12	
Teenagers	5	28	12	
Total		*		

2. A middle school student surveyed middle school and high school teachers on whether they preferred to have their students write in pen. *(Lesson 8.2)*

Grade Level	Prefer Students Use Pen		
	Yes	No	Total
Middle School	3	18	21
High School	7	12	19
Total	10	30	40

Are middle school teachers or high school teachers more likely to prefer that their students use pen? Explain.

MODULE PERFORMANCE TASK

Survey Says?

Students in grades 7–12 were surveyed about which of the following they would most like to do during 2 weeks of a summer vacation: visit a foreign country, attend camp, or visit a national park. The students were divided into two groups, Grades 7–9 and Grades 10–12. Here are the results:

	Visit a Foreign Country	Attend Camp	Visit a National Park
Grades 7–9	25	40	15
Grades 10–12	70	20	30

- Make a table showing the relative frequency of each of the six categories in the table compared to the results for the entire table.
- Make a circle graph, histogram, or bar graph showing the frequencies or relative frequencies of each of the six categories in the table.
- Write and answer at least five questions involving conditional relative probability that can be answered by referring to the table.
- Describe any trends you see in the data.

Use your own paper to work on the task. Use numbers, words, or algebra to explain how you reached your conclusion.

8.1–8.2 Multi-Variable Categorical Data

• Online Homework
• Hints and Help
• Extra Practice

1. A researcher surveyed 135 people, 85 females and 50 males. The researcher asked each person which of the following types of movies they preferred: action, comedy, or drama. Complete the table. *(Lesson 8.1)*

| Gender | Favorite Type of Movie | | | |
	Action	Comedy	Drama	Total
Female	35		18	
Male	12	28		
Total			28	

2. Based on the data given in the frequency table below, does a greater percent of 11th or 12th graders surveyed like tennis? Use conditional relative frequencies to support your answer. *(Lesson 8.2)*

| Grade | Like Tennis | | |
	Yes	No	Total
11th	55	55	110
12th	64	32	96
Total	119	87	206

ESSENTIAL QUESTION

3. How can you compare values in tables of two-variable categorical data?

Assessment Readiness

1. Look at each variable. Is the variable best represented by categorical data? Select Yes or No for each variable.

   A. Favorite song   ○ Yes   ○ No

   B. Car color   ○ Yes   ○ No

   C. Weight   ○ Yes   ○ No

2. Mazin asked his classmates whether they like soccer and whether they like running. The table shows the results of his survey.

Like Soccer	Like Running		
	Yes	No	Total
Yes	12		
No		6	18
Total	24	31	

   Complete the table. Choose True or False for each statement.

   A. 12 students like soccer but not running.   ○ True   ○ False

   B. Mazin surveyed 55 students in all.   ○ True   ○ False

   C. 25 students like soccer.   ○ True   ○ False

Use the following information for questions 3 and 4.

Samantha is preparing to do a survey of the language classes taken by ninth and tenth graders at her high school. Each student in ninth and tenth grade takes one language class. From school records, she knows there are 158 students in the ninth grade, as shown in the table.

Grade	Language			
	French	Mandarin	Spanish	Total
9	r	s	t	158
10	x	y	z	
Total				

3. Write an expression to represent the conditional relative frequency that a student takes Mandarin, given that the student is a tenth grader. Explain how you created the expression.

4. Based on school records, Samantha finds out that there are 65 students in ninth grade who take Spanish and 35 students in ninth grade that take French. Find the conditional probability that a student takes Mandarin, given that the student is a ninth grader. Show your work.

One-Variable Data Distributions

Essential Question: How can you use one-variable data distributions to solve real-world problems?

REAL WORLD VIDEO
In baseball, there are many options for how a team executes a given play. The use of statistics for in-game decision making sometimes reveals surprising strategies that run counter to the common wisdom.

MODULE PERFORMANCE TASK PREVIEW
Baseball Stats

Most baseball fans keep track of a few statistics relating to their favorite team—the number of home runs their favorite player has hit, for example. An entire field of statistics called sabermetrics goes much farther, keeping track of incredibly detailed data about teams and their players. One website lists 111 such statistics. In this module, you'll study ways to analyze these numbers and then apply what you've learned to some actual baseball stats.

Are YOU Ready?

Complete these exercises to review skills you will need for this module.

Measures of Center

Example 1   Find the mode, median, and mean of these data.

8, 4, 16, 8, 12, 19, 35, 8, 4, 11

4, 4, 8, 8, 8, 11, 12, 16, 19, 35   Order the data.

The mode is 8.

The middle two entries are 8 and 11.

Their mean is $\dfrac{8 + 11}{2} = 9.5$.

The median is 9.5.

The sum of all the data is 125.

There are 10 entries.

The mean is $\dfrac{125}{10}$, or 12.5.

Mode: The number with the greatest frequency is the mode.

Median: Find the middle entry or the mean of the two middle entries of the ordered data.

Mean: Find the sum of all the entries and divide it by the number of entries.

Use these data to find the measures of center.
26, 19, 14, 30, 12, 21, 30, 4

1. What is the mean?

_____

2. What is the mode?

_____

3. What is the median?

_____

Box Plots

Example 2   The box plot shown represents the ages people of a certain community were when they purchased their first automobile. What is the range of ages?

The box plot extends from 22 to 31, so the range of ages is 31 − 22, or 9 years.

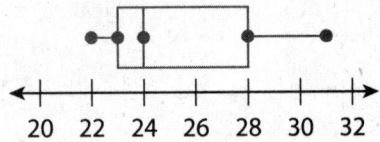

Use the box plot shown to answer the questions.

4. What is the median?

_____

5. What is the first quartile?

_____

6. What is the third quartile?

_____

9.1 Measures of Center and Spread

Essential Question: How can you describe and compare data sets?

Resource
Locker

Explore   Exploring Data

Caleb and Kim have bowled three games. Their scores are shown in the chart below.

Name	Game 1	Game 2	Game 3	Average Score
Caleb	151	153	146	
Kim	122	139	189	

Complete the table.

(A) Find Caleb's average score over the three games and enter it in the table.

$$\frac{151 + 153 + 146}{3} = \frac{\boxed{}}{3} = \boxed{}$$

(B) Find Kim's average score over the three games and enter it in the table.

$$\frac{122 + 139 + 189}{3} = \frac{\boxed{}}{3} = \boxed{}$$

(C) How do their average scores compare?

_____

(D) Caleb's / Kim's scores are more consistent.

(E) Caleb's scores are farther from / closer to the average than Kim's.

They bowl a fourth game, where Caleb scores 150 and Kim scores a 175.
How does this affect their averages?

(F) Caleb's average _____.   (G) Kim's average _____.

(H) Does the Game 4 score affect the consistency of their scores? Explain.

_____

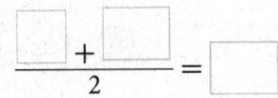

3. **Discussion** For the data on tips, which measure of center is more accurate in describing the typical value? Explain.

_____

_____

Find the mean and median of each data set.

4. Niles scored 70, 74, 72, 71, 73, and 96 on his 6 geography tests.

5. Raul recorded the following golf scores in his last 7 games.
84, 94, 93, 89, 94, 81, 90

⚙ Explain 2 Measures of Spread: Range and IQR

Measures of spread are used to describe the consistency of data values. They show the distance between data values and their distance from the center of the data. Two commonly used measures of spread for a set of numerical data are the *range* and *interquartile range (IQR)*. The **range** is the difference between the greatest and the least data values. **Quartiles** are values that divide a data set into four equal parts. The **first quartile** (Q_1) is the median of the lower half of the set, the **second quartile** (Q_2) is the median of the whole set, and the **third quartile** (Q_3) is the median of the upper half of the set. The **interquartile range** (IQR) of a data set is the difference between the third and first quartiles. It represents the range of the middle half of the data.

$$\text{Range}: 9 - 1 = 8$$
$$\text{IQR}: 7 - 3 = 4$$

1, 2, 2, 3, 3, 4, 4 5, 6, 6, 7, 7, 8, 8, 9

First quartile (Q_1): 3 | Third quartile (Q_3): 7

Median (Q_2): 5

Example 2 Find the median, range, and interquartile range for the given data set.

Ⓐ The April high temperatures for 5 years in Boston are 77 °F, 86 °F, 84 °F, 93 °F, and 90 °F

Order the data values.

Median: 77, 84, 86, 90, 93   Range: $93 - 77 = 16$
             median

Interquartile range:

lower half   upper half
77, 84, 86, 90, 93 $Q_1 = \dfrac{77 + 84}{2} = 80.5$ and $Q_3 = \dfrac{90 + 93}{2} = 91.5$
     median

$IQR = Q_3 - Q_1 = 91.5 - 80.5 = 11$

B The numbers of runs scored by a softball team in 20 games are given.

3, 4, 8, 12, 7, 5, 4, 12, 3, 9, 11, 4, 14, 8, 2, 10, 3, 10, 9, 7

Order the data values.

2, 3, 3, 3, 4, 4, 4, ☐ , ☐ , ☐ , ☐ , ☐ , ☐ , 9, 10, 10, 11, 12, 12, 14

$\underbrace{}_{\text{median}}$

Median $= \dfrac{\boxed{} + \boxed{}}{2} = \boxed{}$

Range $= 14 - 2 = \boxed{}$

Interquartile range.

$Q_1 = \dfrac{\boxed{} + \boxed{}}{2} = 4$ and $Q_3 = \dfrac{\boxed{} + \boxed{}}{2} = \boxed{}$

$IQR = Q_3 - Q_1$

$\quad = \boxed{} - \boxed{}$

$\quad = \boxed{}$

The median is _____.

The range is _____.

The IQR is _____.

Reflect

6. Discussion Why is the IQR less than the range?

_____

_____

_____

_____

Your Turn

Find the median, range, and interquartile range for the given data set.

7. 21, 31, 26, 24, 28, 26

8. The high temperatures in degrees Fahrenheit on 11 days were 68, 71, 75, 74, 75, 71, 73, 71, 72, 74, and 79.

⏺ Explain 3 Measures of Spread: Standard Deviation

Another measure of spread is the **standard deviation**, which represents the average of the distance between individual data values and the mean.

The formula for finding the standard deviation of the data set $\{x_1, x_2, x_2, x_2 \cdots, x_n\}$, with n elements and mean x, is shown below.

$$\text{standard deviation} = \sqrt{\frac{(x_1 - \bar{x})^2 + (x_2 - \bar{x})^2 + \cdots + (x_n - \bar{x})^2}{n}}$$

Example 3

(A) Find the standard deviation of 77, 86, 84, 93, 90.

Find the mean.

$$\text{mean} = \frac{77 + 86 + 84 + 93 + 90}{5}$$
$$= \frac{430}{5}$$
$$= 86$$

Complete the table.

Data Value, x	Deviation from Mean, $x - \bar{x}$	Squared Deviation, $(x - \bar{x})^2$
77	$77 - 86 = -9$	$(-9)^2 = 81$
86	$86 - 86 = 0$	$0^2 = 0$
84	$84 - 86 = -2$	$(-2)^2 = 4$
93	$93 - 86 = 7$	$7^2 = 49$
90	$90 - 86 = 4$	$4^2 = 16$

Find the mean of the squared deviations.

$$\text{mean squared deviation} = \frac{81 + 0 + 4 + 49 + 16}{5}$$
$$= \frac{150}{5}$$
$$= 30$$

Find the square root of the mean of the squared deviations, rounding to the nearest tenth. $\sqrt{30} = 5.5$

The standard deviation is approximately 5.5.

(B) Find the standard deviation of 3, 4, 8, 12, 7, 5, 4, 12, 3, 9, 11, 4, 14, 8, 2, 10, 3, 10, 9, 7.

Find the mean.

$$\text{mean} = \frac{2 + 3 + 3 + 3 + 4 + 4 + 4 + 5 + 7 + 7 + 8 + 8 + 9 + 9 + 10 + 10 + 11 + 12 + 12 + 14}{20}$$
$$= \frac{\boxed{}}{20}$$
$$= \boxed{}$$

Complete the table.

Data Value, x	Deviation from Mean, $x - \bar{x}$	Squared Deviation, $(x - \bar{x})^2$
2	$2 - \boxed{} = \boxed{}$	$\left(\boxed{}\right)^2 = \boxed{}$
3	$3 - \boxed{} = \boxed{}$	$\left(\boxed{}\right)^2 = \boxed{}$
3		
3		
4	$4 - \boxed{} = \boxed{}$	$\left(\boxed{}\right)^2 = \boxed{}$
4		
4		
5	$5 - \boxed{} = \boxed{}$	$\left(\boxed{}\right)^2 = \boxed{}$
7	$7 - \boxed{} = \boxed{}$	$\left(\boxed{}\right)^2 = \boxed{}$
7		
8	$8 - \boxed{} = \boxed{}$	$\left(\boxed{}\right)^2 = \boxed{}$
8		
9	$9 - \boxed{} = \boxed{}$	$\left(\boxed{}\right)^2 = \boxed{}$
9		
10	$10 - \boxed{} = \boxed{}$	$\left(\boxed{}\right)^2 = \boxed{}$
10		
11	$11 - \boxed{} = \boxed{}$	$\left(\boxed{}\right)^2 = \boxed{}$
12	$12 - \boxed{} = \boxed{}$	$\left(\boxed{}\right)^2 = \boxed{}$
12		
14	$14 - \boxed{} = \boxed{}$	$\left(\boxed{}\right)^2 = \boxed{}$

Find the mean of the squared deviations.

$$\text{mean squared deviation} = \frac{\boxed{}}{20}$$

$$= \frac{\boxed{}}{20}$$

$$= \boxed{}$$

Find the square root of the mean of the squared deviations, rounding to the nearest tenth.

$$\sqrt{\boxed{}} = \boxed{}$$

The standard deviation is approximately _____.

Reflect

9. In terms of data values used, what makes calculating the standard deviation different from calculating the range?

_____

_____

Your Turn

10. Find the standard deviation of 21, 31, 26, 24, 28, 26.

Data Value, x	Deviation from Mean, $x - \bar{x}$	Squared Deviation, $(x - \bar{x})^2$
21		
24		
26		
26		
28		
31		

11. Find the standard deviation of 68, 71, 75, 74, 75, 71, 73, 71, 72, 74, and 79.

12. In Your Turn 11, what is the mean of the deviations before squaring? Use your answer to explain why squaring the deviations is helpful.

_____

_____

13. How can you determine the first and third quartiles of a data set?

_____

_____

_____

14. How can you determine the standard deviation of a data set?

_____

_____

_____

15. Essential Question Check-In What does the measure of center of a data set indicate?

_____

_____

 # Evaluate: Homework and Practice

- Online Homework
- Hints and Help
- Extra Practice

1. The data set {13, 24, 14, 15, 14} gives the times of Tara's one-way ride to school (in minutes) for one week. Is the average (mean) of the times a good description of Tara's ride time? Explain.

Find the mean and median of each data set.

2. The numbers of hours Cheri works each day are 3, 7, 4, 6, and 5.

3. The weights in pounds of 6 members of a basketball team are 125, 136, 150, 119, 150, and 143.

4. 36, 18, 12, 10, 9

5. The average yearly gold price for the period from 2000–2009:

$279.11, $271.04, $309.73, $363.38, $409.72, $444.74, $603.46, $695.39, $871.96, $972.35

6. There are 28, 30, 29, 26, 31, and 30 students in a school's six Algebra 1 classes.

7. 13, 14, 18, 13, 12, 17, 15, 12

8. The numbers of members in five karate classes are 13, 12, 10, 16, and 19.

9. Find the range and interquartile range for 3, 7, 4, 6, and 5.

10. Find the range and interquartile range for 125, 136, 150, 119, 150, and 143.

11. Find the range and interquartile range for 36, 18, 12, 10, and 9.

12. Find the range and interquartile range for $279.11, $271.04, $309.73, $363.38, $409.72, $444.74, $603.46, $695.39, $871.96, and $972.35.

13. Find the range and interquartile range for 28, 30, 29, 26, 31, and 30.

14. Find the range and interquartile range for 13, 14, 18, 13, 12, 17, 15, and 12.

15. Find the range and interquartile range for 13, 12, 15, 17, and 9.

16. Find the standard deviation of 3, 7, 4, 6, and 5.

17. Find the standard deviation of 125, 136, 150, 119, 150, and 143.

18. Find the standard deviation of 36, 18, 12, 10, and 9.

19. Find the standard deviation of $279.11, $271.04, $309.73, $363.38, $409.72, $444.74, $603.46, $695.39, $871.96, and $972.35. Round the mean to the nearest $0.01 and the squared deviations to the nearest whole number.

20. Find the standard deviation of 28, 30, 29, 26, 31, and 30.

21. Find the standard deviation of 13, 14, 18, 13, 12, 17, 15, and 12.

22. Determine whether or not the third quartile has the same value as a member of the data set. Select the correct answer for each lettered part.

    A. {79, 91, 90, 99, 91, 80, 80, 90} ☐ Yes ☐ No

    B. {98, 96, 96, 95, 91, 81, 87} ☐ Yes ☐ No

    C. {88, 95, 89, 93, 88, 93, 84, 93, 85, 92} ☐ Yes ☐ No

    D. {97, 84, 96, 82, 93, 88, 82, 91, 94} ☐ Yes ☐ No

    E. {94, 85, 95, 80, 97} ☐ Yes ☐ No

    F. {85, 89, 81, 89, 85, 84} ☐ Yes ☐ No

Use this data for Exercises 23 and 24. The numbers of members in 6 yoga clubs are 80, 74, 77, 71, 75, and 91.

23. Find the standard deviation of the numbers of members to the nearest tenth.

H.O.T. Focus on Higher Order Thinking

24. Explain the Error Suppose a person in the club with 91 members transfers to the club with 71 members. A student claims that the measures of center and the measures of spread will all change. Correct the student's error.

25. What If? If all the values in a set are increased by 10, does the range also increase by 10? Explain.

26. Communicate Mathematical Ideas Jorge has a data set with the following values: 92, 80, 88, 95, and x. If the median value for this set is 88, what must be true about x? Explain.

27. Critical Thinking If the value for the median of a set is not found in the data set, what must be true about the data set? Explain.

Lesson Performance Task

The table lists the ages of the soprano and bass singers in a town choir. Find the mean, median, range, interquartile range, and standard deviation for each type of singer in the data set. Interpret each result. What can you conclude about the ages of the different types of singers?

Age of Soprano Singers	63	42	28	45	36	48	32	40	57	49
Age of Bass Singers	32	34	53	35	43	41	29	35	24	34

9.2 Data Distributions and Outliers

Essential Question: What statistics are most affected by outliers, and what shapes can data distributions have?

⊘ Explore   Using Dot Plots to Display Data

A **dot plot** is a data representation that uses a number line and Xs, dots, or other symbols to show frequency. Dot plots are sometimes called *line plots*.

Finance Twelve employees at a small company make the following annual salaries (in thousands of dollars): 25, 30, 35, 35, 35, 40, 40, 40, 45, 45, 50, and 60.

Ⓐ Choose the number line with the most appropriate scale for this problem. Explain your reasoning.

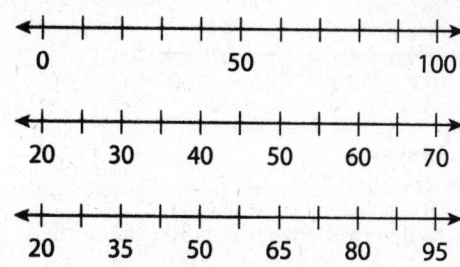

_____

_____

_____

_____

Ⓑ Create and label a dot plot of the data. Put an X above the number line for each time that value appears in the data set.

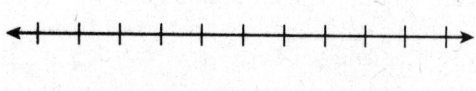

Salary (thousands of dollars)

Reflect

1. **Discussion** Recall that quantitative data can be expressed as a numerical measurement. Categorical, qualitative data is expressed in categories, such as attributes or preferences. Is it appropriate to use a dot plot for displaying quantitative data, qualitative data, or both? Explain.

_____

⚙ Explain 1 The Effects of an Outlier in a Data Set

An **outlier** is a value in a data set that is much greater or much less than most of the other values in the data set. Outliers are determined by using the first or third quartiles and the IQR.

How to Identify an Outlier
A data value x is an outlier if $x < Q_1 - 1.5(\text{IQR})$ or if $x > Q_3 + 1.5(\text{IQR})$.

Example 1 Create a dot plot for the data set using an appropriate scale for the number line. Determine whether the extreme value is an outlier.

Ⓐ Suppose that the list of salaries from the Explore is expanded to include the owner's salary of $150,000. Now the list of salaries is 25, 30, 35, 35, 35, 40, 40, 40, 45, 45, 50, 60, and 150.

To choose an appropriate scale, consider the minimum and maximum values, 25 and 150.

A number line from 20 to 160 will contain all the values. A scale of 5 will be convenient for the data. Label tick marks by 20s.

Plot each data value to see the distribution.

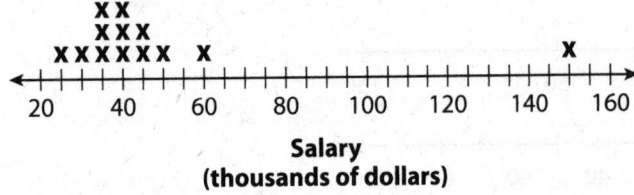

Salary
(thousands of dollars)

Find the quartiles and the IQR to determine whether 150 is an outlier.

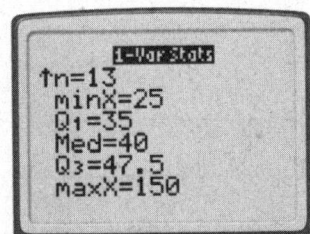

$$150 \overset{?}{>} Q_3 + 1.5(\text{IQR})$$

$$150 \overset{?}{>} 47.5 + 1.5(47.5 - 35)$$

$$150 > 66.25 \text{ True}$$

150 is an outlier.

Ⓑ Suppose that the salaries from Part A were adjusted so that the owner's salary is $65,000.

Now the list of salaries is 25, 30, 35, 35, 35, 40, 40, 40, 45, 45, 50, 60, and 65.

To choose an appropriate scale, consider the minimum and maximum data values, _____ and _____.

A number line from _____ to _____ will contain all the data values.

A scale of _____ will be convenient for the data.

Label tick marks by _____.

Plot each data value to see the distribution.

Salary (thousands of dollars)

20   70

Find the quartiles and the IQR to determine whether 65 is an outlier.

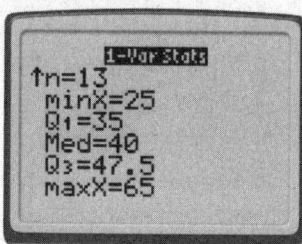

$$65 \overset{?}{>} Q_3 + 1.5(\text{IQR})$$

$$65 \overset{?}{>} \boxed{} + 1.5\left(\boxed{} - \boxed{}\right)$$

$$65 > \boxed{} \quad \text{True / False}$$

Therefore, 65 is / is not an outlier.

Reflect

2. Explain why the median was NOT affected by changing the max data value from 150 to 65.

_____

_____

Your Turn

3. **Sports** Baseball pitchers on a major league team throw at the following speeds (in miles per hour): 72, 84, 89, 81, 93, 100, 90, 88, 80, 84, and 87.

   Create a dot plot using an appropriate scale for the number line. Determine whether the extreme value is an outlier.

⚷ Explain 2   Comparing Data Sets

Numbers that characterize a data set, such as measures of center and spread, are called **statistics**. They are useful when comparing large sets of data.

Example 2   Calculate the mean, median, interquartile range (IQR), and standard deviation for each data set, and then compare the data.

Ⓐ **Sports** The tables list the average ages of players on 15 teams randomly selected from the 2010 teams in the National Football League (NFL) and Major League Baseball (MLB). Describe how the average ages of NFL players compare to those of MLB players.

NFL Players' Average Ages, by Team
25.8, 26.0, 26.3, 25.7, 25.1, 25.2, 26.1, 26.4, 25.9, 26.6, 26.3, 26.2, 26.8, 25.6, 25.7

MLB Players' Average Ages, by Team
28.5, 29.0, 28.0, 27.8, 29.5, 29.1, 26.9, 28.9, 28.6, 28.7, 26.9, 30.5, 28.7, 28.9, 29.3

On a graphing calculator, enter the two sets of data into L_1 and L_2.

Use the "1-Var Stats" feature to find statistics for the data in lists L_1 and L_2. Your calculator may use the following notations: mean $\bar{x}$, standard deviation σ_x.

Scroll down to see the median (Med), Q_1, and Q_3. Complete the table.

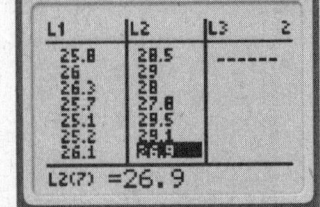

	Mean	Median	IQR ($Q_3 - Q_1$)	Standard deviation
NFL	25.98	26.00	0.60	0.46
MLB	28.62	28.70	1.10	0.91

Compare the corresponding statistics.

The mean age and median age are lower for the NFL than for the MLB, which means that NFL players tend to be younger than MLB players. In addition, the IQR and standard deviation are smaller for the NFL than for the MLB, which means that the ages of NFL players are closer together than those of MLB players.

(B) The tables list the ages of 10 contestants on 2 game shows.

Game Show 1
18, 20, 25, 48, 35, 39, 46, 41, 30, 27

Game Show 2
24, 29, 36, 32, 34, 41, 21, 38, 39, 26

On a graphing calculator, enter the two sets of data into L_1 and L_2.

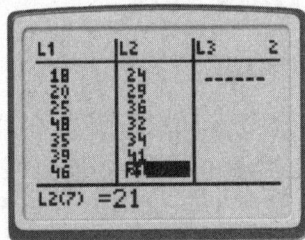

Complete the table. Then circle the correct items to compare the statistics.

	Mean	Median	IQR ($Q_3 - Q_1$)	Standard deviation
Show 1				
Show 2				

The mean is lower for the 1st / 2nd game show, which means that contestants in the 1st / 2nd game show are on average younger than contestants in the 1st / 2nd game show. However, the median is lower for the 1st / 2nd game show, which means that although contestants are on average younger on the 1st / 2nd game show, there are more young contestants on the 1st / 2nd game show. Finally, the IQR and standard deviation are higher for the 1st / 2nd game show, which means that the ages of contestants on the 1st / 2nd game show are further apart than the age of contestants on the 1st/ 2nd game show.

4. The tables list the age of each member of Congress in two randomly selected states. Complete the table and compare the data.

Illinois
26, 24, 28, 46, 39, 59, 31, 26, 64, 40, 69, 62, 31, 28, 26, 76, 57, 71, 58, 35, 32, 49, 51, 22, 33, 56

Arizona
42, 37, 58, 32, 46, 42, 26, 56, 27

	Mean	Median	IQR ($Q_3 - Q_1$)	Standard deviation
Illinois				
Arizona				

Explain 3   **Comparing Data Distributions**

A data distribution can be described as **symmetric**, **skewed to the left**, or **skewed to the right**, depending on the general shape of the distribution in a dot plot or other data display.

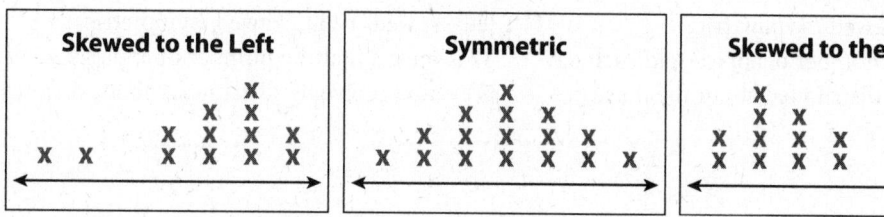

Example 3 For each data set, make a dot plot and determine the type of distribution. Then explain what the distribution means for each data set.

(A) **Sports** The data table shows the number of miles run by members of two track teams during one day.

Miles	3	3.5	4	4.5	5	5.5	6
Members of Team A	2	3	4	4	3	2	0
Members of Team B	1	2	2	3	3	4	3

Team A

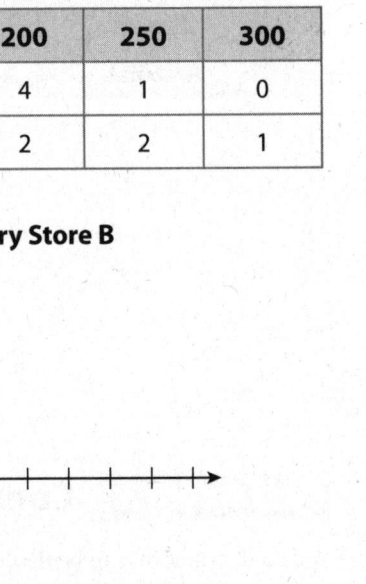

Team B

The data for team A show a symmetric distribution. This means that the distances run are evenly distributed about the mean.

The data for team B show a distribution skewed to the left. This means that more than half the team members ran a distance greater than the mean.

Ⓑ The table shows the number of days, over the course of a month, that specific numbers of apples were sold by competing grocers.

Number of Apples Sold	0	50	100	150	200	250	300
Grocery Store A	1	4	8	8	4	1	0
Grocery Store B	3	6	8	8	2	2	1

Grocery Store A

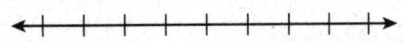

Grocery Store B

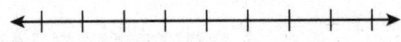

The distribution for grocery store A is: left-skewed/right-skewed / symmetric.
This means that the number of apples sold each day is evenly / unevenly distributed about the mean.

The distribution for grocery store B is: left-skewed/ right-skewed /symmetric.
This means that the number of apples sold each day is evenly/ unevenly distributed about the mean.

Reflect

7. Will the mean and median in a symmetric distribution always be approximately equal? Explain.

_____

_____

8. Will the mean and median in a skewed distribution always be approximately equal? Explain.

_____

_____

_____

9. **Sports** The table shows the number of free throws attempted during a basketball game. Make a dot plot and determine the type of distribution. Then explain what the distribution means for the data set.

Free Throws Shot	0	2	4	6	8
Members of Team A	2	2	4	2	2
Members of Team B	3	4	2	2	1

Team A

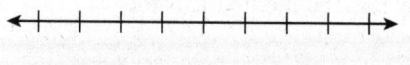

Number of Free Throws

Team B

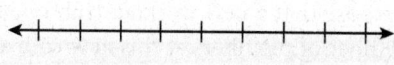

Number of Free Throws

Elaborate

10. If the mean increases after a single data point is added to a set of data, what can you tell about this data point?

_____

_____

11. How can you use a calculation to decide whether a data point is an outlier in a data set?

_____

_____

_____

_____

12. **Essential Question Check-In** What three shapes can data distributions have?

_____

• Online Homework
• Hints and Help
• Extra Practice

Fitness The numbers of members in 8 workout clubs are 100, 95, 90, 85, 85, 95, 100, and 90. Use this information for Exercises 1–2.

1. Create a dot plot for the data set using an appropriate scale for the number line.

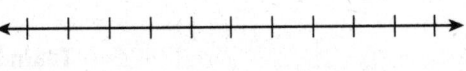

Number of Members

2. Suppose that a new workout club opens and immediately has 150 members. Is the number of members at this new club an outlier?

Sports The number of feet to the left outfield wall for 10 randomly chosen baseball stadiums is 315, 325, 335, 330, 330, 330, 320, 310, 325, and 335. Use this information for Exercises 3–4.

3. Create a dot plot for the data set using an appropriate scale for the number line.

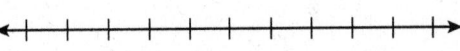

Number of Feet

4. The longest distance to the left outfield wall in a baseball stadium is 355 feet. Is this stadium an outlier if it is added to the data set?

Education The numbers of students in 10 randomly chosen classes in a high school are 18, 22, 26, 31, 25, 20, 23, 26, 29, and 30. Use this information for Exercises 5–6.

5. Create a dot plot for the data set using an appropriate scale for the number line.

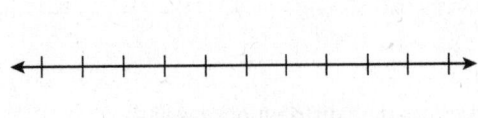

Number of Students

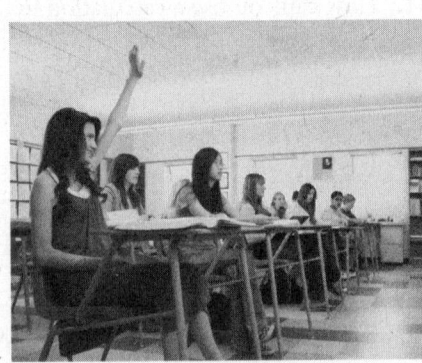

6. Suppose that a new class is opened for enrollment and currently has 7 students. Is this class an outlier if it is added to the data set?

© Houghton Mifflin Harcourt Publishing Company • Image Credits: ©Blend Images/Alamy

Sports The average bowling scores for a group of bowlers are 200, 210, 230, 220, 230, 225, and 240. Use this information for Exercises 7–8.

7. Create a dot plot for the data set using an appropriate scale for the number line.

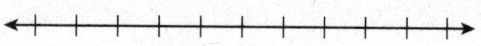

Bowling Scores

8. Suppose that a new bowler joins this group and has an average score of 275. Is this bowler an outlier in the data set?

The tables describe the average ages of employees from two randomly chosen companies. Use this information for Exercises 9–10.

Company A
23, 29, 35, 46, 51, 50, 42, 37, 30

Company B
24, 23, 45, 45, 42, 52, 55, 47, 55

9. Calculate the mean, median, interquartile range (IQR), and standard deviation for each data set.

	Mean	Median	IQR $(Q_3 - Q_1)$	Standard deviation
Company A				
Company B				

10. Compare the data sets.

The tables describe the size of microwaves, in cubic feet, chosen randomly from two competing companies. Use this information for Exercises 11–12.

Company A
1.8, 2.1, 3.1, 2.0, 3.3, 2.9, 3.3, 2.1, 3.2

Company B
1.9, 2.6, 1.8, 3.0, 2.5, 2.8, 2.0, 3.6, 3.1

11. Calculate the mean, median, interquartile range (IQR), and standard deviation for each data set.

	Mean	Median	IQR $(Q_3 - Q_1)$	Standard deviation
Company A				
Company B				

12. Compare the data sets.

For each data set, make a dot plot and determine the type of distribution. Then explain what the distribution means for each data set.

13. Sports The data table shows the number of miles run by members of two teams running a marathon.

Miles	5	10	15	20	25
Members of Team A	3	5	10	5	3
Members of Team B	6	10	4	1	5

Team A

Team B

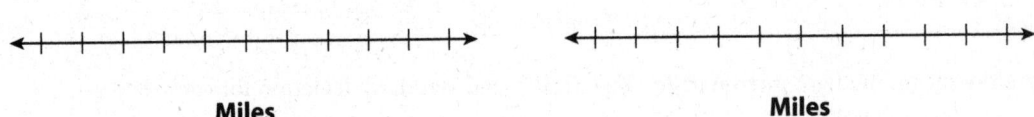

Miles

Miles

14. Sales The data table shows the number of days that specific numbers of turkeys were sold. These days were in the two weeks before Thanksgiving.

Number of Turkeys	10	20	30	40
Grocery Store A	2	5	5	2
Grocery Store B	5	5	1	3

Grocery Store A

Grocery Store B

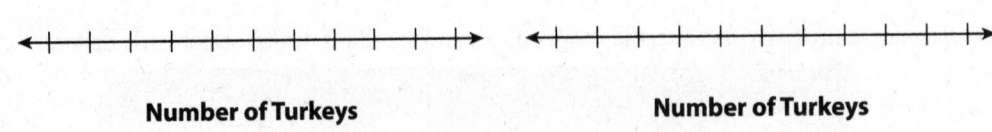

Number of Turkeys

Number of Turkeys

15. State whether each set of data is left-skewed, right-skewed, or symmetrically distributed.

    A. 3, 5, 5, 3

    B. 1, 1, 3, 1

    C. 7, 9, 9, 11

    D. 5, 5, 3, 3

    E. 19, 21, 21, 19

H.O.T. Focus on Higher Order Thinking

16. What If? Given the data set 8, 15, 12, 10, and 5, what happens to the mean if you add a data value of 40? Is 40 an outlier of the new data set?

17. Critical Thinking Can an outlier be a data value between Q_1 and Q_3? Justify your answer.

18. Justify Reasoning If the distribution has outliers, why will they always have an effect on the range?

19. Education The data table describes the average testing scores in 20 randomly selected classes in two randomly selected high schools, rounded to the nearest ten. For each data set, make a dot plot, determine the type of distribution, and explain what the distribution means in context.

Average Scores	0	10	20	30	40	50	60	70	80	90	100
School A	0	1	2	2	3	4	3	2	2	1	0
School B	0	1	1	1	2	4	5	4	2	0	0

School A

School B

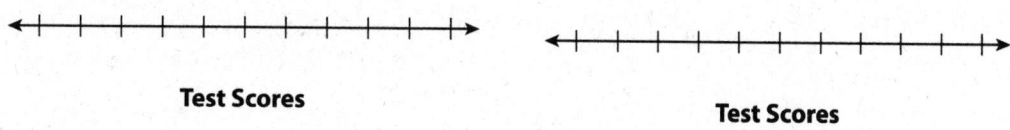

Test Scores

Test Scores

Lesson Performance Task

The tables list the daily car sales of two competing dealerships.

Dealer A			
14	13	15	12
15	16	15	17
17	12	16	14
15	16	14	16
13	14	18	15

Dealer B			
16	17	15	20
18	19	18	17
19	10	19	18
15	17	20	19
18	18	16	17

A. Calculate the mean, median, interquartile range (IQR), and standard deviation for each data set. Compare the measures of center for the two dealers.

	Mean	Median	IQR ($Q_3 - Q_1$)	Standard deviation
Dealer A				
Dealer B				

_____

_____

B. Create a dot plot for each data set. Compare the distributions of the data sets.

Dealer A   **Dealer B**

C. Determine if there are any outliers in the data sets. If there are, remove the outlier and find the statistics for that data set(s). What was affected by the outlier?

9.3 Histograms and Box Plots

Essential Question: How can you interpret and compare data sets using data displays?

Resource
Locker

⊘ Explore Understanding Histograms

A **histogram** is a bar graph that is used to display the frequency of data divided into equal intervals. The bars must be of equal width and should touch but not overlap. The heights of the bars indicate the frequency of data values within each interval.

(A) Look at the histogram of "Scores on a Math Test." Which axis indicates the frequency?

The _____ axis shows the frequency for each interval.

(B) What does the horizontal axis indicate?

The horizontal axis shows the _____.

(C) How is the horizontal axis organized?

It is organized in groups of _____.

(D) How many had scores in the interval 60–69? ☐

(E) How many had scores in the interval 70–79? ☐

(F) How many had scores in the interval 80–89? ☐

(G) How many had scores in the interval 90–99? ☐

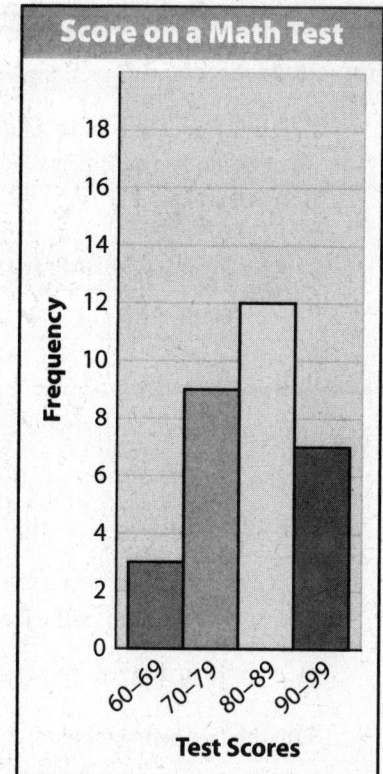

Score on a Math Test

Test Scores

Reflect

1. What statistical information can you tell about a data set by looking at a histogram? What statistical information cannot be determined by looking at a histogram?

_____

_____

2. How many test scores were collected? How do you know?

_____

_____

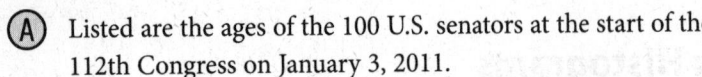

Explain 1 Creating Histograms

When creating a histogram, make sure that the bars are of equal width and that they touch without overlapping. Create a frequency table to help organize the data before constructing the histogram. Consider the range of the data values when creating intervals.

Example 1 Create a frequency table from the data. Then use the frequency table to create a histogram.

Ⓐ Listed are the ages of the 100 U.S. senators at the start of the 112th Congress on January 3, 2011.

39, 39, 42, 44, 46, 47, 47, 47, 48, 49, 49, 49, 50, 50, 51, 51,
52, 52, 53, 53, 54, 54, 55, 55, 55, 55, 55, 55, 56, 56, 57, 57,
57, 58, 58, 58, 58, 58, 59, 59, 59, 59, 60, 60, 60, 60, 60, 60,
60, 61, 61, 62, 62, 62, 63, 63, 63, 63, 64, 64, 64, 64, 66, 66,
66, 67, 67, 67, 67, 67, 67, 67, 68, 68, 68, 68, 69, 69, 69, 70,
70, 70, 71, 71, 73, 73, 74, 74, 74, 75, 76, 76, 76, 76, 77, 77,
78, 86, 86, 86

Create a frequency table. The data values range from 39 to 86, so use an interval width of 10 and start the first interval at 30.

Age Interval	Frequency
30–39	2
40–49	10
50–59	30
60–69	37
70–79	18
80–89	3

Check that the sum of the frequencies is 100.

$2 + 10 + 30 + 37 + 18 + 3 = 100$

Use the frequency table to create a histogram.

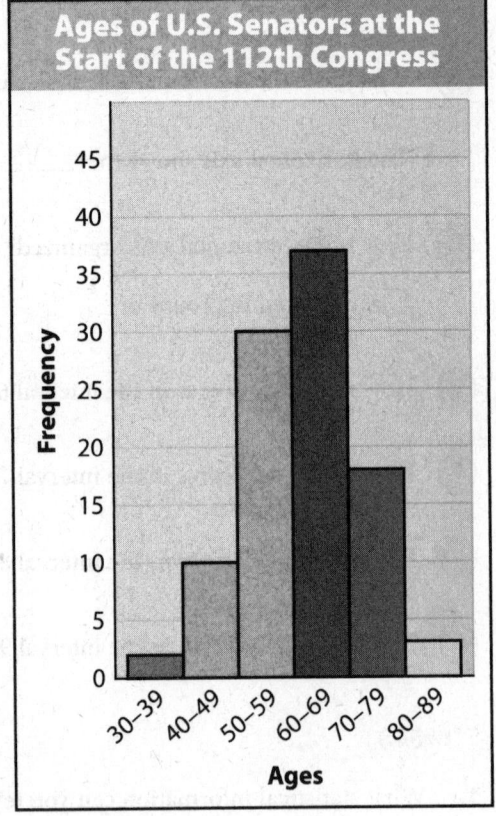

Ages of U.S. Senators at the Start of the 112th Congress

Ⓑ Listed are the scores from a golf tournament.

68, 78, 76, 71, 69, 73, 72, 74, 76, 70, 77, 74, 75, 76, 71, 74

Create a frequency table. The data values range from [ ] to [ ],

so use an interval width of 3, and start the first interval at [ ].

Score Interval	Frequency
68– [ ]	[ ]
71– [ ]	[ ]
74– [ ]	[ ]
77– [ ]	[ ]

Check that the sum of the frequencies is [ ].

$3 + 4 + 7 + 2 =$ [ ]

Use the frequency table to create a histogram.

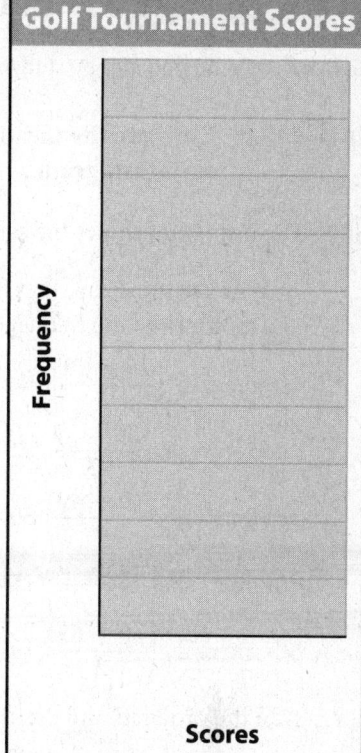

Golf Tournament Scores

Reflect

3. Describe the shape of the distribution of senators' ages. Interpret the meaning.

_____

_____

Your Turn

4. Listed are the heights of players, in inches, on a basketball team. Create a frequency table from the data. Then use the frequency table to create a histogram.

79, 75, 74, 68, 63, 76, 74, 73, 69, 65, 71, 68, 74, 73, 70

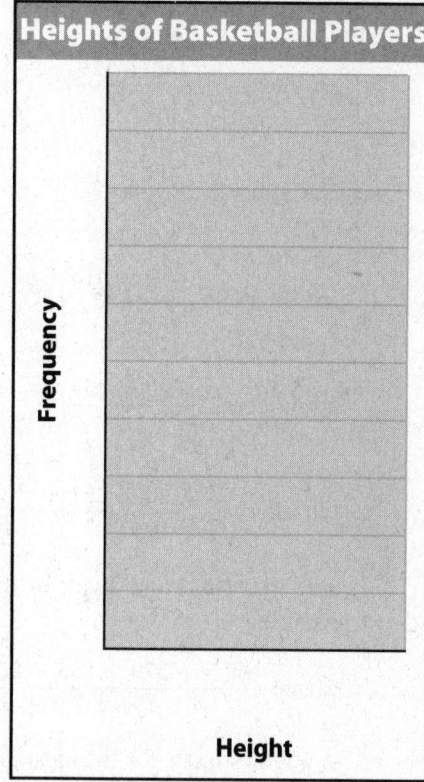

Heights of Basketball Players

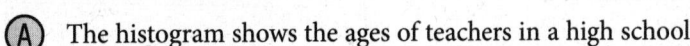

Explain 2 Estimating from Histograms

You can estimate statistics by studying a histogram.

Example 2 Estimate the mean of the data set displayed in each histogram.

Ⓐ The histogram shows the ages of teachers in a high school.

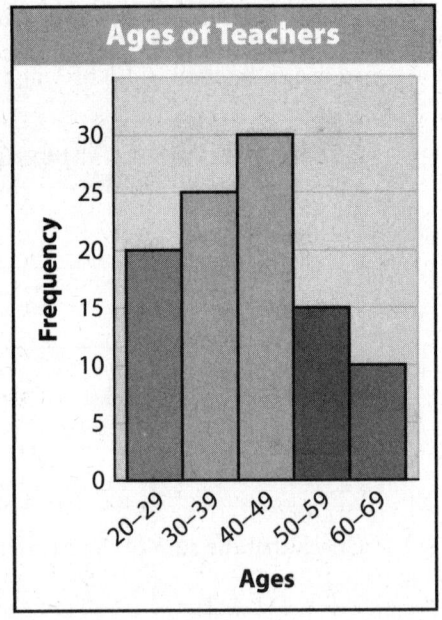

To estimate the mean, first find the midpoint of each interval, and multiply by the frequency.

1st interval: $\left(\dfrac{20+29}{2}\right)(20) = (24.5)(20) = 490$

2nd interval: $\left(\dfrac{30+39}{2}\right)(25) = (34.5)(25) = 862.5$

3rd interval: $\left(\dfrac{40+49}{2}\right)(30) = (44.5)(30) = 1335$

4th interval: $\left(\dfrac{50+59}{2}\right)(15) = (54.5)(15) = 817.5$

5th interval: $\left(\dfrac{60+69}{2}\right)(10) = (64.5)(10) = 645$

Add the products and divide by the sum of the frequencies.

Mean: $\dfrac{490+862.5+1335+817.5+645}{20+25+30+15+10} = \dfrac{4150}{100} = 41.5$

A good estimate for the mean of this data set is an age of 41.5.

Ⓑ The histogram shows the 2012 Olympic results for women's weightlifting.

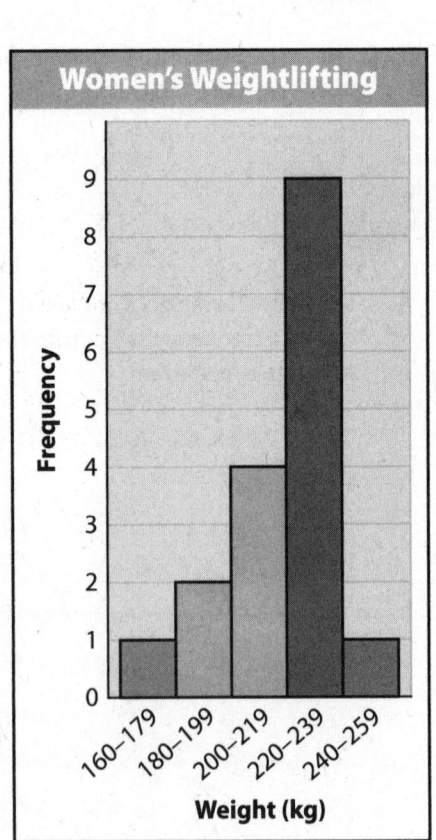

To estimate the mean, first find the midpoint of each interval, and multiply by the frequency.

1st interval: $\left(\dfrac{160+179}{2}\right)\Box = \boxed{}\ \Box = \boxed{}$

2nd interval: $\left(\dfrac{180+199}{2}\right)\Box = \boxed{}\ \Box = \boxed{}$

3rd interval: $\left(\dfrac{200+219}{2}\right)\Box = \boxed{}\ \Box = \boxed{}$

4th interval: $\left(\dfrac{220+239}{2}\right)\Box = \boxed{}\ \Box = \boxed{}$

5th interval: $\left(\dfrac{240+259}{2}\right)\Box = \boxed{}\ \Box = \boxed{}$

Add the results and divide by the total number of values in the data set.

Mean: $\dfrac{169.5+379+838+2065.5+249.5}{1+2+4+9+1} = \dfrac{\boxed{}}{17} \approx \boxed{}$

A good estimate for the mean of this data set is $\boxed{}$ kg.

5. The histogram shows the length, in days, of Maria's last vacations. Estimate the mean of the data set displayed in the histogram.

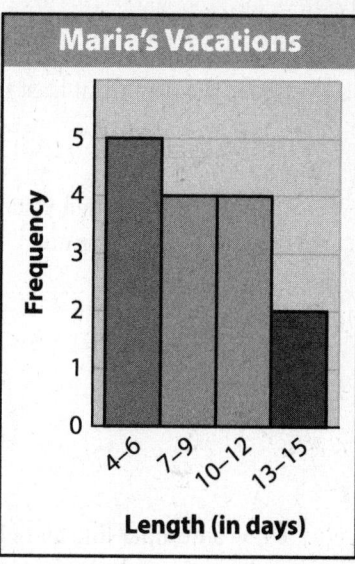

Maria's Vacations

Frequency

Length (in days)

4-6   7-9   10-12   13-15

🎵 Explain 3   Constructing Box Plots

A box plot can be used to show how the values in a data set are distributed. You need 5 values to make a box plot: the minimum (or least value), first quartile, median, third quartile, and maximum (or greatest value).

Example 3   Use the data to make a box plot.

Ⓐ The numbers of runs scored by a softball team in 20 games are given.

3, 4, 8, 12, 7, 5, 4, 12, 3, 9, 11, 4, 14, 8, 2, 10, 3, 10, 9, 7

Order the data from least to greatest.

2, 3, 3, 3, 4, 4, 4, 5, 7, 7, 8, 8, 9, 9, 10, 10, 11, 12, 12, 14

Identify the 5 needed values. Those values are the minimum, first quartile, median, third quartile, and maximum.

2, 3, 3, 3, 4, 4, 4, 5, 7, 7, 8, 8, 9, 9, 10, 10, 11, 12, 12, 14

Minimum	Q_1	Median	Q_3	Maximum
2	4	7.5	10	14

Draw a number line and plot a point above each of the 5 needed values. Draw a box whose ends go through the first and third quartiles, and draw a vertical line segment through the median. Draw horizontal line segments from the box to the minimum and maximum.

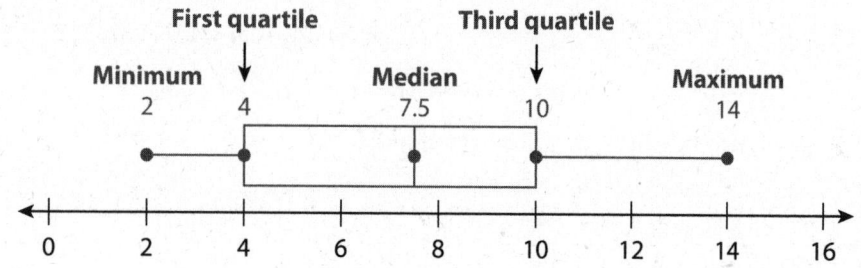

First quartile   Third quartile

Minimum   Median   Maximum
2   4   7.5   10   14

0   2   4   6   8   10   12   14   16

Ⓑ 13, 14, 18, 13, 12, 17, 15, 12, 13, 19, 11, 14, 14, 18, 22, 23

Order the data from least to greatest.

[ ], 12, 12, [ ], [ ], 13, 14, [ ], [ ], 15, 17, [ ], [ ], 19, 22 [ ]

Identify the 5 needed values. Those values are the minimum, first quartile, median, third quartile, and maximum.

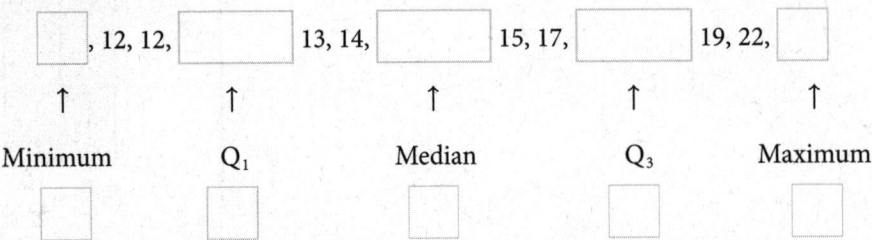

[ ], 12, 12, [ ] 13, 14, [ ] 15, 17, [ ] 19, 22, [ ]

↑ ↑ ↑ ↑ ↑

Minimum   Q₁   Median   Q₃   Maximum

[ ]   [ ]   [ ]   [ ]   [ ]

Draw a number line and plot a point above each of the 5 needed values. Draw a box whose ends go through the first and third quartiles, and draw a vertical line through the median. Draw horizontal lines from the box to the minimum and maximum.

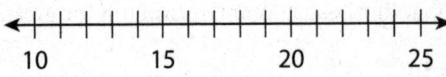

10   15   20   25

Reflect

6. The lines that extend from the box in a box plot are sometimes called "whiskers." What part (lower, middle, or upper) and about what percent of the data does the box represent? What part and about what percent does each "whisker" represent?

_____

_____

7. Which measures of spread can be determined from the box plot, and how are they found? Calculate each measure.

_____

_____

Your Turn

Use the data to make a box plot.

8. 25, 28, 26, 16, 18, 15, 25, 28, 26, 16

9. The numbers of goals scored by Lisa's soccer team in 13 games are listed below.

2, 3, 4, 1, 1, 3, 4, 2, 6, 2, 2, 3, 2

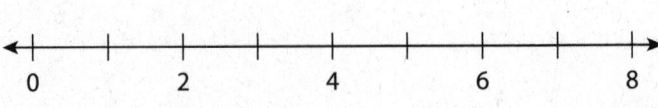

15   20   25   30   0   2   4   6   8

⊘ Explain 4 Comparing Box Plots

You can plot two box plots above a single number line to compare two data sets.

Example 4 Construct two box plots, one for each data set. Compare the medians and measures of variation for each distribution.

Ⓐ The tables show the total gross earnings, in dollars, for the top 10 movies of 2013 and 2012.

Total Gross Earnings by the Top 25 Movies of 2013 & 2012				
Rank	**Total Gross in 2013**		**Rank**	**Total Gross in 2012**
1	$420,468,544		1	$623,357,910
2	$409,013,994		2	$448,139,099
3	$368,061,265		3	$408,010,692
4	$352,946,000		4	$304,360,277
5	$291,045,518		5	$303,003,568
6	$268,492,764		6	$292,324,737
7	$262,547,000		7	$262,030,663
8	$253,029,814		8	$237,283,207
9	$238,679,850		9	$218,815,487
10	$234,911,825		10	$216,391,482

🧩 Analyze Information

For each set of data, identify the five values you need to make a box plot: the

minimum, _____. In this

case, the data is from least to _____ reading from the bottom to the top.

🧩 Formulate a Plan

With the _____ needed values for each data set, construct 2 _____

on the same number line. The number line for both plots can go from $ _____

million to $ _____ million. Interpret the box plots to compare the gross
earnings for the top 10 movies in 2012 and 2013.

Solve

Using the statistics feature of a graphing calculator, find the five needed values, rounded to the nearest hundred million.

	2013 Top 10 Movies Gross Earnings ($100,000,000s)	2012 Top 10 Movies Gross Earnings ($100,000,000s)
Minimum		
Q_1		
Median		
Q_3		
Maximum		

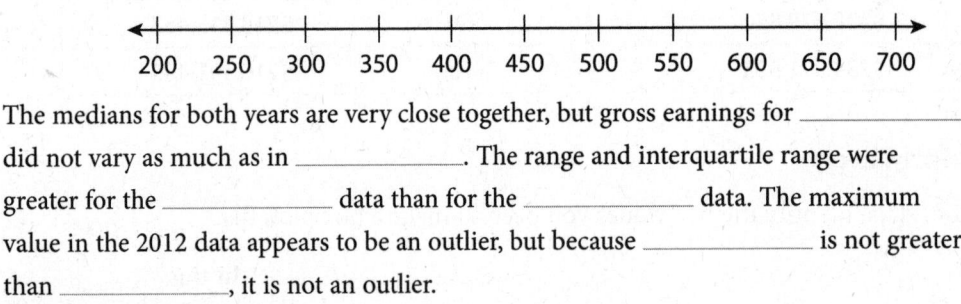

The medians for both years are very close together, but gross earnings for _____ did not vary as much as in _____. The range and interquartile range were greater for the _____ data than for the _____ data. The maximum value in the 2012 data appears to be an outlier, but because _____ is not greater than _____, it is not an outlier.

Justify and Evaluate

Considering the little difference between minimum values but the great difference between maximum values the data sets, it makes sense that their measures of variation would / would not be alike.

Your Turn

Construct two box plots, one for each data set. Compare the medians and measures of variation for each distribution.

10. The net worth of the 10 richest people in the world for 2012 and 2013 (in billions) are:
    2012: 69, 61, 44, 41, 37.5, 36, 30, 26, 25.5, 25.4   **2013:** 73, 67, 57, 53.5, 43, 34, 34, 31, 30, 29

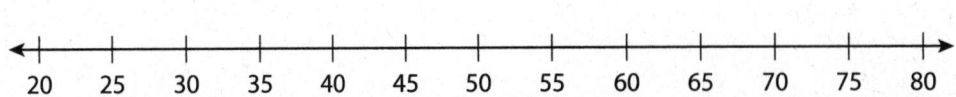

11. The ages of the 10 richest people in the world for 2012 and 2013 (in years) are:

2012: 72, 56, 81, 63, 75, 67, 55, 64, 83, 92   **2013**: 72, 57, 76, 82, 68, 77, 72, 84, 90, 63

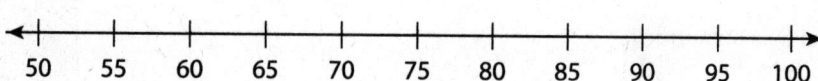

⊙ **Elaborate**

12. How can you create a histogram from a data set?

_____

_____

_____

13. How can you create a box plot from a data set?

_____

_____

_____

14. **Essential Question Check-In** How can you use histograms and box plots to interpret and compare data sets?

_____

_____

• Online Homework
• Hints and Help
• Extra Practice

Use the histogram to answer the following questions.

1. What does each axis indicate?

2. How is the horizontal axis organized?

3. How many bowlers competed?

4. Describe the general shape of the distribution.

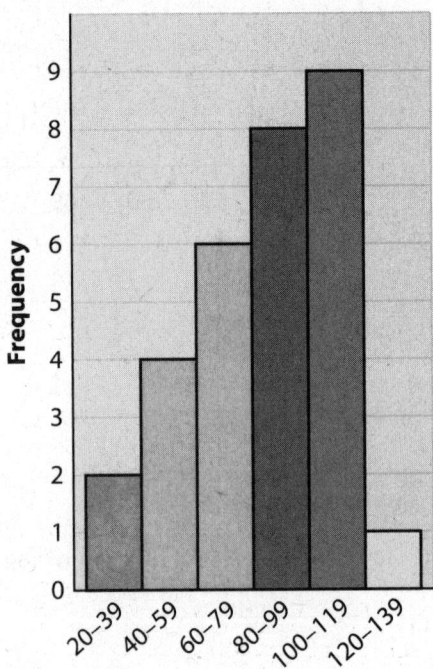

Create a histogram for the given data.

5. Listed are the ages of the first 44 U.S. presidents on the date of their first inauguration.

57, 61, 57, 57, 58, 57, 61, 54, 68, 51, 49, 64, 50, 48, 65, 52, 56, 46, 54, 49, 51, 47, 55, 55, 54, 42, 51, 56, 55, 51, 54, 51, 60, 62, 43, 55, 56, 61, 52, 69, 64, 46, 54, 47

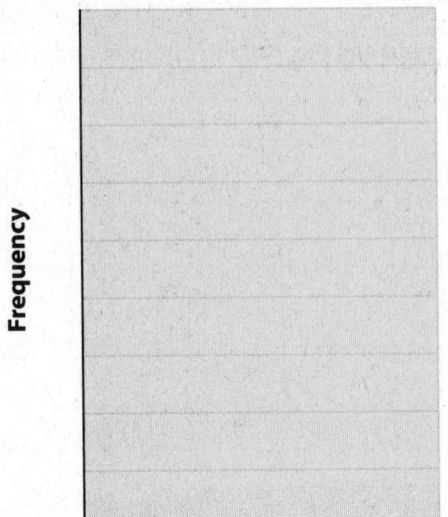

6. Listed are the breathing intervals, in minutes, of gray whales.

8, 5, 13, 7, 16, 9, 15, 11, 8, 6, 10, 9, 9, 11, 14, 12, 13, 15, 16, 11, 14, 9, 15, 6, 14

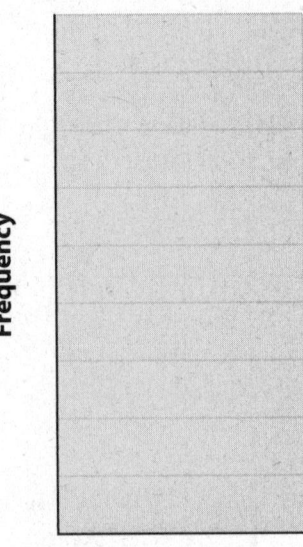

7. Listed are the heights, in inches, of the students in Marci's karate class.

42, 44, 47, 50, 51, 53, 53, 55, 56, 57, 57, 58, 59, 60, 66

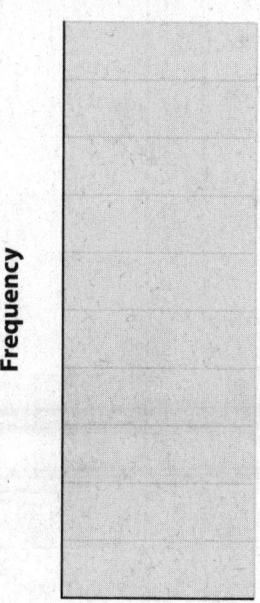

Height (in.)

8. Listed are the starting salaries, in thousands of dollars, for college graduates.

34, 20, 32, 45, 32, 48, 34, 32, 20, 35, 34, 32, 40, 47, 21, 37, 21, 47, 30, 31, 40, 31, 21, 22, 30, 22, 34, 48, 35, 37, 22, 46, 38, 39, 45, 37, 52, 25, 26, 26, 27, 43, 34, 28, 55, 29, 31, 42, 24, 21, 42, 42, 31, 30, 20, 39, 23, 41, 24, 33, 49, 24, 36, 36, 23, 38, 33, 33, 54

Salary Range (thousands $)

Estimate the mean of the data set displayed in each histogram.

9. The histogram shows the GPAs of the students in George's class.

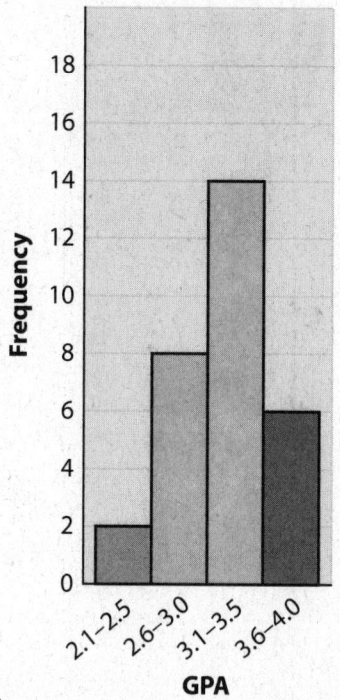

GPA

10. The histogram shows long jump distances, in feet, for a track and field team.

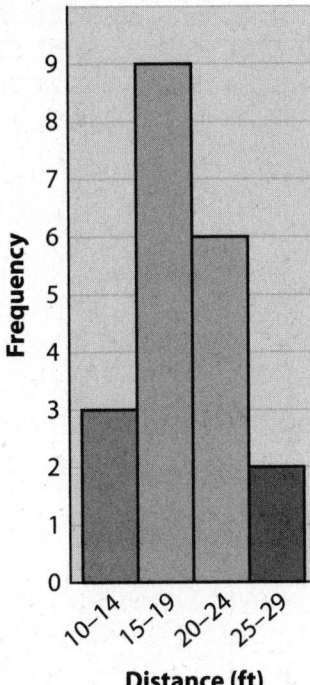

Distance (ft)

11. The histogram shows the speeds of downhill skiers, in miles per hour, during a competition.

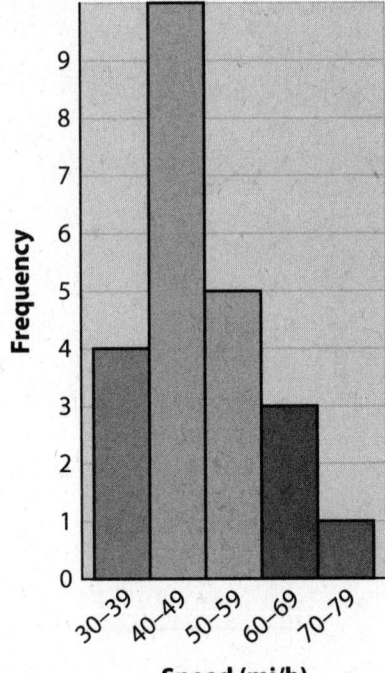

Speed (mi/h)

12. The histogram shows the depths a diver has been to, in meters.

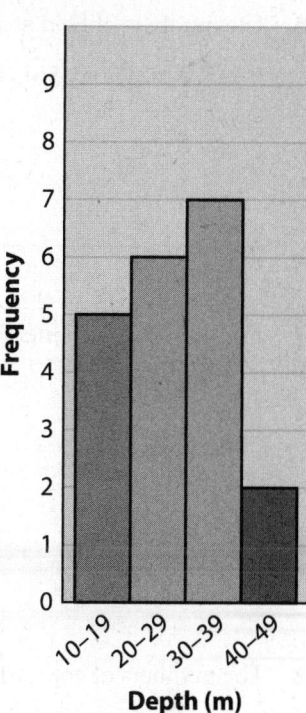

Use the data to make a box plot.

13. The numbers of points Julia's basketball team scored in 11 games are listed below.

50, 62, 37, 36, 34, 44, 44, 36, 37, 42, 36

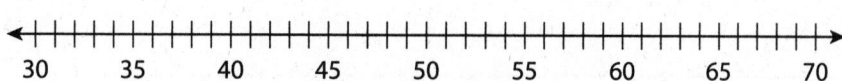

14. The numbers of baskets Kelly's team scored in 9 games are listed below.

14, 24, 29, 15, 16, 20, 24, 15, 15

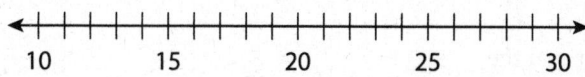

15. The numbers of runs Jane's baseball team scored in 9 games are listed below.

0, 2, 3, 2, 4, 11, 3, 4, 3

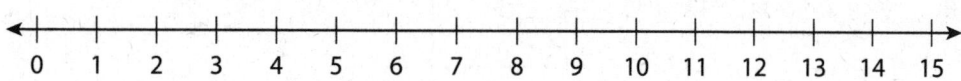

16. The numbers of field goals James' football team scored in 12 games are listed below.

3, 2, 5, 3, 5, 2, 1, 0, 5, 4, 4, 2

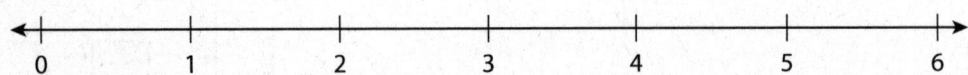

17. The numbers of points scored by Jane in 8 basketball games are listed below.

0, 13, 12, 2, 0, 16, 3, 14

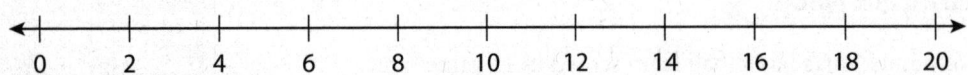

18. The numbers of goals Claudia's soccer team scored in 21 games are shown below.

0, 5, 4, 3, 3, 2, 1, 1, 6, 2, 2, 1, 1, 1, 2, 2, 0, 1, 0, 1, 4

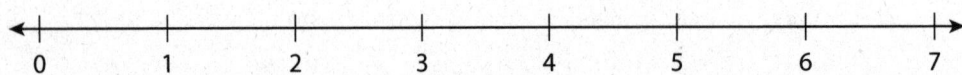

19. Mario and Carlos, two brothers, play for the same basketball team. Here are the points they scored in 10 games:

Game	1	2	3	4	5	6	7	8	9	10
Mario	15	X	X	12	7	11	12	11	10	11
Carlos	10	X	9	12	15	X	19	11	12	12

(Xs mark games each one missed.) Which brother had the highest-scoring game? How many more points did he score in that game than the other brother did in his highest-scoring game?

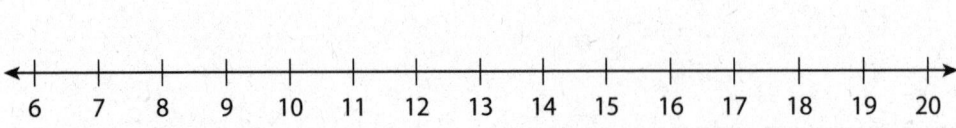

20. Communicate Mathematical Ideas Describe how you could estimate the IQR of a data set from a histogram.

21. Critical Thinking Suppose the minimum in a data set is the same as the first quartile. How would this affect a box plot of the data? Explain.

22. Draw Conclusions Dolly and Willie's scores are shown. Dolly claims that she is the better student, but Willie claims that he is the better student. What statistics make either Dolly or Willie seem like the better student? Explain.

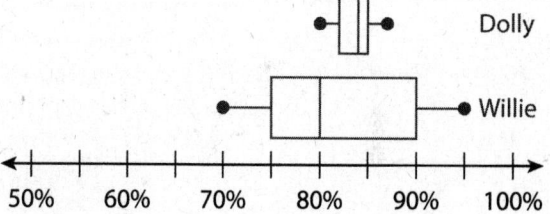

Lesson Performance Task

The batting averages for the starting lineup of two competing baseball teams are given in the table.

Batting Averages for Team A	0.270	0.260	0.300	0.290	0.260	0.280	0.280	0.240	0.270	0.280
Batting Averages for Team B	0.290	0.270	0.240	0.280	0.230	0.280	0.230	0.270	0.250	0.270

a. Create a box plot for each data set on the same number line.

Batting Averages

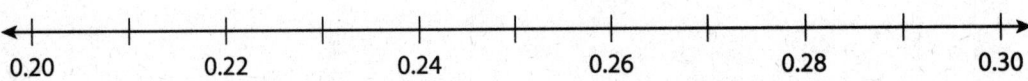

b. Compare the distributions of the batting averages for each team.

c. Which team has a better starting lineup? Explain.

9.4 Normal Distributions

Essential Question: How can you use characteristics of a normal distribution to make estimates and probability predictions about the population that the data represents?

🧭 Explore 1 Investigating Symmetric Distributions

A bell-shaped, symmetric distribution with a tail on each end is called a **normal distribution**.

Use a graphing calculator and the infant birth mass data in the table below to determine if the set represents a normal distribution.

Birth Mass (kg)				
3.3	3.6	3.5	3.4	3.7
3.6	3.5	3.4	3.7	3.5
3.4	3.5	3.2	3.6	3.4
3.8	3.5	3.6	3.3	3.5

Ⓐ Enter the data into a graphing calculator as a list. Calculate the "1-Variable Statistics" for the distribution of data.

Mean, $\bar{x} \approx$ ☐   Standard deviation, $\sigma_x \approx$ ☐

Median = ☐   IQR = $Q_3 - Q_1$ = ☐

Ⓑ Sketch the histogram. Always include labels for the axes and the bar intervals.

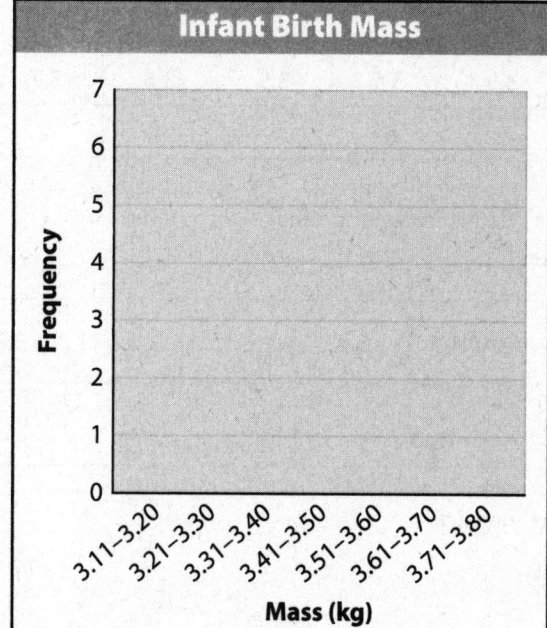

(C) Could this data be described by a normal distribution? Explain.

_____

_____

1. Which intervals on the histogram had the fewest values? Which interval had the greatest number of values?

_____

_____

2. **Make a Conjecture** For the normal distribution, the mean and the median are the same. Is this true for every normal distribution? Explain.

_____

_____

_____

3. **Counterexamples** Allison thinks that every symmetric distribution must be bell-shaped. Provide a counterexample to show that she is incorrect.

_____

_____

⊚ Explore 2 Investigating Symmetric Relative Frequency Histograms

The table gives the frequency of each mass from the data set used in the first Explore.

Mass (kg)	3.2	3.3	3.4	3.5	3.6	3.7	3.8
Frequency	1	2	4	6	4	2	1

(A) Use the frequency table to make a relative frequency table. Notice that there are 20 data values.

Mass (kg)	3.2	3.3	3.4	3.5	3.6	3.7	3.8
Relative Frequency	$\frac{1}{20} = 0.05$						

What is the sum of the relative frequencies? _____

(B) Sketch a relative frequency histogram. The heights of the bars now indicate relative frequencies.

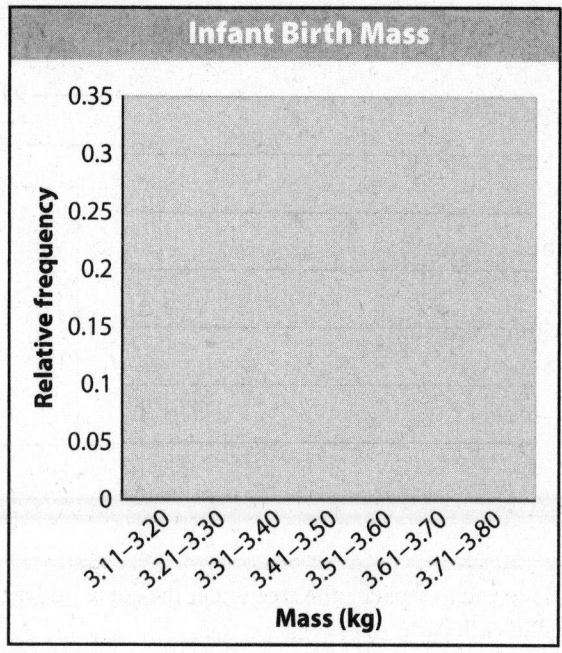

Infant Birth Mass

(C) Recall from the first Explore that the mean of this data set is 3.5 and the standard deviation is 0.14. By how many standard deviations does a birth mass of 3.2 kg differ from the mean? Round to one decimal place. Justify your answer.

$3.5 - 3.2 =$ ☐ and ☐ $\div 0.14 =$ ☐ , so a birth mass of 3.2 kg is _____ standard deviations below the mean.

Reflect

4. Identify the interval of values that are within one standard deviation of the mean. Use the frequency table to determine what percent of the values in the set are in this interval.

_____

_____

5. Identify the interval of values that are within two standard deviations of the mean. Use the frequency table to determine what percent of values in the set are in this interval.

_____

_____

⏺ Explain 1 Using Properties of Normal Distributions

The smaller the intervals are in a symmetric, bell-shaped relative frequency histogram, the closer the shape of the histogram is to a curve called a *normal curve*. Let σ represent the standard deviation.

A **normal curve** has the following properties:

- about 68% of the data fall within 1 standard deviation of the mean.

- about 95% of the data fall within 2 standard deviations of the mean.

- about 99.7% of the data fall within 3 standard deviations of the mean.

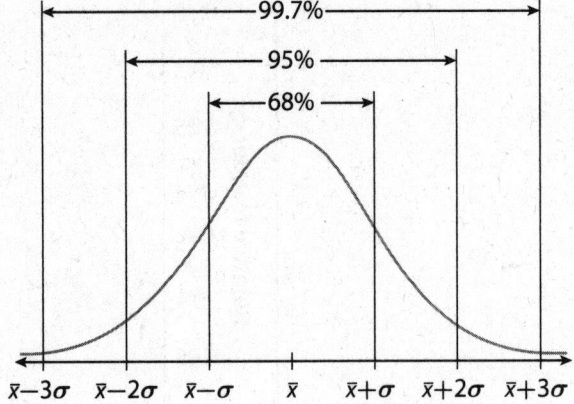

The symmetry of a normal curve allows you to separate the area under the curve into eight parts and know what percent of the data is contained in each part.

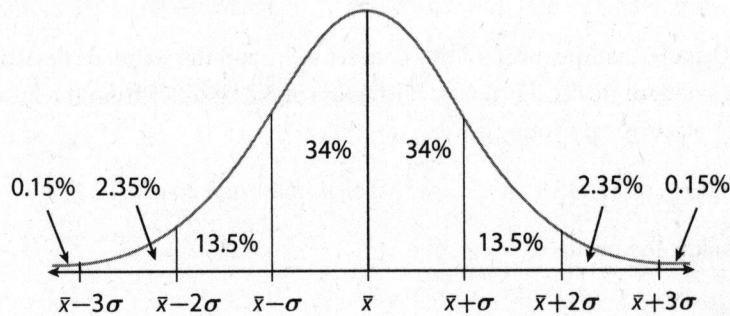

Example 1 The masses (in grams) of pennies minted in the United States after 1982 are normally distributed with a mean of 2.50 g and a standard deviation of 0.02 g.

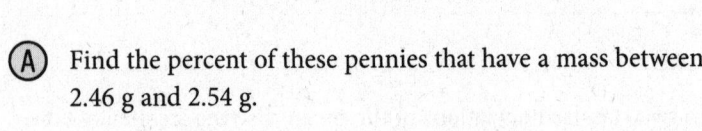

Ⓐ Find the percent of these pennies that have a mass between 2.46 g and 2.54 g.

Find the percent between 2.46 g and the mean, 2.50 g.

2.50 g − 2.46 g = 0.04 g

This is 2 standard deviations below the mean.

Find the percent between 2.54 g and the mean, 2.50 g.

2.54 g − 2.50 g = 0.04 g

This is 2 standard deviations above the mean.

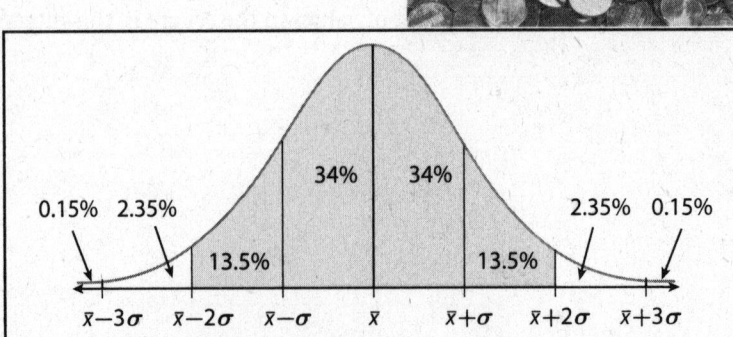

The shaded area represents pennies between 2.46 g and 2.54 g.

95% of the data in a normal distribution fall within 2 standard deviations of the mean.

95% of pennies minted in the United States after 1982 have a mass between 2.46 g and 2.54 g.

B Find the percent of pennies that have a mass between 2.48 g and 2.52 g.

Find the percent between 2.48 g and the mean, 2.50 g.

$2.50 \text{ g} - 2.48 \text{ g} = \boxed{} \text{ g}$

This is $\boxed{}$ standard deviation(s) above/below the mean.

Find the distance between 2.52 g and the mean, 2.50 g.

$2.52 \text{ g} - 2.50 \text{ g} = \boxed{} \text{ g}$

This is $\boxed{}$ standard deviation(s) above/below the mean.

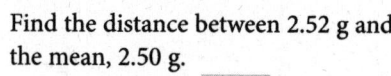

0.15%   2.35%   34%   34%   2.35%   0.15%

13.5%   13.5%

$\bar{x}-3\sigma$ $\bar{x}-2\sigma$ $\bar{x}-\sigma$ $\bar{x}$ $\bar{x}+\sigma$ $\bar{x}+2\sigma$ $\bar{x}+3\sigma$

Shade the area for pennies between 2.48 g and 2.52 g.

$\boxed{}$ % of the data in a normal distribution fall within $\boxed{}$ standard deviation(s) of the mean.

So, $\boxed{}$ % of pennies minted in the United States after 1982 have a mass between 2.48 g and 2.52 g.

Your Turn

6. Find the percent of these pennies that have a mass between 2.44 g and 2.56 g.

7. Find the percent of these pennies that have a mass between 2.46 g and 2.50 g.

Estimating Probabilities in Approximately Normal Distributions

You can use the properties of a normal distribution to make estimations about the larger population that the distribution represents.

Example 2 The masses (in grams) of pennies minted in the United States after 1982 are normally distributed with a mean of 2.50 g and a standard deviation of 0.02 g.

(A) Estimate the probability that a randomly chosen penny has a mass greater than 2.52 g.

Find the percent greater than 2.52 g.
2.52 g − 2.50 g = 0.02 g
2.52 g is 1 standard deviation above the mean.

Shade in the percent of data greater than 1 standard deviation above the mean.

13.5% + 2.35% + 0.15% = 16%

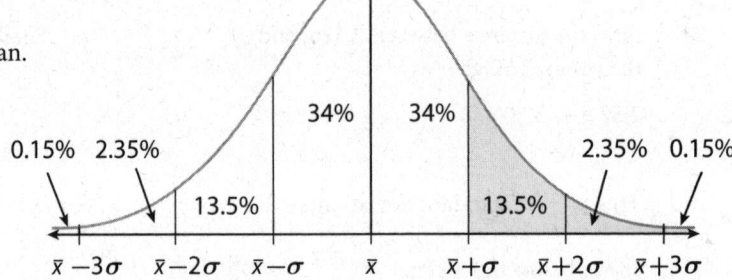

The probability that a randomly chosen penny has a mass greater than 2.52 g is about 16%.

(B) Estimate the probability that a randomly chosen penny has a mass greater than 2.56 g.

Find the percent greater than 2.56 g.

[   ] g − [   ] g = [   ] g

[   ] g is [   ] standard deviation(s) above/below the mean.

Shade in the percent of data greater/less than [   ] standard deviation(s) above/below the mean.

[   ] %

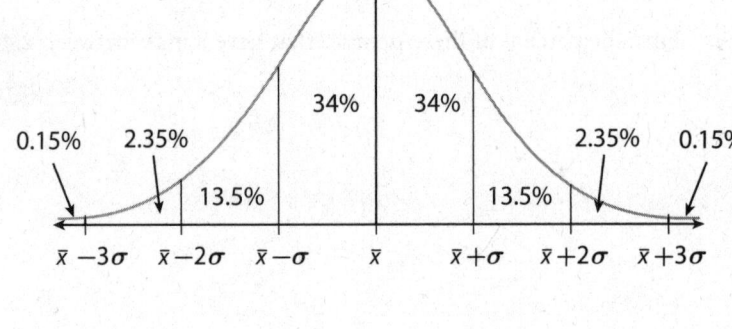

The probability that a randomly chosen penny has a mass greater than 2.56 g is about [   ] %.

8. Find the probability that a randomly chosen penny has a mass less than 2.54 g.

9. Find the probability that a randomly chosen penny has a mass greater than 2.44 g.

10. For data described by a normal distribution, how do the mean and median compare?

_____

11. What does the symmetry of the normal distribution tell you about the areas above and below the mean?

_____

_____

12. How can you tell if data follow a normal distribution by looking at a histogram of the data?

_____

_____

13. **Essential Question** How do you find percents of data and probabilities of events associated with normal distributions?

_____

_____

_____

_____

⭐ Evaluate: Homework and Practice

• Online Homework
• Hints and Help
• Extra Practice

The scores on a test given to all juniors in a school district are normally distributed with a mean of 74 and a standard deviation of 8.

1. Find the percent of juniors whose score is no more than 90.

2. Find the percent of juniors whose score is between 58 and 74.

3. Find the percent of juniors whose score is at least 74.

4. Find the percent of juniors whose score is below 66.

5. Find the probability that a randomly chosen junior has a score above 82.

6. Find the probability that a randomly chosen junior has a score between 66 and 90.

7. Find the probability that a randomly chosen junior has a score below 74.

8. Find the probability that a randomly chosen junior has a score above 98.

A normal distribution has a mean of 10 and a standard deviation of 1.5.

9. Between which two values do 95% of the data fall?

10. Between which two values do 68% of the data fall?

Suppose the heights (in inches) of adult males in the United States are normally distributed with a mean of 72 inches and a standard deviation of 2 inches.

11. Find the percent of men who are no more than 68 inches tall.

12. Find the percent of men who are between 70 and 72 inches tall.

13. Find the percent of men who are at least 76 inches tall.

14. Find the probability that a randomly chosen man is more than 72 inches tall.

15. Find the probability that a randomly chosen man is between 68 and 76 inches tall.

16. Find the probability that a randomly chosen man is less than 76 inches tall.

17. Multi-Step Ten customers at Fielden Grocery were surveyed about how long they waited in line to check out. Their wait times, in minutes, are shown.

16	15	10	7	5
5	4	3	3	2

   a. What is the mean of the data set?

   b. How many data points are below the mean, and how many are above the mean?

   c. Does the data appear to be normally distributed? Explain.

18. Kori is analyzing a normal data distribution, but the data provided is incomplete. Kori knows that the mean of the data is 120 and that 84% of the data values are less than 130. Find the standard deviation for this data set.

19. Suppose compact fluorescent light bulbs last, on average, 10,000 hours. The standard deviation is 500 hours. What percent of light bulbs burn out within 11,000 hours?

20. The numbers of raisins per box in a certain brand of cereal are normally distributed with a mean of 339 raisins and a standard deviation of 9 raisins. Find the percent of boxes of this brand of cereal that have fewer than 330 raisins. Explain how you solved this problem.

Suppose the heights of professional basketball players in the United States are distributed normally, with a mean of 79 inches and a standard deviation of 4 inches.

21. How far below the mean is 71 inches and how many standard deviations is this?

22. How far below the mean is 75 inches and how many standard deviations is this?

Suppose the upper-arm length (in centimeters) of adult males in the United States is normally distributed with a mean of 39.4 cm and a standard deviation of 2.3 cm.

23. Justify Reasoning What percent of adult males have an upper-arm length between 34.8 cm and 41.7 cm? Explain how you got your answer.

24. Communicate Mathematical Ideas Explain how you can determine whether a set of data is approximately normally distributed.

25. Critical Thinking The distribution titled "Heads Up" shows results of many trials of tossing 6 coins and counting the number of "heads" that land facing up. The distribution titled "Number 1s Up" shows results of many trials of tossing 6 number cubes and counting the number of 1s that land facing up. For which distribution is it reasonable to use a normal distribution as an approximation? Justify your answer.

Heads Up

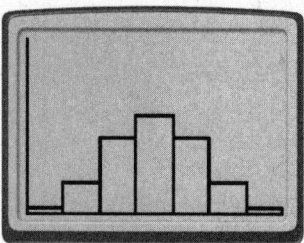

Number 1s Up

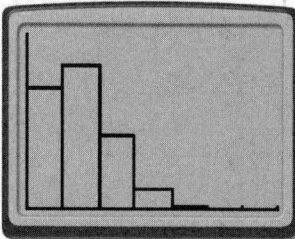

Lesson Performance Task

During a series of 100-meter races, the times of the runners are normally distributed with a mean of 12.5 seconds and a standard deviation of 0.3 seconds.

a. Find the percent of runners that have a time between 11.6 seconds and 12.8 seconds. Explain how you got your answer.

b. Find the probability that a randomly selected runner has a time greater than 12.8 seconds and less than 13.4 seconds.

One-Variable Data Distributions

Essential Question: How can you use one-variable data distributions to solve real-world problems?

KEY EXAMPLE   (Lesson 9.2)

The dot plot given shows the high score of 12 members of a bowling club. A new member joins whose high score is 294. Determine if the new score is an outlier.

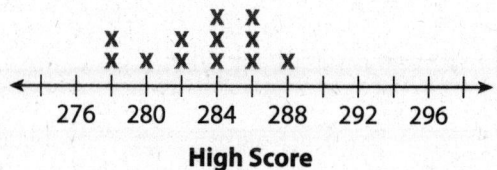

High Score

The scores are 278, 278, 280, 282, 282, 284, 284, 284, 286, 286, 286, 288, and 294.

Median $= 284$ $Q_1 = \dfrac{280 + 282}{2} = 281$ $Q_3 = \dfrac{286 + 286}{2} = 286$ IQR $= 286 - 281 = 5$

A data value is an outlier if $x < Q_1 - 1.5(\text{IQR})$ or if $x > Q_3 + 1.5(\text{IQR})$.

Since $294 > 286 + 1.5(5)$, the new score is an outlier.

© Houghton Mifflin Harcourt Publishing Company

KEY EXAMPLE   (Lesson 9.4)

A machine produces plastic skateboard wheels with diameters that are normally distributed with a mean diameter of 52 mm and a standard deviation of 0.15 mm. Find the percent of wheels made by the machine that have a diameter of less than 51.7 mm.

$52 - 51.7 = 0.3$ $\dfrac{0.3}{0.15} = 2$

51.7 is 2 standard deviations below the mean.

The percent of data that is 2 standard deviations below the mean is $0.15\% + 2.35\% = 2.5\%$.

2.5% of the wheels have a diameter less than 51.7 mm.

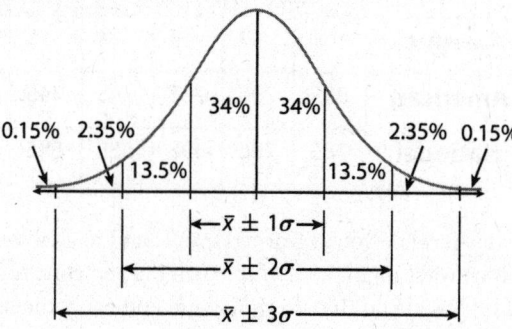

Key Vocabulary

histogram *(histograma)*

interquartile range IQR
   (rango entre cuartiles)

mean *(media)*

median *(mediana)*

normal curve *(curva normal)*

normal distribution
   (distribución normal)

outlier *(valor extremo)*

range *(rango de un conjunto
   de datos)*

EXERCISES

Find the mean, median, range, and interquartile range of each data set. *(Lesson 9.1)*

1. {12, 12, 13, 14, 16, 20, 32}

2. {4, 8, 9, 9, 11, 12, 15, 15}

3. Make a box plot to represent the data set {28, 30, 32, 32, 34, 35, 36, 38}. *(Lesson 9.3)*

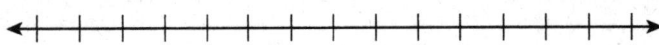

4. The weights of a small box of Healthy Oats are normally distributed with a mean of 8.9 oz and a standard deviation of 0.1 oz. Find the probability that a randomly chosen box of Healthy Oats weighs more than 8.8 oz. Express the probability as a decimal. *(Lesson 9.4)*

MODULE PERFORMANCE TASK

Baseball Stats

The table below gives the total number of runs scored by each of the 15 teams in each of baseball's two major leagues, the American League and the National League, during the 2013 season.

League	Team														
	1	2	3	4	5	6	7	8	9	10	11	12	13	14	15
American	853	796	767	745	745	733	730	712	700	650	648	624	614	610	598
National	783	706	698	688	685	656	649	640	634	629	619	618	610	602	513

In this module you've learned many ways to analyze a set of data, both numerically and graphically. Which ways might be useful in helping someone to make sense of the statistics in the runs-scored table? Decide on the ones you'll use and apply them, either through numerical calculations or pictorial representations or both. You may also explain why you decided not to calculate certain data measures.

Use your own paper to work on the task. Use numbers, words, or algebra to explain how you reached your conclusion.

9.1–9.4 One-Variable Data Distributions

- Online Homework
- Hints and Help
- Extra Practice

1. The dot plot given represents the scores of 10 students on a standardized test. An eleventh student was sick on the test date, took a make-up test, and made a score of 212. Complete the table. If necessary, round to the nearest tenth. *(Lesson 9.1)*

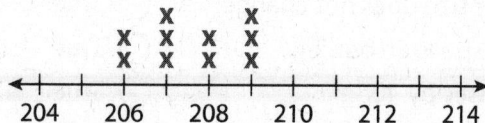

	Mean	Median	Range	IQR	Standard Deviation
Without Make-up Test					
With Make-up Test					

2. The ages of students in a tango class are represented by the data set {24, 41, 33, 36, 28, 30, 32, 22, 26, 44}. Complete the frequency table and make a histogram to represent the data. *(Lesson 9.3)*

Age Interval	Frequency
20–24	
25–29	
30–34	
35–39	
40–44	

ESSENTIAL QUESTION

3. When is it better to use a histogram than a dot plot?

Assessment Readiness

1. The dot plot shown represents the number of students enrolled in each of the 16 courses at a community college. A new course has started and has 65 enrolled students. Consider the effect of the addition of the new course to the data set. Choose True or False for each statement.

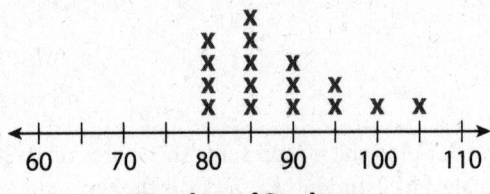

Number of Students

A. The median class size does not change. ◯ True ◯ False

B. The new course size is an outlier. ◯ True ◯ False

C. The range increases by 40. ◯ True ◯ False

2. The histogram shows the number of tomato plants Susan has in each height range. Select True or False for each statement.

A. Susan has 11 plants. ◯ True ◯ False

B. Susan has the same number of plants that are 7 to 9 inches high as plants that are 10 to 12 inches high. ◯ True ◯ False

C. The median height of the plants could be about 11 inches. ◯ True ◯ False

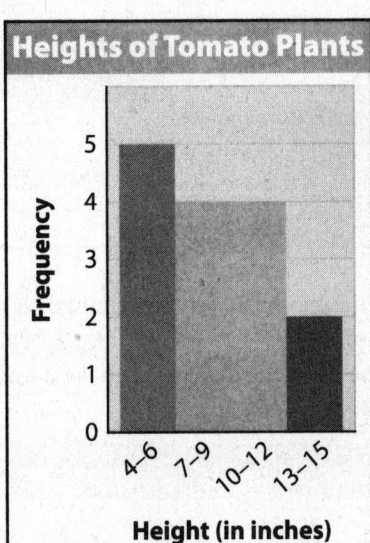

Heights of Tomato Plants

Frequency

Height (in inches)

3. The high temperature, in °F, for the past 4 days was 45, 38, 46, and 35. Carlos knows that the mean high temperature for the past 5 days was 42°F. Write and solve an equation to find the high temperature on the first day. Show your work.

4. Write an equation in slope-intercept form to represent a line that includes the points $(3, -4)$ and $(5, 2)$. Explain how you wrote the equation.

Linear Modeling and Regression

Essential Question: How can you use linear modeling and regression to solve real-world problems?

REAL WORLD VIDEO
A fossil is a remnant or trace of an organism from a past geologic age that has been preserved in the earth's crust. Fossils are often dated by using interpolation, a type of calculation that uses an observed pattern to estimate a value between two known values.

MODULE PERFORMANCE TASK PREVIEW

How Does Wingspan Compare with Weight in Birds?

The wingspan of a bird is the distance from one wingtip to the other wingtip. Birds that fly have to support their body weight when in flight. What, if any, relationship exists between the wingspan and body weight for different species of birds? Let's use math to find out!

Are (YOU) Ready?

Complete these exercises to review skills you will need for this module.

Scatter Plots

Example 1   Tell whether the correlation is positive or negative, or if there is no correlation.

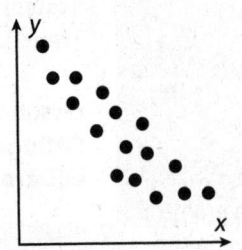

Scatter plots can help you see relationships between two variables.

- In a positive correlation, as the value of one variable increases, the value of the other variable increases.

- In a negative correlation, as the value of one variable decreases, the value of the other variable increases.

- Sometimes there is no correlation, meaning there is no relationship between the variables.

The scatter plot has a negative correlation.

Tell whether the correlation is positive or negative, or if there is no correlation.

1.

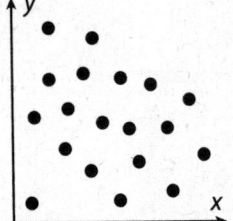

_____

2.

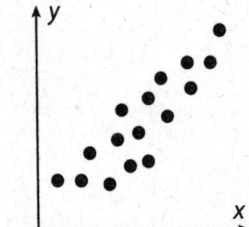

_____

Linear Associations

Example 2   Estimate the correlation coefficient.

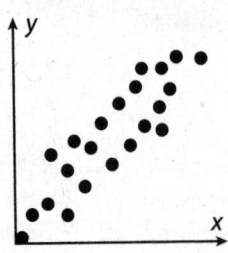

One measure of the strength and direction of a correlation is the correlation coefficient, denoted by *r*. The stronger the correlation, the closer the correlation coefficient will be to −1 or 1. The weaker the correlation, the closer *r* will be to zero.

The points lie close to a line with positive slope. *r* is close to 1.

Estimate the correlation coefficient.

3.

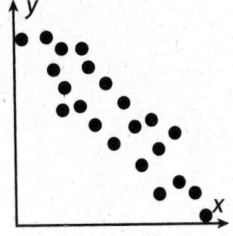

_____

4.

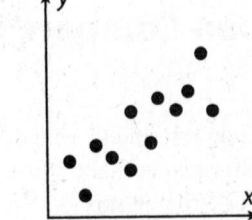

_____

10.1 Scatter Plots and Trend Lines

Essential Question: How can you describe the relationship between two variables and use it to make predictions?

Explore **Describing How Variables Are Related in Scatter Plots**

Two-variable data is a collection of paired variable values, such as a series of measurements of air temperature at different times of day. One method of visualizing two-variable data is called a **scatter plot**: a graph of points with one variable plotted along each axis. A recognizable pattern in the arrangement of points suggests a mathematical relationship between the variables.

Correlation is a measure of the strength and direction of the relationship between two variables. The correlation is positive if both variables tend to increase together, negative if one decreases while the other increases, and we say there is "no correlation" if the change in the two variables appears to be unrelated.

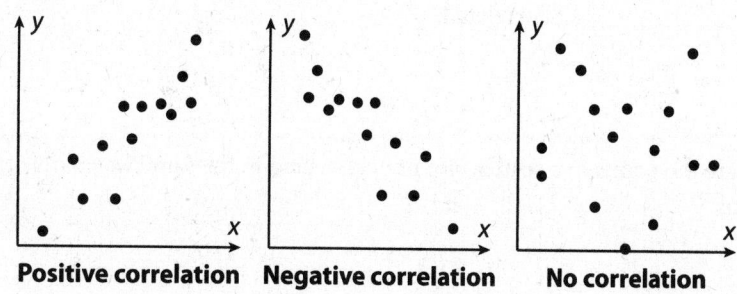

Positive correlation **Negative correlation** **No correlation**

(A) The table below presents two-variable data for seven different cities in the Northern hemisphere.

City	Latitude (°N)	Average Annual Temperature (°F)
Bangkok	13.7	82.6
Cairo	30.1	71.4
London	51.5	51.8
Moscow	55.8	39.4
New Delhi	28.6	77.0
Tokyo	35.7	58.1
Vancouver	49.2	49.6

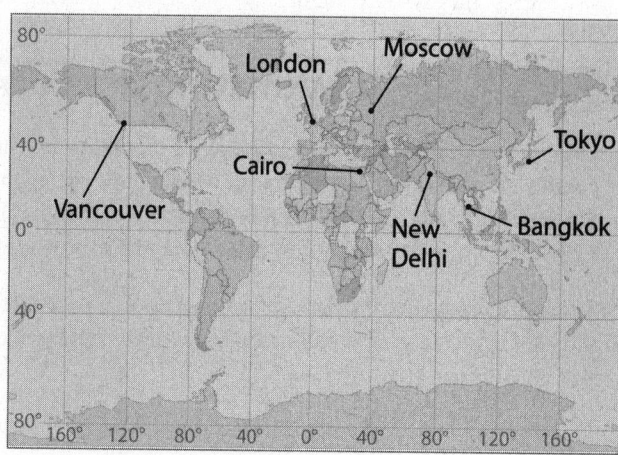

The two variables are _____ and _____.

(B) Plot the data on the grid provided.

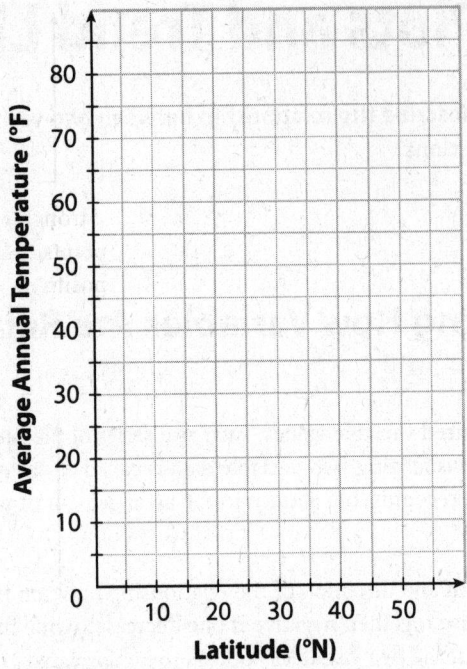

(C) The variables are _____ correlated.

1. **Discussion** Why are the points in a scatter plot not connected in the same way plots of linear equations are?

_____

_____

_____

_____

_____

🎻 Explain 1   Estimating the Correlation Coefficient of a Linear Fit

One way to quantify the correlation of a data set is with the **correlation coefficient**, denoted by r. The correlation coefficient varies from -1 to 1, with the sign of r corresponding to the type of correlation (positive or negative). Strongly correlated data points look more like points that lie in a straight line, and have values of r closer to 1 or -1. Weakly correlated data will have values closer to 0.

There is a precise mathematical formula that can be used to calculate the correlation coefficient, but it is beyond the scope of this course. It is still useful to learn the qualitative relationship between the appearance of the data and the value of r. The chart below shows examples of strong correlations, with r close to -1 and 1, and weak correlations with r close to 0.5. If there is no visible correlation, it means r is closer to 0.

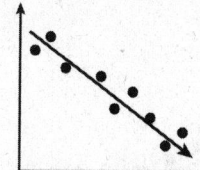

Strong negative correlation; points lie close to a line with negative slope. r is close to -1.

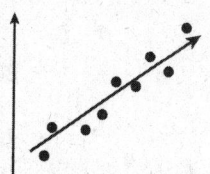

Strong positive correlation; points lie close to a line with positive slope. r is close to 1.

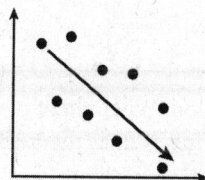

Weak negative correlation; points loosely follow a line with negative slope. r is between 0 and -1.

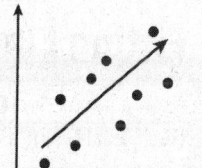

Weak positive correlation; points loosely follow a line with positive slope. r is between 0 and 1.

Example 1 Use a scatter plot to estimate the value of r. Indicate whether r is closer to $-1, -0.5, 0, 0.5,$ or 1.

(A) Estimate the r-value for the relationship between city latitude and average temperature using the scatter plot you made previously.

This is strongly correlated and has a negative slope, so r is close to -1.

(B)

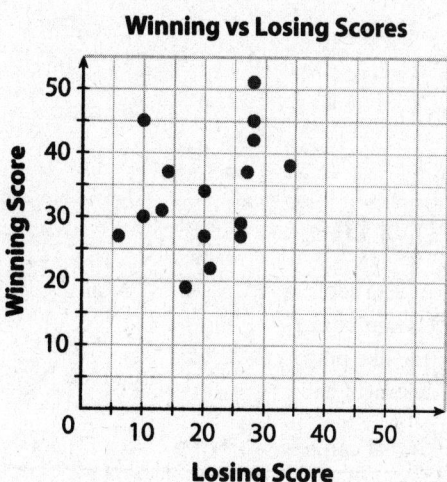

This data represents the football scores from one week with winning score plotted versus losing score.

r is close to ☐ .

2.

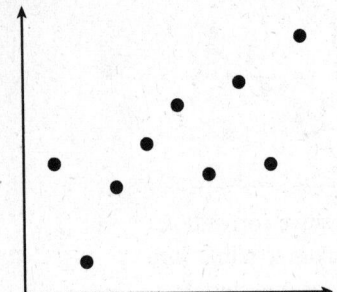

3.

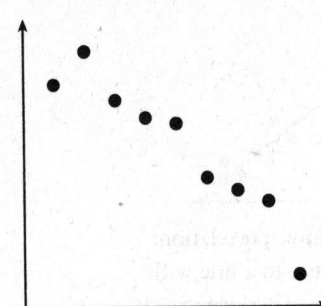

⚙ Explain 2   Fitting Linear Functions to Data

A **line of fit** is a line through a set of two-variable data that illustrates the correlation. When there is a strong correlation between the two variables in a set of two-variable data, you can use a line of fit as the basis to construct a linear model for the data.

There are many ways to come up with a line of fit. This lesson addresses a visual method: Using a straight edge, draw the line that the data points appear to be clustered around. It is not important that any of the data points actually touch the line; instead the line should be drawn as straight as possible and should go through the middle of the scattered points.

Once a line of fit has been drawn onto the scatter plot, you can choose two points on the line to write an equation for the line.

Example 2   **Determine a line of fit for the data, and write the equation of the line.**

Ⓐ   Go back to the scatter plot of city temperatures and latitudes and add a line of fit.

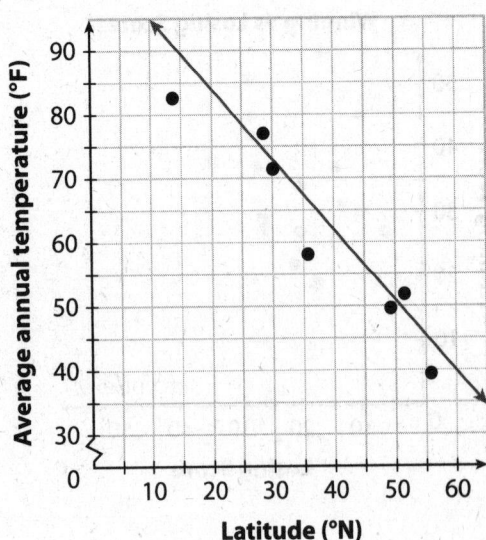

A line of fit has been added to the graph. The points (10, 95) and (60, 40) appear to be on the line.

$$m = \frac{40 - 95}{60 - 10} = -1.1$$

$$y = mx + b$$

$$95 = -1.1(10) + b$$

$$106 = b$$

The model is given by the equation

$$y = -1.1x + 106$$

(B) The boiling point of water is lower at higher elevations because of the lower atmospheric pressure. The boiling point of water in some different cities is given in the table.

City	Altitude (feet)	Boiling Point (°F)
Chicago	597	210
Denver	5300	201
Kathmandu	4600	205
Madrid	2188	207
Miami	6	210

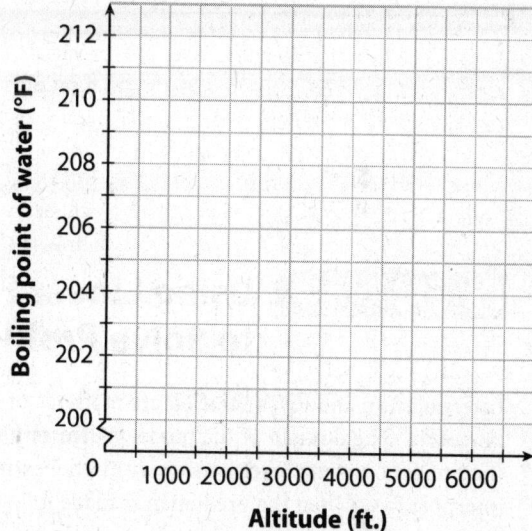

A line of fit may go through points $\left(\boxed{}, \boxed{} \right)$ and $\left(\boxed{}, \boxed{} \right)$.

$$m = \frac{\boxed{}}{\boxed{}} \qquad b = \boxed{}$$

The equation is of this line of fit is $y = \boxed{} \, x + \boxed{}$.

Reflect

4. In the model from Example 2A, what do the slope and y-intercept of the model represent?

_____

_____

_____

5. Aoiffe plants a tree sapling in her yard and measures its height every year. Her measurements so far are shown. Make a scatter plot and find a line of fit if the variables have a correlation. What is the equation of your line of fit?

Years after Planting	Height (ft)
0	2.1
1	4.3
2	5
3	7.3
4	8.1
5	10.2

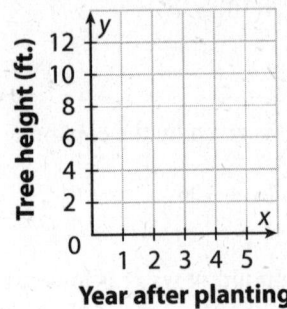

Explain 3 Using Linear Functions Fitted to Data to Solve Problems

Interpolation and **extrapolation** are methods of predicting data values for one variable from another based on a line of fit. The domain of the model is determined by the minimum and maximum values of the data set. When the prediction is made for a value within the extremes (minimum and maximum) of the original data set, it is called interpolation. When the prediction is made for a value outside the extremes, it is called extrapolation. Extrapolation is not as reliable as interpolation because the model has not been demonstrated, and it may fail to describe the relationship between the variables outside the domain of the data. Extrapolated predictions will also vary more with different lines of fit.

Example 3 Use the linear fit of the data set to make the required predictions.

(A) Use the model constructed in Example 2A to predict the average annual temperatures for Austin (30.3°N) and Helsinki (60.2°N).

$$y = -1.1x + 106$$

Austin: $y = -1.1 \cdot 30.3 + 106 = 72.67\ °F$

Helsinki: $y = -1.1 \cdot 60.2 + 106 = 39.78\ °F$

(B) Use the model of city altitudes and water boiling points to predict the boiling point of water in Mexico City (altitude = 7943 feet) and in Fargo, North Dakota (altitude = 3000 feet)

Mexico City: $y = \boxed{} \cdot 7943 + \boxed{} = 197.74$

Fargo: $y = \boxed{} \cdot 3000 + \boxed{} = 205.99$

Reflect

6. **Discussion** Which prediction made in Example 3B would you expect to be more reliable? Why?

_____

_____

Your Turn

7. Use the model constructed in YourTurn 5 to predict how tall Aoiffe's tree will be 10 years after she planted it.

⏱ Explain 4 Distinguishing Between Correlation and Causation

A common error when interpreting paired data is to observe a correlation and conclude that causation has been demonstrated. Causation means that a change in the one variable results directly from changing the other variable. In that case, it is reasonable to expect the data to show correlation. However, the reverse is not true: observing a correlation between variables does not necessarily mean that the change to one variable caused the change in the other. They may both have a common cause related to a variable not included in the data set or even observed (sometimes called lurking variables), or the causation may be the reverse of the conclusion.

Example 4 **Read the description of the experiments, identify the two variables and describe whether changing either variable is likely, doubtful, or unclear to cause a change in the other variable.**

(A) The manager of an ice cream shop studies its monthly sales figures and notices a positive correlation between the average air temperature and how much ice cream they sell on any given day.

The two variables are ice cream sales and average air temperatures.

It is likely that warmer air temperatures cause an increase in ice cream sales.

It is doubtful that increased ice cream sales cause an increase in air temperatures.

Ⓑ A traffic official in a major metropolitan area notices that the more profitable toll bridges into the city are those with the slowest average crossing speeds.

The variables are _____ and _____.

It is [likely | doubtful | unclear] that increased profit causes slower crossing speed.

It is [likely | doubtful | unclear] that slower crossing speeds cause an increase in profits.

Reflect

8. Explain your reasoning for your answers in Example 4B and suggest a more likely explanation for the observed correlation.

_____

_____

Your Turn

9. HDL cholesterol is considered the "good" cholesterol as it removes harmful bad cholesterol from where it doesn't belong. A group of researchers are studying the connection between the number of minutes of exercise a person performs weekly and the person's HDL cholesterol count. The researchers surveyed the amount of physical activity each person did each week for 10 weeks and collected a blood sample from 67 adults. After analyzing the data, the researchers found that people who exercised more per week had higher HDL cholesterol counts. Identify the variables in this situation and determine whether it describes a positive or negative correlation. Explain whether the correlation is a result of causation.

💬 **Elaborate**

10. Why is extrapolating from measured data likely to result in a less accurate prediction than interpolating?

_____

_____

11. What will the effect be on the correlation coefficient if additional data is collected that is farther from the line of fit? What will the effect be if the newer data lies along the line of fit? Explain your reasoning.

_____

_____

12. **Essential Question Check-In** How does a scatter plot help you make predictions from two-variable data?

_____

_____

_____

Estimate the value of *r*. Indicate whether *r* is closest to −1, −0.5, 0, 0.5 or 1 for the following data sets.

1.

x	y
1	8
2	4.037522
3	7.200593
4	4.180245
5	4.763788
6	1
7	1.047031
8	2.436249
9	1.844607

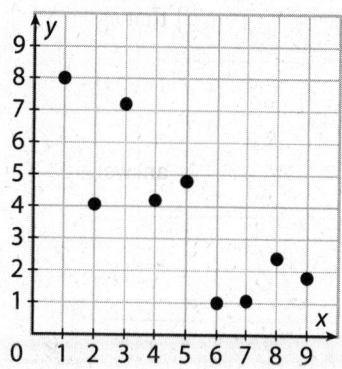

2. The table below presents exam scores earned by six students and how long they each studied.

Hours of Study	Exam Score
2	63
2	71
2.5	75
3	67
4.5	82
5	95

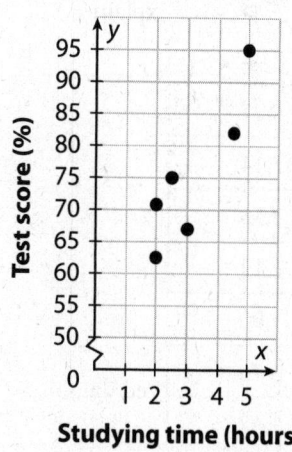

3. Raymond opens a car wash and keeps track of his weekly earnings, as shown in the table

Weeks after Opening	Earnings ($)
0	1050
1	1700
2	2400
3	2000
4	3500
5	3600

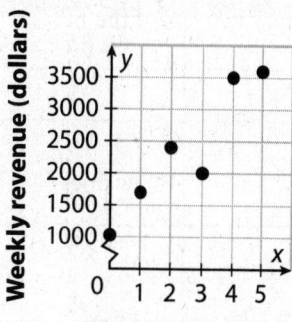

4. Rafael is training for a race by running a mile each day. He tracks his progress by timing each trial run.

Trial	Run Time (min)
1	8.2
2	8.1
3	7.5
4	7.8
5	7.4
6	7.5
7	7.1
8	7.1

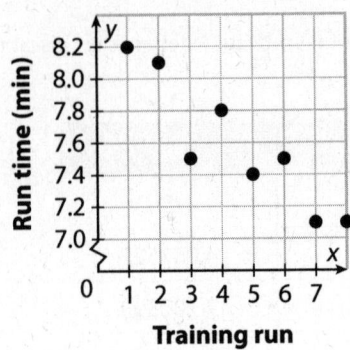

Determine a line of fit for the data, and write the equation of your line.

5.

x	y
1	7.15
2	8.00
3	4.81
4	7.14
5	3.56
6	2.12
7	1.00
8	3.76
9	1.42

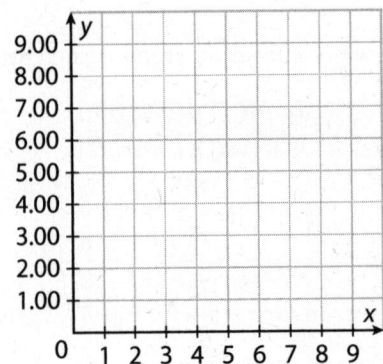

6.

Studying Time (Hours)	Test Score (%)
2	63
2	71
2.5	75
3	67
4.5	82
5	95

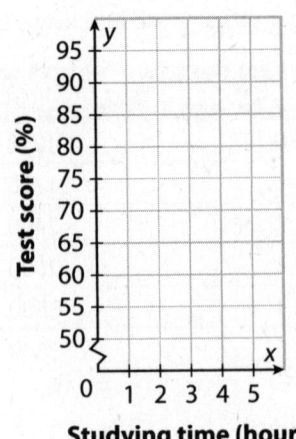

7.

Weeks After Opening	Weekly Revenue (dollars)
0	1050
1	1700
2	2400
3	2000
4	3500
5	3600

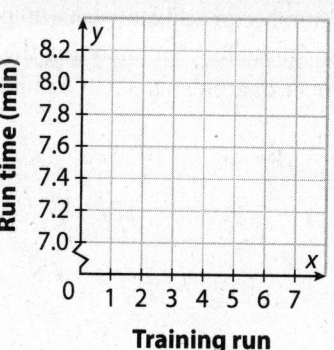

8.

Training Run	Run Time (min)
1	8.2
2	8.1
3	7.5
4	7.8
5	7.4
6	7.5
7	7.1
8	7.1

Use the linear models found in problems 5–8 for 9–12, respectively, to make predictions, and classify each prediction as an interpolation or an extrapolation.

9. Find y when $x = 4.5$.

10. What grade might you expect after studying for 4 hours?

11. How much money might Raymond hope to earn 8 weeks after opening if the trend continues?

12. What mile time does Rafael expect for his next run?

Read each description. Identify the variables in each situation and determine whether it describes a positive or negative correlation. Explain whether the correlation is a result of causation.

13. A group of biologists is studying the population of wolves and the population of deer in a particular region. The biologists compared the populations each month for 2 years. After analyzing the data, the biologists found that as the population of wolves increases, the population of deer decreases.

14. Researchers at an auto insurance company are studying the ages of its policyholders and the number of accidents per 100 policyholders. The researchers compared each year of age from 16 to 65. After analyzing the data, the researchers found that as age increases, the number of accidents per 100 policyholders decreases.

15. Educational researchers are investigating the relationship between the number of musical instruments a student plays and a student's grade in math. The researchers conducted a survey asking 110 students the number of musical instruments they play and went to the registrar's office to find the same 110 students' grades in math. The researchers found that students who play a greater number of musical instruments tend to have a greater average grade in math.

16. Researchers are studying the relationship between the median salary of a police officer in a city and the number of violent crimes per 1000 people. The researchers collected the police officers' median salary and the number of violent crimes per 1000 people in 84 cities. After analyzing the data, researchers found that a city with a greater police officers' median salary tends to have a greater number of violent crimes per 1000 people.

17. The owner of a ski resort is studying the relationship between the amount of snowfall in centimeters during the season and the number of visitors per season. The owner collected information about the amount of snowfall and the number of visitors for the past 30 seasons. After analyzing the data, the owner determined that seasons that have more snowfall tend to have more visitors.

18. Government researchers are studying the relationship between the price of gasoline and the number of miles driven in a month. The researchers documented the monthly average price of gasoline and the number of miles driven for the last 36 months. The researchers found that the months with a higher average price of gasoline tend to have more miles driven.

19. Interpret the Answer Each time Lorelai fills up her gas tank, she writes down the amount of gas it took to refill her tank, and the number of miles she drove between fill-ups. She makes a scatter plot of the data with miles driven on the y-axis and gallons of gas on the x-axis, and observes a very strong correlation. The slope is 35 and the y-intercept is 0.83. Do these numbers make sense, and what do they mean (besides being the slope and intercept of the line)?

20. Multi-Step The owner of a maple syrup farm is studying the average winter temperature in Fahrenheit and the number of gallons of maple syrup produced. The relationship between the temperature and the number of gallons of maple syrup produced for the past 8 years is shown in the table.

a. Make a scatter plot of the data and draw a line of fit that passes as close as possible to the plotted points.

Temperature (°F)	Number of gallons of maple syrup
24	154
26	128
25	141
22	168
28	104
21	170
24	144
22	160

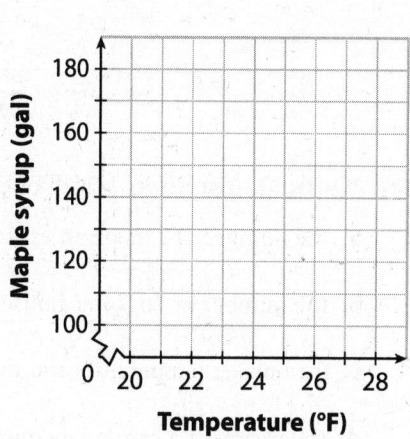

b. Find the equation of this line of fit.

c. Identify the slope and y-intercept for the line of fit and interpret it in the context of the problem.

21. The table below shows the number of boats in a marina during the years 2007 to 2014.

Years Since 2000	7	8	9	10	11	12	13	14
Number of Boats	26	25	27	27	39	38	40	39

a. Make a scatterplot by using the data in the table as the coordinates of points on the graph. Use the calendar year as the *x*-value and the number of boats as the *y*-value.

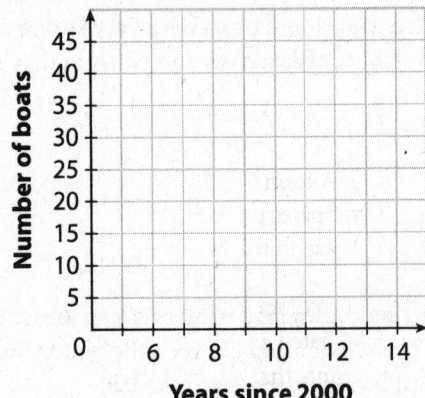

b. Use the pattern of the points to determine whether there is a positive correlation, negative correlation, or no correlation between the number of boats in the marina and the year. What is the trend?

22. Multiple Response Which of the following usually have a positive correlation? Select all that apply.

a. the number of cars on an expressway and the cars' average speed

b. the number of dogs in a house and the amount of dog food needed

c. the outside temperature and the amount of heating oil used

d. the weight of a car and the number of miles per gallon

e. the amount of time studying and the grade on a science exam

23. Justify Reasoning Does causation always imply linear correlation? Explain.

24. Explain the Error Olivia notices that if she picks a very large scale for her *y*-axis, her data appear to lie more along a straight line than if she zooms the scale all the way in. She concludes that she can use this to increase her correlation coefficient and make a more convincing case that there is a correlation between the variables she is studying. Is she correct?

25. What if? If you combined two data sets, each with *r* values close to 1, into a single data set, would you expect the new data set to have an *r* value between the original two values?

Lesson Performance Task

A 10-team high school hockey league completed its 20-game season. A team in this league earns 2 points for a win, 1 point for a tie, and 0 points for a loss. One of the team's coaches compares the number of goals each team scored with the number of points each team earned during the season as shown in the table.

a. Plot the points on the scatter plot, and use the scatterplot to describe the correlation and estimate the correlation coefficient. If the correlation coefficient is estimated as −1 or 1, draw a line of fit by hand and then find an equation for the line by choosing two points that are close to the line. Identify and interpret the slope and y-intercept of the line in context of the situation.

Goals Scored	Points
46	15
48	11
49	17
51	20
57	18
58	21
59	25
60	23
62	27
64	24

b. Use the line of fit to predict how many points a team would have if it scored 35 goals, 54 goals, and 70 goals during the season.

c. Use the results to justify whether the coach should only be concerned with the number of goals his or her team scores.

10.2 Fitting a Linear Model to Data

Essential Question: How can you use the linear regression function on a graphing calculator to find the line of best fit for a two-variable data set?

Resource Locker

⊘ Explore 1 Plotting and Analyzing Residuals

For any set of data, different lines of fit can be created. Some of these lines will fit the data better than others. One way to determine how well the line fits the data is by using residuals. A **residual** is the signed vertical distance between a data point and a line of fit.

After calculating residuals, a residual plot can be drawn. A **residual plot** is a graph of points whose x-coordinates are the variables of the independent variable and whose y-coordinates are the corresponding residuals.

Looking at the distribution of residuals can help you determine how well a line of fit describes the data. The plots below illustrate how the residuals may be distributed for three different data sets and lines of fit.

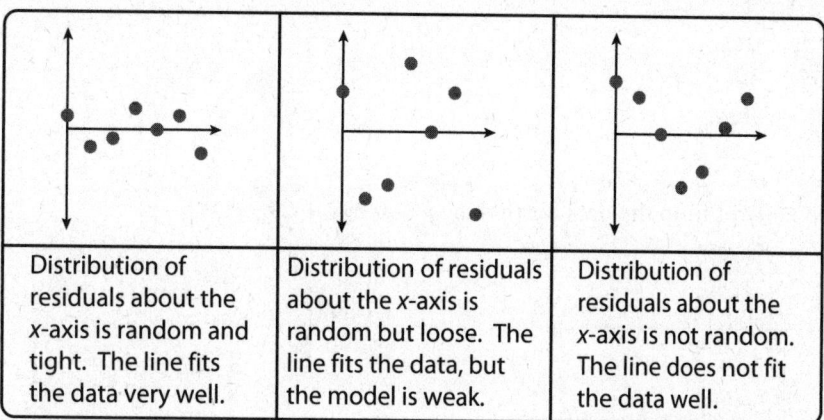

| Distribution of residuals about the x-axis is random and tight. The line fits the data very well. | Distribution of residuals about the x-axis is random but loose. The line fits the data, but the model is weak. | Distribution of residuals about the x-axis is not random. The line does not fit the data well. |

The table lists the median age of females living in the United States, based on the results of the United States Census over the past few decades. Follow the steps listed to complete the task.

(A) Use the table to create a table of paired values for x and y. Let x represent the time in years after 1970 and y represent the median age of females.

Year	Median Age of Females
1970	29.2
1980	31.3
1990	34.0
2000	36.5
2010	38.2

x					
y					

B Use residuals to calculate the quality of fit for the line $y = 0.25x + 29$, where y is median age and x is years since 1970.

x	Actual y	Predicted y based on $y = 0.25x + 29$	Residual Subtract Predicted from Actual to Find the Residual.
0	29.2		
10	31.3		
20	34.0		
30	36.5		
40	38.2		

C Plot the residuals.

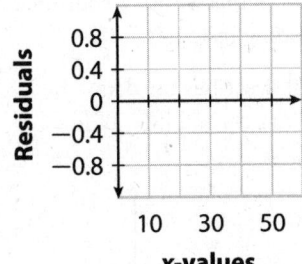

D Evaluate the quality of fit to the data for the line $y = 0.25x + 29$.

_____

_____

Reflect

1. **Discussion** When comparing two lines of fit for a single data set, how does the residual size show which line is the best model?

_____

_____

2. **Discussion** What would the residual plot look like if a line of fit is a weak model for a data set?

_____

_____

When different people fit lines to the same data set, they are likely to choose slightly different lines. Another way to compare the quality of a line of fit is by squaring residuals. In this model, the closer the sum of the squared residuals is to 0, the better the line fits the data.

In the previous section, a line of data was fit for the median age of females over time. After performing this task, two students came up with slightly different results. Student A came up with the equation $y = 0.25x + 29.0$ while Student B came up with the equation $y = 0.25x + 28.8$, where x is the time in years since 1970 and y is the median age of females in both cases.

(A) Complete each table below.

$y = 0.25x + 29.0$				
x	**y (Actual)**	**y (Predicted)**	**Residual**	**Square of Residual**
0	29.2			
10	31.3			
20	34.0			
30	36.5			
40	38.2			

$y = 0.25x + 28.8$				
x	**y (Actual)**	**y (Predicted)**	**Residual**	**Square of Residual**
0	29.2			
10	31.3			
20	34.0			
30	36.5			
40	38.2			

(B) Find the sum of squared residuals for each line of fit.

$y = 0.25x + 29.0$: ☐

$y = 0.25x + 28.8$: ☐

(C) Which line has the smaller sum of squared residuals?

_____

Reflect

3. How does squaring a residual affect the residual's value?

_____

_____

4. Are the sums of residuals or the sum of the squares of residuals a better measure of quality of fit?

_____

_____

✏️ Explain 1   Assessing the Fit of Linear Functions from Residuals

The quality of a line of fit can be evaluated by finding the sum of the squared residuals. The closer the sum of the squared residuals is to 0, the better the line fits the data.

Example 1 The data in the tables are given along with two possible lines of fit. Calculate the residuals for both lines of fit and then find the sum of the squared residuals. Identify the lesser sum and the line with better fit.

(A)

x	2	4	6	8
y	7	8	4	8

$y = x + 2.2$

$y = x + 2.4$

a. Find the residuals of each line.

x	y (Actual)	y Predicted by $y = x + 2.4$	Residual for $y = x + 2.4$	y Predicted by $y = x + 2.2$	Residual for $y = x + 2.2$
2	7	4.4	2.6	4.2	2.8
4	8	6.4	1.6	6.2	1.8
6	4	8.4	−4.4	8.2	−4.2
8	8	10.4	−2.4	10.2	−2.2

b. Square the residuals and find their sum.

$y = x + 2.4: (2.6)^2 + (1.6)^2 + (-4.4)^2 + (-2.4)^2 = 6.76 + 2.56 + 19.36 + 5.76 = 34.44$

$y = x + 2.2: (2.8)^2 + (1.8)^2 + (-4.2)^2 + (-2.2)^2 = 7.84 + 3.24 + 17.64 + 4.84 = 33.56$

The sum of the squared residuals for $y = x + 2.2$ is smaller, so it provides a better fit for the data.

(B)

x	1	2	3	4
y	5	4	6	10

$y = 2x + 3$

$y = 2x + 2.5$

a. Find the residuals of each line.

x	y (Actual)	y Predicted by $y = 2x + 3$	Residual for $y = 2x + 3$	y Predicted by $y = 2x + 2.5$	Residual for $y = 2x + 2.5$
1	5				
2	4				
3	6				
4	10				

b. Square the residuals and find their sum.

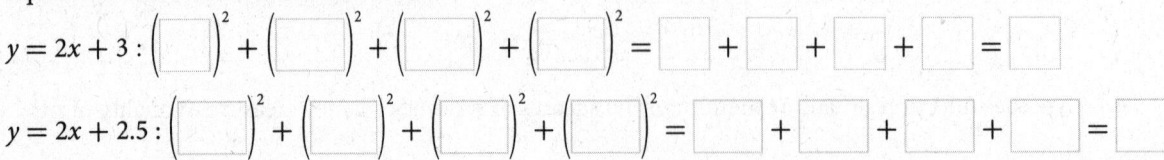

The sum of the squared residuals for $y = \boxed{} x + \boxed{}$ is smaller, so it provides a better fit for the data.

5. How do negative signs on residuals affect the sum of squared residuals?

_____

6. Why do small values for residuals mean that a line of best fit has a tight fit to the data?

_____

_____

Your Turn

7. The data in the table are given along with two possible lines of fit. Calculate the residuals for both lines of fit and then find the sum of the squared residuals. Identify the lesser sum and the line with better fit.

x	1	2	3	4
y	4	7	8	6

$y = x + 4$

$y = x + 4.2$

✏ Explain 2 Performing Linear Regression

The least-squares line for a data set is the line of fit for which the sum of the squared residuals is as small as possible. Therefore the least-squares line is a line of best fit. A **line of best fit** is the line that comes closest to all of the points in the data set, using a given process. **Linear regression** is a method for finding the least-squares line.

Example 2 Given latitudes and average temperatures in degrees Celsius for several cities, use your calculator to find an equation for the line of best fit. Then interpret the correlation coefficient and use the line of best fit to estimate the average temperature of another city using the given latitude.

Ⓐ

City	Latitude	Average Temperature (°C)
Barrow, Alaska	71.2°N	−12.7
Yakutsk, Russia	62.1°N	−10.1
London, England	51.3°N	10.4
Chicago, Illinois	41.9°N	10.3
San Francisco, California	37.5°N	13.8
Yuma, Arizona	32.7°N	22.8
Tindouf, Algeria	27.7°N	22.8
Dakar, Senegal	14.0°N	24.5
Mangalore, India	12.5°N	27.1

Estimate the average temperature in Vancouver, Canada at 49.1°N.

Enter the data into data lists on your calculator. Enter the latitudes in column **L1** and the average temperatures in column **L2**.

Create a scatter plot of the data.

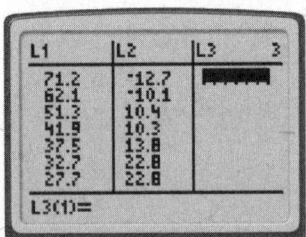

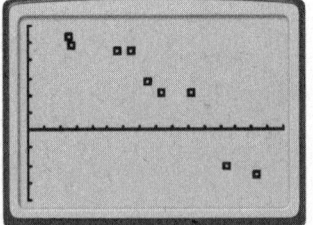

Use the Linear Regression feature to find the equation for the line of best fit using the lists of data you entered. Be sure to have the calculator also display values for the correlation coefficient r and r^2.

The correlation coefficient is about −0.95, which is very strong. This indicates a strong correlation, so we can rely on the line of fit for estimating average temperatures for other locations within the same range of latitudes.

The equation for the line of best fit is $y \approx -0.693x + 39.11$.

Graph the line of best fit with the data points in the scatter plot.

Use the TRACE function to find the approximate average temperature in degrees Celsius for a latitude of 49.1°N.

The average temperature in Vancouver should be around 5°C.

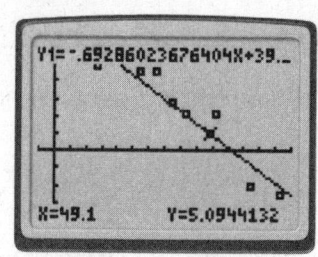

B

City	Latitude	Average Temperature (°F)
Fairbanks, Alaska	64.5°N	30
Moscow, Russia	55.5°N	39
Ghent, Belgium	51.0°N	46
Kiev, Ukraine	50.3°N	49
Prague, Czech Republic	50.0°N	50
Winnipeg, Manitobia	49.5°N	52
Luxembourg	49.4°N	53
Vienna, Austria	48.1°N	56
Bern, Switzerland	46.6°N	59

Estimate the average temperature in degrees Fahrenheit in Bath, England, at 51.4°N.

Enter the data into data lists on your calculator.

Use the Linear Regression feature to find the equation for the line of best fit using the lists of data you entered. Be sure to have the calculator also display values for the correlation coefficient r and r^2.

The correlation coefficient is about _____, which indicates a _____ correlation. The correlation coefficient indicates that the line of best fit [is/ is not] reliable for estimating temperatures of other locations within the same range of latitudes.

The equation for the line of best fit is $y \approx -$ ⬚ $x +$ ⬚ .

Use the equation to estimate the average temperature in Bath, England at 51.4°N.

$y \approx -$ ⬚ $x +$ ⬚

The average temperature in degrees Fahrenheit in Bath, England, should be around ⬚ °F.

Graph the line of best fit with the data points in the scatter plot. Then use the TRACE function to find the approximate average temperature in degrees Fahrenheit for a latitude of 51.4°N.

8. Interpret the slope of the line of best fit in terms of the context for Example 2A.

_____

_____

9. Interpret the *y*-intercept of the line of best fit in terms of the context for Example 2A.

_____

_____

Your Turn

10. Use the given data and your calculator to find an equation for the line of best fit. Then interpret the correlation coefficient and use the line of best fit to estimate the average temperature of another city using the given latitude.

City	Latitude	Average Temperature (°F)
Anchorage, United States	61.1°N	18
Dublin, Ireland	53.2°N	29
Zurich, Switzerland	47.2°N	34
Florence, Italy	43.5°N	37
Trenton, New Jersey	40.1°N	
Algiers, Algeria	36.5°N	46
El Paso, Texas	31.5°N	49
Dubai, UAE	25.2°N	56
Manila, Philippines	14.4°N	61

💬 Elaborate

11. What type of line does linear regression analysis make?

_____

_____

12. Why are squared residuals better than residuals?

_____

_____

13. **Essential Question Check-In** What four keys are needed on a graphing calculator to perform a linear regression?

_____

_____

• Online Homework
• Hints and Help
• Extra Practice

The data in the tables below are shown along with two possible lines of fit. Calculate the residuals for both lines of fit and then find the sum of the squared residuals. Identify the lesser sum and the line with better fit.

1.

x	2	4	6	8
y	1	3	5	7

$y = x + 5$

$y = x + 4.9$

2.

x	1	2	3	4
y	1	7	3	5

$y = 2x + 1$

$y = 2x + 1.1$

3.

x	2	4	6	8
y	2	8	4	6

$y = 3x + 4$

$y = 3x + 4.1$

4.

x	1	2	3	4
y	2	1	4	3

$y = x + 1$

$y = x + 0.9$

5.

x	2	4	6	8
y	1	5	4	3

$y = 3x + 1.2$

$y = 3x + 1$

6.

x	1	2	3	4
y	4	1	3	2

$y = x + 5$

$y = x + 5.3$

7.

x	2	4	6	8
y	3	6	4	5

$y = 2x + 1$

$y = 2x + 1.4$

8.

x	1	2	3	4
y	5	3	6	4

$y = x + 2$

$y = x + 2.2$

9.

x	2	4	6	8
y	1	5	7	3

$y = x + 3$

$y = x + 2.6$

10.

x	1	2	3	4
y	2	5	4	3

$y = x + 1.5$

$y = x + 1.7$

11.

x	1	2	3	4
y	2	9	7	12

$y = 2x + 3.1$

$y = 2x + 3.5$

12.

x	1	3	5	7
y	2	6	8	13

$y = 1.6x + 4$

$y = 1.8x + 4$

13.

x	1	2	3	4
y	7	5	11	8

$y = x + 5$

$y = 1.3x + 5$

14.

x	1	2	3	4
y	4	11	5	15

$y = 2x + 3$

$y = 2.4x + 3$

Use the given data and your calculator to find an equation for the line of best fit. Then interpret the correlation coefficient and use the line of best fit to estimate the average temperature of another city using the given latitude.

15.

City	Latitude	Average Temperature (°F)
Calgary, Alberta	51.0°N	24
Munich, Germany	48.1°N	26
Marseille, France	43.2°N	29
St. Louis, Missouri	38.4°N	34
Seoul, South Korea	37.3°N	36
Tokyo, Japan	35.4°N	38
New Delhi, India	28.4°N	43
Honolulu, Hawaii	21.2°N	52
Bangkok, Thailand	14.2°N	58
Panama City, Panama	8.6°N	

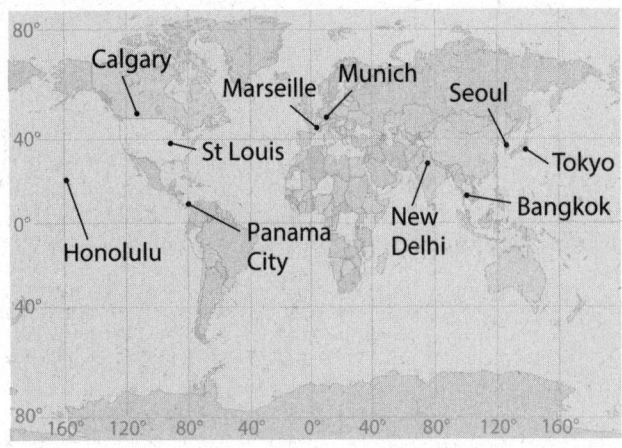

16.

City	Latitude	Average Temperature (°F)
Oslo, Norway	59.6°N	21
Warsaw, Poland	52.1°N	28
Milan, Italy	45.2°N	34
Vatican City, Vatican City	41.5°N	41
Beijing, China	39.5°N	42
Tel Aviv, Israel	32.0°N	48
Kuwait City, Kuwait	29.2°N	
Key West, Florida	24.3°N	55
Bogota, Columbia	4.4°N	64
Mogadishu, Somalia	2.0°N	66

17.

City	Latitude	Average Temperature (°F)
Tornio, Finland	65.5°N	28
Riga, Latvia	56.6°N	36
Minsk, Belarus	53.5°N	39
Quebec City, Quebec	46.5°N	45
Turin, Italy	45.0°N	47
Pittsburgh, Pennsylvania	40.3°N	49
Lisbon, Portugal	38.4°N	52
Jerusalem, Israel	31.5°N	
New Orleans, Louisiana	29.6°N	60
Port-au-Prince, Haiti	18.3°N	69

18.

City	Latitude (°N)	Average Temperature (°F)
Juneau, Alaska	58.2	15
Amsterdam, Netherlands	52.2	24
Salzburg, Austria	47.5	36
Belgrade, Serbia	44.5	38
Philadelphia, Pennsylvania	39.6	41
Tehran, Iran	35.4	44
Nassau, Bahamas	25.0	52
Mecca, Saudi Arabia	21.3	56
Dakar, Senegal	14.4	
Georgetown, Guyana	6.5	65

Demographics Each table lists the median age of people living in the United States, based on the results of the United States Census over the past few decades. Use residuals to calculate the quality of fit for the line $y = 0.5x + 20$, where y is median age and x is years since 1970.

19.

Year	Median age of men
1970	25.3
1980	26.8
1990	29.1
2000	31.4
2010	35.6

20.

Year	Median Age of Texans
1970	27.1
1980	29.3
1990	31.1
2000	33.8
2010	37.6

21. State the residuals based on the actual y and predicted y values.

    a. Actual: 23, Predicted: 21

    b. Actual: 25.6, Predicted: 23.3

    c. Actual: 24.8, Predicted: 27.4

    d. Actual: 34.9, Predicted: 31.3

H.O.T. Focus on Higher Order Thinking

22. Critical Thinking The residual plot of an equation has x-values that are close to the x-axis from $x = 0$ to $x = 10$, but has values that are far from the axis from $x = 10$ to $x = 30$. Is this a strong or weak relationship?

23. Communicate Mathematical Ideas In a squared residual plot, the residuals form a horizontal line at $y = 6$. What does this mean?

24. Interpret the Answer Explain one situation other than those in this section where squared residuals are useful.

Lesson Performance Task

The table shows the latitudes and average temperatures for the 10 largest cities in the Southern Hemisphere.

City	Latitude (°S)	Average Temperature (°F)
Sao Paulo, Brazil	23.9	69
Buenos Aires, Argentina	34.8	64
Rio de Janeiro, Brazil	22.8	76
Jakarta, Indonesia	6.3	81
Lodja, DRC	3.5	73
Lima, Peru	12.0	68
Santiago de Chile, Chile	33.2	58
Sydney, Australia	33.4	64
Melbourne, Australia	37.7	58
Johannesburg, South Africa	26.1	61

   a. Use a graphing calculator to find a line of best fit for this data set. What is the equation for the best-fit line? Interpret the meaning of the slope of this line.

   b. The city of Piggs Peak, Swaziland, is at latitude 26.0°S. Use the equation of your best-fit line to predict the average temperature in Piggs Peak. The actual average temperature for Piggs Peak is 65.3 °F. How might you account for the difference in predicted and actual values?

   c. Assume that you graphed the latitude and average temperature for 10 cities in the Northern Hemisphere. Predict how the line of best fit for that data set might compare with the best-fit line for the Southern Hemisphere cities.

Linear Modeling and Regression

Essential Question: How can you use linear modeling and regression to solve real-world problems?

Key Vocabulary

correlation *(correlación)*

line of best fit *(línea de mejor ajuste)*

linear regression *(regresión lineal)*

scatter plot *(diagrama de dispersión)*

KEY EXAMPLE   *(Lesson 10.1)*

The boiling point of water is lower at higher elevations because of the lower atmospheric pressure. The boiling point of water at some different elevations is given in the table.

Altitude (feet)	Boiling Point (°F)
500	211
1500	209
5250	202
3650	205.5
2000	207.5

Determine a line of fit for the data, and write the equation of the line. Then use your model to predict the boiling point of water at an altitude of 6400 feet.

Plot the points and sketch a line of fit. One possible line of fit goes through points (0, 212) and (5250, 202).

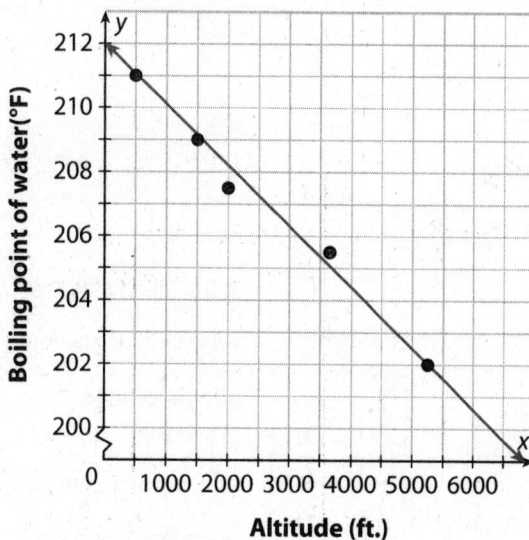

Altitude (ft.)

$m = -\dfrac{10}{5250}, b = 212$

The equation of this line of fit is $y = -0.0019x + 212$.

Substituting 6400 feet for x gives you $y = 199.84$. So the boiling point of water at 6400 feet is approximately 199.84°F.

EXERCISES

Estimate the correlation coefficient for the following data sets, indicating whether it is closest to –1, –0.5, 0, 0.5, or 1. *(Lesson 10.1)*

1.

x	y
1	2.569
2	4.236
3	3.49
4	5.62
5	4.3
6	6.1

2.

x	y
1	9.6
2	6.3
3	2.8
4	8.73
5	5.9
6	1.2

3. The data in the table below is shown along with a possible line of fit.

x	1	3	5	7
y	4	6	9	10

$y = 2x - 1$

Calculate the residuals and give the sum of the squared residuals for your answer. *(Lesson 10.2)*

MODULE PERFORMANCE TASK

How Does Wingspan Compare with Weight in Birds?

How can we use a mathematical model to describe the relationship between wingspan and weight for birds? The table shows the weights and wingspans of several small birds. Use the data to explore a possible mathematical model, and explain how you can use your model to predict weight or wingspan of different birds.

Use your own paper to complete the task. Be sure to write down all your data and assumptions. Then use graphs, numbers, words, or algebra to explain how you reached your conclusion.

Bird	Weight (ounces)	Wingspan (inches)
Blue Jay	3	16
Black-Billed Magpie	6	25
Red-Winged Blackbird	1.8	13
Brown-Headed Cowbird	1.5	12
European Starling	2.9	16
Rusty Blackbird	2.1	14
Brewer's Blackbird	2.2	15.5
Yellow-Headed Blackbird	2.3	15

(Ready) to Go On?

10.1–10.2 Linear Modeling and Regression

• Online Homework
• Hints and Help
• Extra Practice

1. The table shows test averages of eight students.

U.S. History Test Average	88	68	73	98	88	83	78	88
Science Test Average	78	73	70	93	90	80	78	90

If $x =$ the U.S. History Test Average, and $y =$ the Science Test Average, the equation of the least-squares line for the data is $y \approx 0.77x + 17.65$ and $r \approx 0.87$. Discuss correlation and causation for the data set. *(Lesson 10.1)*

2. The table shows numbers of books read by students in an English class over a summer and the students' grades for the following semester.

Books	0	0	0	0	1	1	1	2	2	3	5	8	10	14	20
Grade	64	68	69	72	71	74	76	75	79	85	86	91	94	99	98

Find an equation for the line of best fit. Calculate and interpret the correlation coefficient. Then use your equation to predict the grade of a student who read 7 books. *(Lessons 10.1, 10.2)*

ESSENTIAL QUESTION

3. How can you use statistical methods to find relationships between sets of data?

© Houghton Mifflin Harcourt Publishing Company

Assessment Readiness

1. Some students were surveyed about how much time they spent playing video games last week and their overall test averages. The equation of the least-squares line for the data is $y \approx -2.82x + 87.50$ and $r \approx -0.89$. Choose True or False for each statement.

   A. The variables are time spent playing games and test averages. ○ True ○ False

   B. The variables have a negative correlation. ○ True ○ False

   C. The variables have a weak correlation. ○ True ○ False

2. Consider $f(x) = -3x - 12$. Choose True or False for each statement.

   A. The slope is -3. ○ True ○ False

   B. The y-intercept is -12. ○ True ○ False

   C. The x-intercept is 4. ○ True ○ False

3. Look at each equation. Does the equation have a solution of $x = 3$? Select Yes or No for each statement.

   A. $2x - 8 = 19 - 7x$ ○ Yes ○ No

   B. $-2(3x - 4) = 10$ ○ Yes ○ No

   C. $\dfrac{-6x}{2} = -9$ ○ Yes ○ No

4. Use your calculator to write an equation for the line of best fit for the following data.

x	12	15	19	31	43	57
y	36	41	44	61	72	94

   Calculate and interpret the correlation coefficient. Use your equation to predict the value of y when $x = 25$.

Personal
**Math
Trainer**
• Online Homework
• Hints and Help
• Extra Practice

The data plot shown represents the age of the members of a jogging club.

1. Find the median, range, and interquartile range of the data.
   Is each statement True?

   A. The median age is 36. ⃝ Yes ⃝ No

   B. The range of ages is 8. ⃝ Yes ⃝ No

   C. The interquartile range is 4. ⃝ Yes ⃝ No

2. A new member who is 30 joins the jogging club. Determine if each statement is True or False.

   A. The range increases by 2. ⃝ True ⃝ False

   B. The median decreases by 1. ⃝ True ⃝ False

   C. The age of the new member is an outlier. ⃝ True ⃝ False

3. Is each of the following a linear function?

   A. $y = -\dfrac{4}{5}x$ ⃝ Yes ⃝ No

   B. $y = 5x^2 - 2$ ⃝ Yes ⃝ No

   C. $y = -7$ ⃝ Yes ⃝ No

4. Several hundred people were surveyed about their salary and the length of their commute to work. The equation of the line of best fit for the data is $y \approx 1.14x + 1.45$ and $r \approx 0.45$. Does each phrase accurately describe the data set?

   A. The variables have a strong correlation. ⃝ Yes ⃝ No

   B. The variables have a positive correlation. ⃝ Yes ⃝ No

   C. This study shows that there is no correlation between the length of a person's commute and their salary. ⃝ Yes ⃝ No

5. A student notices that as the town population has gone up steadily over several years, the price of a quart of milk has also gone up steadily. Describe the correlation, if any. Then explain whether you think the situation implies causation.

6. Vivian surveyed 10th and 11th graders about whether they like reading comics. Some of the results are shown in the frequency table shown. Complete the table. Find the conditional relative frequency that a student enjoys reading comics given that the student is an 11th grader. Explain how you solved this problem.

Grade	Enjoy Reading Comics		
	Yes	No	Total
10th	45	53	
11th	72		110
Total		91	208

7. Thomas drew a line of best fit for the scatter plot as shown.

Write an equation for the line of best fit in slope-intercept form. Show your work.

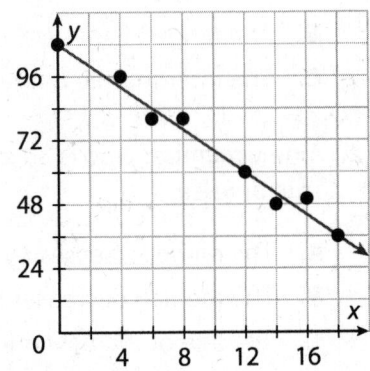

Performance Tasks

★ **8.** Gail counted the number of cars passing a certain store on Tuesday from 4 P.M. to 4:05 P.M. and on Saturday from 4 P.M. to 4:05 P.M. for 6 weeks. Her data sets are shown below.

Week	1	2	3	4	5	6
Cars on Tuesday	10	8	12	3	9	15
Cars on Saturday	24	8	31	36	29	32

A. Use the most appropriate measure of central tendency to compare the centers of these two data sets. Explain your choice.

B. Draw two box plots on the same number line to represent the data.

★★ **9.** A total of 150 students in two grades at Lowell High School were asked whether they usually ate lunch in the cafeteria. If they did not, they were asked if they would or would not eat lunch in the cafeteria if it had a salad bar.

	Now eat in cafeteria	Would eat if salad bar	Would not eat if salad bar
9th graders	36	14	32
10th graders	25	10	28

A. Use the given frequency table to make a new table showing the joint and marginal relative frequencies. Round to the nearest tenth of a percent.

B. The school board has decided that a salad bar should be added to the cafeteria if at least 30% of the students who currently do not eat in the cafeteria would start doing so. Should the salad bar be added?

★★★**10.** A scientist theorizes that you can estimate the temperature by counting how often crickets chirp. The scientist gathers the data in the table shown.

Number of chirps in a 14-second interval	37	32	42	37	46	35	34
Temperature (°F)	78	72	81	77	88	75	76

A. How many cricket chirps would you expect to indicate a temperature of 85 degrees? Include a graph and an equation as part of the justification of your answer.

B. What might be the lowest temperature your model could be applied to? Explain your reasoning.

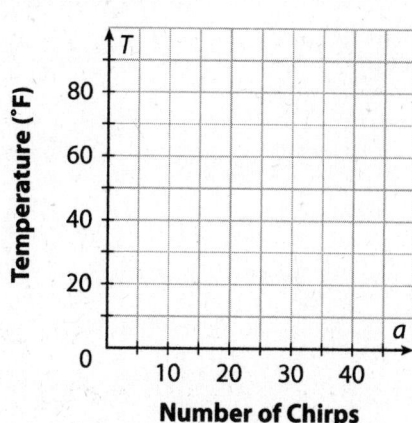

Geologist A geologist is studying the sediment discharged from several U.S. rivers, as shown in the table.

River	Amount of Sediment Discharged (millions of tons)
Mississippi River	230
Copper River	80
Yukon River	65
Columbia River	40
Susitna River	25
Eel River	15
Brazos River	11

For Parts **a–c**, round your answers to the nearest whole number, if necessary.

a. Find the mean and the median of the data for all seven rivers. Which measure represents the data better? Explain.

b. Find the mean of the data for the six rivers, excluding the Mississippi River. Does this mean represent the data better than the mean you found in part a? Explain.

c. Find the range and standard deviation of the data of all seven rivers. Describe what the measures tell you about the dispersion of the data.

Linear Systems and Piecewise-Defined Functions

MATH IN CAREERS

Personal Shopper Personal shoppers assist clients in their needs for a variety of merchandise, which can include furniture, clothing, groceries, or gifts. Personal shoppers must have a good understanding of financial math, including percentages. They must be able to stay within the budgetary constraints of their clients. They must also be able to calculate expenses such as transportation costs and reasonable rates for their services.

If you are interested in a career as a personal shopper, you should study these mathematical subjects:
- Algebra
- Business Math

Research other careers that require staying within the constraints of a budget. Check out the career activity at the end of the unit to find out how **personal shoppers** use math.

Reading Start-Up

© Houghton Mifflin Harcourt Publishing Company

Vocabulary

Review Words

✔ greater than *(mayor que)*

✔ greater than or equal to *(mayor que o igual a)*

✔ less than *(menor que)*

✔ less than or equal to *(menor que o igual a)*

✔ *x*-intercept *(intersección con el eje x)*

✔ *y*-intercept *(intersección con el eje y)*

Preview Words

absolute-value function *(función de valor absolute)*

consistent system *(sistema consistente)*

dependent system *(sistema dependiente)*

independent system *(sistema independiente)*

piecewise function *(función a trozos)*

system of linear equations *(sistema de ecuaciones lineales)*

system of linear inequalities *(sistema de desigualdades lineales)*

Visualize Vocabulary

Use the ✔ words to complete the chart.

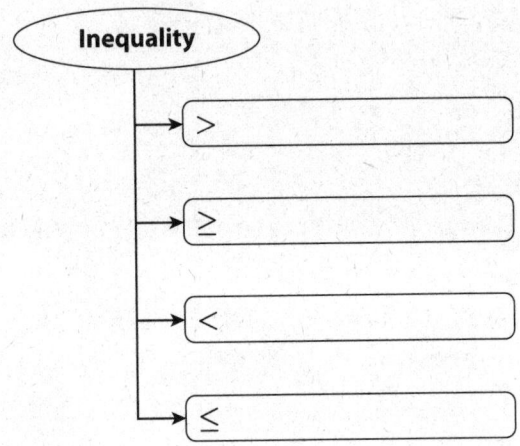

Understand Vocabulary

Complete the sentences using the preview words. Match the term on the left to the example on the right.

1. __ independent system

2. __ consistent system

3. __ dependent system

A. a system of equations that has an infinite number of solutions

B. a system of equations or inequalities that has at least one solution

C. a system of equations that has exactly one solution

Active Reading

Three-Panel Flip Chart Create a three-panel flip chart to help you understand the concepts in this unit. Label one flap "Solving Systems of Linear Equations," another "Modeling with Linear Systems," and the last flap "Piecewise-Defined Functions." As you study each module, write important ideas under the appropriate flap. Include any sample equations, inequalities, and functions that will help you remember the concepts later when you look back at your notes.

Solving Systems of Linear Equations

★

Essential Question: How can you use a system of linear equations to solve real-world problems?

REAL WORLD VIDEO
A Mars rover is sent into space to land on Mars. This feat requires planning the trajectory of the rover to intersect with the orbit of Mars. Systems of equations are used to find the intersection of graphs.

MODULE PERFORMANCE TASK PREVIEW
Do Hybrid Cars Pay for Themselves?

Hybrid cars often get better gas mileage than traditional cars, which can lead to savings on gas money. The longer you drive a hybrid car, the more you are likely to save on gas. In this module, you will explore the question of how many years it would take to save enough money on gas to pay for the extra cost of a hybrid car. Buckle up and let's find out!

Complete these exercises to review skills you will need for this module.

Graphing Linear Relationships

Example 1
Tell whether the graph represents a linear nonproportional or proportional relationship.

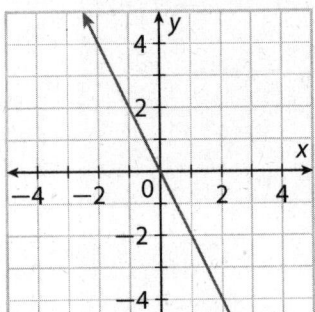

The graph of a linear nonproportional relationship is a straight line that does not pass through the origin.

The graph of a linear proportional relationship is a straight line that passes through the origin.

The graph is a straight line that passes through the origin, so it represents a linear proportional relationship.

Tell whether the graph represents a linear nonproportional or proportional relationship.

1.

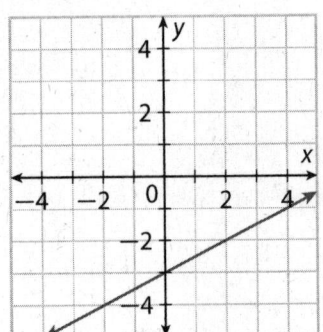

_____

2.

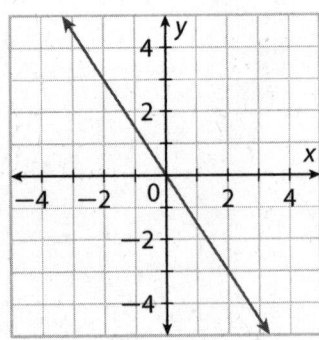

_____

Algebraic Expressions

Example 2
Evaluate $3x + 4y$ for $x = -2$ and $y = 4$.

$3x + 4y$

$3(-2) + 4(4)$ Substitute -2 for x and 4 for y.

$-6 + 16$ Multiply.

10 Add.

Evaluate each expression for the given values of the variables.

3. $6p - 2q$ for $p = 3$ and $q = -7$

_____

4. $5a - 2b$ for $a = -2$ and $b = 5$

_____

5. $8m + 5n$ for $m = 3$ and $n = -5$

_____

6. $7x + 9y$ for $x = -3$ and $y = 2$

_____

11.1 Solving Linear Systems by Graphing

Essential Question: How can you find the solution of a system of linear equations by graphing?

🧭 Explore   Types of Systems of Linear Equations

A **system of linear equations,** also called a *linear system,* consists of two or more linear equations that have the same variables. A **solution of a system of linear equations** with two variables is any ordered pair that satisfies all of the equations in the system.

Ⓐ Describe the relationship between the two lines in Graph A.

_____

_____

Graph A

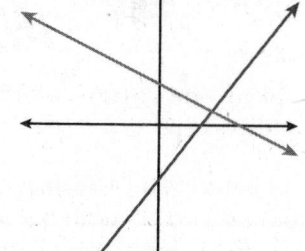

Ⓑ What do you know about every point on the graph on a linear equation?

_____

_____

Ⓒ How many solutions does a system of two equations have if the graphs of the two equations intersect at exactly one point?

_____

_____

Ⓓ Describe the relationship between the two lines that coincide in Graph B.

_____

_____

Graph B

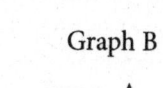

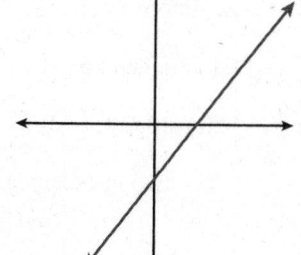

Ⓔ How many solutions does a system of two equations have if the graphs of the two equations intersect at infinitely many points?

_____

_____

(F) Describe the relationship between the two lines in Graph C.

_____

_____

(G) How many solutions does a system of two equations have if the graphs of the two equations do not intersect?

_____

Graph C

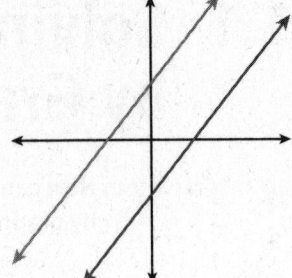

Reflect

1. **Discussion** Explain why the solution of a system of two equations is represented by any point where the two graphs intersect.

_____

_____

🔧 **Explain 1** ## Solving Consistent, Independent Linear Systems by Graphing

A **consistent system** is a system with at least one solution. Consistent systems can be either independent or dependent.

An **independent system** has exactly one solution. The graph of an independent system consists of two lines that intersect at exactly one point. A **dependent system** has infinitely many solutions. The graph of a dependent system consists of two coincident lines, or the same line.

A system that has no solution is an **inconsistent system**.

Example 1 Solve the system of linear equations by graphing. Check your answer.

(A) $\begin{cases} 2x + y = 6 \\ -x + y = 3 \end{cases}$

Find the intercepts for each equation, plus a third point for a check. Then graph.

$2x + y = 6$	$-x + y = 3$
x-intercept: 3	x-intercept: -3
y-intercept: 6	y-intercept: 3
third point: $(-1, 8)$	third point: $(3, 6)$

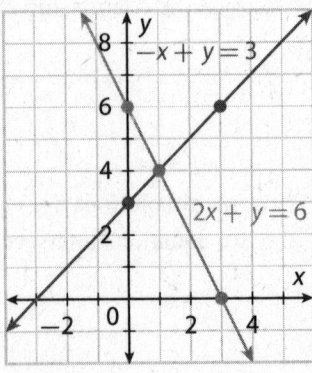

The two lines appear to intersect at $(1, 4)$. Check.

$2x + y = 6$ $\qquad$ $-x + y = 3$

$2(1) + 4 \overset{?}{=} 6$ $\qquad$ $-(1) + 4 \overset{?}{=} 3$

$6 = 6$ $\qquad\qquad$ $3 = 3$

The point satisfies both equations, so the solution is $(1, 4)$.

Ⓑ $\begin{cases} y = 2x - 2 \\ 3y + 6x = 18 \end{cases}$

Find the intercepts for each equation, plus a third point for a check. Then graph.

$y = 2x - 2$ $3y + 6x = 18$

x-intercept: ☐   x-intercept: ☐

y-intercept: ☐   y-intercept: ☐

third point: $\left(3, \boxed{}\right)$ third point: $\left(1, \boxed{}\right)$

The two lines appear to intersect at ☐ . Check.

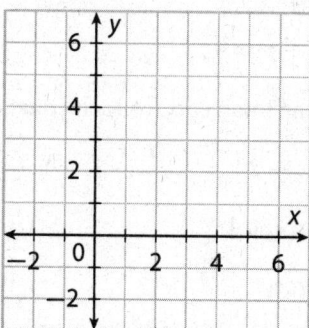

$y = 2x - 2$ $y + 2x = 6$

$\boxed{} \stackrel{?}{=} 2\left(\boxed{}\right) - 2$ $\boxed{} + 2\left(\boxed{}\right) \stackrel{?}{=} 6$

$\boxed{} = \boxed{}$ $\boxed{} = 6$

The point satisfies both equations, so the solution is ☐ .

Reflect

2. How do you know that the systems of equations are consistent? How do you know that they are independent?

_____

_____

Your Turn

Solve the system of linear equations by graphing. Check your answer.

3. $\begin{cases} y = -2x - 2 \\ x + 2y = 2 \end{cases}$ 4. $\begin{cases} y = 2x + 8 \\ -x + y = 6 \end{cases}$

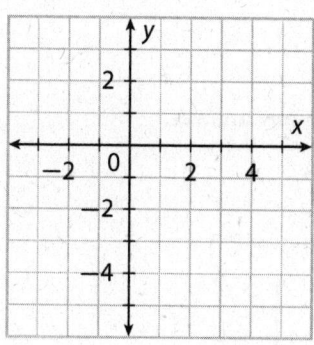   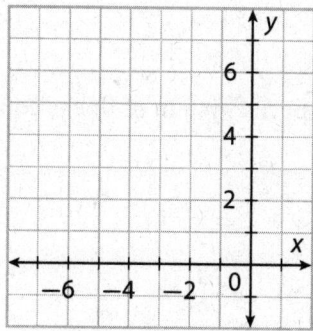

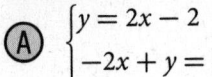 **Explain 2** **Solving Special Linear Systems by Graphing**

Example 2 Solve the special system of equations by graphing and identify the system.

Ⓐ $\begin{cases} y = 2x - 2 \\ -2x + y = 4 \end{cases}$

Find the intercepts for each equation, plus a third point for a check.

$y = 2x - 2$	$-2x + y = 4$
x-intercept: 1	x-intercept: -2
y-intercept: -2	y-intercept: 4
third point: $(2, 2)$	third point: $(2, 8)$

The two lines don't intersect, so there is no solution.
The two lines have the same slope and different y-intercepts
so they will never intersect. This is an inconsistent system.

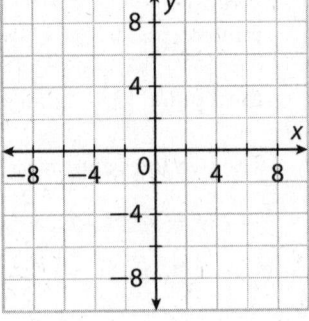

Ⓑ $\begin{cases} y = 3x - 3 \\ -3x + y = -3 \end{cases}$

Find the intercepts for each equation, plus a third point for a check.

$y = 3x - 3$	$-3x + y = -3$
x-intercept: ☐	x-intercept: ☐
y-intercept: ☐	y-intercept: ☐
third point: $\left(2, \boxed{}\right)$	third point: $\left(2, \boxed{}\right)$

The two lines coincide, so there are _____ solutions.

They have the same slope and y-intercept; therefore, they are _____ line(s) / equation(s).

This is a _____ and _____ system.

Your Turn

Solve the special system of linear equations by graphing. Check your answer.

5. $\begin{cases} y = -x - 2 \\ x + y + 2 = 0 \end{cases}$

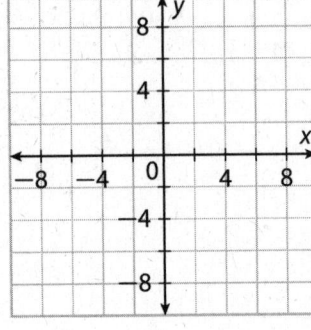

6. $\begin{cases} y = \frac{2}{3}x - 1 \\ -\frac{2}{3}x + y = 1 \end{cases}$

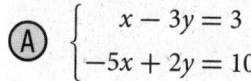 **Explain 3** **Estimating Solutions of Linear Systems by Graphing**

You can estimate the solution of a linear system of equations by graphing the system and finding the approximate coordinates of the intersection point.

Example 3 Estimate the solution of the linear system by graphing.

(A) $\begin{cases} x - 3y = 3 \\ -5x + 2y = 10 \end{cases}$

Graph the equations using a graphing calculator.

Y1 = (3 − X)/(−3) and Y2 = (10 + 5X)/2

Find the point of intersection.

The two lines appear to intersect at about $(-2.8, -1.9)$.

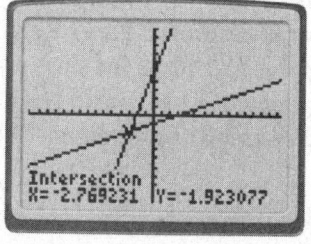

(B) $\begin{cases} 6 - 2y = 3x \\ y = 4x + 8 \end{cases}$

Graph each equation by finding intercepts.

The two lines appear to intersect at about $\boxed{}$.

Check to see if $\boxed{}$ makes both equations true.

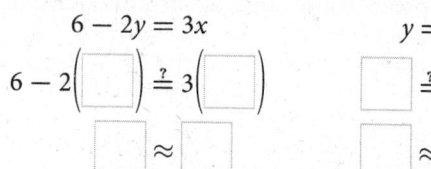

$6 - 2y = 3x$ \qquad $y = 4x + 8$

$6 - 2\left(\boxed{}\right) \stackrel{?}{=} 3\left(\boxed{}\right)$ \qquad $\boxed{} \stackrel{?}{=} 4\left(\boxed{}\right) + 8$

$\boxed{} \approx \boxed{}$ \qquad $\boxed{} \approx \boxed{}$

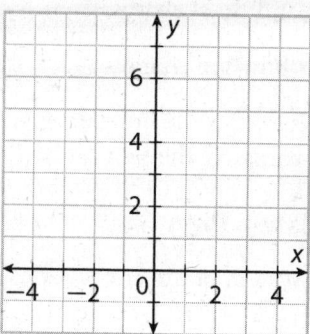

The point does not satisfy both equations, but the results are close.

So, $\boxed{}$ is an approximate solution.

Your Turn

Estimate the solution of the linear system of equations by graphing.

7. $\begin{cases} 2y = -5x + 10 \\ -15 = -3x + 5y \end{cases}$

8. $\begin{cases} 3x + 3y = -9 \\ y = \dfrac{1}{2}x - 1 \end{cases}$

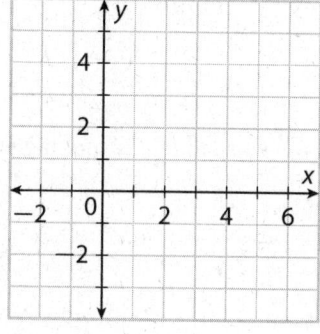

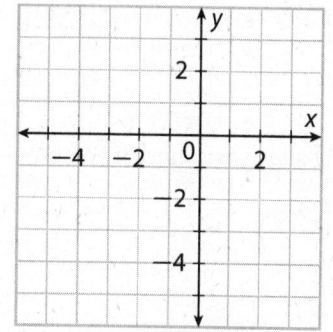

Interpreting Graphs of Linear Systems to Solve Problems

You can solve problems with real-world context by graphing the equations that model the problem and finding a common point.

Example 4 Rock and Bowl charges $2.75 per game plus $3 for shoe rental. Super Bowling charges $2.25 per game and $3.50 for shoe rental. For how many games will the cost to bowl be approximately the same at both places? What is that cost?

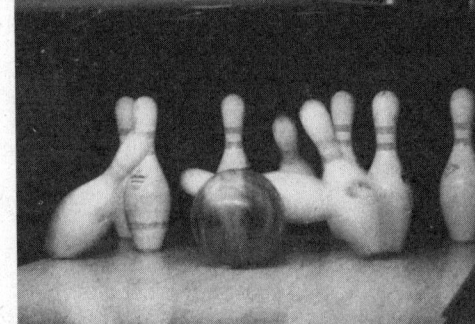

 Analyze Information

Identify the important information.

- Rock and Bowl charges $ [ ] per game plus $ [ ] for shoe rental.
- Super Bowling charges $ [ ] per game and $ [ ] for shoe rental.
- The answer is the number of games played for which the total cost is approximately the same at both bowling alleys.

Formulate a Plan

Write a system of linear equations, where each equation represents the price at each bowling alley.

_____

Solve

Graph $y = 2.75x + 3$ and $y = 2.25x + 3.50$.

The lines appear to intersect at _____. So, the cost at both places will be the same for _____ game(s) bowled and that cost will be _____.

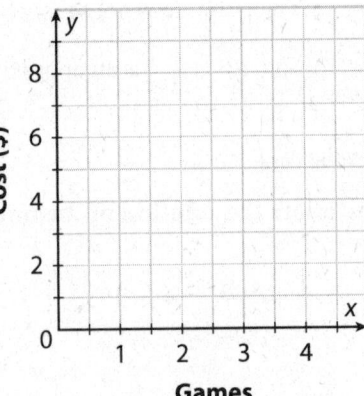

Justify and Evaluate

Check _____ using both equations.

$$2.75\left(\boxed{}\right) + 3 = \boxed{} \qquad 2.25\left(\boxed{}\right) + 3.5 = \boxed{}$$

Reflect

9. Which bowling alley costs more if you bowl more than 1 game? Explain how you can tell by looking at the graph.

_____

_____

Your Turn

10. Video club A charges $10 for membership and $4 per movie rental. Video club B charges $15 for membership and $3 per movie rental. For how many movie rentals will the cost be the same at both video clubs? What is that cost? Write a system and solve by graphing.

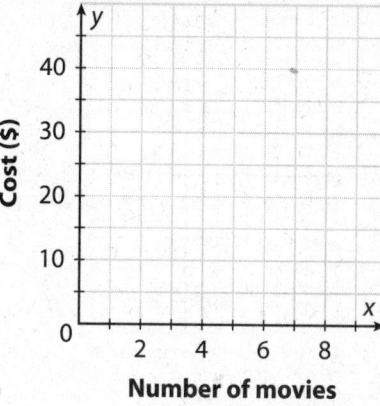

Cost ($)

Number of movies

Elaborate

11. When a system of linear equations is graphed, how is the graph of each equation related to the solution(s) of that system?

_____

12. **Essential Question Check-In** How does graphing help you solve a system of linear equations?

_____
_____
_____

⊛ Evaluate: Homework and Practice

- Online Homework
- Hints and Help
- Extra Practice

1. Is the following statement correct? Explain.

   A system of two equations has no solution if the graphs of the two equations are coincident lines.

Solve the system of linear equations by graphing. Check your answer.

2. $\begin{cases} y = 2x - 4 \\ x + 2y = 12 \end{cases}$

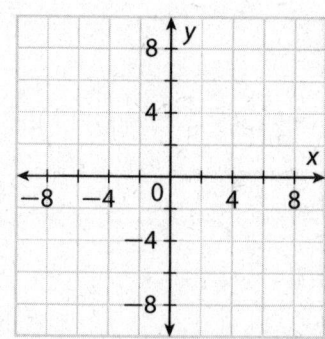

3. $\begin{cases} y = -\frac{1}{3}x + 2 \\ y + 4 = -\frac{4}{3}x \end{cases}$

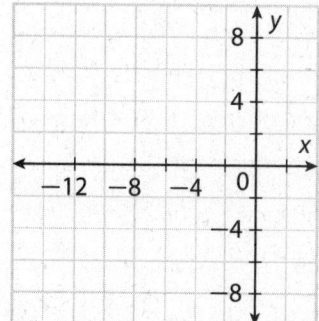

4. $\begin{cases} y = -x - 6 \\ y = x \end{cases}$

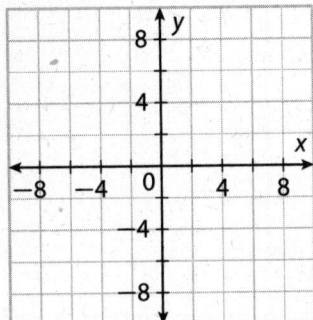

5. $\begin{cases} y = \frac{4}{3}x - 4 \\ y = 4 \end{cases}$

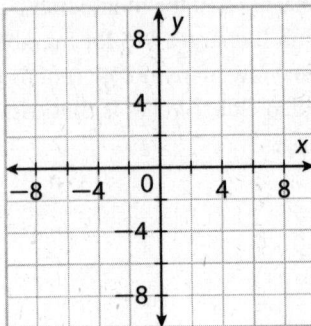

6. $\begin{cases} y = -2x + 2 \\ y + 2 = 2x \end{cases}$

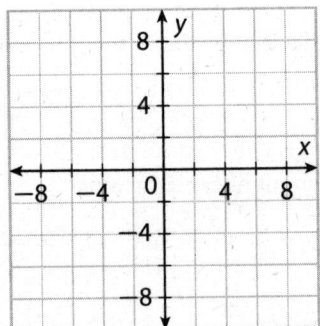

7. $\begin{cases} y = \frac{1}{2}x + 5 \\ \frac{2}{3}x + y = -2 \end{cases}$

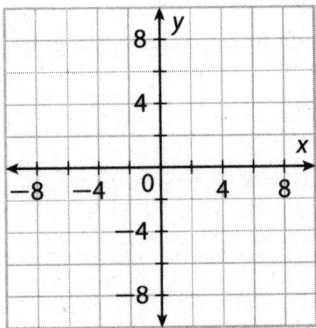

8. $\begin{cases} y = \frac{1}{2}x - 2 \\ -\frac{1}{2}x + y - 3 = 0 \end{cases}$

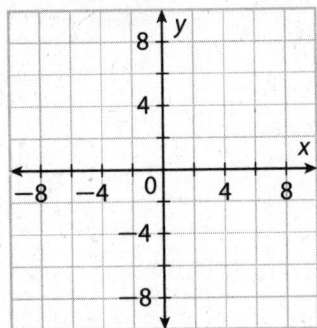

9. $\begin{cases} y = 2x + 4 \\ -4x + 2y = 8 \end{cases}$

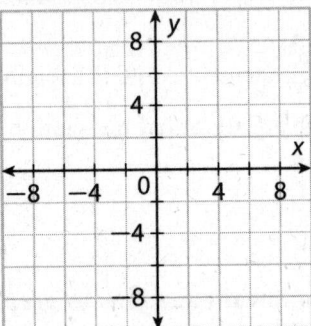

10. $\begin{cases} y = -3x + 1 \\ 12x + 4y = 4 \end{cases}$

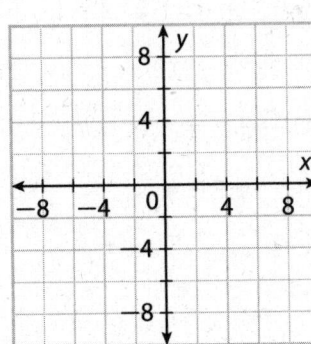

11. $\begin{cases} y = 4x + 4 \\ -4x + y + 4 = 0 \end{cases}$

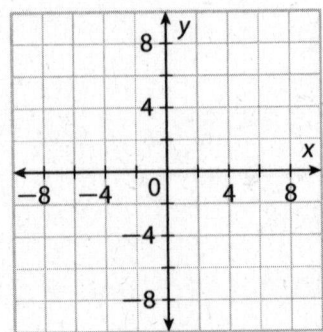

12. $\begin{cases} y = -\dfrac{3}{4}x + \dfrac{1}{4} \\ \dfrac{3}{4}x + y - 2 = 0 \end{cases}$

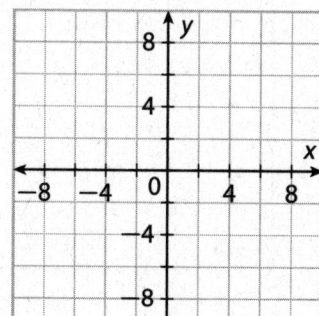

13. $\begin{cases} y = 5x - 1 \\ -5x + y + 4 = 3 \end{cases}$

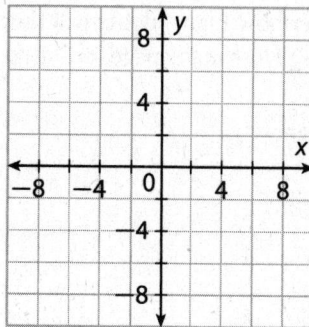

Estimate the solution of the linear system of equations by graphing.

14. $\begin{cases} 3y = -5x + 15 \\ -14 = -2x + 7y \end{cases}$

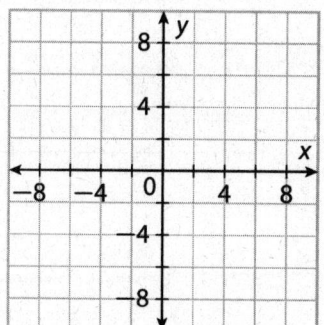

15. $\begin{cases} 2y + 5x = 14 \\ -35 = -5x + 7y \end{cases}$

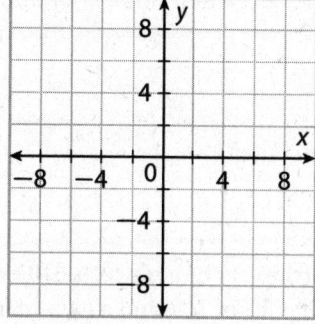

16. $\begin{cases} \dfrac{4}{7}y = x + 4 \\ 2x - 5y = 10 \end{cases}$

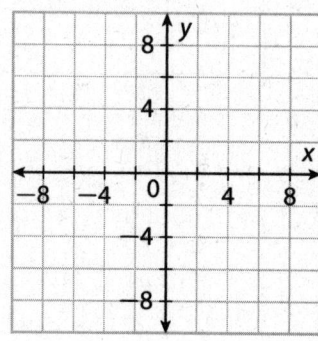

17. $\begin{cases} 6y = 5x + 30 \\ 2 = -\dfrac{2}{7}x + y \end{cases}$

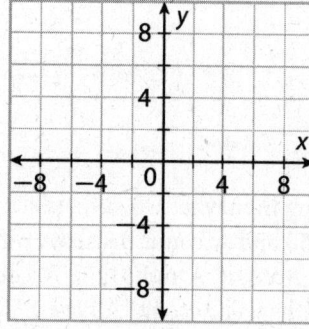

Solve by graphing. Give an approximate solution if necessary.

18. Wren and Jenni are reading the same book. Wren is on page 12 and reads 3 pages every night. Jenni is on page 7 and reads 4 pages every night. After how many nights will they have read the same number of pages? How many pages will that be?

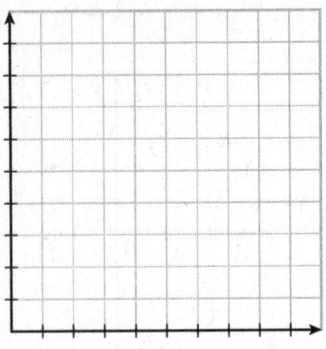

19. Rusty burns 6 calories per minute swimming and 10 calories per minute jogging. In the morning, Rusty burns 175 calories walking and swims for x minutes. In the afternoon, Rusty will jog for x minutes. How many minutes must he jog to burn at least as many calories y in the afternoon as he did in the morning? Round your answer up to the next whole number of minutes.

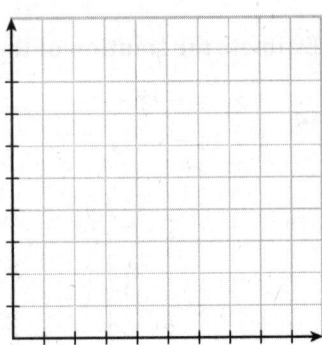

20. A gym membership at one gym costs $10 every month plus a one-time membership fee of $15, and a gym membership at another gym costs $4 every month plus a one-time $40 membership fee. After about how many months will the gym memberships cost the same amount?

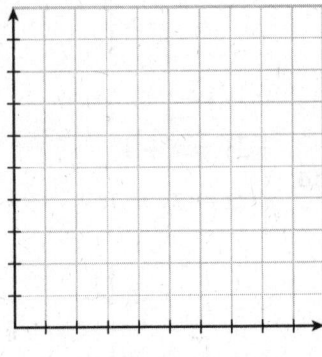

21. Malory is putting money in two savings accounts. Account A started with $150 and Account B started with $300. Malory deposits $16 in Account A and $12 in Account B each month. In how many months will Account A have a balance at least as great as Account B? What will that balance be?

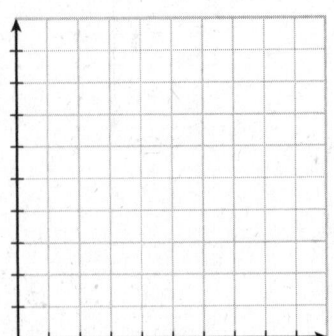

22. Critical Thinking Write *sometimes*, *always*, or *never* to complete the following statements.

a. If the equations in a system of linear equations have the same slope,

there are _____ infinitely many solutions for the system.

b. If the equations in a system of linear equations have different slopes, there

is _____ one solution for the system.

c. If the equations in a system of linear equations have the same slope and a different

y-intercept, there is _____ any solution for the system.

H.O.T. Focus on Higher Order Thinking

23. Critique Reasoning Brad classifies the system below as inconsistent because the equations have the same y-intercept. What is his error?

$$\begin{cases} y = 2x - 4 \\ y = x - 4 \end{cases}$$

24. Explain the Error Alexa solved the system

$$\begin{cases} 5x + 2y = 6 \\ x - 3y = -4 \end{cases}$$

by graphing and estimated the solution to be about $(1.5, 0.6)$.
What is her error? What is the correct answer?

25. Represent Real-World Problems Cora ran 3 miles last week and will run 7 miles per week from now on. Hana ran 9 miles last week and will run 4 miles per week from now on. The system of linear equations $\begin{cases} y = 7x + 3 \\ y = 4x + 9 \end{cases}$ can be used to represent

this situation. Explain what x and y represent in the equations. After how many weeks will Cora and Hana have run the same number of miles? How many miles? Solve by graphing.

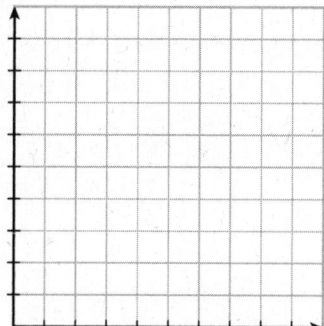

Lesson Performance Task

A boat takes 7.5 hours to make a 60-mile trip upstream and 6 hours on the 60-mile return trip. Let v be the speed of the boat in still water and c be the speed of the current. The upstream speed of the boat is $v - c$ and the downstream boat speed is $v + c$.

a. Use the distance formula to write a system of equations relating boat speed and time to distance, one equation for the upstream part of the trip and one for the downstream part.

b. Graph the system to find the speed of the boat in still water and the speed of the current.

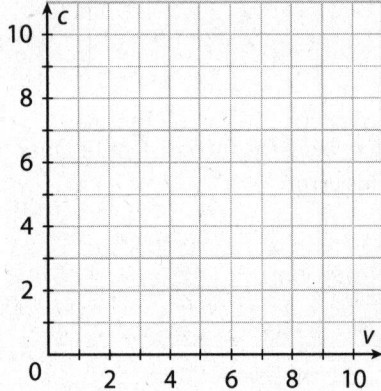

c. How long would it take the boat to travel the 60 miles if there were no current?

11.2 Solving Linear Systems by Substitution

Essential Question: How can you solve a system of linear equations by using substitution?

Resource Locker

🧭 Explore Exploring the Substitution Method of Solving Linear Systems

Another method to solve a linear system is by using the substitution method.

In the system of linear equations shown, the value of y is given. Use this value of y to find the value of x and the solution of the system.

$$\begin{cases} y = 2 \\ x + y = 6 \end{cases}$$

(A) Substitute the value of y in the second equation and solve for x.

$$x + y = 6$$

$$x + \boxed{} = 6$$

$$x = \boxed{}$$

(B) The values of x and y are known. What is the solution of the system?

Solution: $\left(\boxed{}, \boxed{} \right)$

(C) Graph the system of linear equations. How do your solutions compare?

(D) Use substitution to find the values of x and y in this system of linear equations. Substitute $4x$ for y in the second equation and solve for x. Once you find the value for x, substitute it into either original equation to find the value for y.

$$\begin{cases} y = 4x \\ 5x + 2y = 39 \end{cases}$$

Solution: $\left(\boxed{}, \boxed{} \right)$

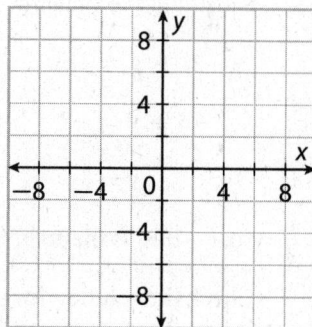

Reflect

1. **Discussion** For the system in Step D, what equation did you get after substituting $4x$ for y in $5x + 2y = 39$ and simplifying?

_____

_____

2. **Discussion** How could you check your solution in part D?

_____

_____

Explain 1 **Solving Consistent, Independent Linear Systems by Substitution**

The **substitution method** is used to solve a system of equations by solving an equation for one variable and substituting the resulting expression into the other equation. The steps for the substitution method are as shown.

1. Solve one of the equations for one of its variables.
2. Substitute the expression from Step 1 into the other equation and solve for the other variable.
3. Substitute the value from Step 2 into either original equation and solve to find the value of the other variable.

Example 1 Solve each system of linear equations by substitution.

(A) $\begin{cases} 3x + y = -3 \\ -2x + y = 7 \end{cases}$

Solve an equation for one variable.

$3x + y = -3$	Select one of the equations.
$y = -3x - 3$	Solve for y. Isolate y on one side.

Substitute the expression for y in the other equation and solve.

$-2x + (-3x - 3) = 7$	Substitute the expression for y.
$-5x - 3 = 7$	Combine like terms.
$-5x = 10$	Add 3 to both sides.
$x = -2$	Divide each side by -5.

Substitute the value for x into one of the equations and solve for y.

$3(-2) + y = -3$	Substitute the value of x into the first equation.
$-6 + y = -3$	Simplify.
$y = 3$	Add 6 to both sides.

So, $(-2, 3)$ is the solution of the system.

Check the solution by graphing.

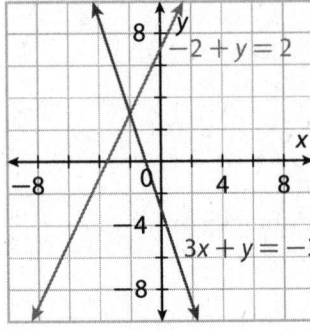

$3x + y = -3$

x-intercept: -1

y-intercept: -3

$-2x + y = 7$

x-intercept: $-\dfrac{7}{2}$

y-intercept: 7

The point of intersection is $(-2, 3)$.

Ⓑ $\begin{cases} x - 3y = 9 \\ x + 4y = 2 \end{cases}$

Solve an equation for one variable.

$x - 3y = 9$ \qquad\qquad Select one of the equations.

$x = \boxed{}$ \qquad Solve for x. Isolate x on one side.

Substitute the expression for ____ in the other equation and solve.

$\left(\boxed{}\right) + 4y = 2$ \qquad Substitute the expression for ____.

$\boxed{} = 2$ \qquad Combine like terms.

$\boxed{} = \boxed{}$ \qquad Subtract $\boxed{}$ from both sides.

$y = \boxed{}$ \qquad Divide each side by $\boxed{}$.

Substitute the value for y into one of the equations and solve for x.

$x - 3\left(\boxed{}\right) = 9$ \qquad Substitute the value of y into the first equation.

$\boxed{} = 9$ \qquad Simplify.

$x = \boxed{}$ \qquad Subtract $\boxed{}$ from both sides.

So, $\left(\boxed{}, \boxed{}\right)$ is the solution by graphing.

Check the solution by graphing.

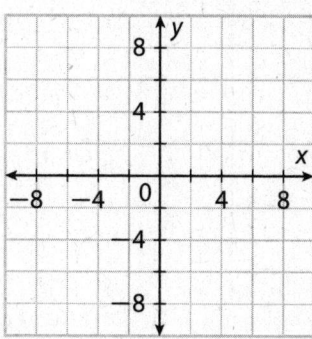

$x - 3y = 9$ \qquad\qquad $x + 4y = 2$

x-intercept: $\boxed{}$ \qquad x-intercept: $\boxed{}$

y-intercept: $\boxed{}$ \qquad y-intercept: $\boxed{}$

The point of intersection is $\left(\boxed{}, \boxed{}\right)$.

Reflect

3. Explain how a system in which one of the equations is of the form $y = c$, where c is a constant, is a special case of the substitution method.

_____

4. Is it more efficient to solve $-2x + y = 7$ for x than for y? Explain.

_____

_____

5. Solve the system of linear equations by substitution.

$$\begin{cases} 3x + y = 14 \\ 2x - 6y = -24 \end{cases}$$

⚙ Explain 2 Solving Special Linear Systems by Substitution

You can use the substitution method for systems of linear equations that have infinitely many solutions and for systems that have no solutions.

Example 2 Solve each system of linear equations by substitution.

 Ⓐ $\begin{cases} x + y = 4 \\ -x - y = 6 \end{cases}$

Solve $x + y = 4$ for x.

$$x = -y + 4$$

Substitute the resulting expression into the other equation and solve.

$-(-y + 4) - y = 6$ Substitute.

$-4 = 6$ Simplify.

The resulting equation is false, so the system has no solutions.

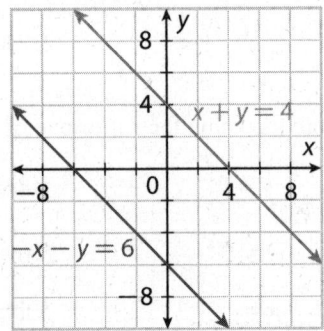

The graph shows that the lines are parallel and do not intersect.

 Ⓑ $\begin{cases} x - 3y = 6 \\ 4x - 12y = 24 \end{cases}$

Solve $x - 3y = 6$ for _____.

$$x = \boxed{}$$

Substitute the resulting expression into the other equation and solve.

$4\left(\boxed{}\right) - 12y = 24$ Substitute.

$\boxed{} = 24$ Simplify.

The resulting equation is _____, so the

system has _____.

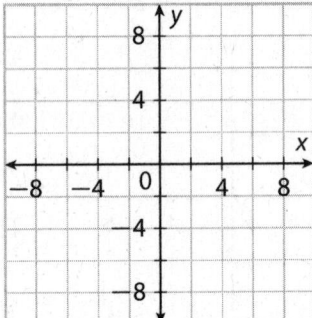

The graphs are _____,

so the system has _____.

6. Provide two possible solutions of the system in Example 2B. How are all the solutions of this system related to one another?

_____

_____

Solve each system of linear equations by substitution.

7. $\begin{cases} -2x + 14y = -28 \\ x - 7y = 14 \end{cases}$

8. $\begin{cases} -3x + y = 12 \\ 6x - 2y = 18 \end{cases}$

🔑 Explain 3 Solving Linear System Models by Substitution

You can use a system of linear equations to model real-world situations.

Example 3 Solve each real-world situation by using the substitution method.

Ⓐ Fitness center A has a $60 enrollment fee and costs $35 per month. Fitness center B has no enrollment fee and costs $45 per month. Let t represent the total cost in dollars and m represent the number of months. The system of equations $\begin{cases} t = 60 + 35m \\ t = 45m \end{cases}$ can be used to represent this situation. In how many months will both fitness centers cost the same? What will the cost be?

$60 + 35m = 45m$	Substitute $60 + 35m$ for t in the second equation.
$60 = 10m$	Subtract $35m$ from each side.
$6 = m$	Divide each side by 10.
$t = 45m$	Use one of the original equations.
$= 45(6) = 270$	Substitute 6 for m.
$(6, 270)$	Write the solution as an ordered pair.

Both fitness centers will cost $270 after 6 months.

Ⓑ High-speed Internet provider A has a $100 setup fee and costs $65 per month. High-speed internet provider B has a setup fee of $30 and costs $70 per month. Let t represent the total amount paid in dollars and m represent the number of months. The system of equations $\begin{cases} t = 100 + 65m \\ t = 30 + 70m \end{cases}$ can be used to represent this situation. In how many months will both providers cost the same? What will that cost be?

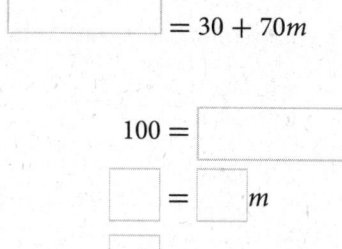

$\boxed{} = 30 + 70m$ Substitute $\boxed{}$ for t in the second equation.

$100 = \boxed{}$ Subtract $\boxed{}\ m$ from each side.

$\boxed{} = \boxed{}\ m$ Subtract $\boxed{}$ from each side.

$\boxed{} = m$ Divide each side by $\boxed{}$.

$t = 30 + 70m$ Use one of the original equations.

$t = 30 + 70\left(\boxed{}\right)$ Substitute $\boxed{}$ for m.

$t = \boxed{}$

$\left(\boxed{}, \boxed{}\right)$ Write the sulotion as an ordered pair.

Both Internet providers will cost $_____ after _____ months.

Reflect

9. If the variables in a real-world situation represent the number of months and cost, why must the values of the variables be greater than or equal to zero?

_____

_____

Your Turn

10. A boat travels at a rate of 18 kilometers per hour from its port. A second boat is 34 kilometers behind the first boat when it starts traveling in the same direction at a rate of 22 kilometers per hour to the same port. Let d represent the distance the boats are from the port in kilometers and t represent the amount of time in hours. The system of equations $\begin{cases} d = 18t + 34 \\ d = 22t \end{cases}$ can be used to represent this situation. How many hours will it take for the second boat to catch up to the first boat? How far will the boats be from their port? Use the substitution method to solve this real-world application.

💬 Elaborate

11. When given a system of linear equations, how do you decide which variable to solve for first?

_____

_____

12. How can you check a solution for a system of equations without graphing?

_____

_____

13. **Essential Question-Check-In** Explain how you can solve a system of linear equations by substitution.

_____

_____

_____

1. In the system of linear equations shown, the value of y is given. Use this value of y to find the value of x and the solution of the system.

$$\begin{cases} y = 12 \\ 2x - y = 4 \end{cases}$$

a. What is the solution of the system?

b. Graph the system of linear equations. How do the solutions compare?

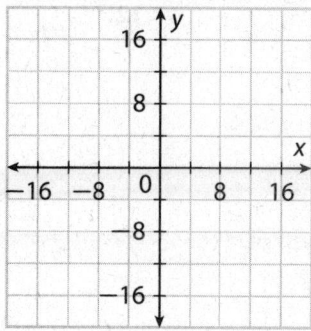

Solve each system of linear equations by substitution.

2. $\begin{cases} 5x + y = 8 \\ 2x + y = 5 \end{cases}$

3. $\begin{cases} x - 3y = 10 \\ x + 5y = -22 \end{cases}$

4. $\begin{cases} 5x - 3y = 22 \\ -4x + y = -19 \end{cases}$

5. $\begin{cases} x + 7y = -11 \\ -2x - 5y = 4 \end{cases}$

6. $\begin{cases} 2x + 6y = 16 \\ 3x - 5y = -18 \end{cases}$

7. $\begin{cases} 7x + 2y = 24 \\ -6x + 3y = 3 \end{cases}$

Solve each system of linear equations by substitution.

8. $\begin{cases} x + y = 3 \\ -4x - 4y = 12 \end{cases}$

9. $\begin{cases} 3x - 3y = -15 \\ -x + y = 5 \end{cases}$

10. $\begin{cases} x - 8y = 17 \\ -3x + 24y = -51 \end{cases}$

11. $\begin{cases} 5x - y = 18 \\ 10x - 2y = 32 \end{cases}$

12. $\begin{cases} -2x - 3y = 12 \\ -4x - 6y = 24 \end{cases}$

13. $\begin{cases} 3x + 4y = 36 \\ 6x + 8y = 48 \end{cases}$

Solve each real-world situation by using the substitution method.

14. The number of DVDs sold at a store in a month was 920 and the number of DVDs sold decreased by 12 per month. The number of Blu-ray discs sold in the same store in the same month was 502 and the number of Blu-ray discs sold increased by 26 per month. Let d represent the number of discs sold and t represent the time in months.

The system of equations $\begin{cases} d = 920 - 12t \\ d = 502 + 26t \end{cases}$ can be used to represent this situation. If this trend continues, in how many months will the number of DVDs sold equal the number of Blu-ray discs sold? How many of each is sold in that month?

15. One smartphone plan costs $30 per month for talk and messaging and $8 per gigabyte of data used each month. A second smartphone plan costs $60 per month for talk and messaging and $3 per gigabyte of data used each month. Let c represent the total cost in dollars and d represent the amount of data used in gigabytes. The system of equations $\begin{cases} c = 30 + 8d \\ c = 60 + 3d \end{cases}$ can be used to represent this situation. How many gigabytes would have to be used for the plans to cost the same? What would that cost be?

16. A movie theater sells popcorn and fountain drinks. Brett buys 1 popcorn bucket and 3 fountain drinks for his family, and pays a total of $9.50. Sarah buys 3 popcorn buckets and 4 fountain drinks for her family, and pays a total of $19.75. If p represents the number of popcorn buckets and d represents the number of drinks, then the system of equations $\begin{cases} 9.50 = p + 3d \\ 19.75 = 3p + 4d \end{cases}$ can be used to represent this situation. Find the cost of a popcorn bucket and the cost of a fountain drink.

17. Jen is riding her bicycle on a trail at the rate of 0.3 kilometer per minute. Michelle is 11.2 kilometers behind Jen when she starts traveling on the same trail at a rate of 0.44 kilometer per minute. Let d represent the distance in kilometers the bicyclists are from the start of the trail and t represent the time in minutes. The system of equations $\begin{cases} d = 0.3t + 11.2 \\ d = 0.44t \end{cases}$ can be used to represent this situation. How many minutes will it take Michelle to catch up to Jen? How far will they be from the start of the trail? Use the substitution method to solve this real-world application.

18. Geometry The length of a rectangular room is 5 feet more than its width. The perimeter of the room is 66 feet. Let L represent the length of the room and W represent the width in feet. The system of equations $\begin{cases} L = W + 5 \\ 66 = 2L + 2W \end{cases}$ can be used to represent this situation. What are the room's dimensions?

19. A cable television provider has a $55 setup fee and charges $82 per month, while a satellite television provider has a $160 setup fee and charges $67 per month. Let c represent the total cost in dollars and t represent the amount of time in months. The system of equations $\begin{cases} c = 55 + 82t \\ c = 160 + 67t \end{cases}$ can be used to represent this situation.

a. In how many months will both providers cost the same? What will that cost be?

b. If you plan to move in 12 months, which provider would be less expensive? Explain.

20. Determine whether each of the following systems of equations have one solution, infinitely many solutions, or no solution. Select the correct answer for each lettered part.

a. $\begin{cases} x + y = 5 \\ -6y - 6y = 30 \end{cases}$

b. $\begin{cases} x + y = 7 \\ 5x + 2y = 23 \end{cases}$

c. $\begin{cases} 3x + y = 5 \\ 6x + 2y = 12 \end{cases}$

d. $\begin{cases} 2x + 5y = -12 \\ x + 7y = -15 \end{cases}$

e. $\begin{cases} 3x + 5y = 17 \\ -6x - 10y = -34 \end{cases}$

21. Finance Adrienne invested a total of $1900 in two simple-interest money market accounts. Account A paid 3% annual interest and account B paid 5% annual interest. The total amount of interest she earned after one year was $83. If a represents the amount invested in dollars in account A and b represents the amount invested in dollars in account B, the system of equations $\begin{cases} a + b = 1900 \\ 0.03a + 0.05b = 83 \end{cases}$ can represent this situation. How much did Adrienne invest in each account?

H.O.T. **Focus on Higher Order Thinking**

22. Real-World Application The Sullivans are deciding between two landscaping companies. Evergreen charges a $79 startup fee and $39 per month. Eco Solutions charges a $25 startup fee and $45 per month. Let c represent the total cost in dollars and t represent the time in months. The system of equations $\begin{cases} c = 39t + 79 \\ c = 45t + 25 \end{cases}$ can be used to represent this situation.

a. In how many months will both landscaping services cost the same? What will that cost be?

b. Which landscaping service will be less expensive in the long term? Explain.

23. Multiple Representations For the first equation in the system of linear equations below, write an equivalent equation without denominators. Then solve the system.

$$\begin{cases} \dfrac{x}{5} + \dfrac{y}{3} = 6 \\ x - 2y = 8 \end{cases}$$

24. Conjecture Is it possible for a system of three linear equations to have one solution? If so, give an example.

25. Conjecture Is it possible to use substitution to solve a system of linear equations if one equation represents a horizontal line and the other equation represents a vertical line? Explain.

Lesson Performance Task

A company breaks even from the production and sale of a product if the total revenue equals the total cost. Suppose an electronics company is considering producing two types of smartphones. To produce smartphone A, the initial cost is $20,000 and each phone costs $150 to produce. The company will sell smartphone A at $200. Let $C(a)$ represent the total cost in dollars of producing a units of smartphone A. Let $R(a)$ represent the total revenue, or money the company takes in due to selling a units of smartphone A. The system of

equations $\begin{cases} C(a) = 20{,}000 + 150a \\ R(a) = 200a \end{cases}$ can be used to represent the situation for phone A.

To produce smartphone B, the initial cost is $44,000 and each phone costs $200 to produce. The company will sell smartphone B at $280. Let $C(b)$ represent the total cost in dollars of producing b units of smartphone B and $R(b)$ represent the total revenue from

selling b units of smartphone B. The system of equations $\begin{cases} C(b) = 44{,}000 + 200b \\ R(b) = 280b \end{cases}$ can be

used to represent the situation for phone B.

Solve each system of equations and interpret the solutions. Then determine whether the company should invest in producing smartphone A or smartphone B. Justify your answer.

11.3 Solving Linear Systems by Adding or Subtracting

Essential Question: How can you solve a system of linear equations by adding and subtracting?

⊘ Explore   Exploring the Effects of Adding Equations

Systems of equations can be solved by graphing, substitution, or by a third method, called **elimination.**

Ⓐ Look at the system of linear equations.

$$\begin{cases} 2x - 4y = -10 \\ 3x + 4y = 5 \end{cases}$$

What do you notice about the coefficients of the y-terms?

_____

Ⓑ What is the sum of $-4y$ and $4y$? How do you know?

_____

_____

Ⓒ Find the sum of the two equations by combining like terms.

$$\begin{array}{ccccc} 2x & -4y & = & -10 \\ +3x & +4y & = & +5 \\ \hline \boxed{} & + \boxed{} & = & \boxed{} \end{array}$$

Ⓓ Use the equation from Step C to find the value of x.

$x = \boxed{}$

Ⓔ Use the value of x to find the value of y. What is the solution of the system?

$y = \boxed{}$

Solution: _____

Reflect

1. **Discussion** How do you know that when both sides of the two equations were added, the resulting sums were equal?

_____

_____

2. **Discussion** How could you check your solution?

_____

_____

⚙ Explain 1 · Solving Linear Systems by Adding or Subtracting

The **elimination method** is a method used to solve systems of equations in which one variable is eliminated by adding or subtracting two equations in the system.

Steps in the Elimination Method
1. Add or subtract the equations to eliminate one variable, and then solve for the other variable.
2. Substitute the value into either original equation to find the value of the eliminated variable.
3. Write the solution as an ordered pair.

Example 1 Solve each system of linear equations using the indicated method. Check your answer by graphing.

(A) Solve the system of linear equations by adding.

$$\begin{cases} 4x - 2y = 12 \\ x + 2y = 8 \end{cases}$$

Add the equations.

$$4x - 2y = 12$$
$$\underline{x + 2y = 8}$$
$$5x + 0 = 20$$
$$5x = 20$$
$$x = 4$$

Substitute the value of x into one of the equations and solve for y.

$$x + 2y = 8$$
$$4 + 2y = 8$$
$$2y = 4$$
$$y = 2$$

Write the solution as an ordered pair.

$$(4, 2)$$

Check the solution by graphing.

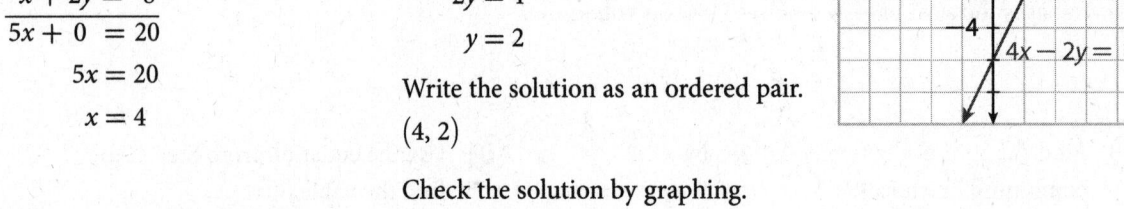

(B) Solve the system of linear equations by subtracting.

$$\begin{cases} 2x + 6y = 6 \\ 2x - y = -8 \end{cases}$$

Subtract the equations.

$$2x + 6y = 6$$
$$\underline{2x - y = -8}$$
$$\boxed{}\;\boxed{} = \boxed{}$$

Substitute the value of y into one of the equations and solve for x.

Write the solution as an ordered pair.

_____

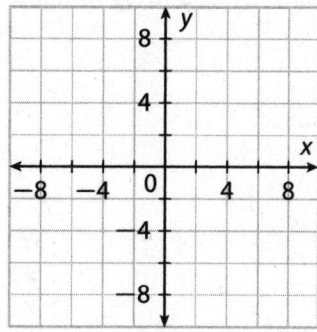

Check the solution by graphing.

3. Can the system in part A be solved by subtracting one of the original equations from the other? Why or why not?

_____

_____

4. In part B, what would happen if you added the original equations instead of subtracting?

_____

_____

Your Turn

Solve each system of linear equations by adding or subtracting.

5. $\begin{cases} 2x + 5y = -24 \\ 3x - 5y = 14 \end{cases}$

6. $\begin{cases} 3x + 2y = 5 \\ x + 2y = -1 \end{cases}$

⏺ Explain 2 Solving Special Linear Systems by Adding or Subtracting

Example 2 Solve each system of linear equations by adding or subtracting.

(A) $\begin{cases} -4x - 2y = 4 \\ 4x + 2y = -4 \end{cases}$

Add the equations.

$$\begin{array}{r} -4x - 2y = 4 \\ +4x + 2y = -4 \\ \hline 0 + 0 = 0 \\ 0 = 0 \end{array}$$

The resulting equation is true, so the system has infinitely many solutions.

Graph the equations to provide more information.

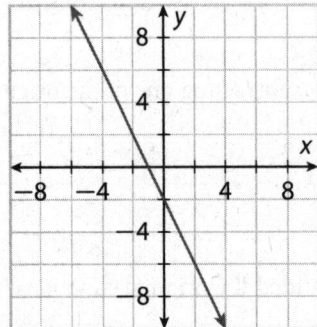

The graphs are the same line, so the system has infinitely many solutions.

(B) $\begin{cases} x + y = -2 \\ x + y = 4 \end{cases}$

Subtract the equations.

$$\begin{array}{r} x + y = -2 \\ -(x + y = 4) \\ \hline \end{array}$$

Graph the equations to provide more information.

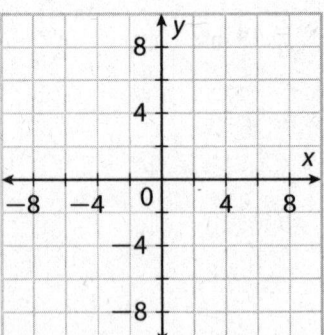

The resulting equation is _____ ,

so the system has _____ solutions.

The graph shows that the lines are _____

and _____ .

Solve each system of linear equations by adding or subtracting.

7. $\begin{cases} 4x - y = 3 \\ 4x - y = -2 \end{cases}$

8. $\begin{cases} x - 6y = 7 \\ -x + 6y = -7 \end{cases}$

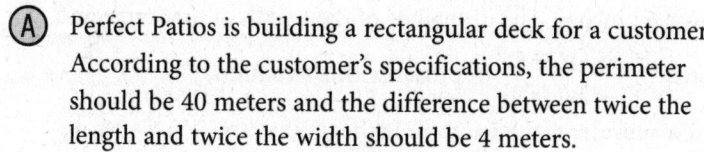 **Explain 3** **Solving Linear System Models by Adding or Subtracting**

Example 3 Solve by adding or subtracting.

(A) Perfect Patios is building a rectangular deck for a customer. According to the customer's specifications, the perimeter should be 40 meters and the difference between twice the length and twice the width should be 4 meters.

The system of equations $\begin{cases} 2\ell + 2w = 40 \\ 2\ell - 2w = 4 \end{cases}$ can be used to

represent this situation, where ℓ is the length and w is the width. What will be the length and width of the deck?

Add the equations.

$$2\ell + 2w = 40$$
$$\underline{2\ell - 2w = 4}$$
$$4\ell + 0 = 44$$
$$4\ell = 44$$
$$\ell = 11$$

Substitute the value of ℓ into one of the equations and solve for w.

$$2\ell + 2w = 40$$
$$2(11) + 2w = 40$$
$$22 + 2w = 40$$
$$2w = 18$$
$$w = 9$$

Write the solution as an ordered pair.

$$(\ell, w) = (11, 9)$$

The length of the deck will be 11 meters and the width will be 9 meters.

B A video game and movie rental kiosk charges \$2 for each video game rented, and \$1 for each movie rented. One day last week, a total of 114 video games and movies were rented for a total of \$177. The system of equations $\begin{cases} x + y = 114 \\ 2x + y = 177 \end{cases}$ represents this situation, where x represents the number of video games rented and y represents the number of movies rented. Find the numbers of video games and movies that were rented.

Subtract the equations.

$x + y = 114$

$-(2x + y = 177)$
_____

Substitute the value of x into one of the equations and solve for y.

Write the solution as an ordered pair.

_____ video games and _____ movies were rented.

Your Turn

9. The perimeter of a rectangular picture frame is 62 inches. The difference of the length of the frame and twice its width is 1. The system of equations $\begin{cases} 2\ell + 2w = 62 \\ \ell - 2w = 1 \end{cases}$ represents this situation, where ℓ represents the length in inches and w represents the width in inches. What are the length and the width of the frame?

💬 Elaborate

10. How can you decide whether to add or subtract to eliminate a variable in a linear system? Explain your reasoning.

_____

_____

11. **Discussion** When a linear system has no solution, what happens when you try to solve the system by adding or subtracting?

_____

_____

12. **Essential Question Check-In** When you solve a system of linear equations by adding or subtracting, what needs to be true about the variable terms in the equations?

_____

1. Which method of elimination would be best to solve the system of linear equations? Explain.

$$\begin{cases} \frac{1}{2}x + \frac{3}{4}y = -10 \\ -x - \frac{3}{4}y = 1 \end{cases}$$

Solve each system of linear equations by adding or subtracting.

2. $\begin{cases} 3x + 2y = 10 \\ 3x - y = 22 \end{cases}$

3. $\begin{cases} -2x + y = 3 \\ 3x - y = -2 \end{cases}$

4. $\begin{cases} x + y = 5 \\ x - 3y = 3 \end{cases}$

5. $\begin{cases} 7x + y = -4 \\ 2x - y = 1 \end{cases}$

6. $\begin{cases} -5x + y = -3 \\ 5x - 3y = -1 \end{cases}$

7. $\begin{cases} 2x + y = -6 \\ -5x + y = 8 \end{cases}$

8. $\begin{cases} 6x - 3y = 15 \\ 4x - 3y = -5 \end{cases}$

9. $\begin{cases} 8x - 6y = 36 \\ -2x + 6y = 0 \end{cases}$

10. $\begin{cases} \dfrac{1}{2}x - \dfrac{7}{9}y = -\dfrac{20}{3} \\ -\dfrac{1}{2}x + \dfrac{7}{9}y = 6\dfrac{2}{3} \end{cases}$

11. $\begin{cases} -10x + 2y = -7 \\ -10x + 2y = -2 \end{cases}$

12. $\begin{cases} -2x + 5y = 7 \\ 2x - 5y = -7 \end{cases}$

13. $\begin{cases} x + y = 0 \\ -x - y = 0 \end{cases}$

14. $\begin{cases} -5x - y = -3 \\ -5x - y = -2 \end{cases}$

15. $\begin{cases} ax - by = c \\ ax - by = c \end{cases}$

16. The sum of two numbers is 65, and the difference of the numbers is 27. The system of linear equations $\begin{cases} x + y = 65 \\ x - y = 27 \end{cases}$ represents this situation, where x is the larger number and y is the smaller number. Solve the system to find the two numbers.

17. A rectangular garden has a perimeter of 120 feet. The length of the garden is 24 feet greater than twice the width. The system of linear equations $\begin{cases} 2\ell + 2w = 120 \\ \ell - 2w = 24 \end{cases}$ represents this situation, where ℓ is the length of the garden and w is its width. Find the length and width of the garden.

18. The sum of two angles is 90°. The difference of twice the larger angle and the smaller angle is 105°. The system of linear equations $\begin{cases} x + y = 90 \\ 2x - y = 105 \end{cases}$ represents this situation where x is the larger angle and y is the smaller angle. Find the measures of the two angles.

19. Max and Sasha exercise a total of 20 hours each week. Max exercises 15 hours less than 4 times the number of hours Sasha exercises. The system of equations $\begin{cases} x + y = 20 \\ x - 4y = -15 \end{cases}$ represents this situation, where x represents the number of hours Max exercises and y represents the number of hours Sasha exercises. How many hours do Max and Sasha exercise per week?

20. The sum of the digits in a two-digit number is 12. The digit in the tens place is 2 more than the digit in the ones place. The system of linear equations $\begin{cases} x + y = 12 \\ x - y = 2 \end{cases}$ represents this situation, where x is the digit in the tens place and y is the digit in the ones place. Solve the system to find the two-digit number.

21. A pool company is installing a rectangular pool for a new house. The perimeter of the pool must be 94 feet, and the length must be 2 feet more than twice the width.

The system of linear equations
$$\begin{cases} 2\ell + 2w = 94 \\ \ell = 2w + 2 \end{cases}$$
represents
this situation, where ℓ is the length and w is the width. What are the dimensions of the pool?

22. Use one solution, no solutions, or infinitely many solutions to complete each statement.

a. When the solution of a system of linear equations yields the

equation $4 = 4$, the system has _____.

b. When the solution of a system of linear equations yields the

equation $x = 4$, the system has _____.

c. When the solution of a system of linear equations yields the

equation $0 = 4$, the system has _____.

H.O.T. **Focus on Higher Order Thinking**

23. **Multiple Representations** You can use subtraction to solve the system of linear equations shown.

$$\begin{cases} 2x + 4y = -4 \\ 2x - 2y = -10 \end{cases}$$

Instead of subtracting $2x - 2y = -10$ from $2x + 4y = -4$, what equation can you add to get the same result? Explain.

© Houghton Mifflin Harcourt Publishing Company • Image Credits: ©Marlene Ford/Alamy

24. Explain the Error Liang's solution of a system of linear equations is shown. Explain Liang's error and give the correct solution.

$$\begin{cases} 3x - 2y = 12 \\ -x - 2y = -20 \end{cases}$$

$$3x - 2y = 12$$
$$\underline{-x - 2y = -20}$$
$$2x = -8$$
$$x = -4$$

$$3x - 2y = 12$$
$$3(-4) - 2y = 12$$
$$-12 - 2y = 12$$
$$-2y = 24$$
$$y = -12$$

Solution: $(-4, -12)$

25. Represent Real-World Problems For a school play, Rico bought 3 adult tickets and 5 child tickets for a total of $40. Sasha bought 1 adult ticket and 5 child tickets for a total of $25.

The system of linear equations represents this $$\begin{cases} 3x + 5y = 40 \\ x + 5y = 25 \end{cases}$$

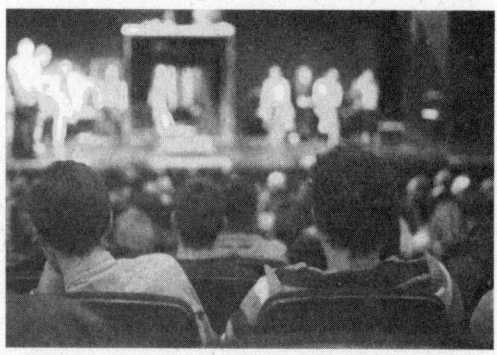

situation, where x is the cost of an adult ticket and y is the cost of a child ticket. How much will Julia pay for 5 adult tickets and 3 child tickets?

Lesson Performance Task

A local charity run has a Youth Race for runners under the age of 12. The entry fee is $5 for an individual or $4 each for two runners from the same family. Carter is collecting the registration forms and fees. After everyone has registered, he picks up the cash box and finds a dollar on the ground. He checks the cash box and finds that it contains $200 and the registration slips for 47 runners. Does the dollar belong in the cash box or not? Explain your reasoning. (Hint: You can use the system of equations $i + f = 47$ and $5i + 4f = 200$, where i equals the number of individual tickets and f equals the number of family tickets.)

11.4 Solving Linear Systems by Multiplying First

Essential Question: How can you solve a system of linear equations by using multiplication and elimination?

⊘ Explore 1 Understanding Linear Systems and Multiplication

A system of linear equations in which one of the like terms in each equation has either the same or opposite coefficients can that be readily solved by elimination.

How do you solve the system if neither of the pairs of like terms in the equations have the same or opposite coefficients?

(A) Graph and label the following system of equations.
$$\begin{cases} 2x - y = 1 \\ 4x + 4y = 8 \end{cases}$$

(B) The solution to the system is _____.

(C) When both sides of an equation are multiplied by the same value, the equation [is/is not] still true.

(D) Multiply both sides of the first equation by 2.

_____

(E) Write the resulting system of equations.
$$\begin{cases} \boxed{} \\ 4x + 4y = 8 \end{cases}$$

(F) Graph and label the new system of equations.

Solution: _____

(G) Can the new system of equations be solved using elimination now that $4x$ appears in each equation?

_____

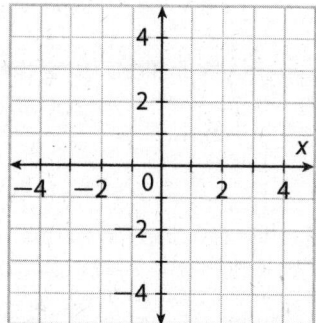

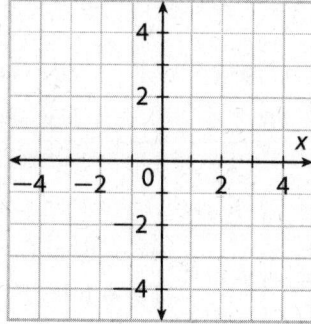

1. **Discussion** How are the graphs of $2x - y = 1$ and $4x - 2y = 2$ related?

_____

2. **Discussion** How are the equations $2x - y = 1$ and $4x - 2y = 2$ related?

_____

⊘ Explore 2   Proving the Elimination Method with Multiplication

The previous example illustrated that rewriting a system of equations by multiplying a constant term by one of the equations does not change the solutions for the system. What happens if a new system of equations is written by adding this new equation to the untouched equation from the original system?

(A) Original System → New System

$$\begin{cases} 2x - y = 1 \\ 4x + 4y = 8 \end{cases} \rightarrow \begin{cases} 4x - 2y = 2 \\ 4x + 4y = 8 \end{cases}$$

Add the equations in the new system.

$4x - 2y = 2$
$4x + 4y = 8$

⬚

(B) Write a new system of equations using this new equation.

$$\begin{cases} 2x - y = 1 \\ \end{cases}$$

(C) Graph and label the equations from this new system of equations.

(D) Is the solution to this new system of equations the same as the solution to the original system of equations? Explain.

_____

_____

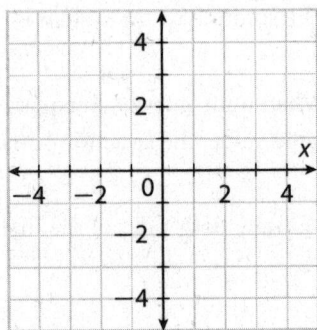

(E) If the original system is $Ax + By = C$ and $Dx + Ey = F$, where A, B, C, D, E, and F are constants, then multiply the second equation by a nonzero constant k to get $kDx + kEy = kF$. Add this new equation to $Ax + By = C$.

$$\begin{array}{rcll} Ax + & By & = & C \\ + \quad kDx + & kEy & = & kF \\ \hline \boxed{} + & \boxed{} & = & \boxed{} \end{array}$$

(F) So, the original system is $\begin{cases} Ax + By = C \\ Dx + Ey = F \end{cases}$, and the new system is

$$\begin{cases} Ax + By = C \\ \underline{} \end{cases}.$$

Ⓖ Let (x_1, y_1) be the solution to the original system. Fill in the missing parts of the following proof to show that (x_1, y_1) is also the solution to the new system.

Ⓗ $Ax_1 + By_1 = \boxed{}$ Given.

Ⓘ $Dx_1 + Ey_1 = \boxed{}$ Given.

Ⓙ $\boxed{}(Dx_1 + Ey_1) = kF$ _____ Property of Equality

Ⓚ $kDx_1 + kEy_1 = kF$ _____

Ⓛ $\boxed{} + kDx_1 + kEy_1 = C + kF$ _____ Property of Equality

Ⓜ $Ax_1 + \boxed{} + kDx_1 + kEy_1 = C + kF$ Substitute $Ax_1 + \boxed{}$ for $\boxed{}$ on the left.

Ⓝ $Ax_1 + \boxed{} + By_1 + kEy_1 = C + kF$ _____ Property of Addition

Ⓞ $(Ax_1 + kDx_1) + (By_1 + kEy_1) = C + kF$ _____ Property of Addition

Ⓟ $(A + kD)x_1 + \left(\boxed{}\right)y_1 = C + kF$ _____

Ⓠ Therefore, (x_1, y_1) is the solution to the new system.

Reflect

3. **Discussion** Is a proof required using subtraction? What about division?

_____

_____

_____

🔑 Explain 1 Solving Linear Systems by Multiplying First

In some systems of linear equations, neither variable can be eliminated by adding or subtracting the equations directly. In these systems, you need to multiply one or both equations by a constant so that adding or subtracting the equations will eliminate one or more of the variables.

Steps for Solving a System of Equations by Multiplying First
1. Decide which variable to eliminate.
2. Multiply one or both equations by a constant so that adding or subtracting the equations will eliminate the variable.
3. Solve the system using the elimination method.

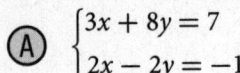 **Example 1** **Solve each system of equations by multiplying. Check the answers by graphing the systems of equations.**

A $\begin{cases} 3x + 8y = 7 \\ 2x - 2y = -10 \end{cases}$

Multiply the second equation by 4.

$4(2x - 2y = -10) \Rightarrow 8x - 8y = -40$

Add the result to the first equation.

$$\begin{array}{r} 3x + 8y = 7 \\ + \ 8x - 8y = -40 \\ \hline 11x = -33 \end{array}$$

Solve for x.

$11x = -33$

$x = -3$

Substitute -3 for x in one of the original equations, and solve for y.

$3x + 8y = 7$

$3(-3) + 8y = 7$

$-9 + 8y = 7$

$8y = 16$

$y = 2$

The solution to the system is $(-3, 2)$.

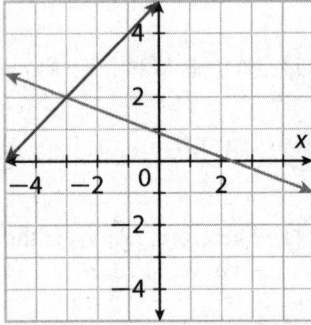

B $\begin{cases} -3x + 2y = 4 \\ 4x - 13y = 5 \end{cases}$

Multiply the first equation by _____ and multiply the second equation by _____ so the x terms in the system have coefficients of -12 and 12 respectively.

$\boxed{} (-3x + 2y = 4)$ $-12x + \boxed{} y = \boxed{}$
$ \Rightarrow$
$\boxed{} (4x - 13y = 5)$ $12x - \boxed{} y = \boxed{}$

Add the resulting equations.

$-12x + \boxed{} y = \boxed{}$

$+12x - \boxed{} y = \boxed{}$

$\boxed{} y = \boxed{}$

Solve for y.

$\boxed{} y = \boxed{}$

$y = \boxed{}$

Solve the first equation for x when $y =$ ☐.

$$-3x + 2y = 4$$

$$-3x + 2\left(\boxed{}\right) = 4$$

$$-3x + \boxed{} = 4$$

$$-3x = \boxed{}$$

$$x = \boxed{}$$

The solution to the system is $\boxed{}$.

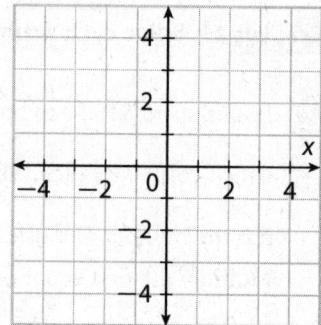

Your Turn

Solve each system of equations by multiplying. Check the answers by graphing the systems of equations.

4. $\begin{cases} -3x + 4y = 12 \\ 2x + y = -8 \end{cases}$

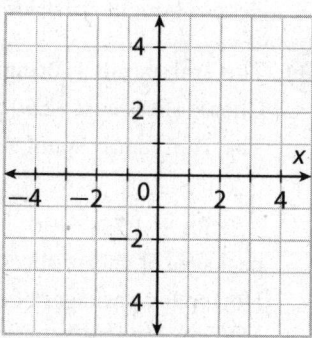

5. $\begin{cases} 2x + 3y = -1 \\ 5x - 2y = -12 \end{cases}$

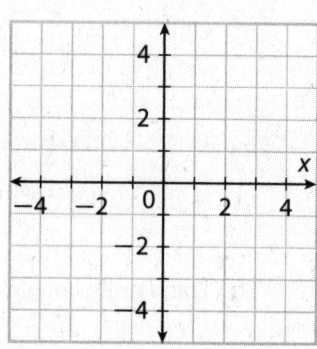

Explain 2 Solving Linear System Models by Multiplying First

You can solve a linear system of equations that models a real-world example by multiplying first.

Example 2 Solve each problem by multiplying first.

Ⓐ Jessica spent $16.30 to buy 16 flowers. The bouquet contained daisies, which cost $1.75 each, and tulips, which cost $0.85 each. The system of equations $\begin{cases} d + t = 16 \\ 1.75d + 0.85t = 16.30 \end{cases}$ models this situation, where

d is the number of daisies and t is the number of tulips. How many of each type of flower did Jessica buy?
Multiply the first equation by -0.85 to eliminate t from each equation. Then, add the equations.

$$\begin{cases} -0.85(d + t) = -0.85(16) \\ 1.75d + 0.85t = 16.30 \end{cases} \Rightarrow$$

$$\begin{array}{r} -0.85d - 0.85t = -13.60 \\ +1.75d + 0.85t = \ \ \ 16.30 \\ \hline 0.9d \ \ \ \ \ \ \ \ \ \ = \ \ \ \ 2.70 \\ d = 3 \end{array}$$

Find t. $d + t = 16$
$\ \ \ \ \ \ \ \ \ \ \ \ \ \ \ 3 + t = 16$
$\ t = 13$ The solution is (3, 13).
Jessica bought 3 daisies and 13 tulips.

Ⓑ The Tran family is bringing 15 packages of cheese to a group picnic. Cheese slices cost $2.50 per package. Cheese cubes cost $1.75 per package. The Tran family spent a total of $30 on cheese. The system of equations
$\begin{cases} s + c = 15 \\ 2.50s + 1.75c = 30 \end{cases}$ represents this situation, where s is the number of
packages of cheese slices and c is the number of packages of cheese cubes. How many packages of each type of cheese did the Tran family buy? Multiply the first equation by a constant so that c can be eliminated from both equations, and then subtract the equations.

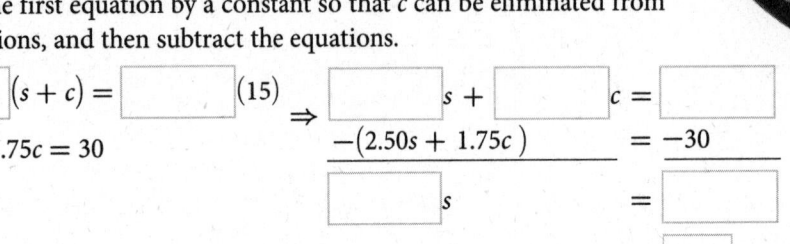

$$\begin{cases} \boxed{}(s + c) = \boxed{}(15) \\ 2.50s + 1.75c = 30 \end{cases} \Rightarrow$$

$$\begin{array}{r} \boxed{}s + \boxed{}c = \boxed{} \\ -(2.50s + 1.75c) \ \ \ \ \ \ \ \ = -30 \\ \hline \boxed{}s \ \ \ \ \ \ \ \ \ \ \ = \boxed{} \\ s = \boxed{} \end{array}$$

Find c. $s + c = 15$
$\ \ \ \ \ \ \ \ \ \ \ \boxed{} + c = 15$
$\ \ \ \ \ \ \ \ \ \ \ \ \ \ \ \ \ \ c = \boxed{}$ The solution is $\boxed{}$.

The Tran family bought _____ packages of sliced cheese and _____ packages of cheese cubes.

Your Turn

6. Jacob's family bought 4 adult tickets and 2 student tickets to the school play for $64. Tatianna's family bought 3 adult tickets and 3 students tickets for $60. The system of equations $\begin{cases} 4a + 2s = 64 \\ 3a + 3s = 60 \end{cases}$ models this situation, where a is the cost of an adult ticket and s is the cost of a student ticket. How much does each type of ticket cost?

7. When would you solve a system of linear equations by multiplying?

_____

_____

8. How can you use multiplication to solve a system of linear equations if none of the coefficients are multiples or factors of any of the other coefficients?

_____

_____

9. **Essential Question Check-In** How do you solve a system of equations by multiplying?

_____

_____

_____

⭐ Evaluate: Homework and Practice

- Online Homework
- Hints and Help
- Extra Practice

For each linear equation,

a. find the product of 3 and the linear equation;

b. solve both equations for y.

1. $2y - 4x = 8$

2. $-5y + 7x = 12$

3. $4x + 7y = 18$

4. $x - 2y = 13$

For each linear system, multiply the first equation by 2 and add the new equation to the second equation. Then, graph this new equation along with both of the original equations.

5. $\begin{cases} 2x + 4y = 24 \\ -12x + 8y = -16 \end{cases}$

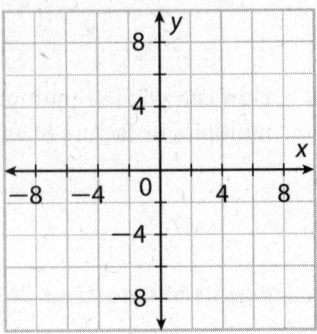

6. $\begin{cases} 2x + 2y = 16 \\ -15x + 3y = -12 \end{cases}$

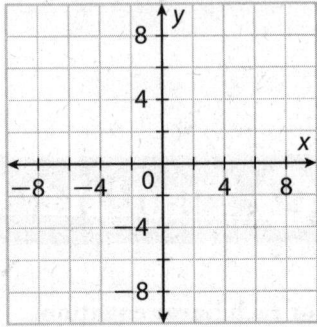

Solve each system of linear equations by multiplying. Verify each answer by graphing the system of equations.

7. $\begin{cases} 5x - 2y = 11 \\ 3x + 5y = 19 \end{cases}$

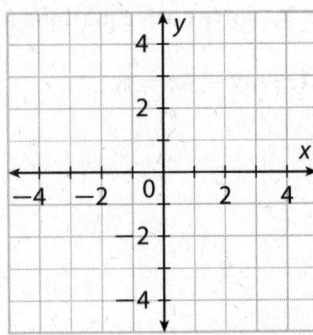

8. $\begin{cases} -2x + 2y = 2 \\ -4x + 7y = 16 \end{cases}$

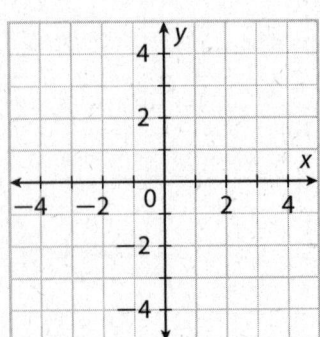

9. $\begin{cases} 3x + 4y = 13 \\ 2x - 2y = -10 \end{cases}$

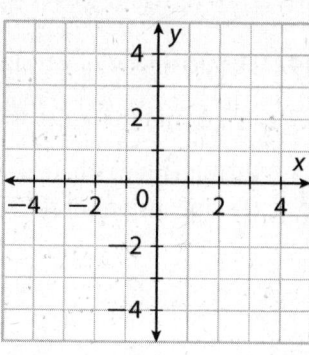

10. $\begin{cases} x - 4y = -1 \\ 5x + 2y = 17 \end{cases}$

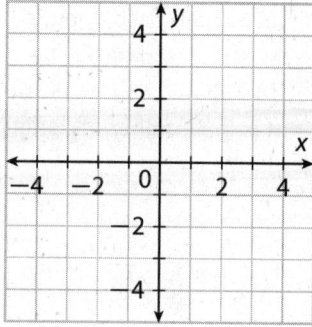

Solve each system of linear equations using multiplication.

11. $\begin{cases} -3x + 2y = 4 \\ 5x - 3y = 1 \end{cases}$

12. $\begin{cases} 3x + 3y = 12 \\ 6x + 11y = 14 \end{cases}$

Solve each problem by multiplying first.

13. The sum of two angles is 180°. The difference between twice the larger angle and three times the smaller angle is 150°. The system of equations $\begin{cases} x + y = 180 \\ 2x - 3y = 150 \end{cases}$ models this situation, where x is the measure of the larger angle and y is the measure of the smaller angle. What is the measure of each angle?

14. The perimeter of a rectangular swimming pool is 126 feet. The difference between the length and the width is 39 feet. The system of equations $\begin{cases} 2x + 2y = 126 \\ x - y = 39 \end{cases}$ models this situation, where x is the length of the pool and y is the width of the pool. Find the dimensions of the swimming pool.

15. Jamian bought a total of 40 bagels and donuts for a morning meeting. He paid a total of $33.50. Each donut cost $0.65 and each bagel cost $1.15. The system of equations $\begin{cases} b + d = 40 \\ 1.15b + 0.65d = 33.50 \end{cases}$ models this situation, where b is the number of bagels and d is the number of donuts. How many of each did Jamian buy?

16. A clothing store is having a sale on shirts and jeans. 4 shirts and 2 pairs of jeans cost $64. 3 shirts and 3 pairs of jeans cost $72. The system of equations $\begin{cases} 4s + 2j = 64 \\ 3s + 3j = 72 \end{cases}$ models this situation, where s is the cost of a shirt and j is the cost of a pair of jeans. How much does one shirt and one pair of jeans cost?

17. Jayce bought 5 bath towels and returned 2 hand towels. His sister Jayna bought 3 bath towels and returned 4 hand towels. Jayce paid a total of $124 and Jayna paid a total of $24. The system of equations $\begin{cases} 5b - 2h = 124 \\ 3b - 4h = 24 \end{cases}$ models this situation, where b is the price of a bath towel and h is the price of a hand towel. How much does each kind of towel cost?

18. Apples cost $0.95 per pound and bananas cost $1.10 per pound. Leah bought a total of 8 pounds of apples and bananas for $8.05.

The system of equations $\begin{cases} a + b = 8 \\ 0.95a + 1.10b = 8.05 \end{cases}$ models this

situation, where a is the number of pounds of apples and b is the number of pounds of bananas. How many pounds of each did Leah buy?

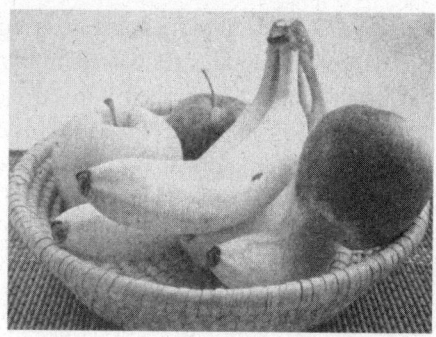

19. Which of the following are possible ways to eliminate a variable by multiplying first? $\begin{cases} -x + 2y = 3 \\ 4x - 5y = -3 \end{cases}$

    a. Multiply the first equation by 4.

    b. Multiply the first equation by 5 and the second equation by 2.

    c. Multiply the first equation by 4 and the second equation by 2.

    d. Multiply the first equation by 5 and the second equation by 4.

    e. Multiply the first equation by 2 and the second equation by 5.

    f. Multiply the second equation by 4.

20. **Explain the Error** A linear system has two equations $Ax + By = C$ and $Dx + Ey = F$. A student begins to solve the equation as shown. What is the error?

$$Ax + By = C$$
$$\underline{+\ k(Dx + Ey) = F}$$
$$(A + kD)x + (B + kE)y = C + F$$

21. **Critical Thinking** Suppose you want to eliminate y in this system: $\begin{cases} 2x + 11y = -3 \\ 3x + 4y = 8 \end{cases}$

By what numbers would you need to multiply the two equations in order to eliminate y? Why might you choose to eliminate x instead?

22. **Justify Reasoning** Solve the following system of equations by multiplying.

$\begin{cases} x + 3y = -14 \\ 2x + y = -3 \end{cases}$ Would it be easier to solve the system by using substitution? Explain your reasoning.

23. Multi-Step The school store is running a promotion on school supplies. Different supplies are placed on two shelves. You can purchase 3 items from shelf A and 2 from shelf B for $16. Or you can purchase 2 items from shelf A and 3 from shelf B for $14. This can be represented by the following system of equations.

a. Solve the system of equations $\begin{cases} 3A + 2B = 16 \\ 2A + 3B = 14 \end{cases}$ by multiplying first.

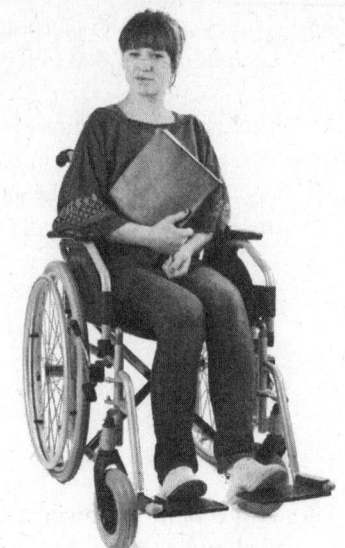

b. If the supplies on shelf A are normally $6 each and the supplies on shelf B are normally $3 each, how much will you save on each package plan from part A?

Lesson Performance Task

A chemist has a bottle of 1% acid solution and a bottle of 5% acid solution. She wants to mix the two solutions to get 100 mL of a 4% acid solution.

a. Complete the table to write the system of equations.

	1% Solution	+	5% Solution	=	4% Solution
Amount of Solution (mL)	x	+	y	=	
Amount of Acid (mL)	0.01x	+		=	0.04(100)

b. Solve the system of equations to find how much she will use from each bottle to get 100 mL of a 4% acid solution.

Essential Question: How can you use a system of linear equations to solve real-world problems?

Key Vocabulary

elimination method
(eliminación)

substitution method
(sustitución)

system of linear equations
(sistema de ecuaciones lineales)

KEY EXAMPLE   (Lesson 11.2)

Solve $\begin{cases} 4x + y = 7 \\ -6x + y = -3 \end{cases}$ by substitution.

Solve an equation for one variable.

$-6x + y = -3$ Select one of the equations.

$y = 6x - 3$ Solve for y. Isolate y on one side.

Substitute the expression for y in the other equation and solve.

$4x + (6x - 3) = 7$ Substitute the expression for y.

$10x - 3 = 7$ Combine like terms.

$10x = 10$ Add 3 to both sides.

$x = 1$ Divide each side by 10.

Substitute the value for x into one of the equations and solve for y.

$4(1) + y = 7$ Substitute the value of x into the first equation.

$4 + y = 7$ Simplify.

$y = 3$ Subtract 4 from both sides.

So, (1, 3) is the solution of the system.

KEY EXAMPLE   (Lesson 11.3)

Solve $\begin{cases} -6x + 8y = 19 \\ 6x - 8y = -19 \end{cases}$ by adding.

Add the equations.

$$-6x + 8y = 19$$
$$+6x - 8y = -19$$
$$\overline{0 + 0 = 0}$$
$$0 = 0$$

The resulting equation is always true, so the system has infinitely many solutions.

EXERCISES

Solve each system of equations. *(Lessons 11.1, 11.2, 11.3, 11.4)*

1. $\begin{cases} 3x + 7y = -5 \\ 8x + 9y = 6 \end{cases}$

2. $\begin{cases} -5x + 2y = 13 \\ 3x - 2y = -11 \end{cases}$

3. $\begin{cases} 9x - 2y = -5 \\ -6x + y = -1 \end{cases}$

4. $\begin{cases} 7x - 9y = -11 \\ 7x - y = -9 \end{cases}$

5. $\begin{cases} -3x + 5y = 8 \\ 3x - 5y = -8 \end{cases}$

6. $\begin{cases} -2x + 6y = 6 \\ -4x - 8y = 12 \end{cases}$

MODULE PERFORMANCE TASK

Do Hybrid Cars Pay for Themselves?

Your family wants to buy a specific model of new car and is considering buying the hybrid version. Use the information shown for the two cars to determine how long it will take to save enough money on gas to pay for the extra cost of the hybrid. Then make a recommendation on which car to buy.

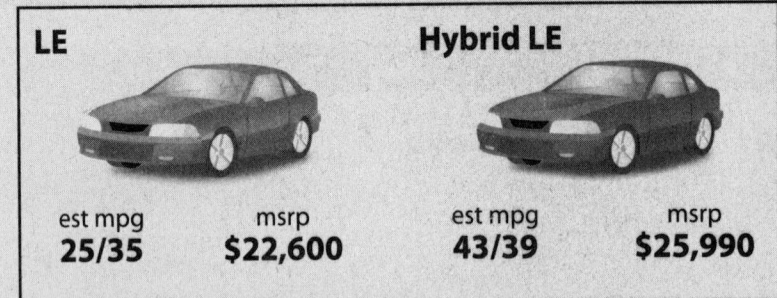

LE		Hybrid LE	
est mpg	msrp	est mpg	msrp
25/35	**$22,600**	**43/39**	**$25,990**

Start by listing in the space below the information you will need to solve the problem. Then use your own paper to complete the task. Be sure to write down all your data and assumptions. Then use graphs, numbers, words, or algebra to explain how you reached your conclusion.

(Ready) to Go On?

11.1–11.4 Solving Systems of Linear Equations

• Online Homework
• Hints and Help
• Extra Practice

Solve each system of equations using the given method. *(Lessons 11.1, 11.2, 11.3, 11.4)*

1. $\begin{cases} -3x + y = 6 \\ 5x + 2y = 23 \end{cases}$; substitution

2. $\begin{cases} -4x + 9y = 14 \\ 12x - 10y = -8 \end{cases}$; multiplication

3. $\begin{cases} 7x + 2y = 8 \\ -5x - 2y = -12 \end{cases}$; addition

4. $\begin{cases} 6x - 12y = 15 \\ 2x - 4y = 6 \end{cases}$; multiplication

5. $\begin{cases} 5x - 3y = 3 \\ 3x - y = 9 \end{cases}$; graphing

6. $\begin{cases} 9x - 2y = 8 \\ -2x + 2y = 6 \end{cases}$; addition

ESSENTIAL QUESTION

7. When must a system of linear equations be solved algebraically, not graphically?

Assessment Readiness

1. A system of equations is represented on the graph. Is each equation part of the system? Select Yes or No for each equation.

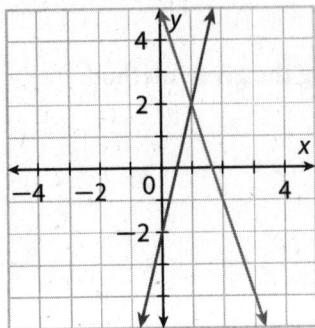

A. $3x + y = 5$ ◯ Yes   ◯ No

B. $2x + 3y = 8$ ◯ Yes   ◯ No

C. $-8x + 2y = -4$ ◯ Yes   ◯ No

2. Consider the lines and solution set of the system of equations $\begin{cases} -8x - 6y = 8 \\ 4x + 3y = 2 \end{cases}$.

Determine if each of the following statements is True or False.

A. The lines have the same y-intercept.   ◯ True   ◯ False

B. The lines have the same slope.   ◯ True   ◯ False

C. The system has no solutions.   ◯ True   ◯ False

3. Solve the system of equations $\begin{cases} 5x + y = 10 \\ 2x + 3y = -9 \end{cases}$. Explain how you solved this system.

4. The perimeter of a picture frame is 68 inches. The difference between the length of the frame and three times its width is 2. The system of equations $\begin{cases} 2\ell + 2W = 68 \\ 2\ell - 6W = 4 \end{cases}$ represents this situation, where ℓ represents the length in inches and W represents the width in inches. What is the width of the frame? What is the length of the frame?

Modeling with Linear Systems

Essential Question: How can you model with linear systems to solve real-world problems?

REAL WORLD VIDEO
When you're playing an arcade game, chances are that you don't have math on your mind. But you might be surprised to find that mathematical reasoning can sometimes help you figure out the best strategy for the winning the game.

MODULE PERFORMANCE TASK PREVIEW

How to Win at an Arcade Game

Many arcades have a game that is somewhat like bowling. Players roll a hand-sized ball up an inclined lane so that the ball lands in one of several different holes, each with varying point values. The goal is to collect as many points as possible. How can you use mathematics to help you win at this game? Let's find out!

Are YOU Ready?

Complete these exercises to review skills you will need for this module.

• Online Homework
• Hints and Help
• Extra Practice

One-Step Inequalities

Example 1   Solve.

$$x + 13 \leq 9$$

$$x + 13 - 13 \leq 9 - 13$$ Isolate the variable by subtracting 13 from both sides of the inequality.

$$x \leq -4$$

Solve each inequality.

1. $k - 12 \geq 5$

2. $y + 2 < -9$

3. $\dfrac{n}{4} > -7$

Two-Step Equations and Inequalities

Example 2   Solve.

$$4b - 19 = 17$$

$$4b - 19 + 19 = 17 + 19$$ Add 19 to both sides of the equation.

$$4b = 36$$

$$\dfrac{4b}{4} = \dfrac{36}{4}$$ Divide both sides of the equation by 4.

$$b = 9$$

Solve each equation.

4. $3a + 17 = 38$

5. $27 - 5c = 12$

6. $\dfrac{3}{4}m - 8 = 10$

Example 3   Solve.

$$11 - 7t < 67$$

$$11 - 11 - 7t < 67 - 11$$ Subtract 11 from both sides of the inequality.

$$-7t < 56$$

$$\dfrac{-7t}{-7} > \dfrac{56}{-7}$$ Divide both sides of the inequality by –7.

$$t > -8$$ Reverse the inequality symbol.

Solve each inequality.

7. $9p + 23 < 41$

8. $-6w - 16 \geq 44$

9. $\dfrac{v}{3} + 12 > 7$

12.1 Creating Systems of Linear Equations

Essential Question: How do you use systems of linear equations to model and solve real-world problems?

Resource Locker

🧭 Explore   Creating Linear System Models by Changing Parameters

Investigate how a system of equations can help you compare and interpret situations where rates of change affect the outcome.

After leaving her hotel, a student is walking to a café to have breakfast and do some sightseeing. On the way, she passes two stores that rent bicycles. The first shop charges an initial fee of $7.00 and $2.75 for each hour. The second shop charges a flat fee of $3.00 per hour. Over breakfast, the student needs to decide which rental agency to use. How should she start?

(A) Begin by finding functions that represent the cost of each rental. Let $f(t)$ represent the cost of renting a bicycle for t hours from the first shop, and let $g(t)$ represent the cost of renting a bicycle from the second shop.

(B) What is the initial cost of renting a bicycle from the first shop? _____

(C) This represents the _____ of the model for the first business.

(D) The slope of this linear model represents the _____ of the cost, as a function of time.

(E) The slope of the first model is _____.

(F) This makes $f(t) =$ _____.

(G) Similarly, the function modeling the cost for renting a bicycle from the

second shop is $g(t) =$ _____.

(H) Once the student decides the length of time she plans to spend on her bike ride, she can

solve the linear system of the two functions, _____, to determine from which company she wants to rent a bicycle.

1. **Discussion** Under what conditions would this type of real-world situation have no solution?

_____

_____

_____

2. **Discussion** Under what conditions would this type of real-world situation have infinitely many solutions?

_____

_____

_____

⚙ Explain 1 Creating Linear System Models from Verbal Descriptions

Often, a company will charge a start-up fee for its services, followed by a monthly or per unit cost. This can be written as a linear function in slope-intercept form.

When the costs of the same services from two different companies must be compared, the variable amount for each must represent the same thing, and both models should produce values with the same type of unit. For example, if one function models yearly income in terms of thousands of dollars and the other function models monthly income in terms of hundreds of dollars, the comparison will not be accurate.

Example 1 **Determine when the cost of the two services will be the same amount, and what the price will be.**

Video streaming service Atomic Stream charges $10 for membership and $1.00 for each movie download. Blitz Video charges $15 for a membership and $0.50 per movie download. How many movies would you need to download for the services to have identical costs? What is that cost?

⊞ Analyze Information

Identify the important information.

Atomic Stream has a _____ membership fee.

Atomic Stream has a _____ per download fee.

Blitz Video has a _____ membership fee.

Blitz Video has a _____ per download fee.

⊞ Formulate a Plan

Create two functions to model the cost of each service, $A(x)$ and $B(x)$, where x represents the _____.

The solution can be found by setting up an equation so that the function $A(x)$ is _____ to the function $B(x)$ and then solving for _____.

The model for Atomic Stream is $A(x) =$ ☐ .

The model for Blitz Video is $B(x) =$ ☐ .

The two functions are $\left\{\rule{0pt}{30pt}\right.$ ☐ .

Solve using substitution. You can use substitution because you are solving for the value where $A(x)$ ☐ $B(x)$.

☐ $=$ ☐ $A(x) =$ ☐

$0.5x = 5$

$x =$ ☐ $A\left(\boxed{}\right) =$ ☐

$=$ ☐

The cost of each service is _____ when _____ movies are screened.

 **Justify and Evaluate**

It is reasonable to expect the cost of the services to be the same after a number of uses. The businesses are in the same market but can appeal to different customers.

Atomic Stream is more affordable for customers who stream _____

movies a month, while Blitz Video is a better deal for people who stream _____ movies a month.

Your Turn

Determine when the cost of the two services will be the same amount, and what the price will be.

3. One cable television provider has a $60 setup fee and charges $80 per month, and another cable provider has a $160 equipment fee and charges $70 per month.

4. The Strauss family is deciding between two lawn-care services. Green Lawn charges a $49 startup fee plus $29 per month. Yard Guard charges a $25 startup fee plus $37 per month.

⊘ Explain 2   Creating Linear System Models from Tables

Sometimes, there is not enough information to model an equation. Businesses may have a table of rates posted to explain their pricing. To compare the cost of items or services from two or more businesses, table entries can be used to create and solve a linear system.

Example 2 Use the cost tables for two services to create a linear system of equations. Then solve the system to determine when the cost of the two services will be equal.

Ⓐ Two garden supply companies deliver mulch according to the following table.

Mulch (Cubic Yards)	Yard Depot	Lawn & Garden
1	$60	$80
2	$90	$105
3	$120	$130
4	$150	$155

Yard Depot	Lawn & Garden
Use points $(1, 60)$ and $(2, 90)$.	Use points $(1, 80)$ and $(2, 105)$.
$m = \dfrac{90 - 60}{2 - 1} = 30$	$m = \dfrac{105 - 80}{2 - 1} = 25$
Write the equation.	Write the equation.
$y - 60 = 30(x - 1)$	$y - 80 = 25(x - 1)$
$y = 30x + 30$	$y = 25x + 55$

The system of equations is: $\begin{cases} f(x) = 30s + 30 \\ g(x) = 25x + 55 \end{cases}$

Solve for x when $f(x) = g(x)$ to find the amount of cubic yards, x, for which both companies charge the same amount.

$$30s + 30 = 25x + 55$$

$$x = 5 \Rightarrow f(5) = 30(5) + 30 = 180$$

Both companies charge $180 for 5 cubic yards of mulch.

B The table shows canoe rental prices for two companies.

Time t (in hours)	Canoe Depot	Paddle and Oar
1	$14	$20
2	$19	$23
3	$24	$26

Canoe Depot	Paddle & Oar
Use points $\left(1, \boxed{}\right)$ and $\left(2, \boxed{}\right)$.	Use points $\left(1, \boxed{}\right)$ and $\left(2, \boxed{}\right)$.
$m = \dfrac{\boxed{} - \boxed{}}{2 - 1} = \boxed{}$	$m = \dfrac{\boxed{} - \boxed{}}{2 - 1} = \boxed{}$
Write the equation.	Write the equation.
$y - \boxed{} = \boxed{}(x - 1)$	$y - \boxed{} = \boxed{}(x - 1)$
$y = \boxed{}\,x + \boxed{}$	$y = \boxed{}\,x + \boxed{}$

The system of equations is $\begin{cases} C(x) = \boxed{}\,x + \boxed{} \\ P(x) = \boxed{}\,x + \boxed{} \end{cases}$

Solve for x when $C(x) = P(x)$ to find the number of hours, x, for which both canoe rental places charge the same amount.

$$\boxed{}\,x + \boxed{} = \boxed{}\,x + \boxed{}$$

$$x = \boxed{} \quad \Rightarrow \quad C\left(\boxed{}\right) = \boxed{}$$

Both companies charge $\boxed{}$ for $\boxed{}$ hours of canoe rental.

Your Turn

5. Two garden supply companies deliver pea stone according to the following table.

Pea Stone x (in cubic yards)	Yard Depot	Lawn & Garden
1	$75	$45
2	$110	$85
3	$145	$125

6. Two beachfront stores rent surfboards according to the following table.

Time t (in hours)	Hang Ten	Waverider
1	$28	$46
2	$48	$63
3	$68	$80
4	$88	$97

⊘ Explain 3 Creating Linear System Models from Graphs

In newspapers and magazines, information is often displayed in the form of a graph. You can use the graph of a linear system to write the function models that are represented.

Example 3 Use the graph to make a linear model of each function. Describe the meaning of the terms in the models. Then create the linear system, and state what the solution represents.

 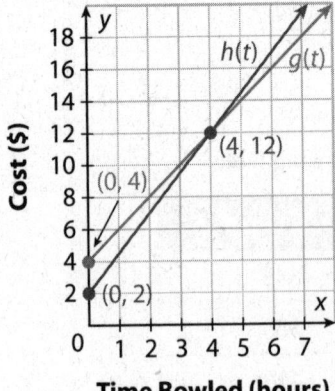

Time Bowled (hours)

$g(x)$	$h(x)$
The y-intercept b is 4.	The y-intercept b is 2.
Initial cost is $4.	Initial cost is $2.
Use $(0, 4)$ and $(4, 12)$:	Use $(0, 2)$ and $(4, 12)$:
$m = \dfrac{12 - 4}{4 - 0} = 2$	$m = \dfrac{12 - 2}{4 - 0} = 2.5$
Charge per hour: $2.00/h	Charge per hour: $2.50/h
$y = 2x + 4$	$y = 2.5x + 2$

The system of equations is: $\begin{cases} g(x) = 2x + 4 \\ h(x) = 2.5x + 2 \end{cases}$

The solution $(4, 12)$ represents the same charge of $12 for 4 hours that both bowling alleys charge.

Ⓑ

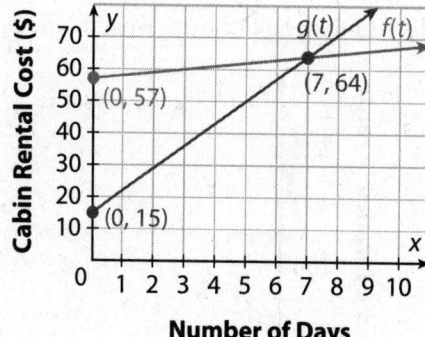

Cost ($) vs Trail Mix (pounds)

Points shown: (0, 8), (0, 1), (7, 15)

f(x)	g(x)
The y-intercept b is ☐.	The y-intercept b is ☐.
Initial cost is $ ☐.	Initial cost is $ ☐.
Use $\left(0, \boxed{}\right)$ and (7, 15):	Use $\left(0, \boxed{}\right)$ and (7, 15):
$m = \dfrac{15 - \boxed{}}{\boxed{} - 0} = \boxed{}$	$m = \dfrac{15 - \boxed{}}{\boxed{} - 0} = \boxed{}$
Rate of change: $ ☐ /lb	Rate of change: $ ☐ /lb
$y = \boxed{}x + \boxed{}$	$y = \boxed{}x + \boxed{}$

The system of equations is
$$\begin{cases} f(x) = \boxed{}x + \boxed{} \\ g(x) = \boxed{}x + \boxed{} \end{cases}$$

The solution (7, 15) represents the same charge of $ ☐ for ☐ pounds of trail mix.

Your Turn

7. Use the graph to make a linear model of each function. Describe the meaning of terms in the models. Then create the linear system and state what the solution represents.

Cabin Rental Cost ($) vs Number of Days

Curves labeled g(t) and f(t). Points shown: (0, 57), (0, 15), (7, 64)

8. When writing a linear model of a situation, what does the slope represent?

_____

_____

9. **Discussion** Compare and contrast the system of equations that can be determined from a verbal description of a relationship, a table of values, and a graph.

_____

_____

_____

10. **Essential Question Check-In** How do you use systems of linear equations to model and solve real-world problems?

_____

_____

⭐ **Evaluate: Homework and Practice**

1. In the graph shown, what do the parameters of each line represent?

• Online Homework
• Hints and Help
• Extra Practice

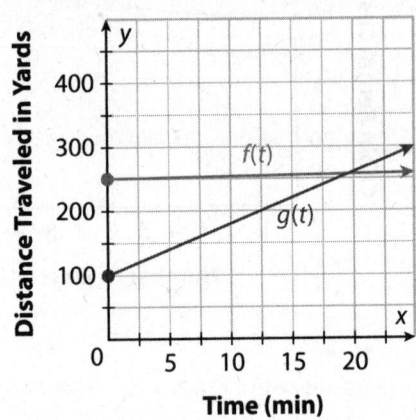

Set up and solve a system of equations to solve the problem.

2. Casey wants to buy a gym membership. One gym has a $150 joining fee and costs $35 per month. Another gym has no joining fee and costs $60 per month. When would Casey pay the same amount to be a member of either gym? How much would he pay?

3. A jar contains n nickels and d dimes. There are 20 coins in the jar, and the total value of the coins is $1.40. How many nickels and how many dimes are in the jar?

4. Helene invested a total of $1000 in two simple-interest bank accounts. One account paid 5% annual interest; the other paid 6% annual interest. The total amount of interest she earned after 1 year was $58. Find the amount invested in each account.

5. A local boys club sold 176 bags of mulch and made a total of $520. It sold two types of mulch: hardwood for $3.50 a bag and pine bark for $2.75 a bag. How many bags of each kind of mulch did it sell?

6. The school band sells carnations on Valentine's Day for $2 each. It buys the carnations from a florist for $0.50 each, plus a $16 delivery charge. When will the cost of the carnations be equal to the revenue from selling them? How many carnations does it need to sell to reach this point?

Use the given cost tables for the same product from two different companies to create a linear system. Then solve the system to determine when the cost of the product will be the same and what the price will be.

7. Two online spice retailers sell paprika by the pound using the following pricing chart.

Paprika(lb)	iSpice	Spice Magic
1	$15.75	$26.25
2	$27.50	$36.50
3	$39.25	$46.75
4	$51	$57

8. Two online retailers sell organic vanilla extract by the ounce using the following pricing chart.

Vanilla Extract (oz)	Chef Mate	Grocery Gourmet
2	$12.50	$17
3	$17.25	$21
4	$22	$25
5	$26.75	$29

9. Two dry cleaning companies offer a home pick-up and delivery service. The monthly cost depends on the number of garments laundered, and is shown in the following table.

Number of Garments	Company 1	Company 2
5	$55.25	$31.25
10	$75.50	$57.50
15	$95.75	$83.75

10. A small town in the mountains needs to buy road salt for the coming winter. It has found two companies that use the following pricing table.

Road Salt (tons)	Company 1	Company 2
5	$1775	$2750
10	$3350	$4000
15	$4925	$5250

11. A restaurant needs to stock paper towels in its kitchen and bathrooms. It has found two vendors using the following case price chart.

Paper Towels (cases)	Restaurant Warehouse	Supply Side
5	$300.20	$220.20
10	$480.15	$420.15
15	$660.10	$620.10

Use the graph to make a linear model of each function. Describe the meaning of the terms in the models. Then create the linear system, and state what the solution represents.

12.

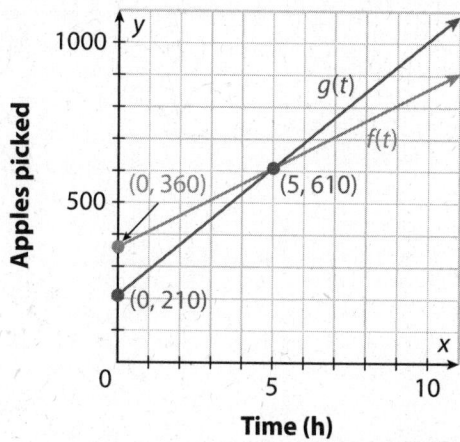

13.

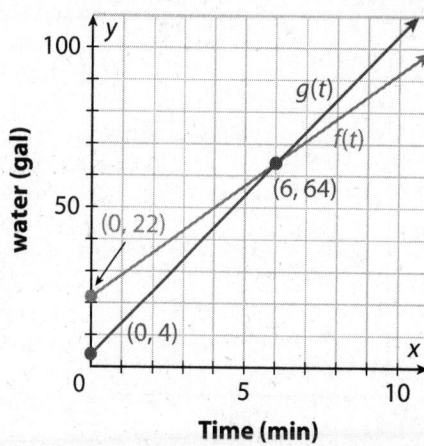

14.

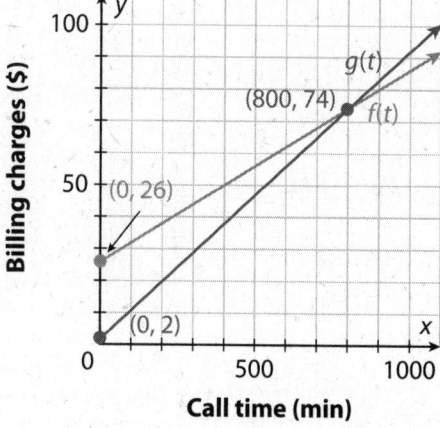

15.

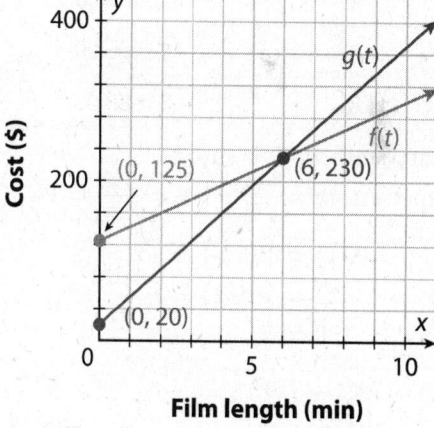

16. Two office supply stores sell their brand of copy paper by the pound. One company offers a flat rate shipping charge and the other offers free shipping. Use the graph provided to construct a linear system to model this situation. Solve the system to determine the amount of copy paper for which the cost is the same at both stores. Use the graph to verify that your answer is reasonable.

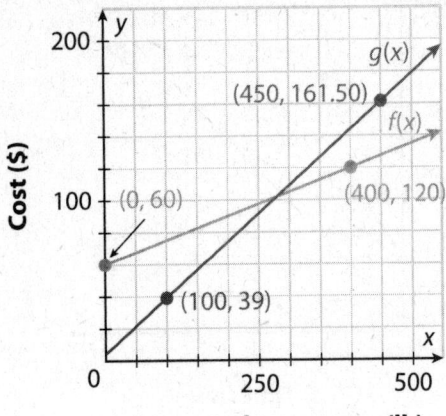

17. Find the Error A student is given the following problem:

A painter can buy 5-gallon containers of paint from two different stores based on the following pricing table.

Containers of Paint	Company A	Company B
2	$512.00	$422.00
4	$904.00	$834.00
6	$1296.00	$1246.00
8	$1688.00	$1658.00

The student's work is shown.

Company A: $m = \frac{904 - 512}{4 - 2} = \frac{392}{2} = 196$ Company B: $m = \frac{1246 - 834}{6 - 2} = \frac{412}{4} = 103$

$$A(x) = 196x + b \qquad\qquad B(x) = 103x + b$$
$$512 = 196(2) + b \qquad\qquad 834 = 103(2) + b$$
$$120 = b \qquad\qquad\qquad 628 = b$$

$$\begin{cases} A(x) = 196x + 120 \\ B(x) = 103x + 628 \end{cases}$$

$$196x + 120 = 103x + 628$$
$$93x = 508$$
$$x = 5.5$$

The student knows that the function values for Company A would be less than those of Company B for x-values greater than that of the intersection. This is not true if the x-coordinate of the intersection is 5.5, so he concludes that his results must contain an error. Find the error and the correct solution.

18. Two friends, Jorge and Mark, are taking a trip to the mountains for a camping trip, but they are not leaving together. Both friends separately record the distance they each have traveled from home every hour on the second day. The distance each friend is from his home can be modeled by a linear function of the hours spent traveling. Determine if the linear system created by the models for each situation has a unique solution with a positive value for time.

a. Jorge and Mark traveled the same distance on the first day and they are traveling at the same speed on the second day.

◯ Yes ◯ No

b. Jorge travels 25 miles on the first day and drives 65 miles per hour on the second day. Mark travels 100 miles on the first day and also drives 65 miles per hour on the second day.

◯ Yes ◯ No

c. Jorge travels 25 miles on the first day and drives 65 miles per hour on the second day. Mark travels 100 miles on the first day and drives 45 miles per hour on the second day.

◯ Yes ◯ No

d. Jorge traveled 45 miles on the first day and drives 55 miles per hour on the second day. Mark arrived at the campsite on the first day after traveling 300 miles. Assume Jorge lives at least 300 miles from the campsite and that he keeps driving on the second day until he gets there.

◯ Yes ◯ No

e. Jorge gets sick before the trip and doesn't get in touch with Mark. Mark travels 40 miles on the first day and drives 67 miles per hour on the second day.

◯ Yes ◯ No

19. Communicate Mathematical Ideas Given a set of data measuring the distance two planes have traveled after takeoff as a function of when they both passed over the same point, how would you find when they have both traveled the same distance since takeoff?

20. Analyze Relationships How can you use the slope and the y-intercept of each model in a linear system to determine whether or not there will be a solution?

Lesson Performance Task

A family is going on vacation and they need to bring their dog to a kennel. Alpha Kennel charges an initial fee of $75 and a daily rate of $30. Beta Kennel charges a flat fee of $34.95 a day. Find linear functions modeling the cost of boarding a dog for n days in each kennel. Set up and solve a system of linear equations. Then interpret the solution.

What if the family has two dogs? Alpha Kennel runs a special where you receive a 10% discount if you board more than one pet. Modify the linear models to give the price of boarding two dogs. Set up, solve, and interpret the linear system covering this case.

12.2 Graphing Systems of Linear Inequalities

Essential Question: How do you solve a system of linear inequalities?

⊘ Explore **Determining Solutions of Systems of Linear Inequalities**

A **system of linear inequalities** consists of two or more linear inequalities that have the same variables. The **solutions of a system of linear inequalities** are all the ordered pairs that make all the inequalities in the system true.

Solve the system of equations by graphing.

$$\begin{cases} x + 3y > 3 \\ -x + y \leq 6 \end{cases}$$

(A) First look at $x + 3y > 3$. The equation of the boundary line is _____.

(B) What are the x-and y-intercepts?

(C) The inequality symbol is $>$ so use a _____ line.

(D) Shade _____ the boundary line for solutions that are greater than the inequality.

(E) Graph $x + 3y > 3$.

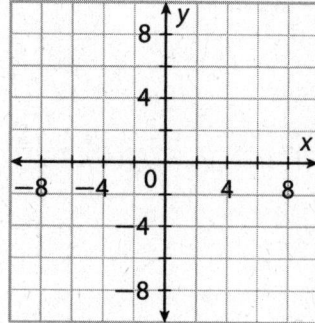

(F) Look at $-x + y \leq 6$. The equation of the boundary line is _____.

(G) What are the x-and y-intercepts?

(H) The inequality symbol is $\leq$ so use a _____ line.

I. Shade _____ the boundary line for solutions that are less than the inequality.

J. Graph $-x + y \leq 6$ on the same graph as $x + 3y > 3$.

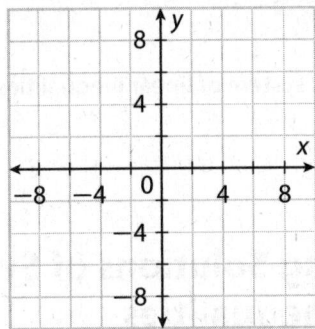

K. Identify the solutions. They are represented by the _____ shaded regions.

L. Check your answer by using a point in each region. Complete the table.

Ordered Pair	Satisfies $x + 3y > 3$?	Satisfies $-x + y \leq 6$?	In the overlapping shaded regions?
(0, 0)			
(2, 3)			
(−8, 2)			
(−4, 6)			

Reflect

1. **Discussion** Why is (0, 0) a good point to use for checking the answer to this system of linear inequalities?

_____

_____

_____

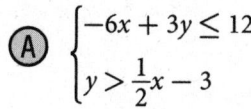

You can use a graph of a system of linear inequalities to determine and identify solutions to the system of linear inequalities.

Example 1 Graph the system of linear inequalities. Give two ordered pairs that are solutions and two that are not solutions.

Ⓐ $\begin{cases} -6x + 3y \le 12 \\ y > \frac{1}{2}x - 3 \end{cases}$

Solve the first inequality for y.   Graph the system.

$-6x + 3y \le 12$ $\begin{cases} y \le 2x + 4 \\ y > \frac{1}{2}x - 3 \end{cases}$

$\qquad 3y \le 6x + 12$

$\qquad\quad y \le 2x + 4$

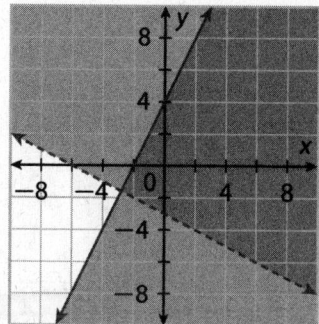

$(0, 0)$ and $(2, 8)$ are solutions. $(-6, -4)$ and $(-4, 4)$ are not solutions.

Ⓑ $\begin{cases} 3x + y \le 1 \\ y > \frac{2}{3}x - 2 \end{cases}$

Solve the first inequality for y.   Graph the system.

$3x + y \le 1$ $\begin{cases} y \le \boxed{} \\ y > \frac{2}{3}x - 2 \end{cases}$

$\qquad y \le \boxed{}$

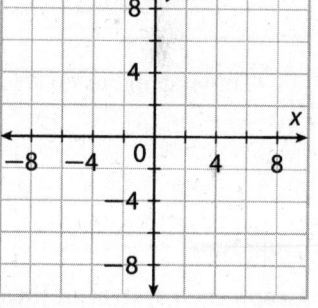

_____ and _____ are solutions. _____ and _____ are not solutions.

Reflect

2. Is $(-6, -6)$ a solution of the system?

_____

Your Turn

Graph the system of linear inequalities. Give two ordered pairs that are solutions and two that are not solutions.

3. $\begin{cases} y \le x + 3 \\ y < -3 \end{cases}$

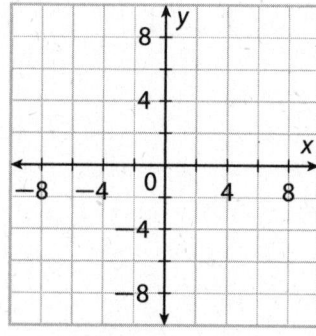

4. $\begin{cases} y > x - 8 \\ 2x + 4y < 16 \end{cases}$

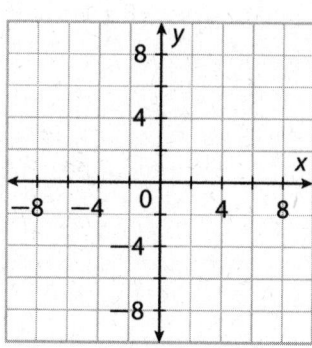

If the lines in a system of linear equations are parallel, there are no solutions. However, if the boundary lines in a system of linear inequalities are parallel, the system may or may not have solutions.

Example 2 Graph each system of linear inequalities. Describe the solutions.

Ⓐ $\begin{cases} y < 4x - 3 \\ y > 4x + 2 \end{cases}$

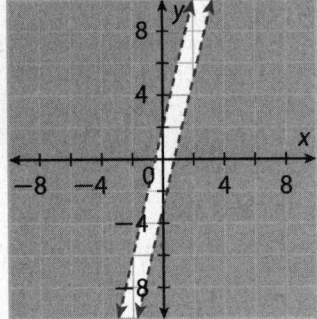

This system has no solution.

Ⓑ $\begin{cases} y > x - 2 \\ y \le x + 4 \end{cases}$

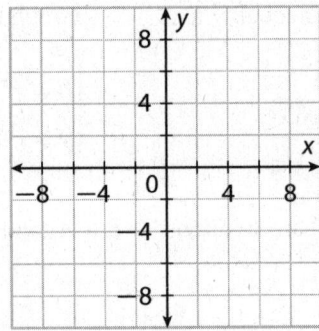

The solutions are all points

_____ the parallel lines

and on the _____ line.

Your Turn

Graph each system of linear inequalities. Describe the solutions.

5. $\begin{cases} y \le -2x - 3 \\ y \le -2x + 1 \end{cases}$

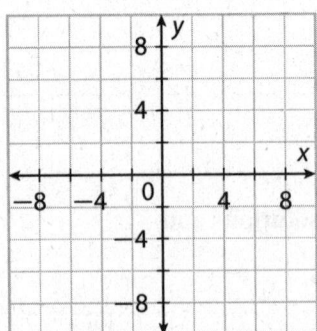

6. $\begin{cases} y < \frac{1}{3}x - 6 \\ y \ge \frac{1}{3}x + 5 \end{cases}$

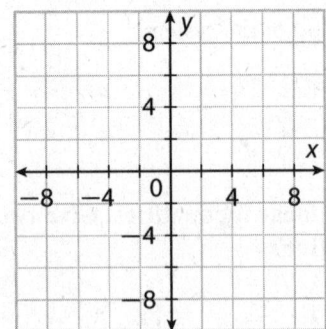

7. Is it possible for a system of two linear inequalities to have every point in the plane as solutions? Why or why not?

_____

_____

_____

8. **Discussion** How would you write a system of linear inequalities from a graph?

_____

_____

_____

9. **Essential Question Check-In** How does testing specific ordered pairs tell you that the solution you graphed is correct?

_____

_____

_____

⭐ Evaluate: Homework and Practice

- Online Homework
- Hints and Help
- Extra Practice

1. Match the inequality with the correct boundary line. Answers may be used more than once.

a. $y = 3x$ _____ $-x + 3y \leq 0$

b. $y = \frac{1}{3}x$ _____ $y > -x + \frac{1}{2}$

c. $y = x - 0.5$ _____ $y \leq \frac{1}{3}x$

d. $y = -x + \frac{1}{2}$ _____ $\frac{2}{3} + \frac{1}{3}y \geq x$

e. $y = 3x - 2$ _____ $-y > x - 0.5$

f. $y = x$ _____ $\frac{1}{3}y \geq x$

Determine if the given point satisfies either equation and is a solution of the system of inequalities.

2. $\begin{cases} 4y - 20x < 6 \\ \dfrac{5}{2}y \geq 5x - 10 \end{cases}$; $(0, 0)$

3. $\begin{cases} x + 5y > -10 \\ x - y \leq 4 \end{cases}$; $(2.5, -1.5)$

Determine if the given point is a solution of the system of inequalities. If not, find a point that is.

4. $(-9, 4)$

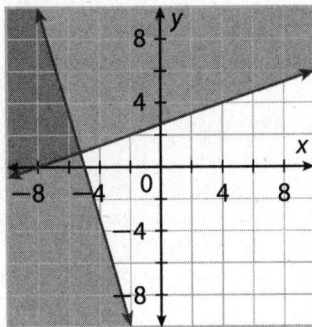

5. $(6, -2)$

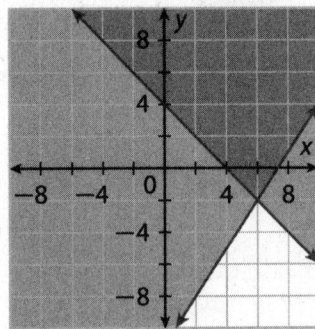

6. $(0, -4)$

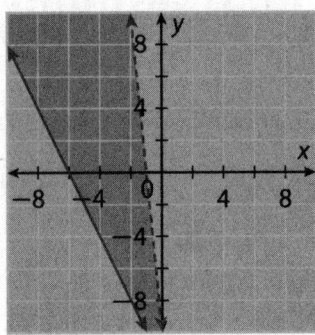

Graph the system of linear inequalities. Give two ordered pairs that are solutions and two that are not solutions.

7. $\begin{cases} x > 2 \\ y \leq -\dfrac{1}{2}x - 2 \end{cases}$

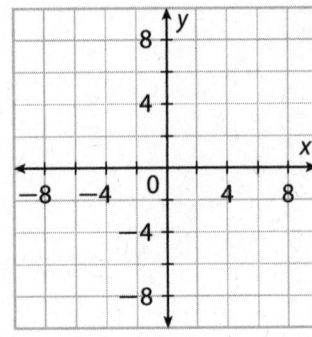

8. $\begin{cases} y > -x \\ y \geq x \end{cases}$

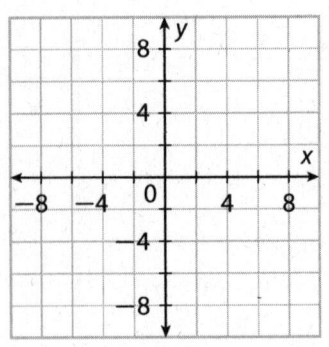

9. $\begin{cases} y < -x + 10 \\ y < \dfrac{1}{10}x + 7 \end{cases}$

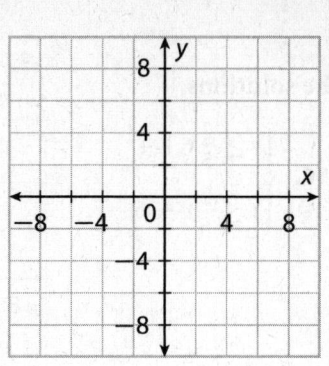

10. $\begin{cases} y \le \dfrac{1}{2}x - 5 \\ y \ge -2x + 12 \end{cases}$

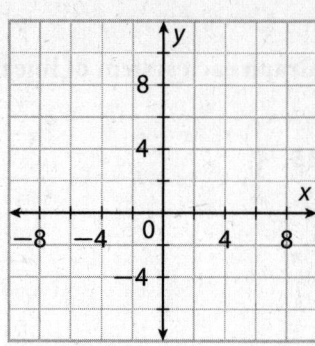

11. $\begin{cases} y \le -\dfrac{3}{5}x \\ y > -x - 4 \end{cases}$

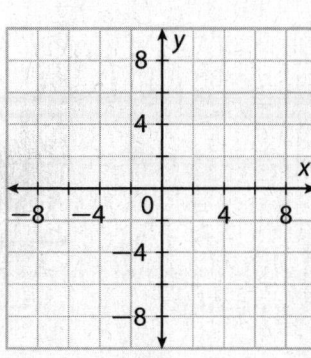

12. $\begin{cases} y \ge 2x + 6 \\ y < -\dfrac{1}{2}x - 1 \end{cases}$

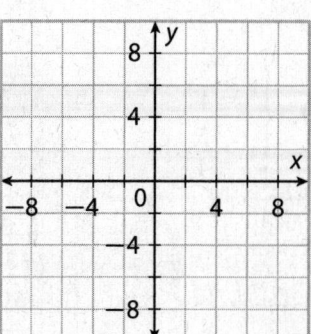

13. $\begin{cases} y \le \dfrac{4}{5}x - 4 \\ y < 2x - 8 \end{cases}$

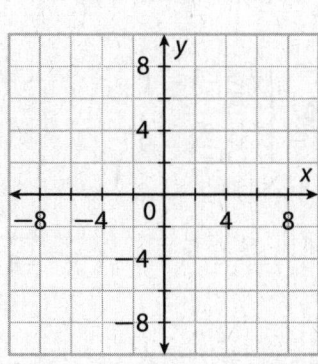

14. $\begin{cases} x \ge -6 \\ y < 3 \end{cases}$

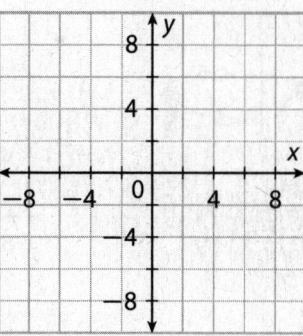

Graph each system of linear inequalities. Describe the solutions.

15. $\begin{cases} y \leq 3x + 6 \\ y < 3x - 8 \end{cases}$

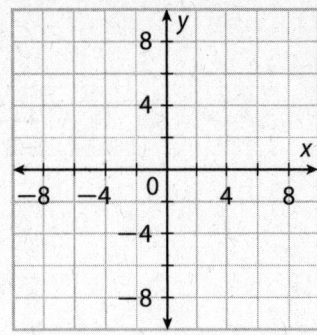

16. $\begin{cases} y \geq \frac{2}{5}x + 4 \\ y \leq \frac{2}{5}x - 6 \end{cases}$

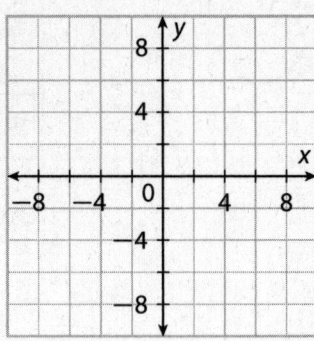

17. $\begin{cases} y \geq \frac{5}{4}x - 6 \\ y \geq \frac{5}{4}x \end{cases}$

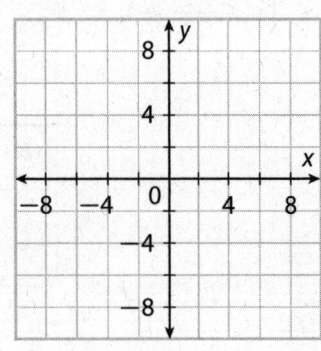

18. $\begin{cases} y \geq -\frac{3}{2}x - 3 \\ y \leq -\frac{3}{2}x + 10 \end{cases}$

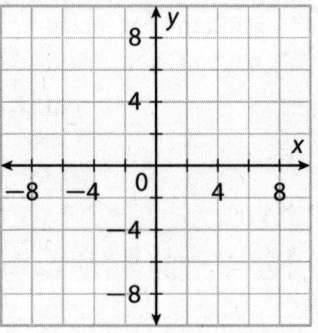

19. $\begin{cases} x < 6 \\ x \geq -3 \end{cases}$

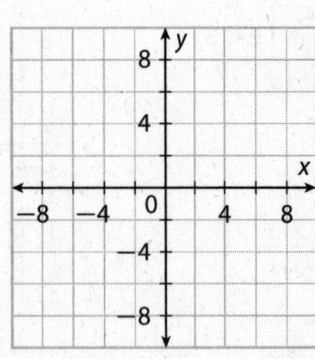

20. $\begin{cases} y \geq \frac{9}{4}x - 1 \\ y < \frac{9}{4}x - 9 \end{cases}$

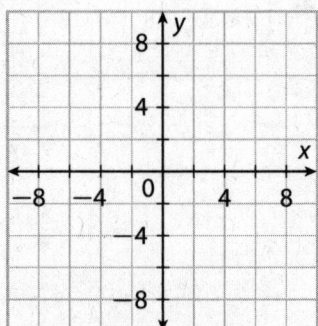

21. $\begin{cases} y < -\dfrac{3}{5}x + 3 \\ y \geq -\dfrac{3}{5}x - 4 \end{cases}$

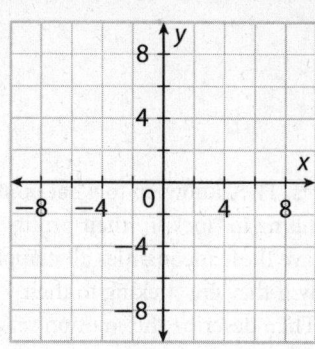

22. $\begin{cases} y > -\dfrac{1}{2}x + 5 \\ y > -\dfrac{1}{2}x - 1 \end{cases}$

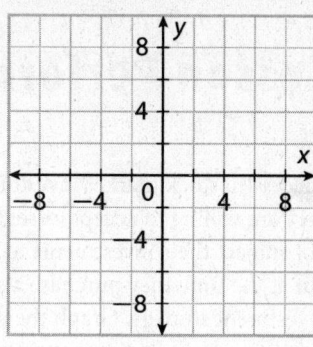

H.O.T. Focus on Higher Order Thinking

23. Persevere in Problem Solving Write and graph a system of linear inequalities for which the solutions are all the points in the second quadrant, not including points on the axes.

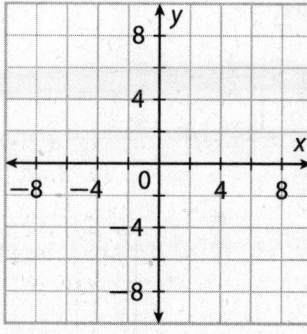

24. Critical Thinking Can the solutions of a system of linear inequalities be the points on a line? Explain.

25. Explain the Error A student was asked to graph the system $\begin{cases} y < \dfrac{3}{2}x - 8 \\ y \leq \dfrac{3}{2}x + 2 \end{cases}$ and describe the solution set. The student gave the following answer. Explain what the student did wrong, then give the correct answer.

The solutions are the same as the solutions of $y \leq \dfrac{3}{2}x + 2$.

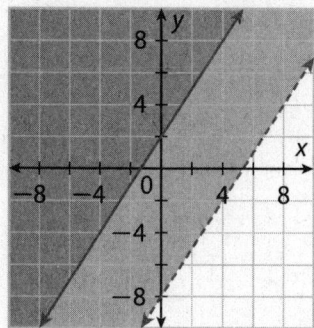

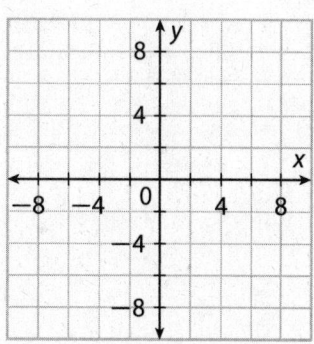

Lesson Performance Task

Successful stock market investors know a lot about inequalities. They know up to what point they are willing to accept losses, and at what point they are willing to "lock in" their profits and not subject their investments to additional risk. They often have these inequalities all mapped out at the time they purchase a stock, so they can tell instantly if they are sticking to their investment strategy. Graph the system of linear inequalities. Then describe the solution set and give two ordered pairs that are solutions and two that are not. Is there anything particular to note about the shape of this system?

$$\begin{cases} y < -\frac{3}{5}x + 4 \\ y \le \frac{3}{2}x + 8 \\ y > -\frac{3}{5}x - 8 \\ y > \frac{3}{2}x - 6 \end{cases}$$

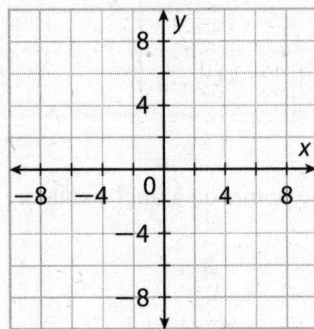

12.3 Modeling with Linear Systems

Essential Question: How can you use systems of linear equations or inequalities to model and solve contextual problems?

Resource
Locker

⊘ Explore   Modeling Real-World Constraints with Systems

Real-world situations can often be modeled by systems of equations. Usually, information about prices and the total number of items purchased is given, and the system is solved to find the number of each item purchased.

Joe goes to the store to buy jeans and some T-shirts. The jeans cost $40 each and the T-shirts cost $20 each. If Joe spends $160 on 5 items, how many pairs of jeans and how many T-shirts did he buy?

(A) Write an expression to represent the amount that Joe spent on x pairs of jeans. _____

(B) Write an expression to represent the amount that Joe spent on y T-shirts. _____

(C) Now write an equation that represents the total amount spent on jeans and T-shirts.

Amount spent on jeans	+	Amount spent on T-shirts	=	Total amount spent
☐	+	☐	=	☐

(D) What variable represents the number of jeans purchased? _____

(E) What variable represents the number of T-shirts purchased? _____

(F) Write an equation to represent the total number of items purchased. _____

(G) Write the system that represents the situation.

☐ = 160

☐ = 5

Reflect

1. What units are associated with the two expressions that you wrote in steps A and B?

_____

_____

2. When you add the units for the expressions representing the amounts spent on jeans and T-shirts, what units do you get for the total amount spent?

_____

Explain 1   Modeling Real-World Constraints with Systems of Linear Equations

You can model real-world constraints, such as the number of items needed and the amount of money one has to spend, with systems of linear equations.

Example 1   Write a system of equations to represent the situation, and then solve the system.

Ⓐ   Bobby will buy coffee and hot chocolate for his co-workers. Each cup of coffee costs \$2.25 and each cup of hot chocolate costs \$1.50. If he pays a total of \$15.75 for 8 cups, how many of each did he buy?

Create a table to organize the information.

	Coffee	Hot Chocolate	Total
Number of Cups	c	h	8
Cost	\$2.25c	\$1.50h	\$15.75

Use the information to write a system of equations.

$2.25c + 1.50h = 15.75$ Total amount spent on c cups of coffee and h cups of hot chocolate

$c + h = 8$ Total number of cups bought

Multiply the second equation by -2.25 to get opposite coefficients for c.

$-2.25(c + h = 8)$

$-2.25c - 2.25h = 18$

Add the new equation to the first equation.

$$2.25c + 1.50h = 15.75$$
$$\underline{+(-2.25c - 2.25h = -18)}$$
$$-0.75h = -2.25$$

Solve for h.

$-0.75h = -2.25$

$h = 3$

Substitute the value found for h back into one of the original equations and solve for c.

$c + h = 8$

$c + 3 = 8$

$c = 5$

So Bobby bought 5 cups of coffee and 3 cups of hot chocolate.

(B) A student is buying pens and markers for school. Packs of pens cost $2.75 each and packs of markers cost $3.25 each. If she bought a total of 6 packs and spent $17.50, how many of each did she buy?

Create a table to organize the information.

	Pens	Markers	Total
Number of packs	p	m	
Cost			$17.50

Use the information to write a system of equations.

$\boxed{} + \boxed{} = 17.50$ Total amount spent on p packs of pens and m packs of markers

$p + m = \boxed{}$ Total number of packs bought

Multiply the second equation by _____ to get opposite coefficients for p.

$\boxed{} \left(p + m = \boxed{} \right)$

$\boxed{} p + \boxed{} m = \boxed{}$

Add the new equation to the first equation.

$\boxed{} p + \boxed{} m = 17.50$

$+ \boxed{} p + \boxed{} m = \boxed{}$

$ \boxed{} m = \boxed{}$

Solve for m, the number of markers.

$m = \boxed{}$

Substitute the value found for m back into one of the original equations and solve for p.

$p + m = \boxed{}$

$p + \boxed{} = \boxed{}$

$p = \boxed{}$

So the student bought _____ packs of pens and _____ packs of markers.

Reflect

3. What's another possible way to solve the problem?

_____

_____

Write a system of equations to represent the situation, and then solve the system.

4. A company has to buy computers and printers. Each computer costs $550 and each printer costs $390. If the company spends $8160 and buys a total of 16 machines, how many of each did it buy?

🔑 **Explain 2** **Modeling Real-World Constraints with Systems of Linear Inequalities**

You can use a system of linear inequalities and its graph to model many real-world situations.

Example 2 Set up and solve the system of linear equalities.

(A) Sue is buying T-shirts and shorts. T-shirts cost $14 and shorts cost $21. She plans on spending no more than $147 and buy at least 5 items. Show and describe all combinations of the number of T-shirts and shorts she could buy.

First write the system. Let x represent the number of T-shirts, and let y represent the number of shorts.

$x + y \geq 5$ She wants to buy at least 5 items.

$14x + 21y \leq 147$ She wants to spend no more than $147.

Graph the system of inequalities: $\begin{cases} x + y \geq 5 \\ 14x + 21y \leq 147 \end{cases}$

T-shirts and Shorts

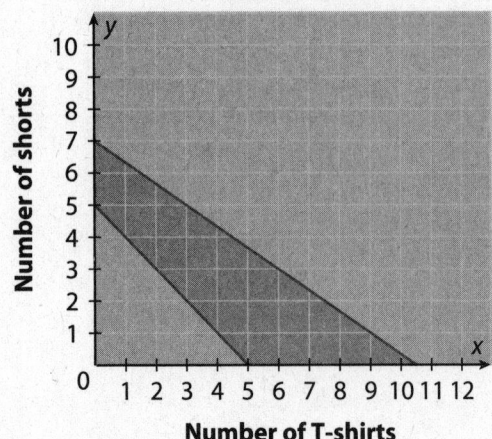

The possible solutions are where the shaded regions overlap. So, a possible solution is 5 T-shirts and 2 shorts. Substitute this value into the inequalities to make sure it is a reasonable solution.

$\begin{cases} x + y \geq 5 \\ 14x + 21y \leq 147 \end{cases} \rightarrow \begin{cases} 5 + 2 \overset{?}{\geq} 5 \\ 14(5) + 21(2) \overset{?}{\leq} 147 \end{cases} \rightarrow \begin{cases} 7 \geq 5 \\ 112 \leq 147 \end{cases}$

The result is two inequalities that are true, so this is a reasonable answer.

Ⓑ John has to buy two different kinds of rope. Rope A costs $0.60 per foot and Rope B costs $0.90 per foot. John needs to buy at least 15 feet of rope, but he wants to spend no more than $18. Show and describe all combinations of the number of feet of each type of rope John can buy.

First write the system. Let x represent the amount of Rope A, and let y represent the amount of Rope B.

$\boxed{} + \boxed{} \geq 15$

$\boxed{} + 0.9y \boxed{} \ 18$

Graph the system.

Buying Rope

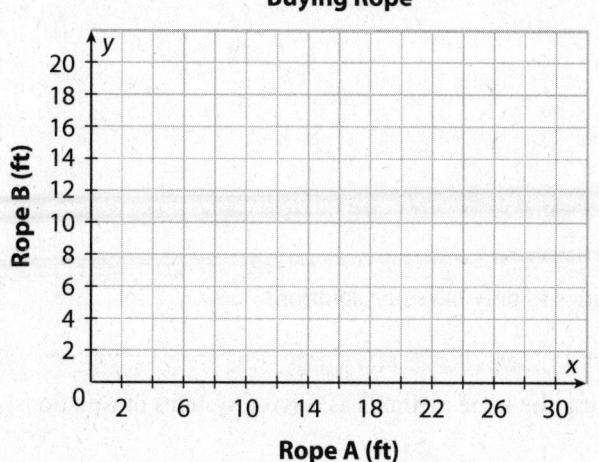

Describe the solutions to the system.

The possible solutions are _____

_____

_____

_____

Your Turn

Write a system of inequalities for the given situation and graph the system. Then determine if the point (8, 4) is a solution to the system.

5. A student has to buy graph paper and printer paper. The printer paper costs $2 a pack, while the graphing paper costs $3 a pack. She wants to buy at least 6 packs of paper but wants to spend at most $27.

Buying Paper

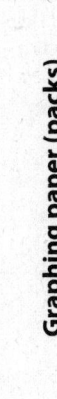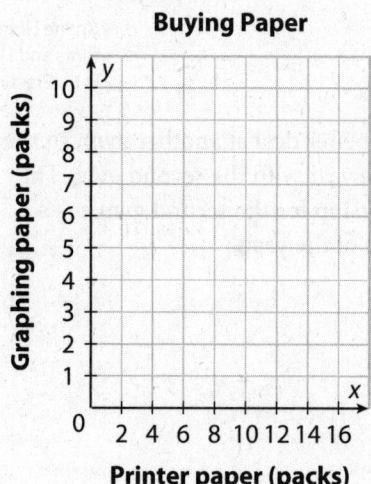

6. Now assume that she wants to buy at least 7 packs and will spend at most $30.

Buying Paper

(Graph with x-axis labeled "Printer paper (packs)" ranging from 0 to 16 in increments of 2, and y-axis labeled "Graphing paper (packs)" ranging from 0 to 10.)

7. Is it possible for a system of two linear inequalities to only have one solution?

_____

8. Why can't a system of inequalities be solved using the same methods as solving systems of equations?

_____

9. **Essential Question Check-In** When writing a system of equations or inequalities from a situation, how do you know that you have possibly written the system correctly?

_____

⭐ **Evaluate: Homework and Practice**

• Online Homework
• Hints and Help
• Extra Practice

Write a system of equations that corresponds to the situation. Do not solve.

1. Lisa spends part of her year as a member of a gym. She then finds a better deal at another gym, so she cancels her membership with the first gym and spends the rest of the year with the second gym. The membership to the first gym costs $75 per month, while the membership for the second gym costs $50 per month. She ends up spending a total of $775 over the course of the year.

2. Jack is selling tickets to an event. Attendees can either buy a general admission ticket or a VIP ticket. The general adimission tickets are $60 and the VIP tickets are $90. He doesn't know how many of each type he has sold, but he knows he sold a total of 29 tickets and made $2100.

3. There are 200 adults and 300 children at a zoo. The zoo makes a total of $7000 from the entrance fees, and the cost for an adult and a child to attend is $30.

4. A local fish market is selling fish and lobsters by the pound. The fish costs $4.50 a pound, while the lobster costs $9.50 a pound. The fish market sells 25.5 pounds and makes $189.75.

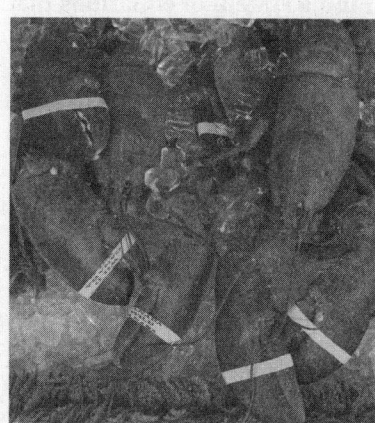

5. Jennifer has 12 nickels and dimes. The value of her coins is $1.

6. The sum of 5 times one number and 2 times a second number is 57. The sum of the two numbers is 18.

7. Gary goes to the grocery store to buy hot dogs and hamburgers for a cookout. He buys a total of 8 packages for a total of $28.52. A package of hot dogs costs $2.29 and a package of hamburgers costs $5.69.

8. The sum of two numbers is 28, and the sum of 6 times the first number and 3 times the second number is 105.

Find a system of equations that corresponds to the situation and then solve the resulting system.

9. Jan spends part of her year as a member of a gym. She then finds a better deal at another gym, so she cancels her membership with the first gym and spends the rest of the year with the second gym. The membership to the first gym costs $80 per month, while the membership for the second gym costs $45 per month. If she ends up spending a total of $645 over the course of the year, how much time did she spend at each gym?

10. John is selling tickets to an event. Attendees can either buy a general admission ticket or a VIP ticket. The general adimission tickets are $70 and the VIP tickets are $105. If he knows he sold a total of 33 tickets and made $2730, how many of each type did he sell?

11. There are 150 adults and 225 children at a zoo. If the zoo makes a total of $5100 from the entrance fees, and the cost of an adult and a child to attend is $31, how much does it cost each for a parent and a child?

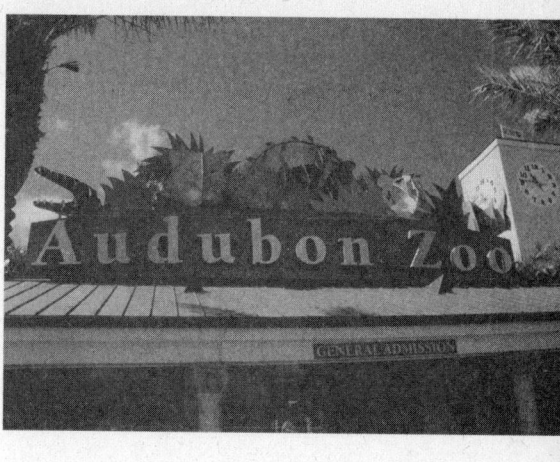

12. A local fish market is selling fish and lobsters by the pound. The fish costs $5.25 a pound, while the lobster costs $10.50 a pound. The fish market sells 28.5 pounds and makes $215.25.

13. Nicole has 15 nickels and dimes. If the value of her coins is $1.20, how many of each coin does she have?

14. The sum of 4 times one number and 3 times a second number is 64. If the sum of the two numbers is 19, find the two numbers.

15. Meaghan goes to the grocery store to buy hot dogs and hamburgers for a cookout. She buys a total of 6 packages for a total of $30.46. If a package of hot dogs costs $2.65 and a package of hamburgers costs $6.29, determine how many packages of each she bought.

16. The sum of two numbers is 33, and the sum of 7 times the first number and 5 times the second number is 197.

Write the system of inequalities that represents the situation. Then graph the system and describe the solutions. Give one possible solution.

17. Angelique is buying towels for her apartment. She finds some green towels that cost $8 each and blue towels that cost $10 each. She wants to buy at least 4 towels but doesn't want to spend more than $70. How many of each towel can she purchase?

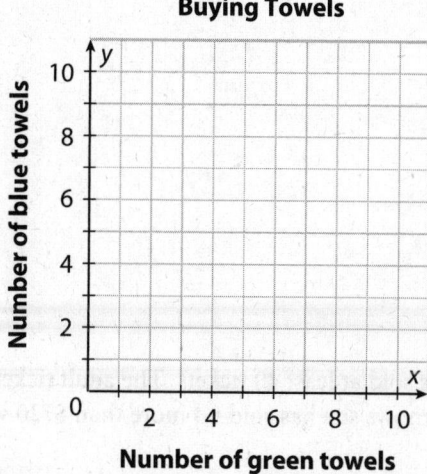

Buying Towels

Number of blue towels (y-axis)
Number of green towels (x-axis)

18. The sum of two numbers is at least 8, and the sum of one of the numbers and 3 times the second number is no more than 15.

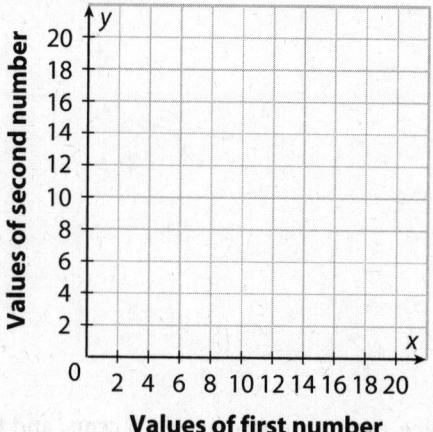

Values of second number (y-axis)
Values of first number (x-axis)

19. The sum of two numbers is at most 12, and the sum of 3 times the first number and 8 times the second number is at least 48.

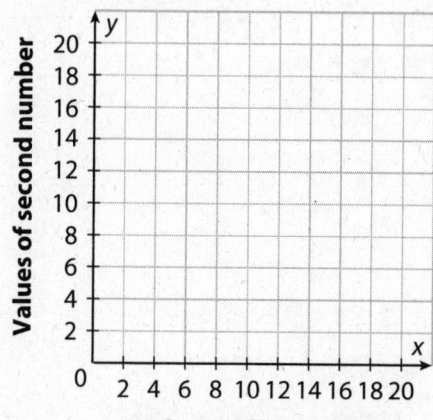

Values of second number (y-axis)
Values of first number (x-axis)

20. Katie is purchasing plates and mugs for her house. She would like to buy at least 8 items. Determine the possibilities if the plates cost $8 each and the mugs cost $7 each, and she plans to spend no more than $112.

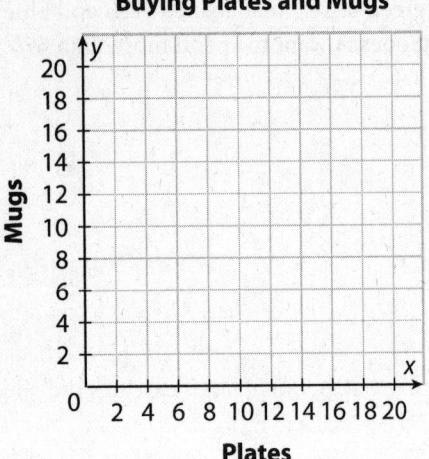

Buying Plates and Mugs

21. Christine is selling tickets at a museum. She knows that she has sold at least 40 tickets. The adult tickets cost 14 dollars and the children's tickets cost 12 dollars. If she knows she has sold no more than $720 worth of tickets, what are the possible combinations?

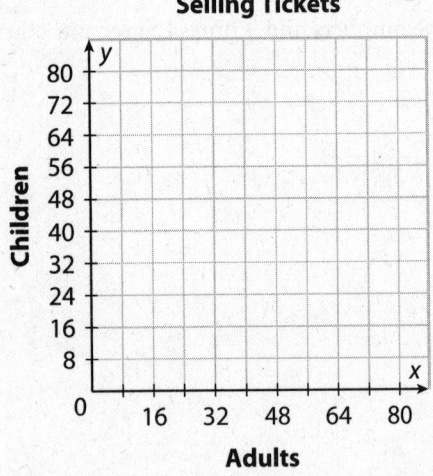

Selling Tickets

22. Mike is bringing cans and bottles to a recycling center. For a type A can or bottle he gets 5 cents, and for a type B can or bottle he gets 10 cents. He knows that he has redeemed at least 11 cans but has no more than 95 cents. What are the possible combinations?

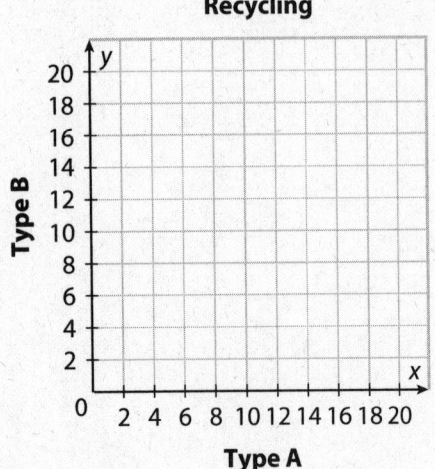

Recycling

23. Explain the Error A student is given the following system. He graphs the system as shown and determines that a solution is $(7, 0)$. Where did the student go wrong? What should the correct answer be?

$$x + y = 6$$
$$x + 2y = 8$$

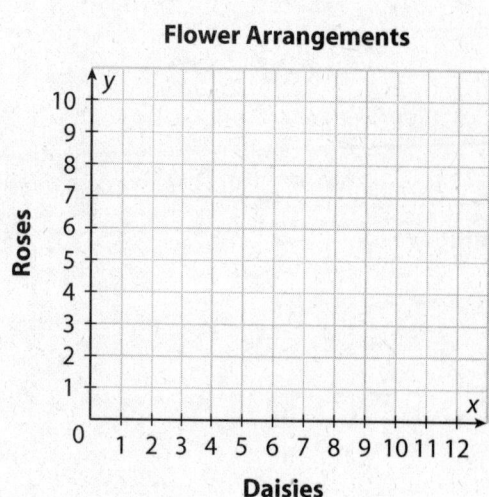

24. Justify Reasoning Molly went shopping to buy jewelry. All of the earrings cost $15.25 and the necklaces cost $40.75. If she spends $127.25 and buys 5 items, how many necklaces and pairs of earrings did she buy? Justify your answer.

25. Check for Reasonableness Chris is at the florist and has to buy flowers. Arrangements of daisies are $4.25 and arrangements of roses are $6.50. He wants to spend less than $39 and wants to buy more than 4 arrangements. What are possible combinations that Chris can buy? Check to make sure your answer is reasonable.

Flower Arrangements

Roses (y-axis, 0 to 10)
Daisies (x-axis, 1 to 12)

Lesson Performance Task

Amy is at the store to buy shirts and pants. The shirts cost $40 each and the pants cost $50 each. She plans to spend no more than $400 and buy at least 5 items. Find a possible combination of shirts and pants she can buy. How do you know this is a solution? What are two possible ways to show that this is a solution?

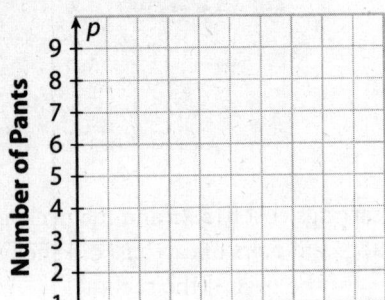

Possible Options

Number of Pants

Number of Shirts

Modeling with Linear Systems

Essential Question: How can you model with linear systems to solve real-world problems?

KEY EXAMPLE (Lesson 12.1)

One cable television provider has a $50 setup fee and charges $90 per month, and another cable provider has a $150 equipment fee and charges $80 per month. Determine when the cost of the two services will be the same amount, and what the price will be.

Let $f(t)$ represent the cost for the first cable company and let $g(t)$ represent the cost of the second cable company, where t is the number of months.

The system of equations is $\begin{cases} f(t) = 50 + 90t \\ g(t) = 150 + 80t \end{cases}$.

Solve the system when $f(t) = g(t)$.

$50 + 90t = 150 + 80t$

$90t - 80t = 150 - 50$

$10t = 100$

$t = 10$

$f(t) = 50 + 90t$

$f(10) = 50 + 90(10)$

$f(10) = 950$

A subscriber would have paid either company $950 for 10 months of service.

KEY EXAMPLE (Lesson 12.2)

Graph the system of linear inequalities $\begin{cases} y \leq 2x - 2 \\ y > 0.5x + 1 \end{cases}$.

Graph the line $y = 2x - 2$. Use a solid line because the inequality symbol is $\leq$. Lightly shade below the line.

Graph the line $y = 0.5x + 1$. Use a dashed line because the inequality symbol is $>$. Lightly shade above the line.

The intersection of the two shaded areas contains the solution set to the system of linear inequalities. For example, (4, 4) is within the intersection and satisfies both inequalities.

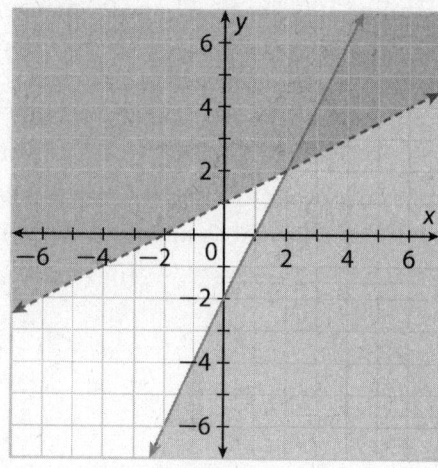

EXERCISES

1. Jacob wants to buy a gym membership. The table below shows the total cost of two gyms after several months, including any startup fees.

Month	2	4	6	8
Tony's Gym	$220	$300	$380	$460
Mickey's Gym	$120	$240	$360	$480

Use the data to write a system of equations. Then solve to find out in how many months both memberships will cost the same. What will that cost be? *(Lesson 12.1)*

2. Graph $\begin{cases} y \le -2x + 3 \\ 3y \ge 9x - 6 \end{cases}$. Give two ordered pairs that are

solutions and two that are not solutions. *(Lesson 12.2)*

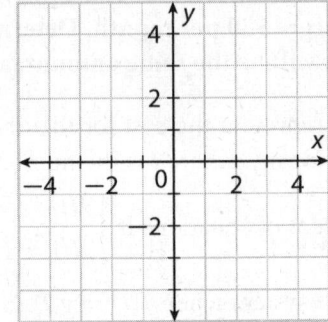

3. A local fish market is selling fish and lobster by the pound. The fish costs $5.00 a pound, while the lobster costs $10.50 a pound. The fish market sells 30 total pounds and makes $194. Represent this situation with a system of equations and solve it to find how many pounds of fish and lobster were sold. *(Lesson 12.3)*

MODULE PERFORMANCE TASK

How to Win at an Arcade Game

You are playing an arcade game that involves rolling a ball up a ramp. If you earn at least 450 points, you win the grand prize. You want to figure out a winning strategy. Here is some background information that will help you to formulate your plan.

- One round of the game uses 9 balls.
- Earning 100, 50, 40, 30, and 20 points is fairly obvious as the ball has to go down the corresponding hole. However, if you miss all of those holes, a big curve catches the balls and empties into the 10-points hole. So, you will almost always earn at least 10 points.

Use your own paper to complete the task. Be sure to write down all your data and assumptions. Then use graphs, numbers, words, or algebra to explain how you reached your conclusion.

(Ready) to Go On?

12.1–12.3 Modeling with Linear Systems

- Online Homework
- Hints and Help
- Extra Practice

1. A jar contains n nickels and d dimes. There are 30 coins in the jar, and the total value of the coins is $2.10. Set up and solve a system of equations to find how many nickels and how many dimes are in the jar. *(Lesson 12.1)*

Tell whether each ordered pair is a solution of $\begin{cases} y < 2x + 5 \\ 4y > -4x-8 \end{cases}$. *(Lesson 12.2)*

2. $(1, 2)$

3. $(0, 6)$

4. $(-1, -2)$

5. $(-1, 2)$

6. Nathan buys coffee and hot chocolate for his co-workers. Each cup of coffee costs $1.75 and each cup of hot chocolate costs $1.20. If he pays a total of $11.15 for 7 cups, how many of each does he buy? *(Lesson 12.3)*

ESSENTIAL QUESTION

7. How can the graph of a system of linear equations help you find the solution to a real-world problem?

Assessment Readiness

1. Consider each ordered pair. Is the ordered pair a solution of $\begin{cases} y \le 3x + 5 \\ y \ge -\frac{2}{3}x + 5 \end{cases}$?

   A. $(-1, 4)$ ⃝ Yes ⃝ No

   B. $(0, 5)$ ⃝ Yes ⃝ No

   C. $(2, 9)$ ⃝ Yes ⃝ No

2. Consider the graph of $y - 5 = \frac{1}{5}(x + 2)$.
   Determine whether each statement is True or False.

   A. The slope of the graph is $\frac{1}{5}$. ⃝ True ⃝ False

   B. The graph includes the point $(0, 2)$. ⃝ True ⃝ False

   C. The graph includes the point $(2, -5)$. ⃝ True ⃝ False

3. The sum of 4 times one number and 3 times a second number is 65. The sum of the two numbers is 18. Write and solve a system of equations to find the two numbers. Show your work.

4. Steven wants to buy a couch that costs $475. He has already saved $120. He plans to save $25 a week. Write a function to represent the amount Steven will have saved in x weeks. Will he have enough to buy the couch in 10 weeks? Explain your answer.

Piecewise-Defined Functions

Essential Question: How can you use piecewise-defined functions to solve real-world problems?

REAL WORLD VIDEO
Optimizing sales prices is key to running a successful retail business. Cost and pricing structures are rarely linear, instead taking "jumps" at certain price points.

MODULE PERFORMANCE TASK PREVIEW

A Taxing Situation

United States citizens pay sales taxes on items they buy, gasoline taxes when they fill up their cars at the pump, and property taxes if they own a home. Everyone who earns more than a certain minimum amount also pays the federal government a tax on their income. The amount paid is defined not as a percent of income but by a "piecewise" function. You'll learn about these functions in this module and then use them to analyze the income tax system.

© Houghton Mifflin Harcourt Publishing Company • ©Fuse/Getty Images

Are 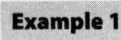 Ready?

Complete these exercises to review skills you will need for this module.

Multi-Step Equations

Example 1   Solve. $\frac{3}{4}b + 2 = 38$

$\quad\quad\quad\quad \frac{3}{4}b = 36$ Subtract 2 from both sides.

$\quad\quad\quad\quad\quad b = 48$ Multiply both sides by $\frac{4}{3}$.

• Online Homework
• Hints and Help
• Extra Practice

Solve each equation.

1. $10x - 15 = -4$

2. $5x - 7 = 2(3x + 1)$

3. $5(8v - 4) = -2$

Two-Step Inequalities

Example 2   Solve. $-2w + 3 \leq 4$

$\quad\quad\quad\quad\quad -2w \leq 1$ Subtract 3 from both sides.

$\quad\quad\quad\quad\quad w \geq -0.5$ Divide both sides by –2 and flip the sign.

Solve.

4. $n - 7 \geq -4$

5. $\frac{3x}{2} < -6$

6. $5 - 9a \leq 32$

Absolute Value

Example 3   Use the definition of absolute value to write two equations that represent the equation $|3x - 11| = 1$.

If $3x - 11 > 0$, then $3x - 11 = 1$.

If $3x - 11 < 0$, then $3x - 11 = -1$.

The two equations are $3x - 11 = 1$ and $3x - 11 = -1$.

Write two equations that represent the given function.

7. $\left|\frac{k}{9} + \frac{1}{3}\right| = 12$

8. $\left|6(r - 4)\right| = 4.8$

9. $\left|\frac{n}{22}\right| = 16$

13.1 Understanding Piecewise-Defined Functions

Essential Question: How are piecewise-defined functions different from other functions?

Explore Exploring Piecewise-Defined Function Models

A **piecewise function** has different rules for different parts of its domain. The following situation can be modeled by a piecewise function.

Armando drives from his home to the grocery store at a speed of 0.9 mile per minute for 4 minutes, stops for 2 minutes to buy snacks, and then drives to the soccer field at a speed of 0.7 mile per minute for 3 minutes. The graph shows Armando's distance from home.

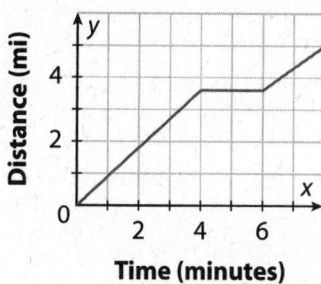

Time (minutes)

The three different sections in the graph show that there are three different parts to the function. The function for this graph will have three function rules, each for a different range of values for *x*.

The following steps can be used to build the piecewise function to model this situation.

(A) Determine the function rule for the first 4 minutes for the domain, $0 \leq x \leq 4$. The rate of change is Armando's speed in miles per minute.

$$m = \frac{\boxed{} \text{ mi}}{\boxed{} \text{ min}} = \boxed{}$$

The *y*-intercept is _____.

The function for the first 4 minutes is $y = \boxed{}$.

(B) Determine the function rule for the next 2 minutes for the domain, $4 < x \leq 6$.

Because the distance is not changing, the rate of change is $m = \dfrac{\boxed{} \text{ mi}}{\boxed{} \text{ min}} = \boxed{}$.

The function for the next 2 minutes is a constant function. The constant y-value is Armando's distance from home at the end of the first 4 minutes.

$y = 0.9x$

$y = 0.9(4) = \boxed{}$

Ⓒ Determine the function rule for the last 3 minutes.
The rate of change is Armando's speed in miles per minute.

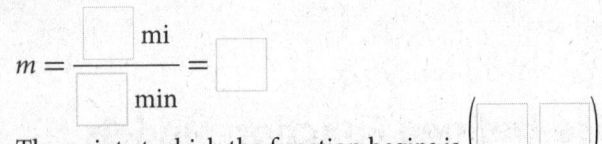

The point at which the function begins is $\left(\boxed{}, \boxed{} \right)$.

Use the point and slope to construct the function rule for the last 3 minutes.

$y - \boxed{} = \boxed{} \left(x - \boxed{} \right)$

$y - \boxed{} = \boxed{} x - \boxed{}$

$y = \boxed{} x - \boxed{}$

Ⓓ Use all three parts to build the piecewise function that represents this situation.

$$f(x) = \begin{cases} \boxed{} & \text{if } 0 \leq x \leq 4 \\ \boxed{} & \text{if } 4 < x \leq 6 \\ \boxed{} & \text{if } 6 < x \leq 9 \end{cases}$$

Reflect

1. **Discussion** Describe how the domain is constructed so that the piecewise function is a function with no more than one value of the dependent variable for any value of the independent variable.

_____

_____

_____

✏ Explain 1 Evaluating Piecewise-Defined Functions

The **greatest integer function** is a piecewise function whose rule is denoted by $\lfloor x \rfloor$, which represents the greatest integer less than or equal to x. The greatest integer function is an example of a **step function**, a piecewise function in which each function rule is a constant function. To evaluate a piecewise function for a given value of x, substitute the value of x into the rule for the part of the domain that includes x.

Example 1 Evaluate each piecewise function for the given values.

Ⓐ Find $f(-3)$, $f(-2.9)$, $f(0.7)$, and $f(1.06)$ for $f(x) = \lfloor x \rfloor$.

The greatest integer function $f(x) = \lfloor x \rfloor$ can also be written in the form below.

$$f(x) = \begin{cases} \vdots \\ -3 & \text{if } -3 \le x < -2 \\ -2 & \text{if } -2 \le x < -1 \\ -1 & \text{if } -1 \le x < 0 \\ 0 & \text{if } 0 \le x < 1 \\ 1 & \text{if } 1 \le x < 2 \\ 2 & \text{if } 2 \le x < 3 \\ \vdots \end{cases}$$

-3 is in the interval $-3 \le x < -2$, so $f(-3) = -3$.

-2.9 is in the interval $-3 \le x < -2$, so $f(-2.9) = -3$.

0.7 is in the interval $0 \le x < 1$, so $f(0.7) = 0$.

1.06 is in the interval $1 \le x < 2$, so $f(1.06) = 1$.

Ⓑ Find $f(-3)$, $f(-0.2)$, $f(0)$, and $f(2)$ for $f(x) = \begin{cases} -x & \text{if } x < 0 \\ x+1 & \text{if } x \ge 0 \end{cases}$

$-3 < 0$, so $f(-3) = -(-3) = \boxed{}$

$0 \ge 0$, so $f(0) = \boxed{} + 1 = \boxed{}$

$-0.2 < 0$, so $f(-0.2) = \boxed{} = \boxed{}$

$2 \ge 0$, so $f(2) = \boxed{} + \boxed{} = \boxed{}$

Reflect

2. For positive numbers, how is applying the greatest integer function different from the method of rounding to the nearest whole number?

Your Turn

3. Find $f(-2)$, $f(-0.4)$, $f(3.7)$, and $f(5)$ for $f(x) = \begin{cases} -x & \text{if } x < 2 \\ 2x+3 & \text{if } 2 \le x < 4. \\ x^2 & \text{if } x \ge 4 \end{cases}$

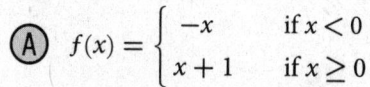 **Explain 2** **Graphing Piecewise-Defined Functions**

You can graph piecewise-defined functions to illustrate their behavior.

Example 2 Graph each function.

Ⓐ $f(x) = \begin{cases} -x & \text{if } x < 0 \\ x+1 & \text{if } x \ge 0 \end{cases}$

Make a table of values.

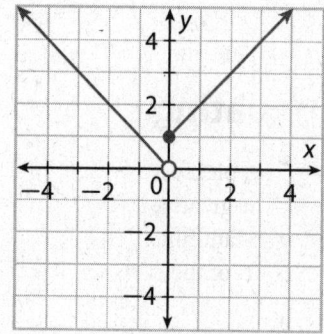

x	−3	−2	−1	0	1	2
f(x)	3	2	1	1	2	3

Ⓑ $f(x) = \lfloor x \rfloor$

Make a table of values.

x	−3	−2.9	−2.1	−2	−1.5	−1	0	1	1.5	2
f(x)	−3			−2			0			

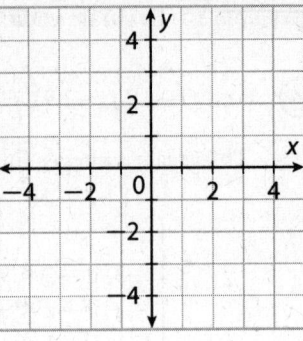

Reflect

4. Why does the graph in Example 2A use rays and not lines?

_____

_____

5. Use the graph of the greatest integer function from Example 2B to explain why this function is called a step function.

_____

_____

Your Turn

6. $f(x) = \begin{cases} x & \text{if} & x < 2 \\ 2x + 3 & \text{if} & 2 \le x < 4 \\ x^2 & \text{if} & x \ge 4 \end{cases}$

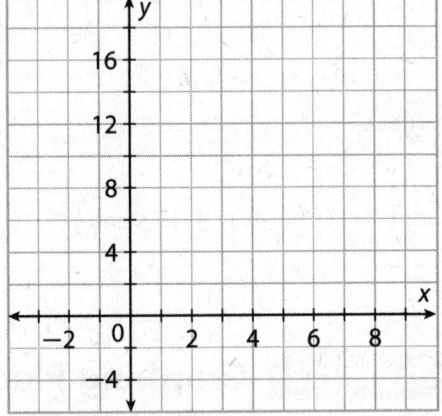

🔑 Explain 3 Modeling with Piecewise-Defined Functions

Some real-world situations can be described by piecewise functions.

Example 3 Write a piecewise function for each situation. Then graph the function.

(A) **Travel** On her way to a concert, Maisee walks at a speed of 0.03 mile per minute from her car for 5 minutes, waits in line for a ticket for 3 minutes, and then walks to her seat for 4 minutes at a speed of 0.01 mile per minute.

Express the Maisee's distance traveled d (in miles) as a function of time t (in minutes).

For $0 \leq t \leq 5$, $m = 0.03$ and $b = 0$, so $d(t) = 0.03t$.

For $5 < t \leq 8$, $m = 0$ and $b = 0.15$, so $d(t) = 0.15$.

For $8 < t \leq 12$, $m = 0.01$ beginning at $(8, 0.15)$, so $d(t) = 0.01t + 0.07$.

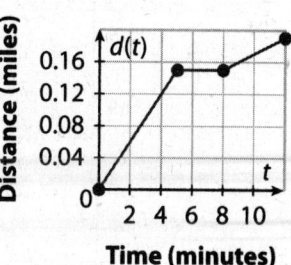

$$d(t) = \begin{cases} 0.03t & \text{if } 0 \leq t \leq 5 \\ 0.15 & \text{if } 5 < t \leq 8 \\ 0.01t + 0.07 & \text{if } 8 < t \leq 12 \end{cases}$$

(B) **Travel** On his way to class from his dorm room, a college student walks at a speed of 0.05 mile per minute for 3 minutes, stops and talks to a friend for 1 minute, and then to avoid being late for class, runs at a speed of 0.10 mile per minute for 2 minutes.

Express the student's distance traveled d (in miles) as a function of time t (in minutes).

For $0 \leq t \leq 3$, $m = $ [____] and $b = 0$, so $d(t) = $ [____] t.

For $3 < t \leq $ [____], $m = 0$ and $b = 0.15$, so $d(t) = 0.15$.

For $4 < t \leq 6$, $m = $ [____] beginning at [____], so $y = $ [____] $x - $ [____].

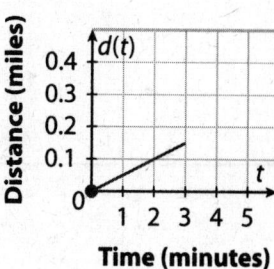

$$d(t) = \begin{cases} \boxed{}\, t & \text{if } 0 \leq t \leq 3 \\ 0.15 & \text{if } 3 < t \leq \boxed{} \\ \boxed{}\, t - \boxed{} & \text{if } 4 < t \leq 6 \end{cases}$$

Your Turn

7. **Finance** A savings account earns 1.4% simple interest annually for balances of $100 or less, 2.4% simple interest for balances greater than $100 and up to $500, and 3.4% simple interest for balances greater than $500. Write a function rule for the interest paid by the account and graph the function.

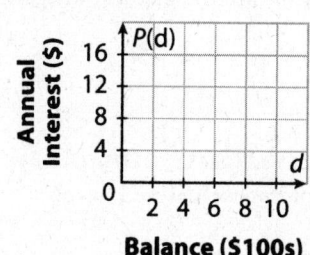

Explain 4 Building Piecewise-Defined Functions from Graphs

You can find the function rules for a piecewise function when you are given the graph of the function.

Example 4 Write an equation for each graph.

(A)

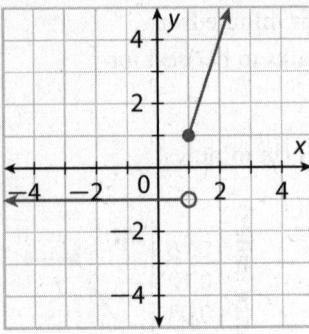

Find the equation of the ray on the right.

$$m = \frac{1-4}{1-2} = \frac{-3}{-1} = 3$$

Because the point $(1, 1)$ is on the ray, $y - 1 = 3(x - 1)$, so $y = 3x - 2$

The equation of the line that contains the horizontal ray is $y = -1$.

The equation for the function is $y = \begin{cases} -1 & \text{if } x < 1. \\ 3x - 2 & \text{if } x \geq 1 \end{cases}$

(B)

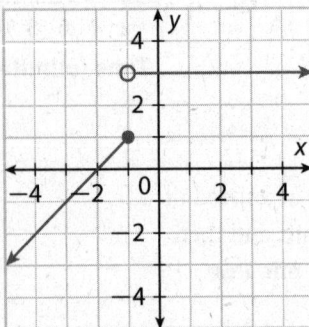

Find the equation for the ray on the left.

$$m = \frac{1 - \boxed{}}{-1 - \boxed{}} = \frac{\boxed{}}{\boxed{}} = \boxed{}$$

Because the point $(-1, 1)$ is on the ray, $y \boxed{} = \boxed{}\left(x \boxed{}\right)$,

so $y = \boxed{}$

The equation of the horizontal ray is $y = \boxed{}$.

The equation for the function is $y = \begin{cases} \boxed{}x + \boxed{} & \text{if } x \leq -1 \\ \boxed{} & \text{if } x > -1 \end{cases}$

Your Turn

8.

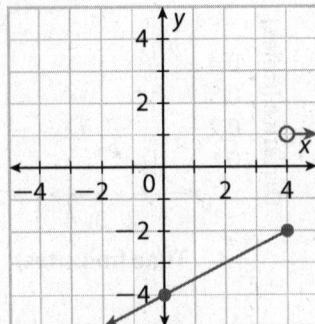

Elaborate

9. How are the greatest integer function and $f(x) = 2\lfloor x \rfloor$ related?

_____

_____

10. **Essential Question Check-In** How many function rules do functions that are not piecewise-defined have?

_____

☆ Evaluate: Homework and Practice

Evaluate each piecewise function for the given values.

1. Find $f(-4)$, $f(-3.1)$, $f(1.2)$, and $f(2.8)$ for $f(x) = \lfloor x \rfloor$.

2. Find $f(-3)$, $f(-2.1)$, $f(0.6)$, and $f(3.3)$ for $f(x) = \begin{cases} -1 & \text{if } x \le 0 \\ 3x & \text{if } 0 < x < 1 \\ x + 3 & \text{if } x \ge 1 \end{cases}$.

3. Find $f(-4)$, $f(-2.9)$, and $f(1.9)$ for $f(x) = \begin{cases} -5 & \text{if } x \le -3 \\ x + 2 & \text{if } -3 < x \le 0 \\ x^2 + 7 & \text{if } x \ge 0 \end{cases}$.

4. Find $f(-6)$, $f(-2.2)$, $f(1.4)$ and $f(3.6)$ for $f(x) = -2\lfloor x \rfloor$.

5. Find $f(-3)$, $f(-1)$, and $f(1)$ for $f(x) = \begin{cases} \dfrac{2}{x} & \text{if } x \le -2 \\ x & \text{if } -2 < x \le 0 \\ 1 & \text{if } x \ge 0 \end{cases}$

6. Find $f(-2)$, $f(-1)$, $f(0)$, $f(4)$, and $f(9)$ for $f(x) = \begin{cases} -x^2 & \text{if } x \le -2 \\ 2x & \text{if } -2 < x < 2 \\ x + 6 & \text{if } 2 \le x \le 4 \\ \sqrt{x} + 8 & \text{if } x > 4 \end{cases}$.

7. Find $f(-2.8)$, $f(-1.2)$, $f(0.4)$, and $f(1.6)$ for $f(x) = \lfloor x \rfloor^2$

8. Find $f(0)$, $f(2)$, and $f(4)$ for $f(x) = \begin{cases} 8 & \text{if } x \le 0 \\ 0 & \text{if } x > 0 \end{cases}$.

Graph each piecewise function.

9. $f(x) = \begin{cases} -x + 1 & \text{if } x < 0 \\ x & \text{if } x \ge 0 \end{cases}$

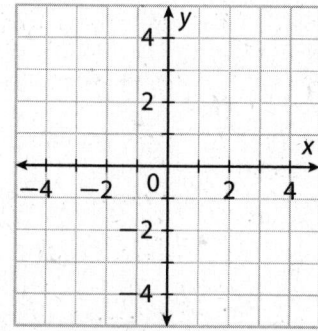

10. $f(x) = \begin{cases} -1 & \text{if } x < 1 \\ 2x - 2 & \text{if } x \ge 1 \end{cases}$

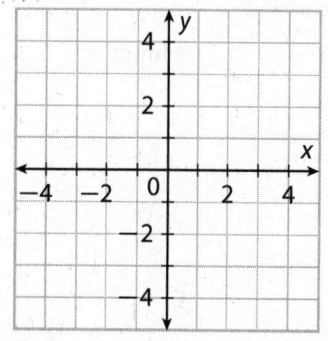

11. $f(x) = \lfloor x \rfloor + 1$

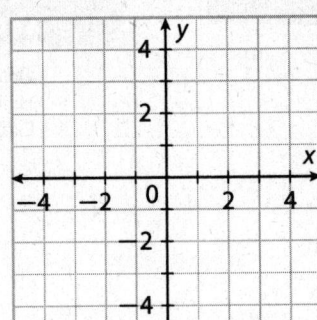

12. $f(x) = 2\lfloor x \rfloor - 2$

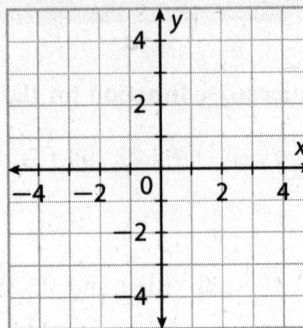

Write an equation for each graph.

13.

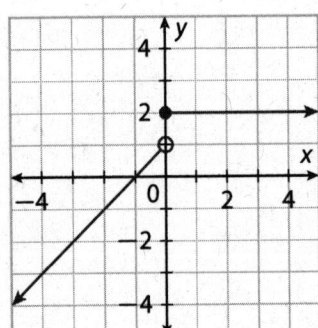

14.

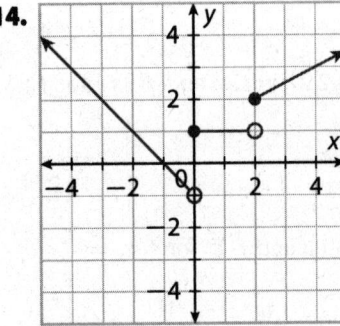

15.

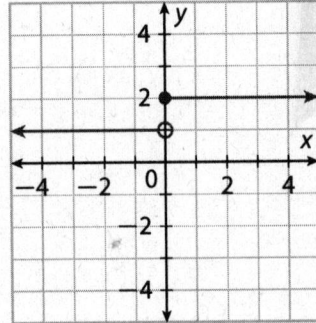

16.

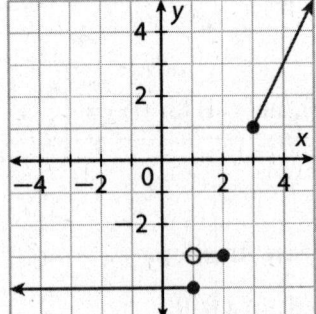

Write a piecewise function for each situation. Then complete the table and the graph.

17. Finance A garage charges the following rates for parking (with an 8 hour limit):

$4 per hour for the first 2 hours

$2 per hour for the next 4 hours

No additional charge for the next 2 hours

Express the cost C (in dollars) as a function of the time t (in hours) that a car is parked in the garage.

$C(t) =$

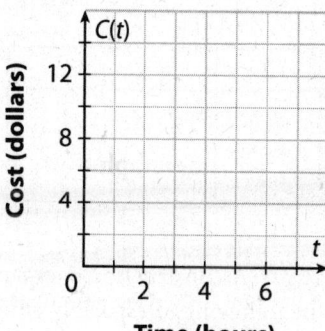

t	0	1	2	3	4
$C(t)$					

t	5	6	7	8
$C(t)$				

18. Cost Analysis The cost to send a package between two cities is $8.00 for any weight less than 1 pound. The cost increases by $4.00 when the weight reaches 1 pound and again each time the weight reaches a whole number of pounds after that.

Express the shipping cost C (in dollars) as a function of the weight (in pounds). Express your answer in terms of the greatest integer function $\lfloor w \rfloor$.

$C(w) =$

w	0.5	1	1.5	2	2.5
$C(w)$					

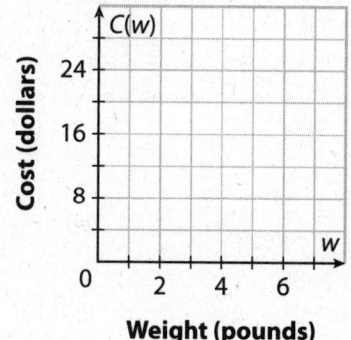

19. Golfing A local golf course charges members $30 an hour for the first three hours, $35 an hour for the next five hours, and nothing for the last 2 hours, for a maximum of 10 hours.

Express the cost C (in dollars) as a function of the time t (in hours) that a member plays golf at this golf course.

$C(t) =$

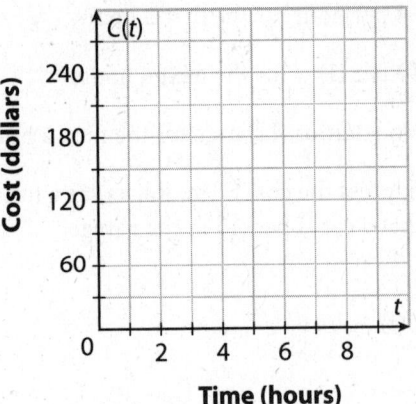

t	2	4	6	8	10
$C(t)$					

20. Construction A construction company is building a new parking garage and is charging the following rates: $5000 a month for the first 2 months; $8000 a month for the next 4 months; $6000 in total for the last 4 months, when the garage will be completed. This amount will be paid in a lump sum at the end of the 6th month.

Express the cost C (in thousands of dollars) as a function of the time t (in months) that the construction company works on the parking garage.

$C(t) =$

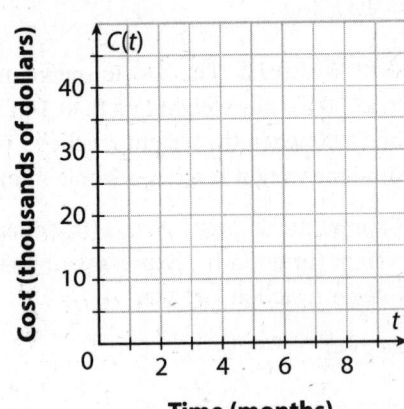

t	2	4	6	8	10
$C(t)$					

21. State the domain and range of each piecewise function.

A. $y = \begin{cases} 5 & \text{if } 0 < x \leq 1 \\ 0 & \text{if } x > 1 \end{cases}$

B. $y = \begin{cases} -x & \text{if } x \leq 0 \\ x & \text{if } x > 0 \end{cases}$

C. $y = \begin{cases} x^2 & \text{if } x \leq 4 \\ x^3 & \text{if } x > 4 \end{cases}$

D. $y = \begin{cases} x^2 + 1 & \text{if } x \leq -2 \\ x^3 & \text{if } -2 < x < 4 \\ x^x & \text{if } x \geq 4 \end{cases}$

E. $y = \begin{cases} 1 & \text{if } x \leq -3 \\ 1 & \text{if } -3 < x < 8 \\ 1 & \text{if } x \geq 8 \end{cases}$

22. **Critical Thinking** Rewrite the piecewise function into a function of the greatest integer function.

$$f(x) = \begin{cases} -6 & \text{if } -2 \le x < -1 \\ -3 & \text{if } -1 \le x < 0 \\ 0 & \text{if } 0 \le x < 1 \\ 3 & \text{if } 1 \le x < 2 \\ 6 & \text{if } 2 \le x < 3 \end{cases}$$

23. **Explain the Error** Clara was given the following situation and told to write a piecewise function to describe it.

While exercising, a person loses weight in the following manner:
0.5 pound per hour for the first hour
0.7 pound per hour for the next three hours
0.1 pound per hour until the workout is finished

Clara produced the following result. What did she do wrong and what is the correct answer?

$$W(t) = \begin{cases} 0.5t & \text{if } 0 \le t \le 1 \\ 0.7t & \text{if } 1 \le t < 4 \\ 0.1t & \text{if } t \ge 4 \end{cases}$$

24. **Critical Thinking** Write an equation for the shown graph. Express the answer in terms of $\lfloor x \rfloor$.

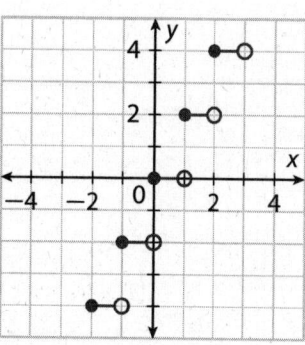

25. **Communicate Mathematical Ideas** Is a piecewise function still a function if it contains a vertical line? Explain why or why not.

Lesson Performance Task

Suppose someone is traveling from New York City to Miami, Florida. The following table describes the average speeds at various intervals on this 1200-mile trip.

Distance Traveled (hundreds of miles)	Average Speed (mi/h)
$0 < d \leq 2$	37.7
$2 < d \leq 4$	46.6
$4 < d \leq 6$	63.3
$6 < d \leq 8$	45.5
$8 < d \leq 10$	64.4
$10 < d \leq 12$	49.9

A. Graph the distance function. Make sure to use appropriate labels.

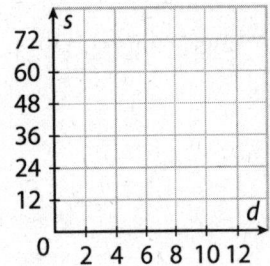

B. Write the piecewise function that is given by the table.

C. Suppose the destination was changed from Miami, Florida to Minneapolis, Minnesota instead. Explain why it is not okay to use the piecewise function created for the trip from New York to Miami when traveling to Minneapolis, even though the distance is comparable.

© Houghton Mifflin Harcourt Publishing Company

13.2 Absolute Value Functions and Transformations

Resource
Locker

Essential Question: What are the effects of parameter changes on the graph of
$$y = a|x - h| + k?$$

⊘ Explore   Understanding the Parent Absolute Value Function

The most basic **absolute value function** is a piecewise function given by the following rule.

$$f(x) = |x| = \begin{cases} x & \text{if } x \geq 0 \\ -x & \text{if } x < 0 \end{cases}$$

This function is sometimes called the parent absolute value function. Complete each step to graph this function.

(A) Complete the table of values.

x	$f(x) = |x|$
−3	3
−2	
−1	
0	
1	
2	
3	3

(B) Plot these points on a graph and using two rays, connect them to display the absolute value function.

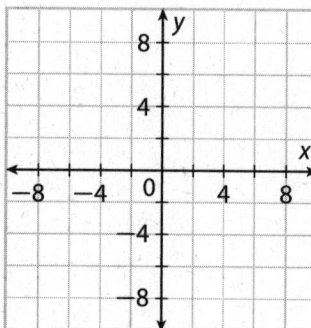

(C) The vertex of an absolute value function is the single point that both rays have in common. Identify the vertex of the parent absolute value function.

_____

Reflect

1. What is the domain of $f(x) = |x|$? What is the range?

_____

2. For what values of x is the function $f(x) = |x|$ increasing? decreasing?

_____

🔧 Explain 1   Graphing Translations of Absolute Value Functions

You can compare the graphs of absolute value functions in the form $g(x) = |x - h| + k$, where h and k are real numbers, with the graph of the parent function $f(x) = |x|$ to see how h and k affect the parent function.

Example 1   Graph each absolute value function with respect to the parent function $f(x) = |x|$.

(A) $g(x) = |x + 3| - 5$

First, create a table of values for x and $g(x)$.

x	$g(x) = |x + 3| - 5$
−6	−2
−3	−5
−1	−3
0	−2
1	−1
3	1
6	4

Now graph the function along with the parent function.

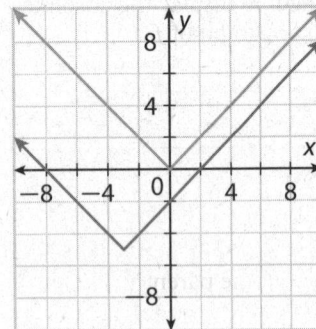

Ⓑ $g(x) = |x - 4| + 2$

First, create a table of values for x and $g(x)$.

x	$g(x) = |x - 4| + 2$
-5	
-3	
-1	
0	
1	
3	
5	

Now graph the function along with the parent function.

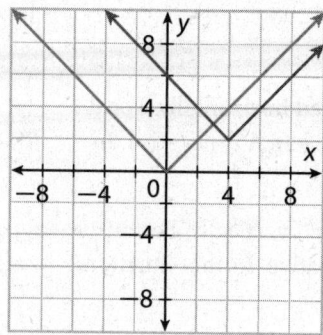

Reflect

3. How is the graph of $g(x) = |x - 4| + 2$ related to the graph of the parent function $f(x) = |x|$?

_____

_____

4. In general, how is the graph of $g(x) = |x - h| + k$ related to the graph of $f(x) = |x|$?

_____

_____

YourTurn

5. Graph the absolute value function $g(x) = |x + 1| + 2$ along with the parent function $f(x) = |x|$.

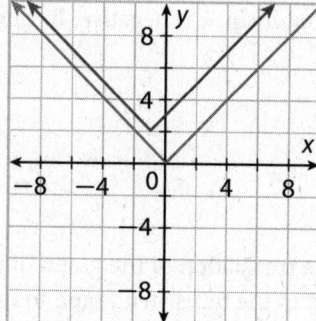

Constructing Functions for Given Graphs of Absolute Value Functions

You can write an absolute value function from a graph of the function.

Example 2 Write an equation for each absolute value function whose graph is shown.

(A)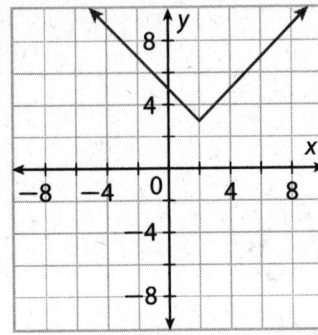

- *h* is the number of units that the parent function is translated horizontally. For a translation to the right, *h* is positive; for a translation to the left, *h* is negative. In this situation, $h = 2$.

- *k* is the number of units that the parent function is translated vertically. For a translation up, *k* is positive; for a translation down, *k* is negative. In this situation, $k = 3$.

The function is $g(x) = |x - 2| + 3$.

(B)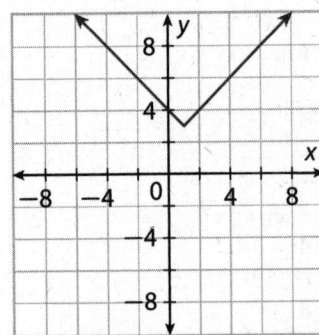

- *h* is the number of units that the parent function is translated horizontally. For a translation to the right, *h* is positive; for a translation to the left, *h* is negative. In this situation, $h = \boxed{}$.

- *k* is the number of units that the parent function is translated vertically. For a translation up, *k* is positive; for a translation down, *k* is negative. In this situation, $k = \boxed{}$.

The function is $g(x) = \left| x - \boxed{} \right| + \boxed{}$.

Reflect

6. If the graph of an absolute value function is a translation of the graph of the parent function, explain how you can use the vertex of the translated graph to help you determine the equation for the function.

YourTurn

7.

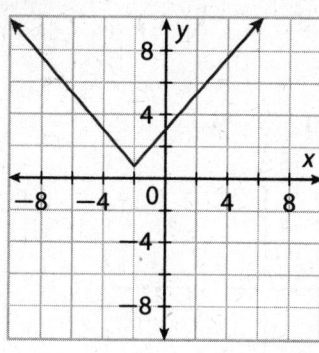

🎸 Explain 3 Graphing Stretches and Compressions of Absolute Value Functions

You can compare the graphs of absolute value functions in the form $g(x) = a|x|$, where a is a real number, with the graph of the parent function $f(x) = |x|$ to see how a affects the absolute value function.

Example 3 Graph each absolute value function.

(A) $g(x) = -2|x|$

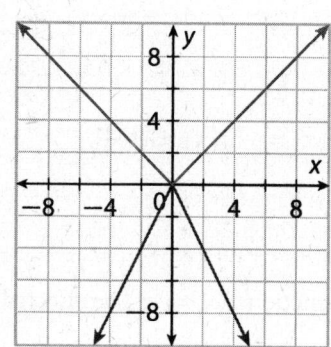

(B) $g(x) = \frac{1}{4}|x|$

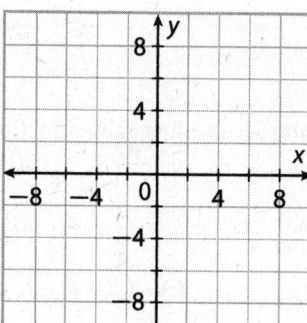

Reflect

8. Describe how the graphs of $g(x) = \frac{1}{4}|x|$ and $h(x) = -2|x|$ compare with the graph of $f(x) = |x|$. Use either the word *stretch* or *shrink*, and include the directions of movement.

_____

_____

9. What other transformation occurs when the value of a in $g(x) = a|x|$ is negative?

_____

Graph each absolute value function.

10. $g(x) = -\frac{1}{2}|x|$

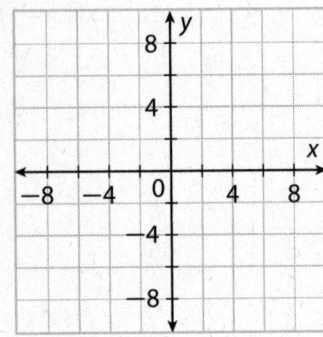

11. $g(x) = 4|x|$

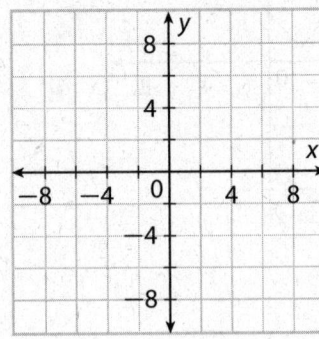

💬 Elaborate

12. Why is it important to note both the direction and the distance that a point has been translated either vertically or horizontally?

_____

_____

_____

13. How does knowing a point in the graph other than the vertex help you find the value of a?

_____

_____

_____

14. When graphing an absolute value function, how are $g(x) = a|x|$ and $h(x) = -a|x|$ related?

_____

_____

_____

15. Essential Question Check-In How would the graph of the parent function $f(x) = |x|$ be affected if $h > 0$, $k < 0$ and $a > 1$?

_____

_____

Personal
Math
Trainer

• Online Homework
• Hints and Help
• Extra Practice

Graph each absolute value function.

1. $g(x) = |x + 1| + 1$

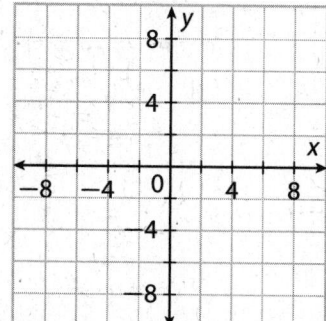

2. $g(x) = |x - 4| + 2$

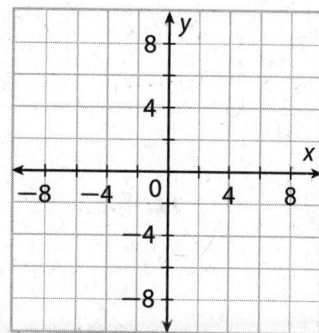

3. $g(x) = |x - 3| - 5$

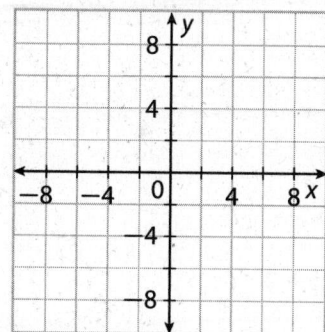

4. $g(x) = |x + 7| - 1$

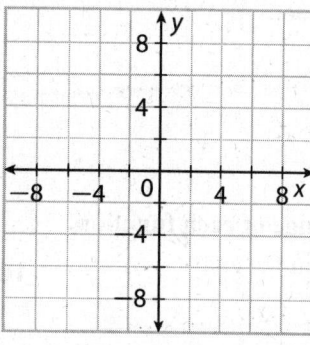

5. $g(x) = |x + 3| - 1$

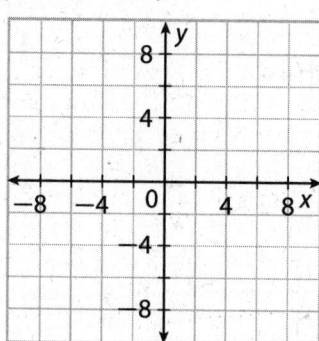

6. $g(x) = |x + 5| - 3$

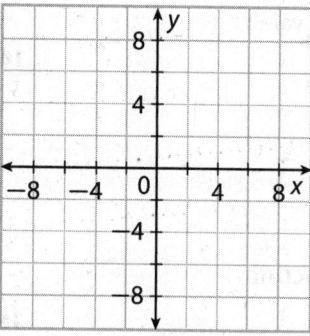

Write an equation for each absolute value function whose graph is shown.

7.

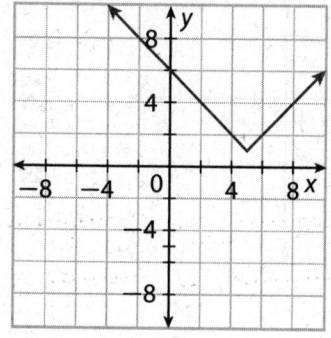

8.

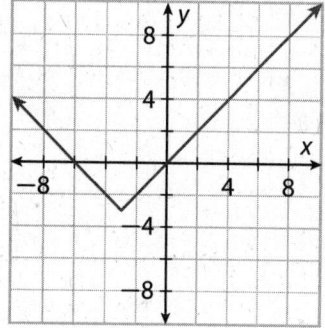

9.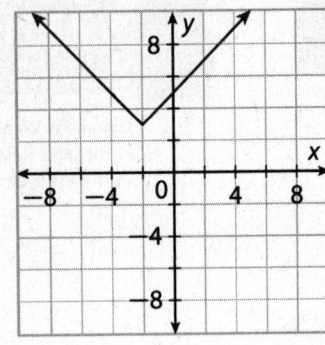

10.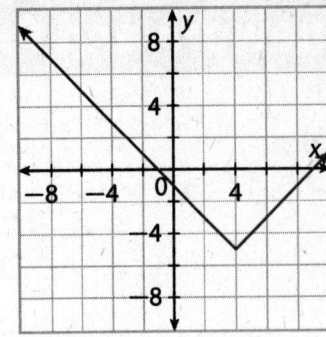

11.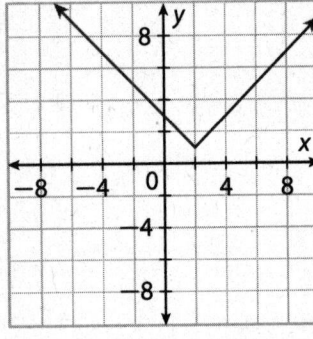

12.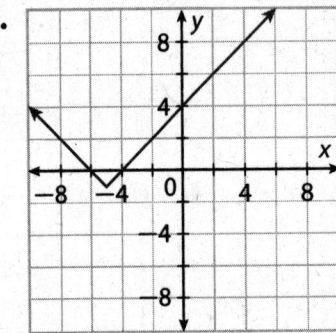

Determine the domain and range of each function.

13. $g(x) = |x + 3| - 1$

14. $g(x) = |x + 2| + 2$

15. $g(x) = |x| + 1$

16. $g(x) = |x - 9| + 6$

Graph each absolute value function.

17. $g(x) = 3|x|$

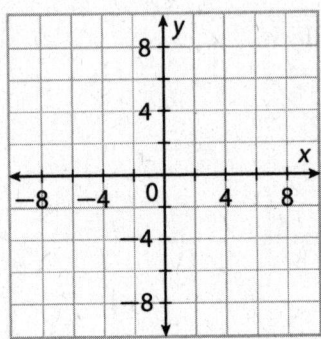

18. $g(x) = -2.5|x|$

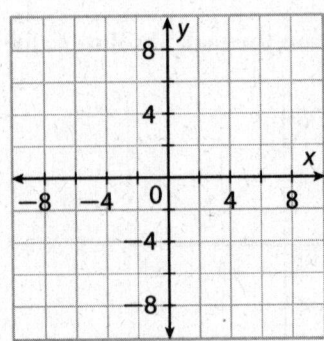

19. $g(x) = \frac{1}{2}|x|$

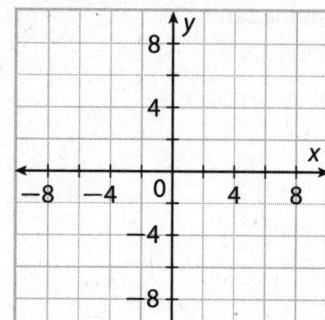

20. $g(x) = -\frac{2}{3}|x|$

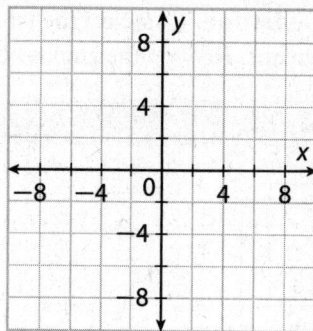

21. Identify the values of h, k, and a given each absolute value function.

   A. $f(x) = 3|x - 2| + 2$

   B. $f(x) = -0.2|x - 3| + 4$

   C. $f(x) = -5|x + 6| - 1$

   D. $f(x) = 0.5|x + 2| - 7$

   E. $f(x) = 0.8|x| + 3$

22. Body Temperature The average body temperature of a human is generally accepted to be 98.6 °F. Complete the absolute value function below describing the difference $d(x)$ in degrees Fahrenheit of the temperature x of an individual human and the average temperature of a human. How is the graph of $d(x)$ related to the graph of the parent function $f(x) = |x|$?

$d(x) = |x - \boxed{}|$

23. Population Statistics The average height of an American man is 69.3 inches. Complete the absolute value function below describing the difference $d(x)$ in inches of the height x of an individual American man and the average height of an American man. How is the graph of $d(x)$ related to the graph of the parent function $f(x) = |x|$?

$d(x) = |x - \boxed{}|$

24. Make a Prediction Complete the table and graph all the functions on the same coordinate plane. How do the graphs of $f(x) = a|x|$ and $g(x) = |ax|$ compare?

x	−6	−3	0	3	6
$g(x) = \frac{1}{3}|x|$					
$g(x) = \left|\frac{1}{3}x\right|$					
$g(x) = -\frac{1}{3}|x|$					
$g(x) = \left|-\frac{1}{3}x\right|$					

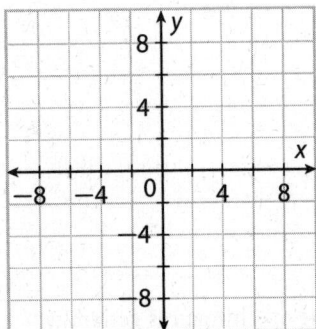

Multiple Representations Write an equation for each absolute value function whose graph is shown.

25.

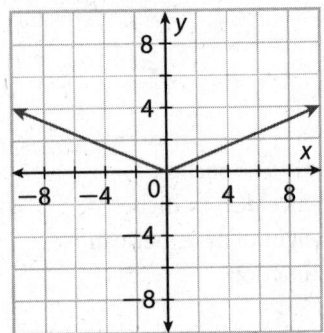

Note: One point on this graph is $(10, 4)$.

26.

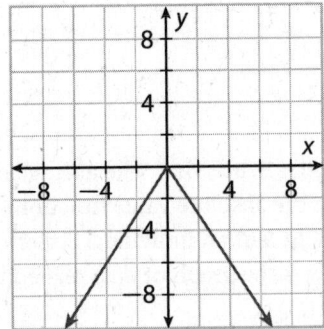

Note: One point on this graph is $(6, -9)$.

© Houghton Mifflin Harcourt Publishing Company

27. Represent Real-World Problems From his driveway at point $(4, 6)$, Kerry is adjusting his rearview mirror before backing out onto the street. The farthest object behind him to the left he can see is a neighbor's mailbox at $(-4, 12)$. The farthest object behind him to the right he can see is a telephone pole at $(20, 18)$. Create an absolute value function in the form $f(x) = a|x - h| + k$, with Kerry at the vertex, to represent the boundaries of Kerry's visual field in the rearview mirror. Graph the function, and label Kerry, the mailbox, and the telephone pole.

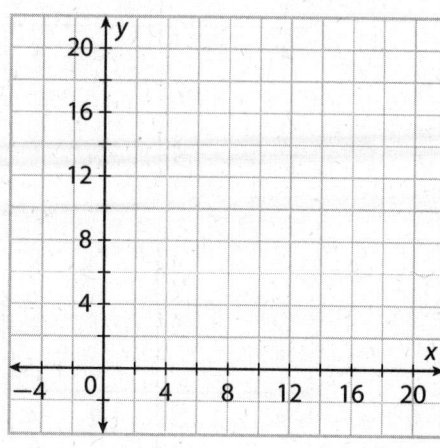

Lesson Performance Task

Geese are initially flying south in a V-shaped pattern that can be modeled by the absolute value function $f(x) = a|x - h| + k$, where a represents the growth or shrinkage of the distance between geese, k represents the height change of the flock, and h represents a left or right shift in the flock.

A. Graph the original flock function, $g(x) = |x|$. State the function's domain and range in words.

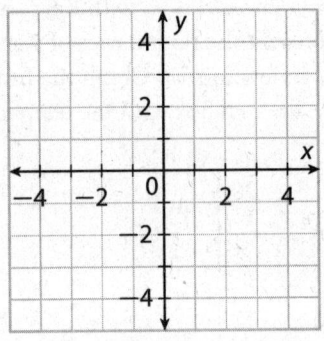

B. While flying south, the flock encounters a jet stream and is forced to drop 2 feet. Write the new equation and graph this function along with the original. State the new function's domain and range in words.

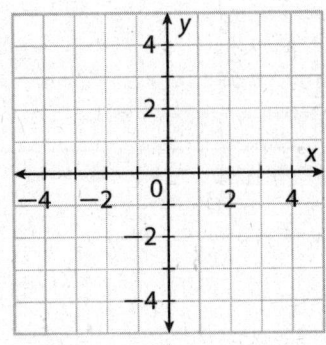

C. A short while after passing through the jet stream, the flock of geese encounters a rain storm and is forced to double the distance between each of its members in order to avoid colliding with one another. Write the new equation and graph all three functions. State the new function's domain and range in words.

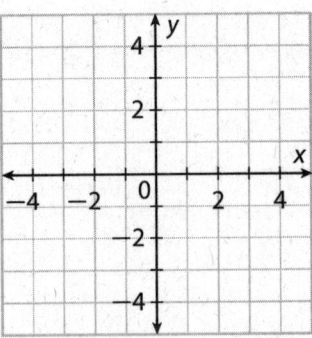

13.3 Solving Absolute Value Equations

Essential Question: How can you solve an absolute value equation?

⊙ Explore **Solving Absolute Value Equations Graphically**

Absolute value equations differ from linear equations in that they may have two solutions. This is indicated with a **disjunction**, a mathematical statement created by a connecting two other statements with the word "or." To see why there can be two solutions, you can solve an absolute value equation using graphs.

(A) Solve the equation $2|x - 5| - 4 = 2$.

Plot the function $f(x) = 2|x - 5| - 4$ on the grid. Then plot the function $g(x) = 2$ as a horizontal line on the same grid, and mark the points where the graphs intersect.

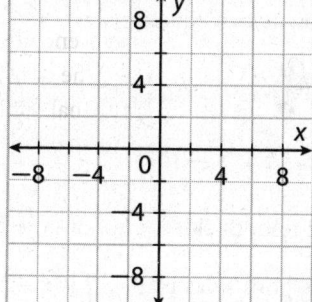

(B) Write the solution to this equation as a disjunction:

$x =$ _____ or $x =$ _____

Reflect

1. Why might you expect most absolute value equations to have two solutions? Why not three or four?

_____

_____

_____

_____

2. Is it possible for an absolute value equation to have no solutions? one solution? If so, what would each look like graphically?

_____

_____

_____

_____

Explain 1 — Solving Absolute Value Equations Algebraically

To solve absolute value equations algebraically, first isolate the absolute value expression on one side of the equation the same way you would isolate a variable. Then use the rule:

If $|x| = a$ (where a is a positive number), then $x = a$ OR $x = -a$.

Notice the use of a **disjunction** here in the rule for values of x. You cannot know from the original equation whether the expression inside the absolute value bars is positive or negative, so you must work through both possibilities to finish isolating x.

Example 1 Solve each absolute value equation algebraically. Graph the solutions on a number line.

(A) $|3x| + 2 = 8$

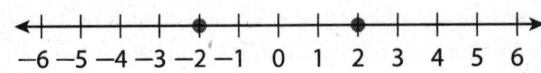

Subtract 2 from both sides. $|3x| = 6$

Rewrite as two equations. $3x = 6$ or $3x = -6$

Solve for x. $x = 2$ or $x = -2$

(B) $3|4x - 5| - 2 = 19$

Add 2 to both sides. $3|4x - 5| = \boxed{}$

Divide both sides by 3. $|4x - 5| = \boxed{}$

Rewrite as two equations. $4x - 5 = \boxed{}$ or $4x - 5 = \boxed{}$

Add 5 to all four sides. $4x = \boxed{}$ or $4x = \boxed{}$

Solve for x. $x = \boxed{}$ or $x = -\dfrac{\boxed{}}{\boxed{}}$

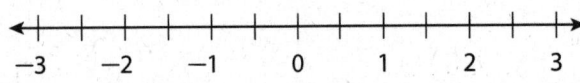

Your Turn

Solve each absolute value equation algebraically. Graph the solutions on a number line.

3. $\frac{1}{2}|x + 2| = 10$

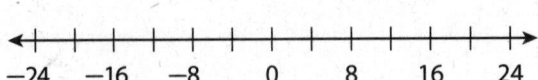

4. $-2|3x - 6| + 5 = 1$

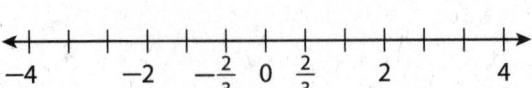

Explain 2   Absolute Value Equations with Fewer than Two Solutions

You have seen that absolute value equations have two solutions when the isolated absolute value expression is equal to a positive number. When the absolute value is equal to zero, there is a single solution because zero is its own opposite. When the absolute value expression is equal to a negative number, there is no solution because absolute value is never negative.

Example 2   Isolate the absolute value expression in each equation to determine if the equation can be solved. If so, finish the solution. If not, write "no solution."

(A) $-5|x + 1| + 2 = 12$

Subtract 2 from both sides. $-5|x + 1| = 10$

Divide both sides by -5. $|x + 1| = -2$

Absolute values are never negative.   No Solution

(B) $\frac{3}{5}|2x - 4| - 3 = -3$

Add 3 to both sides. $\frac{3}{5}|2x - 4| = \boxed{}$

Multiply both sides by $\frac{5}{3}$. $|2x - 4| = \boxed{}$

Rewrite as one equation. $2x - 4 = \boxed{}$

Add 4 to both sides. $2x = \boxed{}$

Divide both sides by 2. $x = \boxed{}$

Your Turn

Isolate the absolute value expression in each equation to determine if the equation can be solved. If so, finish the solution. If not, write "no solution."

5. $3\left|\frac{1}{2}x + 5\right| + 7 = 5$

6. $9\left|\frac{4}{3}x - 2\right| + 7 = 7$

7. Why is important to solve both equations in the disjunction arising from an absolute value equation? Why not just pick one and solve it, knowing the solution for the variable will work when plugged backed into the equation?

_____

_____

_____

_____

_____

8. **Discussion** Discuss how the range of the absolute value function differs from the range of a linear function. Graphically, how does this explain why a linear equation always has exactly one solution while an absolute value equation can have one, two, or no solutions?

_____

_____

_____

_____

_____

_____

_____

9. **Essential Question Check-In** Describe, in your own words, the basic steps to solving absolute value equations and how many solutions to expect.

_____

_____

_____

_____

_____

_____

_____

Solve the following absolute value equations by graphing.

1. $|x - 3| + 2 = 5$

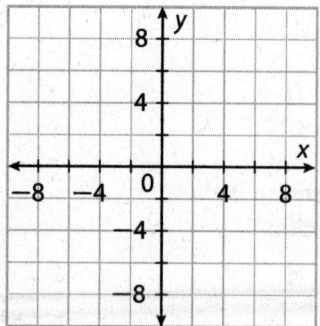

2. $2|x + 1| + 5 = 9$

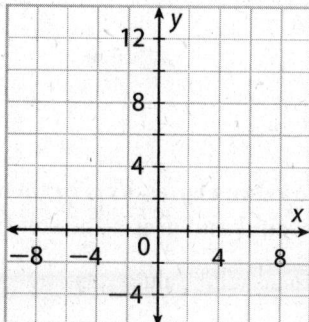

3. $-2|x + 5| + 4 = 2$

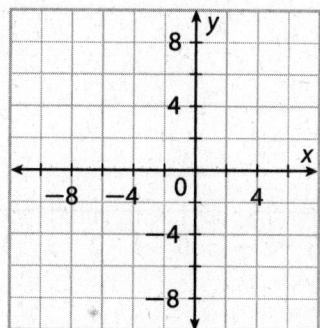

4. $\left|\dfrac{3}{2}(x - 2)\right| + 3 = 2$

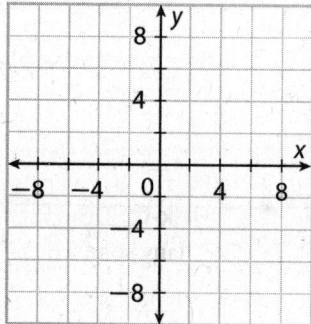

Solve each absolute value equation algebraically. Graph the solutions on a number line.

5. $|2x| = 3$

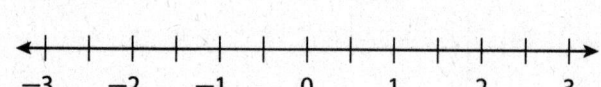

6. $\left|\dfrac{1}{3}x + 4\right| = 3$

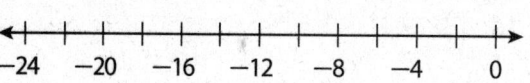

7. $3|2x - 3| + 2 = 3$

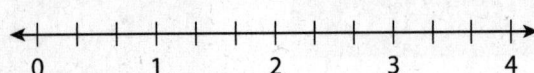

8. $-8|-x - 6| + 10 = 2$

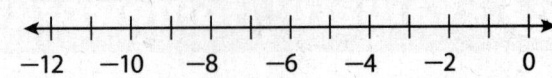

Isolate the absolute value expressions in the following equations to determine if they can be solved. If so, find and graph the solution(s). If not, write "no solution".

9. $\frac{1}{4}|x + 2| + 7 = 5$

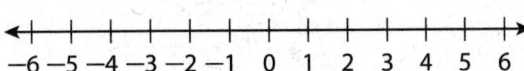

10. $-3|x - 3| + 3 = 6$

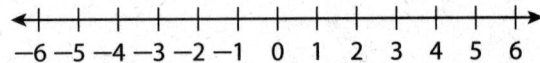

11. $2\left(|x + 4| + 3\right) = 6$

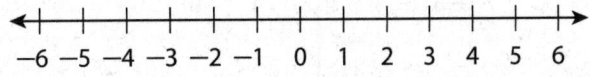

12. $5|2x + 4| - 3 = -3$

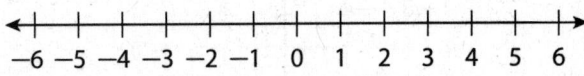

Solve the absolute value equations.

13. $|3x - 4| + 2 = 1$

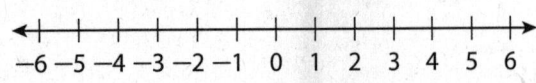

14. $7\left|\frac{1}{2}x + 3\frac{1}{2}\right| - 2 = 5$

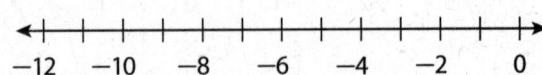

15. $\left|2(x+5)-3\right|+2=6$

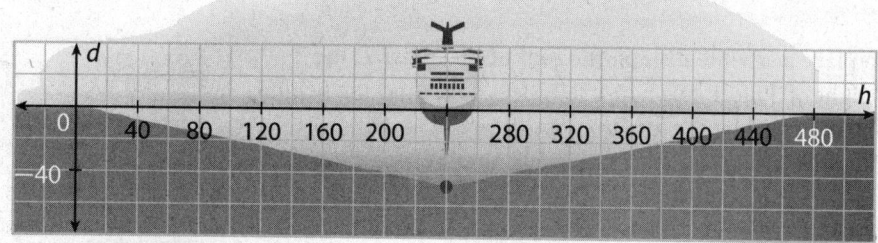

16. $-5\left|-3x+2\right|-2=-2$

17. The bottom of a river makes a V-shape that can be modeled with the absolute value function, $d(h)=\frac{1}{5}\left|h-240\right|-48$, where d is the depth of the river bottom (in feet) and h is the horizontal distance to the left-hand shore (in feet).

A ship risks running aground if the bottom of its keel (its lowest point under the water) reaches down to the river bottom. Suppose you are the harbormaster and you want to place buoys where the river bottom is 30 feet below the surface. How far from the left-hand shore should you place the buoys?

18. A flock of geese is flying past a photographer in a V-formation that can be described using the absolute value function $b(d)=\frac{3}{2}\left|d-50\right|$, where $b(d)$ is the distance (in feet) of a goose behind the leader, and d is the distance from the photographer. If the flock reaches 27 feet behind the leader on both sides, find the distance of the nearest goose to the photographer.

19. Geometry Find the points where a circle centered at (3, 0) with a radius of 5 crosses the x-axis. Use an absolute value equation and the fact that all points on a circle are the same distance (the radius) from the center.

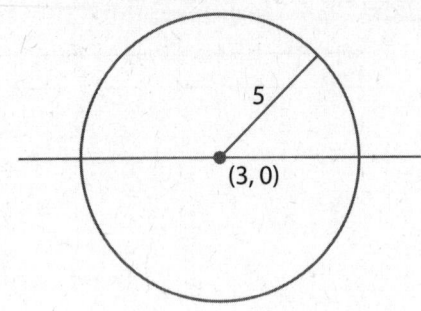

(3, 0)

20. Select the value or values of x that satisfy the equation $-\frac{1}{2}|3x - 3| + 2 = 1$.

A. $x = \frac{5}{3}$ B. $x = -\frac{5}{3}$

C. $x = \frac{1}{3}$ D. $x = -\frac{1}{3}$

E. $x = 3$ F. $x = -3$

G. $x = 1$ H. $x = -1$

21. Terry is trying to place a satellite dish on the roof of his house at the recommended height of 30 feet. His house is 32 feet wide, and the height of the roof can be described by the function $h(x) = -\frac{3}{2}|x - 16| + 24$, where x is the distance along the width of the house. Where should Terry place the dish?

H.O.T. Focus on Higher Order Thinking

22. **Explain the Error** While attempting to solve the equation $-3|x - 4| - 4 = 3$, a student came up with the following results. Explain the error and find the correct solution:

$$-3|x - 4| - 4 = 3$$

$$-3|x - 4| = 7$$

$$|x - 4| = -\frac{7}{3}$$

$$x - 4 = -\frac{7}{3} \quad \text{or} \quad x - 4 = \frac{7}{3}$$

$$x = \frac{5}{3} \quad \text{or} \quad x = \frac{19}{3}$$

23. Communicate Mathematical Ideas Solve this absolute value equation and explain what algebraic properties make it possible to do so.

$$3|x-2| = 5|x-2| - 7$$

24. Justify Your Reasoning This absolute value equation has nested absolute values. Use your knowledge of solving absolute value equations to solve this equation. Justify the number of possible solutions.

$$\left| |2x+5| - 3 \right| = 10$$

25. Check for Reasonableness For what type of real-world quantities would the negative answer for an absolute value equation not make sense?

Lesson Performance Task

A snowball comes apart as a child throws it north, resulting in two halves traveling away from the child. The child is standing 12 feet south and 6 feet east of the school door, along an east-west wall. One fragment flies off to the northeast, moving 2 feet east for every 5 feet north of travel, and the other moves 2 feet west for every 5 feet north of travel. Write an absolute value function that describes the northward position, $n(e)$, of both fragments as a function of how far east of the school door they are. How far apart are the fragments when they strike the wall?

13.4 Solving Absolute Value Inequalities

Resource
Locker

Essential Question: What are two ways to solve an absolute value inequality?

⊘ Explore Visualizing the Solution Set of an Absolute Value Inequality

You know that when solving an absolute value equation, it's possible to get two solutions. Here, you will explore what happens when you solve absolute value inequalities.

Ⓐ Determine whether each of the integers from −5 to 5 is a solution of the inequality $|x| + 2 < 5$. Write *yes* or *no* for each number in the table. If a number is a solution, plot it on the number line.

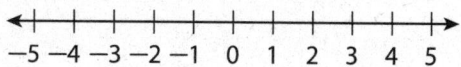

Number	Solution?
$x = -5$	
$x = -4$	
$x = -3$	
$x = -2$	
$x = -1$	
$x = 0$	
$x = 1$	
$x = 2$	
$x = 3$	
$x = 4$	
$x = 5$	

Ⓑ Determine whether each of the integers from −5 to 5 is a solution of the inequality $|x| + 2 > 5$. Write *yes* or *no* for each number in the table. If a number is a solution, plot it on the number line.

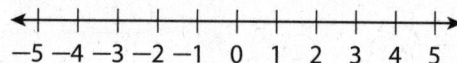

Number	Solution?
$x = -5$	
$x = -4$	
$x = -3$	
$x = -2$	
$x = -1$	
$x = 0$	
$x = 1$	
$x = 2$	
$x = 3$	
$x = 4$	
$x = 5$	

Ⓒ State the solutions of the equation $|x| + 2 = 5$ and relate them to the solutions you found for the inequalities in Steps A and B.

_____

_____

Ⓓ If x is any real number and not just an integer, graph the solutions of $|x| + 2 < 5$ and $|x| + 2 > 5$.

Graph of all real solutions of $|x| + 2 < 5$:

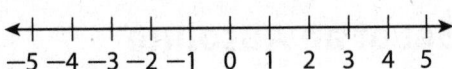
−5 −4 −3 −2 −1 0 1 2 3 4 5

Graph of all real solutions of $|x| + 2 > 5$:

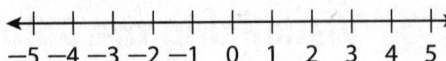
−5 −4 −3 −2 −1 0 1 2 3 4 5

Reflect

1. It's possible to describe the solutions of $|x| + 2 < 5$ and $|x| + 2 > 5$ using inequalities that don't involve absolute value. For instance, you can write the solutions of $|x| + 2 < 5$ as $x > -3$ and $x < 3$. Notice that the word *and* is used because x must be both greater than -3 and less than 3. How would you write the solutions of $|x| + 2 > 5$? Explain.

_____

_____

2. Describe the solutions of $|x| + 2 \leq 5$ and $|x| + 2 \geq 5$ using inequalities that don't involve absolute value.

_____

_____

🔧 Explain 1   Solving Absolute Value Inequalities Graphically

You can use a graph to solve an absolute value inequality of the form $f(x) > g(x)$ or $f(x) < g(x)$, where $f(x)$ is an absolute value function and $g(x)$ is a constant function. Graph each function separately on the same coordinate plane and determine the intervals on the x-axis where one graph lies above or below the other. For $f(x) > g(x)$, you want to find the x-values for which the graph $f(x)$ is above the graph of $g(x)$. For $f(x) < g(x)$, you want to find the x-values for which the graph of $f(x)$ is below the graph of $g(x)$.

Example 1   Solve the inequality graphically.

Ⓐ $|x + 3| + 1 > 4$

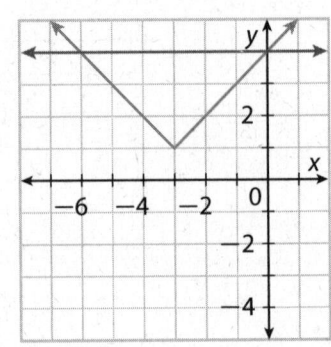

The inequality is of the form $f(x) > g(x)$, so determine the intervals on the x-axis where the graph of $f(x) = |x + 3| + 1$ lies above the graph of $g(x) = 4$.

The graph of $f(x) = |x + 3| + 1$ lies above the graph of $g(x) = 4$ to the left of $x = -6$ and to the right of $x = 0$, so the solution of $|x + 3| + 1 > 4$ is $x < -6$ or $x > 0$.

Ⓑ $|x-2|-3<1$

The inequality is of the form $f(x) < g(x)$, so determine the intervals

on the x-axis where the graph of $f(x) = |x-2|-3$ lies _____
the graph of $g(x) = 1$.

The graph of $f(x) = |x-2|-3$ lies _____ the graph of

$g(x) = 1$ between $x =$ ☐ and $x =$ ☐ , so the solution of

$|x-2|-3<1$ is $x >$ ☐ and $x <$ ☐ .

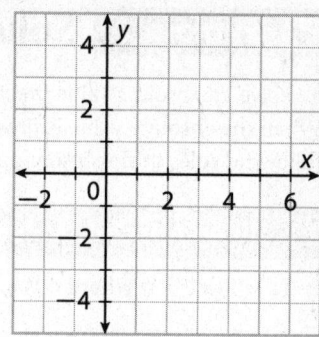

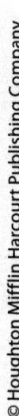
© Houghton Mifflin Harcourt Publishing Company

Reflect

3. Suppose the inequality in Part A is $|x+3|+1 \geq 4$ instead of $|x+3|+1 > 4$. How does the solution change?

_____

4. In Part B, what is another way to write the solution $x > -2$ and $x < 6$?

_____

5. **Discussion** Suppose the graph of an absolute value function $f(x)$ lies entirely above the graph of the constant function $g(x)$. What is the solution of the inequality $f(x) > g(x)$? What is the solution of the inequality $f(x) < g(x)$?

_____

_____

_____

_____

Your Turn

6. Solve $|x+1|-4 \leq -2$ graphically.

Explain 2 Solving Absolute Value Inequalities Algebraically

To solve an absolute value inequality algebraically, start by isolating the absolute value expression. When the absolute value expression is by itself on one side of the inequality, apply one of the following rules to finish solving the inequality for the variable.

> **Solving Absolute Value Inequalities Algebraically**
>
> **1.** If $|x| > a$ where a is a positive number, then $x < -a$ or $x > a$.
>
> **2.** If $|x| < a$ where a is a positive number, then $-a < x < a$.

Example 2 Solve the inequality algebraically. Graph the solution on a number line.

Ⓐ $|4 - x| + 15 > 21$

$|4 - x| > 6$

$4 - x < -6$ or $4 - x > 6$

$-x < -10$ or $-x > 2$

$x > 10$ or $x < -2$

The solution is $x > 10$ or $x < -2$.

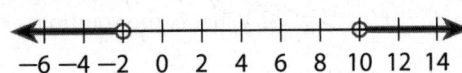

Ⓑ $|x + 4| - 10 \le -2$

$|x + 4| \le \boxed{}$

$x + 4 \ge \boxed{}$ and $x + 4 \le \boxed{}$

$x \ge \boxed{}$ and $x \le \boxed{}$

The solution is $x \ge \boxed{}$ and $x \le \boxed{}$,

or $\boxed{} \le x \le \boxed{}$.

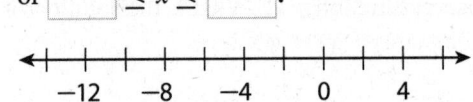

Reflect

7. In Part A, suppose the inequality were $|4 - x| + 15 > 14$ instead of $|4 - x| + 15 > 21$. How would the solution change? Explain.

_____

_____

_____

8. In Part B, suppose the inequality were $|x + 4| - 10 \le -11$ instead of $|x + 4| - 10 \le -2$. How would the solution change? Explain.

_____

_____

_____

_____

Solve the inequality algebraically. Graph the solution on a number line.

9. $3|x-7| \geq 9$

10. $|2x+3| < 5$

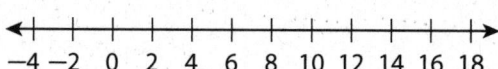

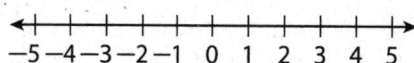

⏱ Explain 3   Solving a Real-World Problem with Absolute Value Inequalities

Absolute value inequalities are often used to model real-world situations involving a margin of error or *tolerance*. Tolerance is the allowable amount of variation in a quantity.

Example 3

A machine at a lumber mill cuts boards that are 3.25 meters long. It is acceptable for the length to differ from this value by at most 0.02 meters. Write and solve an absolute value inequality to find the range of acceptable lengths.

🧩 Analyze Information

Identify the important information.

- The boards being cut are [   ] meters long.
- The length can differ by at most 0.02 meters.

🧩 Formulate a Plan

Let the length of a board be ℓ. Since the sign of the difference between ℓ and 3.25 doesn't matter, take the absolute value of the difference. Since the absolute value of the difference can be at most 0.02, the inequality that models the situation is

$$\left| \ell - \boxed{} \right| \leq \boxed{}.$$

🧩 Solve

$$|\ell - 3.25| \leq 0.02$$

$$\ell - 3.25 \geq -0.02 \text{ and } \ell - 3.25 \leq 0.02$$

$$\ell \geq \boxed{} \text{ and } \qquad \ell \leq \boxed{}$$

So, the range of acceptable lengths is $\boxed{} \leq \ell \leq \boxed{}$.

Justify and Evaluate

The bounds of the range are positive and close to [ ], so this is a reasonable answer.

The answer is correct since [ ] $+ 0.02 = 3.25$ and [ ] $- 0.02 = 3.25$.

11. A box of cereal is supposed to weigh 13.8 oz, but it's acceptable for the weight to vary as much as 0.1 oz. Write and solve an absolute value inequality to find the range of acceptable weights.

Elaborate

12. Describe the values of x that satisfy the inequalities $|x| < a$ and $|x| > a$ where a is a positive constant.

_____

_____

_____

13. How do you algebraically solve an absolute value inequality?

_____

_____

_____

14. Explain why the solution of $|x| > a$ is all real numbers if a is a negative number.

_____

_____

15. **Essential Question Check-In** How do you solve an absolute value inequality graphically?

_____

_____

_____

✪ Evaluate: Homework and Practice

• Online Homework
• Hints and Help
• Extra Practice

1. Determine whether each of the integers from −5 to 5 is a solution of the inequality $|x - 1| + 3 \geq 5$. If a number is a solution, plot it on the number line.

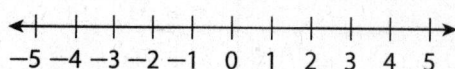

2. Determine whether each of the integers from −5 to 5 is a solution of the inequality $|x + 1| - 2 \leq 1$. If a number is a solution, plot it on the number line.

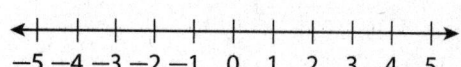

Solve each inequality graphically.

3. $2|x| \leq 6$

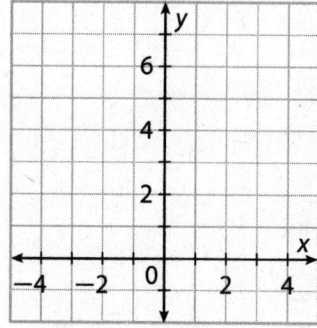

4. $|x - 3| - 2 > -1$

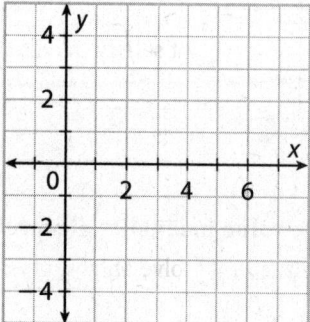

5. $\frac{1}{2}|x| + 2 < 3$

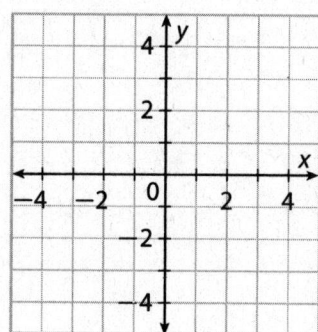

6. $|x + 2| - 4 \geq -2$

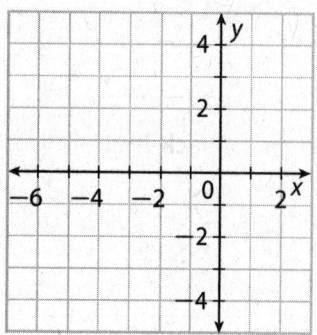

Match each graph with the corresponding absolute value inequality. Then give the solution of the inequality.

A. $2|x| + 1 > 3$　　　B. $2|x+1| < 3$　　　C. $2|x| - 1 > 3$　　　D. $2|x-1| < 3$

7.

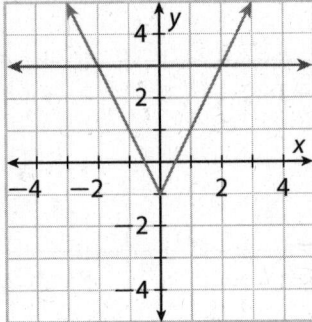

8.

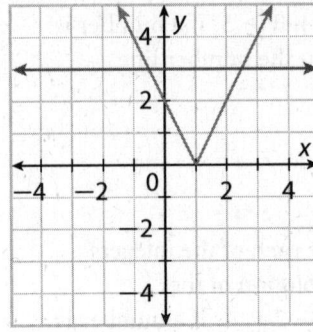

9.

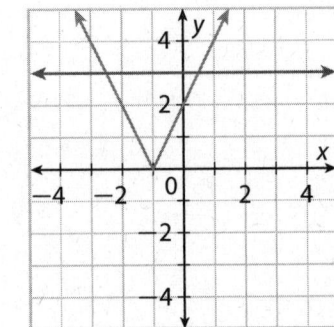

10.

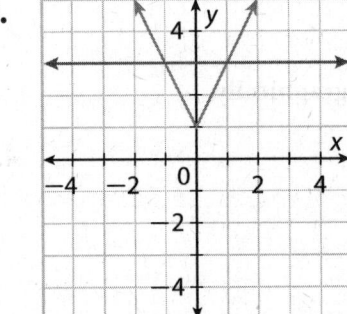

Solve each absolute value inequality algebraically. Graph the solution on a number line.

11. $2\left|x - \dfrac{7}{2}\right| + 3 > 4$

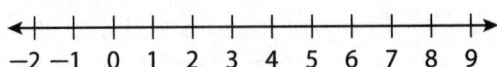

12. $|2x + 1| - 4 < 5$

13. $3|x + 4| + 2 \geq 5$

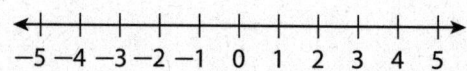

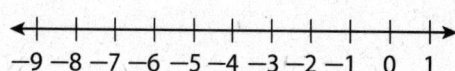

14. $|x + 11| - 8 \leq -3$

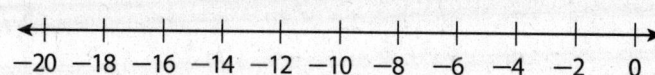

15. $-5|x - 3| - 5 < 15$

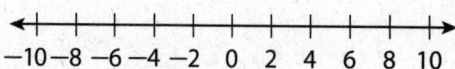

16. $8|x + 4| + 10 < 2$

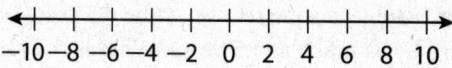

Solve each problem using an absolute value inequality.

17. The thermostat for a house is set to 68 °F, but the actual temperature may vary by as much as 2 °F. What is the range of possible temperatures?

18. The balance of Jason's checking account is $320. The balance varies by as much as $80 each week. What are the possible balances of Jason's account?

19. On average, a squirrel lives to be 6.5 years old. The lifespan of a squirrel may vary by as much as 1.5 years. What is the range of ages that a squirrel lives?

20. You are playing a history quiz game where you must give the years of historical events. In order to score any points at all for a question about the year in which a man first stepped on the moon, your answer must be no more than 3 years away from the correct answer, 1969. What is the range of answers that allow you to score points?

21. The speed limit on a road is 30 miles per hour. Drivers on this road typically vary their speed around the limit by as much as 5 miles per hour. What is the range of typical speeds on this road?

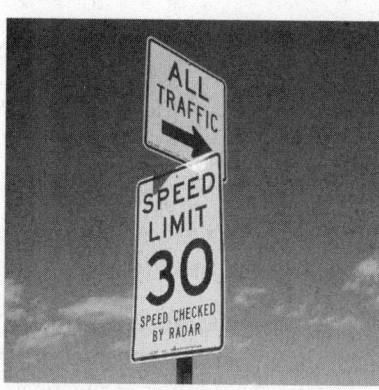

22. Represent Real-World Problems A poll of likely voters shows that the incumbent will get 51% of the vote in an upcoming election. Based on the number of voters polled, the results of the poll could be off by as much as 3 percentage points. What does this mean for the incumbent?

23. Explain the Error A student solved the inequality $|x - 1| - 3 > 1$ graphically. Identify and correct the student's error.

I graphed the functions $f(x) = |x - 1| - 3$ and $g(x) = 1$. Because the graph of $g(x)$ lies above the graph of $f(x)$ between $x = -3$ and $x = 5$, the solution of the inequality is $-3 < x < 5$.

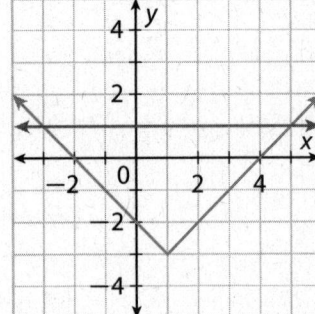

24. Multi-Step Recall that a literal equation or inequality is one in which the constants have been replaced by letters.

    a. Solve $|ax + b| > c$ for x. Write the solution in terms of a, b, and c. Assume that $a > 0$ and $c \geq 0$.

    b. Use the solution of the literal inequality to find the solution of $|10x + 21| > 14$.

    c. Explain why you must assume that $a > 0$ and $c \geq 0$ before you begin solving the literal inequality.

Lesson Performance Task

The distance between the Sun and each planet in our solar system varies because the planets travel in elliptical orbits around the Sun. Here is a table of the average distance and the variation in the distance for the five innermost planets in our solar system.

	Average Distance	Variation
Mercury	36 million miles	7.5 million miles
Venus	67.2 million miles	0.5 million miles
Earth	92.75 million miles	1.75 million miles
Mars	141 million miles	13 million miles
Jupiter	484 million miles	24 million miles

a. Write and solve an inequality to represent the range of distances that can occur between the Sun and each planet.

b. Calculate the percentage variation (variation divided by average distance) in the orbit of each of the planets. Based on these percentages, which planet has the most elliptical orbit?

Piecewise-Defined Functions

Essential Question: How can you use piecewise-defined functions to solve real-world problems?

Key Vocabulary

absolute-value equation
   (ecuación de valor absoluto)
absolute-value function
   (función de valor absoluto)
mean *(media)*
greatest integer function
   (función de entero mayor)
piecewise function *(función a trozos)*
step function *(función escalón)*

KEY EXAMPLE   (Lesson 13.1)

Graph the piecewise function $f(x) = \begin{cases} -2x & \text{if } x \le 2 \\ \frac{1}{2}x + 1 & \text{if } x > 2 \end{cases}$.

x	−4	−2	0	2	4	6
f(x)	−2(−4) = 8	−2(−2) = 4	−2(0) = 0	−2(2) = −4	$\frac{1}{2}(4) + 1 = 3$	$\frac{1}{2}(6) + 1 = 4$

The transition from one rule to the other occurs at $x = 2$. Show a closed dot at $(2, -4)$, since this point is part of the graph. Show an open dot at $(2, 2)$, since this is not part of the graph.

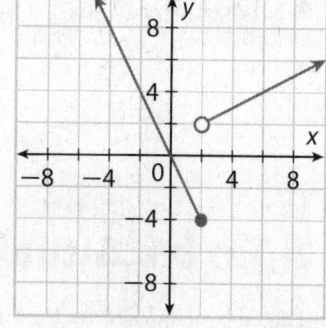

KEY EXAMPLE   (Lesson 13.3)

Solve $-4\left|x + 5\right| = -2$.

$\left|x + 5\right| = \frac{1}{2}$ Divide both sides by −4.

$x + 5 = \frac{1}{2}$ or $x + 5 = -\frac{1}{2}$ Write as two equations.

$x = -4\frac{1}{2}$ or $x = -5\frac{1}{2}$ Subtract 5 from both sides.

KEY EXAMPLE   (Lesson 13.4)

Solve $\frac{1}{2}|x| - 3 \le 1$ graphically.

Let $f(x) = \frac{1}{2}|x| - 3$ and $g(x) = 1$.

Graph $f(x)$ and $g(x)$.

Determine when $f(x) \le g(x)$.

The solution is $x \ge -8$ and $x \le 8$.

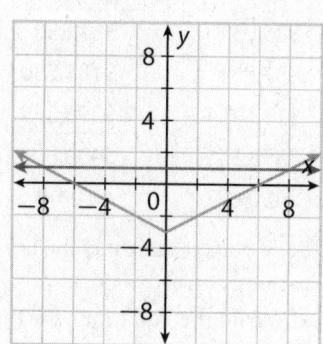

EXERCISES

1. Complete the table of values for $f(x) = \begin{cases} x - 3 & \text{if } x < -1 \\ -2x + 4 & \text{if } x \geq -1 \end{cases}$. Graph the function. *(Lesson 13.1)*

x	f(x)
−3	
−2	
−1	
0	
1	
2	
3	

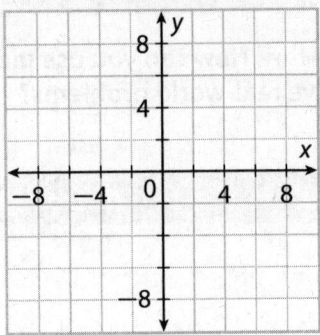

Solve each equation and inequality. *(Lesson 13.3)*

2. $6|x| + 4 = -2$

3. $2|4x - 1| = 6$

4. $|2x + 3| + 7 = 7$

5. $|x + 4| - 12 \leq 20$

MODULE PERFORMANCE TASK

A Taxing Situation

The table below defines the amount of income tax a single U.S. taxpayer must pay to the federal government for income earned in 2013.

If taxable income is over	but not over	the tax is
$0	$8,925	10% of the amount over $0
$8,926	$36,250	$892.50 plus 15% of the amount over $8,925
$36,251	$87,850	$4,991.25 plus 25% of the amount over $36,250
$87,851	$183,250	$17,891.25 plus 28% of the amount over $87,850
$183,251	$398,350	$44,603.25 plus 33% of the amount over $183,250
$398,351	$400,000	$115,586.25 plus 35% of the amount over $398,350
$400,001	no limit	$116,163.75 plus 39.6% of the amount over $400,000

So, if your taxable income is $30,000, you owe $892.50 plus 15% of the amount by which your earnings exceed $8,925.

- Write the equations for the piecewise-defined function that gives the income tax y on taxable income of x (where $x \leq \$100,000$).
- Graph the function.
- Find the percent of total taxable income that a person making $50,000 and a person making $100,000 pay in income tax.

Use your own paper to work on the task. Then use numbers, words, or algebra to explain how you reached your conclusion.

(Ready) to Go On?

13.1–13.4 Piecewise-Defined Functions

- Online Homework
- Hints and Help
- Extra Practice

Write a function to represent each graph shown. *(Lesson 13.1)*

1.

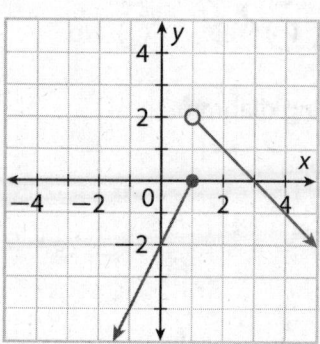

2.

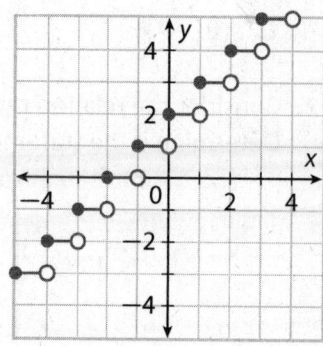

3. The graph of $g(x)$ is a transformation of the graph of $f(x) = |x|$ left 2 units and reflected across the x-axis. Write a function for $g(x)$, and graph $g(x)$. *(Lesson 13.2)*

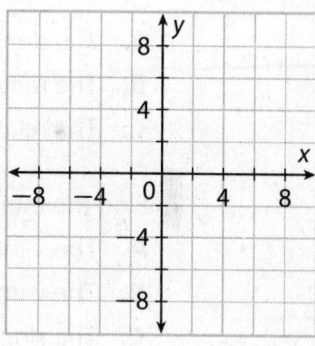

Solve each equation and inequality. *(Lessons 13.3, 13.4)*

4. $|5x| + 4 = 19$

5. $|2x| + 3 \geq 11$

6. $|4x + 2| - 2 = -18$

7. $|x + 8| - 5 < 2$

ESSENTIAL QUESTION

8. Write a real-world situation that could be modeled by $|x - 14| \leq 3$.

Assessment Readiness

1. Consider the function $f(x) = \begin{cases} 3 & \text{if } x < 2 \\ -x + 1 & \text{if } 2 \le x < 6 \\ x & \text{if } x \ge 6 \end{cases}$. Determine if each of the following is a solution of f(x). Select Yes or No for each possible solution.

   A. $(-5, 3)$ ◯ Yes ◯ No

   B. $(2, -1)$ ◯ Yes ◯ No

   C. $(8, -7)$ ◯ Yes ◯ No

2. Consider the relation represented by the mapping diagram. Determine if the statement is True or False.

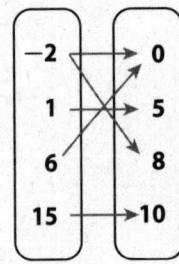

   A. The domain is $\{-2, 1, 6, 15\}$. ◯ True ◯ False

   B. The range is $\{0, 5, 8, 10\}$. ◯ True ◯ False

   C. The relation is a function. ◯ True ◯ False

3. Find the intercepts and slope of $8x - \frac{1}{2}y = 12$. Is the given statement True or False?

   A. The x-intercept is 4. ◯ True ◯ False

   B. The y-intercept is −24. ◯ True ◯ False

   C. The slope is 8. ◯ True ◯ False

4. How many solutions does the equation $|x + 6| - 4 = c$ have if $c = 5$? If $c = -10$? Justify your answers.

1. One equation of a system of two equations is $y = \frac{2}{5}x - 3$. If the second equation is one of the following, is the given number of solutions correct? Select Yes or No for each pair.

   A. $y = \frac{2}{5}x + 1$; no solutions ⃝ Yes ⃝ No

   B. $y = -2x - 3$; 1 solution ⃝ Yes ⃝ No

   C. $y = -\frac{2}{5}x - 3$; infinite number of solutions ⃝ Yes ⃝ No

2. Solve the system of equations $\begin{cases} 2x + 3y = 18 \\ x + y = 6 \end{cases}$.
   Determine if the given statement below is True or False.

   A. $x = 0$. ⃝ True ⃝ False

   B. $y = 6$. ⃝ True ⃝ False

   C. The only solution is $(0, 6)$. ⃝ True ⃝ False

3. Is the following a solution of the system $\begin{cases} y < 2x + 5 \\ y \geq -\frac{1}{2}x - 2 \end{cases}$?
   Select Yes or No for each possible solution.

   A. $(-1, 3)$ ⃝ Yes ⃝ No

   B. $(5, 2)$ ⃝ Yes ⃝ No

   C. $(0, 8)$ ⃝ Yes ⃝ No

4. Asif spent $745.10 on 13 new file cabinets for his office. Small file cabinets cost $43.50 and large file cabinets cost $65.95. Write and solve a system of equations to find the number of small cabinets and large cabinets he purchased.

   Determine if each statement is True or False.

   A. He purchased 5 small cabinets. ⃝ Yes ⃝ No

   B. He purchased 7 large cabinets. ⃝ Yes ⃝ No

   C. He spent $527.60 on large cabinets. ⃝ Yes ⃝ No

5. Solve $\frac{2}{3}|x - 6| \leq 8$. Is each of the following a solution of the inequality?
   Select Yes or No for each possible solution.

   A. $x = -6$ ⃝ Yes ⃝ No

   B. $x = 0$ ⃝ Yes ⃝ No

   C. $x = 20$ ⃝ Yes ⃝ No

6. Graph $y = \frac{1}{2}|x - 2| - 6$. Is the relation a function? Explain why or why not.

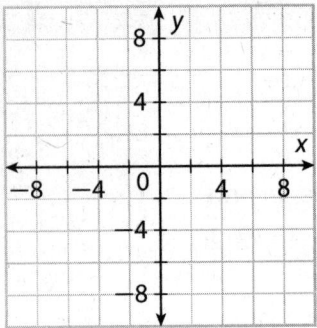

7. Write the system represented on the graph below. Find and explain the meaning of the point of intersection of the lines.

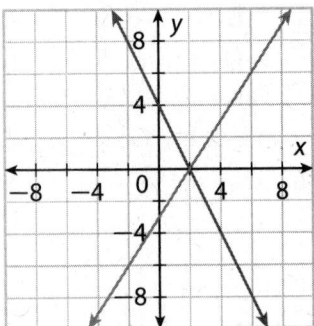

Performance Tasks

★ **8.** A coffee shop purchased 60 pounds of Guatemalan coffee beans and 90 pounds of Nicaraguan coffee beans. The total purchase price was $180. The next week it purchased 80 pounds of Guatemalan coffee and 20 pounds of Nicaraguan coffee, and the cost was $100. Write and solve a system of equations to find the cost per pound for both the Guatemalan and Nicaraguan coffee beans.

★★ **9.** A boat takes 6.5 hours to make a 70-mile trip upstream and 5 hours on the 70-mile return trip. Let v be the speed of the boat in still water and c be the speed of the current. Therefore, the upstream speed of the boat is $v - c$, and the downstream boat speed is $v + c$.

    A. Write two equations, one for the upstream part of the trip and one for the downstream part, relating boat speed, distance, and time.

    B. Solve the equations in part **A** for the speed of the current.

    C. How long would it take the boat to travel the 70 miles if there were no current? How did you determine your answer?

★★★**10.** Students are raising money for a field trip by selling scented candles and specialty soap. The candles cost $0.75 each and will be sold for $1.75. The soap costs $1.25 per bar and will be sold for $3.25. The students need to raise at least $200 to cover their trip costs.

    A. What is the profit per item for the candles and soap?

    B. Write an inequality that relates the number of candles c and the number of bars of soap s to the needed income.

    C. The wholesaler can supply no more than 80 bars of soap and no more than 140 candles. Graph the inequality from part **B** and these constraints, using number of candles for the vertical axis.

    D. What does the shaded area of your graph represent?

Personal Shopper Delia is a personal shopper and is tasked with purchasing jeans and T-shirts for her client. Jeans cost $35 and T-shirts cost $15.

a. Write an equation to represent the total amount Delia will pay for x pairs of jeans and y T-shirts if her client wants to spend $115.

b. Delia's client wants a total of 5 items. Write an equation in x and y representing the total number of items Delia will purchase.

c. Solve the system of equations found in parts **a** and **b** algebraically. Show your work.

d. Graph the system, and state the point of intersection.

e. Was it easier to solve the system algebraically or by graphing? Explain your reasoning.

Glossary/Glosario

A

ENGLISH	SPANISH	EXAMPLES

absolute value The absolute value of x is the distance from zero to x on a number line, denoted $|x|$.

$$|x| = \begin{cases} x & \text{if } x \geq 0 \\ -x & \text{if } x < 0 \end{cases}$$

valor absoluto El valor absoluto de x es la distancia de cero a x en una recta numérica, y se expresa $|x|$.

$$|x| = \begin{cases} x & \text{si } x \geq 0 \\ -x & \text{si } x < 0 \end{cases}$$

$|3| = 3$
$|-3| = 3$

---

accuracy The closeness of a given measurement or value to the actual measurement or value.

exactitud Cercanía de una medida o un valor a la medida o el valor real.

Addition Property of Equality For real numbers a, b, and c, if $a = b$, then $a + c = b + c$.

Propiedad de igualdad de la suma Dados los números reales a, b y c, si $a = b$, entonces $a + c = b + c$.

$$\begin{array}{rr} x - 6 = & 8 \\ +6 & +6 \\ \hline x \quad = & 14 \end{array}$$

Addition Property of Inequality For real numbers a, b, and c, if $a < b$, then $a + c < b + c$. Also holds true for $>$, $\leq$, $\geq$, and $\neq$.

Propiedad de desigualdad de la suma Dados los números reales a, b y c, si $a < b$, entonces $a + c < b + c$. Es válido también para $>$, $\leq$, $\geq$ y $\neq$.

$$\begin{array}{rr} x - 6 < & 8 \\ +6 & +6 \\ \hline x \quad < & 14 \end{array}$$

---

additive inverse The opposite of a number. Two numbers are additive inverses if their sum is zero.

inverso aditivo El opuesto de un número. Dos números son inversos aditivos si su suma es cero.

The additive inverse of 5 is -5.
The additive inverse of -5 is 5.

---

adjacent angles Two angles in the same plane with a common vertex and a common side, but no common interior points.

ángulos adyacentes Dos ángulos en el mismo plano que tienen un vértice y un lado común pero no comparten puntos internos.

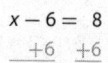

$\angle 1$ and $\angle 2$ are adjacent angles.

---

algebraic expression An expression that contains at least one variable.

expresión algebraica Expresión que contiene por lo menos una variable.

---

alternate exterior angles For two lines intersected by a transversal, a pair of angles that lie on opposite sides of the transversal and outside the other two lines.

ángulos alternos externos Dadas dos líneas cortadas por una transversal, par de ángulos no adyacentes ubicados en los lados opuestos de la transversal y fuera de las otras dos líneas.

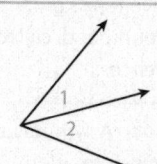

$\angle 4$ and $\angle 5$ are alternate exterior angles.

ENGLISH	SPANISH	EXAMPLES

alternate interior angles For two lines intersected by a transversal, a pair of nonadjacent angles that lie on opposite sides of the transversal and between the other two lines.

ángulos alternos internos Dadas dos líneas cortadas por una transversal, par de ángulos no adyacentes ubicados en los lados opuestos de la transversal y entre las otras dos líneas.

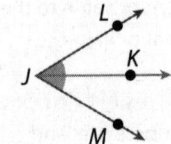

∠3 and ∠6 are alternate interior angles.

---

altitude of a triangle A perpendicular segment from a vertex to the line containing the opposite side.

altura de un triángulo Segmento perpendicular que se extiende desde un vértice hasta la línea que forma el lado opuesto.

AND A logical operator representing the intersection of two sets.

Y Operador lógico que representa la intersección de dos conjuntos.

$A = \{2, 3, 4, 5\}$ $B = \{1, 3, 5, 7\}$
The set of values that are in A AND B is $A \cap B = \{3, 5\}$.

---

angle bisector A ray that divides an angle into two congruent angles.

bisectriz de un ángulo Rayo que divide un ángulo en dos ángulos congruentes.

$\overrightarrow{JK}$ is an angle bisector of ∠LJM.

---

angle of rotation An angle formed by a rotating ray, called the terminal side, and a stationary reference ray, called the initial side.

ángulo de rotación Ángulo formado por un rayo rotativo, denominado lado terminal, y un rayo de referencia estático, denominado lado inicial.

Terminal side   135°   45°   0 | Initial side
The angle of rotation is 135°.

---

arithmetic sequence A sequence whose successive terms differ by the same nonzero number d, called the common difference.

sucesión aritmética Sucesión cuyos términos sucesivos difieren en el mismo número distinto de cero d, denominado *diferencia común*.

4, 7, 10, 13, 16, …
$+3 +3 +3 +3$
$d = 3$

---

arrow notation A symbol used to describe a transformation.

notación de flecha Símbolo utilizado para describir una transformación.

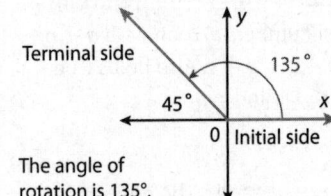

Preimage   Image
$\triangle ABC \longrightarrow \triangle A'B'C'$

Associative Property of Addition For all numbers a, b, and c, $(a + b) + c = a + (b + c)$.

Propiedad asociativa de la suma Dados tres números cualesquiera a, b y c, $(a + b) + c = a + (b + c)$.

$(5 + 3) + 7 = 5 + (3 + 7)$

Associative Property of Multiplication For all numbers a, b, and c, $(a \cdot b) \cdot c = a \cdot (b \cdot c)$.

Propiedad asociativa de la multiplicación Dados tres números cualesquiera a, b y c, $(a \cdot b) \cdot c = a \cdot (b \cdot c)$.

$(5 \cdot 3) \cdot 7 = 5 \cdot (3 \cdot 7)$

ENGLISH	SPANISH	EXAMPLES
asymptote A line that a graph gets closer to as the value of a variable becomes extremely large or small.	**asíntota** Línea recta a la cual se aproxima una gráfica a medida que el valor de una variable se hace sumamente grande o pequeño.	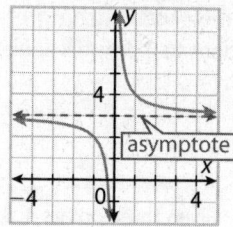
auxiliary line A line drawn in a figure to aid in a proof.	**línea auxiliar** Línea dibujada en una figura como ayuda en una demostración.	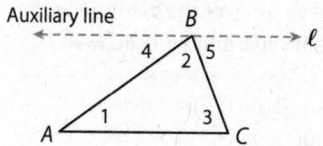
axiom *See* postulate.	**axioma** *Ver* postulado.	

B

base angle of a trapezoid One of a pair of consecutive angles whose common side is a base of the trapezoid.	**ángulo base de un trapecio** Uno de los dos ángulos consecutivos cuyo lado en común es la base del trapecio.	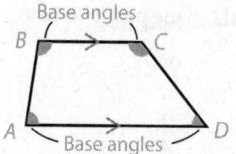
base angle of an isosceles triangle One of the two angles that have the base of the triangle as a side.	**ángulo base de un triángulo isósceles** Uno de los dos ángulos que tienen como lado la base del triángulo.	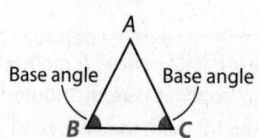
base of a power The number in a power that is used as a factor.	**base de una potencia** Número de una potencia que se utiliza como factor.	$3^4 = 3 \cdot 3 \cdot 3 \cdot 3 = 81$ 3 is the base.
base of a trapezoid One of the sides in a pair of parallel sides of the trapezoid.	**base de un trapecio** Uno de los lados en un par de lados paralelos del trapecio.	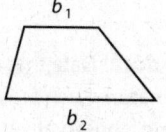
base of a triangle Any side of a triangle.	**base de un triángulo** Cualquier lado de un triángulo.	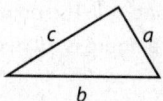
base of an exponential function The value of b in a function of the form $f(x) = ab^x$, where a and b are real numbers with $a \neq 0$, $b > 0$, and $b \neq 1$.	**base de una función exponencial** Valor de b en una función del tipo $f(x) = ab^x$, donde a y b son números reales con $a \neq 0$, $b > 0$ y $b \neq 1$.	In the function $f(x) = 5(2)^x$, the base is 2.

Glossary/Glosario

ENGLISH	SPANISH	EXAMPLES

base of an isosceles triangle
The side opposite the vertex angle.

base de un triángulo isósceles Lado opuesto al ángulo del vértice.

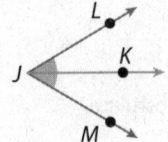

---

between Given three points A, B, and C, B is between A and C if and only if all three of the points lie on the same line, and $AB + BC = AC$.

entre Dados tres puntos A, B y C, B está entre A y C si y sólo si los tres puntos se encuentran en la misma línea y $AB + BC = AC$.

A ——— B ——————— C

---

bisect To divide into two congruent parts.

trazar una bisectriz Dividir en dos partes congruentes.

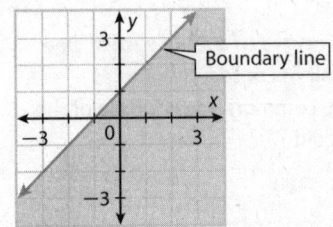

$\overrightarrow{JK}$ bisects $\angle LJM$.

---

boundary line A line that divides a coordinate plane into two half-planes.

línea de límite Línea que divide un plano cartesiano en dos semiplanos.

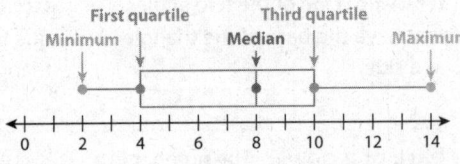

---

box-and-whisker plot A method of showing how data are distributed by using the median, quartiles, and minimum and maximum values; also called a *box plot*.

gráfica de mediana y rango Método para mostrar la distribución de datos utilizando la mediana, los cuartiles y los valores mínimo y máximo; también llamado *gráfica de caja*.

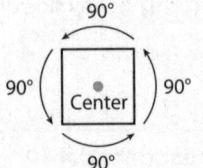

C

categorical data Data that are qualitative in nature, such as "liberal," "moderate," and "conservative."

datos categóricos Datos de índole cualitativa, como "liberal", "moderado" y "conservador".

---

center of rotation The point around which a figure is rotated.

centro de rotación Punto alrededor del cual rota una figura.

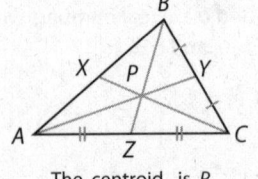

---

centroid of a triangle The point of concurrency of the three medians of a triangle. Also known as the *center of gravity*.

centroide de un triángulo Punto donde se encuentran las tres medianas de un triángulo. También conocido como *centro de gravedad*.

The centroid is P.

Glossary/Glosario

circumcenter of a triangle The point of concurrency of the three perpendicular bisectors of a triangle.	**circuncentro de un triángulo** Punto donde se cortan las tres mediatrices de un triángulo.	 The circumcenter is *P*.
Circumcircle *See* circumscribed circle.	**circuncírculo** Véase círculo circunscrito.	
closure A set of numbers is said to be closed, or to have closure, under a given operation if the result of the operation on any two numbers in the set is also in the set.	**cerradura** Se dice que un conjunto de números es cerrado, o tiene cerradura, respecto de una operación determinada, si el resultado de la operación entre dos números cualesquiera del conjunto también está en el conjunto.	The natural numbers are closed under addition because the sum of two natural numbers is always a natural number.
coefficient A number that is multiplied by a variable.	**coeficiente** Número que se multiplica por una variable.	In the expression $2x + 3y$, 2 is the coefficient of x and 3 is the coefficient of y.
collinear Points that lie on the same line.	**colineal** Puntos que se encuentran sobre la misma línea.	 *K,L*, and *M* are collinear points.
common difference In an arithmetic sequence, the nonzero constant difference of any term and the previous term.	**diferencia común** En una sucesión aritmética, diferencia constante distinta de cero entre cualquier término y el término anterior.	In the arithmetic sequence 3, 5, 7, 9, 11, …, the common difference is 2.
common factor A factor that is common to all terms of an expression or to two or more expressions.	**factor común** Factor que es común a todos los términos de una expresión o a dos o más expresiones.	Expression: $4x^2 + 16x^3 - 8x$ Common factor: $4x$ Expressions: 12 and 18 Common factors: 2, 3, and 6
common ratio In a geometric sequence, the constant ratio of any term and the previous term.	**razón común** En una sucesión geométrica, la razón constante entre cualquier término y el término anterior.	In the geometric sequence 32, 16, 8, 4, 2, …, the common ratio is $\frac{1}{2}$.
Commutative Property of Addition For any two numbers a and b, $a + b = b + a$.	**Propiedad conmutativa de la suma** Dados dos números cualesquiera a y b, $a \cdot b = b \cdot a$.	$3 + 4 = 4 + 3 = 7$
Commutative Property of Multiplication For any two numbers a and b, $a \cdot b = b \cdot a$.	**Propiedad conmutativa de la multiplicación** Dados dos números cualesquiera a y b, $a \cdot b = b \cdot a$	$3 \cdot 4 = 4 \cdot 3 = 12$

Glossary/Glosario

	ENGLISH	SPANISH	EXAMPLES

complement of an angle The sum of the measures of an angle and its complement is 90°.

complemento de un ángulo La suma de las medidas de un ángulo y su complemento es 90°.

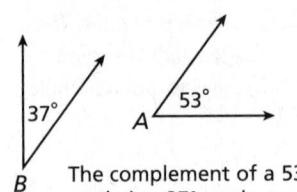

The complement of a 53° angle is a 37° angle.

---

complementary angles Two angles whose measures have a sum of 90°.

ángulos complementarios Dos ángulos cuyas medidas suman 90°.

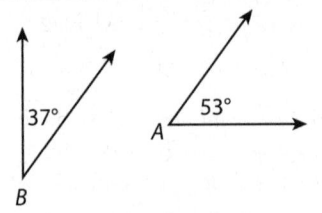

---

component form The form of a vector that lists the vertical and horizontal change from the initial point to the terminal point.

forma de componente Forma de un vector que muestra el cambio horizontal y vertical desde el punto inicial hasta el punto terminal.

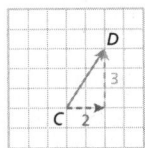

The component form of $\overrightarrow{CD}$ is $\langle 2, 3 \rangle$.

---

composition of transformations One transformation followed by another transformation.

composición de transformaciones Una transformación seguida de otra transformación.

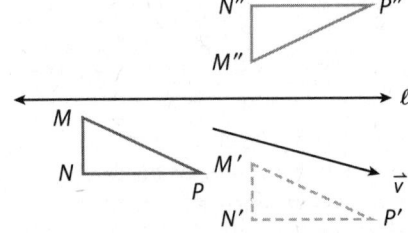

---

compound inequality Two inequalities that are combined into one statement by the word *and* or *or*.

desigualdad compuesta Dos desigualdades unidas en un enunciado por la palabra *y* u *o*.

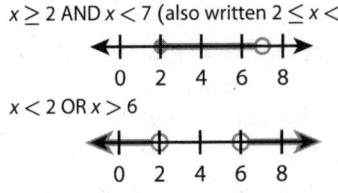

$x \geq 2$ AND $x < 7$ (also written $2 \leq x < 7$)

$x < 2$ OR $x > 6$

---

compound interest Interest earned or paid on both the principal and previously earned interest. The formula for compound interest is $A = P\left(1 + \frac{r}{n}\right)^{nt}$, where A is the final amount, P is the principal, r is the interest rate expressed as a decimal, n is the number of times interest is compounded, and t is the time.

interés compuesto Intereses ganados o pagados sobre el capital y los intereses ya devengados. La fórmula de interés compuesto es $A = P\left(1 + \frac{r}{n}\right)^{nt}$, donde A es la cantidad final, P es el capital, r es la tasa de interés expresada como un decimal, n es la cantidad de veces que se capitaliza el interés y t es el tiempo.

If $100 is put into an account with an interest rate of 5% compounded monthly, then after 2 years, the account will have $100\left(1 + \frac{0.05}{12}\right)^{12 \cdot 2} = \$110.49$.

---

compound statement Two statements that are connected by the word *and* or *or*.

enunciado compuesto Dos enunciados unidos por la palabra *y* u *o*.

The sky is blue and the grass is green.
I will drive to school or I will take the bus.

ENGLISH	SPANISH	EXAMPLES
conditional relative frequency The ratio of a joint relative frequency to a related marginal relative frequency in a two-way table.	**frecuencia relativa condicional** Razón de una frecuencia relativa conjunta a una frecuencia relativa marginal en una tabla de doble entrada.	
conditional statement A statement that can be written in the form "if p, then q," where p is the hypothesis and q is the conclusion.	**enunciado condicional** Enunciado que se puede expresar como "si p, entonces q", donde p es la hipótesis y q es la conclusión.	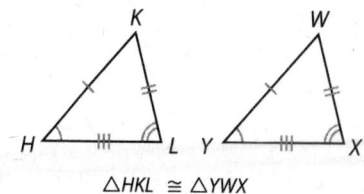
congruence statement A statement that indicates that two polygons are congruent by listing the vertices in the order of correspondence.	**enunciado de congruencia** Enunciado que indica que dos polígonos son congruentes enumerando los vértices en orden de correspondencia.	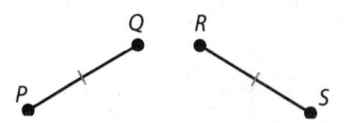
congruent Having the same size and shape, denoted by $\cong$.	**congruente** Que tiene el mismo tamaño y la misma forma, expresado por $\cong$.	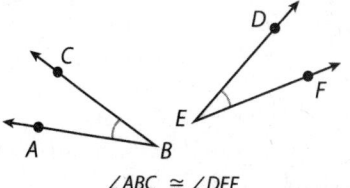
congruent angles Angles that have the same measure.	**ángulos congruentes** Ángulos que tienen la misma medida.	
congruent polygons Two polygons whose corresponding sides and angles are congruent.	**polígonos congruentes** Dos polígonos cuyos lados y ángulos correspondientes son congruentes.	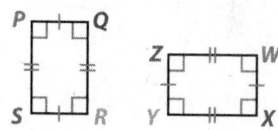
congruent segments Two segments that have the same length.	**segmentos congruentes** Dos segmentos que tienen la misma longitud.	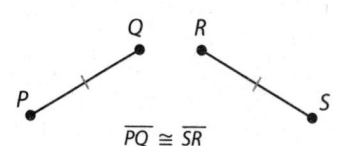
consecutive interior angles See same-side interior angles.	**ángulos internos consecutivos** *Ver* ángulos internos del mismo lado.	
consistent system A system of equations or inequalities that has at least one solution.	**sistema consistente** Sistema de ecuaciones o desigualdades que tiene por lo menos una solución.	$\begin{cases} x+y=6 \\ x-y=4 \end{cases}$ solution: $(5, 1)$
constant A value that does not change.	**constante** Valor que no cambia.	$3, 0, \pi$
constant of variation The constant k in direct and inverse variation equations.	**constante de variación** La constante k en ecuaciones de variación directa e inversa.	$y = 5x$ ↑ constant of variation

Glossary/Glosario

ENGLISH	SPANISH	EXAMPLES
construction A method of creating a figure that is considered to be mathematically precise. Figures may be constructed by using a compass and straightedge, geometry software, or paper folding.	**construcción** Método para crear una figura que es considerado matemáticamente preciso. Se pueden construir figuras utilizando un compás y una regla, un programa de computación de geometría o plegando papeles.	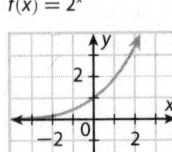
continuous function A function whose graph is an unbroken line or curve with no gaps or breaks.	**función continua** Función cuya gráfica es una línea recta o curva continua, sin espacios ni interrupciones.	$f(x) = 2^x$ 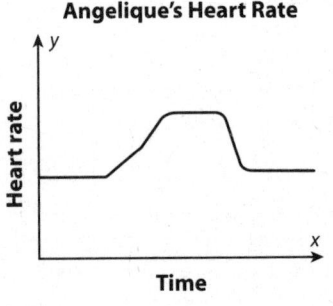
continuous graph A graph made up of connected lines or curves.	**gráfica continua** Gráfica compuesta por líneas rectas o curvas conectadas.	**Angelique's Heart Rate** 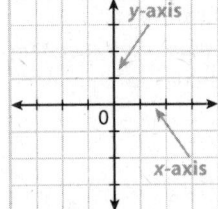
conversion factor The ratio of two equal quantities, each measured in different units.	**factor de conversión** Razón entre dos cantidades iguales, cada una medida en unidades diferentes.	$\dfrac{12 \text{ inches}}{1 \text{ foot}}$
coordinate plane A plane that is divided into four regions by a horizontal line called the x-axis and a vertical line called the y-axis.	**plano cartesiano** Plano dividido en cuatro regiones por una línea horizontal denominada eje x y una línea vertical denominada eje y.	
coordinate proof A style of proof that uses coordinate geometry and algebra.	**prueba de coordenadas** Tipo de demostración que utiliza geometría de coordenadas y álgebra.	
coplanar Points that lie in the same plane.	**coplanar** Puntos que se encuentran en el mismo plano.	
corollary A theorem whose proof follows directly from another theorem.	**corolario** Teorema cuya demostración proviene directamente de otro teorema.	

correlation A measure of the strength and direction of the relationship between two variables or data sets.

correlación Medida de la fuerza y dirección de la relación entre dos variables o conjuntos de datos.

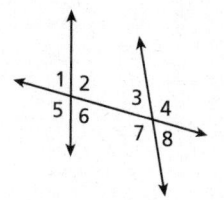

Positive correlation

No correlation

Negative correlation

correlation coefficient A number *r*, where $-1 \leq r \leq 1$, that describes how closely the points in a scatter plot cluster around the least-squares line.

coeficiente de correlación Número *r*, donde $-1 \leq r \leq 1$, que describe a qué distancia de la recta de mínimos cuadrados se agrupan los puntos de un diagrama de dispersión.

An *r*-value close to 1 describes a strong positive correlation.
An *r*-value close to 0 describes a weak correlation or no correlation.
An *r*-value close to −1 describes a strong negative correlation.

corresponding angles of lines intersected by a transversal For two lines intersected by a transversal, a pair of angles that lie on the same side of the transversal and on the same sides of the other two lines.

ángulos correspondientes de líneas cortadas por una transversal Dadas dos líneas cortadas por una transversal, el par de ángulos ubicados en el mismo lado de la transversal y en los mismos lados de las otras dos líneas.

∠1 and ∠3 are corresponding.

corresponding angles of polygons Angles in the same relative position in polygons with an equal number of angles.

ángulos correspondientes de los polígonos Ángulos que se ubican en la misma posición relativa en polígonos que tienen el mismo número de ángulos.

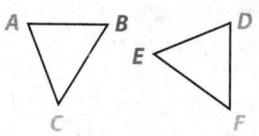

∠A and ∠D are corresponding angles.

corresponding sides of polygons Sides in the same relative position in polygons with an equal number of sides.

lados correspondientes de los polígonos Lados que se ubican en la misma posición relativa en polígonos que tienen el mismo número de lados.

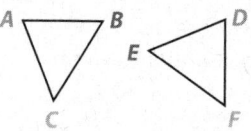

$\overline{AB}$ and $\overline{DE}$ are corresponding sides.

counterexample An example that proves that a conjecture or statement is false.

contraejemplo Ejemplo que demuestra que una conjetura o enunciado es falso.

CPCTC An abbreviation for "Corresponding Parts of Congruent Triangles are Congruent," which can be used as a justification in a proof after two triangles are proven congruent.

PCTCC Abreviatura que significa "Las partes correspondientes de los triángulos congruentes son congruentes", que se puede utilizar para justificar una demostración después de demostrar que dos triángulos son congruentes (CPCTC, por sus siglas en inglés).

Glossary/Glosario

ENGLISH	SPANISH	EXAMPLES

cross products In the statement $\frac{a}{b} = \frac{c}{d}$, bc and ad are the cross products.

productos cruzados En el enunciado $\frac{a}{b} = \frac{c}{d}$, bc y ad son productos cruzados.

$\frac{1}{2} = \frac{3}{6}$
Cross products: $2 \cdot 3 = 6$ and $1 \cdot 6 = 6$

Cross Product Property For any real numbers a, b, c, and d, where $b \neq 0$ and $d \neq 0$, if $\frac{a}{b} = \frac{c}{d}$, then $ad = bc$.

Propiedad de productos cruzados Dados los números reales a, b, c y d, donde $b \neq 0$ y $d \neq 0$, si $\frac{a}{b} = \frac{c}{d}$, entonces $ad = bc$.

If $\frac{4}{6} = \frac{10}{x}$, then $4x = 60$, so $x = 15$.

---

cube root A number, written as $\sqrt[3]{x}$, whose cube is x.

raíz cúbica Número, expresado como $\sqrt[3]{x}$, cuyo cubo es x.

$\sqrt[3]{64} = 4$, because $4^3 = 64$; 4 is the cube root of 64.

---

cumulative frequency The frequency of all data values that are less than or equal to a given value.

frecuencia acumulativa Frecuencia de todos los valores de los datos que son menores que o iguales a un valor dado.

For the data set 2, 2, 3, 5, 5, 6, 7, 7, 8, 8, 8, 9, the cumulative frequency table is shown below.

Data	Frequency	Cumulative Frequency
2	2	2
3	1	3
5	2	5
6	1	6
7	2	8
8	3	11
9	1	12

D

data Information gathered from a survey or experiment.

datos Información reunida en una encuesta o experimento.

---

deductive reasoning The process of using logic to draw conclusions.

razonamiento deductivo Proceso en el que se utiliza la lógica para sacar conclusiones.

---

degree measure of an angle A unit of angle measure; one degree is $\frac{1}{360}$ of a circle.

medida en grados de un ángulo Unidad de medida de los ángulos; un grado es $\frac{1}{360}$ de un círculo.

---

dependent system A system of equations that has infinitely many solutions.

sistema dependiente Sistema de ecuaciones que tiene infinitamente muchas soluciones.

$\begin{cases} x + y = 2 \\ 2x + 2y = 4 \end{cases}$

---

dependent variable The output of a function; a variable whose value depends on the value of the input, or independent variable.

variable dependiente Salida de una función; variable cuyo valor depende del valor de la entrada, o variable independiente.

For $y = 2x + 1$, y is the dependent variable.
input: x output: y

---

diagonal of a polygon A segment connecting two nonconsecutive vertices of a polygon.

diagonal de un polígono Segmento que conecta dos vértices no consecutivos de un polígono.

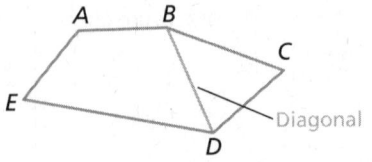

Glossary/Glosario

ENGLISH	SPANISH	EXAMPLES

dimensional analysis A process that uses rates to convert measurements from one unit to another.

análisis dimensional Un proceso que utiliza tasas para convertir medidas de unidad a otra.

$$12 \text{ pt} \cdot \frac{1 \text{ qt}}{2 \text{ pt}} = 6 \text{ qt}$$

---

direct variation A linear relationship between two variables, x and y, that can be written in the form $y = kx$, where k is a nonzero constant.

variación directa Relación lineal entre dos variables, x e y, que puede expresarse en la forma $y = kx$, donde k es una constante distinta de cero.

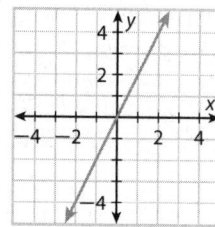

---

discrete function A function whose graph is made up of unconnected points.

función discreta Función cuya gráfica compuesta de puntos no conectados.

---

discrete graph A graph made up of unconnected points.

gráfica discreta Gráfica compuesta de puntos no conectados.

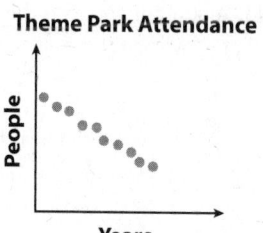

Theme Park Attendance

People / Years

Distance Formula In a coordinate plane, the distance from (x_1, y_1) to (x_2, y_2) is

$$d = \sqrt{(x_2 - x_1)^2 + (y_2 - y_1)^2}.$$

Fórmula de distancia En un plano cartesiano, la distancia desde (x_1, y_1) hasta (x_2, y_2) es

$$d = \sqrt{(x_2 - x_1)^2 + (y_2 - y_1)^2}.$$

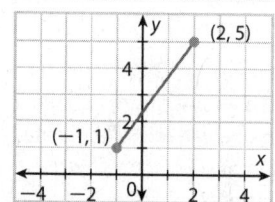

The distance from $(2, 5)$ to $(-1, 1)$ is
$$d = \sqrt{(-1 - 2)^2 + (1 - 5)^2}$$
$$= \sqrt{(-3)^2 + (-4)^2}$$
$$= \sqrt{9 + 16} = \sqrt{25} = 5.$$

---

distance from a point to a line The length of the perpendicular segment from the point to the line.

distancia desde un punto hasta una línea Longitud del segmento perpendicular desde el punto hasta la línea.

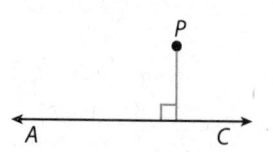

The distance from P to $\overleftrightarrow{AC}$ is 5 units.

Distributive Property For all real numbers a, b, and c, $a(b + c) = ab + ac$, and $(b + c)a = ba + ca$.

Propiedad distributiva Dados los números reales a, b y c, $a(b + c) = ab + ac$, y $(b + c)a = ba + ca$.

$3(4 + 5) = 3 \cdot 4 + 3 \cdot 5$
$(4 + 5)3 = 4 \cdot 3 + 5 \cdot 3$

Division Property of Equality For real numbers a, b, and c, where $c \neq 0$, if $a = b$, then $\frac{a}{c} = \frac{b}{c}$.

Propiedad de igualdad de la división Dados los números reales a, b y c, donde $c \neq 0$, si $a = b$, entonces $\frac{a}{c} = \frac{b}{c}$.

$4x = 12$
$\frac{4x}{4} = \frac{12}{4}$
$x = 3$

Glossary/Glosario

Division Property of Inequality
If both sides of an inequality are divided by the same positive quantity, the new inequality will have the same solution set. If both sides of an inequality are divided by the same negative quantity, the new inequality will have the same solution set if the inequality symbol is reversed.

Propiedad de desigualdad de la división Cuando ambos lados de una desigualdad se dividen entre el mismo número positivo, la nueva desigualdad tiene el mismo conjunto solución. Cuando ambos lados de una desigualdad se dividen entra el mismo número negativo, la nueva desigualdad tiene el mismo conjunto solución si se invierte el símbolo de desigualdad.

$$4x \geq 12$$
$$\frac{4x}{4} \geq \frac{12}{4}$$
$$x \geq 3$$

$$-4x \geq 12$$
$$\frac{-4x}{-4} \leq \frac{12}{-4}$$
$$x \leq -3$$

domain The set of all first coordinates (or x-values) of a relation or function.

dominio Conjunto de todos los valores de la primera coordenada (o valores de x) de una función o relación.

The domain of the function $\{(-5, 3), (-3, -2), (-1, -1), (1, 0)\}$ is $\{-5, -3, -1, 1\}$.

dot plot A number line with marks or dots that show frequency.

diagrama de puntos Recta numérica con marcas o puntos que indican la frecuencia.

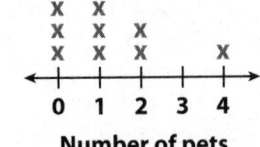
Number of pets

E

elimination method A method used to solve systems of equations in which one variable is eliminated by adding or subtracting two equations of the system.

eliminación Método utilizado para resolver sistemas de ecuaciones por el cual se elimina una variable sumando o restando dos ecuaciones del sistema.

empty set A set with no elements.

conjunto vacío Conjunto sin elementos.

The solution set of $|x| < 0$ is the empty set, $\{\,\}$, or $\varnothing$.

endpoint A point at an end of a segment or the starting point of a ray.

extremo Punto en el final de un segmento o punto de inicio de un rayo.

A B

D

equal vectors Two vectors that have the same magnitude and the same direction.

vectores iguales Dos vectores de la misma magnitud y con la misma dirección.

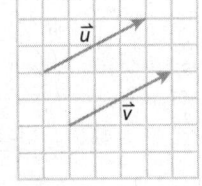

$$|\vec{u}| = |\vec{v}| = 2\sqrt{5}$$

Equality of Bases Property Two powers with the same positive base other than 1 are equal if and only if the exponents are equal.

Propiedad de igualdad de las bases Dos potencias con la misma base positiva distinta de 1 son iguales si y solo si los exponentes son iguales.

If $b > 0$ and, $b \neq 1$, then $b^x = b^y$ if and only if $x = y$.

ENGLISH	SPANISH	EXAMPLES
equation A mathematical statement that two expressions are equivalent.	**ecuación** Enunciado matemático que indica que dos expresiones son equivalentes.	$x + 4 = 7$ $2 + 3 = 6 - 1$ $(x - 1)^2 + (y + 2)^2 = 4$
equiangular polygon A polygon in which all angles are congruent.	**polígono equiangular** Polígono cuyos ángulos son todos congruentes.	
equiangular triangle A triangle with three congruent angles.	**triángulo equiangular** Triángulo con tres ángulos congruentes.	
equidistant The same distance from two or more objects.	**equidistante** Igual distancia de dos o más objetos.	*X* is equidistant from *A* and *B*.
equilateral polygon A polygon in which all sides are congruent.	**polígono equilátero** Polígono cuyos lados son todos congruentes.	
equilateral triangle A triangle with three congruent sides.	**triángulo equilátero** Triángulo con tres lados congruentes.	
equivalent ratios Ratios that name the same comparison.	**razones equivalentes** Razones que expresan la misma comparación.	$\frac{1}{2}$ and $\frac{2}{4}$ are equivalent ratios.
evaluate To find the value of an algebraic expression by substituting a number for each variable and simplifying by using the order of operations.	**evaluar** Calcular el valor de una expresión algebraica sustituyendo cada variable por un número y simplificando mediante el orden de las operaciones.	Evaluate $2x + 7$ for $x = 3$. $2x + 7$ $2(3) + 7$ $6 + 7$ 13
explicit rule for *n*th term of a sequence A rule that defines the *n*th term a_n, or a general term, of a sequence as a function of *n*.	**fórmula explícita** Fórmula que define el enésimo término a_n, o término general, de una sucesión como una función de *n*.	
exponent The number that indicates how many times the base in a power is used as a factor.	**exponente** Número que indica la cantidad de veces que la base de una potencia se utiliza como factor.	$3^4 = 3 \cdot 3 \cdot 3 \cdot 3 = 81$ 4 is the exponent.

Glossary/Glosario

Glossary/Glosario *(side tab)*

exponential decay An exponential function of the form $f(x) = ab^x$ in which $0 < b < 1$. If r is the rate of decay, then the function can be written $y = a(1 - r)^t$, where a is the initial amount and t is the time.

decremento exponencial Función exponencial del tipo $f(x) = ab^x$ en la cual $0 < b < 1$. Si r es la tasa decremental, entonces la función se puede expresar como $y = a(1 - r)^t$, donde a es la cantidad inicial y t es el tiempo.

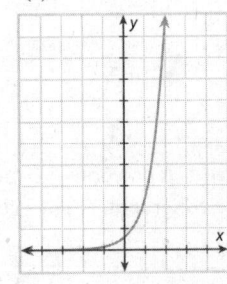

exponential expression An algebraic expression in which the variable is in an exponent with a fixed number as the base.

expresión exponencial Expresión algebraica en la que la variable está en un exponente y que tiene un número fijo como base.

2^{x+1}

exponential function A function of the form $f(x) = ab^x$, where a and b are real numbers with $a \neq 0$, $b > 0$, and $b \neq 1$.

función exponencial Función del tipo $f(x) = ab^x$, donde a y b son números reales con $a \neq 0$, $b > 0$ y $b \neq 1$.

$f(x) = 3 \cdot 4^x$

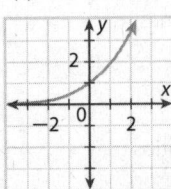

exponential growth An exponential function of the form $f(x) = ab^x$ in which $b > 1$. If r is the rate of growth, then the function can be written $y = a(1 + r)^t$, where a is the initial amount and t is the time.

crecimiento exponencial Función exponencial del tipo $f(x) = ab^x$ en la que $b > 1$. Si r es la tasa de crecimiento, entonces la función se puede expresar como $y = a(1 + r)^t$, donde a es la cantidad inicial y t es el tiempo.

$f(x) = 2^x$

exponential regression A statistical method used to fit an exponential model to a given data set.

regresión exponencial Método estadístico utilizado para ajustar un modelo exponencial a un conjunto de datos determinado.

expression A mathematical phrase that contains operations, numbers, and/or variables.

expresión Frase matemática que contiene operaciones, números y/o variables.

$6x + 1$

exterior angle of a polygon An angle formed by one side of a polygon and the extension of an adjacent side.

ángulo externo de un polígono Ángulo formado por un lado de un polígono y la prolongación del lado adyacente.

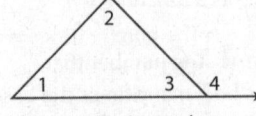

$\angle 4$ is an exterior angle.

exterior of an angle The set of all points outside an angle.

exterior de un ángulo Conjunto de todos los puntos que se encuentran fuera de un ángulo.

Exterior

ENGLISH	SPANISH	EXAMPLES
exterior of a polygon The set of all points outside a polygon.	**exterior de un polígono** Conjunto de todos los puntos que se encuentran fuera de un polígono.	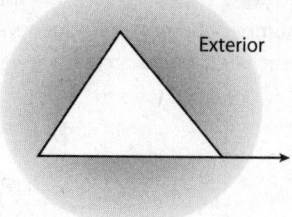 Exterior
extrapolation Making a prediction using a value of the independent variable outside of a model's domain.	**extrapolación** Hacer una predicción con un valor de la variable independiente que esté fuera del dominio de un modelo.	

F

ENGLISH	SPANISH	EXAMPLES
factor A number or expression that is multiplied by another number or expression to get a product. *See also factoring.*	**factor** Número o expresión que se multiplica por otro número o expresión para obtener un producto. *Ver también* factoreo.	$12 = 3 \cdot 4$ 3 and 4 are factors of 12. $x^2 - 1 = (x - 1)(x + 1)$ $(x - 1)$ and $(x + 1)$ are factors of $x^2 - 1$.
factoring The process of writing a number or algebraic expression as a product.	**factorización** Proceso por el que se expresa un número o expresión algebraica como un producto.	$x^2 - 4x - 21 = (x - 7)(x + 3)$
first quartile The median of the lower half of a data set, denoted Q_1. Also called *lower quartile*.	**primer cuartil** Mediana de la mitad inferior de un conjunto de datos, expresada como Q_1. También se llama *cuartil inferior*.	Lower half Upper half 18, (23,) 28, 29, 36, 42 **First quartile**
flowchart proof A style of proof that uses boxes and arrows to show the structure of the proof.	**demostración con diagrama de flujo** Tipo de demostración que se vale de cuadros y flechas para mostrar la estructura de la prueba.	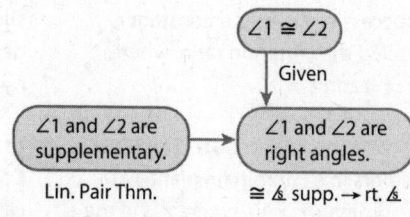
formula A literal equation that states a rule for a relationship among quantities.	**fórmula** Ecuación literal que establece una regla para una relación entre cantidades.	$A = \pi r^2$
frequency The number of times the value appears in the data set.	**frecuencia** Cantidad de veces que aparece el valor en un conjunto de datos.	In the data set 5, 6, 6, 7, 8, 9, the data value 6 has a frequency of 2.

frequency table A table that lists the number of times, or frequency, that each data value occurs.

tabla de frecuencia Tabla que enumera la cantidad de veces que ocurre cada valor de datos, o la frecuencia.

Data set: 1, 1, 2, 2, 3, 4, 5, 5, 5, 6, 6, 6, 6
Frequency table:

Data	Frequency
1	2
2	2
3	1
4	1
5	3
6	4

function A relation in which every domain value is paired with exactly one range value.

función Relación en la que a cada valor de dominio corresponde exactamente un valor de rango.

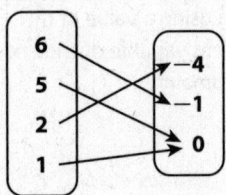

function notation If x is the independent variable and y is the dependent variable, then the function notation for y is $f(x)$, read "f of x," where f names the function.

notación de función Si x es la variable independiente e y es la variable dependiente, entonces la notación de función para y es $f(x)$, que se lee "f de x," donde f nombra la función.

equation: $y = 2x$
function notation: $f(x) = 2x$

function rule An algebraic expression that defines a function.

regla de función Expresión algebraica que define una función.

$f(x) = \underset{\uparrow}{2x^2 + 3x - 7}$

function rule

G

geometric sequence A sequence in which the ratio of successive terms is a constant r, called the common ratio, where $r \neq 0$ and $r \neq 1$.

sucesión geométrica Sucesión en la que la razón de los términos sucesivos es una constante r, denominada razón común, donde $r \neq 0$ y $r \neq 1$.

1, 2, 4, 8, 16, …
$\cdot 2 \; \cdot 2 \; \cdot 2 \; \cdot 2$ $r = 2$

graph of a function The set of points in a coordinate plane with coordinates (x, y), where x is in the domain of the function f and $y = fx$.

gráfica de una función Conjunto de los puntos de un plano cartesiano con coordenadas (x, y), donde x está en el dominio de la función f e $y = f(x)$.

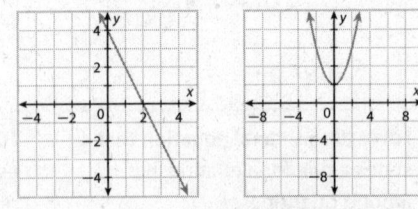

graph of a system of linear inequalities The region in a coordinate plane consisting of points whose coordinates are solutions to all of the inequalities in the system.

gráfica de un sistema de desigualdades lineales Región de un plano cartesiano que consta de puntos cuyas coordenadas son soluciones de todas las desigualdades del sistema.

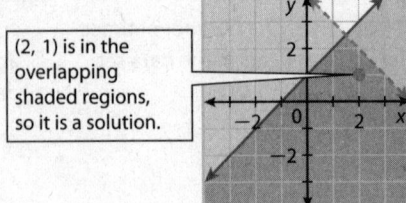

(2, 1) is in the overlapping shaded regions, so it is a solution.

ENGLISH	SPANISH	EXAMPLES
graph of an inequality in one variable The set of points on a number line that are solutions of the inequality.	**gráfica de una desigualdad en una variable** Conjunto de los puntos de una recta numérica que representan soluciones de la desigualdad.	$x \geq 2$ 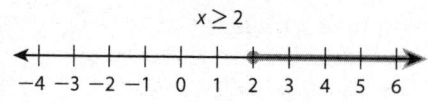
graph of an inequality in two variables The set of points in a coordinate plane whose coordinates (x, y) are solutions of the inequality.	**gráfica de una desigualdad en dos variables** Conjunto de los puntos de un plano cartesiano cuyas coordenadas (x, y) son soluciones de la desigualdad.	$y \leq x + 1$ 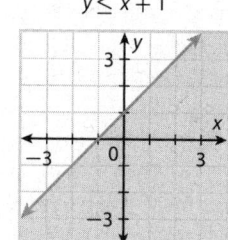
greatest common factor (numbers) (GCF) The largest common factor of two or more given numbers.	**máximo común divisor (números) (MCD)** El mayor de los factores comunes compartidos por dos o más números dados.	The GCF of 27 and 45 is 9.
greatest integer function A function denoted by $f(x) = [x]$ in which the number x is rounded down to the greatest integer that is less than or equal to x.	**función de entero mayor** Función expresada como $f(x) = [x]$ en la cual el número x se redondea hacia abajo hasta el entero mayor que sea menor o igual a x.	
grouping symbols Symbols such as parentheses ( ), brackets [ ], and braces { } that separate part of an expression. A fraction bar, absolute-value symbols, and radical symbols may also be used as grouping symbols.	**símbolos de agrupación** Símbolos tales como paréntesis ( ), corchetes [ ] y llaves { } que separan parte de una expresión. La barra de fracciones, los símbolos de valor absoluto y los símbolos de radical también se pueden utilizar como símbolos de agrupación.	$6 + \{3 - [(4 - 3) + 2] + 1\} - 5$ $6 + \{3 - [1 + 2] + 1\} - 5$ $6 + \{3 - 3 + 1\} - 5$ $6 + 1 - 5$ 2

H

half-plane The part of the coordinate plane on one side of a line, which may include the line.	**semiplano** La parte del plano cartesiano de un lado de una línea, que puede incluir la línea.	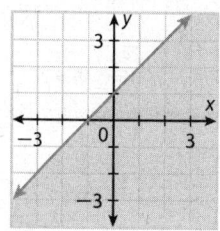
height of a figure The length of an altitude of the figure.	**altura de una figura** Longitud de la altura de la figura.	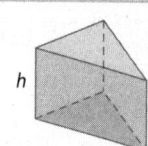 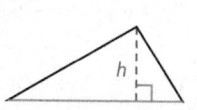

Glossary/Glosario

Glossary/Glosario

height of a triangle
A segment from a vertex that forms a right angle with a line containing the base.

altura de un triángulo
Segmento que se extiende desde el vértice y forma un ángulo recto con la línea de la base.

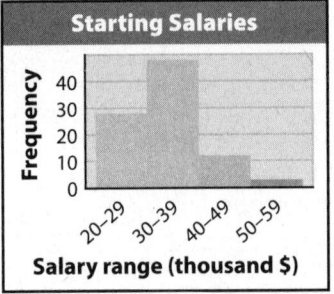

Heron's Formula A triangle with side lengths a, b, and c has area $A = \sqrt{s(s-a)(s-b)(s-c)}$, where s is one-half the perimeter, or $s = \frac{1}{2}(a+b+c)$.

fórmula de Herón Un triángulo con longitudes de lado a, b y c tiene un área $A = \sqrt{s(s-a)(s-b)(s-c)}$, donde s es la mitad del perímetro ó $s = \frac{1}{2}(a+b+c)$.

histogram A bar graph used to display data grouped in intervals.

histograma Gráfica de barras utilizada para mostrar datos agrupados en intervalos de clases.

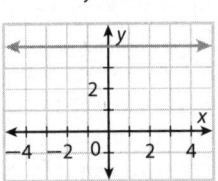

horizontal line A line described by the equation $y = b$, where b is the y-intercept.

línea horizontal Línea descrita por la ecuación $y = b$, donde b es la intersección con el eje y.

$y = 4$

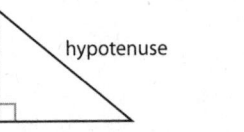

horizontal translation (of a parabola) is a shift of the parabola left or right, with no change in the shape of the parabola.

traslación horizontal (de una parábola) Desplazamiento de la parábola hacia la izquierda o hacia la derecha, sin producir cambios en la forma de la parábola.

hypotenuse The side opposite the right angle in a right triangle.

hipotenusa Lado opuesto al ángulo recto de un triángulo rectángulo.

hypotenuse

hypothesis The part of a conditional statement following the word *if*.

hipótesis La parte de un enunciado condicional que sigue a la palabra *si*.

If $x + 1 = 5$, then $x = 4$.

Hypothesis

I

identity An equation that is true for all values of the variables.

identidad Ecuación verdadera para todos los valores de las variables.

$3 = 3$
$2(x - 1) = 2x - 2$

image A shape that results from a transformation of a figure known as the preimage.

imagen Forma resultante de la transformación de una figura conocida como imagen original.

incenter of a triangle The point of concurrency of the three angle bisectors of a triangle.

incentro de un triángulo Punto donde se encuentran las tres bisectrices de los ángulos de un triángulo.

P is the incenter.

incircle *See* inscribed circle.

incírculo *Véase* círculo inscrito.

included angle The angle formed by two adjacent sides of a polygon.

ángulo incluido Ángulo formado por dos lados adyacentes de un polígono.

$\angle B$ is the included angle between $\overline{AB}$ and $\overline{BC}$.

included side The common side of two consecutive angles of a polygon.

lado incluido Lado común de dos ángulos consecutivos de un polígono.

$\overline{PQ}$ is the included side between $\angle P$ and $\angle Q$.

inconsistent system A system of equations or inequalities that has no solution.

sistema inconsistente Sistema de ecuaciones o desigualdades que no tiene solución.

$\begin{cases} x+y=0 \\ x+y=1 \end{cases}$

independent system A system of equations that has exactly one solution.

sistema independiente Sistema de ecuaciones que tiene sólo una solución.

$\begin{cases} x+y=7 \\ x-y=1 \end{cases}$
Solution: $(4, 3)$

independent variable The input of a function; a variable whose value determines the value of the output, or dependent variable.

variable independiente Entrada de una función; variable cuyo valor determina el valor de la salida, o variable dependiente.

For $y = 2x + 1$, x is the independent variable.

index In the radical $\sqrt[n]{x}$, which represents the nth root of x, n is the index. In the radical $\sqrt{x}$, the index is understood to be 2.

índice En el radical $\sqrt[n]{x}$, que representa la enésima raíz de x, n es el índice. En el radical $\sqrt{x}$, se da por sentado que el índice es 2.

The radical $\sqrt[3]{8}$ has an index of 3.

indirect measurement A method of measurement that uses formulas, similar figures, and/or proportions.

medición indirecta Método de medición en el que se usan fórmulas, figuras semejantes y/o proporciones.

Glossary/Glosario

indirect proof A proof in which the statement to be proved is assumed to be false and a contradiction is shown.

demostración indirecta Prueba en la que se supone que el enunciado a demostrar es falso y se muestra una contradicción.

inductive reasoning The process of reasoning that a rule or statement is true because specific cases are true.

razonamiento inductivo Proceso de razonamiento por el que se determina que una regla o enunciado son verdaderos porque ciertos casos específicos son verdaderos.

inequality A statement that compares two expressions by using one of the following signs: $<$, $>$, $\leq$, $\geq$, or $\neq$.

desigualdad Enunciado que compara dos expresiones utilizando uno de los siguientes signos: $<$, $>$, $\leq$, $\geq$, o $\neq$.

$$x \geq 2$$

initial point of a vector The starting point of a vector.

punto inicial de un vector Punto donde comienza un vector.

Initial point

input A value that is substituted for the independent variable in a relation or function.

entrada Valor que sustituye a la variable independiente en una relación o función.

For the function $f(x) = x + 5$, the input 3 produces an output of 8.

input-output table A table that displays input values of a function or expression together with the corresponding outputs.

tabla de entrada y salida Tabla que muestra los valores de entrada de una función o expresión junto con las correspondientes salidas.

Input	x	1	2	3	4
Output	y	4	7	10	13

intercept See x-intercept and y-intercept.

intersección Ver intersección con el eje x e intersección con el eje y.

interior angle An angle formed by two sides of a polygon with a common vertex.

ángulo interno Ángulo formado por dos lados de un polígono con un vértice común.

$\angle 1$ is an interior angle.

interior of an angle The set of all points between the sides of an angle.

interior de un ángulo Conjunto de todos los puntos entre los lados de un ángulo.

Interior

interest The amount of money charged for borrowing money or the amount of money earned when saving or investing money. *See also* compound interest, simple interest.

interés Cantidad de dinero que se cobra por prestar dinero o cantidad de dinero que se gana cuando se ahorra o invierte dinero. *Ver también* interés compuesto, interés simple.

Glossary/Glosario

interpolation Making a prediction using a value of the independent variable from within a model's domain.

interpolación Hacer una predicción con un valor de la variable independiente a partir del dominio de un modelo.

---

interquartile range (IQR) The difference of the third (upper) and first (lower) quartiles in a data set, representing the middle half of the data.

rango entre cuartiles Diferencia entre el tercer cuartil (superior) y el primer cuartil (inferior) de un conjunto de datos, que representa la mitad central de los datos.

Lower half   Upper half
18, (23), 28, 29, (36), 42
First quartile   Third quartile
Interquartile range: $36 - 23 = 13$

---

intersection The intersection of two sets is the set of all elements that are common to both sets, denoted by ∩.

intersección de conjuntos La intersección de dos conjuntos es el conjunto de todos los elementos que son comunes a ambos conjuntos, expresado por ∩.

$A = \{1, 2, 3, 4\}$
$B = \{1, 3, 5, 7, 9\}$
$A \cap B = \{1, 3\}$

---

inverse of a function The relation that results from exchanging the input and output values of a function.

inverso de una función La relación que se genera al intercambiar los valores de entrada y de salida de una función.

---

inverse operations Operations that undo each other.

operaciones inversas Operaciones que se anulan entre sí.

Addition and subtraction of the same quantity are inverse operations: $5 + 3 = 8, 8 - 3 = 5$
Multiplication and division by the same quantity are inverse operations: $2 \cdot 3 = 6$, $6 \div 3 = 2$

---

inverse relation The relation that results from exchanging the input and output values of a relation.

relación inversa La relación que se genera al intercambiar los valores de entrada y de salida de una relación.

---

inverse variation A relationship between two variables, x and y, that can be written in the form $y = \frac{k}{x}$, where k is a nonzero constant and $x \neq 0$.

variación inversa Relación entre dos variables, x e y, que puede expresarse en la forma $y = \frac{k}{x}$, donde k es una constante distinta de cero y $x \neq 0$.

$y = \frac{8}{x}$

---

irrational number A real number that cannot be expressed as the ratio of two integers.

número irracional Número real que no se puede expresar como una razón de enteros.

$\sqrt{2}, \pi, e$

---

isometry A transformation that does not change the size or shape of a figure.

isometría Transformación que no cambia el tamaño ni la forma de una figura.

Reflections, translations, and rotations are all examples of isometries.

---

isosceles trapezoid A trapezoid in which the legs are congruent but not parallel.

trapecio isósceles Trapecio cuyos lados no paralelos son congruentes.

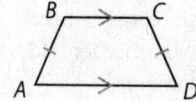

Glossary/Glosario

ENGLISH	SPANISH	EXAMPLES
isosceles triangle A triangle with at least two congruent sides.	**triángulo isósceles** Triángulo que tiene al menos dos lados congruentes.	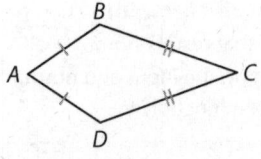

J

joint relative frequency The ratio of the frequency in a particular category divided by the total number of data values.	**frecuencia relativa conjunta** La línea de ajuste en que la suma de cuadrados de los residuos es la menor.	

K

kite A quadrilateral with exactly two pairs of congruent consecutive sides.	**cometa o papalote** Cuadrilátero con exactamente dos pares de lados congruentes consecutivos.	

Kite *ABCD* |

L

least common denominator (LCD) The least common multiple of the denominators of two or more given fractions or rational expressions.	**mínimo común denominador (MCD)** Mínimo común múltiplo de los denominadores de dos o más fracciones dadas o expresionnes racionales.	The LCD of $\frac{3}{4}$ and $\frac{5}{6}$ is 12.
least common multiple (numbers) (LCM) The smallest whole number, other than zero, that is a multiple of two or more given numbers.	**mínimo común múltiplo (números) (MCM)** El menor de los números cabales, distinto de cero, que es múltiplo de dos o más números dados.	The LCM of 10 and 18 is 90.
least-squares line The line of fit for which the sum of the squares of the residuals is as small as possible	**línea de mínimos cuadrados** La línea de ajuste en que la suma de cuadrados de los residuos es la menor.	
leg of a right triangle One of the two sides of the right triangle that form the right angle.	**cateto de un triángulo rectángulo** Uno de los dos lados de un triángulo rectángulo que forman el ángulo recto.	
leg of an isosceles triangle One of the two congruent sides of the isosceles triangle.	**cateto de un triángulo isósceles** Uno de los dos lados congruentes del triángulo isósceles.	

ENGLISH	SPANISH	EXAMPLES
legs of a trapezoid The sides of the trapezoid that are not the bases.	**catetos de un trapecio** Los lados del trapecio que no son las bases.	
length The distance between the two endpoints of a segment.	**longitud** Distancia entre los dos extremos de un segmento.	$$AB = |a - b| = |b - a|$$
like terms Terms with the same variables raised to the same exponents.	**términos semejantes** Términos con las mismas variables elevadas a los mismos exponentes.	
line An undefined term in geometry, a line is a straight path that has no thickness and extends forever.	**línea** Término indefinido en geometría; una línea es un trazo recto que no tiene grosor y se extiende infinitamente.	
line graph A graph that uses line segments to show how data changes.	**gráfica lineal** Gráfica que se vale de segmentos de recta para mostrar cambios en los datos.	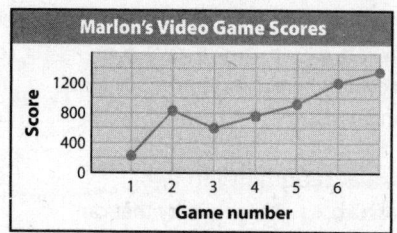
line of best fit The line that comes closest to all of the points in a data set.	**línea de mejor ajuste** Línea que más se acerca a todos los puntos de un conjunto de datos.	
line of fit *See* trend line.	**línea de ajuste** *Ver línea de tendencia.*	
line of symmetry A line that divides a plane figure into two congruent reflected halves.	**eje de simetría** Línea que divide una figura plana en dos mitades reflejas congruentes.	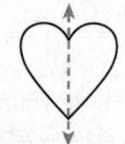
line plot A number line with marks or dots that show frequency.	**diagrama de acumulación** Recta numérica con marcas o puntos que indican la frecuencia.	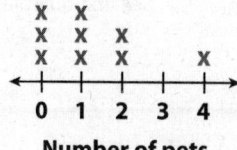
line segment *See* segment of a line.	**segmento** *Véase* segmento de recta.	
line symmetry A figure that can be reflected across a line so that the image coincides with the preimage.	**simetría axial** Figura que puede reflejarse sobre una línea de forma tal que la imagen coincida con la imagen original.	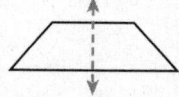

GL23

Glossary/Glosario

ENGLISH	SPANISH	EXAMPLES
linear equation in one variable An equation that can be written in the form $ax = b$ where a and b are constants and $a \neq 0$.	**ecuación lineal en una variable** Ecuación que puede expresarse en la forma $ax = b$ donde a y b son constantes y $a \neq 0$.	$x + 1 = 7$
linear equation in two variables An equation that can be written in the form $Ax + By = C$ where A, B, and C are constants and A and B are not both 0.	**ecuación lineal en dos variables** Ecuación que puede expresarse en la forma $Ax + By = C$ donde A, B y C son constantes y A y B no son ambas 0.	$2x + 3y = 6$
linear function A function that can be written in the form $y = mx + b$, where x is the independent variable and m and b are real numbers. Its graph is a line.	**función lineal** Función que puede expresarse en la forma $y = mx + b$, donde x es la variable independiente y m y b son números reales. Su gráfica es una línea.	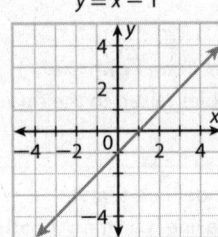 $y = x - 1$
linear inequality in one variable An inequality that can be written in one of the following forms: $ax < b, ax > b, ax \leq b, ax \geq b$, or $ax \neq b$, where a and b are constants and $a \neq 0$.	**desigualdad lineal en una variable** Desigualdad que puede expresarse de una de las siguientes formas: $ax < b, ax > b, ax \leq b,$ $ax \geq b$ o $ax \neq b$, donde a y b son constantes y $a \neq 0$.	$3x - 5 \leq 2(x + 4)$
linear inequality in two variables An inequality that can be written in one of the following forms: $Ax + By < C, Ax + By > C, Ax +$ $By \leq C, Ax + By \geq C$, or $Ax + By \neq C$, where A, B, and C are constants and A and B are not both 0.	**desigualdad lineal en dos variables** Desigualdad que puede expresarse de una de las siguientes formas: $Ax + By < C, Ax + By > C,$ $Ax + By \leq C, Ax + By \geq C$ o $Ax + By$ $\neq C$, donde A, B y C son constantes y A y B no son ambas 0.	$2x + 3y > 6$
linear regression A statistical method used to fit a linear model to a given data set.	**regresión lineal** Método estadístico utilizado para ajustar un modelo lineal a un conjunto de datos determinado.	
literal equation An equation that contains two or more variables.	**ecuación literal** Ecuación que contiene dos o más variables.	$d = rt$ $A = \frac{1}{2}h(b_1 + b_2)$
lower quartile *See* first quartile.	**cuartil inferior** *Ver* primer cuartil.	

M

ENGLISH	SPANISH	EXAMPLES
mapping diagram A diagram that shows the relationship of elements in the domain to elements in the range of a relation or function.	**diagrama de correspondencia** Diagrama que muestra la relación entre los elementos del dominio y los elementos del rango de una función.	**Mapping Diagram** 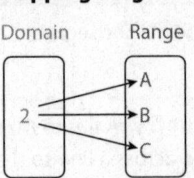 Domain Range

ENGLISH	SPANISH	EXAMPLES
marginal relative frequency The sum of the joint relative frequencies in a row or column of a two-way table.	**frecuencia relativa marginal** La suma de las frecuencias relativas conjuntas en una fila o columna de una tabla de doble entrada.	
mean The sum of all the values in a data set divided by the number of data values. Also called the *average*.	**media** Suma de todos los valores de un conjunto de datos dividida entre el número de valores de datos. También llamada *promedio*.	Data set: 4, 6, 7, 8, 10 Mean: $\frac{4+6+7+8+10}{5} = \frac{35}{5} = 7$
measure of an angle Angles are measured in degrees. A degree is $\frac{1}{360}$ of a complete circle.	**medida de un ángulo** Los ángulos se miden en grados. Un grado es $\frac{1}{360}$ de un círculo completo.	
measure of central tendency A measure that describes the center of a data set.	**medida de tendencia dominante** Medida que describe el centro de un conjunto de datos.	mean, median, or mode
median For an ordered data set with an odd number of values, the median is the middle value. For an ordered data set with an even number of values, the median is the average of the two middle values.	**mediana** Dado un conjunto de datos ordenado con un número impar de valores, la mediana es el valor medio. Dado un conjunto de datos con un número par de valores, la mediana es el promedio de los dos valores medios.	8, 9, ⑨, 12, 15 Median: 9 4, 6, ⑦, ⑩, 10, 12 Median: $\frac{7+10}{2} = 8.5$
median of a triangle A segment whose endpoints are a vertex of the triangle and the midpoint of the opposite side.	**mediana de un triángulo** Segmento cuyos extremos son un vértice del triángulo y el punto medio del lado opuesto.	
midpoint The point that divides a segment into two congruent segments.	**punto medio** Punto que divide un segmento en dos segmentos congruentes.	Point *B* is the midpoint of $\overline{AC}$.
midsegment of a trapezoid The segment whose endpoints are the midpoints of the legs of the trapezoid.	**segmento medio de un trapecio** Segmento cuyos extremos son los puntos medios de los catetos del trapecio.	
midsegment of a triangle A segment that joins the midpoints of two sides of the triangle.	**segmento medio de un triángulo** Segmento que une los puntos medios de dos lados del triángulo.	
midsegment triangle The triangle formed by the three midsegments of a triangle.	**triángulo de segmentos medios** Triángulo formado por los tres segmentos medios de un triángulo.	Midsegment triangle: $\triangle XYZ$

Glossary/Glosario

mode The value or values that occur most frequently in a data set; if all values occur with the same frequency, the data set is said to have no mode.	**moda** El valor o los valores que se presentan con mayor frecuencia en un conjunto de datos. Si todos los valores se presentan con la misma frecuencia, se dice que el conjunto de datos no tiene moda.	Data set: 3, 6, 8, 8, 10 Mode: 8 Data set: 2, 5, 5, 7, 7 Modes: 5 and 7 Data set: 2, 3, 6, 9, 11 No mode
Multiplication Property of Equality If a, b, and c are real numbers and $a = b$, then $ac = bc$.	**Propiedad de igualdad de la multiplicación** Si a, b y c son números reales y $a = b$, entonces $ac = bc$.	$\frac{1}{3}x = 7$ $(3)\left(\frac{1}{3}x\right) = (3)(7)$ $x = 21$
Multiplication Property of Inequality If both sides of an inequality are multiplied by the same positive quantity, the new inequality will have the same solution set. If both sides of an inequality are multiplied by the same negative quantity, the new inequality will have the same solution set if the inequality symbol is reversed.	**Propiedad de desigualdad de la multiplicación** Si ambos lados de una desigualdad se multiplican por el mismo número positivo, la nueva desigualdad tendrá el mismo conjunto solución. Si ambos lados de una desigualdad se multiplican por el mismo número negativo, la nueva desigualdad tendrá el mismo conjunto solución si se invierte el símbolo de desigualdad.	$\frac{1}{3}x > 7$ $(3)\left(\frac{1}{3}x\right) > (3)(7)$ $x > 21$ $-x \leq 2$ $(-1)(-x) \geq (-1)(2)$ $x \geq -2$
multiplicative inverse The reciprocal of the number.	**inverso multiplicativo** Recíproco de un número.	The multiplicative inverse of 5 is $\frac{1}{5}$.

N

negative correlation Two data sets have a negative correlation if one set of data values increases as the other set decreases.	**correlación negativa** Dos conjuntos de datos tienen una correlación negativa si un conjunto de valores de datos aumenta a medida que el otro conjunto disminuye.	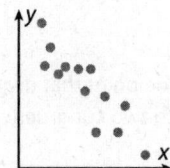
negative exponent For any nonzero real number x and any integer n, $x^{-n} = \frac{1}{x^n}$.	**exponente negativo** Para cualquier número real distinto de cero x y cualquier entero n, $x^{-n} = \frac{1}{x^n}$.	$x^{-2} = \frac{1}{x^2}$; $3^{-2} = \frac{1}{3^2}$
negative number A number that is less than zero. Negative numbers lie to the left of zero on a number line.	**número negativo** Número menor que cero. Los números negativos se ubican a la izquierda del cero en una recta numérica.	-2 is a negative number. ←+—+—●—+—+—+—+—+—+—→ -4 -3 -2 -1 $\ 0\ $ 1 $\ 2\ $ 3 $\ 4$
no correlation Two data sets have no correlation if there is no relationship between the sets of values.	**sin correlación** Dos conjuntos de datos no tienen correlación si no existe una relación entre los conjuntos de valores.	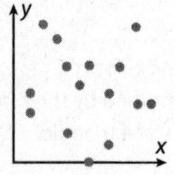

Glossary/Glosario

normal curve The graph of a probability density function that corresponds to a normal distribution; bell-shaped and symmetric about the mean, with the *x*-axis as a horizontal asymptote.

curva normal La gráfica de una función de densidad de probabilidad que corresponde a la distribución normal; con forma de campana y simétrica con relación a la media, el eje *x* es una asíntota horizontal.

---

normal distribution A distribution of data that varies about the mean in such a way that the graph of its probability density function is a normal curve.

distribución normal Distribución de datos que varía respecto de la media de tal manera que la gráfica de su función de densidad de probabilidad es una curva normal.

---

nth root The *n*th root of a number *a*, written as $\sqrt[n]{a}$ or $a^{\frac{1}{n}}$, is a number that is equal to *a* when it is raised to the *n*th power.

enésima raíz La enésima raíz de un número *a*, que se escribe $\sqrt[n]{a}$ o $a^{\frac{1}{n}}$, es un número igual a *a* cuando se eleva a la enésima potencia.

$\sqrt[5]{32} = 2$, because $2^5 = 32$.

---

numerical expression An expression that contains only numbers and operations.

expresión numérica Expresión que contiene únicamente números y operaciones.

O

obtuse triangle A triangle with one obtuse angle.

triángulo obtusángulo Triángulo con un ángulo obtuso.

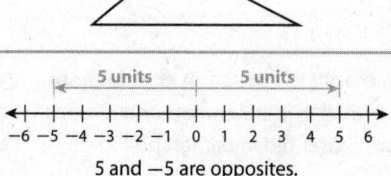

---

opposite The opposite of a number *a*, denoted −*a*, is the number that is the same distance from zero as *a*, on the opposite side of the number line. The sum of opposites is 0.

opuesto El opuesto de un número *a*, expresado −*a*, es el número que se encuentra a la misma distancia de cero que *a*, del lado opuesto de la recta numérica. La suma de los opuestos es 0.

5 and −5 are opposites.

---

opposite reciprocal The opposite of the reciprocal of a number. The opposite reciprocal of any nonzero number *a* is $-\frac{1}{a}$.

recíproco opuesto Opuesto del recíproco de un número. El recíproco opuesto de *a* es $-\frac{1}{a}$.

The opposite reciprocal of $\frac{2}{3}$ is $-\frac{3}{2}$.

OR A logical operator representing the union of two sets.

O Operador lógico que representa la unión de dos conjuntos.

$A = \{2, 3, 4, 5\}$ $B = \{1, 3, 5, 7\}$
The set of values that are in *A* OR *B* is $A \cup B$
$= \{1, 2, 3, 4, 5, 7\}$.

---

order of rotational symmetry The number of times a figure with rotational symmetry coincides with itself as it rotates 360°.

orden de simetría de rotación Cantidad de veces que una figura con simetría de rotación coincide consigo misma cuando rota 360°.

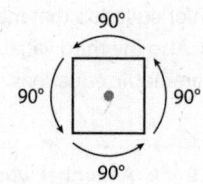

Order of rotational symmetry: 4

Glossary/Glosario

orthocenter of a triangle
The point of concurrency of the
three altitudes of a triangle.

ortocentro de un triángulo
Punto de intersección de las tres
alturas de un triángulo.

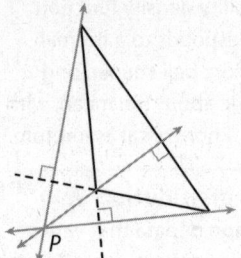

P is the orthocenter.

outlier A data value that is far
removed from the rest of the data.

valor extremo Valor de datos
que está muy alejado del resto
de los datos.

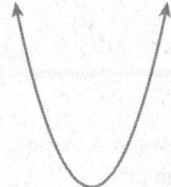

Most of data Mean   Outlier

output The result of substituting a
value for a variable in a function.

salida Resultado de la sustitución
de una variable por un valor en una
función.

For the function $f(x) = x^2 + 1$, the input 3
produces an output of 10.

P

parabola The shape of the graph
of a quadratic function.

parábola Forma de la gráfica de
una función cuadrática.

paragraph proof A style of proof
in which the statements and reasons
are presented in paragraph form.

**demostración con
párrafos** Tipo de demostración en
la cual los enunciados y las razones
se presentan en forma de párrafo.

parallel lines Lines in the same
plane that do not intersect.

líneas paralelas Líneas en el
mismo plano que no se cruzan.

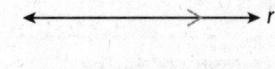

r

s

parallelogram A quadrilateral
with two pairs of parallel sides.

paralelogramo Cuadrilátero con
dos pares de lados paralelos.

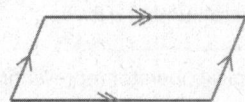

parameter One of the constants
in a function or equation that may
be changed. Also the third variable
in a set of parametric equations.

parámetro Una de las constantes
en una función o ecuación que
se puede cambiar. También es la
tercera variable en un conjunto de
ecuaciones paramétricas.

perfect square A number whose
positive square root is a whole
number.

cuadrado perfecto Número cuya
raíz cuadrada positiva es un número
cabal.

36 is a perfect square because $\sqrt{36} = 6$.

ENGLISH	SPANISH	EXAMPLES
permutation An arrangement of a group of objects in which order is important.	**permutación** Arreglo de un grupo de objetos en el cual el orden es importante.	For objects A, B, C, and D, there are 12 different permutations of 2 objects. AB, AC, AD, BC, BD, CD BA, CA, DA, CB, DB, DC
perpendicular Intersecting to form 90° angles.	**perpendicular** Que se cruza para formar ángulos de 90°.	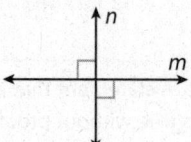
perpendicular bisector of a segment A line perpendicular to a segment at the segment's midpoint.	**mediatriz de un segmento** Línea perpendicular a un segmento en el punto medio del segmento.	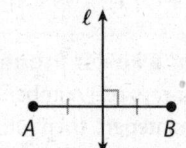 ℓ is the perpendicular bisector of $\overline{AB}$.
perpendicular lines Lines that intersect at 90° angles.	**líneas perpendiculares** Líneas que se cruzan en ángulos de 90°.	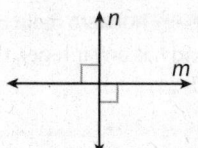
piecewise function A function that is a combination of one or more functions.	**función a trozos** Función que es una combinación de una o más funciones.	
plane An undefined term in geometry, it is a flat surface that has no thickness and extends forever.	**plano** Término indefinido en geometría; un plano es una superficie plana que no tiene grosor y se extiende infinitamente.	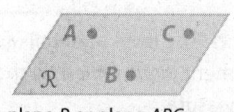 plane R or plane ABC
point An undefined term in geometry, it names a location and has no size.	**punto** Término indefinido de la geometría que denomina una ubicación y no tiene tamaño.	P • point P
point-slope form The point-slope form of a linear equation is $y - y_1 = m(x - x_1)$, where m is the slope and (x_1, y_1) is a point on the line.	**forma de punto y pendiente** La forma de punto y pendiente de una ecuación lineal es $y - y_1 = m(x - x_1)$, donde m es la pendiente y (x_1, y_1) es un punto en la línea.	$y - 3 = 2(x - 3)$
point of concurrency A point where three or more lines coincide.	**punto de concurrencia** Punto donde se cruzan tres o más líneas.	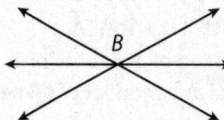
population The entire group of objects or individuals considered for a survey.	**población** Grupo completo de objetos o individuos que se desea estudiar.	In a survey about the study habits of high school students, the population is all high school students.

Glossary/Glosario

positive correlation Two data sets have a positive correlation if both sets of data values increase.

correlación positiva Dos conjuntos de datos tienen correlación positiva si los valores de ambos conjuntos de datos aumentan.

---

postulate A statement that is accepted as true without proof. Also called an *axiom*.

postulado Enunciado que se acepta como verdadero sin demostración. También denominado *axioma*.

Power of a Power Property If *a* is any nonzero real number and *m* and *n* are integers, then $(a^m)^n = a^{mn}$.

Propiedad de la potencia de una potencia Dado un número real *a* distinto de cero y los números enteros *m* y *n*, entonces $(a^m)^n = a^{mn}$.

$$(6^7)^4 = 6^{7 \cdot 4}$$
$$= 6^{28}$$

Power of a Product Property If *a* and *b* are any nonzero real numbers and *n* is any integer, then $(ab)^n = a^n b^n$.

Propiedad de la potencia de un producto Dados los números reales *a* y *b* distintos de cero y un número entero *n*, entonces $(ab)^n = a^n b^n$.

$$(2 \cdot 4)^3 = 2^3 \cdot 4^3$$
$$= 8 \cdot 64$$
$$= 512$$

Power of a Quotient Property If *a* and *b* are any nonzero real numbers and *n* is an integer, then $\left(\frac{a}{b}\right)^n = \frac{a^n}{b^n}$.

Propiedad de la potencia de un cociente Dados los números reales *a* y *b* distintos de cero y un número entero *n*, entonces $\left(\frac{a}{b}\right)^n = \frac{a^n}{b^n}$.

$$\left(\frac{3}{5}\right)^4 = \frac{3}{5} \cdot \frac{3}{5} \cdot \frac{3}{5} \cdot \frac{3}{5}$$
$$= \frac{3 \cdot 3 \cdot 3 \cdot 3}{5 \cdot 5 \cdot 5 \cdot 5}$$
$$= \frac{3^4}{5^4}$$

---

precision The level of detail of a measurement, determined by the unit of measure.

precisión Detalle de una medición, determinado por la unidad de medida.

A ruler marked in millimeters has a greater level of precision than a ruler marked in centimeters.

---

prediction An estimate or guess about something that has not yet happened.

predicción Estimación o suposición sobre algo que todavía no ha sucedido.

---

preimage The original figure in a transformation.

imagen original Figura original en una transformación.

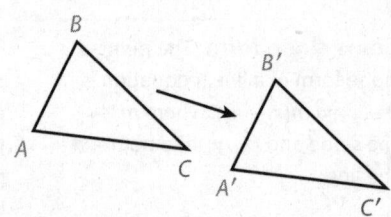

---

prime factorization A representation of a number or a polynomial as a product of primes.

factorización prima Representación de un número o de un polinomio como producto de números primos.

The prime factorization of 60 is $2 \cdot 2 \cdot 3 \cdot 5$.

---

prime number A whole number greater than 1 that has exactly two positive factors, itself and 1.

número primo Número cabal mayor que 1 que es divisible únicamente entre sí mismo y entre 1.

5 is prime because its only positive factors are 5 and 1.

ENGLISH	SPANISH	EXAMPLES
principal An amount of money borrowed or invested.	**capital** Cantidad de dinero que se pide prestado o se invierte.	
Product of Powers Property If a is any nonzero real number and m and n are integers, then $a^m \cdot a^n = a^{m+n}$.	**Propiedad del producto de potencias** Dado un número real a distinto de cero y los números enteros m y n, entonces $a^m \cdot a^n = a^{m+n}$.	$6^7 \cdot 6^4 = 6^{7+4}$ $= 6^{11}$
proof An argument that uses logic to show that a conclusion is true.	**demostración** Argumento que se vale de la lógica para probar que una conclusión es verdadera.	
proof by contradiction *See* indirect proof.	**demostración por contradicción** *Ver* demostración indirecta.	
proportion A statement that two ratios are equal; $\frac{a}{b} = \frac{c}{d}$.	**proporción** Ecuación que establece que dos razones son iguales; $\frac{a}{b} = \frac{c}{d}$.	$\frac{2}{3} = \frac{4}{6}$
Pythagorean Theorem If a right triangle has legs of lengths a and b and a hypotenuse of length c, then $a^2 + b^2 = c^2$.	**Teorema de Pitágoras** Dado un triángulo rectángulo con catetos de longitudes a y b y una hipotenusa de longitud c, entonces $a^2 + b^2 = c^2$.	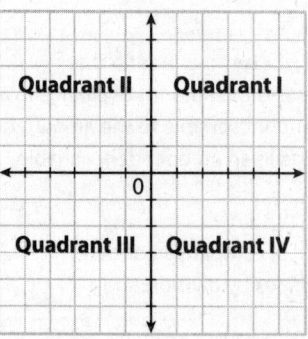 $5^2 + 12^2 = 13^2$ $25 + 144 = 169$
Pythagorean triple A set of three positive integers a, b, and c such that $a^2 + b^2 = c^2$.	**Tripleta de Pitágoras** Conjunto de tres enteros positivos a, b y c tal que $a^2 + b^2 = c^2$.	The numbers 3, 4, and 5 form a Pythagorean triple because $3^2 + 4^2 = 5^2$.

Q

quadrant One of the four regions into which the x- and y-axes divide the coordinate plane.	**cuadrante** Una de las cuatro regiones en las que los ejes x e y dividen el plano cartesiano.	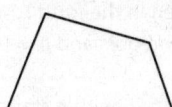
quadrilateral A four-sided polygon.	**cuadrilátero** Polígono de cuatro lados.	
quantitative data Numerical data.	**datos cuantitativos** Datos numéricos.	

Glossary/Glosario

Glossary/Glosario

quartile The median of the upper or lower half of a data set. *See also* first quartile, third quartile.

cuartil La mediana de la mitad superior o inferior de un conjunto de datos. *Ver también* primer cuartil, tercer cuartil.

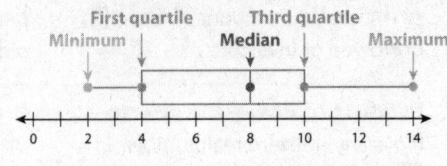

Quotient of Powers Property If a is a nonzero real number and m and n are integers, then $\frac{a^m}{a^n} = a^{m-n}$.

Propiedad del cociente de potencias Dado un número real a distinto de cero y los números enteros m y n, entonces $\frac{a^m}{a^n} = a^{m-n}$.

$\frac{6^7}{6^4} = 6^{7-4} = 6^3$

R

radical symbol The symbol $\sqrt{\ }$ used to denote a root. The symbol is used alone to indicate a square root or with an index, $\sqrt[n]{\ }$, to indicate the nth root.

símbolo de radical Símbolo $\sqrt{\ }$ que se utiliza para expresar una raíz. Puede utilizarse solo para indicar una raíz cuadrada, o con un índice, $\sqrt[n]{\ }$, para indicar la enésima raíz.

$\sqrt{36} = 6$
$\sqrt[3]{27} = 3$

radicand The expression under a radical sign.

radicando Número o expresión debajo del signo de radical.

Expression: $\sqrt{x+3}$
Radicand: $x + 3$

range of a data set The difference of the greatest and least values in the data set.

rango de un conjunto de datos La diferencia del mayor y menor valor en un conjunto de datos.

The data set {3, 3, 5, 7, 8, 10, 11, 11, 12} has a range of $12 - 3 = 9$.

range of a function or relation The set of all second coordinates (or y-values) of a function or relation.

rango de una función o relación Conjunto de todos los valores de la segunda coordenada (o valores de y) de una función o relación.

The range of the function $\{(-5, 3), (-3, -2), (-1, -1), (1, 0)\}$ is $\{-2, -1, 0, 3\}$.

rate A ratio that compares two quantities measured in different units.

tasa Razón que compara dos cantidades medidas en diferentes unidades.

$\frac{55 \text{ miles}}{1 \text{ hour}} = 55$ mi/h

rate of change A ratio that compares the amount of change in a dependent variable to the amount of change in an independent variable.

tasa de cambio Razón que compara la cantidad de cambio de la variable dependiente con la cantidad de cambio de la variable independiente.

The cost of mailing a letter increased from 22 cents in 1985 to 25 cents in 1988. During this period, the rate of change was
$\frac{\text{change in cost}}{\text{change in year}} = \frac{25 - 22}{1988 - 1985} = \frac{3}{3}$
$= 1$ cent per year.

ratio A comparison of two quantities by division.

razón Comparación de dos cantidades mediante una división.

$\frac{1}{2}$ or $1:2$

rational number A number that can be written in the form $\frac{a}{b}$, where a and b are integers and $b \neq 0$.

número racional Número que se puede expresar como $\frac{a}{b}$, donde a y b son números enteros y $b \neq 0$.

$3, 1.75, 0.\overline{3}, -\frac{2}{3}, 0$

ray A part of a line that starts at an endpoint and extends forever in one direction.

rayo Parte de una recta que comienza en un extremo y se extiende infinitamente en una dirección.

Glossary/Glosario

real number A rational or irrational number. Every point on the number line represents a real number.

número real Número racional o irracional. Cada punto de la recta numérica representa un número real.

reciprocal For a real number $a \neq 0$, the reciprocal of a is $\frac{1}{a}$. The product of reciprocals is 1.

recíproco Dado el número real $a \neq 0$, el recíproco de a es $\frac{1}{a}$. El producto de los recíprocos es 1.

Number	Reciprocal
2	$\frac{1}{2}$
1	1
−1	−1
0	No reciprocal

rectangle A quadrilateral with four right angles.

rectángulo Cuadrilátero con cuatro ángulos rectos.

recursive rule for nth term of a sequence A rule for a sequence in which one or more previous terms are used to generate the next term.

fórmula recurrente para hallar el enésimo término de una sucesión Fórmula para una sucesión en la cual uno o más términos anteriores se usan para generar el término siguiente.

reflection A transformation across a line, called the line of reflection, such that the line of reflection is the perpendicular bisector of each segment joining each point and its image.

reflexión Transformación sobre una línea, denominada la línea de reflexión. La línea de reflexión es la mediatriz de cada segmento que une un punto con su imagen.

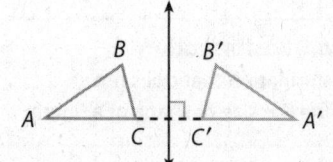

reflection symmetry *See* line symmetry.

simetría de reflexión *Ver* simetría axial.

relation A set of ordered pairs.

relación Conjunto de pares ordenados.

$\{(0, 5), (0, 4), (2, 3), (4, 0)\}$

relative frequency The relative frequency of a category is the frequency of the category divided by the total of all frequencies.

frecuencia relativa La frecuencia relativa de una categoría es la frecuencia de la categoría dividido por el total de todas las frecuencias.

remote interior angle An interior angle of a polygon that is not adjacent to the exterior angle.

ángulo interno remoto Ángulo interno de un polígono que no es adyacente al ángulo externo.

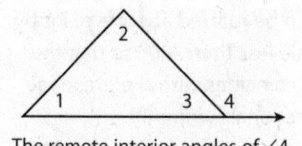

The remote interior angles of $\angle 4$ are $\angle 1$ and $\angle 2$.

resultant vector The vector that represents the sum of two given vectors.

vector resultante Vector que representa la suma de dos vectores dados.

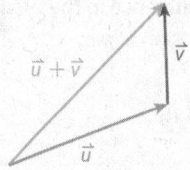

Glossary/Glosario

Glossary/Glosario

ENGLISH	SPANISH	EXAMPLES
repeating decimal A rational number in decimal form that has a nonzero block of one or more digits that repeat continuously.	**decimal periódico** Número racional en forma decimal que tiene un bloque de uno o más dígitos que se repite continuamente.	$1.\overline{3}$, $0.\overline{6}$, $2.1\overline{4}$, $6.77\overline{3}$
replacement set A set of numbers that can be substituted for a variable.	**conjunto de reemplazo** Conjunto de números que pueden sustituir una variable.	
residual The signed vertical distance between a data point and a line of fit.	**residuo** La diferencia vertical entre un dato y una línea de ajuste.	
residual plot A scatter plot of points whose *x*-coordinates are the values of the independent variable and whose *y*-coordinates are the corresponding residuals.	**diagrama de residuos** Diagrama de dispersión de puntos en el que la coordenada *x* representa los valores de la variable independiente y la coordenada *y* representa los residuos correspondientes.	
rhombus A quadrilateral with four congruent sides.	**rombo** Cuadrilátero con cuatro lados congruentes.	
rigid motion *See* isometry.	**movimiento rígido** *Ver* isometría.	
rigid transformation A transformation that does not change the size or shape of a figure.	**transformación rígida** Transformación que no cambia el tamaño o la forma de una figura.	
rise The difference in the *y*-values of two points on a line.	**distancia vertical** Diferencia entre los valores de *y* de dos puntos de una línea.	For the points $(3, -1)$ and $(6, 5)$, the rise is $5 - (-1) = 6$.
rotation A transformation about a point *P*, also known as the center of rotation, such that each point and its image are the same distance from *P*. All of the angles with vertex *P* formed by a point and its image are congruent.	**rotación** Transformación sobre un punto *P*, también conocido como el centro de rotación, tal que cada punto y su imagen estén a la misma distancia de *P*. Todos los ángulos con vértice *P* formados por un punto y su imagen son congruentes.	
rotational symmetry A figure that can be rotated about a point by an angle less than 360° so that the image coincides with the preimage has rotational symmetry.	**simetría de rotación** Una figura que puede rotarse alrededor de un punto en un ángulo menor de 360° de forma tal que la imagen coincide con la imagen original tiene simetría de rotación.	Order of rotational symmetry: 4
run The difference in the *x*-values of two points on a line.	**distancia horizontal** Diferencia entre los valores de *x* de dos puntos de una línea.	For the points $(3, -1)$ and $(6, 5)$, the run is $6 - 3 = 3$.

S

same-side interior angles For two lines intersected by a transversal, a pair of angles that lie on the same side of the transversal and between the two lines.

ángulos internos del mismo lado Dadas dos líneas cortadas por una transversal, el par de ángulos ubicados en el mismo lado de la transversal y entre las dos líneas.

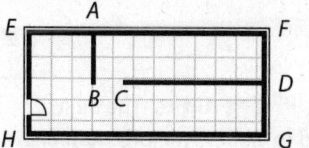

∠2 and ∠3 are same-side interior angles.

---

sample A part of the population.

muestra Una parte de la población.

In a survey about the study habits of high school students, a sample is a survey of 100 students.

---

scale The ratio between two corresponding measurements.

escala Razón entre dos medidas correspondientes.

1 cm : 5 mi

---

scale drawing A drawing that uses a scale to represent an object as smaller or larger than the actual object.

dibujo a escala Dibujo que utiliza una escala para representar un objeto como más pequeño o más grande que el objeto original.

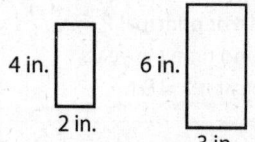

A blueprint is an example of a scale drawing.

---

scale factor The multiplier used on each dimension to change one figure into a similar figure.

factor de escala El multiplicador utilizado en cada dimensión para transformar una figura en una figura semejante.

4 in.   6 in.
2 in.   3 in.

Scale factor: $\frac{3}{2} = 1.5$

---

scale model A three-dimensional model that uses a scale to represent an object as smaller or larger than the actual object.

modelo a escala Modelo tridimensional que utiliza una escala para representar un objeto como más pequeño o más grande que el objeto real.

---

scatter plot A graph with points plotted to show a possible relationship between two sets of data.

diagrama de dispersión Gráfica con puntos que se usa para demostrar una relación posible entre dos conjuntos de datos.

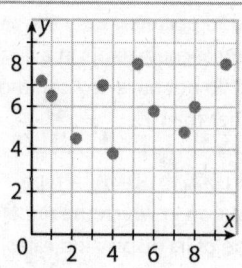

---

second quartile The median of an entire data set, denoted Q_2.

segundo cuartil Mediana de un conjunto de datos completo, expresada como Q_2.

8, 9, ⑨, 12, 15 Q_2 : 9

4, 6, ⑦, ⑩, 10, 12

$Q_2 : \frac{7 + 10}{2} = 8.5$

Glossary/Glosario

segment bisector A line, ray, or segment that divides a segment into two congruent segments.

bisectriz de un segmento Línea, rayo o segmento que divide un segmento en dos segmentos congruentes.

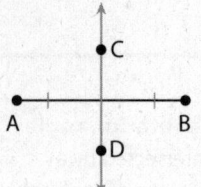

---

segment of a line A part of a line consisting of two endpoints and all points between them.

segmento de una línea Parte de una línea que consiste en dos extremos y todos los puntos entre éstos.

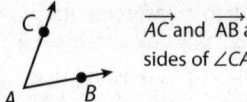

---

sequence A list of numbers that often form a pattern.

sucesión Lista de números que generalmente forman un patrón.

1, 2, 4, 8, 16, …

---

side of an angle One of the two rays that form an angle.

lado de un ángulo Uno de los dos rayos que forman un ángulo.

$\overrightarrow{AC}$ and $\overrightarrow{AB}$ are sides of $\angle CAB$.

---

significant digits The digits used to express the precision of a measurement.

dígitos significativos Dígitos usados para expresar la precisión de una medida.

---

simple interest A fixed percent of the principal. For principal P, interest rate r, and time t in years, the simple interest is $I = Prt$.

interés simple Porcentaje fijo del capital. Dado el capital P, la tasa de interés r y el tiempo t expresado en años, el interés simple es $I = Prt$.

---

simplest form of an exponential expression An exponential expression is in simplest form if it meets the following criteria:
1. There are no negative exponents.
2. The same base does not appear more than once in a product or quotient.
3. No powers, products, or quotients are raised to powers.
4. Numerical coefficients in a quotient do not have any common factor other than 1.

forma simplificada de una expresión exponencial Una expresión exponencial está en forma simplificada si reúne los siguientes requisitos:
1. No hay exponentes negativos.
2. La misma base no aparece más de una vez en un producto o cociente.
3. No se elevan a potencias productos, cocientes ni potencias.
4. Los coeficientes numéricos en un cociente no tienen ningún factor común que no sea 1.

Not Simplest Form	Simplest Form
$7^8 \cdot 7^4$	7^{12}
$\left(x^2\right)^{-4} \cdot x^5$	$\dfrac{1}{x^3}$
$\dfrac{a^5 b^9}{(ab)^4}$	ab^5

---

skewed distribution A type of distribution in which the right or left side of its display indicates frequencies that are much greater than those of the other side. In a distribution skewed to the left, more than half the data are greater than the mean. In a distribution skewed to the right, more than half the data are less than the mean.

distribución sesgada Tipo de distribución en la que el lado derecho o izquierdo muestra frecuencias mucho mayores que las del otro lado. En una distribución sesgada a la izquierda, más de la mitad de los datos son menores que la media. En una distribución sesgada a la derecha, más de la mitad de los datos son menores que la media.

Glossary/Glosario

slope A measure of the steepness of a line. If (x_1, y_1) and (x_2, y_2) are any two points on the line, the slope of the line, known as m, is represented by the equation $m = \frac{y_2 - y_1}{x_2 - x_1}$.

pendiente Medida de la inclinación de una línea. Dados dos puntos (x_1, y_1) y (x_2, y_2) en una línea, la pendiente de la línea, denominada m, se representa con la ecuación $m = \frac{y_2 - y_1}{x_2 - x_1}$.

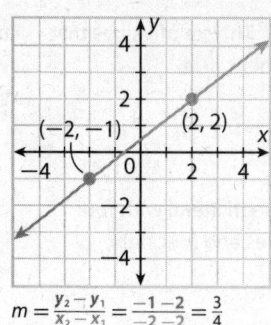

$$m = \frac{y_2 - y_1}{x_2 - x_1} = \frac{-1 - 2}{-2 - 2} = \frac{3}{4}$$

---

slope formula If (x_1, y_1) and (x_2, y_2) are any two points on a line, the slope of the line is $m = \frac{y_2 - y_1}{x_2 - x_1}$.

fórmula de la pendiente Dados dos puntos (x_1, y_1) y (x_2, y_2) en una línea, la pendiente de la línea es $m = \frac{y_2 - y_1}{x_2 - x_1}$.

---

slope-intercept form The slope-intercept form of a linear equation is $y = mx + b$, where m is the slope and b is the y-intercept.

forma de pendiente-intersección La forma de pendiente-intersección de una ecuación lineal es $y = mx + b$, donde m es la pendiente y b es la intersección con el eje y.

$y = -2x + 4$
The slope is -2.
The y-intercept is 4.

---

solution of a linear inequality in one variable A value or values that make the inequality true.

solución de una desigualdad lineal en una variable Valor o valores que hacen que la desigualdad sea verdadera.

Inequality: $x + 2 < 6$
Solution: $x < 4$

---

solution of a linear equation in two variables An ordered pair or ordered pairs that make the equation true.

solución de una ecuación lineal en dos variables Un par ordenado o pares ordenados que hacen que la ecuación sea verdadera.

$(4, 2)$ is a solution of $x + y = 6$.

---

solution of a system of linear equations Any ordered pair that satisfies all the equations in a linear system.

solución de un sistema de ecuaciones lineales Cualquier par ordenado que resuelva todas las ecuaciones de un sistema lineal.

$$\begin{cases} x + y = -1 \\ -x + y = -3 \end{cases}$$

---

solution of a system of linear inequalities Any ordered pair that satisfies all the inequalities in a linear system.

solución de un sistema de desigualdades lineales Cualquier par ordenado que resuelva todas las desigualdades de un sistema lineal.

$$\begin{cases} y \leq x + 1 \\ y < -x + 4 \end{cases}$$

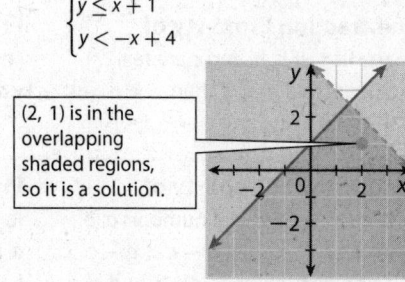

$(2, 1)$ is in the overlapping shaded regions, so it is a solution.

---

solution of an inequality in two variables An ordered pair or ordered pairs that make the inequality true.

solución de una desigualdad en dos variables Un par ordenado o pares ordenados que hacen que la desigualdad sea verdadera.

$(3, 1)$ is a solution of $x + y < 6$.

Glossary/Glosario

Glossary/Glosario

ENGLISH	SPANISH	EXAMPLES
solution set The set of values that make a statement true.	**conjunto solución** Conjunto de valores que hacen verdadero un enunciado.	Inequality: $x + 3 \geq 5$ Solution set: $\{x \mid x \geq 2\}$ 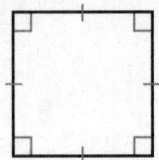
square A quadrilateral with four congruent sides and four right angles.	**cuadrado** Cuadrilátero con cuatro lados congruentes y cuatro ángulos rectos.	
square root A number that is multiplied by itself to form a product is called a square root of that product.	**raíz cuadrada** El número que se multiplica por sí mismo para formar un producto se denomina la raíz cuadrada de ese producto.	A square root of 16 is 4, because $4^2 = 4 \cdot 4 = 16$. Another square root of 16 is -4 because $(-4)^2 = (-4)(-4) = 16$.
standard form of a linear equation $Ax + By = C$, where A, B, and C are real numbers and A and B are not both 0.	**forma estándar de una ecuación lineal** $Ax + By = C$, donde A, B y C son números reales y A y B no son ambos cero.	$2x + 3y = 6$
standard deviation A measure of dispersion of a data set. The standard deviation σ is the square root of the variance	**desviación estándar** Medida de dispersión de un conjunto de datos. La desviación estándar σ es la raíz cuadrada de la varianza	Data set: $\{6, 7, 7, 9, 11\}$ Mean: $\frac{6+7+7+9+11}{5} = 8$ Variance: $\frac{1}{5}(4 + 1 + 1 + 1 + 9) = 3.2$ Standard deviation: $\sigma = \sqrt{3.2} \approx 1.8$
statistics Numbers that describe a sample or samples.v	**estadísticas** Números que describen una o varias muestras.	
straight angle A 180° angle.	**ángulo llano** Ángulo que mide 180°.	
substitution method A method used to solve systems of equations by solving an equation for one variable and substituting the resulting expression into the other equation(s).	**sustitución** Método utilizado para resolver sistemas de ecuaciones resolviendo una ecuación para una variable y sustituyendo la expresión resultante en las demás ecuaciones.	
Subtraction Property of Equality If a, b, and c are real numbers and $a = b$, then $a - c = b - c$.	**Propiedad de igualdad de la resta** Si a, b y c son números reales y $a = b$, entonces $a - c = b - c$.	$\begin{aligned} x + 6 &= 8 \\ -6 \quad &-6 \\ x \quad &= 2 \end{aligned}$
Subtraction Property of Inequality For real numbers a, b, and c, if $a < b$, then $a - c < b - c$. Also holds true for $>$, $\leq$, $\geq$, and $\neq$.	**Propiedad de desigualdad de la resta** Dados los números reales a, b y c, si $a < b$, entonces $a - c < b - c$. Es válido también para $>$, $\leq$, $\geq$ y $\neq$.	$\begin{aligned} x + 6 &< 8 \\ -6 \quad &-6 \\ x \quad &< 2 \end{aligned}$
supplementary angles Two angles whose measures have a sum of 180°.	**ángulos suplementarios** Dos ángulos cuyas medidas suman 180°.	30° 150°

ENGLISH	SPANISH	EXAMPLES
symmetric distribution A type of distribution in which the right and left sides of its display indicate frequencies that are mirror images of each other.	**distribución simétrica** Tipo de distribución en la que los lados derecho e izquierdo muestran frecuencias que son idénticas.	
system of linear equations A system of equations in which all of the equations are linear.	**sistema de ecuaciones lineales** Sistema de ecuaciones en el que todas las ecuaciones son lineales.	$\begin{cases} 2x + 3y = -1 \\ x - 3y = 4 \end{cases}$
system of linear inequalities A system of inequalities in which all of the inequalities are linear.	**sistema de desigualdades lineales** Sistema de desigualdades en el que todas las desigualdades son lineales.	$\begin{cases} 2x + 3y > -1 \\ x - 3y \le 4 \end{cases}$

T

ENGLISH	SPANISH	EXAMPLES
term of a sequence An element or number in the sequence.	**término de una sucesión** Elemento o número de una sucesión.	5 is the third term in the sequence 1, 3, 5, 7, …
term of an expression The parts of the expression that are added or subtracted.	**término de una expresión** Parte de una expresión que debe sumarse o restarse.	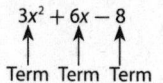
terminal point of a vector The endpoint of a vector.	**punto terminal de un vector** Extremo de un vector.	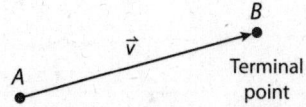
theorem A statement that has been proven.	**teorema** Enunciado que ha sido demostrado.	
third quartile The median of the upper half of a data set. Also called *upper quartile*.	**tercer cuartil** La mediana de la mitad superior de un conjunto de datos. También se llama *cuartil superior*.	Lower half Upper half 18, 23, 28, 29, (36,) 42 Third quartile
tolerance The amount by which a measurement is permitted to vary from a specified value.	**tolerancia** La cantidad por que una medida se permite variar de un valor especificado.	
transformation A change in the position, size, or shape of a figure or graph.	**transformación** Cambio en la posición, tamaño o forma de una figura o gráfica.	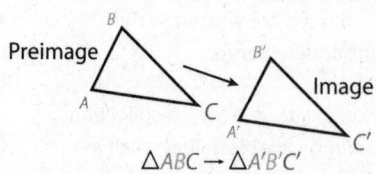
translation A transformation that shifts or slides every point of a figure or graph the same distance in the same direction.	**traslación** Transformación en la que todos los puntos de una figura o gráfica se mueven la misma distancia en la misma dirección.	

Glossary/Glosario

translation symmetry A figure has translation symmetry if it can be translated along a vector so that the image coincides with the preimage.

simetría de traslación Una figura tiene simetría de traslación si se puede trasladar a lo largo de un vector de forma tal que la imagen coincida con la imagen original.

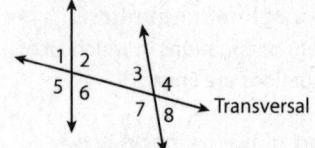

transversal A line that intersects two coplanar lines at two different points.

transversal Línea que corta dos líneas coplanares en dos puntos diferentes.

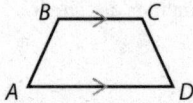

trapezoid A quadrilateral with at least one pair of parallel sides.

trapecio Cuadrilátero con al menos un par de lados paralelos.

trend line A line on a scatter plot that helps show the correlation between data sets more clearly.

línea de tendencia Línea en un diagrama de dispersión que sirve para mostrar la correlación entre conjuntos de datos más claramente.

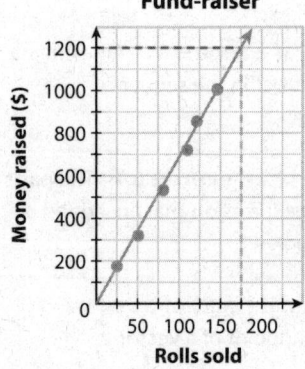

triangle A three-sided polygon.

triángulo Polígono de tres lados.

triangle rigidity A property of triangles that states that if the side lengths of a triangle are fixed, the triangle can have only one shape.

rigidez del triángulo Propiedad de los triángulos que establece que, si las longitudes de los lados de un triángulo son fijas, el triángulo puede tener sólo una forma.

two-column proof A style of proof in which the statements are written in the left-hand column and the reasons are written in the right-hand column.

demostración a dos columnas Estilo de demostración en la que los enunciados se escriben en la columna de la izquierda y las razones en la columna de la derecha.

two-variable data A collection of paired variable values, such as a series of measurements of air temperature at different times of day.

datos de dos variables Conjunto de valores variables agrupados en pares, como una serie de mediciones de la temperatura del aire en diferentes momentos del día.

Time	Temperature (°F)
8 A.M.	65
9 A.M.	69
10 A.M.	72

ENGLISH	SPANISH	EXAMPLES

two-way frequency table A frequency table that displays two-variable data in rows and columns.

table de frecuencia de doble entrada Una tabla de frecuencia que muestra los datos de dos variables organizados en filas y columnas.

		Preference		
		Inside	Outside	*Total*
Pet	**Cats**	35	15	50
	Dogs	20	30	50
	Total	55	45	100

U

undefined term A basic figure that is not defined in terms of other figures. The undefined terms in geometry are point, line, and plane.

término indefinido Figura básica que no está definida en función de otras figuras. Los términos indefinidos en geometría son el punto, la línea y el plano.

unit rate A rate in which the second quantity in the comparison is one unit.

tasa unitaria Tasa en la que la segunda cantidad de la comparación es una unidad.

$\frac{30 \text{ mi}}{1 \text{ h}} = 30 \text{ mi/h}$

unlike terms Terms with different variables or the same variables raised to different powers.

términos distintos Términos con variables diferentes o las mismas variables elevadas a potencias diferentes.

$4xy^2$ and $6x^2y$

upper quartile *See* third quartile.

cuartil superior *Ver* tercer cuartil.

V

value of a function The result of replacing the independent variable with a number and simplifying.

valor de una función Resultado de reemplazar la variable independiente por un número y luego simplificar.

The value of the function $f(x) = x + 1$ for $x = 3$ is 4.

value of a variable A number used to replace a variable to make an equation true.

valor de una variable Número utilizado para reemplazar una variable y hacer que una ecuación sea verdadera.

In the equation $x + 1 = 4$, the value of x is 3.

value of an expression The result of replacing the variables in an expression with numbers and simplifying.

valor de una expresión Resultado de reemplazar las variables de una expresión por un número y luego simplificar.

The value of the expression $x + 1$ for $x = 3$ is 4.

variable A symbol used to represent a quantity that can change.

variable Símbolo utilizado para representar una cantidad que puede cambiar.

In the expression $2x + 3$, x is the variable.

vector A quantity that has both magnitude and direction.

vector Cantidad que tiene magnitud y dirección.

Glossary/Glosario

Glossary/Glosario

Glossary/Glosario

vertex angle of an isosceles triangle The angle formed by the legs of an isosceles triangle.

ángulo del vértice de un triángulo isósceles Ángulo formado por los catetos de un triángulo isósceles.

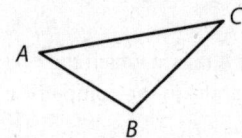

---

vertex of a polygon The intersection of two sides of the polygon.

vértice de un polígono La intersección de dos lados del polígono.

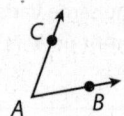

A, B, C, D, and E are vertices of the polygon.

---

vertex of a triangle The intersection of two sides of the triangle.

vértice de un triángulo Intersección de dos lados del triángulo.

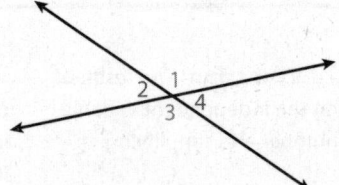

A, B, and C are vertices of △ABC.

---

vertex of an angle The common endpoint of the sides of the angle.

vértice de un ángulo Extremo común de los lados del ángulo.

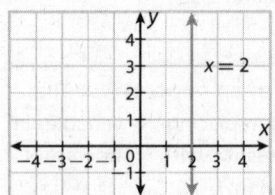

A is the vertex of ∠CAB.

---

vertical angles The nonadjacent angles formed by two intersecting lines.

ángulos opuestos por el vértice Ángulos no adyacentes formados por dos líneas que se cruzan.

∠1 and ∠3 are vertical angles.
∠2 and ∠4 are vertical angles.

---

vertical line A line whose equation is $x = a$, where a is the x-intercept.

línea vertical Línea cuya ecuación es $x = a$, donde a es la intersección con el eje x.

$x = 2$

---

vertical-line test A test used to determine whether a relation is a function. If any vertical line crosses the graph of a relation more than once, the relation is not a function.

prueba de la línea vertical Prueba utilizada para determinar si una relación es una función. Si una línea vertical corta la gráfica de una relación más de una vez, la relación no es una función.

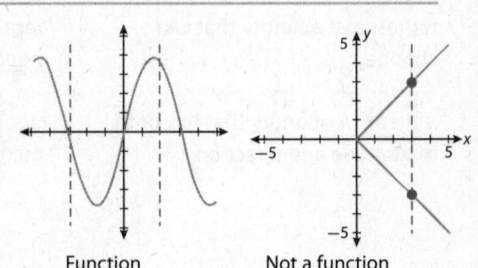

Function   Not a function

ENGLISH	SPANISH	EXAMPLES

X

x-intercept The x-coordinate(s) of the point(s) where a graph intersects the x-axis.

intersección con el eje x Coordenada(s) x de uno o más puntos donde una gráfica corta el eje x.

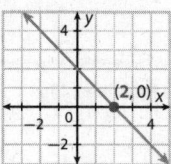

The x-intercept is 2.

Y

y-coordinate The second number in an ordered pair, which indicates the vertical distance of a point from the origin on the coordinate plane.

coordenada y Segundo número de un par ordenado, que indica la distancia vertical de un punto desde el origen en un plano cartesiano.

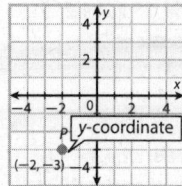

y-intercept The y-coordinate(s) of the point(s) where a graph intersects the y-axis.

intersección con el eje y Coordenada(s) y de uno o más puntos donde una gráfica corta el eje y.

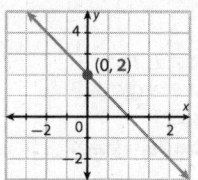

The y-intercept is 2.

Z

zero exponent For any nonzero real number x, $x^0 = 1$.

exponente cero Dado un número real distinto de cero x, $x^0 = 1$.

$5^0 = 1$

Zero Product Property For real numbers p and q, if $pq = 0$, then $p = 0$ or $q = 0$.

Propiedad del producto cero Dados los números reales p y q, si $pq = 0$, entonces $p = 0$ o $q = 0$.

If $(x - 1)(x + 2) = 0$, then $x - 1 = 0$ or $x + 2 = 0$, so $x = 1$ or $x = -2$.

Glossary/Glosario

Glossary/Glosario

Index

Index locator numbers are in Module. Lesson form. For example, 2.1 indicates Module 2, Lesson 1 as listed in the Table of Contents.

Index

Table of Measures

LENGTH

1 inch = 2.54 centimeters

1 meter = 39.37 inches

1 mile = 5,280 feet

1 mile = 1760 yards

1 mile = 1.609 kilometers

1 kilometer = 0.62 mile

MASS/WEIGHT

1 pound = 16 ounces

1 pound = 0.454 kilograms

1 kilogram = 2.2 pounds

1 ton = 2000 pounds

CAPACITY

1 cup = 8 fluid ounces

1 pint = 2 cups

1 quart = 2 pints

1 gallon = 4 quarts

1 gallon = 3.785 liters

1 liter = 0.264 gallons

1 liter = 1000 cubic centimeters

Symbols

$\neq$	is not equal to	π	pi: (about 3.14)
$\approx$	is approximately equal to	$\perp$	is perpendicular to
10^2	ten squared; ten to the second power	$\parallel$	is parallel to
		$\overleftrightarrow{AB}$	line AB
$2.\overline{6}$	repeating decimal 2.66666...	$\overrightarrow{AB}$	ray AB
$\lvert -4 \rvert$	the absolute value of negative 4	$\overline{AB}$	line segment AB
$\sqrt{}$	square root	$m\angle A$	measure of $\angle A$

Formulas

GEOMETRY	
Triangle	$A = \frac{1}{2}bh$
Parallelogram	$A = bh$
Circle	$A = \pi r^2$
Circle	$C = \pi d$ or $C = 2\pi r$
Pythagorean Theorem	$a^2 + b^2 = c^2$

LINEAR EQUATIONS	
Standard form	$Ax + By = C$
Slope-intercept form	$y = mx + b$
Point-slope form	$y - y_1 = m(x - x_1)$
Slope of a line	$m = \dfrac{y_2 - y_1}{x_2 - x_1}$

SEQUENCES	
Arithmetic Sequence	$a_n = a_1 + (n - 1)d$
Geometric Sequence	$a_n = a_1 r^{n-1}$